G000022296

Welcome...

Whether you've lived in Dublin all your life, or you've just r̶ the right book. It's not meant for tourists who are just looking for a bit of 'Paddy' – it's written for you, the savvy resident who knows that on a good day, not many cities can beat Dublin for its energy, its friendliness and, most important of all, its craic.

The Dublin Explorer has been meticulously researched and written by a team of nine Dubliners who not only know the city, but love it too. These intrepid Explorers have scoured all areas to bring you the lowdown on the things that are important to a resident of Dublin.

Flick through the **General Information** chapter (p.2) to brush up on Dublin facts – handy for when you want to impress visitors with your encyclopaedic knowledge on the city's geography, history, politics and more. The **Residents** chapter (p.53) is the meaty section of this book, and covers all the red tape you'll have to cut through when finding a job, getting a work permit, moving house, furnishing your home, getting a pet, connecting your phone or having a baby.

Reading through **Exploring** (p.161) is like having your own personal tour guide, except without the annoying voice and the inflated prices. It will also steer you away from all the usual tourist traps and take you to places off that old beaten track. The **Activities** chapter (p.225) lists hundreds of things to do – whether sporty, arty or intellectual – and will definitely ensure you spend less time on your own in your room.

Turn to **Shopping** on p.279 for some ideas on how to flash your cash, or at least survive if you've only got a fiver left until payday. It features an A-Z listing of everything you might ever need to buy (from art to wedding stationery), and where you can buy it. It also has a rundown of the best malls, markets and shopping streets. Finally, the **Going Out** chapter (p.335) lists 200 restaurants, bars and nightclubs that have been personally recommended by our team of Dublin experts (just remember to get your round in). And if you've overindulged and can't face another night in the pub, it also lists more genteel entertainment options like theatre, cinema and comedy gigs.

Phew! That's a lot of stuff packed into one book. If you can't figure out where to start, turn to the **Maps** section at the back of the book to get your bearings.

So there you have it – a book that covers just about everything. But if you find something we've missed out (like your neighbourhood Guinness appreciation society or your naked Liffey swimming club), then go to www.explorerpublishing.com, fill in the Reader Response Form, and share the knowledge with your fellow Explorers.

Enjoy the journey,

The Explorer Team

Explorer's Dublin

No time in Dublin is ever too much - while we were there we couldn't get enough of the following:

Brunch, lunch or dinner in Gruel (p.384): just goes to show that great food doesn't have to be pretentious, or expensive.

Hanging out in Howth (p.172) – quaint village, lovely harbour, great Sunday market – what's not to like?

Eating and drinking in Temple Bar (p.335) – sure you'll see lots of bridezillas on their hen night, but the area has so much energy and some amazing restaurants and bars.

Kilmainham Gaol (p.187): a poignant yet fascinating glimpse into the past.

Dundrum Town Centre (p.329): a lovely bus ride, some brilliant shopping, and a restaurant terrace that can't be beaten on a sunny day.

Beth Morrissey American-born Beth arrived in Dublin long before Starbucks and Borders, and has seen big changes. As a busy freelance writer and blogger, Beth spends her time shopping, people-watching and going to the theatre, all in the name of 'research', naturally. **City must-do:** Dublin Writer's Museum (p.190) **Best thing about Dublin:** the people - you'll never be lonely in Dublin!

Brian Finnegan Brian is the editor of GCN, Ireland's leading gay magazine, and is a regular contributor to Irish media on the topics of gay politics and culture. He is currently writing his first musical. **City must-do:** Dublin Pride (p.48), when thousands of gorgeous queers take over the city the second-last weekend in June. **Best view:** Lough Dan in Wicklow - heavenly on a clear day.

Carina Scheuringer Although Carina is not Irish by birth, she has adopted the culture heartily and now knows that the crisps go inside the sandwich and beer can only be enjoyed by the pint. **Best thing about living in Dublin:** anything is possible, and life is never dull! **Favourite daytrip:** Glendalough (p.209). **Best view:** from the top of Killiney hill, providing panoramic views of Dublin.

Ellen Brickley Having lived in Dublin for eight years (four of which were spent studying literature at UCD) but with no sense of direction, Ellen has discovered most of the city's best spots by accident. When she's not writing, she can be found reading, browsing street markets or drinking too much tea. **Best view:** take the Dart (southbound) for amazing views of the coast.

Liz Farsaci Liz works as a journalist in Dublin. Originally from the west and east coasts of America, she came to Dublin to study for a term at university, drank too much and stayed on. **Favourite cultural experience:** Impressionists exhibit at the National Gallery (p.182). **City must-do:** check out live performances by any of the modern Dublin bands.

*Having trouble navigating your way around Dublin? Look no further than the **Dublin Mini Map**, an indispensable pocket-sized aid to getting to grips with the roads, areas and attractions of this lovely little city.*

*You live in Dublin. It's brilliant. That means that everybody, from random Facebook friends to relatives you've never met, will be wanting to come and visit you. No problem - give them a copy of the **Dublin Mini Explorer,** which is so packed full of fascinating information for tourists that you'll hardly ever see them. Yippee!*

Lucy White After leaving sunny Dubai for a rather damp Dublin, Lucy finds that Prozac is helping with the S.A.D., particularly when washed down with Guinness. As a lifestyle writer for Metro, she gets to dine out, go to the theatre, and just generally live the high life, all for free of course. **Best cultural experience:** losing a couple of hours at the IMMA (p.181). **Favourite restaurant:** Café Bar Deli (p.358).

Mary Conneely Mary is a freelance journalist and author and spent five years in Paris, buying shoes and translating knitting patterns. Despite recently becoming a mum, she still loves impractical dresses, sky-high heels, and copious cocktails in Cafe En Seine (p.372) **Best cultural experience:** comedy improv night at the International Bar (p.391). **Favourite restaurant:** Chez Max (p.346).

Mundy Walsh After five years in Italy, Mundy is back in Dublin and loves being home. She enjoys discovering unusual shops, restaurants and galleries. She also writes a column for a local paper, and has ambitions to conquer the world. **City must-do:** live music in St Stephens Green in the summer. **Best cultural experience:** St Patrick's Cathedral (p.186). **Best view:** Guinness Storehouse (p.199).

Yvonne Gordon Yvonne was born and raised in Dublin, and although she's lived in other countries, she has always returned to Ireland. Apart from being a freelance travel and features writer, she is also a keen sailor and accomplished musician. **Best thing about living in Dublin:** accessibility to the sea, mountains and beautiful scenery. **Favourite daytrip:** a walk in the Wicklow mountains.

Thanks...

A lot of people got involved in this book, so big thanks to: star deputy editor and genuine Irish lass Katie Drynan, not just for her editing but also because she wrote various sections of the book; Tony & Anand from Emirates Printing Press; Alan & Sandra Chapman for daytrips, admin, accommodation and everything else; Claire & Kevin and Richard & Greta; Shelley Gibbs for Thai food, champagne and company in Dublin; Ann Jordan for the photo on p.220; Grainne O'Connell of Christies Estates for valuable info; the Dubai Irish contingent: Mandy & Dermot Kelly and Regina & Mike Long; and finally, honourary Irishman Justin, little leprechaun Hannah, and the rogue Celt, Stuart.

Where are we exploring next?

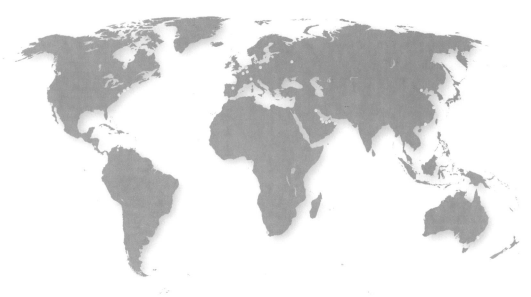

- Abu Dhabi
- Amsterdam
- Bahrain
- Barcelona
- Beijing*
- Berlin*
- Boston*
- Brussels*

- Cape Town*
- Dubai
- Dublin
- Geneva
- Hong Kong
- Kuala Lumpur*
- Kuwait
- London

- Los Angeles*
- Moscow*
- New York
- New Zealand
- Oman
- Paris
- Qatar
- San Francisco*

- Shanghai
- Singapore
- Sydney
- Tokyo*
- Vancouver*
- Washington DC*

* Available 2008

Where do you live?

Is your home city missing from our list? If you'd love to see a residents' guide for a location not currently on Explorer's horizon please email editorial@explorerpublishing.com.

Advertise with Explorer...

If you're interested in advertising with us, please contact sales@explorerpublishing.com.

Make Explorer your very own...

We offer a number of customisation options for bulk sales. For more information and discount rates please contact corporatesales@explorerpublishing.com.

Contract Publishing

Have an idea for a publication or need to revamp your company's marketing material? Contact designlab@explorerpublishing to see how our expert contract publishing team can help.

www.explorerpublishing.com

Life can move pretty fast, so to make sure you can stay up to date with all the latest goings on in your city, we've revamped our website to further enhance your time in the city, whether long or short.

Keep in the know…

Our Complete Residents' Guides and Mini Visitors' series continue to expand, covering destinations from Amsterdam to New Zealand and beyond. Keep up to date with our latest travels and hot tips by signing up to our monthly newsletter, or browse our products section for info on our current and forthcoming titles.

Make friends and influence people…

…by joining our Communities section. Meet fellow residents in your city, make your own recommendations for your favourite restaurants, bars, childcare agencies or dentists, plus find answers to your questions on daily life from long-term residents.

Discover new experiences…

Ever thought about living in a different city, or wondered where the locals really go to eat, drink and be merry? Check out our regular features section, or submit your own feature for publication!

Want to find a badminton club, the number for your bank, or maybe just a restaurant for a hot first date?

Check out city info on various destinations around the world in our residents' section – from finding a Pilates class to contact details for international schools in your area, or the best place to buy everything from a spanner set to a Spandau Ballet album, we've got it all covered.

Let us know what you think!

All our information comes from residents which means you! If we missed out your favourite bar or market stall, or you know of any changes in the law, infrastructure, cost of living or entertainment scene, let us know by using our Feedback form.

The Dubliner

IRELAND'S BEST CITY MAGAZINE

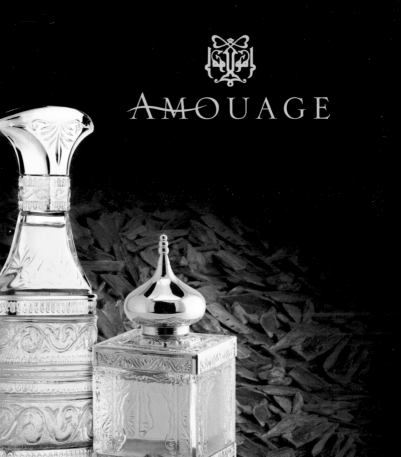

Contents

Contents

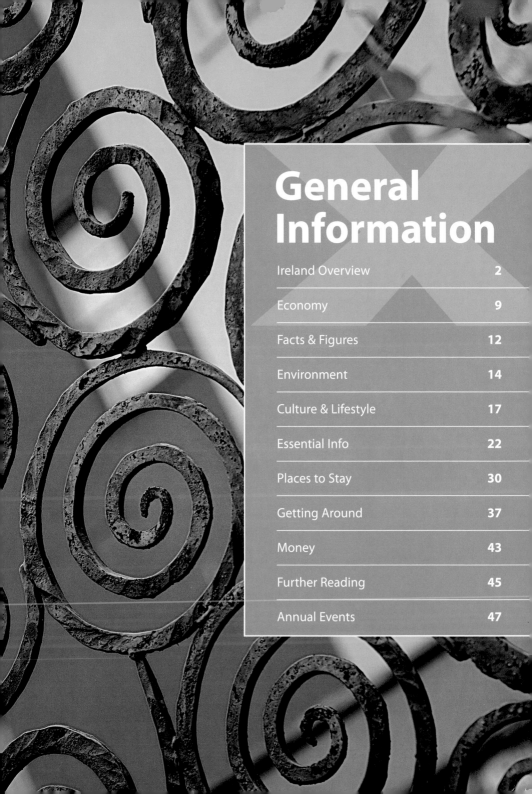

General Information

Dublin At A Glance

Dublin is bordered by County Meath to the north, County Kildare to the west, County Wicklow to the south and the Irish Sea to the east. Its total area is 11,496 hectares, and its main rivers are the Liffey, Poddle, Dodder and Tolka.

Geography

An island located on the western fringe of Europe, Ireland is situated 53° north of the equator and 8° west of the Greenwich Meridian. It covers an area of 84,412 square kilometres, with 3,172 kilometres of coastline bordering the Irish Sea, St George's Channel and the Atlantic Ocean.

Since the declaration of the Irish Free State in 1921, the island has been divided administratively into two parts: what is now called the Republic of Ireland, and Northern Ireland, governed by the United Kingdom. The country as a whole is divided up into four ancient provinces Connacht, Leinster, Munster and Ulster. Each one of these provinces is further split into counties, of which there are 26 in the Republic in total. Ulster is divided between Northern Ireland and the Republic, with six of the nine counties of Ulster being under British rule. In 2006, the Republic of Ireland's population stood at 4,239,848.

While the country's natural biodiversity of wildlife is relatively low, reflecting the fact that it is indeed an island, its diverse landscapes cover everything from beaches to bogland, and from hills to lush forests. Peering down upon the rest of the country at 1,041 metres is Ireland's highest mountain, Carrantuohill in County Kerry, while the river Shannon, the longest river at 340km, bisects it. Lough Neagh in Northern Ireland is the largest of the many lakes, covering an area of 396 square kilometres.

The main concentration of larger settlements and industry is in the east and south of Ireland, with Dublin being the chief commercial, industrial, administrative, educational and cultural centre. The west boasts a more rugged, unspoiled landscape. County Dublin has the highest population density (home to 1,187,176 people in 2006), and is home to Ireland's beloved capital city.

Ireland Fact File

Coordinates 53° north of the equator and 8° west of the Greenwich Meridian
Number of provinces: 4
Number of counties: 26
Borders: Northern Ireland to the north and north-east, the Irish Sea and St George's channel to the east and south-east, Atlantic Ocean to the west and north-west
Total area: 84,412 sq km
Coastline: 3,172km
Highest Point: Carrantouhill, Kerry (1,041m)
Longest River: Shannon (340km)
Largest lake: Lough Neagh (396 sq km)

History

In 1988, the authorities announced Dublin's thousandth anniversary (counting from the year that taxes were first introduced to the city). Yet, as Dubliners raised their glasses to their home, historians were quick to remind them that Dublin – in one form or another – had been around for much longer, with its history closely interwoven with that of the whole island.

A Walk Down Memory Lane

Although Ireland may have been populated as early as 8000BC, it was only around 5000BC that the first big chapter of early Irish history was written. Cultivating the land systematically for the first time, Neolithic farmers laid the foundations for a later economy, and went down in history for their megalithic monuments, many of which stand as witnesses of their existence all over Ireland today.

However, the race which was to leave the most prominent stamp on Ireland and is thought to have given Dublin its first name, 'Dubh Linn' (literally 'black pool'), arrived roughly 4,500 years later in the shape of powerful Iron Age warriors – the Celts. Speaking a language akin to modern Irish, these tribes began to structure their newfound territory socially, culturally and politically, creating provinces and kingdoms as well introducing early law (Brehon Law). Dublin's modern Irish name, Baile Átha Cliath (the town of the ford of the hurdles), is believed to be of Celtic origin.

Land Of Saints & Scholars

While legend has it that St Patrick introduced Christianity to Ireland, the religion of Rome had already taken hold to some extent before the patron saint of Ireland started spreading the word of God. By the sixth century, Ireland had entered the golden age of Christianity, with monasteries flourishing and developing into cultural and learning centres. Some of the country's finest artwork can be traced back to this era, with the Book of Kells and the Ardagh Chalice being the most prominent examples.

The Origins Of The Viking Adventure

Dublin remained little more than a seasonal, small settlement until the arrival of another war-faring lot, this time from the north of Europe – the Vikings. Choosing the area around the tidal pool in the estuary as a base from which to raid the wealthy monasteries, they set the cornerstone for a future capital. By the end of the ninth century, Dublin had grown into a powerful and permanent stronghold and the Vikings as the saying goes 'were becoming more Irish than the Irish themselves', intermarrying and embracing Christianity. However, under constant attack from the Gaelic Irish since 936, the Vikings, despite their growing influence and power, were finally defeated in the Battle of Clontarf on Good Friday 1014. The victors were led by Brian Ború, a high king who referred to himself as the 'Emperor of the Irish'. Sadly, he was slain at the moment of victory by a fleeing Norseman, but his bravery turned him into a household name.

Strongbow's Legacy & The Anglo-Norman Invasion

Former Vikings themselves, the Normans had Britain under firm control by the mid 12th century but showed little interest in expanding to the neighbouring island which, following the death of Brian Ború, had become a battlefield for conflicting dynasties. Things changed however when, deposed by a neighbouring king, the King of Leinster

The Hapenny Bridge

approached the King of England (Henry II) for help to regain his throne, offering in return to make his kingship subject to Henry II's overlordship.

Answering the call, the Normans arrived in 1169, led by the Earl of Pembroke, Richard de Clare (better known as Strongbow). Within a year, they had seized Dublin. After Stongbow inherited the kingship of Leinster, it was not a far leap for Henry II to proclaim Dublin to be under his control. The reconstruction and fortification of the captured city began immediately, leading to the erection of some of Dublin's best-known landmarks, such as Christchurch Cathedral, St Patrick's Cathedral and Dublin Castle.

The Anglican City & Its Golden Age

Until the Tudor period (1485-1603), Dublin remained a typical medieval town, rising and falling with the tides of overcrowding and related problems such as epidemics and famines. The Anglo-Norman dominance was limited to an area known as 'the Pale', loosely corresponding to the area known as Greater Dublin today (this is where the saying 'beyond the pale' comes from, meaning beyond convention). Beyond those boundaries, Ireland remained untamed until Henry VIII consolidated his power across the island. Having split England from the Roman Catholic Church in 1531, he declared himself the head of an Anglicised Irish Church and in 1541, the King of Ireland. Decades of persecution of Catholics followed under Henry VIII's youngest daughter Elizabeth I, leaving a former majority pushed to the margins of society, dispossessed of their houses of worship and often their employment. As the resentment among the oppressed Catholic majority grew against the 'English' capital, Oliver Cromwell appeared on the scene, obsessed with the idea that Ireland could be a threat to England and thus aiming to personally reassert English control throughout. It was a period that was forever going to cast a shadow over neighbourly relations and would see Cromwell go down in history as a perpetrator of shameful acts of military action – around 3,000 Irish soldiers were killed in just one night, some of them burnt alive in a church. The first plantations followed the 'flight of the Earls', with nearly 15 million acres of land being taken from Catholic owners and redistributed amongst Cromwell's supporters (www.flight of the earls.ie).

Meanwhile, Anglican Dublin, having escaped Cromwell's reign largely unharmed, entered its 'belle epoque' in the 17th century, during which time the arts were celebrated and the city's face took the shape we know today, with the construction of Temple Bar, Customs House and the Four Courts to name but a few. Yet, as the likes of G F Handel and Oliver Goldsmith walked Dublin's new broad and neoclassical streets, they had little idea that in the underbelly of their redesigned city, an explosive mix of anger and resentment was coming to the boil.

William Of Orange & The Decline Of The Capital

In 1690, as William of Orange took to the throne following his defeat of King James II at the Battle of the Boyne, all hopes for a Catholic England were destroyed. The new Protestant monarch wasted no time in leaving an imprint on the neighbouring island, issuing laws that deprived Catholics of many rights, most crucially the right to own or buy land. With the majority being countryside farmers, many Irish Catholics suddenly found themselves stripped of their land, with little choice but to either become tenants of their former homes or move to the capital.

Unprecedented migration meant that by the second half of the 18th century, the Protestant community of Dublin found itself greatly outnumbered by newly arrived, disenfranchised Catholics. As rumblings of discontent resulted in rebellion and violence, the Anglican aristocracy did not wait around to see the outcome. Pouring out of the capital, they left Dublin open to decline.

Aware of the necessity to give the city some sort of direction, reformist politician Henry Grattan made a case for legislative autonomy and, after months of negotiations, was

Live, Work, Play

If you're new to Dublin and still trying to figure out which areas are cool, which are dangerous, or which are just miles out of your price range, check out the comprehensive guides to areas in this book. Find your ideal living space using the area guide in the Residents chapter (starting on p.53), and discover where all the hipsters hang out in the Exploring chapter (p.161).

rewarded for his efforts. In 1782, the Irish Parliament was granted temporary independence from England and, as a first action, abolished some of the Penal Laws against Catholics. Yet, as the capital entered another age of turmoil with Wolfe Tone and Robert Emmet becoming the talk of the town, England felt the need to restore direct rule from London. Passed in 1801, the Act of Union, which was intended to ally Britain and Ireland even further, had the complete opposite effect, and only initiated yet another wave of social and economic decline.

The Potato Famine & The Rise Of Nationalism

England's disinterested response to the disastrous potato famine of 1845-1849, which caused a mass exodus and claimed the lives of a great proportion of the population, reducing Ireland's population from eight million to just four and a half million, enraged the country. While natives died from starvation, exports to England did not only continue, but even increased by 30% in what became known as 'Black '47'. Rations, when they finally did arrive in the form of cheap Indian cornmeal (Irish corn was still being exported), were not handed out to those who needed them the most, with the excuse that such an action may encourage laziness and thus have a negative impact on the Irish economy. After all, according to British Prime Minister Robert Peel, the Irish had 'a tendency to exaggerate.' This only served to strengthen opposition against the powerful neighbour, as well as forever imbedding a deep scar on English-Irish relations.

While Dublin escaped the worst of it, it found itself swamped with desperate migrants, so that by the early 20th century, slum dwellings had taken over the city and death rates were at an all-time high. An estimated 20,000 families found themselves living in one-room dwellings, with no adequate water supply and making them vulnerable to diseases. Against this background rose the Fenians, with factions in both Dublin and the US. They were a pro-Irish group who, in the aftermath of the Great Famine, aimed to restore national pride by reminding the people what being Irish entailed. Celebrating national history, language and culture, Dublin saw the establishment of the Gaelic Athletic Association (GAA), the Gaelic League and later the Celtic Revival Movement (under WB Yeats and Lady Gregory) among others.

The Famine Memorial

The Road To Independence

Home Rule was within reach just as the first world war shook Europe, suspending it indefinitely, yet already laying the foundations for a partitioned Ireland. As the war was well underway, a group of Dubliners (including Connolly, Pearse, Clarke, Mac Donagh and Plunkett) started plotting a rebellion, the Easter Rising, which was to initiate the war of independence and later the establishment of the Irish Free State. On Easter Monday 1916, together with an army of nationalists, they occupied five strategic buildings in Dublin, declaring the GPO (General Post Office) the headquarters for their 'provisional government of the Irish Republic'. While there was no unified support for the rebellion, Dubliners were united in their anger following the British response to hand down executions and imprisonments. And so it happened that although the uprising failed, it created unprecedented support for the national question and Sinn Fein won a landslide victory in the general elections in 1918. They went on to proclaim the Irish Republic in 1919, create a separatist Irish parliament (Dáil Eireann), and to plan the war of independence. The war of independence began in 1919. Years of insurgency, led by Michael Collins, began against the British government. It was not until a truce – was agreed upon with the signing of the Anglo-Irish Treaty on December 6, 1921, which granted Ireland limited independence – that it came to an end. Under this treaty, members of parliament were obliged to swear allegiance to the British crown, and the island was partitioned, with 26 counties forming the Irish Free State. This split the country even further, and relations within the Dáil deteriorated rapidly. Feelings of gross betrayal among those against the treaty (De Valera) towards those in favour of it (Collins), led to the civil war in 1922.

The civil war claimed the lives of 3,000 people in the first eleven months, including Michael Collins, who was assassinated by an IRA hitman in 1922. Following Collins' death, and due to a lack of general support, the treaty was finally accepted and approved by the elected officials of the breakaway government, (including de Valera). Two political parties emerged as a result of this war, Fianna Fáil, founded by de Valera in 1926, and Fianna Gael. Fianna Fail went on to win the general election and started penning an Irish constitution. In 1949, under a coalition government, Ireland was finally declared a Republic, although still without six counties.

The Rise Of A Cosmopolitan Capital

As the country was struggling towards a modern democracy and Sean Lemass succeeded De Valera as taoiseach (prime minister) of Ireland in 1959, the country's leaders turned their attention once again to the Irish economy, which was badly in need of redirection. Its dependence on agriculture throughout history had proven detrimental. Looking outwards, Ireland took the first steps towards becoming a player in the international market joined the European Economic Community in 1973. While violence began to shake Northern Ireland once again, with Bloody Sunday (1972) leaving another sad legacy, Ireland was looking ahead at a brighter future – an unprecedented economic boom, which was to become known as the Celtic Tiger (see p.9 for more). As Ireland's economy prospered and unemployment plummeted, Dublin grew into a proud, vibrant and fast-changing cosmopolitan centre, which was dealing with its legacies and finding its place in the modern world. It was certainly not all plain sailing and Dublin was faced with a whole new set of problems from drug-related to immigration issues, but as it stumbled back onto its feet, it was entering a new era; one that would see the rise of Dublin as we know it today.

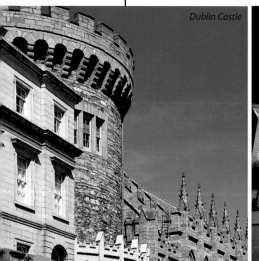
Dublin Castle

The GPO on O'Connell Street

Jim Larkin & the GPO

Key Figures In Ireland's History

Ireland's colourful past has thrown focus on some fairly colourful characters who have become key figures in Irish history.

In the gallery of Catholic patron saints, St Patrick is certainly the centrepiece. Yet his story remains a confusing web of fact and fiction, still largely a mystery to scholars 1,500 years on. Traditional dates set St Patrick's mission to Ireland from 432 to 461. While he was neither the first nor the only significant missionary to walk the Emerald Isle, today's national patron saint was indisputably at the heart of the rise of Christianity in Ireland. He founded numerous churches during his lifetime, most notably perhaps the Cathedral which bears his name today, St Patrick's Cathedral (p.186). He is also famously reputed to have banished snakes from Ireland. His legacy includes two documents, among them the famous Confessions, written in his old age. While these writings provide some insights into the man behind the legends, they do not enable historians to put together all the pieces of the puzzle – they know that St Patrick was the son of a Roman official and was captured by Irish raiders at the age of 16 and taken to Ireland, where he worked as a slave for six years. Where exactly he had come from, however, remains a mystery, although the general consensus among historians is that he lived in Wales. He is believed to have enjoyed such great popularity that landowners fought over the right to bury him after his death.

Another important figure in the history of Ireland is Padraic Pearse. Born in Dublin in 1879, the chosen president of the provisional Republic, proclaimed at the Easter Rising 1916, went down in history as a martyr for his country. At the funeral of a fellow Fenian, he is reported to have said: 'Life springs from death; and from the graves of patriot men and women spring living nations'. Stirring stuff.

Michael Collins was a legendary figure synonymous with the war of independence. Cork-born Collins frustrated the opposition with his ability to elude capture. When signing the Anglo-Irish Treaty he is known to have said 'I have signed my own death warrant'. He was ambushed and killed by an IRA assassin in 1922, just 20 miles from his birthplace.

Eamon de Valera, the son of Irish-Spanish immigrants, was born in New York in 1882 and brought up in Limerick. One of the commanders of the Easter Rising, he opposed the Treaty of 1921 and was the leader of the 'emergency government' during the Civil War. He founded the Fianna Fáil Party and won the elections of 1932, which put him in charge of the country for the best part of 27 years. In 1959, he was elected president of Ireland and re-elected for a second term in 1966. He died two years after retiring from his office in 1975.

These figures, and many others besides, are commemorated in Dublin's many statues and monuments. In fact, one thing that may strike you is the sheer number of statues and monuments in the city. It seems that on every street or in every park you will see a statue of a famous Irish literary, political or religious figure. Most have an accompanying plaque explaining the figure's importance in Ireland's past. You can also get a better understanding of some of Ireland's key political figures by visiting Kilmainham Gaol – see p.187 for more information.

7

Dublin Timeline

8000 BC	Neolithic farmers populate Ireland and erect monuments of early spiritual architecture
from 500BC	The arrival of the Celts
from 300AD	Advent and the golden age of Christianity in Ireland
from 800AD	The Vikings arrive
1014	The Battle of Clontarf led by the King of Munster; BrianBorú puts an end to the Viking era
1169	The first Anglo-Normans arrive under the leadership of Strongbow and take over Dublin
1171	King Henry II creates an area of English power, known as 'the Pale'
1536-1540	Henry VIII initiates the Reformation, dissolves all monasteries and abbeys
1541	Henry VIII declares himself the first English King of Ireland
1607	The 'flight of the Earls' results in Protestant settlements in the northern provinces of Ireland
1690	William of Orange wins the Battle of the Boyne and Penal Laws are introduced. Catholic Irish, now deprived of the right to own land, migrate to Dublin, outnumbering the Protestant population.
1782	Grattan succeeds in securing Irish parliamentary independence. Anglo-Irish relations enter a turbulent state and rebellions lay the foundation for Irish republicanism
1801	The Act of Union (1 January) joins Ireland to the United Kingdom of Great Britain and Ireland
1823	Founding the Catholic Association, Daniel O'Connell starts a campaign for Catholic emancipation
1845-1849	The potato famine sees millions die
1858	Foundation of the Fenian movement
1870	Charles Stewart Parnell, the head of the Irish Land League, fights for the right of tenant farmers to obtain land
1880s	Celtic Revival sees the foundation of the GAA, the Gaelic League and the Irish Literary Theatre
1900s	Housing conditions in Dublin are appalling, with many residing in slums
1914	Irish Home Rule finally reaches the statute-books in the Government of Ireland Act, but is suspended indefinitely with the arrival of the first world war
1916	The Easter Rising: Irish nationalists proclaim the Irish Republic, paving the way for the War for Independence (1919-1921)
1922	The Ango-Irish Treaty provides 'dominion status' to the Irish Free State, although six counties in the north remain under English rule. Civil war breaks out between pro- and anti-treaty sides
1931	The Public Safety Act restores some peace on the streets of Dublin
1932	Eamon de Valera gains power
1937	A new constitution is penned for the Irish Free State
1949	The Republic of Ireland is officially inaugurated on Easter Monday
1972	Bloody Sunday
1973	Ireland joins the European Economic Community
1985	The Anglo-Irish Agreement is signed and followed by IRA bombings
1990s	The Celtic Tiger transforms Ireland
1992	The 'X-case' wins the right to perform the first abortion in Ireland if there is risk to the mother's life
1993	Homosexuality is decriminalised
1995	Divorce is legalised
1996	Organised and drug related crime is on the up in Dublin, culminating in the murder of journalist Veronica Guerin. Legislation is passed which ensures that formerly untouchable criminals are brought to justice
1998	Good Friday Agreement is signed and followed by Omagh bombing by the Real IRA
2002	Ireland introduces the euro
2004	Ireland assumes presidency of the EU. The smoking ban is introduced.

Ireland Overview

In 2003, Dublin was rated the sixth best city to live and work in by Mercer Human Resources. Sipping a latte in one of the many trendy cafes in the city centre and watching the smartly dressed and confident residents of Dublin rush by, it is hard to imagine that not too long ago it was known as the capital of Europe's 'poorhouse'. With only a few indigenous industries, such as leather, silk, glass, hardware and wool, Ireland remained economically underdeveloped until well into the 19th century and was almost completely dependent on agriculture. In 1801, the Act of Union put Ireland under direct rule from London as well as establishing a free trade area between the two countries. While Britain was on its way to becoming a powerful capitalist nation, Ireland – vulnerable to the capers of nature and changes in the market – was heading for disaster. This arrived in the shape of the Great Famine. Millions died of starvation and many more were forced to emigrate, and the country was crippled by poverty and lack of opportunity.

Indeed, one of the greatest challenges facing the Irish Free State from the outset was how to establish a strong and diversified economy that could compete in the world market. Protectionism and self-sufficiency were tried, and although successful in establishing a base for new industries, did not yield the aspired results. However, in 1959, Sean Lemass came to power and recognised the need to open up the Irish economy to foreign investment, in the hope that it would stimulate the domestic market and boost employment. And the rest is history, as they say. Initiatives like the IDA Ireland (Industrial Development Agency) helped revolutionise and transform the economy in the 1990s into what was fondly dubbed the 'Celtic Tiger'.

While growth has certainly slowed down, the Irish economy remains in great shape, mainly thanks to trade and tourism. In 2006, the Gross Domestic Product (GDP) increased by 5.7% in constant prices compared with 2005. While foreign penetration of business in Ireland is still the highest in Europe, with foreign-owned firms controlling 50% of the total turnover and employing almost 40% of the workforce, Ireland's indigenous industry has started to catch up. The emergence of Irish entrepreneurs in the high-tech sector, which was formerly completely dependent on foreign capital, has meant that Ireland is now less dependent on its main foreign investors, the US, Great Britain and Germany.

Agriculture remains an important sector, although it only added €2,875 million to Net National Income, compared to the €79,746 million generated by other industries in 2006. The light industry is the top contributor to Ireland's healthy trade figures, followed by pharmaceuticals, luxury textiles, beverages and crystals. In 2004, the GDP came in at €36,354 per inhabitant.

Ireland was the only English-speaking EU member state to adopt the euro, making it particularly attractive for US investment. Although the common currency has certainly contributed to the fact that Dublin now ranks 13th in the list of the word's most expensive cities, the euro was a success. As the euro is strong and inflation varies between 4.8% and 5.2% (2007), Ireland's employment rate is still increasing (3.8% in the first quarter of 2007) and according to an EU survey, the risk of poverty for those over 65 is falling substantially by the year. In 2005, the average gross household income was just over €51,000 per annum, a 3.6% increase compared to 2004. Unemployment is expected to be between 4.1% and 4.4% in 2007. Overall, the future certainly looks promising, although certain inflation trends are a cause for concern, particularly within the property market.

Gross Domestic Product

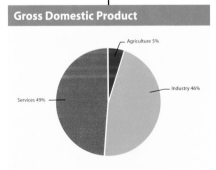

Agriculture 5%

Industry 46%

Services 49%

It will be interesting to see what the next few years have in store for Ireland and indeed the EU, to which it is now closely tied. For now though, Ireland remains the fastest growing of the 15 original EU member states.

Dublin Overview

Dublin has emerged as a cosmopolitan and self-assured city. In the aftermath of unprecedented economic growth, Dublin today is a contemporary hub to rival most other European cities. At the turn of the century the city experienced a sudden influx of foreigners, tourists and refugees alike. While this created its own set of problems (see Race Relations on p.18), Dublin's attractiveness as a tourist destination ensured that the sector was pumping money into the city as well as providing employment for its people. With 5.6 million people travelling to Dublin in 2006, tourism remains a significant sector and together with other primary industries, such as retail trade, construction and financial and other business services, contributes to a steady growth in employment (currently around 3%). Dublin is one of the fastest growing cities in Europe and in spite of it all, still has an excess of jobs. Dublin is vastly wealthier than the rest of the country and the widening gap between the rich and the poor is a growing concern. A high proportion of new millionaires are starkly contrasted by increased, and evermore visible, homelessness.

Tourism

In the first quarter of 2007, Ireland noted a 6% increase in overseas visitors compared to the same period in 2006, totalling an impressive 1,478,000 visitors. While numbers coming in from the outer European countries had risen by 33%, there were 6% less Brits crossing over the Irish Sea. Contributing €819 million to the national earnings between January and March 2007 alone, tourism remains a leading component of the economy.

Dublin is somewhat of a tourist hub, largely due to its sights, the people and a great nightlife. Between 1990 and 1997, the city witnessed an increase in tourist growth of 85%. Although numbers continue to rise every year, it's at a much slower rate. In 2006, 5,676,000 visitors descended upon the capital, raising the tourism revenue up to €1,670.2 million.

The majority of visitors were British or from continental Europe and spent an average of nearly five nights in the capital, typically lodging at hotels, with friends or in a guesthouse or B&B. Over half of them had chosen Ireland as a holiday destination, a trend that Tourism Ireland has picked up on with their campaign 'Discover your very own Ireland' (www.tourismireland.com). Finally, the EFL (English as a foreign language) courses contribute almost €300 million to the Irish economy, with over 130,000 students travelling to Ireland each year to study English or just to practise.

International Relations

Constitutional principles, such as Ireland's neutrality and the rule of law in international relations, determine Irish foreign policy. Ireland has a good standing in the United Nations (which it joined in 1955), due to its contribution to peacekeeping missions and its support for human rights and development. As such, it has been on the UN Security Council a number of times. In its belief that it is beneficial to foster ties with international partners, Ireland strives to continually build new relationships based on respect and tolerance. These relationships are particularly special with countries like the US, where there are a large number of people with Irish ancestry.

Ireland is strongly involved in development cooperation, and private entities and government bodies come together in their efforts to contribute to and support the development of the world's poorest countries. When disaster strikes elsewhere, Irish agencies are always quick on the scene, with the public often generously backing them with donations.

Government & Politics

In a nutshell, Ireland is an independent, post-colonial, capitalist state based on a parliamentary democracy. Responsible for the executive power of the state, the Irish government consists of a cabinet of no less than seven and not more than 15 members and is led by the taoiseach (prime minister). The taoiseach is nominated by the Dáil (the more significant house of parliament, which also passes laws) and is formally appointed by the President.

On 14 June, 2007, Bertie Ahern of Fianna Fáil was re-elected to serve his third term as taoiseach and assumed a coalition government with the Progressive Democrats and The Green Party. At Ahern's side is the tánaiste (Vice-President) and Finance Minister, Brian Cowen, also of Fianna Fáil, who acts on his behalf in absence or in illness.

The taoiseach nominates the members of government, all of which must be in the Oireachtas (National Parliament), which consists of the Irish President (An tUachtaran), the Dáil Eireann (the Irish House of Representatives) and the less significant Seanad Eireann (Irish Senate). It derives its power from the Constitution of Ireland as well as Irish and EU law. Elected by direct vote by the people for a term of seven years, the role of the President is largely ceremonial, although Mary Robinson did illustrate that some influence can be exercised even from this apolitical office. Robinson resigned on September 12, 1997 in order to become the United Nations High Commissioner for Human Rights. She was succeeded by the second female President (and eighth President) of Ireland, Mary McAleese, a Belfast-born barrister and former Professor of Law who was re-elected unopposed in 2004.

Enacted in 1937 (and penned by Fianna Fáil and Eamon de Valera), Bunreacht na hÉireann (the Irish Constitution) comprises a total of 50 Articles (both in Irish and English) which set out the 'basic law of Ireland', and describe how the country should be governed. Although based on the British model, it differs from it in the fact that it is written down and that it contains provision for a US-style judicial review. In short, it

Dublin City Council

describes the nature of the Irish state, its main institutions as well as outlining the fundamental rights of the citizens. In contrast to other countries, Irish politics are fairly homogeneous, with the result that personality and local issues are more significant than party ideologies. Founded by Eamon de Valera, Fianna Fáil has dominated Irish politics for the best part of 75 years. Other parties include the Progressive Democrats, the Green Party, the Labour Party, Fine Gael, the Socialist Party and Sinn Féin. The electoral system is based on a single transferable vote and those registered to vote can participate in elections on a local, national and European government level.

Dublin is governed by the Dublin City Council (formerly known as the Dublin Corporation) and three county councils: South Dublin County Council, Dun Laoghaire-Rathdown County Council and Fingal County Council. With a staff of 6,200 people, Dublin City Council elects the Lord Mayor of the city, who assumes office in the Mansion House for a year and receives very little public attention or regard. You will be hard pushed to find someone who can name Dublin's current Lord Mayor (it's Paddy Bourke, by the way).

11

Dublin Population Age Breakdown

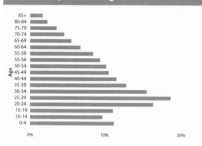

Foreign Population – Nationality

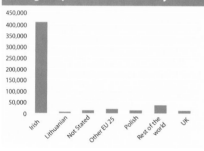

Population

Dublin has developed from a largely mono-cultural society into an international and cosmopolitan capital in the past decade or so. Population structures started to shift as the Celtic Tiger sank its claws deep into the old values. As marriage rates dropped in the 1990s, and divorce was legalised following a referendum in 1995, the cornerstone of Irish society, the family, seemed under threat. Yet, although birth rates reached an all time low in 2005 at 14.8 per thousand of the population and the number of divorces increased from 12.7 per thousand of the population to a rate of 16% from 2003 to 2004, Ireland is neither an isolated case in the European Union nor is it the country which experienced the most drastic changes. In fact, some of the most problematic figures have now either stabilised or actually reversed their trends. Compared to other European countries, Ireland's divorce rate remains low and its marriage rate has now stabilised at 5.2 per thousand. In line with their neighbours, the Irish now marry later, with the average age being 28.4 years for women and 33.1 for men. In 2006, there were 1,053,180 family units in Ireland with a total of 1,486,431 children, including 1,854 families with seven children.

In general, population numbers are on the rise. The 2006 census put the population of County Dublin just shy of 1.2 million, of which Dublin City claimed 506,211. The ratio of male to female is pretty balanced, with slightly more women than men. The average life expectancy is slowly rising too. In 2002, the average age for women was 80.3 years, and 75.1 for men, slightly below EU averages.

National Flag

Vertically disposed and of equal size, the colours green, white and orange on the national flag of Ireland symbolise the truce (white) between the older Gaelic traditions (green) and the supporters of William of Orange (orange). Although the design, which was based on the French flag, was introduced by Thomas Francis Meagher as early as 1848, the tricolour was only acclaimed as the official national flag after the Easter Rising of 1916 (p.5), when it was hoisted above the GPO in Dublin. Holding undisputed sway to date, it is typically flown daily at all military posts and from a number of significant state buildings. It is also used to acknowledge the importance of special events, such as St Patrick's Day, Easter Sunday and Easter Monday (in commemoration of the Rising of 1916), and the National Day of Commemoration of the Anglo-Irish Truce (1921).

The Dublin City flag shows the official coat of arms of the city (three double-towered, blazing castles) on a green background and is not to be confused with the blue version often used at sporting events. The three castles, which were originally three watchtowers, were adapted to bear three battlements, and have been the official symbol of Dublin since the middle ages. Rather than suggesting that Dublin is on fire, the flames leaping from the castles represent the zeal of the citizens in the defence of their city.

Time Zones

Dublin	12:00*
New York	07:00*
London	12:00*
Sydney	21:00
Paris	13:00*
Dubai	15:00
Mumbai	16:30
Toronto	07:00*
Wellington	23:00
Los Angeles	04:00*
Denver	05:00*
Rio de Janeiro	08:00
Perth	19:00
Dallas	06:00*
Mexico City	06:00*
Moscow	15:00*
Munich	13:00*
Prague	13:00*
Rome	13:00*

*daylight savings in effect

Local Time

Ireland is on UCT, Universal Coordinated Time (formerly known as GMT). Daylight savings add one hour from the last Sunday in March (clocks change at 01:00 local standard time) until the last Sunday in October when the clocks go back one hour (clocks change at 02:00 local daylight time). As the clocks go back one hour, evening daylight is reduced to the extent that in the heart of winter, it starts getting dark shortly after 16:30. In the summer, however, the days seem blissfully endless, with the sun only setting at 22:30.

Social & Business Hours

With most shops and businesses opening at 09:00 or 09:30, the city is relatively quiet in the early morning hours (if you discount the many commuters crisscrossing it on their way to work). However, once Dublin has sprung to life, there is no stopping it. As the majority of businesses shut their doors at 17:00, followed by shops at 18:00 or 19:00 (some centres have late night openings on Thursdays until 20:00), the action then moves to the many restaurants, bars, pubs, cafes and finally nightclubs. On a Thursday, Friday and Saturday night, the city is buzzing until well into the early hours. Many clubs charge an admission fee after a certain hour, which can be anywhere between a couple of euros up to a hefty €25, depending on the venue, the time and the DJ spinning the discs.

The days when the city was dead on a Sunday are long over. Many establishments and shops now open their doors to customers on Sunday afternoons and big chains, such as Tesco or Dunnes, have long introduced 24 hour shopping.

Public Holidays

There are nine annual public holidays that commemorate either a special day in the Christian calendar or an event in national history. On a public holiday, the country falls into Sunday mode – pubs, bars, restaurants and cafes are open for business while everything else is closed. Public transport operates on a restricted service. As an employee, the Organisation of Working Time Act 1997, sets out your entitlement to public holidays and determines whether or not you are entitled to paid leave. Bear in mind that although schools are off and many businesses shut down for the day, Good Friday is not officially a public holiday in Ireland.

Public Holidays

New Year's Day	1 Jan
St Patrick's Day	17 Mar
Easter Monday	variable
May Day	first Mon in May
June Bank Holiday	first Mon in Jun
August Bank Holiday	first Mon in Aug
October Bank Holiday	last Mon in Oct
Christmas Day	25 Dec
St Stephen's Day	26 Dec

Time Please!

Many inner-city bars now have a licence to stay open until 02:30 on weekdays and Saturdays. On Sundays, however, last orders are well before midnight, as pubs have to close by 23:30. You'll likely hear the barman shout 'Time please' when it's time to finish up and hit the road. Most cafes are long closed by this time, although caffeine-junkies may get lucky in the Temple Bar area, where the odd establishment serves a delicious hot brew until midnight.

Photography

If you and your SLR are inseparable, you will be happy to hear that it is perfectly acceptable to follow your urge to hunt down the perfect shot while in Dublin. Most sights permit photography and the few that don't (such as Dublin Castle) display an array of signs to make sure that no mistakes are made. Unless they believe it steals their soul, people are usually more than willing to pose for you, as long as you ask for their permission first. Outside of Dublin though, be warned that people are very much aware of the fact that picturesque settings and old horse-drawn carriages sell on for big bucks and may expect a cut!

13

Climate

They say that you can experience all the different nuances of Irish weather in a day and fortunate or not, this is no exaggeration. The weather is variable throughout the year, which means that even in Dublin, one of the driest counties, you can expect rain 185 days in an average year (732.7mm of rain in total). Like the Eskimos have many words for snow, the Irish have an extended vocabulary for the wet stuff that constantly puts a dampener on their day. Indeed, there are many things that the rain does in Ireland, but it rarely just 'falls'. Sometimes it 'spits', 'pours', 'lashes', 'drizzles', 'teems' or 'buckets it down'. And quite often, it is not really rain at all but 'mizzle', that soft drizzle that while visible, barely seems to have any effect when you pass through. This is what the Irish will often cheerfully refer to as 'a fine Irish mist' if you happen to complain that it is raining.

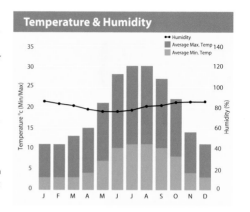

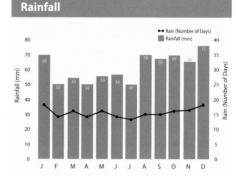

While it is rare you get soaked to the skin, it's best to carry a brolly at all times – a sturdy one, mind you. After a particularly turbulent spell, you'll see the remains of umbrellas that have become the victims of strong coastal winds all over the city.

On a more positive note, the good news is that Ireland should be a lot colder. The North Atlantic drift and the Gulf Stream keeps the climate a lot milder than its mere geographical location would dictate. With temperatures ranging from 2.5°C (January) to 18.9°C (July) in an average year, Ireland never really experiences any real heat or extreme cold. Yet, when the sun does come out and leads to a scorcher, the Irish certainly know how to appreciate it. Although June often has a good share of dry spells, a day when the sun is splitting the skies in Ireland is as predictable as Dublin buses – not very, in other words.

This doesn't deter residents from engaging in amateur predictions or lengthy discussions though. Even before climate change made the weather the talk of the town around the globe, the moods of the heavens were already a favourite topic with the locals here. And who would blame them, where else do you get a 'lá breá báistiúil' – 'a fine, rainy day?'

Flora & Fauna

Considering its size, Ireland has a relatively wide diversity of habitats, ranging from native woodland and grassland to coastal and freshwater. However, as a result of human activity, some are now better represented than others. Centuries of

Need Some Direction?

The *Explorer Mini Maps* pack a whole city into your pocket and once unfolded are excellent navigational tools for exploring. Not only are they handy in size, with detailed information on the sights and sounds of the city, but also their fabulously affordable price mean they won't make a dent in your holiday fund. Wherever your travels take you, from the Middle East to Europe and beyond, grab a mini map and you'll never have to ask for directions.

14

Enjoying the greenery

deforestation have taken their toll on Ireland's woodland areas, diminishing them almost beyond recognition. In April 2002, the National Biodiversity Plan (legislated by the Wildlife Acts) was launched in order to ensure the conservation of, as well as regulate the sustainable use of, Ireland's biological treasures, including Europe's cleanest rivers and some of the world's most sensitive habitats.

It is largely due to biogeographical factors that Ireland boasts habitats of particular scarcity. Its exposed location at the western fringe of Europe provides excellent conditions for a windy climate. Gale-force winds have limited the growth of trees in certain areas, creating soft coastal plains ideal for grazing and machair systems. The latter, a patchwork of sandy calcareous dunes, grassland and wetland, have been listed in the EU Habitats Directive as 'priority habitats', providing a home for three Red Data Book bird species. Ireland's marine life, although repeatedly under threat from oil spillages, is characterised by a great diversity of plants and animals, with spectator favourites such as seals and dolphins spotted feeding in inshore waters. Radioactive pollution has taken its toll on the Irish Sea too, limiting marine life in the waters around Dublin Bay. Wildlife in the area has been threatened by urban sprawl and intense traffic congestion, and many natural habitats have been lost. Except for the coastal areas, nature in Dublin is limited for the most part to its parks and designated refuges. Among the havens for nature are Phoenix Park, Rockabill Island (with its protected Roseate Tern) and almost 4,000 acres of green zone (including parks and protected zones) in south county Dublin.

The National Botanical Gardens (www.botanicgardens.ie) estimate that 120 of Ireland's modest 850 native flowering plants are under threat today. The rarest species are protected under the 1999 Flora Protection Order.

Environmental Issues

Ireland's traditional dependence on agriculture and its late industrialisation meant that its environment remained relatively unspoilt until well into the 20th century. By the time modern industry took a foothold and urban sprawl emerged, the Irish were able to exercise at least some damage control based on the experiences of their European neighbours. Low population density and a climate that tends to wash everything away facilitated their efforts, as did the fact that the predominant industries to gain ground were considered 'clean', but the task was no less daunting. Despite great measures, a number of Irish native plants remain under threat today, with at least six species on the brink of extinction.

Successive governments have made it their objective to protect the Irish environment, working closely with the EU in strategies like the Wild Bird Directive and the Habitat Directive. Every year, the Department of Environment, Heritage and Local Government (www.environ.ie) and the EPA (Environmental Protection Agency, www.epa.ie) jointly host the conference 'Environment Ireland', creating a platform for environmental organisations to discuss the most pressing issues.

15

Do Something
If you want to do more to help the environment than just recycle your old newspapers, you could join an environmental group as a volunteer. See p.237 in the Activities chapter for a list of organisations.

In practical terms, however, the difficult task of conserving Ireland's natural gems rests with the Department of Arts, Heritage, Gaeltacht and the Islands, which acts within the legal framework provided by EU and Irish law.

James Joyce's 'dear, dirty Dublin' itself is refreshingly clean as far as European capitals go. Rather than choking with air pollution or drowning in waste, Dublin's biggest problem is the lack of space. Instead of playfully curling along the mouth of the Liffey, the city is bursting at the seams and spilling over into neighbouring counties. As house prices and availability drive Dubliners further afield, its residents are becoming increasingly dependent on their own set of wheels (thanks to a very lacking transport system), with the result that Dublin is now riddled with congestion.

While the continuing growth raises environmental concerns, Dublin has acted the vanguard in a number of green initiatives, proving to the prophets of doom that change is not always bad – even if you are a smoker (it's outdoors only these days) and don't like paying €0.15 for a plastic bag (it's best to remember to bring your own!). Addressing an increase in waste, the old flat rate system was replaced by a new scheme in 2005, whereby residents are charged according to the amount of waste they produce (for instance, you will be charged less if your bin is emptied every second week, rather than every week). The idea as such was received positively, but the costs involved still give Dubliners a headache. While they don't mind doing their bit for the environment, they are certainly getting tired of having to empty out their pockets every time they do so.

Dublin Zoo

Dublin Explorer 1st Edition

Culture

They used to say that Dublin 'carries its soul on its sleeve'. However, in recent years the capital has undergone such staggering change that it is only once you have scratched away at its shiny new surface that you reveal the true culture, identity and history that makes the city. Although Dublin's transformation has been severe, with changes implemented on many levels and some of the foundations of Irish society rocked to the core, the city has retained its essence. And Dubliners, despite their newfound wealth, are still Dubs with their 'howaya's' and their 'what's da storeeey's'.

With colourful collages of adjectives, many outsiders have tried to paint a picture of the elusive nature of a Dubliner, often losing themselves in stereotypes and all too simplistic generalisations. However, since an attempt to unravel Dublin, or indeed Irish culture, in its complexity would go well beyond the scope of a modest few paragraphs, the best thing to do is highlight some of the cornerstones of Irish culture. Deeply rooted in Catholicism, Irish society centres on the family, with marriage and fertility traditionally high. While previously, Irish men were often accused that they 'couldn't boil an egg between them', gender strictures have loosened in the course of the past few decades, with many women juggling a career as well as a family. Two incomes are often as much of an economic necessity as a personal choice. Although wealth creation is a driving force of Irish society now, it remains less of a priority than in other nations. The Irish as individuals regularly surpass their western European neighbours in their willingness to part with a considerable proportion of their earnings for a charitable cause.

As much as generosity is considered a desirable virtue, so is politeness. Not only will you hear Dubliners thank their bus driver after finally delivering them to their destination an hour late, but they will thank them 'a mil'. Also, if you carelessly bump into someone, you can be sure that they will say sorry before you have had a chance to figure out what has happened.

Social life and the infamous pub culture are other defining aspects. Since the weather imposes certain restrictions on leisure activities, there is a long tradition of providing one's own entertainment, and music, dance, literature and the performing arts are omnipresent. You won't struggle to find a busker who can strike the right note in Dublin, and finding a worthy show or gig is effortless, unless there's a sporting interference. Dubliners are keen sports enthusiasts, whether they're getting grubby on the field or cheering their team on from afar. And while you certainly would not want to expose a young child to the range of colloquialisms used on such occasions, you can learn a lot about Irish culture by listening to the highly articulate local lingo. Don't take it all too seriously, though. Renowned for having a good sense of humour, Dubs certainly like to have a 'bita *craic*'.

How Now Brown Cow
Even within Dublin, there is a distinct difference between accents. Check out www.overheardin dublin.com for a taste of the local vernacular.

Language

Other options **Language Schools** p.242

It may not have been their native tongue, but the Irish have certainly made English their own – and many of them could talk for Ireland any day. Renowned for their eloquence (the gift of the gab), the Irish are confident orators; always carrying a good few stories up their sleeves. While this certainly adds to their charm and their reputation for being great company, their love of a good joke and their readiness to be at the receiving end all but makes them.

The English spoken in Ireland today is known as Hiberno English. The Irish language, (gaeilge) despite all the government's efforts to revive it, has been marginalised in the capital, but lives on in the way Dubliners speak English. It has entwined itself into the grammar, pronunciation and vocabulary of the new national tongue, moulding

17

Basic Irish Slang

Slang	Meaning
Sláinte!	Cheers!
Gas	Funny
Grand	Good
He is after leaving	He has just left
Well	Hello
How's it going?	How are you?
What's da storeey?	How are you?
I'm only messin' wit ya	I am only teasing you
eejit	idiot
wet the tea	make tea
Gardaí	Police
jacks	toilet
What are you like?	Used to express surprise in response to something that's been said or done
Your wan	Used to refer to any female
Brutal	Very bad

English into a different shape. Phrases like 'she is after going out' (she has just gone out) are as typical as the avoidance of simple monosyllabic 'yes' and 'no' answers.

For a relatively small country, Ireland – thanks to Irish – also has more than its fair share of regional accents and dictionary loads of slang expressions and colloquial sayings that will leave other native English speakers utterly confused, and barely give non-native speakers a chance. Ireland has a massive literary and cultural surplus. There is hardly another nation of similar size with more internationally successful writers, poets or comedians to its name, and all in the relatively short period in which it adopted English as a national tongue. James Joyce still has scholars puzzled with his unique stream-of-consciousness work Ulysses, and works by Oscar Wilde, Seamus Heaney, Patrick Kavanagh and W.B. Yeats, to name but a few, have all made their mark.

While Irish, by constitution, is the first official language of Ireland, it only really survives as a mother tongue in Gaeltacht areas (Irish-speaking areas), most of which are located in the west of Ireland. While the 2006 census put the number of Irish speakers at 1,656,790 (41.9% of the total population), one fourth of this total stated that they never speak it outside the educational system, with just 53,471 using it on a daily basis for private and business needs. However, as Dublin has undergone major changes in the past decade, many people now feel the need to return to their roots and embrace all things traditional. And the Irish language has jumped on the bandwagon. An increasing number of parents now send their children to all-Irish primary and secondary schools, and Irish language radio (Raidió na Gaeltachta), television (TG4) and a growing number of Irish language books and films, as well as the odd Irish-Irish pub, are all doing their bit to improve things. Irish is also the 21st working language of the EU, which is creating more Irish language jobs, and most importantly, raising the native tongue's profile internationally.

Race Relations

Although the Irish have set sail for foreign lands for centuries and have happily mingled with other cultures, they are fairly new to the idea of encountering a whole mix of nationalities on home turf. In the wake of the Celtic Tiger, not only tourists have flocked across the Irish Sea. Almost overnight, Ireland, (and Dublin in particular) became home to thousands of economic, humanitarian and political refugees. Overwhelmed and swamped with foreign faces, the country renowned for being welcoming and friendly, saw its first racial attacks. In response to this the Garda Síochana set up a Racial and Intercultural office, located in Harcourt Square, which aims to advise, monitor and coordinate police activity around racial, ethnic, religious and cultural diversity in Ireland (www.garda.ie/angarda/racial.html, 01 666 3150). It will certainly take time to adjust to this new situation, but while cynics are quick to point out the irony in the Irish developing a race-relation problem, many of the new groups have already started to assimilate into Irish society, at the forefront of which are the Poles, who currently form the biggest foreign community in Dublin.

The Liffey

Religion

Religious Traditions
Churches of various styles and types are dotted all over Ireland, and there are often small grottos dedicated to the Virgin Mary in the outskirts of villages. You'll often see people crossing themselves when passing a church, and even those who no longer actively practise their faith still believe in the symbolism of the cross as well as having a little holy water font by the front door.

The right of Irish citizens to religious liberty is manifested in Article 44 of the Irish constitution, Bunreacht na hÉireann, including the freedom to practice any religion as well as the freedom of conscience. Consequently, an Irish citizen cannot be discriminated against on the grounds of religion unless in an effort to protect public order or morality. The state is obliged to refrain from endowing or favouring any religion, and the same aid has to be granted to schools of different denominations. Roman Catholics accounted for roughly 88% of the population in 2002. The figures speak volumes about the identities the majority of Irish citizens assume, but they bear little evidence to the changing nature of religious conviction in Ireland.

Dublin's move towards a cosmopolitan European capital has come hand-in-hand with a departure from traditional views often associated with the Catholic Church. Feeling that the church has missed the bandwagon to the 21st century in key issues such as divorce, contraception or homosexuality, many Dubliners have distanced themselves from everything it represents. The results are plummeting church attendances and an increase in the number of purely nominal Christians. The last straw for many was the series of well-publicised scandals relating to child abuse and embezzlement that shook the foundations of the Irish religious establishments in the 1990s and aroused a sense of betrayal in many followers. While some have turned their backs on the institutional side of things and have started to view religion as a spiritual quest from within, others have grown so disillusioned that they have completely drifted away. Today, a strong Catholic Polish community joins those still firmly devoted to the church and Christian values in regular attendance at church services.

Other denominations in Ireland include the Church of Ireland (followed by 3% of the population in 2002), Presbyterians (0.5%) and Methodists (0.25%). Smaller minorities, such as Jews and Muslims make up the rest.

Outside of Ireland, the Irish church retains its strong missionary outreach with around 3,000 priests, brothers and nuns following their vocation in over 90 countries.

Places of Worship

Christ Church Cathedral	Christchurch Place	Dublin 8	01 677 8099	Church of Ireland
ChristChurch Presbyterian	Rathgar Road	Dublin 6	01 497 6985	Presbyterian
Dublin Jewish Progressive Congregation, Knessett Orach Chayim	7 Leicester Road	Dublin 6	01 490 7605	Liberal/ Progressive
Dublin Machzikei Hadass Congregation	Rathmore Villas, Rear of 77 Terenure Road North	Dublin 6	01 493 8991	Ashkenazi Orthodox
Dublin Mosque	South Circular Road	Dublin 8	01 453 3242	Islam
Dublin Terenure Hebrew Congregation	Rathfarnham Road	Dublin 6	01 497 2351	Ashkenazi Orthodox
Dun Laoghaire Evangelical Church	Lower Glenageary Road	Dun Laoghaire	01 280 5099	Evangelical
Dundrum Methodist Church	Ballinteer Road	Dundrum	01 295 1940	Methodist
Greek Orthodox Church of the Annunciation	46 Arbour Hill	Dublin 7	01 677 9020	Orthodox
Romanian Orthodox Church – Exaltation of the Holy Cross	Christ Church, Leeson Park	Dublin 4	087 614 8140	Orthodox
Saint Patrick's Cathedral	Saint Patrick's Close	Dublin 8	01 475 4817	Roman Catholic
St Bartholomew's with Christ Church, Leeson Park	Clyde Rd & Elgin Road	Dublin 4	01 668 8522	Church of Ireland
St Columcille	Dublin Airport	Dublin 9	01 840 7277	Roman Catholic
St Mark's Family Worship Centre	42a Pearse Street	Dublin 2	01 671 4276	Pentecostal
St Mary's	Main Street	Tallaght	01 404 8188	Roman Catholic
St Mary's Pro Cathedral	Marlborough Street	Dublin 1	01 874 5441	Roman Catholic
St Matthias' Church	Church Road, Ballybrack	Killiney	01 285 6180	Church of Ireland
St Michael's	Marine Road	Dun Laoghaire	01 280 4969	Roman Catholic
St Patrick's Cathedral	St Patrick's Close	Dublin 8	01 475 4817	Church of Ireland
St Vincent de Paul	Griffith Avenue	Dublin 9	01 833 2772	Roman Catholic
Swords Baptist Church	Jugback Lane	Swords	01 808 5313	Baptist

19

National Dress

It has travelled the world – the green dress adorned with intricate embroidery, a type of cloak attached to its shoulders and worn in combination with dancing pumps and white socks. Yet, contrary to the belief of many non-nationals, this attire is not the national dress of Ireland but rather traditional Irish dancing wear. In fact, nobody seems quite sure whether or not a national dress exists! The Museum of Decorative Arts and History at Collins Barracks (see p.190) has put an end to some of the mystery with its exhibition 'The way we wore: 300 years of Irish clothing and jewellery', while The National Museum of Ireland on Kildare Street (see p.190) traces the development of Irish civilisation to its very beginnings, offering an insight into different Irish clothing styles throughout history.

Food & Drink

Other options **Eating Out** p.336

It's Your Round
One major faux pas when out in a pub is not getting your round in, but readily accepting other people buying drinks for you. Being such a generous lot, the Irish don't appreciate tightfistedness. While they will make great allowances for anyone in financial difficulties, they don't stand for anyone taking advantage of the round system. A new round starts when the first person has finished their pint so if you're a lightweight, you may be well advised to exclude yourself. Apart from being out of pocket, you may end up with a fleet of pints lined up in front of you, and that's just a blatant waste!

Ireland is blessed with an array of high-quality ingredients, including a wealth of dairy products, seafood and meat, the standard of which the rest of Europe cannot really compete with. The island has some of the purest fresh water rivers and, in addition to some of the best wild trout and salmon, it harbours excellent mussel and trout farms. However, while products like Kerrygold's finest butter are gracing dinner tables around the globe, Irish cuisine has a bad name. In the past chefs and homesteads were seen to be almost consciously cooking their glorious local produce 'to death', and the common joke amongst cynics was 'Irish food is great – until it's cooked'.

Today however, Irish cuisine has witnessed something of a revival and has taken its fate into its own hands, and in a new direction. New Irish Cuisine, quite contrary to its name, describes a return to the old recipes, applied with the best ingredients and simple cooking techniques (as well as adequate cooking times). While the flavours of the world have made their mark in some of the dishes, the age-old combination of meat, veg and spuds still ranks high on the list of dinner favourites. Supermarkets (see p.296) stock almost anything a globalised soul could desire. Aldi and Lidl are sprouting up all over the city and filling Irish households with German brand names while delicatessens and specialist food stores cater to everything else (see p.297).

A Drinking Culture

If liquid food was any more popular, the Irish would be in all sorts of trouble. And although *Ceol agus Craic* (music and fun) is no longer the theme of most establishments, the pub remains the hub of social life. With over a thousand pubs scattered all over Dublin, there is more than one for every occasion, from the quiet local down the road to the more lively weekend destination.

While you won't attract attention enjoying a pint at the bar by yourself, you will rarely be alone for long unless you are socially awkward. The Irish are a friendly bunch and will happily adopt a stranger on a night out, and every local pub has its share of flat-capped regulars who will be more than pleased to give you the ins and outs of how the city has changed in the past few decades. Pubs remain popular even with the young crowd, but money and changing times have brought about the establishment of modern bars and high-end night clubs that will be packed to the gills on weekends. A drink is no such thing in Ireland if it isn't alcoholic (it's a beverage then) and you will find people staring at you in pure disbelief if you ask them for water in a pub or bar. Sometimes, they may simply refuse (these are people who even put whiskey in their coffee, after all!) but stick with it and they'll come round eventually. The Irish like their beer and Irish men, unlike their continental friends, would rather be seen dead than caught drinking a half pint (they will pour it into their pint glass instead). Popular brews include Guinness, Smithwicks and Bulmers, as well as international brands such as Becks or Bud. Some establishments, such as The Porterhouse Central (see p.377) or Messers Maguire (01 670 5777) offer house brews at a reduced price. *Uisce beatha*, 'the water of life' or whiskey, is also considered a national drink, yet in contrast to its Scottish counterpart, it is not only spelt differently but is distilled three times.

Sitting Pretty
Finding seats in city centre restaurants can be a bit of a challenge from 21:00 onwards on a Friday or Saturday night, so if you're planning on a big night out or have a group in tow, it's best to get there early.

Favourite Dishes

The Irish and their potatoes are a story of their own. Potatoes are eaten and cooked in countless ways in Ireland and every mother can list the merits of the different local varieties – be they Wexford's new potatoes or Kerr's Pinks. Spuds appear on the Irish dinner table in all sorts of shapes and forms – boiled, roasted, mashed, or fried as chips, hash browns or croquettes; made into potato bread, champ (mashed potatoes with scallions and melted butter), colcannon (champ with cabbage and leeks) or Dublin's favourite meat and potato dish, coddle. Often, a meal is not complete without at least two kinds of potatoes, so expect to get mash with your chips.

While some dishes have been kept alive purely thanks to the tourism industry, others have been adapted to suit everyday life. While a full Irish breakfast may be on the menu in an Irish guesthouse every day of the week, you will struggle to find many Dubliners who savour it with such regularity. Come Sunday morning though and the rashers, eggs, sausages, tomatoes and black and white pudding will likely make an appearance on most breakfast tables, and may even be eaten as an evening meal during the week. Similarly, it's rare to find a household not cooking up the comforting Sunday roast for lunch, the leftovers of which are often reheated in new formations for meals the next day.

Home baking is another Irish specialty and you'll find expatriates around the globe gloomily reminiscing about soda or potato bread and those deliciously fluffy and varied scones (note that in Ireland, scone rhymes with stone). Barm brack (fruit cake associated with Halloween) and Christmas pudding and Christmas cake are all fixtures on the annual culinary calendar.

Drinking for Ireland

21

In Emergency

It always pays to be prepared in case disaster strikes. Luckily, in Ireland, you only have to remember two numbers to cover all eventualities. Call 999 or 112 (toll free) for any type of emergency assistance and you will be connected to the relevant service. Services include the police (Gardaí), fire, ambulance, lifeboat and coastguard. Take the time to locate your closest emergency hospital and 24-hour Garda station when you move to a new area, as this may save you precious time when it is most needed. If you lose your passport, contact your local embassy immediately (see p.24), as well as your nearest police station.

Emergency Numbers	
Anne's Lane Dental Centre	01 671 8581
Baggot Street Hospital	01 668 1577
Confidential Line Freephone	1800 666 111
Dame House Dental Surgery	01 679 9256
Garda Station, Dublin Airport	01 666 4950
Garda Station, Pearse Street	01 666 9000
Hickey's Pharmacies	01 873 1077
Mater Misericordiae Hospital	01 830 1122
Rape Crises Centre	1800 778 888
Samaritans	1850 609 090
Senior Helpline	1850 440 444
St James Late Night Pharmacy	01 473 4022
St James's Hospital	01 453 7941
Walsh's Late Night Pharmacy	01 492 3769
Women's Aid	1800 341 900
Women's Refuge & Helpline	01 496 1002

Electricity

Electricity runs on 220 volts AC, with sockets fitting into the same three-pin plugs as in the UK. Adapters are available at the airport, in electrical shops and wherever travel equipment is for sale.

Post

The General Post Office, a key location in the 1916 Easter Rising, is located on O'Connell Street and is open for business from 08:00 to 20:00 Monday to Saturday (most other branches close at 17:30). The national postal service is largely reliable and sufficient and you will never have to look too hard to find a post box. Usually green in colour, they mostly come with two signature slots: 'Dublin Only' and 'All Other Places'.

Drinking Water

The Office of Environmental Enforcement regularly publishes reports on the quality of drinking water in Ireland based on a set of 48 standards. In 2005, 96.7% of the public water supplied by sanitary authorities complied with these standards.

Children

The Irish attitude towards the young and restless resembles that of Southern Europe. Children are welcome at social events, with most places going all out to cater for them, and it's usually not too big a deal if they make a bit of noise either.

The majority of restaurants and cafes supply high chairs and children's menus and most will happily provide you with hot water to heat up a bottle. While there is still a general lack of public amenities in the city, some of the newer establishments have finally responded to the need for baby changing facilities. Children under 5 years travel free on public transport, but beware if you are taking a pram, as only the newer, wheelchair friendly buses provide easy access.

Family tickets help to keep the costs down at attractions, such as interactive museums, sports facilities, workshops or the zoo. And the numerous parks and playgrounds around the city, as well as the local beaches, provide plenty of free entertainment for youngsters as soon as they can walk; all you need is the weather on your side. Dublin Tourism regularly brings out a brochure with suggestions for new activities in and around Dublin and many newspapers (especially the Sunday papers) have a special family section.

Most hotels and shopping malls provide childcare facilities, often including babysitting services and kids' clubs. Professional childcare agencies can arrange nannies, babysitters or childminders for a fee. Check out South County Dublin Childcare

Dry Cleaners p.74
Divorce Lawyers p.108

Written by residents, these unique guidebooks are packed with insider info, from arriving in a new destination to making it your home and everything in between.

Explorer Residents' Guides
We Know Where You Live

Embassies & Consulates

Name	Phone	Map	
Argentina	01 269 1546	421 E1	281
Australia	01 664 5300	416 C3	304
Austria	01 269 4577	421 E1	284
Belgium	01 205 7100	417 E4	274
Brazil	01 475 6000	416 B3	292
Britain	01 205 3700	417 E4	273
Bulgaria	01 660 3293	416 C4	299
Canada	01 234 4000	416 B3	289
China	01 260 1119	421 E1	278
Croatia	01 476 7181	429 F2	294
Cuba	01 475 0899	416 B4	291
Czech Republic	01 668 1135	417 D3	306
Denmark	01 475 6404	416 B3	293
Finland	01 478 1344	430 A2	295
France	01 260 1666	421 E1	279
Germany	01 269 3011	421 F2	282
Greece	01 676 7254	416 C3	309
Hungary	01 661 2902	416 C3	301
India	01 496 6792	416 C4	297
Iran	01 288 0252	422 A3	287
Israel	01 230 9400	417 D4	276
Italy	01 660 1744	417 D3	298
Japan	01 202 8300	421 F1	272
Mexico	01 260 0699	421 E1	277
Morocco	01 660 9449	417 D4	300
Norway	01 662 1800	416 C3	303
Pakistan	01 261 3032	421 E1	280
Poland	01 283 0855	421 E1	285
Portugal	01 289 4416	na	
Romania	01 668 1085	431 E4	305
Russia	01 492 2048	420 A2	296
Slovenia	01 670 5240	416 B2	308
South Africa	01 661 5553	416 B3	302
Spain	01 283 9900	421 F1	286
Sweden	01 474 4400	416 B2	290
Switzerland	01 218 6382	421 E1	275
The Netherlands	01 269 3444	421 F1	283
USA	01 668 8777	417 D4	307

(www.southdublinchildcare.ie), the babysitting club Mindersfinders (www.minderfinders.ie), Cocoon Childcare (www.cocoonchildcare.ie), or Nanny Solutions (www.nannysolutions.com) for details. While there are numerous parents groups in Dublin, Parent Plus, a registered charity under the auspices of the Mater Hospital, is a good address if you need professional support (086 172 1902, www.parentsplus.ie).

Women

Dublin is a city in which most people keep to themselves and you're not going to be harassed going about your business. However, as in any major city, keep your wits about you. Be streetwise, especially at night and on dark winter evenings, and don't go wandering down dark alleyways or avenues alone. Be aware of the areas that are reputed to be less salubrious and either avoid them or be on your guard. It's advisable to keep valuables, including mobile phones and iPods, out of sight. A good tip is to always give the impression that you know where you're going – so keep those maps hidden unless absolutely necessary.

Travelling on public transport or in a taxi is usually safe at any time of the day, but you may want to stay downstairs on late-night services such as the Nitelink – not only will you be more comfortable, but you may also avoid the more unpleasant signs of an all too successful Saturday night out.

You can wear whatever you like in Dublin and you'll see all sorts of wild outfits going around, but like anywhere, the more skin you show, the more attention you'll attract, harmless or not.

People With Disabilities

According to the 2002 Census by the Statistical Office Ireland, the number of people with disabilities in Dublin city and county is 90,867, with the majority aged 60 or over. Following the Special Olympics World Games which Dublin hosted in 2003 (see p.253), the government recognised that the needs of this large group of people had not been adequately addressed and approved the first Irish National Disability Survey to be carried out after the next Census. In September 2006, the survey, based on a questionnaire covering all age groups and including comprehensive sections on aids and impairments, was carried out. While the results are due for publication in October/November 2007 (see www.cso.ie), the recognition of the necessity for such a survey is a milestone in itself. For the first time, service providers and policymakers will have the necessary data to make informed decisions on improvements.

Although many restaurants, hotels and attractions now cater to people with disabilities, Dublin is by no means as well adapted as it could be. However, the city has significantly developed its accessibility over the past number of years. Dublin Bus operates wheelchair accessible buses on an increasing number of routes and the majority of Dart stations are now equipped with ramps or lifts. While each Enterprise rail service has a customer services attendant on hand, Iarnród Éireann's Mobility Impaired Liaison Office has been created especially to accommodate any mobility-impaired passengers requiring further assistance. Contact them at least 24 hours before your journey (1850 366 222, www.iarnrodeireann.ie). Guide dogs are welcome on all rail services.

Parking can still prove difficult, although newer outlets usually reserve spots for challenged drivers near the entrance to the main shopping area.

For tourists with special needs, Fáilte Ireland has developed an accommodation rating scheme, featuring four categories including access for wheelchairs and access for ambulant people incapable of climbing stairs, see www.visitdublin.com/disabled for more. All state airports are obliged to provide facilities for people with special needs, and Dublin airport strives to continually update its services. For further information, refer to www.dublinairport.ie. See also schools (p.150), and activities(p.293).

Dress

Hey Smarty Pants ◄
If you're going to a wedding or religious service, you should dress respectfully (at least until the reception where you can feel free to drink a skinful and dance with your tie around your head). If you're unsure about what constitutes appropriate dress, it's always better to check ahead to avoid any embarrassment.

It is really only the weather that imposes restrictions on what you can and can't wear in Ireland. That said, on a Saturday night, short mini-skirts and halter-necks are common, irrespective of conditions. You may also be fooled into believing that the summer has arrived just because the sun is shining, but stick your nose out and check for that cold breeze before you head out in just a T-shirt. Stock up on rain gear and keep an umbrella handy throughout the year.

Smart-casual is usually the look for company executives and for top-end restaurants. Some clubs and bars have dress codes (see p.368), though rumour has it that it's all down to the bouncer on the night. However, if you're wearing runners (trainers), don't be surprised if you're refused entry to some of the classier establishments. In general, people tend to dress up before hitting the town on a Saturday night and while the guys usually keep it down to jeans and a shirt, the girls can be seen in all sorts of fashionable attire, whether its appropriate for the weather conditions or not.

Dos & Don'ts

Drink-driving, though sadly still practised by some, is no minor offence in Ireland and the law comes down heavily on those who are found intoxicated behind the wheel. You can be stopped and breathalysed at any point in time, as alcohol testing is now mandatory. The Road Traffic Bill 2006 highlights disqualification from driving as the sanction to be expected when convicted for drink driving, with the period varying according to the alcohol levels detected. You may face a hefty fine or even a prison sentence. Driving while holding a mobile phone is also an offence.

While there is no national legislation prohibiting drinking in public, local authority areas are entitled to pass by-laws to that effect. To avoid a fine, it is recommended that you check before you are caught in the act. If you are perceived to be in a state in which you could be of harm to yourself or others, you are liable for a €127 fine.

The minimum legal drinking age is 18. It is illegal to buy alcohol for a minor and it is illegal for them to be on a premises that sells alcohol during extended hours (exceptions apply). One thing that will not get you into trouble with the law but with fellow Dubliners, is not playing according to the rules of the round system. An Irish saying goes: 'It's impossible for two men to go to a pub for one drink.' If somebody buys you a drink, you are expected to get the next one in.

In March 2004, the Irish government introduced a ban on smoking in the workplace, including office blocks, pubs/bars, restaurants and company vehicles. While certain places, such as hotels, maternity homes and prisons, are exempt from this rule, all employers have the right to enforce the ban if they wish. If you want to smoke, you'll need to check out the outdoor smoking areas.

Crime & Safety

Other options **In Emergency** p.22

Other options **In Emergency** p.22

Are You A Bad Driver?
Check how many
penalty points you're
likely to rack up for
various offences by
visiting the website of
the Department of
Transport
(www.transport.ie).

Traffic Accidents & Violations

The penalty point system for driving offences was introduced on 31 October 2002 under the Road Traffic Act. Identifying 36 offences, including careless driving, tailgating, speeding and drink driving. The system aimed to improve road safety and driver behaviour.

Road fatalities in Ireland have decreased as a result, but figures in Ireland are still higher than the EU average with a recorded 368 deaths in 2006.

The system is pretty straightforward. A point is essentially an official reprimand on your driving licence, which states that you have committed a driving offence. Every point may raise your insurance, but if you accumulate twelve of them within a period of three years, you face disqualification from driving for six months.

On 3 April, 2006, the complete Fixed Charge Penalty System (FCPS) came into operation, computerising a previously manual payment system. It also links the Garda pulse system to the courts.

When involved in an accident in which somebody is injured or even killed, contact the Gardaí immediately. Unless you plead guilty in advance, you will be heard in the Circuit Court before a judge and jury.

Getting Arrested

In the majority of cases, an arrest is on foot of a warrant, with the Criminal Law Act 1997 outlining the conditions under which a person can be arrested without a warrant. Such instances include when an arrestable offence has been or is about to be committed and an officer has reasonable cause to suspect a certain individual to be guilty of the offence.

Unless you are arrested under Section 30 of the Offences Against the State Act the Gardaí is obliged to inform you about your offence. You cannot be arrested simply because the Gardaí needs your assistance with their inquiries and if you voluntarily help the Gardaí at one of their stations, you must be informed that you can leave at any point in time and can only be prohibited from doing so with an arrest. You must also be immediately informed that you are entitled to consult a solicitor as well as to notify another person that you are in custody. If you are a minor (under 18 years of age), you must be told that your parent or guardian has been informed and asked to come to the station.

Once arrested and charged, you are on remand, meaning that the District Court will decide whether you will be released on bail or detained in custody before your trial. Refer to criminal law, such as the Criminal Justice (Legal Aid) Act (1962), with questions on maximum detention and conditions for bail. The Irish Statue Book is available online at www.irishstatutebook.ie.

Victims Of Crime

Victims play a significant role in the criminal justice system and their position is continually under review (refer to the Department of Justice, Equality and Law Reform for the most recent developments).

In 2005, the Commission for the Support of Victims was established with a three year remit to fund organisations supporting those affected by criminal activity as well as creating a framework for future services directed at victims. Within the first year, €1.5 million was allocated in funds. Victims of crime should contact the National Helpline (1850 211 407, www.crimevictimshelpline.ie). They're available from 10:00 to 17:00 Monday to Friday and from 14:00 to 16:00 on Saturday (if you leave a message after hours, they'll contact you as soon as possible). The helpline is run by trained volunteers and is independent from the Garda Síochána. All calls are confidential.

Prison Time

In 2005, 8,686 people were sentenced to prison, the majority for violent offences against a person or property; most of them were to serve more than one year in the establishment closest to their home (to facilitate contact with their families). The average yearly costs per offender amounted to €90,900.

There are 14 prisons and places of detention in Ireland, 11 of which are closed institutions with internal and perimeter security. Section 35 of the Prison Acts outlines the prison rules, including admission, registration and visiting rights. See www.citizensinformation.ie for details of prisoner's rights.

Prison safety is a priority, especially in the wake of incidences related to overcrowding in Mountjoy. In early summer 2007, an inmate was stabbed to death on a night when there were 568 offenders in a jail with a bed capacity of just 454. Aware of the alarming conditions at Mountjoy, a 150 acre site was purchased at Thornton Hall in the hope of creating new facilities. The Irish Prison Service in Clondalkin (01 461 6000, www.irishprisons.ie) is in charge of prison safety and works on rehabilitation and creating efficient organisation and management structures.

Police

The national police force of Ireland, the Garda Síochána (literally 'The Guardians of the Peace'), was formed following the foundation of the Irish Free State. It has its headquarters in Phoenix Park. With a personnel strength of 12,265 today, the Gardaí exercises all police functions from state security to prosecuting any type of criminal offence. There are 1,700 detectives in civilian attire and over a thousand civilian support staff.

Uniformed offers are traditionally unarmed and are only equipped with a wooden truncheon. Detectives, however, carry firearms. A male officer is called a garda, a female officer a ban garda and a group of officers is referred to as the gardaí.

Many gardaí stations operate 24 hours a day and can be called in all circumstances involving criminal activity. For a list of stations in the Dublin Metropolitan Area, please check the section on emergencies.

Lost/Stolen Property

As anywhere, the police should be notified immediately if any kind of crime occurs. Call emergency services or seek assistance at any of the Garda Síochána stations. If you have lost important travel documents, you also need to inform the police and file a report, before contacting your embassy for replacements. If your credit card is lost or stolen, report it immediately to prevent the new 'owner' going on a massive spending spree on your account. See p.44.

Lost/Stolen Property	
Airport Police Station	01 814 4481
Busáras	01 836 6111
Dublin Bus	01 873 4222

City Information

There are plenty of tourist information centres scattered all over Ireland, with Dublin itself claiming its fair share of them. Conveniently located at points of entry (the airport, the ferry terminal, the heart of the city), they are easily spotted and usually filled with friendly staff who will go out of their way to help you with anything from accommodation to domestic travel.

The new main inner city tourism office is located in a beautifully restored church, formerly known as St Andrew's, in Suffolk Street (close to Grafton Street). While you wait

---

Was It Good For You?

We've put a lot of sweat, blood and tears (and swear words) into this book, and we'd love to know what you think. Call us brilliant, call us stupid, call us crazy - but just call us. Or rather, visit our website and fill in our reader response form. All feedback is welcome!

27

for your number to be called (queues can be long during high season), you can stroll over to one of the little cafes or grab a bite to eat in O'Brien's sandwich bar. Back in the tourist office, services include all Ireland information and reservations, Ticketmaster, a foreign exchange service (Fexco), tours and transport information and car hire.

Tourist Information

Name	Address	Area	Phone
Irish Country Houses & Restaurants Association	8 Mount Street Cresent	Dublin 2	01 676 9914
Dublin Tourism	Arrivals Hall, Dublin Airport	Dublin 9	01 605 7700
	Ferry Terminal	Dun Laoghaire	01 605 7700
	Suffolk Street	Dublin 2	01 605 7700
	Upper O'Connell Street	Dublin 1	1850 230 330
Dun Laoghaire-Rathdown Tourism Company Limited	Marine Road	Dun Laoghaire	01 205 4855
Fáilte Ireland	Baggot Street	Dublin 1	01 602 4000

Although you may get away with showing up on the day in search of a bed in the country, even the best tourism office will struggle to find accommodation for you in Dublin during high season without prior notice (June to August). Plan ahead and use the online resources provided by Fáilte Ireland and Dublin Tourism to get a good deal in a nice location (http://visitdublin.com, www.ireland.ie, www.tourismireland.com, www.discoverireland.com).

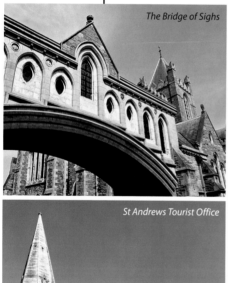

The Bridge of Sighs

St Andrews Tourist Office

The Spire

Life in the fast lane?

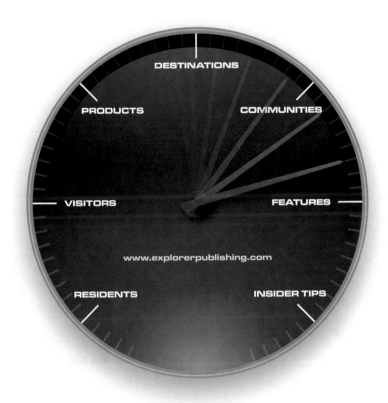

Life can move pretty quickly so make sure you keep in the know with regular updates from **www.explorerpublishing.com**

Or better still, share your knowledge and advice with others, find answers to your questions, or just make new friends in our community area

www.explorerpublishing.com – for life in real time

Places To Stay

Like with everything else, Dublin's accommodation options have changed a lot over the last decade. However, that is not to say that the new has replaced the old; it has simply added to the mix.

With great care, many historic properties have been restored to meet the needs of a 21st century clientele, while still keeping their old charm and retaining that all-important integrity. New builds have added to the range, resulting in a Dublin that now caters to all sorts of tastes and budgets. While the size of your wallet will certainly influence your choice of accommodation, location is a major factor in a city like Dublin, where public transport can be a challenge. There is a lot to be said for the suburbs, such as Dun Laoghaire, if you have the luxury of time and want to avoid the weekend crowds, but if you are only here for a short visit, it pays to be staying as central as possible.

Hotels

Other options **Main Hotels** p.32

In the past decade, cranes and drills have been a common sight on the streets of Dublin, as new hotels have sprung up like mushrooms. The Irish capital is a lucrative city for hoteliers, as last year's Deloitte survey illustrated once again by ranking Ireland at number 16 in an index of 7,000 hotels in 165 cities according to the revenue earned per room. International hotel chains have recognised the appeal, and some big hotel names now form part of Dublin's skyline. But traditional establishments have risen to the challenge, improving their standards and services to match or better those of their competitors. What some of them lack in amenities, they make up for in 'x-factor' – that particular Irish quality that sets them apart from international, often quite indistinguishable chains.

A particularly charming accommodation option is the opportunity to stay in historic establishments that have been converted (such as Clontarf Castle, p.32, or the Schoolhouse, p.34). Charming Georgian conversions and luxurious boutique hotels are also a popular choice.

Fáilte Ireland (www.failteireland.ie) grades hotels according to a star system, with prices starting at around €100 per night for a decent three-star choice. The majority of high-end, celeb favourites are clustered around Dublin 2 and Ballsbridge. While those on a shoestring are usually well advised to stay north of the Liffey, a special hotel B&B deal allows you to taste the life of society's most privileged for a bargain price of as little as €160. Staying in one of the city's top establishments may set you back anywhere from €450, with the penthouse suite at the Clarence Hotel priced at a staggering €2,600 (small change for U2's Bono and The Edge, who are co-owners, no doubt).

View from the Clarence penthouse

Budget Hotels

Keep an eye out for last minute deals and you may save yourself a pretty penny. Also bear in mind that hotel prices often come down to location, location, location so if you are on a budget, look beyond pricy Dublin 2 and Ballsbridge – or plan well ahead and travel during low season. Bewley's Hotel in Ballsbridge is a good example of great value for money in a prime location.

Hotels

Five Star	Phone	Website	Map	
Berkeley Court	01 660 1711	www.jurysdoyle.com	417 D4	338
The Clarence	01 407 0800	www.theclarence.ie	425 F4	3
Conrad Hotel	01 602 8900	www.conrad-international.ie	430 B3	332
Merrion Hotel	01 603 0600	www.merrionhotel.com	430 C2	29
The Shelbourne	01 663 4500	www.marriott.co.uk	430 B2	9
The Westbury	01 679 1122	www.jurysdoyle.com	430 A1	43

Four Star	Phone	Website	Map	
Brooks Hotel	01 670 4000	www.sinnotthotels.com	430 A1	341
Brownes Hotel Dublin	01 638 3939	www.brownesdublin.com	430 B2	360
The Burlington	01 660 5222	www.jurysdole.com	430 C4	45
Clarion Hotel IFSC	01 433 8800	www.clariondublin.com	417 D2	326
Crowne Plaza	01 862 8888	www.cpdublin-airport.com	na	
Fitzpatrick Castle Dublin	01 230 5400	www.fitzpatrickhotels.com	na	
Four Seasons Hotel	01 665 4000	www.fourseasons.com/dublin	417 E4	25
Great Southern Hotel	01 844 6000	www.greatsouthernhotels.com	na	
The Gresham	01 874 6881	www.gresham.ie	426 B2	354
Herbert Park Hotel	01 667 2200	www.herbertparkhotel.ie	417 D4	340
Hilton Dublin	01 402 9988	www.hilton.com	na	
The Morgan	01 679 3939	www.themorgan.com	426 A4	44
The Morrison	01 887 2400	www.morrisonhotel.ie	425 F4	533
O'Callaghan Alexander Hotel	01 607 3700	www.ocallaghanhotels.com	431 D1	334
O'Callaghan Davenport Hotel	01 607 3500	www.ocallaghanhotels.com	431 D1	33
Plaza Hotel	01 462 4200	www.plazahotel.ie	na	
Radisson SAS St Helen's Hotel	01 218 6000	www.radissonsas.com	421 F3	321
Schoolhouse Hotel	01 667 5014	www.schoolhousehotel.com	417 D3	36
Stephen's Green Hotel	01 607 3600	www.ocallaghanhotels.com	430 B3	333
Stillorgan Park Hotel	01 200 1800	www.stillorganpark.ie	422 A4	320

Three Star	Phone	Website	Map	
Arlington Hotel	01 804 9100	www.arlington.ie	426 B3	347
Aston Hotel	01 677 9300	www.aston-hotel.com	426 B4	344
Best Western Ashling Hotel	01 677 2324	www.ashlinghotel.ie	424 B3	109
Bewley's Hotel Ballsbridge	01 668 1111	www.bewleyshotels.com	417 E4	37
Blooms Hotel	01 671 5622	www.blooms.ie	426 A4	40
Camden Court Hotel	01 475 9666	www.camdencourthotel.com	430 A4	330
Cassidys Hotel	01 878 0555	www.cassidyshotel.com	426 A2	356
Drury Court Hotel	01 475 1988	www.drurycourthotel.com	430 A1	328
Hotel Isaacs	01 813 4700	www.hotelisaacs.com	426 C3	348
Jurys Inn Custom House	01 607 5000	www.jurysinn.com	426 C3	335
Mercer Hotel	01 478 2179	www.mercerhotel.ie	430 A2	331
Mespil Hotel	01 488 4600	www.mespilhotel.ie	426 C2	352
Paramount Hotel	01 417 9900	www.paramounthotel.ie	425 F4	325
Parliament Hotel	01 670 8777	www.parliamenthotel.ie	425 F4	343
Quality Hotel Dublin City	01 643 9500	www.qualityhoteldublin.com	427 E4	336
Tara Towers Hotel	01 269 4666	www.taratowers.com	422 A2	323
Trinity Capital Hotel	01 648 1000	www.capital-hotels.com	426 C4	337

Two Star	Phone	Website	Map	
Abbey Hotel	01 872 8188	www.abbey-hotel.ie	426 A3	351
Castle Hotel	01 874 6949	www.castle-hotel.ie	426 A1	355
Dergvale Hotel	01 874 4753	www.dergvalehotel.com	426 A1	353
Fitzsimons Hotel	01 677 9315	www.fitzsimonshotel.com	426 A4	345
Harding Hotel	01 679 6500	www.hardinghotel.ie	425 F4	346
Kingston Hotel	01 280 1810	www.kingstonhotel.com	423 F4	324
Maple Hotel	01 874 0225	www.maplehotel.com	426 C2	352
Portobello Hotel & Bar	01 475 2715	www.portobellohotel.ie	430 A4	329
River House Hotel	01 670 7655	www.riverhousehotel.com	426 A4	342

Main Hotels

Bewley's Hotel Ballsbridge

Merrion Rd
Ballsbridge
Dublin 4
Map 811 E4 **37**

01 668 1111 | *www.bewleyshotels.com*
Bewley's Hotel Ballsbridge, a beautifully restored 19th century Masonic school, has the look of a castle and stands in stark contrast to the Four Seasons Hotel which it is facing. Just like the hotel itself, O'Connells restaurant offers great value for money. Rooms here are consistently reasonably priced, given the high standards.

Burlington Hotel

Upper Leeson St
Dublin 4
Map 824 C4 **45**

01 660 5222 | *www.jurysdoyle.com*
The four-star Burlington Hotel is the Jurys flagship (although not the one with the highest star rating). With 300 classic rooms, 200 executive rooms, suites and conference rooms as well as its own nightclub (Club Anabel), it is a perennial favourite with both leisure and business travellers.

The Clarence

Wellington Quay
Dublin 2
Map 819 F4 **3**

01 407 0800 | *www.theclarence.ie*
Bono and The Edge of U2 are the proud owners of this unique boutique hotel on the Liffey, which they have restored to be the kind of hotel that they would prefer to stay in when visiting Dublin. It's characteristic green dome is a familiar sight along the Quays, and the Tea Room Restaurant is a must-do on the city's dining circuit.

Clontarf Castle Hotel

Castle Av
Clontarf
Dublin 3
Map 409 F4 **359**

01 833 2321 | *www.clontarfcastle.ie*
This hotel is like something out of a fairy tale right in the leafy suburb of Clontarf. A €10 million makeover resulted in a luxurious establishment which keeps an air of history, while being firmly positioned in the 21st century. Knights Bar and Farenheit Grill will keep you fed and watered.

Conrad Hotel

Earlsford Tce
Dublin 2
Map 824 B3 **332**

01 602 8900 | *www.conradhotels.com*
This exquisite five-star hotel is situated just around the corner from St Stephen's Green and shopping haven Grafton Street, so you won't have to carry your bargains far. In-house Alex Restaurant provides a range of delicious seafood, and the National Concert Hall is nearby.

St Stephen's Green
Dublin 2
Map 824 A2 **32**

The Fitzwilliam

01 478 7000 | *www.fitzwilliamhotel.com*
A blend of style, understated luxury and impeccable service makes the Fitzwilliam Hotel one of Dublin's finest establishments. Add to this one of the hippest, state-of-the-art penthouses at 2,000 square feet and an award-winning restaurant (Thornton's) and you will certainly struggle to find a reason to stay elsewhere.

Simmonscourt Rd
Ballsbridge
Dublin 4
Map 811 E4 **25**

Four Seasons Hotel

01 665 4000 | *www.fourseasons.com/dublin*
The luxury chain hotel mingles with ivy-covered embassies in the prestigious community of Ballsbridge, overlooking some of Dublin's most beautiful Georgian houses. It offers all the trappings you would expect from a five-star hotel, including a spa, an excellent fitness centre, a pool and a worthy restaurant.

35 Dawson St
Dublin 2
Map 824 B1 **17**

La Stampa Hotel & Spa

01 677 4444 | *www.lastampa.ie*
La Stampa's 28 luxurious rooms will take you a world away from Dublin with their exotic decor and sumptuous eastern themes. Within this hotel you'll find Balzac (p.347) and Tiger Becs (p.362) restaurants, SamSara Café Bar (p.379) and the ultimate in pampering, Mandala Spa (p.272). It's definitely a place that invites lingering.

54-46 Merrion Rd
Ballsbridge
Dublin 4
Map 811 E4 **358**

Merrion Hall

01 668 1426 | *www.epoquehotels.com*
Who says only big chains can create truly remarkable hotels? This private hotel can easily stand on its own in Dublin's embassy district with its classic, luxury four poster bedrooms, meeting rooms, lounge and spa baths. Bridgestone have repeatedly included this manor house on their list of top hundred properties in Ireland.

Merrion St
Dublin 2
Map 824 C2 **29**

Merrion Hotel

01 603 0600 | *www.merrionhotel.com*
The word 'tranquility' is written in capital letters all over this sensitively restored period property, which is situated opposite the Government Buildings. Beautiful landscaped period gardens, an intimate cocktail bar and The Tethra Spa make this a welcome retreat where you can unwind from the hustle and bustle of the city.

33

Fleet St
Dublin 2
Map 820 A4 **44**

The Morgan

01 679 3939 | *www.themorgan.com*
Pale walls, beechwood furniture and that touch of something special create a stylish ambience in this chic hotel. The contemporary and arty style of Temple Bar is reflected on the inside by the numerous displays of modern Irish art, yet at the same time, it is a welcome retreat from the Temple Bar weekend cacophony.

Merrion Square
Dublin 2
Map 825 D1 **33**

O'Callaghan Davenport Hotel

01 607 3500 | *www.ocallaghanhotels.com*
Situated at Merrion Square, the Davenport is famous for its historic facade built in 1863. Today, the four-star establishment caters for business and leisure travellers, but focuses on the former. The two main meeting facilities, the Gandon Suites and the boardroom, can accommodate up to 200 people.

Northumberland Rd
Ballsbridge
Dublin 4
Map 811 D3 **36**

Schoolhouse Hotel

01 667 5014 | *www.schoolhousehotel.com*
This refurbished 19th century schoolhouse was central during the 1916 Easter Rising and is a unique hotel experience. 31 rooms, each named after a famous Irish literary figure, will make sure you rest well. Some of the former classrooms now host the Schoolhouse Restaurant and the Schoolhouse Bar.

Grafton St
Dublin 2
Map 824 A1 **43**

The Westbury Hotel

01 679 1122 | *www.jurysdole.com*
A recent €12 million refurbishment has added some extra sparkle to this already shiny, chic-modern establishment situated off Grafton Street and frequented by Dublin's beautiful people. Hand-made furniture, silk curtains and sparkling Waterford crystal are extra special touches and the hotel also has its own bistro, bar and lounge.

College Green
Dublin 2
Map 820 B4 **34**

The Westin

01 645 1000 | *www.westin.com/dublin*
Hidden behind a 19th century facade, 163 traditionally decorated guest rooms promise you the best sleep ever in a warm and homey atmosphere. After a good rest, re-energise in the gym or on the dancefloor of the Mint Bar. Situated opposite Trinity College, right in the centre of Dublin, this five-star hotel will fulfil your every wish.

Hotel Apartments

There are various types of self-catering accommodation available in Dublin, ranging from on-campus studios to city centre, luxury apartments, and from town houses to cottages. The majority of short lets are owned and run by smaller companies, sometimes even individuals, although some of the larger hotels chains also offer excellent long-term and corporate rates. Amenities will differ, but typically include a separate bedroom, a living room with television, a kitchen area (or kitchenette), a bathroom and washing facilities. Places like Gogarty even service the apartments on a daily basis. Minimum rental varies according to the establishment, for anything from one night to one month.

Hotel Apartments

Name	Area	Phone	Web
Brookman Townhomes	Various locations	01 283 9088	www.brookman.ie
DCU Summer Accommodation	Dublin 9	01 700 5736	www.summeraccommodation.dcu.ie
Dublin Shortlets	Various locations	01 201 8470	www.dublinshortlets.com,
Gogarty's Apartments	Dublin 2	01 671 1822	www.gogartys.ie
Jacobs Apartments	Dublin 1	01 855 5660	www.isaacs.ie
Premier Apartments	Various locations	01 638 1201	www.premierapartmentsdublin.com

Bed & Breakfasts

There's a fine line between what constitutes a small hotel and what constitutes a guesthouse. Since the distinction is often fairly academic, it is not uncommon to find one and the same establishment listed under both headings in different accommodation guides. Rather than bearing witness to a confused classification system, this speaks for the excellent quality of Dublin's guesthouses, which now typically feature en suite bedrooms with direct dial phones and tea and coffee making facilities. While similar trimmings can be found at many B&Bs, today en suites are not always on offer as the houses are usually smaller and always owner-occupied. Dublin's guesthouses and B&Bs are old-time favourites with visitors to Ireland, due to their reputation of being charming 'homes from home'. Without the fanfare of large establishments, but with 100% personalised service, they cater to the individual needs of each traveller in an informal and comfortable atmosphere. The emphasis is on great value for money and both B&Bs and guesthouses come in all shapes and styles, from ivy-covered Georgian manors to townhouses. Look out for the Fáilte Ireland approved sign.

Bed & Breakfasts

Name	Address	Phone	Web
Ariel House	Lansdowne Road, Ballsbridge	01 668 5512	www.ariel-house.net
Baggot Court	Baggot Street Lower	01 661 2819	www.baggotcourt.com
Butlers Town House	Lansdowne Road, Ballsbridge	01 667 4022	www.butlers-hotel.com
Clifden Guesthouse	Gardiner Place	01 874 6364	www.clifdenhouse.com
Days Inn Talbot Street	Talbot Street	01 874 9202	www.daysinntalbot.com
Donnybrook Lodge	Stillorgan Road, Donnybrook	01 283 7333	www.donnybrooklodge.com
Egan's Guesthouse	Iona Park, Glasnevin	01 830 3611	www.eganshouse.com
Ferryview House	Clontarf Road, Contarf	01 833 5893	www.ferryviewhouse.com
Glenogra House	Merrion Road, Ballsbridge	01 668 3661	www.glenogra.com
Harrington Hall	Harcourt Street	01 475 3497	www.harringtonhall.comr
Kilronan Guesthouse	Adelaide Road	01 475 5266	www.dublinn.com
Number 31	Leeson Close	01 676 5011	www.number31.ie
St Aiden's Guesthouse	Brighton Road, Rathgar	01 490 2011	www.staidens.com
Tavistock House	Ranelagh Road, Ranelagh	01 498 8000	www.tavistockhouse.com
Waterloo House	Waterloo Road, Ballsbridge	01 660 1888	www.waterloohouse.ie

Backpacker Tips ◀

Many hostels provide facilities where you can leave your backpack even after you have checked out. Dublin is a backpacker friendly city, offering a good choice of attractions for those on a shoestring budget, although overall a trip to Dublin will never be cheap. Check www.thebackpacker .net for tips on surviving if you're a bit short of cash.

Hostels

Backpackers and globetrotters can often find a bed in a hostel on the Liffey for as little as €10 per night, although obviously this depends on availability and quality. There is a great range of rooms and facilities, pushing the price over €80 at the top end of the scale (for a single room during high season in Barnacles House). Hostels in Ireland (www.hostels-ireland.com) lists over a hundred Fáilte Ireland approved choices sprinkled all over the country, giving you plenty to choose from.

Like B&Bs and guesthouses, hostels in Dublin come in all shapes, styles and locations. They are usually filled to the brim with people to socialise with and are mostly clean and comfortable.

Hostels

Name	Area	Phone	Web
Abbey Court	Dublin 1	01 878 0700	www.abbey-court.com
Abraham House	Dublin 1	01 855 0600	www.abraham-house.ie
Ashfield House	Dublin 2	01 679 7734	www.ashfieldhouse.ie
Avalon House	Dublin 2	01 475 0001	www.avalon-house.ie
Barnacles House	Dublin 2	01 671 6277	www.barnacles.ie
Dublin International Youth Hostel	Dublin 1	01 830 1766	www.iyhr.org
Four Courts Hostel	Dublin 8	01 672 5839	www.fourcourtshostel.com
Isaacs Hostel	Dublin 1	01 855 6215	www.isaacs.ie/isaacs_hostel
Kinlay House	Dublin 2	01 679 6644	www.kinlaydublin.ie
Litton Lane Hostel	Dublin 1	01 872 8389	www.littonlane.hostel.com
Marina House	Dun Laoghaire	01 284 1524	www.marinahouse.com
Marlborough Hostel	Dublin 1	01 874 7629	www.marlboroughhostel.com
Oliver St John Gogarty's	Dublin 2	01 671 1822	www.gogartys.ie

Campsites

While you won't find a place to pitch your tent in the heart of the city, having your own roof to put up over your head will pay off if you are prepared to venture further afield. Although it is not completely unheard of for people to camp on one of the beaches, a caravan and camping park certainly is the much safer and more convenient option. County Dublin boasts two excellent choices – the award-winning Camac Valley Tourist Caravan & Camping Park in Clondalkin (www.camacvalley.com) and the North Beach Caravan & Camping Park in Rush (www.northbeach.ie). Check out the official website of the Irish caravan and camping council, www.campingireland.ie, for other options in Ireland.

Beautiful Irish landscapes, ideal for camping

Getting Around

Other options **Exploring** p.161

There's no point being overly polite about it – any Dubliner will tell you that getting around in the city is often a time-consuming nightmare. While Dublin's public transport was once fairly advanced compared to other European cities, the absence of an underground or metro system and overburdened roads have made it one of the most frustrating cities to navigate.

It's not all bad though – the Luas is helping to combat commuter blues (although it's pretty congested during rush hour and on the weekends), and the Dart is a quick and scenic trip along the coastline into and out of the city centre. The bus network is certainly extensive, although chat to a few residents and you'll probably hear tales of woe about unreliability and lateness. On the whole though, the bus service seems to be pretty good, most of the time.

However, many Dubliners still rely on their own set of wheels, and therein lies the problem. Traffic jams are a daily occurrence, particularly along the Quays and on the dreaded M50. Seemingly continuous roadworks promise a slightly less congested future, although currently they seem to be adding to the problem.

Air

In 2006, 21 million passengers passed through Ireland's busiest airport, located approximately 10km north of Dublin city centre, near the M50 ring road and the M1 motorway. Served by over 90 airlines and providing scheduled and chartered flights to more than 150 long and short-haul destinations (including Europe, the Middle East and the US), Dublin airport saw a total of 197,000 aircraft movements last year. London ranked top on the 2006 destination charts, followed by Paris, Manchester and New York. Alongside Ryanair (Europe's first budget airline) and Aer Arann (domestic carrier), the national airline Aer Lingus is one of the main operators at Dublin airport. Founded by the Irish government in 1936, the now publicly listed company remains Ireland's flagship airline, set to serve almost a hundred international destinations by the end of 2007.

Dublin Airport

Like many other European airports, Dublin has witnessed an increase in passenger numbers and freight in the past decade. With its capacity at its limits, the 'Capital Development Programme', a 10 year, €1.2 billon project was initiated in 2006, in order to catapult the modestly sized airport into a new era. Major changes include a second terminal, scheduled for completion in 2009.

Airport security complies with the EU Aviation Security Regulations. The hand luggage allowance is one item per passenger and liquids, in containers of 100ml or less, have to snugly fit into one resealable 20x20cm see-through plastic bag of one litre capacity. Shopping facilities on 'The Street', the Airside Airport Shopping, however ensure that you won't be left high and dry, as you can buy a large collection of liquids and other items.

For the latest developments and regulations, as well as flight information, check www.dublinairport.com.

Airport Services

Facilities at Dublin airport include banking and currency exchange, Dublin Airport Church (086 1642 113), meet & greet services (Flight Greeting 01 805 8000, or Platinum Airport Services 01 814 5021), left luggage (01 814 4633) and a trolley service. Depending on your chosen airline, self-service check-in kiosks and internet

Going Somewhere?
When you're off on your hols, don't forget to take the essentials. Tickets? Check. Passport? Check. Toothbrush? Check. Explorer Mini Guide? Check! These pocket-sized marvels really pack a punch, and are the cutest way to make sure you've got the inside track when you arrive at your destination.

check-in options may also be available. For medical assistance, refer to the Airport Pharmacy or the Health & Medicine store. Refer to the Airport Police Public Office (01 814 5555) if retrieving lost items in the airport itself or contact your airline for any items lost on their aircraft.

Airport Buses

The 747 and 748 Airlinks, an express service run by Dublin Bus, will take you to Busáras or Connelly Station in the heart of the city for €6 (adult single). The slightly more expensive private operator Aircoach (www.aircoach.ie, €7 adult single), provides a more comfortable 24 hour service along one north-bound (Belfast) and two south-bound routes (Ballsbridge, Sandyford). For northsiders, Urbus(www.urbus.ie) offers a direct link from Castleknock to Swords via Dublin Airport. If time is a luxury you can afford, but money an issue, there are numerous 'ordinary' buses that serve the airport (16A, 41, 41B, 46X, 58X, 230, or 746). Regardless of your chosen mode of transport, allow plenty of time for your journey, as construction works or heavy traffic may add extra time to the usual 20 minute bus ride from the city centre.

Airlines		
Aer Arann	01 844 7700	www.aerarann.ie
Aer Lingus	01 886 8888	www.aerlingus.com
Air Canada G.S.A.	01 679 3958	www.aircanada.com
Air France	01 605 0383	www.airfrance.ie
American Airlines	01 602 0550	www.aa.com
British Airways	1890 626 747	www.britishairways.com
Etihad Airways	01 477 3479	www.etihadairways.com
KLM Royal Dutch Airlines	1850 747 400	www.klm.com
Lufthansa	01 844 5544	www.lufthansa.com
Ryanair	081 830 3030	www.ryanair.com
Swiss	1890 200 515	www.swiss.com

Boat

For transport of the more watery kind, nip over to Holyhead, Liverpool or Mostyn for a day or two. Connected by a regular bus and taxi service, Dublin port (www.dublinport.ie), the largest harbour in Ireland, is situated in close proximity to Dublin city centre. Six operators offer up to 18 daily crossings to the UK and Continental Europe, transporting over a million passengers across the Irish Sea each year. Dublin's second port at Dun Laoghaire (www.dlharbour.ie) connects the south of Dublin with Holyhead in Wales on a fast-boat service in approximately 100 minutes. Foot passenger day trip passes to Britain start at €28 (www.stenaline.com).

Bus

From 05:40 to after 23:00 on weekdays, Dublin Bus (Bus Átha Cliath) provides an extensive service for Dubliners who don't have their own set of wheels. With a fleet of 950 buses crisscrossing the city and its peripheries on 140 routes, Greater Dublin is dotted with bus stops, marked by tall green or blue lollipop-shaped signs. Since the buses are as predictable as the weather and drivers are renowned for only keeping loosely to their schedules, timetables (www.dublinbus.ie) are rarely reliable – especially at rush hour.

To flag down a bus, signal with your hand. Fare-saver tickets (Rambler passes, Bus or Luas passes) can be purchased at newsagents, tourist offices or directly at Dublin Bus, while single and feeder tickets can be bought upon boarding. If you opt for the latter option, give the exact fare in change or you might award Dublin Bus with an unintentional

Dublin Bus

tip – refunds can only be obtained at the O'Connell Street office. As fares are calculated according to the number of stops travelled, a single adult ticket will set you back between €1.00 and €1.90 within the city zone.

Special services provided by Dublin Bus include the Xpresso (express service), the School Link, the Railink (rail service), the Airlink (airport service) and the Nitelink (a service for night owls).

In recent years, the Department of Transport has granted various private bus companies the licence to operate in Dublin, opening up the market for competition.

Bus Éireann

Although trains are the swiftest means of connecting between towns in Ireland, the comprehensive service by the national coach provider, Bus Éireann, is often the much cheaper alternative. Tickets can be purchased in advance or on the day at Dublin's central bus station Busáras (01 836 6111; behind Custom House) or at any other bus station. Refer to the company website www.buseireann.ie for information on discounted fares.

Car Sharing
www.dublintraffic.ie is a free platform for car commuters.

Car

Other options **Transportation** p.152

In 2002 the Central Statistics Office published findings that Irish people rely heavily on their cars – although this was hardly news to the thousands of commuters in the gridlock every working day. In fact, it was found that the majority of people use their vehicle at least twice a day. With the number of new private car licences reaching a peak last year, this problematic trend is bound to continue.

In 2005, the government launched its 10 year programme Transport 21, a project aimed at improving the life of the Irish motorist considerably. Major objectives include completion of the inter-urban network routes by 2010 (738km motorway or roads of equivalent standard) as well as the creation of 150km high-quality dual carriageways and 300km single carriageway routes by 2015. While this is certainly a step in the right direction, for many Dubliners, it is too little, too late.

With the annual distance covered by Irish motorists now approaching twice the European average, driving in Dublin is as little for the fainthearted as it is for those who watch every penny. The city is choked with traffic and construction, adding to the nightmare of high taxes (www.motortax.ie), pricey parking and toll road fees. Where parking is at a premium, parking meters and 'pay & display' spots can set you back €1.00 per hour, and sometimes almost triple that depending on the zone. Yellow zone parking costs €2.70 per hour, red zone is €2.20 per hour, green zone €1.50 per hour, orange zone €1.00 per hour. Zones are clearly marked and colour coded on the 'pay & display' notices.

Free parking (in metered spots or within single yellow lines) is only available after 19:00 on Saturday but all day Sunday. Supervised car parks are pricey, but constitute a good option if you are staying overnight or

Luxury Car Hire

Many car rental agents offer high-spec models for special occasions, from sleek Mercedes or BMWs to rugged 4WD off-roaders. If, however, you don't settle for less than an Aston Martin, a Porsche, a Bentley or a Ferrari, Elite (www.eliterent.com), Guy Salmon (www.guysalmon.com) or Gorman's Vintage Cars (www.gormansvintagecars.com) will talk cash to you. Tired of taking matters into your own hands? If you'd rather enjoy a glass of bubbly than fight your way through traffic, check out one of the many limousine hire companies (www.dbcsireland.com, www.comfortlinelimos.com, www.dorgans.com).

you have a foreign number plate, as the percentage of break-ins and car theft remains relatively high.

As in the UK, cars drive on the left and the alcohol limit is 80mg per 100ml of blood. EU, US and international driving licences are valid. If not otherwise signposted, speed limits are 30mph in the city, 60mph on primary roads and 70mph on motorways and dual carriageways. Seatbelts must be worn at all times and children under the age of 12 are not allowed to sit in the front (for further regulations, please check with the Department of Transport, www.transport.ie).

Car Hire

While public transport is a more practical solution in the city, a car is essential if you want to explore beyond its borders. Car hire in Ireland is straightforward but usually on the expensive side. As a driver over the age of 21 (sometimes 23) and under the age of 75 (sometimes 70), all you need is a valid driving licence and a credit card. Prices vary greatly, so book in advance if you can. Many rental agencies have offices at the airport as well as in the city centre, so take the time to shop around for the best deal. Typical high-season weekly rates start from €150 for a small manual car. While there is usually a great range of car models, insisting on an automatic car may be costly as they are hard to come by.

Car Rental Agencies		
Argus Car Hire	01 499 9600	www.arguscarhire.com
Avis Car Rental	01 605 7500	www.avis.ie
Budget Rent-a-car	01 837 9611	www.budget.ie
County Car	01 235 2030	www.countycar.ie
Europcar	01 614 2888	www.europcar.ie
Hertz	01 676 7476	www.hertz.ie
National Car Rental	01 260 3771	www.carhire.ie
Nova Car Hire	1800 200 115	www.novacarhire.com
Thrifty	1800 515 800	www.thrifty.ie

Cycling

Other options **Cycling** p.233

Cycling is an economical, healthy and practical way to get around the city. Hundreds of kilometres of cycle tracks cut across the city and new facilities continue to be developed in conjunction with bus priority schemes. The Ranelagh route, in particular, is an example of good design, complete with wide lanes and safe crossings. In recent years, awareness campaigns have promoted cycling as a mode of transport, but even though Dublin city is relatively compact and mostly flat, the majority of Dubliners have taken rather slowly to the idea. Although bike stands now dot the city, parking your two-wheeler safely can be somewhat of a challenge. Lonely locks or random bike parts hanging from the metal posts are hardly an uncommon sight, and serve as a reminder that not much is safe from the long fingers of thieves, especially your trusty bicycle. Take all detachables with you wherever possible. Bike hire remains expensive at €80 per week or €20 a day (www.cycleways.ie). To get your own, see Shopping on p.279.

Taxi

Taxi Companies	
ABC Taxis	01 285 5444
Budget Cabs	01 459 9333
City Cabs	01 872 7272
Direct Taxis	01 839 9999
Dublin Dial a Cab	01 808 0800
Metro Cabs	01 668 3333
National Radio Cabs	01 708 9292
Pony Cabs	01 661 0101
Taxi Taxi	087 781 9770
Trinity Taxis	01 708 2222

With numerous taxi companies working the city, it is usually easy to flag down a cab at any time of the day except for a Friday or Saturday night. Then, taxi ranks are often swarming with people queuing, making waits of over an hour a regular occurrence. On those nights, you are better advised taking the Nitelink, especially between 02:00 and 03:30 when many pubs and clubs have just closed. At this point in the night, phone calls are usually unsuccessful and advance bookings are only accepted for rides to the airport. Whether you hail a taxi on the street or pick it up at one of the many ranks, you will be charged a initial fare of €3.80, followed by a charge per unit (one-sixth of a kilometre or per 30 seconds) which typically amounts to €0.95 per km and €0.34 per minute (from 8:00 to 20:00). Expect extra charges for additional passengers, luggage or phone bookings. Drivers generally have good knowledge of the city and can usually be trusted to take you on the most direct, rather than the scenic route. Never averse to a good chat, they are often a wealth of information and always have an anecdote to share.

Train

In 2004, passenger traffic on Irish Rail (Iarnród Éireann), the national rail network, amounted to a total of 34,550 journeys (1,581,698km). The extensive service provided by Iarnród Éireann connects Dublin's two main train stations with all major cities in Ireland. Euston Station (01 703 3299), a 20 minute walk to the west of the city centre, serves Cork, Tralee, Limerick, Waterford, Galway, Westport, Kildare and Clonmel. Connelly Station (01 703 2358), north-east of Busáras, offers regular trains to Silgo, Belfast, Rosslare, Longford and Arklow. While not all InterCity routes are as efficient as they could be, the Dublin to Belfast service is exemplary – fast, reliable, comfortable and, with a day return costing in the region of €36.50, it is also affordable. Contact Iarnród Éireann (1850 366 222) directly for any type of rail information, from fares to timetables, or refer to their website: www.irishrail.ie.

Most stations provide left-luggage locker facilities and ATMs. Bikes can be taken onboard on most mainline routes for a small fee.

Dart (Dublin Area Rapid Transport)

One of the most reliable modes of public transport for commuters in and out of the city, Iarnród Éireann's electronic rail service along Dublin Bay provides a fast and comfortable alternative to journeys by bus or car. Being supplemented by Suburban Rail lines reaching as far as Dundalk, Arklow or Mullingar, it is also ideal for journeys beyond the city centre. A typical single adult ticket from Dun Laoghaire to Dublin City Centre (Pearse, Tara Street or Connelly Station) will set you back €2 – slightly more than the bus (€1.90) but definitely worth it. Commuter tickets and monthly passes are also available. For more information refer to www.iarnrodeireann.ie/dart.

Before boarding a Dart or Suburban Rail service, make sure to check the noticeboard for a list of stations served or you may accidentally end up on an express service to Bray. Which is fine if you're going to Bray, but not so good if you're after a quick journey!

Tram (Luas)

The Luas (Irish for 'speed'), Dublin's high-capacity and high-frequency light rail system, is a relatively new addition to the city. The green line, which runs every five minutes at peak times, and every 15 minutes at other times, connects St Stephen's Green with Sandyford (a distance of nine kilometres) and has been in operation since June 2004. The red line followed in September 2004, providing a regular service from Connelly to Tallaght (14km) every 20 minutes. While there are plans to extend the current service, at the moment the two systems run independently and there is no easy way of connecting between them. Due to its reliability, its reasonable fares and the comfort provided, the Luas is one of Dublin's most effective and successful modes of transport. Last year, the 40 vehicles run by the operating company, Veolia Transport Ireland, carried 26 million passengers, with an average 80,000 daily. Both the red and the green line run from 05:30 to 00:30 Monday to Friday, from 06:30 to 00:30 on Saturday and from 07:00 to

23:30 on Sunday. Fares are calculated according to zones and start at €1.25 for a single adult ticket, with flexi, combi and other fare saver options available (www.luas.ie, 1800 300 604).

Just a note about safety on the Luas: as good as it is for getting from one point to another in the city centre, at peak times it is absolutely packed, and you may find yourself at uncomfortably close quarters to several perfect strangers. Apart from being annoying if you are picky about your personal space, this also leaves you vulnerable to pickpockets. Try not to keep any cash or valuables in your pockets on the Luas – stash them in your bag if possible. A scam that has caught out several people on the Luas involves a total stranger picking a really loud verbal fight with you, and while you furiously protest your innocence his mates are pinching your bag. These incidents do not happen often, but it is a good idea to stay super alert when the Luas is busy.

Walking
Other options **Hiking** p.241

In 2002, a fifth of all commutes were made on foot. The city centre is compact and there are several pedestrianised areas, making the postal code areas of Dublin 1 and 2 easily accessible on two legs. Most roads leading away from the very centre are flanked with good pavements, but not all are safe – especially at night. Avoid badly lit streets and don't walk through any of the notoriously crime-ridden inner city areas if you can help it. While you may not want to splash out on a taxi, bear in mind that it is always better to be safe than sorry. Keep your eyes open and stay well clear of any gatherings of dodgy-looking characters or any suspicious-looking activity.

During the day, however, walking may be your best and quickest way of getting around the city centre. There are many pedestrian bridges, including Dublin's most famous, the Ha'Penny Bridge, and numerous shortcuts unavailable to your fellow commuters on wheels. You'll be surprised how quickly you can get from Henry Street to Dame Street on foot if you cut through Temple Bar. Jaywalking is common practice among seasoned locals who can nip across busy roads, but unless you know what you're doing it's very dangerous, so don't follow the person in front of you aimlessly. If you happen to forget from which direction to expect traffic, Dublin City has thoughtfully printed 'look right' and 'look left' onto the street for you.

The Luas

Lock up your bike

Dublin Explorer 1st Edition

Sweet Sixteen
Dublin now ranks as number 16 on the list of the world's most expensive places to live, according to Mercer's Cost of Living Survey 2007. It's still a long way behind London, which came second.

Money

Money is what makes the world around – in Ireland as much as anywhere else. A country once considered the 'poorhouse of Europe' has emerged into the 21st century with a thriving economy and new found prosperity. Yet, it has come at a price – if you emigrated from Ireland 10 years ago and are coming back for a short visit, be in for a major shock as you will find that nearly everything will seem to suddenly cost an arm and a leg. But if money is not an issue, it'll get you anywhere, be it cash or plastic, as long as it is euros.

Local Currency

'The heavier the purse, the lighter the heart' claims an Irish saying, illustrating the healthy respect that the Irish have for money. In 2002, Ireland was among the first eleven EU nations to opt for a shared currency, the euro, officially withdrawing the Irish pound with effect from 9 February of the same year. The euro comes in seven notes and eight coins (euros and cents), with each of the latter featuring a communal map on one face and a country-specific sign on the other. With the exception of special editions, all Irish coins display the national emblem, the harp. Notes are available in the denominations of €5 (grey), €10 (red), €20 (blue), €50 (orange), €100 (green), €200 (yellow), €500 (purple). While five euros are commonly referred to as 'a fiver', 'five quid' or 'five squids', and €10 'a tenner', general local slang terms for money include shillings, snots and dillions.

Remember that it can be pretty hard to change a €500 note – not many shops will accept it or have that much change handy. So if a bank teller or money exchange bureau gives you this big purple note, ask them to change it for smaller notes then and there, or you may be stuck with loads of money and no way to spend it!

Banks

Most major international banks are represented in Dublin, including a dense network of the prominent Irish names such as the Allied Irish Bank (AIB), Bank of Ireland and Ulster Bank. While banking hours can vary, in the city centre they are generally from 10:00 to 16:00 Monday to Wednesday and Friday, 10:00 to 17:00 on Thursday. There is no service on Saturday on Sunday. To find your closest branch, check the individual websites or refer to a general directory like Golden Pages (www.goldenpages.ie).

To open a bank account, you are obliged to produce a current, valid form of ID (passport or driving licence) and a recent household bill (phone or electricity bill). Under current Money Laundering legislation, non-residents have to additionally supply a character reference and financial history from your own bank. For more information, please see the Bank Accounts section of the Residents' chapter on p.71.

ATMs

Automatic teller machines (ATMs) are conveniently located outside most banks and building societies and are usually linked to one of the international networks, thus accepting most international credit cards (check the symbols displayed on the machine). Beware that in addition to basic nominal charges, extra charges may be applicable if you are using a foreign card. While it is usually no problem to withdraw small amounts

Exchange Rates

Foreign Currency(FC)	1 Unit FC = x €	€1 = x FC
Australia	0.59	1.68
Bahrain	1.92	0.51
Bangladesh	0.01	94.77
Brazil	0.37	2.7
Canada	0.68	1.45
Cyprus	1.71	0.58
Denmark	0.13	7.44
Hong Kong	0.09	10.72
India	0.02	56.01
Malaysia	0.2	4.84
New Zealand	0.49	2.01
Norway	0.12	7.92
Oman	1.88	0.52
Pakistan	0.01	83.36
Philippines	0.01	64.26
Russia	0.02	35.23
Singapore	0.47	2.1
South Africa	0.09	10.01
Sri Lanka	0.01	156
Sweden	0.106	9.38
Switzerland	0.61	1.63
Thailand	0.02	44.58
United Arab Emirates	0.19	5.05
United Kingdom	1.47	0.67
United States	0.72	1.37

above €10 from any ATM, city centre machines are renowned for running out of the smaller denominations on a Friday night and often, you find yourself stuck with multiples of €20 or even €50. Since cash deposits are not refilled until Monday morning, queues get notoriously long, making it well worth planning ahead and having your finances in place before you hit town for a night out.

Money Exchanges

Bureaux de change are two a penny in Dublin city, giving you the option to shop around for the best deal. As a rule of thumb, banks tend to have the best exchange and commission rates, followed by building societies and post offices. Private companies or hotel exchanges, in turn, typically have the better opening times. Rates are usually displayed outside or at the counter, so take the time to compare and get the most for your foreign currency. Euros can be bought at all major bus and train stations, ferry ports and airports.

Exchange Centres

Name	Phone	Web
AIB	01 679 9222	www.aib.ie
American Express Foreign Exchange Service	01 679 9000	www.americanexpress.co.uk
Bank of Ireland	01 459 8644	www.bankofireland.ie
Foreign Exchange Company of Ireland	01 661 1800	na
ICE (International Currency Exchange) Bureau de Change	na	www.dublinairport.com
Permanent TSB	01 677 9941	www.permanenttsb.ie
Thomas Cook Bureau de Change	01 677 7422	www.thomascook.co.uk
Ulster Bank	01 608 5506	www.ulsterbank.ie

Credit Cards

In The Red

Credit card debt has increased substantially over the past decade, in line with a general increase in personal borrowing. While residential mortgages account for the majority of debts accumulated by the Irish public, the ease with which debt can be run up on credit cards makes them particularly interesting for those requiring limited additional funds.

While Ireland is becoming less of a cash culture, many people still prefer to plastic. However, the majority of larger establishments accept most major credit cards today and Visa or MasterCard should be fine almost anywhere except markets or taxis (American Express and Diners Club cards are more tricky). More often than not you are required to key in your pin (depending on the card), so make sure you get it before you set off on a shopping spree. If your card goes missing, contact the relevant 24 hour service hotline immediately and ask them to block it so that no further transactions can be made.

Credit Card Hotlines

Allied Irish Bank	01 668 5500
American Express	1800 282 728
Bank of Ireland	1890 251 251
Diners Club	1800 709 944
First Active	1800 245 399
MasterCard	1800 557 378
National Irish Bank	1850 700 221
Ulster Bank	1800 245 399
Visa	1800 558 002

Tipping

While tipping in Dublin is certainly less of an undertaking or an obligation as it is in the States, a 12% tip is commonplace in restaurants. To acknowledge good service, some people may even give up to 20%. Whatever the amount you are prepared to part with, beware of automatic service charges, as an additional tip would bring your bill up way above the odds. You can refuse to pay this charge, if they money does not directly go to the waiting staff. You are under no obligation to tip elsewhere (hairdressers, taxi drivers, hotel porters), but many people like to hand over a few coins as a sign of gratitude. Although you can tip on your credit card, leaving a cash tip increases the chances of it definitely reaching your server.

Streetside newsstand

Newspapers & Magazines

The Irish like to be in the know on national and international affairs, making the country a heaven on the news front. A good variety of national or local newspapers and magazines caters to various readerships, as the newsagents stock the shelves with an increasing number of foreign prints.

Although traditionally divided, the majority of newspapers are non-aligned on the religious (and the political) front, with some of them still displaying Anglo-centric or nationalist tendencies in their choice of topics. The oldest daily newsprint, *The Irish Times* (€1.60), is Dublin-centred and features a great selection of reviews and entertainment listings on a Saturday. A lot more serious than its main broadsheet competitor, the *Irish Independent*, it is renowned to be an example of excellent journalism, although some argue that it should limit its extensive selection of foreign news to those that are relevant for Ireland. It is surpassed in sales by the *Irish Independent*, which has a much more domestic focus, but goes to the other extreme in its coverage of foreign news, which can be very sensationalist. Always a good read, but not attracting as big a readership in Dublin as the other two broadsheet papers is *The Irish Examiner*, the former *Cork Examiner*.

On the tabloid front, the *Irish Daily Star* (€0.90) and its evening version (although available just after lunch time) *The Evening Herald* (€1.10), are the biggest sellers. They certainly look to *The Sun* for ideas, although British advocates of the gutter press will be disappointed to find that the Irish versions display a lot less bare flesh. *The Evening Herald* is particularly useful for its entertainment and property listings. Two British publications, *The Sun* and *The Times* both publish Irish editions of their titles.

The Sunday Tribune and *The Sunday Independent* are considered the best Irish Sunday papers, but are said to be somewhat lacking compared to their English rivals. *The Sunday Business Post* is an excellent excuse for workaholics to keep informed about the Irish business world, while the rest of the papers – the majority of which are tabloids– will easily more than fulfil your need for gossip.

Following the example of its European neighbours, Dublin now also has some free morning papers, including *The Metro*. Also adding to the long list of publications is an array of local prints of various sizes and frequencies.

There is also a wide range of magazines, including many specialised prints available monthly or fortnightly. In Dublin, *Dublin Event Guide* and *Slate* provide weekly listings, with the latter two easily surpassing the former (and not only because they are for free). *The Dubliner* and *Social & Personal* both have a distinctive lifestyle focus, although the latter blends out the world of the less fortunate half. *Hot Press* carries details of the city's music scene, while *Phoenix* concentrates on social and political satire.

Books

There are shelves' worth of books on Ireland and the Irish, ranging from general to specific guides and from historical portraits to analyses of the Irish psyche. While a lot of it isn't worth the paper it is printed on, there are some excellent informative and entertaining reads. Lonely Planet's *Irish – Language and Culture* presents an interesting approach to Irish culture and provides great insights into the local lingo, although you may want to confirm any phrases with a native before you add them to your mental dictionary – some are very area specific and others plain strange! Guides to customs and etiquette or generally tackling this elusive theme of 'Irishness' are prone to outrageous generalisations, but can nevertheless tickle out a laugh.

Buy The Book

Borders, Books Upstairs, Cathach Rare Books, Chapters, Easons and Hodges Figgis are just some of the major bookshops that can be found in Dublin. See p.287.

If you are looking for a different kind of read that by no means can be taken seriously, try Paul Howard's latest satirical *Ross O'Carroll-Kelly's Guide to South Dublin. How to get by on, like, €10,000 a day*. Another humorous read that is part travel journal and part outrageous story telling, is Pete McCarthy's *McCarthy's Bar*, recounting his travels around Ireland under the condition that he never pass a pub with his name on it. It gives a great insight into Irish people and their legendary hospitality. There is certainly plenty to choose from, not to forget a whole body of literature which, serving as a platform for social discourse, may teach you a thing or two about Ireland and the Irish.

Websites

There are no limits to the wisdom of the world wide web, or so it seems. The internet is like one vast digital library, producing an incredible amount of information at just one mouse click. If you surf the net patiently, you can pretty much find answers to anything you may want to know about Dublin, yet there are certain sites which may get you to your goal quicker (and also provide information you can definitely rely on). Scoring high points on the list of usefulness are the home pages of the Irish Government (www.irlgov.ie) – with its link to the Citizen Information page – and the (sometimes temperamental) website of Dublin City Council (www.dublincity.ie). Not far behind are the tourism websites: www.visitdublin.com, www.dublintourist.com, www.ireland.ie, www.discoverireland.com and www.tourismireland.com.

Websites	
Dublin Information	
www.dublin-airport.com	Dublin Airport
www.dublinboards.com	Friendly chatboard with various information topics
www.dublincity.ie	Dublin City Council website
www.garda.ie	Irish Police
www.ireland.ie	Fáilte Ireland website
www.irishstatutebook.ie	Irish Statute Book
www.irlgov.ie	Official website of the Irish government
www.ticketmaster.ie	Tickets for concerts, theatre performances and sports matches
www.visitdublin.com	Official online tourist office for Dublin
Leisure	
http://entertainment.ie	Entertainment listings
www.diningtreats.com	Restaurant Listings
www.dublinevents.com	Event Guide
www.irishsportscouncil.ie	Irish Sports Council
www.rte.ie	Ireland's National Television and Radio Broadcaster
Online Publications	
www.hotpress.com	Hot Press online
www.independent.ie	The Irish Independent online
www.ireland.com	The Irish Times online
www.sbpost.ie	Sunday Business Post online
www.thedubliner.ie	The Dubliner Magazine online
www.thestar.ie	The Irish Daily Star online
www.tribune.ie	Irish Tribune online
Transport	
www.cie.ie	Information on all types of public transport
www.dublintraffic.ie	Car Sharing
www.irishferries.com	Official website of Irish Ferries
www.stenaline.ie	Stena Line Ferries
Work/Education	
www.basis.ie	Business Access to State Information and Services
www.dcu.ie	Dublin City University
www.jobs.ie	Job Search
www.ucd.ie	University College Dublin

Annual Events

February
Temple Bar
Dublin 2

Jameson International Film Festival

01 672 8861 | www.dubliniff.com

The colourful programme with its mix of independent and mainstream flicks makes this festival a platform for national as well as international film titles and talents. Screening in various locations in and around Temple Bar, the festival features a 'surprise film', short Irish documentaries, and some upcoming box office hits. The public can vote for their favourite film to win the coveted Audience Award.

February-March
Various Locations

Six Nations Rugby

01 647 3800 | www.irishrugby.ie

Rugby in Ireland is based on an all-Ireland basis, meaning that in international competitions a single team represents Northern Ireland and the Republic of Ireland. One of the most important events on the rugby union calendar is the annual tournament held between Ireland, Scotland, England, Wales, Italy and France with the very creative name of Six Nations Rugby. With the usual Irish venue at Lansdowne Road under major restructuring at the moment, Ireland met England at Europe's fourth largest stadium, Croke Park, in 2007.

March
Various Locations

St Patrick's Festival

01 676 3205 | www.stpatricksfestival.ie

Nobody can throw a party like the Irish, and no party is as big as the one that takes place around the country on St Patrick's Day. No efforts are spared to honour the patron saint of Ireland, and thousands of visitors flock to the capital every year to join in the legendary *craic*.

April
Temple Bar
Dublin 2

Convergence Festival

01 674 5773 | www.sustainable.ie/convergence

Cultivate regularly hosts festivals on sustainable living in its Temple Bar centre on Essex Street West, in the course of which lectures, workshops and exhibitions are being held on the world's most pressing contemporary issues. Topics such as biodiversity and climate change consistently spark lively debate.

April
Temple Bar
Dublin 2

Handel Festival

01 677 2255 | www.temple-bar.ie

Commemorating George Frederic Handel's colourful past and visit to Dublin in 1742, the Temple Bar Cultural Trust annually presents the week-long Handel Festival, including free concerts, workshops, talks and tours. It's a great opportunity to enjoy some beautiful classical music and learn about Handel himself.

Six Nations Rugby

May
Dublin Castle
Dublin 2

Heineken Green Energy Festival

Since the mid 1990s, this festival with its base at Dublin Castle has been held during the May bank holiday weekend in various venues around the city. The 2007 line-up was certainly music to the ears of many, including Kasabian, The Blizzards, Sinead O'Connor and Kila amongst others.

Bloomsday

June
Various Locations
Dublin

01 878 8547 | www.jamesjoyce.ie

Celebrating its 104rd anniversary in June 2008 is Bloomsday – the day that James Joyce's *Ulysses* is set on. Joyce enthusiasts mark the day by dressing in traditional attire and visiting various sites that are featured in the book – including Davy Byrne's on Duke Street for a glass of burgundy and a gorgonzola cheese sandwich. The James Joyce Centre hosts a week-long festival, including activities, music, film, lectures and readings.

Diversions

June-August
Various Locations
Dublin

01 677 2255 | www.temple-bar.ie

Dublin's Cultural Quarter is full of beans during the annual arts and culture festival, involving 100 performers from twelve different countries and traditionally attracting over 300,000 people. Film, music, opera, circus, live performances and markets will even put ideas into the heads of those who usually keep their feet firmly on the ground – true to its name, it provides diversion from the gridlock of every-day life.

Docklands Maritime Festival

June
Customs House Quay
Docklands
Dublin 1

01 818 3300 | www.dublindocklands.ie

This is a great family day out in the Docklands area, which is undergoing extensive and continuing regeneration. Various ships are on display, and you have the chance to go sailing along the River Liffey. There are also plenty of street performers and food markets, as well as an endless list of family entertainment options.

Dublin Pride

June
Various Locations
Dublin

www.dublinpride.org

This yearly gay festival celebrates the triumph of diversity – for two weeks there is a series of workshops, performances, parties and discussion forums, culminating in Parade Day, when thousands of people take the celebration to the streets and later wind up the day in the amphitheatre of the civic offices. The fun continues in the many after parties organised all around the city.

Dublin Writers Festival

June
Various Locations
Dublin

01 222 7848 | www.dublinwritersfestival.com

The Dublin Writers' Festival gives voice to some of the finest creations of non-fiction, fiction and poetry as well as encouraging discussion and debate. Various locations are used throughout the city to host innovative events, discussions and question and answer sessions.

Street Performance World Championships

June
Merrion Square
Dublin 2

01 639 4859 | www.spwc.ie

This festival is probably one of the more unusual festivals in Dublin and promises to be stranger and weirder each year. Street performers from throughout the world gather in Merrion Sqaure and try to out-do each other with their performances on unicylces, juggling and fire eating.

Taste of Dublin

June
Iveagh Gardens
Upper Mount St
Dublin 2

01662 0140 | www.tasteofdublin08.ie

Anyone for food and wine? This is the festival for you. Held over four days in the beautiful Iveagh Gardens, it brings together over 20 of the best restaurants in Dublin and enables you to sample their dishes for a fraction of the price. Just a word of warning, avoid going if it is raining. As it is out door and unsheltered, any rain really takes away from enjoying the food and ambience. One for a fine day.

Annual Events

June
Fitzwilliam Sq
Dublin 2

Women's Mini Marathon

01 293 0984 | www.womensminimarathon.ie

The biggest women only event of its kind in the world, Dublin's Women's Mini Marathon has been going for 14 years, and had over 40,000 runners in 2006. The course is over 10km, and proceeds go to various Irish charities. Around €10m was raised in 2006 alone.

June/July
Howth

Howth Peninsula Festival

www.howthpeninsula.com

From poetry readings to barbecues, and from live jazz music to Punch and Judy shows, there is much to please everyone at the Howth Peninsula Festival. It usually runs during the last weekend in June or the first weekend in July.

July
Punchestown
Racecourse
Co Kildare

Oxegen

www.oxegen.ie

Despite being located outside the city, Oxegen is a very popular event with many Dubliners. It is a weekend of fabulous performances by some of the biggest names in rock and pop – previous acts have included Snow Patrol, Mika, the Scissor Sisters, the Killers, Razorlight and Muse. Oxegen celebrates its fifth anniversary in 2008.

July/August
Irish Film Institute
Temple Bar
Dublin 2

Gay & Lesbian Film Festival

01 671 0939 | www.gcn.ie/dlgff

The second annual film festival to keep an eye on in Dublin caters to the city's gay scene, featuring many previous hits and a series of short films. The programme is usually released shortly before the event, but is always sure to be diverse.

August
RDS, Ballsbridge
Dublin 4

Dublin Horse Show

01 666 0866 | www.dublinhorseshow.com

This five-day celebration of the horse is very popular, with many visitors flying in especially for the occasion. One of the highlights is the nailbiting Nations Cup, which Ireland last won in 2004. If you're more interested in the frivolous side of the horsey world, check out the best dressed lady contest or the shopping area.

September
Various Locations
Dublin

Anna Livia Opera Festival

01 661 7544 | www.dublinopera.com

Lovers of popular opera are all ears at the annual Anna Livia festival, which brings the streets of Dublin alive with the sound of music with an array of events at multiple locations, such as the Olympia Theatre and Gaiety Theatre. Ticket prices start at €12.50.

September
Various Locations
Dublin

Culture Night

01 677 2255 | www.culturenight.ie

Following the success of the 2006 premiere, the organisers, the Temple Bar Cultural Trust, are hoping to draw 80,000 people to the 80 cultural venues spread across the city during this event. Apart from various free events, Dublin's museums, galleries, historic houses, studios and cathedrals stay open for extended hours.

September
Various Locations
Dublin

Dublin Fringe Festival

01 817 1677 | www.fringefest.com

The Fringe festival connects artists to their audience in displays of theatre, dance, music, visual and live arts as well as street and outdoor events and performances. At its heart are those expressions of creativity which would otherwise be unavailable to the public, and in this way, the DFF is a good stepping stone for emerging artists.

49

September
Various Locations
Dublin

Dublin Theatre Festival

01 677 8899 | www.dublintheatrefestival.com

50 years old and not a bit quiet. The world's oldest English-speaking theatre festival, founded in the 1950s by Brendan Smith, returns to Dublin every September for a period of just over two weeks, presenting international as well as national productions. The festival is an opportunity to catch some top quality performances (including some of theatre's biggest names), at various venues around the city.

September
Various Locations
Dublin

International Comedy Festival

081 871 9300 | www.bulmerscomedy.ie

This festival is now in its fourth year and among the world's five largest comedy festivals. For a week during autumn, some of the world's funniest comedians will have you rolling in the aisles of Dublin's premier comedy venues. And book early, because tickets for the main acts disappear quickly.

September
River Liffey
Dublin

Liffey Swim

01 222 2222 | www.dublincity.ie

Since 1920, brave swimmers have participated in this event organised by the Dublin City Council. The total distance is 2.2km, starting from the Watling Street Bridge and finishing at Customs House. You have to qualify for the race by swimming in five other swimming events in the season, so it's not something you can do on the spur of the moment! Last year, well over 300 swimmers took part.

October
Nassau St
Dublin 2

Dublin City Marathon

01 623 2250 | www.dublincitymarathon.ie

Around 10,000 runners ran the 2007 Dublin Marathon. The course measures 42km, starting at Nassau Street and ending in Merrion Square. The marathon starts at 09:00, although wheelchair participants start at 08:50. The course stays open for eight hours, so it is possible to walk the whole way – as long as you set a brisk pace! The entrance fee is €60 for EU residents, and €80 for non-EU residents.

October
Various locations
Dublin

Samhain Parade (Halloween)

01 605 7700 | www.visitdublin.com

Samhain signifies the end of the summer. In true carnival spirit, professional street artists in colourful and intriguing attire roam the streets of Dublin during the Halloween Parade, creating a giant piece of street theatre. Elsewhere, children can be seen walking from house to house dressed up in imaginative costumes as the rest of the city uses the occasion as an excuse for a good party in wacky outfits.

December
Leopardstown
Racecourse
Dublin 18

Christmas Racing Festival

01 289 3607 | www.leopardstown.com

The most high-profile of the 22 race meetings held at Leopardstown Racecourse each year, the Christmas Festival at the end of December rounds off the city events calendar, forming an integral part of the season for many. And if Christmas has left you out of pocket, there is over €1 million in the pot for winning jockeys and trainers.

December-January
RDS, Ballsbridge
Dublin 4

Funderland

01 6141 9988 | www.funderland.com

A saviour for those parents whose thoughtful gifts can't keep their children entertained throughout their Christmas holidays. Funderland, a huge indoor funfair event, has brought all sorts of things to Dublin in the course of its 32 year existence, including performing dolphins and a high wire motorcycle act.

Great things can come in small packages...

Perfectly proportioned to fit in your pocket, these marvellous mini guidebooks make sure you don't just get the holiday you paid for, but rather the one that you dreamed of.

Explorer Mini Visitors' Guides
Maximising your holiday, minimising your hand luggage

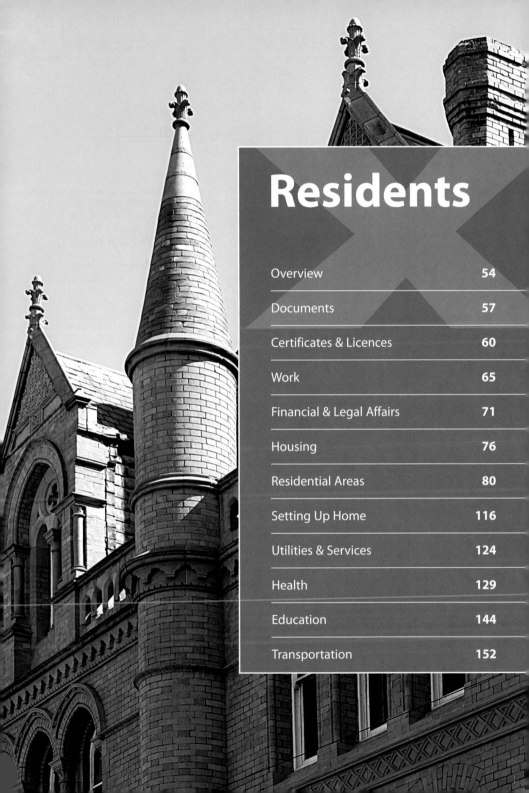

Residents

Residents

A Land Of Boozers

A common misconception is that all Irish people are alcoholics, which, to state the obvious, is not true. Yes, the pub is still very much the centre of social life, and most people go out for drinks, especially at the weekend, but that doesn't make them a nation of alcoholics.

Overview

In the last 10 to15 years, a strong economy has transformed Dublin into a cosmopolitan city. There are plenty of jobs in a variety of sectors and those with shortages, such as the IT and financial services sectors, are particularly interested in recruiting from abroad (see p.68).

Ireland has had a lot of catching up to do since its booming economy, dubbed the Celtic Tiger, launched it as a happening city. Birth control, divorce and homosexuality have only been legalised within the last 20 years or so, and the transport infrastructure is still behind most other European cities (although it is getting better all the time). Ireland's membership of the European Union, and the subsequent funding the country has received, has transformed it into a city which is well regarded for its economic transformation and its political character.

The Irish people, by and large, have taken this newfound wealth in their stride and embraced the transformations that have come with it. Making an honest living, raising strong family units, and enjoying the *craic* are still important priorities, as they were in pre-Tiger years.

It certainly has plenty to offer to the new resident. So whether you are thinking of a move to Dublin, or you are already there and are cutting your way through the red tape, or whether you've lived there for some time, this chapter is full of helpful information on working, living and getting settled in the city.

Where Are All The Redheads?

The myth that Ireland is populated by redheads is common. While red hair only comes from Celtic genes, the majority of Irish people have dark brown or black hair.

Considering Ireland

Dubliners may complain about the weather, the prices and the poor transport system, but everyone agrees on one major advantage: the compact city centre. This makes finding your bearings in Dublin an easy task, and you'll be whizzing about the city streets on foot in no time.

Although there is some fear that the economy is starting to slow down, it is hardly flailing, and there are still more jobs than people so your chances of finding work are pretty good. Particular sectors, such as financial services, IT, engineering, nursing and construction, are especially easy to find a job in. The work ethic tends to be more relaxed than in America or England, with less of an emphasis on working longer hours to impress the boss, and the atmosphere among colleagues usually being friendly and casual.

While the job market is good, it is wise to check it out before you arrive, especially if you work in a field that is not overly specialised or in which there are not labour shortages. In some fields, getting a job is largely based on contacts, so think about whether you are willing to work in a job unrelated to your profession, or maybe do some volunteer work until you find what you're looking for. Salaries are pretty good but the cost of living is high, and you might not save much.

If you are not an EU citizen, or the holder of a highly specialised skill, getting residency in Ireland can be difficult. It is best to read up on the procedures and regulations of gaining legal residence status in the country before you make the move.

However, once you're settled, have made friends (which is easy to do) and regularly make the most of the great nightlife (there's everything you could want in terms of drinking, dancing, theatre and music), you will probably find that Dublin feels like home and that, depsite the ups and downs, you love the 'dirty old town'.

Before You Arrive

Before you arrive in Dublin, be sure to have all your documents, such as your passports, letters from employers or educational institutions and entry visas, if you need them, ready. There are different requirements for EU and non-EU citizens, and various options are open to non-EU citizens, so do some research and find out exactly which category you fall under and which documents you need.

If you do not have a job lined up, check with the relevant professional bodies to see whether any specific qualifications (in law or accountancy, for example) are recognised here. Because living in Dublin is so expensive, it might not be a bad idea to rent out your house in your home country, if you own one, or have some savings, to tide you over while you adjust to Dublin's hefty prices.

Dublin banks, particularly the bigger branches, are well equipped to handle international banking transactions so you don't necessarily have to close your bank account in your home country. However, it is a good idea to set up an Irish bank account as soon as you start work.

You can easily manage without a car in Dublin. Traffic is bad, parking and petrol are expensive and the public transport system is simply far less hassle, despite its shortcomings. If you are keen to have your own wheels though, make sure you have parking with your accomodation (and factor it into your rent calculations) as it is fairly sparse in the city.

If you have children, be sure to research the schools well in advance. The school year starts in the Autumn (usually in early September), so it makes sense to move in time for that, if feasible. Contact a few schools to check for availability and get your kids on the waiting lists as early as possible. Be aware that the waiting list for schools in 'nicer' areas might be long. Another thing to consider is that most non-private schools are Catholic – there are some Protestant and non-denominational schools available, but these usually have the longest waiting lists.

When looking for somewhere to live, you will probably want to rent somewhere first while you feel out the property market. The city is divided in two by the River Liffey, which runs through the city centre. General opinion is that the south side (Dublin 2) is nicer, but the north side has a certain character and offers some more reasonable housing areas. Buying a house is always an option, although most people are advising against it in the current market, in which prices are extremely high. It may be worth waiting a while to see if there is any significant or permanent decrease in the average house prices.

When You Arrive

Don't panic! Whenever you move to a new country, there will always be a few weeks of transitioning and taking care of details. However, remember that in a few weeks everything will be sorted and you will be able to sit back and enjoy Dublin. Here are a few things that need to be taken care of when you arrive:

- Get your Personal Public Service (PPS) number (like a social security number) at your local Social Welfare office so that you can begin work (and start being taxed).
- If you need to, register with the police at the Garda National Immigration Bureau on Burgh Quay and get your GNIB card (an ID card that says you're allowed to live in Ireland).
- Start work (p.65).
- Find a place to live. Having done some research on the internet, you can now go and view houses. Most places are rented furnished, and many are available on short-term leases, so you don't have to find your dream home right away. See p.76.
- Open a bank account (p.71).
- Figure out how to get around the city. See www.dublinbus.ie or www.irishrail.ie (go to the Dart section) to find out routes and timetables or go to the Dublin Bus office on O'Connell Street or the Dublin Tourist Office, just off Grafton Street.
- Sort out a driving licence (p.60). If your country is eligible, you can exchange your existing licence for an Irish one. Even if you come from a non-eligible country, you can still drive for up to 12 months before you need to get your Irish licence.

North Or South?
Many people think that because Dublin is such a small city, there can't be that much difference between the areas. This is not the case. While Dublin is a fairly compact city, there are many neighbourhoods or suburbs, each with its own unique flavour. Locals really identify with – and are very much defined by – the area they grew up in. There is a huge divide between the north and south sides of the city, the south side being more affluent than the north side.

Don't Be Daft
www.daft.ie is one of the most popular property listings websites. It covers rentals and purchase.

- If you have children, take them to their new school to meet the principal, teachers and pupils.
- Make some friends and have fun. Look at newspapers or just wander around Temple Bar, Dublin's cultural quarter (right in the city centre), to find out what's going on.

Going Places

While most areas, particularly the city centre and the south side, are safe during the day, be alert in the north inner city (including O'Connell Street) and the north side of the city, especially after dark. And during the daytime, keep a tight hold on your personal belongings. Dublin is a relatively safe city, but it's still worth being careful.

When You Leave

- Get your P45 document from the Revenue office. This is a summary of the tax that your employer has deducted from your salary, in accordance with tax laws, and also states that you have finished working at your company (and are able to begin work somewhere else). Also, you should leave your forwarding address either with your employer or the local Revenue office so that you can receive your P60, a summary of your tax information for the year, at the end of the tax year.
- Give your landlord a month's notice. This is standard, unless your contract says otherwise, and in doing so you will be able to get back your deposit.
- Utilities: transfer all your utilities out of your name (electricity, gas, phone). Failure to do so could make you liable for charges racked up by the next tenant. An easy solution is to transfer your accounts (once settled) into your landlord's name.
- Bank accounts: If you think you will be returning to Ireland, you can keep your bank account open. However, if you will not be coming back, it's easier to close your account while you're still there.
- Ship, sell or give away your stuff. If you want to ship some of your belongings, ring several companies and get quotes for the best price (p.116). If you don't want to keep it all, you can give almost anything to charity shops. Alternatively, you can try to sell them in the classifieds in most newspapers or through *Buy & Sell*, a classifieds newspaper, or on Craig's List (http://dublin.craigslist.org).

Apartments on St Stephen's Green

Houses in Dublin 4

Apartments along the Liffey

Documents

Access Granted
Countries whose citizens don't need visas to enter Ireland include citizens from all the EU countries, Australia, America, Canada, New Zealand, South Africa and many others. For a full list go to the website of the Irish Department of Foreign Affairs (www.dfa.ie).

Arriving in a new country always entails serious amounts of paperwork, and this is no 'one size fits all' process. The paperwork you need depends on many factors such as your nationality, your age, your profession and your purpose for coming to Ireland. Fortunately there are several very useful websites where you can figure out exactly what you are going to need. The Department of Justice (www.justice.ie) handles immigration. The Department of Foreign Affairs gives you plenty of info on what you need to get in, depending on your nationality (www.dfa.ie). The Department of Enterprise, Trade and Employment (www.entemp.ie) can provide information relating to work permits. The Immigrant Council of Ireland (www.immigrantcouncil.ie) is an advisory and advocacy group for immigrants. And the Office of the Immigration Services Commissioner in the UK (www.workpermit.com) may not be an Irish office, but its website has a lot of helpful information on moving to Ireland.

Residence Visa

In the last decade or so, Ireland, for the very first time in its history, has been a nation of immigration, rather than emigration. This means that most legislation relating to immigrants has been fairly recent or is in the process of being drawn up. The Department of Justice, which handles immigration, is still figuring out how exactly to deal with the relatively large number of people who have moved to Ireland. There are a lot of grey areas, both in legislation itself and in the way different civil servants and gardaí (police officers) treat immigrants and legislation and court cases with regards to immigration are ongoing.

All EU/EEA citizens, except for some Romanians and Bulgarians are allowed to work and live in Ireland without any restrictions.

If you are not an EU citizen, a highly qualified professional with a large earning potential or are not married to an EU citizen (although that has complications of its own, see p.58) it is rather difficult to be able to live and work here. So, before you move here, check whether it would actually be possible for you to work in Ireland. That said, Ireland was one of the few 'old' EU member states to welcome people from the new EU states during the enlargement in 2004, without any restrictions. Some restrictions still apply to people from Romania and Bulgaria (see p.59).

You'll frequently come across, and need to go and visit, the Garda National Immigration Bureau (GNIB). Their office is located on Burgh Quay, between between O'Connell Street Bridge and Tara Street Dart station (01 666 9100, http://www.garda.ie/angarda/gnib.html). They're open from 08:00 to 22:00 Monday to Thursday, and from 08:30 to 16:00 on Fridays. Obtaining a visa and a work permit is a lengthy and complicated process, and there are different procedures and options, and paperwork, depending on whether you are an EU citizen or not so patience and a strong desire to see it through, are a must.

Work Permits For Non-EU Citizens

If, as a non-EU citizen, you are not eligible to get a job under the green card permits scheme (see p.59), you might be able to get one under the Work Permits scheme. This covers jobs for which the annual salary is at least €30,000, excluding bonuses, and in some very rare cases, below €30,000. It is primarily designed for unique jobs that do not fit into a category under the Green Card scheme. Either the employee or the employer can apply for the work permit, which will initially be issued for two years, and is renewable. Once you apply for a work permit, it takes about four to eight weeks to process. The fee for applying for a work permit is €500 to €1,000. If you have a spouse and children, they will not be able to come and live with you in Ireland for 12 months.

Certain workers – including administrative and clerical staff, operations and production staff, general operatives and labourers, retail or sales staff, drivers (excluding HGV drivers), childcare workers, hotel, catering and tourism staff (excluding chefs) and craft workers and apprentice/trainee craft workers are not covered under the work permits scheme and are not allowed to apply for one.

Also, under the work permit scheme, your potential employer must do a labour market needs test – in other words, they must advertise the job to see if there are any suitable EU, Romanian or Bulgarian citizens who can fill it before they can offer it to you.

Inter-Company Transfers

This allows non-EU senior management people and key personnel and trainees who are earning at least €40,000 annually, and have worked at an overseas station of a company for at least 12 months, to work at the company's office in Ireland. The duration of the permit depends on the reason for the transfer, can be granted for up to 24 months and can later be extended for up to five years. The company does not need to advertise the job before giving it to you. Once you come to Ireland, you must register with the GNIB on Burgh Quay. Your spouse and dependents can get their own work permits once you have been given permission to transfer.

Spouses Of EU Citizens

This is a particularly grey area at the moment because of recent legislation. It is possible for non-EU spouses of EU citizens to work in Ireland, based on their marriage. When you enter the country (having organised a visa if you needed one), you will probably be given a temporary stamp to say you can stay in the country for a short period, probably three months.

In the past, the next step would have been to go to the Garda National Immigration Bureau. Along with your spouse, you would have needed to bring the following documents: both of your passports, your marriage certificate, a letter from your EU spouse's employer saying that they work there and possibly shared private health insurance (you are not always asked for this last requirement).

Your passport would either have been stamped, you would have be given a GNIB identification card (which you will need to present anytime you return to Ireland after going on holidays) and you would have been allowed to stay in Ireland for a year, and then get your residency renewed the following year.

Alternatively, you would be asked at the GNIB to send an application to the justice department, with the documents listed above. Then, in about six months, you would (or would not) receive permission from the justice department to remain here on the basis of your marriage. If you received permission you would then go to the GNIB on Burgh Quay and get your GNIB card.

However, this has been complicated by recent legislation which states that a non-EU spouse has to have lived legally with their EU spouse in the spouse's home country. For example, if a Russian woman is married to a French man, she will have needed to live with him legally in France in order to be allowed to live in Ireland on the basis that she is his spouse. If you are a non-EU spouse and you do not fulfill this requirement, it may be easier to work in Ireland on a green card or a work permit, rather than as a spouse (p.59).

Spouses Of Irish Citizens

The process is similar for spouses of Irish citizens as it is for those of non-Irish EU citizens. Although it is not quite as complicated, it may take longer.

The spouse of an Irish citizen can enter with their spouse (be sure to get the relevant visa, if you need one, before you come to Ireland). You will be given a

Working Holiday Visas

Ireland has working holiday visa agreements with four countries: Australia, New Zealand, Canada and Hong Kong. These last for one year and allow citizens from those countries to engage in casual work in Ireland. They cannot be renewed. Full-time tertiary students or recent graduates from America and South Africa can also apply for temporary work visas that last four to six months.

Children

Children under the age of 16 do not need to be registered with the gardai. Once children turn 16, they must register. If you, as a parent, are a non-EU citizen and you are here on a green card or work permit, your child can get a permit as a dependent. This process is the same as that for a non-EU spouse of a non-EU person who has a green card or work permit.

stamp and then need to go to the GNIB office on Burgh Quay with all the relevant documents (see the EU spouse section above). You will either be given your stamp, GNIB card and allowed to stay for at least a year (probably more), with the option to renew this, or you will be asked to apply to the justice department. However, because this is covered under domestic legislation, the queue is longer and your application might not be processed for 18 months. You can always try to get your own work permit or green card (p.57).

Work Permits For Non-EU Spouses

If you are a non-EU spouse of a non-EU citizen who has a work permit or green card, you can apply for a work permit as well. However, the process will be much easier for you than it was for your spouse. You or the employer can apply for a work permit once you have been offered a full-time job in any (legal) sector. Also, the employer does not need to advertise the job before offering it to you and there is no fee. The work permit will be issued for as long as your spouse's work permit or green card is valid.

---

i

Business Permission

If you are a non-EEA citizen who wishes to set up a business in Ireland, these are the requirements: you must have at least €300,000 in capital with which to start the business; must employ at least two EEA citizens; your proposed business must add to commercial activity and competitiveness of Ireland; the business must be viable and able to provide enough money to support you; and you must have a valid passport and be of good character. You apply for business permission to the justice department, and it is granted for a period of 12 months initially. You must present the letter granting permission when you arrive in Ireland and you must then register at the GNIB office on Burgh Quay.

Go For Green

Unlike with the work permit scheme, employers do not need to do a labour market needs test before they offer the job to a non-EU person if that person qualifies for a green card.

Green Card For Non-EU Citizens

The Green Card Permits Act came into effect on 1 February, 2007. It allows people who have been offered a job at a company in Ireland to work for that company. It is granted for two years and is renewable. Years accumulated working on a green card count towards permanent residency and citizenship. Either the employee or the employer can apply for the permit, which will take about four to eight weeks to process. You can download the form online from The Department of Enterprise, Trade and Employment (www.entemp.ie). It will cost you €1,000 the first time you apply for a green card. Both the green cards and work permits (see p.57) tie you to the specific employer with whom you are employed. Your spouse and children will be able to move to Ireland with you (see above).

There are two categories of jobs under which non-EU citizens can apply for a green card permit. The first is for a job in any sector for which the annual salary is at least €60,000, not including bonuses. The other category is for those who have been offered a job in certain sectors – including IT, healthcare, industry, research or science, financial services and marketing and other specialist managing – for which the annual salary is between €30,000 and €59,999.

Romanians & Bulgarians

As of 1 January 2007, Romanian and Bulgarian citizens do not need visas to enter Ireland. However, when it comes to living and working here, citizens from these countries fall into two different categories: those who were legally living in Dublin before 31 December 2006 and those who are not yet resident in Ireland. Those who have been living legally in Ireland for at least 12 continuous months prior to 1 January 2007, can continue working and living here. Those who have not been living in Ireland no longer need a visa to enter the country, as they did in the past, but otherwise they are more or less legally in the same situation as non-EU citizens, needing work permits and other related red tape, if they want to work here.

Driving Licence

Other options **Transportation** p.152

Other options **Transportation** p.152

You'll often hear Irish motorists joke, 'I failed my driving test and then drove home.' This is because drivers here can continue to drive on their provisional licences for a long time, as long as they sit their tests. Also, there is a backlog of motorists who want to take their tests, and some have to wait months to be given a date. Motorists can begin driving when they are 17 years old and must carry their licence with them at all times.

Driving Licence

To obtain a full or permanent Irish driving licence, you must first pass your driver theory test. To apply, and to find the nearest testing centre to you, go to the Driver Theory Test Services website (www.dtts.ie). At this stage you don't need to take any driving lessons, although the more you know about cars and driving, the easier it will be. Once you pass this, you receive your first provisional driving licence. This allows you to drive accompanied by a licensed driver, except on the motorway. However, on your second provisional licence (they last for two years each) you can drive unaccompanied. You can keep on renewing your second provisional licence indefinitely but you must show that you have attempted to pass the test, even if you fail it, before it expires or you can end up in an odd grey area where you no longer have a licence at all. If you pass your driver's test, you can then apply for a full licence.

Permanent Licence

All motorists from the EU/EEA countries, as well as from the other countries mentioned above, who have a full driving licence, can exchange it for an Irish one. You can get an Irish one by filling out an application form (called form A.D401) at your local motor taxation office, post office or garda station. You will also need to have a medical exam and fill out an Exchange of Driving Licence form, which you can download or get at your local motor tax office. The fees are minimal. The length of the licence depends on your age. If you are under 60, you can apply for a 10 year licence.

Motorcycle Licence

If you have a full Irish licence to drive a car, you automatically qualify for a 'Category M' motorcycle licence, which means you can drive two-wheeled vehicles that can't go above 45km per hour, and does not have an engine size exceeding 50 cc. However, if you wish to drive a motorcycle that is faster and more powerful than this (Category A1), or wish to drive a motorcycle with a sidecar or an engine size of more than 125 cc (category A), you need to get a provisional motorcycle licence (and then, after two two-year provisional licences, take your test for the full licence). You can get an application for your provisional motorcycle licence (indicate if you're applying for Category A, A1 or M) at your local Motor Taxation office. You can then apply for your full motorcycle licence.

Driving Schools

Accelerate Driving	01 296 5904	www.acceleratesom.com
Airport Driving School	1890 829 999	www.airportdrivingschool.com
Barabara's School of Motoring	086 362 9988	www.dublindrivinginstructor.com
First Gear Driving School	01 847 4806	www.first-gear.ie
Irish School of Motoring	01 874 6677	www.ism.ie
PassRight School of Motoring	01 838 2479	www.iol.ie/~passright

Christenings ◀

Ireland is still very much a Catholic country, with significant religious events, such as christenings and holy communions marking different stages in a child's development. These tend to turn into social events and are usually followed by a party put on by the proud parents. Most people in Ireland get their child christened. If you wish to christen your child, you can contact your local church and they will make all the necessary arrangements. It is worth noting that children prepare for their holy communion in school, so if your children are not baptised, they will not be able to participate in holy communion and similar religious events.

Birth Certificate & Registration

Within three months of having your baby, you must register his or her birth in the office of the Registrar of Births, Marriages and Deaths. The one in Dublin is located at Joyce House, 8/11 Lombard Street East, Dublin 2 (01 671 1968). You can also get birth certificates here for a small fee.

While still in hospital (after giving birth) you will be given a Birth Notification Form, imaginatively called Form BNF/01. Fill this out and the hospital will forward it on to the local registrar's office, so that the registrar knows that the birth has happened. However, one or both of the parents still needs to go the registrar's office to sign the Register of Births. There are different registration forms depending on whether the parents are married and whether or not both of them are registering the child, or if just one parent is registering the child.

If the parents are not Irish, they register their child according to their nationality. For example, if the parents are Canadian, they register their child as Canadian. If the parents are from different countries, they can register their child under one or both of the nationalities, depending on each country's rules about dual citizenship and the parents' wishes. Once registered, your child is legal and does not need a residency card.

Since 2004, children born in Ireland no longer get automatic Irish citizenship. If you wish to apply for Irish citizenship for your child, you need to apply to the Naturalisation and Immigration Service at the Department of Justice. There is a special form for persons under 18 years.

If your child is not Irish and you wish to apply for a passport, you can do so through your country's embassy. If your child is Irish and you wish to apply for an Irish passport, you can get a form from garda stations, libraries, Citizens Information Centres or post offices. Then send the form to the Passport Office in Dublin, which is on Molesworth Street, Dublin 2 (01 671 1633 or 1890 426 888).

Adoption

The majority of adoptions in Ireland are by stepparents, usually by the biological mother's partner, who is not the father, adopting the child. There is a low placement of children for adoption in Ireland because the State heavily supports single mothers, as do extended families. Couples who cannot have children of their own tend to adopt children from other countries with which Ireland has bilateral agreements.

Adoption in Ireland is a very complicated and drawn-out process – it takes about two years – and there is a thorough vetting system. Adoption legislation is also currently being updated. In order to be eligible to adopt, you must be a resident in Ireland and at least 21 years old. You must also fall into one of the following categories: a married couple; a married person living alone (there are various conditions for this); the mother, father or close relative of the child; a widow or widower; or a sole applicant if they are suitable. Note that an unmarried couple cannot jointly adopt a child.

If you wish to adopt a child, contact the Adoption Board (01 230 9300, www.adoptionboard.ie), which is an independent statutory body that determines the eligibility and suitability of people who want to adopt. They will refer you to an agency. You then attend information classes and start filling out the forms.

Next, you will be assessed by an agency's social worker, and it will involve a number of interviews and home visits. You must also have a medical exam, be checked to see if you have a criminal record, and supply character references. The social worker then makes a report for the adoption agency and a decision is made. This part of the process takes at least a year.

If you are accepted, you will have to wait for a baby to be offered. The length of the wait will depend on whether you are applying for an inter-country or domestic adoption. Once a baby is available, you apply to the Adoption Board for an adoption

Two Daddies? ◀

Gay men and women can adopt as individuals, put not as a couple, which affects the rights of one parent. See www.glen.ie for more information about this anomaly and the efforts to rectify it.

order. This can take quite a long time and the Adoption Board can still turn down your application at this stage.

If you are adopting a child from another country, you have to make sure that the adoption law of that country is recognised under Irish law and the adoption can be registered when you return to Ireland with the child. When you decide upon which country you want to adopt a child from, you must get a referral to an adoption agency or foundation in that country – you can do this through the Irish Adoption Board. There will be paperwork to fill out in the country where the child is from. You must also get permission from the Department of Justice so that the child will be able to come into Ireland. There will be more paperwork when you return to Ireland in order to register the child in the adoption register here.

Marriage Certificate & Registration

Divorce

Divorce only became legal in Ireland in 1995, with the passing of the Divorce Referendum. The subsequent legislation on divorce came out in 1997. This has led to an increase in civil marriage ceremonies, which are often preferred by couples who are re-marrying. It has also had a knock-on affect for lawyers and the courts. Prenuptial agreements are not legally recognised in Ireland.

Weddings in Ireland are usually a grand and expensive affair. You can get married in a short civil ceremony in the Registrar's Office or you can have a full church ceremony (with no need for a civil service as it is recognised by the State). There's also a growing trend for people to have a civil ceremony in Ireland and then take off to the south of France or somewhere else with a sunnier clime for a more lavish celebration in a gothic cathedral or Romanesque church.

Before the wedding day, however, the bride-to-be usually has a hen party with her female friends and the prospective groom has a stag party with his male friends to bid farewell to their single days. These can involve anything from a night at the pub or a day in a spa to a weekend in Prague.

If you opt for a church wedding, you will need to book the church well in advance. You may also have to take a marriage preparation course.

Most ceremonies, whether religious or civil, are then followed by a reception. Again, you will need to book the venue months in advance. People usually opt for restaurants, fancy pubs or hotels, but sometimes chose to hire a marquee.

Guests can be invited for the whole day, or else for just the reception, known as the 'afters'. If you're invited to a wedding you will usually receive a formal invitation by post with RSVP. The dress code is quite formal; although not so lavish that the bride risks being upstaged, and needless to say, wearing white is a major no-no. Men should look to wear trousers and a formal jacket, if not a suit. Tops and tails is rare for guests in Ireland, but the invitation should state so if it's the case.

Civil Ceremonies

To get married in a civil ceremony, the first thing you need to do is obtain an application to get married from the Office of the Registrar of Births, Marriages and Deaths, located at Joyce House, 8/11 Lombard Street East, Dublin 2 (01 671 1968). They can post you an application or you can download one from the General Register Office's website. You then send the application, along with a cheque made out for €40 to the office. Legally, you must give three months' written notice of your intention to marry and you will not be given a date until at least three months from when the office has received your application in writing.

Once the office has received your application, they will contact you and you and your partner can go to the registrar's office and apply in person to get married and fill out the paperwork. You must bring your passport, and divorce papers if you have already been married. This costs €10. It is worth noting that over the summer period the office is incredibly busy, and you may have to wait longer than three months before you can get married.

The actual ceremony takes about 10 minutes and costs €50. You only need to invite two witnesses but the registrar's office in Dublin can seat at least 50 people. You can also have music if you wish. You are given your marriage certificate, which costs €8, after the ceremony.

Tiny Dub
If you've got far-flung relatives heading to Dublin to help you celebrate your wedding, get them a copy of the *Mini Dublin Explorer*. It's a teeny, tiny tome of useful information on the city, meaning they'll be out and about discovering the city, leaving you more time to concentrate on your last minute wedding plans!

Religious Ceremonies

If you want to be married in a church, you must give three months' written notification to the Registrar of Marriages, stating which church your ceremony will be in. The priest conducting the ceremony has the authority to fill out all the paperwork for you, and he can send this on to the Registrar of Marriages for you, so your chosen church should be your first port of call. Alternatively, you can have a civil ceremony and then a church one (only necessary if you plan on having the church one outside of Ireland). Similar rules apply if you wish to get married in a Protestant church or a Jewish synagogue. However, Muslim couples that wish to marry must do so at the Registrar's office in order for their marriage to be legal. Contact your local church/religious organisation for full details and requirements.

Tax Implications For Married Couples

Once you are married, you must inform the Revenue office. They will then send you a form, on which you can change your name and address (if you have moved), giving them both of your PPS numbers and informing them whether you are declaring jointly as a married couple (which is usually the most favourable), or separately. However, for the remainder of the tax year in which you were married, you will be taxed as single people. If you end up paying more tax as two single people than as a married couple, you can claim the difference back.

If You Need Money
In the event of the death of your spouse, if you need access to money you can ring your local social welfare office to talk about what benefits or grants you may be entitled to. Alternatively, you can contact the Money Advice and Budgeting Service (1890 283 438, www.mabs.ie), which can offer support and advice.

Death Certificate & Registration

Death, particularly when you may not have family members close by, is a very difficult time. However, don't feel like you are alone – there are plenty of support services and organisations available to help. If you have children, Sólás (01 473 2110) is a counselling service, provided through Barnardos (www.barnardos.ie), which specifically works with children. If you haven't done so already, it is always a good idea for you and your family to sort out legal matters such as wills and power of attorney so that you don't have to worry about these things should the worst happen.

If your residency was dependent on your marriage (if your spouse was the one who had a green card or was an EU citizen) get advice from the Immigrant Council of Ireland (01 674 0200) or from a solicitor (lawyer) as to your legal status.

If you wish to be an organ donor, you can carry an organ donor card with you, which you can get from your doctor, a chemist, the Irish Kidney Association (1890 456 556, www.ika.ie), the Irish Heart and Lung Transplant Association (01 495 0940, www.ihlta.com) or other members of the Irish Donor Network. You can contact one of these organisations with any questions you might have. Be sure to discuss your wishes with your partner or family. If you wish to donate your body for medical research, contact the medical research schools at University College Dublin, University College Cork, University College Galway, Trinity College or the Royal College of Surgeons, to sort out details. There will be different procedures if a post-mortem examination is needed.

In The Event Of A Death

Two things need to be established when someone dies: their identity and the cause of death. Obviously, if you are the partner or a close relative or friend, the identity can easily be established. To establish the cause of death, you need to ring your local doctor. If the doctor is satisfied as to the cause of death, they will certify the death. You can then call a funeral director or undertaker and they will help you take care of all the

The Irish Wake

The wake is an important ritual following the heart-breaking event of a death. It is a purging affair, when friends and family members of the deceased gather together (traditionally in the home of the deceased), with the deceased's body nearby, to sing, dance, drink, and reminisce about the person who died. Traditionally, a wake was supposed to be held just in case the dead person was actually asleep, and woke up.

funeral arrangements. However, if the doctor is uncertain about the cause of death, they may call the coroner, who will decide whether a postmortem is needed.

Registering A Death

You are legally required to register a death. You must do so as soon as possible, and no later than three months after the person dies. In order to do so, bring the Death Notification Form stating the cause of death, which the doctor who declared the cause of death will give you, to the Office of the Registrar of Births, Marriages and Deaths, located at Joyce House, 8/11 Lombard Street East, Dublin 2 (01 671 1968). You must sign the register in the presence of the registrar. It does not cost anything to register the death, although a death certificate will cost €8.

Inquest & Autopsy

If the doctor is not satisfied as to the cause of death, she/he can call the coroner. Also, if the person died through an accident, or in unexplained or violent circumstances, the coroner must be called. The gardaí (police) must also be called. The coroner will then decide whether a post-mortem examination (autopsy) needs to be done. The State pathologist or the assistant State pathologist will carry out the examination. The coroner will register the death for you if a there is a post-mortem examination or an inquest.

Repatriating The Body

If you would like to repatriate the deceased's body to their home country, the funeral director can help you to organise it. You can also get help from the embassy of the country you are repatriating the body to and from a funeral director in the home country. Repatriating a body is quite expensive. You can opt to cremate the body in Ireland and then send on the ashes.

The documentation you will need to repatriate the body includes the deceased's passport or ID card; a coroner's removal order/non-infectious note, which the funeral director can get for you; an embalming certificate; a funeral director's declaration; a notarisation of documents (where applicable) and an embassy permit. Contact the embassy of the country you are repatriating the body to for full details of what you will need, and any queries.

The funeral home in Dublin will embalm the body and prepare it for travel. A coffin travelling across international borders must be sealed and lead or zinc-lined. These coffins cannot be cremated, and so you must get another coffin, or have the lining removed, if you wish to cremate the body in the deceased's home country.

The funeral director in Ireland can help you make the travel arrangements. The body can travel by plane, ferry or by car although, obviously, time will probably be an issue.

The embassy here will need to be contacted (the funeral director can do this) so they can liaise with authorities in the home country. A funeral director in the home country must also be contacted so that they can take care of arrangements when the body arrives.

The River Liffey

Working in Dublin

On the back of the Celtic Tiger, hundreds of thousands of immigrants from both the EU and around the world have come to work in Dublin, adding strength and skills to the Irish economy. Ireland was one of the very few countries not to impose any restrictions on people from eastern European countries after the 2004 enlargement. Thus, many people from Poland and other 'new' EU member states have come to Dublin, working in various sectors and setting up businesses. Statistically, Ireland needs immigrants, as there are more jobs than people at the moment. If you can get over the frustrations of commuting in Dublin, working in the city is great. There are many professional jobs that offer interesting challenges and opportunities with great possibilities for advancing your career, while a big emphasis is placed on a work/life balance. Professional jobs offer plenty of holidays, sick and maternity leave and there are also nine public holidays or 'bank holidays' throughout the year.

International experience and the ability to speak several languages are highly regarded by employers. Please note that you need to speak English to get a decent job in Dublin. If you have a skill that is particularly specialised, employers will be all the more willing to negotiate and hire you.

In some ways, Dublin is like a small town, and in some sectors, getting the job you want depends on the people you know. So, when you first move to Dublin, stay open-minded – if you can't get your dream job right away, try to get a similar or related job, network and make contacts, and these should help you to eventually snag your dream job.

Job Sectors

The sectors with the most openings, and the ones that immigrants often work in, include construction, IT, accounting, banking and financial services, sales and marketing, engineering, the legal sector and medical professions (nursing in particular). Skills gained abroad – particularly if there is not the infrastructure or equipment available to learn such skills in Ireland – are highly regarded. With the opening up of Ireland to non-English Europeans, there are currently a great deal of opportunities available to people who have strong language skills in other languages.

Business Culture & Etiquette

To someone from the US or other countries with more formal work ethics, conversation between colleagues might seem very casual in the Irish workplace. This is mainly due to the fact that many Irish people become friends with their colleagues and socialise with them outside work. Irish people love to tease (or 'take the piss' out of) each other and this is seen as a sign of affection and friendship. The clothes women wear to work might also seem casual. However, when they need to be, the Irish are very professional and, if you are new to the job and the country, and unsure of how to behave, it is much better to err on the side of too professional rather than not professional enough.

Setting Up Your Own Business Or Being Self Employed

If you are not an EU/EEA citizen, setting up your own business is quite complicated and difficult. However, if you are an EU/EEA citizen, it's easy. There are different rules for citizens of Romania and Bulgaria. Many eastern Europeans have set up successful businesses and, with a growing immigrant population, there is certainly a need for restaurants, shops, salons and other businesses that offer food and products from different countries.

Make sure you read up on all the financial, legal and taxation issues before you start. The Business Access to State Information and Services (www.basis.ie), the

Dublin City Enterprise Board (www.dceb.ie), the Chambers of Commerce Ireland (www.chambers.ie) and other organisations can help you.

If you wish to be self employed and work on a freelance basis, EU citizens can do so freely, except for Romanians and Bulgarians. If you are not an EU citizen, you'll need a bit more perseverance. Again, make sure you are aware of all the tax implications from the start.

Getting Started

In order to work in Ireland, you need a personal public service number (PPS) so that you can be taxed (similar to the US social security number). In order to get a number, go to your local office of the Department of Social and Family Affairs to fill out the required form. Go to www.welfare.ie to find out where your local branch is. If you are a UK citizen, you need to bring along your passport or your birth certificate and a valid form of photo ID when you apply for your PPS number. You will also need proof of address and of either work, claim, education, residency, or tax liability history in the UK. If you do not have any bills or bank statements yet at your new address, a letter from your employer or tenancy agreement is acceptable. If you are from an European Economic Area country, which includes the EU countries as well as Iceland, Norway, Liechtenstein and Switzerland, you need to bring your passport or national identity card, proof of birth, work, unemployment, education, residency, or tax liability in the EEA or Switzerland, and proof of address. You will be sent your new PPS number by post within a few days.

Non-EEA nationals must provide a valid passport or certificate of registration with the Department of Justice, Equality and Law Reform (www.justice.ie), and evidence of either work (including your work permit or letter from the Department of Justice, Equality and Law Reform giving permission to work), unemployment, residency, tax liability or education in the foreign country, and proof of address.

Working Hours

For most professional jobs, the working week is from Monday to Friday, from 09:00 to 17:00 or from 10:00 to 18:00, with an hour for lunch, usually taken between 13:00 and 14:00. If you work in a hospital, the media, retail or manufacturing industry, hospitality or other sectors, your hours may very well differ. Working overtime is not unusual, depending on the sector you work in, but usually your salary will either reflect the long hours you put in or you will be paid overtime. All professional jobs have bank holidays off. While most offices close during weekends, most shops, restaurants, pubs and hotels are open, so those working in these sectors will be required to work weekends. However, under the labour law you will be entitled to overtime pay or time off in lieu.

Finding Work

How you go about finding work really depends on whether you are an EU or non-EU citizen (that is, whether you need a green card or a work permit to work here) and what kind of job you want. No matter what type of job you are looking for, it's a good idea to update your CV and organise references (with English translations, if needed) before you arrive. For most jobs, especially professional jobs, references will be followed up. Also be sure to find out if your qualifications are recognised here. No matter what type of job you are looking for, the better prepared you are, the higher your chances of getting the job you really want.

Finding Work Before You Come

For non-EU citizens (or those not married to EU citizens) who want a professional job, research your sector and contact companies you're interested in a good few months in

Are you always taking the wrong turn?

Whether you're a map person or not, these pocket-sized marvels will help you get to know the city – and its limits.

Explorer Mini Maps
Fit the city in your pocket

advance. Recruitment specialists, such as Brightwater, will be able to give you advice on trends, salaries and jobs. If you find a company that might be interested in hiring you, you will probably do a phone interview and then, if both of you are still interested, they will probably fly you to Ireland so you can do an interview in person. If you are hired, you or the employer will need to get a green card permit (see permits section). If you are an EU citizen, or are allowed to work in Ireland, and you want a professional job in Dublin, it is still a good idea to do your research beforehand and get in touch with recruitment agencies and companies a few weeks before you arrive. Recruitment agencies and specialists can also go through your employment options with you.

A Fine Balance
Although some jobs will require you to work very hard, in general the Irish maintain a healthy balance between work and family life. If you are immigrating to Ireland to work, you will be able to develop your career as well as have a good social and family life outside of work.

Finding Work Online

The internet has opened up job searching possibilities, although there is no substitute for actually being in the country and being available for interviews in relatively short notice. Still, there are some job websites that are particularly worth keeping an eye on if you are on the hunt for your dream job. Some allow you to sign up for updates, so that you will get emails alerting you to potentially suitable jobs. Try www.myjob.ie, www.irishjobsonline.com, www.irishjobs.ie and www.dublincityjobs.ie. Other good websites include www.monster.ie and www.loadzajobs.ie. If you are looking for a job in construction, try www.construction-jobs.ie, and if you are looking for a job in accounts or finance, try www.antsjobs.ie. Do a bit of research into some big corporations that have offices in Dublin, and check their websites regularly for new job postings.

Finding Work While You're Here

If you are looking for casual work, you can temp, or take your CV round to hotels, restaurants and shops once you arrive. The summer months and Christmas are always busy times for these sectors, and shops, restaurants, etc. will put a sign up by their front door if they need staff.

The classifieds section in any of the newspapers, particularly the *Evening Herald*, has a good listing of casual jobs, while *The Irish Times* contains listings for more professional jobs in their Friday business supplement. You can get a job through recruitment specialists and agencies or by getting in touch with organisations in your sector or profession. By reading the newspapers (the main broadsheets are *The Irish Times* and the *Irish Independent*) you will not only see the job

Recruitment Agencies

Accountancy Solutions	01 679 7990	www.accountancysolutions.ie
Ace Personnel Recruitment	01 671 3126	www.acepersonnel.ie
Atlas Personnel Group	01 677 6477	www.atlaspg.ie
Brightwater Recruitment Specialists	01 662 1000	www.brightwater.ie
CMI Engineering and Architectural Recruitment	01 676 5722	www.cmi-recruitment.ie
Grafton Recruitment	01 670 4564	www.grafton-group.com
Griffin Personnel	01 676 2719	www.griffinpersonnel.ie
Marketing People	01 661 9636	www.peoplegroup.ie
Noel Recruitment	01 677 9332	www.noel.ie
Reed Personnel Recruitment	01 670 4466	www.reed.ie

advertisements, but you will also become acquainted with the names of people and organisations within you sector. For those areas where contacts and networking are important, this will prove essential.

Recruitment Agencies

With so many companies looking to employ people and so many people looking for work, there are a lot of recruitment agencies and specialists in Dublin. These will help acquaint you with your sector and will also be able to find you temporary/contract and permanent work, and they offer a wide range of jobs and services. Temping, for which you are paid weekly, can be a great way to start work and get your bearings in Dublin.

Changing Jobs

If you are allowed to work in Ireland without a green card or work permit, you are entitled to change jobs whenever you want, provided you give the appropriate notice. The length of notice that you (and your employer) need to give will be specified in your contract. However, if you are here on a green card or work permit, your permission to stay here is dependent on your specific job and you cannot change jobs unless you find another employer who is willing to apply for a new green card or work permit for you.

Voluntary & Charity Work

Volunteering is a great way to meet new people and feel a part of the community while helping others. If you do not need to work, or cannot work at the moment, it is also a good way to advance your career, gain new experiences and make contact with people who might be able to help you get the job you want in the future.

There is a wide range of charities from which to choose, from those who help children with disabilities or abuse victims to those working with refugees. The Dublin Volunteer Centres throughout the city will be able to provide you with information about the area and charities you are interested in. See www.volunteerdublin.ie for more details.

Working As A Freelancer Or Contractor

Freelance work depends on whether you are legally allowed to do so or not. If you are not an EU citizen, it is nearly impossible to be legally self-employed. Also, a lot of freelance work is based upon your reputation and on people you know, so freelance work might not be the most beneficial option when you first move to Dublin.

That being said, many people from a wide range of sectors, from farming to construction (more than half of those in this sector are self-employed or work for very small businesses) to journalism, do freelance work, and make lots of money too.

In terms of tax, you will need to register as a self-employed person. You can download the appropriate form from the Revenue's website (www.revenue.ie). You will also need to keep records of invoices, bills and expenditures so that you can figure out how much tax you need to pay. 31 October has been named as the 'pay and file' date for self-employed people – when you can pay your estimated tax for the current year and file your tax return for the previous year. On that date you can also pay any income tax you owe from the previous year and pay any capital gains tax. You can get an accountant to help you out if it all seems overwhelming. The Revenue office should also be able to help you with any queries you might have.

Employment Contracts

Once an employer agrees to hire you and you accept the job offer (this is often done verbally), you should receive a written contract. All employers should give you one – if not, insist on one (or find another employer who will give you one). Not only does the

Post-work 'meetings' are popular!

contract protect the employer, it protects you. The contract should include: your job title, responsibilities and working hours; your salary; your probationary period (it's standard to have an initial probation period); sick leave; holidays; maternity leave; grievance procedures; period for notice of termination and pension and health benefits. Although employers do not have to give you basic leave during your probationary period, most do. You may not be eligible to receive pension and health benefits, etc. until after your probation period or after a certain length of time with the company. Also, employers and employees have to give a certain period of notice of termination or resignation, the length of which depends on what your contract says and how long you have been with the company. In most professional jobs, in which you are paid monthly, you must give a month's notice.

Maternity leave in Ireland allows you to spend a fairly generous amount of time with your child in its first year, while retaining your job. Every female worker, regardless of how many hours she works and how long she is in the job, is entitled to a basic period of maternity leave. As a new mother, you are entitled to 26 weeks maternity leave and 16 weeks unpaid maternity leave. Some employers will continue to pay an employee their usual salary when on maternity leave, minus the Maternity Benefit, but this all depends on your company and the terms of your contract. You are also entitled to State maternity benefits, the amount of which will depend on the amount of taxes you have paid, and your job must be kept open for you, see Maternity on p.134 for more. Also note, you have every right under the Irish constitution to join a trade union. The Irish Congress of Trade Unions website (www.ictu.ie) has some very helpful information on joining unions and on labour law in general.

Labour Law

Your basic rights as an employee, including minimum wages and holidays, should all be included in your contract. Your contract should also state grievance procedures and if you have a grievance, you should follow these. However, if you need advice about issues of employment you can contact your trade union or the Department of Enterprise, Trade and Employment (01 631 2121 or 1890 220 222). They will then decide if your case should go to the Rights Commissioner, who will settle the case or decide if it needs to go to the Employment Appeals Tribunal. If it is a really serious issue you can contact a solicitor; however, you should do this only after contacting your trade union and the Department of Enterprise. You can also contact the Equality Authority (01 417 3333, www.equality.ie) if it is an equality or discrimination issue.

Company Closure

If the company you work for closes, you can be entitled to certain payments/redundancy packages. How much depends on whether the company voluntarily closes or whether it has been made insolvent, and also on how long you have worked there. If the company closes voluntarily, and you have been with them for at least two years, you are entitled to a redundancy package of two weeks' pay for every year of service. This is usually more, particularly in sectors with strong trade unions. You are also entitled to a bonus which cannot exceed €600. If you have worked for the company for less than two years, you are only entitled to receive outstanding leave pay. Likewise, if the company closes because of bankruptcy, you are only entitled to outstanding pay. If you have a green card/work permit and the company you work for closes, there is nothing you can do except find a new employer to sponsor you, or leave the country.

You should consult your trade union or the Department of Enterprise, Trade and Employment (01 631 2121 or 1890 220 222, www.entemp.ie) if you need advice or recommendations for solicitors. Colleagues and friends should also be able to recommend a solicitor.

Immigrant Rights
Green card permits are initially given for two years and if it is your first green card permit you are expected to stay in that job for at least 12 months. This situation can leave the employee open to exploitation and immigrant rights groups have been putting pressure on the Government to address this issue.

Business Councils & Groups

Business Access to State Information and Services	www.basis.ie
Chambers of Commerce Ireland	www.chambers.ie
Enterprise Ireland	www.enterprise-ireland.com
Forfás	www.forfas.ie
IDA Ireland	www.idaireland.com
Ireland-Pakistan Business Council	www.irelandpakistan.com
Irish Business and Employment Confederation	www.ibec.ie
Irish Small and Medium Enterprises Association	www.isme.ie

The Financial Regulator

The Financial Regulator (Rialtóir Airgeadais) was established on 1 May 2003, to regulate Ireland's burgeoning financial services sector and to protect consumers and provide them with independent financial advice. Feel free to contact the watchdog if you have any financial query (www.ifsra.ie).

Bank Accounts

The banking sector in Ireland is quite strong and, although the market is dominated by home-grown banks, these are perfectly well-equipped to handle international transactions. The main types of accounts that can be opened are current accounts or savings accounts. A current account is your basic account, in which you can deposit or lodge money and withdraw from it at any time. You usually get a debit card that you can use in ATMs and many shops, and while you do not normally get a cheque book, you can always go to the bank and get a bank draft, which is the equivalent of a cheque, if you ever need one.

With savings accounts there are various interest rates and returns. There are also different types of accounts for students and children. Once you have an account, you can apply for credit cards, loans and overdrafts. All the banks also provide other banking and financial services including mortgages, pensions, investments and business banking.

To open an account you need photo ID and proof of your address, preferably a utilities bill. This can be a bit of a 'catch 22' because you often need a bank account to put household bills in your name when you move into a new home. However, employers often pay directly into your bank account and you can get a letter from your employer saying they do so, which will help you open the account. You might also need to bring in your PPS number.

Banking Comparison Table

Bank	Phone	Website	Online Banking	Tele-Banking
Allied Irish Banks (AIB)	01 679 3211	www.aib.ie	✓	1850 724 724
Anglo Irish Bank	01 616 2000	www.angloirishbank.ie	✓	1850 442 222
Bank of Ireland	01 677 6801	www.boi.ie	✓	1890 365 365
Halifax	1890 818 283	www.halifax.ie	✓	1890 818 283
National Irish Bank	01 484 0800	www.nationalirishbank.ie	✓	1850 200 400
Permanent TSB	01 677 0425	www.permanenttsb.ie	✓	1890 500 121
Ulster Bank	01 702 8600	www.ulsterbank.ie	✓	1850 424 365

Most banks charge fees for transactions, including withdrawing money from an ATM (fees vary depending on which ATM you withdraw from), going into your overdraft and foreign exchange. However, there has been a lot of media coverage about the high fees and banks are increasingly moving away from them.

The opening hours of banks are not very customer friendly and this can be a bit frustrating. Most banks are usually open 10:00 to 16:00 Mondays to Fridays, except for Thursday, when they are open until 17:00. However, opening hours do vary, with some branches open until 17:30 and on Saturday mornings.

Financial Planning

Because everything is so expensive in Dublin, saving money is very difficult. That being said, many people are becoming increasingly aware of the importance of maintaining healthy savings. It is widely accepted that the following financial precautions are ideal: an emergency cash buffer (at least three times your monthly salary), some form of retirement income, and adequate life, property and medical insurance.

Owning a house is very important to Irish people, and many save with the express purpose of buying a home. However, while the housing market has cooled down in Dublin, housing prices are still quite high so there's no guarantee you will see huge returns on your investment. Savvy property investors are looking further afield to eastern Europe and elsewhere for good investments. The golden rule if you are looking for an investment property is to do thorough research.

71

International Banking
If you have moved to Dublin from another country it may be worth keeping your bank accounts back home open, particularly if the charges are lower, the interest is higher, or you have direct debits.

Offshore Accounts
Offshore accounts in locations like the Isle of Man, Jersey and Guernsey often have attractive tax and investment benefits. With an offshore account, you usually get to pick the currency.

Tax Relief
There are a number of items on which you can get tax relief and credits. These can include rent, medical expenses, pension contributions and your union membership dues. Talk to the Revenue office off O'Connell Street to see which ones apply to you (more details on www.revenue.ie).

If you are interested in investing but not sure about which type of investment would suit you best, you can visit a bank or a financial advisor. Some financial advisors offer a free financial review. People who are married with children, who perhaps have big bills to pay, might prefer a low-risk investment. On the other hand, those who are younger and have more disposable income might prefer a higher-risk, higher-return investment. When seeing a financial advisor, make sure they are regulated with the relevant governing body in Ireland (see www.ifsra.ie).

The euro, the main currency of the European Union, is quite strong at the moment and is expected to stay that way over the next few

Bank of Ireland

years, assuming there are no major economic crises. The European Central Bank keeps a very watchful eye over the euro and does its best to stem rising inflation, which it hopes to keep below, but close to, 2% over the medium term. One way it does this is by raising interest rates, which is fairly painful for the average consumer but is theoretically for the greater good.

Pensions

As with many other European countries, Ireland could very well face a pensions crisis when the current working generation retires. Therefore, there has been a push by the Government and financial institutions to encourage pensions. Most companies have pension schemes which you can take advantage of, often after working with the company for a certain length of time. There is also a state pension – how much you will receive depends on how much tax you have paid and how long you have been in the workforce (how many monthly or weekly contributions you have made). You can also set up a private pensions fund on your own (with the help of a bank or financial planning group), which might be especially helpful if you are a freelancer. If you have a pension already at home and you can keep it, you probably want to do so because the longer you have a pension fund, the better return you get. Also, if you leave Ireland, the contributions you have made while you are here will probably be taken into account when you retire, depending on whether it is favourable for you to do so.

Financial Advisors		
Acumen & Trust	01 293 6500	www.acumenandtrust.com
Bluechip Financial Consultants	01 288 0800	www.bluechipfc.ie
Davy	01 679 7788	www.davy.ie
Deloitte Pensions & Investments	01 417 2200	www.deloitte.com
EBS Building Society	01 665 8000	www.ebs.ie
Foresthill Financial Planning	01 469 3716	www.foresthill.ie
Friends First	01 661 0600	www.friendsfirst.ie
Grant Thornton Financial Counselling	01 680 5805	www.grantthornton.ie
Keaney Financial Services	01 660 7566	www.keaneyfinance.ie

Cost of Living

Apples (per kg)	€ 2.49
Aspirin/paracetamol (24)	€ 4
Bananas (per kg)	€ 1.39
Beef (per kg)	€ 14.25
Beer (a pint)	€ 4.95
Beer (six-pack)	€ 10.50
Bread (a loaf)	€ 1.40
Burger (takeaway)	€ 4.50
Bus (10km journey)	€ 1.60
Camera film	€ 1.50
Cappucino	€ 2.75
Car rental (per day)	€ 45
Carrots (per kg)	€ 1.30
CD (new release)	€ 18
Chicken (per kg)	€ 12.95
Chocolate bar	€ 0.75
Cigarettes	€ 7.25
Cinema ticket	€ 9
Dogfood (a can)	€ 0.90
DVD (new release)	€ 20
Eggs (a dozen)	€ 2.55
Film developing	€ 6
Fish (fresh, per kg)	€ 8.80
Golf (18 holes)	€ 25
Milk (1 litre)	€ 0.80
Mobile to mobile call (local)	€0.00-€0.15
Newspaper (international)	€ 2
Newspaper (local)	€ 1.50
Orange juice (1 litre)	€ 2.50
Petrol (per litre)	€ 1.17
Pizza (large, takeaway)	€ 18
Postage stamp (local)	€ 0.48
Postcard	€ 1
Potatoes (per kg)	€ 1.48
Rice (1 kg)	€ 1.50
Salon haircut (female)	€ 60
Salon haircut (male)	€ 40
Soft drink (can)	€ 0.75
Strawberries (punnet)	€ 4.50
Sugar (2 kg)	€ 2.20
Taxi (10km)	€ 20
Text message (local)	€0.00-€0.13
Toothpaste	€ 3
Water (1.5 litres, restaurant)	€ 3.50
Water (1.5 litres, supermarket)	€ 1.45
Wine (bottle, off-licence)	€ 13

Taxation

Everyone who works in Ireland is taxed. How much you earn, as well as personal circumstances, such as your marital status, determines how much tax you pay. Tax is deducted by your employer on behalf of the government. There are two types of tax: pay as you earn, or PAYE, and your pay related social insurance, or PRSI. Your PAYE goes to the tax office and your PRSI goes to the social welfare department, and goes towards such things as pensions, sick benefits and job-seekers benefits.

At the end of the tax year, your employer will sort out your taxes for you, so you don't need to worry about that unless you are a freelancer (see freelance section).

Your employer will let you know what details they need, such as your PPS number, when you begin work, so they can let the tax office know you are working for them. When you start a new job, you will be on emergency tax (which is very high) until everything is sorted out between you, your employer and the Revenue Office, so make sure it gets sorted as quickly as possible.

When you leave a job, be sure to get your P45 form, which your new employer will need. The P45 states that your employer has correctly deducted your PAYE and your PRSI from your pay.

Sales tax, or VAT, is between 12 and 21%, depending on the item, and is included in the displayed prices. So while prices may seem that bit higher in shops, at least there are no nasty surprises at the till – if it says €4 on the price tag, it's going to cost you €4.

There is no local council tax as such. Once a year, you have to pay a fee to your local council but this is minimal and usually for such services as the collection of bins.

Have a good look through the Revenue website (www.revenue.ie), as it explains how much tax you will pay, as well as ways to reduce the amount of tax you pay and how you can earn tax credits.

Legal Issues

Ireland is a constitutional democracy, with the powers of the State coming from the 1937 constitution (Bunreacht na hÉireann). The powers of the State are divided into three branches: the legislative (the Dáil), the executive (the Government) and the judiciary, which is independent. Ireland inherited a common law system from England, which means judgements are based on precedent (previous rulings) although they have to be in accordance with the constitution. European Union law has precedence over Irish law, although EU law is limited and only covers certain areas (for example, the EU can't legislate on tax issues).

Judges realise that prison does not usually do a criminal much good, and are often hesitant to sent someone to jail for a long period. Sentences run low – if you are given a life sentence, you might only have to serve 13 years. Time can also be taken off for such things as good behaviour and pleading guilty (if you did it). This can seem strange and outrageous to the public in some cases, particularly in those cases which are high profile or have been covered extensively in the media. Irish law is strictly enforced by members of An Garda Síochána (the police force) and it remains one of the few European police forces whose members are unarmed.

In Ireland, lawyers are either solicitors or barristers. Solicitors provide members of the public with advice, representation and assistance. They are the ones you go to first if you have a legal issue. Barristers, meanwhile, are the ones who usually argue before the High Court, the Supreme Court and, often, the Circuit Court. Thus, if a case goes to court, a solicitor will usually prepare the file and a barrister will argue it in court. Barristers also give specialist advice on complex legal issues.

The lowest level in the courts system is the District Court, which deals with minor criminal offences. A garda, as opposed to the State in the form of the Director Of Public Prosecutions (DPP), will prosecute. The court, which is busy, is quite lenient on minor offences and can only give a maximum sentence of one year in prison and low level fines. Usually, the judge will give a formal warning but no conviction, a conviction with probation (with conditions), a fine, an order to provide the victim with compensation or an order to make a donation to the poor box (really, that's what it's called!).

The Circuit Court is the next level, and deals with more serious offences, although there is still no jury. This court tries offences on indictment (which means the accusations against you are formal and the prosecution has enough evidence to go to trial), and also handles some appeals. This court deals with more serious offences like assault, sexual crimes and drugs offences.

Then there is the Central Criminal Court, which is also referred to as the High Court when it is dealing with civil matters. This court, which has a jury, deals with offences such as rape, murder, attempted murder, manslaughter and serious drugs offences. The Court of Criminal Appeals handles appeals. It can overturn decisions made in the lower courts and adjust sentences. The highest court is the Supreme Court, which deals with points of law and is the ultimate decider on what is constitutional.

Mind Your Language
Court proceedings are conducted in English, although it is your right to have them conducted in Irish. With the increase in foreign nationals living in Ireland, however, the need for translation of court hearings has increased.

Making A Will

If you wish to make a will in Ireland, it is advisable to use the services of a solicitor. A solicitor will help you use the correct wording (very important in a will), so that there is no confusion over what happens to your assets in the event of your death. The will must also be properly witnessed by someone, preferably the solicitor. Bear in mind that inheritance is taxed in Ireland.

Divorce

The exact procedure for getting divorced in Ireland depends on where you got married and what nationality and religion you are. Irish people who get married in Ireland need to be living apart for three consecutive years, or for four out of the last five years before they can get divorced. Under the Brussels II convention, which most EU countries have signed up to, you can get divorced under the law of the EU country that one or both of you are from. There is also

Law Firms		
Arthur Cox	01 618 0000	www.arthurcox.com
Dixon Quinlan	01 878 8085	info@dixonquinlan.ie
Geraldine Kelly & Co	01 492 1223	na
James O'Higgins	01 865 8800	na
Matheson, Ormsby, Prentice	01 232 2000	www.mop.ie
McCann Fitzgerald	01 829 0000	www.mccannfitzgerald.ie
Murray Flynn Maguire	01 660 0622	www.murrayflynn.ie
O'Connor Bergin	01 873 2411	www.oconnorbergin.ie
Paula Duffy	01 478 4070	pd@pauladuffy.com
Sheehan & Co	01 661 6922	www.sheehanandco.ie

the 'domicile' rule: if you were born here or plan to live here permanently, you can probably get divorced here. You might also be able to get divorced in your home country, even if you are temporarily living in Ireland. Consult your solicitor about your options. The courts will decide on alimony, income distribution and what happens to the children. However, it is highly recommended that, when possible, the couple sort out all these issues with their solicitors – this will usually work out to everyone's advantage. Note that there is no such thing as a prenuptial agreement in Irish law. Thus, if you have one, it can be taken into consideration, but it may not be legally binding. AIM Family Services can offer advice, if you are unsure of where to start (www.aimfamilyservices.ie).

Drink Driving Laws

Ireland has a relatively high road death rate, and the government has implemented strict drinking and driving laws. Up until recently, it was socially acceptable to drink and drive, and some people do find it a hard habit to break. Additionally, in some rural areas there is a lack of alternative transport, so sometimes the only way to get back from the pub is in your car. However, neither of these excuses will be accepted if you are caught driving over the limit. The legal blood alcohol limit for a driver is 80 milligrams of alcohol per 100 millilitres of blood. How many drinks this equates to depends on a lot of different factors but, on average, your body takes about one hour to process a standard drink. Gardaí are allowed to conduct random breath tests at designated checkpoints.

Put That Pint Down
If convicted of drink driving, you will be automatically disqualified from driving. However, the amount by which you were over the limit and whether it is your first offence will affect the length of time for which you are disqualified. You can also be fined.

Graffiti speaks out against crime

Statue of Justice, Dublin Castle

75

Housing

The Irish property market is probably one of the most talked-about subjects (apart from the weather) at dinner gatherings around the city and in the media. The main debate is whether the property market will crash and if so, when. Property prices in Dublin began climbing steadily with the 'Celtic Tiger', the economic boom that began in the late 1990s, transforming the country from being one of the poorest in Europe to one of the wealthiest. During the past 10 years, prices rose on average 15% per year, leading many financial analysts to believe that the market was overheated and over-inflated, predicting a crash. These predictions continue, however some analysts are determined that the economy is strong and that demand for housing is high so they think a crash is unlikely. However in late 2006, price increases began to slow down and in early 2007, prices began to fall, with recorded drops of 1.8% per month at the time of writing.

The Irish have always preferred to own their own home rather than to rent and 'getting on the property ladder' is important to many young people once they are earning regular money. For many potential first-time buyers, property prices have been out of reach, with average house prices in Dublin over €400,000 and a new two-bed apartment in the docklands with parking, costing half a million. However many banks and building societies have been offering 100% mortgages. In 2007, there were a number of mortgage interest rate increases, with more predicted before the year's end, leading to further uncertainty in the market.

Unfortunately, this has had a knock-on effect on rents. With landlords' mortgages increasing, they are passing these increases onto tenants and with such an uncertain property market, many people prefer to rent, meaning high demand is also raising prices.

The Lease

Leases in Ireland are usually drawn up by an estate agent, and both the landlord and tenant sign it. It is a legally binding contract. Many of the conditions are those that legally apply to a tenancy under the Residential Tenancies Act. Typical conditions include that the tenant must pay the rent and deposit, pay local authority and utility charges, not sub-let the property, not alter the property in any way and must leave the premises and all fixtures and fittings clean and tidy at the end of the tenancy. An inventory of contents is sometimes supplied to tenants. Some tenancies forbid smoking and pets.

Most leases are for 12 months, but you can sometimes sign up for shorter or longer periods. If a tenant breaks the terms of a lease before the full term is up, they will lose their deposit.

Dublin housing options

Main Accommodation Options

The main types of property to rent are houses, apartments, and bedsits or studios which combine a bedroom and living room in one, and usually have their own kitchenette with either a private or shared bathroom. House or apartment sharing is also popular.

Prices vary hugely, depending on the condition of the property and on the area. Studios near the city start at €500 or €600 per month, while a one-bedroom apartment on the North Circular Road might start at €850 or €900, rising to €2,000 a month on St Stephen's Green. For sharing, a single room in the suburbs somewhere like Rathfarnham, Lucan or Blanchardstown will start upwards of €300 per month while a high-spec double ensuite room in the docklands can go for up to €800.

Other Rental Costs

If the rent of a property is over €1,600 per month, the lease needs to be stamped by the Revenue Commissioners and the tenant has to pay stamp duty. This is calculated at 1% of the annual rent, plus €12.70 for the counterpart (copy of lease). The landlord or agent usually arranges to have the lease stamped but it is the tenant's responsibility to pay it.

Parking can also add on substantial costs. Most areas near the city are pay and display, which works out at to be a hefty sum if used regularly, but you can apply to the local authority for a residential parking permit. In Dublin City, this costs €70 for one year and €130 for two years and you'll need proof of address such as utility bills and bank statements.

Otherwise, expect to pay deposits on utilities such as telephone and ESB (electricity). Tenants are also liable to pay waste charges for refuse collections.

Buying Property

Demand for residential property in Dublin and the rest of the country, after many years of heightened growth, has fallen off since the start of 2007, with rising interest rates and decreased consumer confidence being two of the key factors. At the time of writing, there had been eight interest rate increases since December 2005, bringing them to a six-year high, with more expected before the end of the year.

This has affected prices, and the market is changing month by month. According to The Daft.ie House Price Report for Quarter 2, 2007, the average price of a second-hand property in Dublin fell by 3.0% during quarter two, down 5.2% for the year to date. However there are still many new developments being released onto the market. Property has always been considered one of the soundest investments you can make – it's not as volatile as stocks and shares and in the short term, investors can be lucky if they are clever.

Buying Property As A Non-Citizen

Non-citizens can buy property in Ireland. If paying by cash, you will need to account for where the money is coming from. If applying for a mortgage, you will need two years' accounts and to have a permanent job here which you have been in for at least six months. It is also possible to buy land to build on, although certain counties such as Wicklow, prohibit non-locals from buying in the area.

The Buying Process

Once you have viewed and selected a property that you are interested in, there are a few steps before completion of the sale. The first step is to make an offer. You usually make an offer to the estate agent who is acting on behalf of the seller, and you can say that your offer is subject to contract and survey – so you can withdraw the offer

77

Real Estate Agents

Douglas Newman Good	01 491 2600	www.dng.ie
Gunne	01 618 5501	www.gunne.com
Hamilton Osborne King	01 663 4300	www.hok.ie
Lisney	01 638 2700	www.lisney.com
Sherry Fitzgerald Group	01 639 9200	www.sherryfitz.ie

later if there are any unforeseen problems. With the offer there might be a bit of negotiating, especially if other parties are also interested and bidding for the property, and you might have to revise your offer upwards, so be sure of your maximum budget and how high you are willing to go.

Once the sale is agreed, you might be asked to pay a booking deposit – usually around 2% of the purchase price, to indicate that you are serious. This is refundable at any time up to the point that the contract is signed, should the sale not go ahead.

You should then appoint your solicitor and instruct them. They will run a number of searches, checking the title to the property and investigating if there are any planning or access issues, before setting the buying process in motion.

You then notify your mortgage lender that you've agreed on a purchase, and they will do a survey and valuation. If you are buying a second hand property, you might also want to have your own survey done, either by a surveyor or architect, to check for structural problems and signs of damp or dry rot.

When your solicitor receives a contract from the seller's solicitor, they will call you in to pay the balance of the deposit (to bring it up to 10%) and to sign the contract. The solicitor will have drawn up a new deed of title, to record the change. This will contain the names of the seller and buyer, the location of the property, the change of ownership and the date. The contracts are then sent back to the seller's solicitor. You will also sign mortgage documents at this stage. As soon as both parties have signed, the contract becomes legally binding – up to this point, either party can pull out.

The closing is then finalised between the two solicitors (seller's and purchaser's) and can take a further week or so after signing. This includes transfer of the full purchase price to the seller. The whole closing process can take a few weeks or months after the sale is initially agreed to become final, to allow time for surveys, loan approval, planning searches on the property, drawing up and signing of contracts.

They're Going Down
At the time of writing, the Economic and Social Research Institute (ESRI) in Ireland, the International Monetary Fund, the OECD and the Central Bank had all agreed that the property market in Ireland was overvalued.

Freehold Or Leasehold?
You can buy both freehold and leasehold property. In Dublin, residential property is mainly freehold – the advantage is that you own it in its entirety, you don't have to pay a yearly fee and you don't have to renegotiate a lease in the future.

Buying To Rent

Buying to rent can be a good idea, depending on the location you buy in and the yield (ratio of monthly rent to purchase price). However at the moment, yields are low and prices are high in Dublin. In the short term, you probably won't be able to rent the property out for enough to cover the mortgage and you may have to subsidise the mortgage yourself. If you are renting, all tenancies must be registered with the Private Residential Tenancies Board by law and landlords are bound by certain obligations and minimum standards. As a landlord, you will also have tax obligations.

Housing Abbreviations

Beds	Bedrooms
Det	Detached house
ECH	Electric central heating
Gdn	Garden
GFCH	Gas-fired central heating
Kit	Kitchen
M/wave	Microwave
N/s	Non-smoker
OFCH	Oil-fired central heating
Pking	Parking
Pm/pw	Per month/per week
Prof	Professional
Refs	References
S/c	Self-contained
Semi or s/d	Semi-detached house
SF or SFCH	Solid fuel central heating
Tce	Terraced house
Twnhse	Townhouse
Utility	Utility room
W/machine or w/dryer	Washing machine or washing machine and dryer
WC	Toilet

Housing

It's Not Sold Until The Money's In The Bank
Approximately one in three sales falls through – either the vendor or the purchaser may pull out. When you sell a property, you are liable for capital gains tax of 20%.

Selling Property

Property is usually sold through an agent rather than privately, and purchasers usually prefer to deal with an agent too. Agents advertise properties by erecting 'For Sale' boards on site, in newspapers and on the internet, arranging viewings and taking offers and bids. Houses can be sold through an auction or sale.

Estate agent fees are usually negotiated – shop around. Typical fees are 1% of the purchase price, plus VAT. Sherry Fitzgerald recently increased its prices to 1.5% but the other agents have not followed suit. The seller pays for advertising so it will be agreed with the agent where the property will be advertised. There will also be solicitor's fees – again approximately 1% of the sale price.

Mortgages

Taking out a mortgage for 25 or 30 years is the most common way to pay for a house. There are two main types of mortgage, annuity and endowment. Annuity mortgages, where the sum is repaid with interest, are the most popular. In the first few years, the payments are mainly interest. It is possible to opt for a fixed rate or variable mortgage. Many people opt to fix the rate for the first year or two of the mortgage and then switch to variable. Fixed rates are usually a little higher than the Central Bank rate. Endowment mortgages are where an insurance policy is taken out, designed to repay the entire loan. Each month, the purchaser pays the insurance policy premium and loan interest. Endowment mortgages have attracted some negative publicity in recent years as nothing is paid off the loan until the policy matures and customers who bought policies years ago found that there was not enough to pay off the loan at the end. When you take out a mortgage, you also need to take out mortgage protection, a type of life assurance policy to cover the mortgage payments if you are taken ill or die. Tax relief on mortgage interest is also available for those making mortgage repayments – you can apply for this at the tax office.

Mortgage Providers

AIB	01 679 9222	www.aib.ie
Bank of Ireland	01 459 8644	www.bankofireland.ie
Halifax	1890 818 283	www.halifax.ie
IIB Bank	01 664 6000	www.iibbank.ie
Irish Mortgage Corporation	1850 444 474	www.irishmortgage.ie
Irish Mortgage Providers	01 260 7070	www.imp.ie
Mortgages Ireland	1850 320 920	www.mortgages.ie
Permanent TSB	01 677 9941	www.permanenttsb.ie

Banks and building societies are the main mortgage providers, and there also are a few specialist mortgage providers and agents in the market. Rates and prices vary according with fluctuating interest rates, so you'll need to shop around.

Mortgage Massive
Some newspapers publish tables of mortgage rate comparisons. The standard mortgage borrowing is two and a half times your annual salary, although many financial institutions give three or four times the salary. You usually need to have saved a deposit of 10% for a property; however some mortgage companies offer 100% mortgages.

Other Purchasing Costs

A lending institution will have a fee. You also need to pay a solicitor for the conveyancing work – legal fees vary and can either be a flat fee or a percentage of the property purchase price (around 1.5%) – shop around to get the best prices. If you are buying a second hand house, you might undertake a survey, which can cost from €150 to €400. Stamp duty is also payable on a second-hand property, or a new one over 125 square metres. Rates vary, depending on whether it is your first property purchase or not (in which case you will be exempt) and on the value of the property; your solicitor will advise you on this. If you buy a property as an owner or occupier, the stamp duty is lower than for an investor, but if you decide to do this, you can't rent the property for a certain period of time.

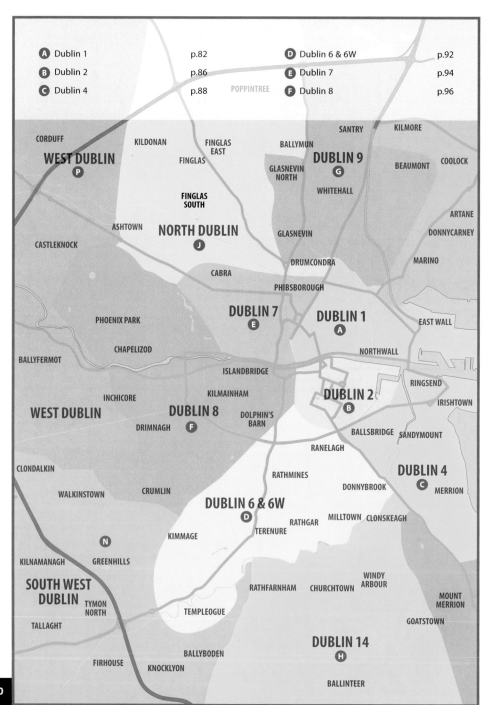

A Dublin 1 — p.82
B Dublin 2 — p.86
C Dublin 4 — p.88
D Dublin 6 & 6W — p.92
E Dublin 7 — p.94
F Dublin 8 — p.96

POPPINTREE

CORDUFF
KILDONAN
FINGLAS EAST
BALLYMUN
SANTRY
KILMORE

WEST DUBLIN
P

FINGLAS
GLASNEVIN NORTH
DUBLIN 9
G
BEAUMONT
COOLOCK

WHITEHALL

FINGLAS SOUTH

ASHTOWN
NORTH DUBLIN
J
GLASNEVIN
ARTANE
DONNYCARNEY

CASTLEKNOCK
MARINO

DRUMCONDRA

CABRA
PHIBSBOROUGH

PHOENIX PARK
DUBLIN 7
E
DUBLIN 1
A
EAST WALL

CHAPELIZOD
NORTHWALL

BALLYFERMOT
ISLANDBRIDGE
RINGSEND

KILMAINHAM
DUBLIN 2
B
IRISHTOWN

INCHICORE
DUBLIN 8
F
DOLPHIN'S BARN

WEST DUBLIN
DRIMNAGH
BALLSBRIDGE
SANDYMOUNT

RANELAGH

CLONDALKIN
DUBLIN 4
C
MERRION

CRUMLIN
RATHMINES
DONNYBROOK

WALKINSTOWN
DUBLIN 6 & 6W
D
RATHGAR
MILLTOWN
CLONSKEAGH

N
KIMMAGE
TERENURE

KILNAMANAGH
GREENHILLS

SOUTH WEST DUBLIN
TYMON NORTH
RATHFARNHAM
CHURCHTOWN
WINDY ARBOUR
MOUNT MERRION

TALLAGHT
TEMPLEOGUE
GOATSTOWN

DUBLIN 14
H

BALLYBODEN

FIRHOUSE
KNOCKLYON
BALLINTEER

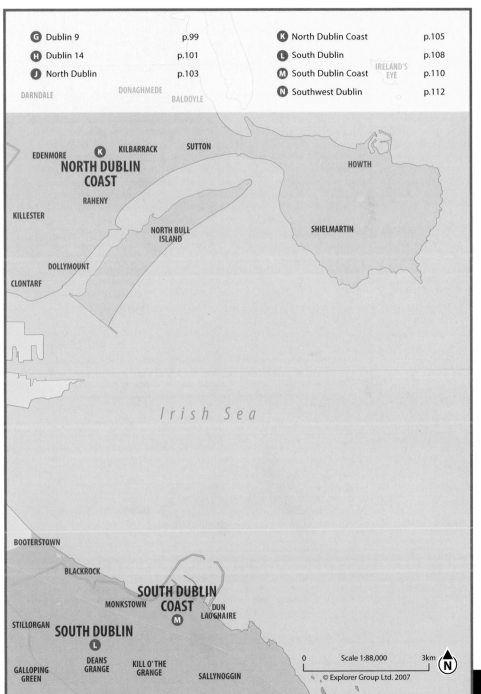

G Dublin 9   p.99

H Dublin 14   p.101

J North Dublin   p.103

K North Dublin Coast   p.105

L South Dublin   p.108

M South Dublin Coast   p.110

N Southwest Dublin   p.112

IRELAND'S EYE

DARNDALE   DONAGHMEDE   BALDOYLE

EDENMORE   K   KILBARRACK   SUTTON

NORTH DUBLIN COAST

HOWTH

RAHENY

KILLESTER

NORTH BULL ISLAND

SHIELMARTIN

DOLLYMOUNT

CLONTARF

Irish Sea

BOOTERSTOWN

BLACKROCK

SOUTH DUBLIN COAST

MONKSTOWN   M   DUN LAOGHAIRE

STILLORGAN   **SOUTH DUBLIN**   L

GALLOPING GREEN   DEANS GRANGE   KILL O' THE GRANGE   SALLYNOGGIN

0   Scale 1:88,000   3km   N

© Explorer Group Ltd. 2007

Map p.425, 426, 427
Area **A** p.80-81

Dublin 1

Dublin 1, the area immediately north of the river Liffey, stretching as far west as the Capel Street area and east past the Irish Financial Services Centre (IFSC) to North Wall and Dublin Port, is right at the heart of Dublin city. The area covers O'Connell St, Parnell Square, Mountjoy Square, Capel Street, the IFSC and the Docklands and has all of the advantages – and nuisances – of city centre living.

Compared to its southside counterpart, Dublin 2, Dublin 1 has a more run-down appearance. However the area hasn't avoided the economic boom and its focal point, O'Connell Street, has undergone major regeneration in recent years with the addition of the Spire, new facades and pedestrian plazas. The smart IFSC (International Financial Services Centre) at Custom House docks is the headquarters for the financial services industry and the docklands area is still being developed, with the €700m Point Village due for completion in 2009. This will include retail outlets, apartments, a 14,000 seat concert venue, a 120m skyscraper and an extension to the Luas tram line from Connolly Station. The National Conference centre on Spencer Dock is also due to open in 2009. Other touches, such as a smart new boardwalk on the River Liffey and three new bridges, the Millennium Bridge (2000), James Joyce Bridge (2003) and the Sean O'Casey Bridge (2005), have all helped to smarten up the area. The Samuel Beckett Bridge, crossing the Liffey at the docklands, is due to open in 2008, and there are proposals to make the area around the Custom House into a public space for cultural events.

With the influx of immigrants to the city in recent years, ethnic areas have also developed in Moore Street and Parnell Street, with restaurants, hair salons and specialist shops from around the world – Polish, African and Asian being the most popular. A new Italian quarter – Quartier Bloom – is also developing between the quays and Jervis Street, which has food shops, restaurants and cafes.

Best Points
The advantages of living so centrally are many – access to public transport such as buses, trams and rail, and easy access to shops, restaurants and services. Property prices are cheaper on the north side too.

Worst Points
A lot of once elegant period buildings are grimy and neglected, home to seedy flats and cheap B&B's. Some areas of the north inner city centre are not pleasant places after dark.

Accommodation

The northside is less affluent than the southside, in general, and property prices are generally cheaper north of the Liffey. Many large period houses in once elegant Georgian squares have become shabby and neglected over the years and are home to budget B&Bs or groups of student flats. However, these are mixed with new apartment developments, which, as in the rest of the city, are changing the character of many areas. Accommodation available to buy in Dublin 1 is mostly one and two-bedroom apartments and at the time of going to print, one-bedroom apartments in developments in Georgian areas Parnell Street and Mountjoy Square, were going for between €240,000 and €285,000, with two-beds going for anything from €300,000 to €350,000.

In the IFSC – a highly sought-after location due to its proximity to offices, the city and the River Liffey – a one-bed with parking can go for around €380,000 to €400,000, or a two-bed for €500,000. Parking spaces alone in the IFSC are worth about €40,000 each. Other options include apartments in period buildings on Capel Street which are nice but pricey – they are often over business premises and do not include parking or balconies.

Shopping & Amenities

Being in the heart of the city centre, there's a wide selection of shops and shopping centres in Dublin 1, as well as travel agents, banks and restaurants. Most retail outlets are concentrated in and around O'Connell Street, which is home to department store Clerys and also around Henry Street, a busy pedestrianised shopping street which has a mix of fashion boutiques and discount shops, department stores Debenhams (formerly Roches Stores) and Arnotts, The Ilac Shopping Centre and access to the Jervis Centre (see Shopping on p.330 for more). The General Post Office is also on O'Connell Street, as is the Revenue Tax Office, headquarters of Dublin Bus and a branch of Dublin Tourism.

Residential Areas

Apartments along the Liffey

Parnell Monument

The Garden of Remembrance

The Spire

Entertainment & Leisure

There are plenty of pubs, cafes and restaurants around O'Connell Street. The Cineworld cinema multiplex is on Parnell Street and there's also the Savoy Cinema on O'Connell Street (see Cinemas on p.390 for more). Theatre buffs will be pleased that some of the city's theatres can be found in Dublin 1, with The Gate on Parnell Square, The Abbey and Peacock on Abbey Street Lower and other small venues such as the Liberty Hall theatre in the landmark Liberty Hall building on Eden Quay. Comedy venue The Laughter Lounge is also on Eden Quay, and further down past the IFSC is The Point Depot for major performances.

Popular large pubs in the north city centre include Zanzibar on Ormond Quay, late night bar Traffic and nightclub Spirit, both on Middle Abbey Street and Pravda on Lower Liffey Street. The Ambassador Theatre on O'Connell Street is a popular venue for gigs. The IFSC's many smart pubs and restaurants are popular with financial types who live and work in the area (see the Going Out chapter for more on all of these). Dublin 1 is within reach of Croke Park, the 80,000 seater GAA stadium, and Phoenix Park, Europe's largest urban park.

Healthcare

The nearest main hospital in Dublin 1 is the Mater Misercordiae University Hospital on Eccles Street, just off Dorset Street Lower, a large, acute hospital with a number of surgical specialities (01 803 2000, www.mater.ie). The Rotunda Maternity Hospital is on Parnell Square (01 873 0700, www.rotunda.ie). Temple Street Children's University Hospital, is an acute hospital for children (01 878 4344, www.childrenshospital.ie). The Hamilton Long pharmacy (01 874 8456) on O'Connell Street stays open until 21:00 on weekdays.

Education

Large secondary schools in the area include boys school Belvedere College (01 858 6600), Mount Carmel for girls (01 873 0958) and Larkin Community College, a mixed school (01 874 1913, www.larkincommunitycollege.ie). Third level colleges include DIT Bolton Street, DIT Cathal Brugha Street and DIT Mountjoy Square (see p.149), and the National College of Ireland (see table, p.148) is located in Mayor Street in the IFSC. Nearby universities include Trinity College and DCU (see p.149).

Transport

Dublin 1 is well serviced by public transport and most major bus routes travel through the city centre. You'll also find Connolly train station; the Luas Red line from Tallaght and Busáras bus station. Parking can be a problem in the city, though there are large car parks in Parnell Street and the Jervis Centre. However, as they are designed for shoppers rather than residents, hourly rates are expensive and they close overnight.

James Joyce Bridge

Safety & Annoyances

Living in the centre of any city has problems – noise and pollution from traffic; few open spaces; difficulty with parking and the anti-social problems associated with late night drinking. Like any busy city centre, pickpockets and bag snatching are a problem. O'Connell Street after 23:00 on a weekend night is not always a savoury place and it is advisable not to walk in certain areas of the city centre alone after dark, particularly behind Connolly Station towards Sheriff Street.

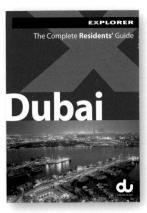

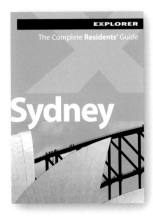

Tired of writing your insider tips…

…in a blog that nobody reads?

The Explorer Complete Residents' Guide series is growing rapidly, and we're always looking for literate, resident writers to help pen our new guides. So whether you live in Tuscany or Timbuktu, if writing's your thing, and you know your city inside out, we'd like to talk to you.

Apply online at www.explorerpublishing.com

Map p.426, 427
430, 431
Area **B** p.80-81

Dublin 2

Dublin 2, immediately south of the River Liffey and stretching between Temple Bar to the west, the Docklands to the east and the Georgian square areas to the south, has all the ingredients of city centre living that make it one of the most desirable places to live in the city. The area covers Temple Bar, Grafton Street, St Stephen's Green, Merrion Square, Pearse Street and the Docklands.

An apartment in the cobblestone streets of cultural quarter Temple Bar will have quirky shops, restaurants, pubs, galleries and arts centres on your doorstep and you're only a stone's throw from Trinity College and Grafton Street. If you choose the Docklands, you'll find brand new riverside apartments in an up and coming area with easy access to the city centre and IFSC, and if you choose areas around Merrion Square and St Stephen's Green, you'll find elegant enclosed parks, period Georgian buildings, museums and galleries – but be prepared to pay a hefty premium for the privilege.

One of the biggest changes in Dublin 2 property in recent years is the development of the Docklands, centred around the Grand Canal docks between the Grand Canal basin and the River Liffey, with around 3,500 new apartments mixed with offices and retail space and with planned restaurants, bars and shops. The area has been under construction for a number of years, with many projects completed in 2007. The U2 tower, when completed, will rise 60m and form one half of a gateway to the city. The former Boland Mill at Grand Canal Dock is to be redeveloped as a major office and hotel complex.

Best Points
The advantages of living in Dublin 2 are many, including the convenience of being near shopping, nightlife and entertainment, admiring the Georgian architectural surrounds and visiting the many cultural institutions on your doorstep.

Worst Points
Temple Bar can be noisy at night and there is still a lot of construction in the docklands area, which will continue for a few more years yet as the area is being developed.

Accommodation

Accommodation is pricier in Dublin 2 compared to its northside counterpart Dublin 1, however you're paying for the area. Accommodation is mostly apartments in either new developments or period houses. Houses come up from time to time around streets to the south, around Adelaide Road or around Pearse Street, one of the traditionally working-class and more run-down areas of the D2 district, with many local authority housing developments. Prices vary in Dublin 2 – a second-hand two-bed apartment in Temple Bar (without parking) will cost from €380,000 to €400,000; a new two-bed apartment in the docklands (with parking) will cost from €500,000 to €650,000 and in Merrion Square, a period apartment can go from €500,000 for a one-bed, up to as much as €4 million.

Shopping & Amenities

Everything you need is on your doorstep – from shopping in Grafton Street and its surrounds full of independent boutiques and quirky shops, to banks, travel agents, post offices and tourist offices. Shopping centres include St Stephen's Green Shopping Centre and the Powerscourt Centre (see Shopping on p.279 for more info).

Entertainment & Leisure

You won't be stuck finding somewhere to eat or drink out in Dublin 2 as it's where the city's nightlife is centred. Choose party-central Temple Bar or the bars, restaurants and pubs around Grafton Street, if you want to be in on the action (see Going Out on p.335 for a listing of bars, restaurants and cafes).

The Gaiety Theatre, National Concert Hall and Olympia Theatre are also in this area, as are the Project Arts Centre (01 881 9613, www.projectarts.ie), Irish Film Institute (IFI) (see p.390), Screen Cinema (see p.390) and music venue Crawdaddy on Harcourt Street (01 662 4305). Around Kildare Street you'll find the National Museum and National Art Gallery. During the day, parks at St Stephen's Green, the Iveagh Gardens and Merrion Square are a quiet escape from the city centre buzz, or take a walk into the enclosed courtyards of Trinity College (see Exploring on p.164). The Markievicz Leisure Centre (p.263) in Townsend Street has a 25m pool and gym. Dublin 2 is close to the sea at Sandymount (Dublin 4) and to the Grand Canal (also Dublin 4).

Healthcare
The nearest main hospitals are St James's hospital in Dublin 8 (01 410 3100, www.stjames.ie), St Vincent's University hospital in Merrion, Dublin 4 (01 277 4000, www.stvincents.ie) or the Mater hospital on the northside's Eccles Street (01 803 2000, www.mater.ie). In Dublin 2, the National Maternity Hospital is at Holles Street, just off Merrion Square (01 637 3100, www.nmh.ie) and the Royal Victoria Eye and Ear hospital is on Adelaide Road, Dublin 2, just off Leeson Street (01 664 4600). The Dublin Dental Hospital (01 612 7200) is on Lincoln Place, beside Trinity College. The Georges Street Pharmacy is open until 22:00 every day.

Education
Girls' secondary schools in Dublin 2 include Loreto College on St Stephen's Green (01 661 8179), while CBS in Westland Row is a mixed school (01 661 4143), as is The Institute of Education on Leeson Street (see p.147). The CUS on Leeson Street is a private boys school (01 676 2586, www.cus.ie), and also has a junior school. Trinity College is the main university in the area (see p.149). Other third-level colleges in the area include the Dublin Business School (see p.148).

Transport
Most buses from the southside of the city pass through Dublin 2, as does the Dart suburban rail. Pearse Station at Westland Row also has connections to inter-city rail services. The Luas Green Line starts at St Stephen's Green and runs to Sandyford. Parking is hard to find and pricey in Dublin 2. There's a choice of parking at pay and display spaces around Grafton Street and carparks in Temple Bar, Drury Street and St Stephens' Green. Don't even think about parking illegally – you'll get clamped, or worse, towed away, both incurring hefty fines. Traffic in the city centre can be heavy, especially during morning and evening rush hours, and there's a one-way system in operation along the quays.

Safety & Annoyances
The lively night scene, especially in Temple Bar, can bring its fair share of noise, disturbance and litter. And general tourist traffic make this a jam-packed area almost year round. As in any city centre, watch your belongings and beware of pickpockets.

Apartments in Temple Bar

Docklands apartments

Map p.417, 421
Area ● p.80-81

Dublin 4

With their wide, leafy roads, large houses, a canal, parks and pretty villages like Sandymount, the residential suburbs of Dublin 4 are among the most exclusive areas of the city to live in and include Donnybrook, Ballsbridge, Sandymount, Ringsend and Irishtown. Long popular with embassies and diplomatic offices – the American Embassy in Ballsbridge is a landmark – the area stretches from the Grand Canal to Ballsbridge and Merrion in the south, Sandymount in the east and Donnybrook in the west, home to UCD and to the national broadcaster, RTÉ. Dublin 4 also includes the traditionally working-class areas Ringsend and Irishtown, though with the economic boom and development in the nearby docklands at Grand Canal Quay, prices in these areas have long been catching up with their counterparts a couple of streets away. Dublin 4 – or 'D4' as it is often known – along with other areas of south Dublin like Foxrock, Dalkey and Killiney, has historically been an area where the elite set up residence. Rich, influential people – lawyers, accountants, stockbrokers, doctors and senior managers – have traditionally preferred D4, which has resulted in some of the highest property prices in the country. The term Dublin 4 or 'D4' is used by people, often as an insult, to refer to people who are elitist upper middle class, and the area is also known for having its own 'D4 accent'.

Best Points

Living in the leafy suburbs of Dublin 4 is a cause for celebration, with beautiful buildings and parks, access to the sea and Dublin Bay and proximity to the city.

Worst Points

These areas are generally safe, however streets and roads can be very quiet at night and houses are far back off the road – not great for walking home alone. You will also probably have to drive to get to a supermarket.

Accommodation

As well as apartments, there are plenty of two, three, four and five-bed houses in Dublin 4 – terraced, semi-detached or detached, gardens, garages, sea-views and as many bedrooms as you want, as long as you can afford to pay. A mid-terrace two-bed former local authority house in Ringsend or Irishtown can go for between €460,000 and €510,000; a large period four or five-bed house in Sandymount will cost between €1.1 and €2.2 million (the higher end of the scale if it has sea views) and on exclusive Ailesbury Road, a large five-bed period semi-detached house can go for as much as €12 million.

Shopping & Amenities

Surprisingly for such a well-to-do area, the shopping in Dublin 4 isn't great. You'll find convenience shops, gourmet food shops and newsagents in the main villages but that's about it. Ballsbridge has a few newsagents, cafes and pubs; Donnybrook village has a few gourmet food stores; Sandymount has lots of little shops and a Tesco supermarket. You'll find the odd boutique, bookshop and cafe, but each village is really only handy for day-to-day essentials – bank branches, pharmacies, post offices and estate agents. There's also a large supermarket at the Merrion Centre, which has a carpark. Fortunately, you're only a stone's throw away from the city centre, where you can shop up a storm.

Entertainment & Leisure

There are lots of open spaces in Dublin 4 – the promenade and beach at Sandymount are popular with walkers, and Herbert Park has a large duck pond, sports pitches, playgrounds, tennis courts and a bowling green. The Grand Canal runs past Leeson Street and Baggot Street to Grand Canal Docks, and the river Dodder runs past Herbert Park and Lansdowne Road Rugby ground also finishing at Grand Canal Docks.

With so much wealth concentrated into the area, it's not surprising that popular sports include rugby, tennis and cricket. The rugby stadium at Lansdowne Road is currently closed for redevelopment until 2009, however other rugby clubs in the area include Bective Rangers, Old Wesley and Old Belvedere, all in Donnybrook, Monkstown Rugby Club (also home to a cricket club) at Sydney Parade and Wanderers in Ballsbridge. Tennis clubs include Donnybrook Lawn Tennis Club and

Residential Areas

Housing options, and the Grand Canal

Lansdowne Tennis Club. Irishtown Stadium (p.264) has a variety of sports including a running track, gym and football pitches and there's a greyhound-racing track at Shelbourne Park (p.262).

The RDS (Royal Dublin Society) in Ballsbridge has show jumping grounds, large halls, a concert hall and library and is popular for exhibitions and outdoor concerts. Pricey, luxurious gyms in the area include Riverview, towards Clonskeagh, and Westwood in Sandymount, and the pool at Marian College school is open to the public. Mespil Swimming Pool on Sussex Road (off Leeson Street, see p.255) has reasonable membership rates.

Get Away

No matter where you live in the city, sometimes you just need a change of scenery. The Exploring chapter features some great daytrips (p.209) and weekend breaks (p.216), all within easy reach of Dublin city.

The best places for eating out in the area are in Sandymount, Ballsbridge and Baggot Street and there are some good pubs in Sandymount, Ballsbridge and Donnybrook, although they lack the buzz and vibrancy of the city centre. There are some late-night pubs in Baggot Street, particularly as you head towards the city end. Club Anabel in the Burlington (see p.32) is popular on weekend nights, although the hotel is due to close in 2008. In Donnybrook, Old Wesley Rugby Club is an institution for teenage discos.

Healthcare

St Vincent's University Hospital in Elm Park (Merrion), is a large acute hospital with many specialities including an accident and emergency department (01 277 4000, www.stvincents.ie). There's a late night pharmacy in Donnybrook and Byrnes pharmacy in Merrion Road is open until 21:00, Monday to Friday. Baggot Street Hospital is a hospital for respite care and has several health board clinics but is not a general hospital (01 668 1577).

Education

Girls' secondary schools include Muckross Park College (01 260 4077), The Teresian School (01 269 1376), and St Mary's Secondary School on Belmont Avenue (01 269 2578). Boys' schools include St Matthew's National School (01 660 3145, www.stmatts.ie) with both Marian College (01 668 4036) and St Conleths College (01 668 0022) taking a small number of girls. Mixed schools include Technical Institute (01 668 4498) in Ringsend and John Scottus Secondary School (01 660 9309). University College Dublin is also situated on a large campus in Belfield, Dublin 4 (see p.150) and there is a College of Further Education in Ballsbridge (see p.148).

Transport

Ballsbridge and Sandymount are well served by the Dart suburban rail which stops at Grand Canal Dock, Lansdowne Road, Sandymount and Sydney Parade. There are also buses to Sandymount and through Ballsbridge, and the efficient 46A route from the city travels through Donnybrook before reaching the quality bus corridor to the south side and Dun Laoghaire. Like many parts of the city, most of the residential roads have speed ramps, so driving in the area can be bumpy, and most roads in the area also have pay and display parking. Gates for the Dart track can leave you stuck at the side of the track at Lansdowne or Ballsbridge for a few minutes. Access to the East Link toll bridge from Irishtown is handy for the northside and airport.

Safety & Annoyances

Most areas around here are safe, though streets can seem quiet and eerie at night, with lots of tall trees and houses set back from the roads. Shopping isn't abundant – you'll need to drive to Merrion or Sandymount to do a decent supermarket shop and to avoid the astronomical prices in the village gourmet food stores. The only other minor annoyance is the abundance of SUVs, Mercedes and the D4 accent – but you will probably get used to them, or even adopt them, if you can afford to live here.

Written by residents, the New York Explorer
is packed with insider info, from arriving in a
new destination to making it your home and
everything in between.

New York Explorer Residents' Guide
We Know Where You Live

Map p.416, 419, 420
Area **D** p.80-81

Dublin 6 & 6W

Dublin 6 stretches beyond the Grand Canal, south of the city centre, from Ranelagh village, west through Rathmines and Rathgar villages. Dublin 6W (The 'w' standing for west) includes Templeogue, Kimmage and Terenure. Dublin 6 was split into 6 and 6W in 1985, when a new sorting office opened and residents of some areas felt their property would be devalued if it was given the code Dublin 26. This will give you a clue as to what the area is like. Rathgar, and parts of Ranelagh, Rathmines and Terenure are quite exclusive, with wide, leafy roads, detached houses on their own grounds similar to those found in neighbouring Dublin 4, and with prices to match. The area covers Milltown, Ranelagh, Rathmines, Rathgar, Harolds Cross, Terenure and Lower Kimmage Road. Overall, Dublin 6 is a pleasant, quiet place to live, well served by pubs and restaurants. Ranelagh is a large village, packed with trendy eateries and a mix of old-style and modernised pubs, all within a 20 minute walk from the city centre. The roads and streets around Ranelagh are mainly residential and well established, with not many new developments. Rathmines is a little shabbier than Ranelagh – its tall houses long popular for cheap student flats and bedsits, with many of the buildings sadly neglected, and former front gardens given over to parking spaces and business premises. Rathgar is more like Dublin 4 – a small village and lots of large houses on substantial grounds. Further west, areas of Dublin 6W like Terenure have many three and four-bedroom settled semi-detached housing estates from the 1950s and 1960s.

Best Points

As with Dublin 4, you have all the convenience of living near the city, but the areas are much quieter, with many long, leafy, residential roads and old-style houses with long gardens.

Worst Points

Rathmines and Harold's Cross are a little run-down compared to some of their adjoining areas, with some ugly shop fronts, neglected houses, litter, and local authority housing estates contrasting with their richer D6 neighbours.

Accommodation

Dublin 6 is quite a mature residential area and there aren't many large new developments. However, the odd small apartment block or townhouses are built in the grounds of a larger house and there has been some development in Rathmines, with the Town Centre apartment complex, and along the Grand Canal towards Harold's Cross. In general, one-bed properties around Rathmines or Rathgar start from around €380,000 and prices can go up to €10 million or even €12 million for a large, period family home with a garden, especially around Rathgar.

Shopping & Amenities

Shopping in Ranelagh isn't great – apart from banks, pharmacies, the odd specialist or charity shop and useful services like newsagents, it's mostly restaurants and cafes, and the small villages of Rathgar or Harold's Cross have very little either, although you will see some exclusive little boutiques dotted about Rathgar. Rathmines has a shopping centre (the Swan Centre) with a large Dunnes Stores and some other assorted shops, but fashion shopping in Rathmines is of the low budget or discount variety and you'll find lots of charity and discount shops. However there's everything else useful from supermarkets (Dunnes, Tesco and Aldi) and shoe repairs to laundrettes and hairdressers, so you won't have to go into the city and you won't break the bank. There's also a large public library in Rathmines (see p.245).

Entertainment & Leisure

If you're looking to eat out in Ranelagh you shouldn't be disappointed. From takeaways, suburban pizza joints and smart restaurants, the choice is there, but it can be hard to get a table mid-week so book ahead. The same goes for Rathmines, though the fare is a little more fast than tasty – long popular with students, the village has every type of takeaway from burgers, kebabs and pizza, to fish and chips and fried chicken, with a couple of 'proper restaurants' dotted in between. Rathgar doesn't have many restaurants though there are a few gourmet shops like the Deli Boutique (01 496 7612) and there are more restaurants in Terenure village.

Pubs in Ranelagh and Rathgar get a good enough crowd on weekends, but if you're looking for live music, DJs spinning tunes or late-night drinking, you're more likely to find it in Rathmines or the city centre.

For the more athletic, there are lots of sporting activities in Dublin 6 and 6W. Clubs like Mount Pleasant Tennis Club (p.256) or LA Fitness (01 491 1675) in Dartry will keep you in shape and meeting new people, as will Rathmines Swimming Pool, a public pool on Lower Rathmines Road (p.255). Bushy Park in Terenure has playing fields, tennis courts, a playground and walks and there are small parks around the area at squares like Kennilworth Square and Eaton Square. Harold's Cross offers a park and a bit of a dabble on the dogs with greyhound racing in Harold's Cross Stadium (see p.262).

Healthcare

The nearest main hospitals to Dublin 6 are St. Vincent's University Hospital in Elm Park (Merrion), Dublin 4 (01 277 4000, www.stvincents.ie), and St James's Hospital, James's Street, Dublin 8 (01 410 3100, www.stjames.ie). Johnston's Pharmacy in Ranelagh is open until 21:00 on weekdays; Bourkes Pharmacy in Rathmines is open until 21:00 Thursday and Friday and McCabe's Pharmacy on Lower Kimmage Road, Dublin 6W (01 490 6011) is open until 21:00 on weekdays. Bradley's in Kimmage is open until 22:00 Monday to Saturday.

Education

Popular girls-only secondary schools in the area include Our Ladys School, Terenure (01 490 3241); Alexandra College, Milltown (p.146); St Louis High School in Rathmines (01 497 5458) and Presentation School, Terenure (01 490 2404). Boys-only schools include Sandford Park, Ranelagh (01 497 1417, www.sandfordparkschool.ie); Gonzaga College, Ranelagh (01 497 2931) and Terenure College (01 490 4621), and mixed schools include The High School, Rathgar (01 492 2611); Rathmines College (01 497 5334); St Mac Dara's Community College, Templeogue (01 456 6216); Templeogue College (01 490 5788, www.templeoguecollege.ie) and St Marys College, Rathmines (01 406 2100).

The Dublin Institute of Technology (DIT) has some faculties in Rathmines, while for evening classes, Sandford Language Institute in Milltown (see p.148) and Rathmines College (see p.148) are both good. Trinity College and UCD are just a couple of miles from the area (see Higher Education on p.147 for more).

Transport

These areas are all well served with bus routes from the city centre, one of the busiest being the number 15 route from the city centre though Rathmines and Rathgar. The Luas from St Stephen's Green also travels through Ranelagh before going on through Milltown and south to Dundrum and Sandyford. Most of the roads around here are residential so spaces are not too hard to find – parking is residential permit or pay and display. There's a taxi rank outside Tesco in Rathmines. A lot of the residential roads have ramps and speed bumps so short cuts are deterred.

Safety & Annoyances

Traffic congestion can be heavy especially during morning rush hour heading towards the city, and evening rush-hour heading out of the city. Side roads around Ranelagh and the canal are locations for some of the city's worst bottlenecks.

Housing in Dublin 6

Map p.408, 416
Area **E** p.80-81

Best Points
Next door to the city centre and close to Phoenix Park, Dublin 7 is also on the Luas line and there's a good community spirit in the area.

Worst Points
The DIT building works around Grangegorman will continue for the next couple of years. As with much of the city centre, car clampers regularly patrol the area so it's advisable not to park illegally, and don't forget to pay and display.

Dublin 7

Dublin 7, on the north quays just west of the city centre, has been undergoing one of the city's biggest transformations, mainly around the Smithfield area. Huge building works and a skyline full of cranes have been a permanent feature in recent years, as the area is being transformed from a rundown inner city area into what is hoped to be a smart, trendy enclave. It's been taking its time, but the ultimate plan will transform its windswept central square (which used to be the Smithfield Market), into a burgeoning area full of shops, cafes and art galleries, surrounded by smart new apartments and offices.

Dublin 7 is also home to the centre of the legal system at the Four Courts, and the country's solicitors and barristers train at nearby King's Inns and Blackhall Place. The Dublin Institute of Technology, currently based in a number of campuses around the city, will move to Grangegorman over the next few years, providing the main campus and bringing a studenty feel to the area. Phibsborough, Smithfield, Stoneybatter and North Circular Road all fall into this area.

Accommodation

In formerly working-class residential areas such as Stoneybatter, which became popular with young, upwardly mobile workers at the start of the economic boom, two-bed cottages sell from between €380,000 and €420,000, and two-storey two-bed houses range from €450,000 to €475,000. In more settled areas such as Phibsborough, houses on roads like Rathdown Road sell from between €750,000 up to €1.2 million, with types of property ranging from three-bed terraced houses built in the 1930s to larger, period houses in Phibsborough and surrounding areas.

Shopping & Amenities

Dublin 7 is extremely close to the city centre so all of the shopping and amenities of Dublin 1 are on the doorstep. There are small shops in Smithfield, a selection of convenience stores and newsagents dotted around the residential areas and Phibsborough Shopping Centre has shops, a gym and a Tesco supermarket. Prussia Street in Dublin 7 has the small Park Shopping Centre with a Tesco, pharmacy, cafe and post office.

Entertainment & Leisure

Dublin 7 is close to the city centre so the main entertainment and leisure options, such as theatres, cinemas and art galleries, will be found there. There are some good pubs in Smithfield, Stoneybatter and along the quays – The Cobblestone (01 872 1799) is popular for traditional music whereas Sin É on Ormond Quay (01 878 7009) and Voodoo Lounge (see p.388 for more information on Voodoo Lounge), on Arran Quay, both have live rock music. There's a viewing chimney at Smithfield and the Old Jameson Distillery is another popular tourist attraction in the area, near Heuston Station (see p.200). The National Museum of Ireland – Decorative Arts and History section is at Collins Barracks and Dublin 7 also borders on Phoenix Park, Europe's largest urban park and home to Dublin Zoo, and the residence of the President of Ireland (Áras an Uachtaráin), with entrances on Conyngham Road and Infirmary Road. Croke Park GAA Stadium and Museum is also nearby (Dublin 3). See Exploring on p.175 for more.

Healthcare

The Mater Misercordiae University Hospital on Eccles Street, just off Dorset Street Lower, is a large, acute hospital with a number of surgical specialities (01 803 2000, www.mater.ie). Collins's pharmacy on the North Circular Road is open until 20:00 Monday to Friday.

Education

Girls secondary schools in Dublin 7 include St Dominics College in Cabra (01 838 5282) and St Josephs Secondary School (01 6710419). St Declan's College in Cabra (01 838 0357) and St Paul's CBS (01 872 0781) are both boys' schools, and mixed schools include Coláiste Eanna in Cabra (01 838 9577) and Coláiste Mhuire (01 868 8996). DIT (see p.149) is to merge its various colleges at a new campus at Grangegorman in the next four years.

Transport

The Luas is extremely convenient to Dublin 7, with easy access to the city centre and IFSC to the east, and Heuston Station to the west. The area is also served by buses and within walking distance to the city centre. There isn't a huge amount of parking in Smithfield and Stoneybatter so if you are thinking about living there and have a car, take the parking situation into consideration.

Safety & Annoyances

This is the north inner city so like any inner city areas, pickpockets and car break-ins are not unheard of, so watch your valuables. There are a number of hostels for the homeless in the area and both the Four Courts and the Juvenile Court at Smithfield attract some dodgy characters from time to time.

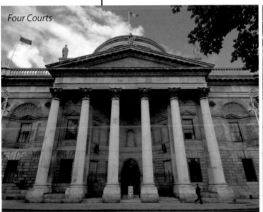

Four Courts

Jameson Distillery

Apartments in Smithfield

Map p.414, 415
Area **F** p.80-81

Dublin 8

Dublin 8, just west of Dublin 2, stretches from the edge of Temple Bar and Christchurch, westwards across to Kilmainham and Islandbridge and southwards towards Portobello Bridge. Covering a large area, namely Portobello, Inchicore, Islandbridge, South Circular Road, The Coombe, Kilmainham and Dolphin's Barn, Dublin 8 includes some of the oldest and most historic components of the city. One of the area's best property features is that it has a great selection of solid, well-built rows of redbrick period houses, in quiet little streets. The area feels settled, is near to the city centre and can be better value than other areas.

However it has been through hardships and some parts are among the poorest and most run-down in the inner city, with some local authority estates earning bad reputations for problems such as high unemployment and drug abuse. Like the rest of the city though, Dublin 8 is experiencing major change. Investment, such as the €2.6bn Liberties and Coombe area development plan for the area south of Heuston Station – to be called 'SoHo' will transform the area. Inchicore village is designated for urban renewal, and developers have been given tax incentives for a lot of previously deprived areas like Cork Street and James Street, so are pouring money in, changing the feel of the area and improving the not so good parts. Developments such as the Digital Hub and Luas light rail have kept prices on the up in recent years. Because it is so close to the city, and accessible to the IFSC by Luas, competition for small terraced houses especially around Portobello, is high and these can generate extremely high prices.

Best Points

The best points about Dublin 8 are its proximity to the city centre and the vibe around Portobello. You can do gourmet breakfast along the canal in a trendy cafe before buying market fresh fruit and flowers to brighten up your cute little red brick house.

Worst Points

If you're living near areas of major redevelopment, check development plans carefully. Rejuvenation plans for Inchicore village, the Coombe-Liberties, the old John Player factory and adjacent sites mean large-scale construction, which might be unpleasant to live near. There are also many houses in the area being refurbished so expect to see skips lining the streets. Traffic can be heavy along the canal, towards Inchicore and out towards the Naas Road, especially during evening rush hour.

Accommodation

Portobello is one of the most sought after parts of Dublin 8, partly due to its rows of cute Victorian houses, many of which run alongside the canal. A typical two bedroom 'two-up two-down' house is priced between €600,000 and €650,000, with a two-storey 4-bed house costing around €1.75m. The South Circular Road (SCR) isn't as pretty as other parts of Dublin 8 as many houses are used as offices, doctors and dentists surgeries and front gardens have given way to car spaces. That said, buying a large house here will still cost a couple of million.

There is a slight price divide when it comes to Clanbrassil Street, reflecting how rapidly Dublin can change from one street to the next. Behind this street, there are some traditionally working-class areas and houses become larger and cheaper and you might get a three-bed or four-bed for €725,000 to €800,000. Corporation flats such as St Teresa's Gardens off Donore Avenue have a bad reputation, which have kept prices in the vicinity low, although there is a proposal to demolish the flats and regenerate the area.

On SCR, there are proposals to build a massive mixed-use development on the former John Player factory site, replacing it with residential, retail, education and office space. There are also proposals for development on the adjoining site for mixed use development, including new streets and a square.

The Tenters area is also good value, with ex-local authority pebbledash 3-bed houses costing from €475,000 to €550,000, or a cottage in Blackpitts around €400,000 to €500,000. Cork Street has been undergoing a lot of investment and regeneration and around Newmarket Square, there are some new two-bed apartments going for €350,000 to €400,000.

The SCR runs to Rialto, Dolphins Barn, Kilmainham and Inchicore, including parts of Islandbridge. These areas are mixed bags. Most housing varies from period redbrick to e-corporation housing from the 1950s and more modern developments built in the last 20 years. In the Liberties/Coombe area, a two bed period redbrick house might cost between €400,000 and €450,000. Ex-corporation houses are prominent in Inchicore too. Fatima Mansions, local-

A Big Garden

The 709 hectare Phoenix Park, with sports grounds, Dublin Zoo and the residence of the President of Ireland, is one of the area's greatest amenities.

authority blocks of flats from the 1950s, which developed major social disorder problems in the 1970s and 80s, are also being regenerated, with a mix of private and public housing. Finally, there has been a lot of building along Conyngham Road and around Islandbridge in recent years (again, developers were given tax incentives), so there's a good supply of modern town houses, duplexes and apartments.

Shopping & Amenities

Inchicore village and Kilmainham offer the usual convenience stores and essential services and there's also a mix of shops along Portobello and Camden Street, including many second hand and charity shops. Thomas Street and Meath Street are popular for market stalls, and the indoor Liberty Market on Meath Street has a number of stalls – selling all manner of discount goods and haberdashery (see Markets on p.328). Francis Street is great for antiques (see Shopping on p.279 for more).

Entertainment & Leisure

One of the city's biggest amenities, the 709 hectare Phoenix Park, on the north side of the Liffey, is classed in the Dublin 8 postcode and is home to sports grounds, Dublin Zoo and the President of Ireland's residence (Áras an Uachtaráin). One of the city's most visited tourist attractions, the Guinness Storehouse, is also in Dublin 8, at St James's Gate, the traditional home of the Guinness Brewery. The area is also home to the Digital Hub, a government initiative to encourage digital and technology enterprises, and the Irish National War Memorial Park runs along the Con Colbert Road and also contains sports grounds.

There's a nice park at St Patrick's Cathedral, and the Grand Canal around Harold's Cross is full of swans. There are rowing clubs at Islandbridge and along the river Liffey and the Irish Museum of Modern Art occupies a unique location in a former military barracks in Kilmainham. Kilmainham Gaol is also here. Richmond Park football stadium is off Emmet Road in Inchicore and the National Stadium is on the South Circular Road. See Exploring on p.161 for more.

For going out, there are some restaurants and bars around Portobello, and the area is also close to the suburbs of Ranelagh and Rathmines and depending on whereabouts you are, a short hop into the city centre. Vicar Street on Thomas Street is a popular venue for live gigs, as are The Village and Whelans's (see p.392), both on Wexford Street in Dublin 2. The lower end of Camden Street (also D2), with its pubs such as Solas (01 478 0583, www.solasbars.com) and Carnival (01 405 3604), are popular nightspots especially with the student crowd. Around Christchurch, leading into Temple Bar and Dame Street, are also heaving nightspots while the pubs around NCAD (National College of Art and Design) on Thomas Street have a studenty feel.

Healthcare

The main hospital for this area is St James's Hospital on James's Street, a large acute hospital with many specialities and an accident and emergency department (01 410 3100, www.stjames.ie). The Coombe Maternity and Women's Hospital is in the Liberties, Dublin 8 (01 408 5200) and Our Lady's Hospital for Sick Children in nearby Crumlin is an acute hospital for children (01 409 6100, www.olhsc.ie). Leonards Corner pharmacy at 108 South Circular Road is open until 22:00 every night.

Education

Girls secondary schools in Dublin 8 include Mercy Secondary College in Goldenbridge (01 453 126) and Presentation College in Warrenmount (01 280 1338). For Boys schools, there's CBS James Street (01 454 7756) and Christian Brothers, Synge Street (01 478 399). Mixed schools include Liberties College (01 454 0044) and St Patrick's

Vive La France

Take a break from Dublin and head over to the capital of fine food, refined fashions and beautiful scenery (and, most importantly, cheap duty free), Paris. Take the *Paris Mini Explorer* with you – it fits in your pocket, yet it's packed with essential city info.

Cathedral GS (01 454 0588) and there's also Inchicore College of Further Education (01 453 5358). Griffith College on SCR is an independent third-level college and Portobello College is another independent college (see p.148). DIT Aungier Street and Kevin Street are both handy for Dublin 8, and NCAD, the National College of Art and Design, is on Thomas Street (see p.149).

No Spending
There isn't much shopping in Dublin 8, but it's accessible to the city centre either by Luas, bus or on foot.

Transport

The Luas light rail Red Line runs from Heuston Station, past St James's Hospital, along Rialto and towards Goldenbridge and Drimnagh before it reaches the end of the line in Tallaght. Heuston Station has intercity rail and commuter train services to surrounding counties and major cities in Ireland, as well as nearly 20 bus connections to various routes. Parking on some of the narrower residential streets can be hard to find and is permit or pay and display parking.

Safety & Annoyances

Like many areas close to the city centre, it's good to be careful everywhere. Dublin 8 includes some of the poorest parts of the inner city and brings with it problems such as unemployment and drug abuse. However, areas such as Fatima Mansions and Saint Teresas's Gardens have been set aside for rejuvenation and are changing for the better. There's no major supermarket shopping area so Jervis Centre (Tesco) or the Sundrive Road (Superquinn) are the nearest decent size supermarkets.

James Street

The Liberties

St James's Gate

Map p.408
Area **G** p.80-81

Best Points

Areas like Drumcondra and Glasnevin are near to the city centre but also mature, residential areas. Dublin 9 is great for easy access to Dublin Airport.

Worst Points

Heavy traffic going to Croke Park can cause severe congestion on match days, which take place on Sundays for about four months of the year, mostly during the summer. Construction on the Metro North route will be disruptive until completion, which is scheduled for 2012.

Dublin 9

Suburbs like Drumcondra, Glasnevin and Griffith Avenue are mature residential areas with a mix of period and early 20th century properties, with easy access to the city centre. Whitehall and Santry are a little less convenient for the city and would have traditionally been more working-class areas. Glasnevin also crosses into the Dublin 11 postcode. Drumcondra, Glasnevin, Griffith Avenue, Whitehall, Beaumont and Santry all fall in to the Dublin 9 area.

Housing in Drumcondra

Accommodation

Dublin 9, just north of the city, is an established area with a mix of period red-brick houses and those built in the 1930s, especially around Mobhi Road and Griffith Avenue. Further out, towards Whitehall, Collins Avenue and Santry, houses date mainly from the 1950s with a lot of three-bed semi detached homes. Whitehall also has some former local authority housing estates and developments from the 1990s include Collinswood and Charlemont.

Like everywhere else in the city, there are some more recent apartment developments, a two-bed costing anywhere from €350,000 to €500,000. A typical 1930s house on Mobhi Road or Griffith Avenue will set you back over €1m and a three-bed or four-bed redbrick house on a road like Iona Road in Drumcondra will cost around €1.5m. Towards Santry and further out, prices come down to between €450,000 and €600,000 for a typical house.

Shopping & Amenities

Small villages such as Drumcondra contain typical convenience stores, fast food outlets, pharmacies and hairdressers. The biggest shopping centre in the area, Omni Park, is further out in Santry and has a supermarket. Other supermarkets include Tesco in Drumcondra.

Entertainment & Leisure

The Botanic Gardens in Glasnevin date back to 1795, and are a popular tourist attraction (see p.195). Other green spaces are supplied by Griffith Park on Botanic Avenue and Ellenfield Park in Whitehall. Sports clubs include Na Fianna GAA club on Mobhi Road, Homefarm Sports Ground off the Swords Road in Whitehall, and Glasnevin Tennis Club. There's a 25m pool nearby in Ballymun Leisure Centre (D11), as well as in St Vincents CBS School on the Finglas Road in Glasnevin.

Hampstead Park between Ballymun Road and DCU, has tennis courts and for GAA matches and the GAA museum, Croke Park, in Dublin 3, is nearby.

The Helix at Dublin City University is the main theatre (see p.394). Drumcondra and Glasnevin are popular for eating out, with good pub grub at Fagan's pub (01 836 9491). Drumcondra has a few fine eateries with Italian restaurant Il Corvo (01 837 5727), the Independent Pizza Company (01 830 2044) and Andersons Food Hall & Café (01 837 8394) off The Rise in Glasnevin, a trendy cafe and wine bar. Nearby Washerwoman's Hill Restaurant (01 837 9199) is also worth a visit.

99

Healthcare

Beaumont Hospital on Beaumont Road, is a large acute hospital with 706 beds (01 809 3000, www.beaumont.ie). Other nearby hospitals include the Mater Misercordiae University Hospital on Eccles Street, Dublin 7 (01 803 2000, www.mater.ie), or Connolly Hospital Blanchardstown, Dublin 15 (01 646 5000, www.connollyhospital.ie). The Bon Secours Hospital, Glasnevin, Dublin 9 is a general private hospital with consultation by appointment only (01 837 5111, www.bonsecours.org/ie).

Education

Girls secondary schools include Dominican College on Griffith Avenue (01 837 6080), Our Lady Of Mercy College in Beaumont (01 837 1478) and Maryfield College in Drumcondra (01 837 3574). Mixed schools include Scoil Chaitriona in Glasnevin (01 837 0762), Rosmini Community School in Drumcondra (01 837 1694, www.pobalscoilrosmini.ie), Plunket College in Whitehall (01 837 1689, www.plunkettcollege.ie) and Trinity Comprehensive School on the Ballymun Road (01 842 1195). Boys schools include St. Aidan's CBS in Whitehall (01 837 7587, www.staidanscbs.com) and St Vincents CBS, Glasnevin (01 830 4375). Dublin City University is on Collins Avenue (see p.149) and teacher training college, St Patrick's College, is located in Drumcondra (see p.148).

Transport

Main routes to Drumcondra, Whitehall, Beaumont and Santry are all well served by buses from the city centre. The western suburban rail service connects Drumcondra to Connolly station and on to the Dart suburban rail in the city centre. The proposed Metro North, a new metro line from St Stephen's Green, will stop at Drumcondra, Griffith Avenue, DCU, Ballymun and Santry, with links to Dublin Airport and further out to Lissenhall. The line is due to be completed in 2012.

Safety & Annoyances

Traffic can be busy on most of the main roads into the city and out to Dublin airport, and like many other areas of the city, construction is ongoing in many areas, which can be a nuisance.

Traffic in Drumcondra

Map p.419, 420
Area **H** p.80-81

Dublin 14

Dublin 14 is a large, mature residential suburb south of Dublin 6, with the village of Dundrum one of its main focal points. The area covers Clonskeagh, Windy Arbour, Churchtown, Dundrum, Goatstown and Rathfarnham. Two new developments in Dundrum, the opening of the Luas light rail line in 2004, and the completion of the Dundrum Town Centre in 2005, along with the area's quiet, tree-lined residential roads and access to the M50 Motorway, have made it one of the south city's most desirable areas to live, along with Clonskeagh and Windy Arbour, with their close proximity to the city.

Best Points

The arrival of the Luas has meant that St Stephen's Green is now just minutes away, although with the Dundrum Town Centre, you won't even have to go shopping in the city centre.

Accommodation

Housing developments in Dublin 14 are mostly mature, with wide, tree-lined roads with names ending in 'avenue', 'grove', 'lawn' and 'park', full of houses built in the 1950s and 60s. Around Weston Park, Dundrum, prices range from €800,000 to €950,000 for a four-bed semi-detached residence. There are also some detached period houses in the area, and on roads such as Sydenham Road, one of most sought after roads, where a 2,000 square foot four or five-bed house will cost you around €2m. Towards Clonskeagh, detached houses in Ardilea or Louvain, with their large gardens, are highly sought after and range from €1.5 up to €3.5 million, depending on what's been done to the house.

Apartments in those areas range from €500,000 to €600,000 for a two-bed and there's a good mix of new and second hand, with new developments such as Wickham Point still under construction.

Worst Points

One of the worst points for residents is traffic congestion caused by access to the M50 motorway or the Dundrum Town Centre. There can be long tailbacks on approaching roads to the shopping centre particularly on Thursday evenings (late night shopping), weekends and rainy days.

Shopping & Amenities

There are a few small shops here and there around the area, but the main focus of shopping is undoubtedly the Dundrum Town Centre (p.329), a €650 million shopping centre which opened in 2005, with a range of fashion brands from Harvey Nichols to House of Fraser, Next, Oasis and H&M as well as a large Tesco, hairdressers, salons and jewellers. Nutgrove Shopping Centre is an older centre with a good range of shops (www.nutgroveshoppingcentre.ie, more information on p.331) and Dundrum village itself has another smaller shopping centre, as well as banks and independent shops.

Entertainment & Leisure

The Mill Theatre (p.395) can be found in Dundrum Town Centre and there's also a multi-screen cinema located here. Another cinema nearby is The Ormonde in Stillorgan (see p.390). There are a few restaurants and bars in Dundrum, in the village itself and around the shopping centre. There isn't much in Clonskeagh but two popular pubs are Ashton's (01 283 0045) and O'Shea's (01 283 0189). In Goatstown, The Goat Grill (01 298 4145) is popular for pub grub and refreshments and in Rathfarnham, Taylors 3 Rock (01 494 2999) runs Irish nights popular with overseas visitors.

There are some nice walks and parklands along the River Dodder, especially through Dartry Park and towards Milltown. Marlay Park in Rathfarnham has 200 acres of parkland, lakes and weirs as well as an 18th century Demesne (land that was once owned by the crown), tennis and picnic areas, and there's a farmers market on Saturdays. The Wicklow Way walk also starts in Marlay Park. Airfield House in Dundrum has five acres of gardens and a cafe and you can visit Rathfarnham Castle, which dates back to the 1580s (see Exploring on p.183 for more). There are four golf courses in Rathfarnham and one at Milltown, and many other tennis and sports clubs in the area (see Activities on p.225).

101

Healthcare

The nearest public hospitals are at either St. Vincent's University Hospital in Elm Park (Merrion), Dublin 4 (01 277 4000, www.stvincents.ie); St James's Hospital, James's Street, Dublin 8, (01 410 3100, www.stjames.ie); St Michael's Hospital, Dun Laoghaire, (01 280 6901, www.stmichaels.ie) or The Adelaide and Meath Hospital Dublin, Tallaght, (01 414 2000, www.amnch.ie). Mount Carmel hospital, Braemor Park, Churchtown, is a private hospital (01 406 3400; www.mt-carmel.com) and the Beacon Hospital in Sandyford is a private hospital with an emergency department where a walk-in consultation costs €120. Rockfield Pharmacy in Dundrum (Balally Luas Stop) is open until 22:00 every night and Mark Ellis (01 495 2135) in Knocklyon (D16) is open until 21:00 on weekdays. McCabe's Pharmacy in Dundrum Town Centre (01 298 6709) is open until 21:00 on weekdays.

Education

Large girls' secondary schools in the area include Mount Anville (01 288 5313, www.mountanville.ie), Our Ladys Grove (01 295 1913), Loreto High School Beaufort (01 493 3052), Notre Dame (01 298 9533) and Sancta Maria College (01 493 4887) in Rathfarnham. Boys' schools include Colaiste Eanna (01 493 1767) and De La Salle College (01 298 1067, www.delasallecollege.com). Mixed secondary schools include Wesley College and St Columba's (see p.147), St Killian's Deutsche Schule (01 288 3323), St Tiernan's Community School (01 295 3224) and Ballinteer Community School (01 298 8195). For colleges, Dundrum College (01 298 2340, www.dundrumcollege.ie) runs adult education courses and the nearest university is UCD (University College Dublin, p.150), which is accessible from Dublin 14 through the Clonskeagh gate.

Transport

The Luas green line from St Stephen's Green passes through Dundrum, over the impressive cable-stayed William Dargan Bridge, on its way to Sandyford. Dundrum is also well served by buses, with routes to Enniskerry and Glencullen as well as to the city centre. Parking is available on many residential roads, though it can be difficult to find parking in Dundrum village itself. However the main Town Centre car park has 3,400 spaces.

Safety & Annoyances

New additions to the Dundrum Town Centre will be under construction for another year or two and construction is still ongoing around developments such as Wickham Point. Dundrum Village is to undergo further regeneration so demolition and construction are yet to take place.

Houses in Dundrum

The Luas track through Dundrum

Map p.407, 408, 409
Area J p.80-81

Best Points
These areas are right beside the airport, and the M1 motorway, with easy access to the M50. Compared with some other areas, you can find some good value property.

Worst Points
Construction and noise are an issue – St Margaret's Road is under development and Metro North will bring its fair share of tunnelling and disruption once it starts. Proximity to the airport brings overhead aircraft noise under flight paths in various areas, especially to the north.

North Dublin

North Dublin suburbs Finglas and Ballymun have seen their fare share of poverty, social deprivation, drugs and anti-social behaviour in the past, especially in the infamous tower blocks of Ballymun Flats and in parts of Finglas. The towers are being demolished as part of a huge regeneration project of the Ballymun area and Finglas has also changed dramatically in the past few years, with new developments and projects outnumbering the problem areas. Further north around Dublin Airport, there are more settled residential suburbs like Santry and Swords. The area covers Finglas, Santry, Ballymun, St Margaret's and Swords.

Accommodation

Property for sale in Finglas consists of a lot of former local authority properties and older, private properties, and in recent years there has been a lot of new development around Ballymun and St Margaret's Road. These areas have seen their fair share of deprivation and problems in the past, especially in local authority estates, however the entire Ballymun area is being regenerated, which is cutting down on the social problems attached to the area.

In Finglas South, a three-bed mid-terrace former council house, measuring about 900 square feet, will cost from €300,000 upwards while in Finglas East, towards Glasnevin, a three-bed mid terrace house will go for €420,000 to €500,000. In Ballymun, in new developments on St Margaret's Road, a two-bed apartment will go for around €350,000 and parking is usually included, although it depends on the particular development. Santry is a more mature residential area with a few new apartments and houses, such as a large development at Northwood Demesne, and older houses off the village. New apartments start at about €260,000 for a one-bed or €330,000 for a two-bed. A three-bed semi-detached house goes for around €520,000, depending on whether it has a garage or extension. In estates which are 15 to 20 years old, for example Knightswood and Royal Oak out towards Coolock, a house might cost between €450,000 and €510,000. Further north in the more settled suburb of Swords, there's a mix of old and new properties. A one-bed apartment might cost around €250,000, while two-bed apartments cost around €365,000 and four-bed houses can go for as much as €575,000. Detached houses can sell for around €1 million.

Shopping & Amenities

Finglas village has all of the essentials – newsagents, banks and services, as well as a Superquinn. Tesco, Clearwater, on the N2 is open 24 hours. Towards St Margaret's Road you'll find budget supermarkets Aldi and Lidl, and a new shopping centre at Charlestown, which is nearly completed and has a Dunnes Stores.

The Omni Park Shopping Centre (01 842 1262) in Santry has a large fashion mall, cafes and a Tesco supermarket, and there's an Aldi off Santry Avenue. Ireland's first IKEA store is proposed for near Santry and Ballymun (rumoured to open in 2009). The Pavilions Shopping Centre (01 840 4601) in Swords has bookshops, pharmacies, phone shops and travel agents, as well as a fashion mall.

Entertainment & Leisure

In Finglas, amenities include Mellowes Park, which has a 25 metre pool and leisure centre (01 837 3891), and the sports grounds behind Janelle Shopping Centre in Poppintree Park (01 837 3891) and also in Johnstown Park (01 834 3656). Ballymun also has a leisure centre (01 862 3510). Green space is provided by Tolka Valley Park, situated on the Tolka River. Morton Stadium, or Santry Stadium (01 837 0278) as it is also known, is the national athletics stadium and home of Clonliffe Harriers Football Club.

103

On the Ballymun Road, behind DCU, there's Hampstead Park and Ellenfield Park is off the Swords Road. There's an Astro Park off Coolock Lane (www.astropark.ie), and a park and golf course at Sillogue Park in Ballymun (01 842 9956). There are plenty of other green areas and places to play sports around estates, for example in small parks such as Kildonan Park.

For nightlife, there isn't a huge number of restaurants in Finglas, but there are plenty of pubs and many do good pub grub. The Full Shilling (01 834 6061) in Finglas village is a late-night bar. Swords and Santry villages have a variety of restaurants and pubs and there are neighbourhood newsagents and shops around various housing estates.

For entertainment and culture, The Helix theatre is in the DCU campus (see p.394) and there's a cinema at the Pavilions, Swords (see p.390). The National Botanic Gardens (see p.195) with their famous Victorian glasshouses, are in Glasnevin, Dublin 11.

Healthcare

Beaumont Hospital on Beaumont Road, is a large acute hospital with 706 beds (01 809 3000, www.beaumont.ie), while Connolly Hospital Blanchardstown is an acute hospital with an accident and emergency department and many other clinics (01 646 5000, www.connollyhospital.ie). The Mater Misercordiae University Hospital on Eccles Street, just off Dorset Street Lower, is a large, acute hospital with a number of surgical specialities (01 803 2000, www.mater.ie). The Bon Secours Hospital, Glasnevin, Dublin 9 is a general private hospital with consultation by appointment only, (01 837 5111, www.bonsecours.org/ie). McCabe's Pharmacy in the Pavilions Swords (01 890 3073, ww.mccabespaharmacy.com) and also on Rathbeale Road (01 840 2111) is open until 21:00 on weekdays. O'Sullivan's Pharmacy (01 842 7784) on the Swords Road is open until 20:00 on weekdays and McCabe's Pharmacy (01 834 2493) on Glasnevin Ave (D11) is open until 21:00 on weekdays.

Education

There are plenty of schools in North Dublin – secondary schools for girls include St Mary's (01 837 4413) in Glasnevin, Mercy College Coolock (01 848 0888, www.mercycoolock.ie), Mater Christi in Cappagh (01 834 1610), Loreto College Swords (01 840 7025) and St Michael's in Finglas (01 834 1767). For boys, there's St Vincents primary school in Glasnevin (01 830 2328, www.stvincentsprimary.com), Beneavin De La Salle College (01 834 1410), Coláiste Choilm (01 840 1420) in Swords, St Kevin's primary Finglas (01 834 3061) and Patrician College (01 834 3067). Mixed schools include Hartstown Community College in Clonsilla (01 820 7863), Coláiste Dhúlaigh in Coolock (01 848 1337), Coláiste Eoin (01 834 1426) and St Finian's (01 840 2623). For further education, Whitehall College (01 837 6011, www.whitehallcollege.com) is in Swords and Dublin City University (DCU) is on Collins Avenue (p.149).

Transport

The north Dublin area is well served by buses and there is a Quality Bus Corridor through Finglas. Dublin Airport is between Santry and Swords and the M1 motorway running north to Belfast and linking with the M50 is also here. The proposed Metro North line will connect Swords to the airport and city centre, running through Lissenhall and Ballymun and linking with the Luas Red and Green lines.

Safety & Annoyances

Some areas around Finglas and Ballymun have bad reputations for drug problems and anti-social behaviour, including gang activities and violence blamed on inter-gang warfare. Other areas are being regenerated in an attempt to shake off their bleak pasts. Check any area out carefully before deciding to live there.

A Great Place For Tee

Golf clubs include Roganstown Golf and Country club in Swords (01 843 3118, www.roganstown. com), St Margaret's Golf and Country Club (01 864 0400, www.stmargarets golf.com), Swords Open Golf Course (p.240), as well as plenty of other courses in Donabate and surrounding areas.

Map p.410, 411
412, 413
Area **K** p.80-81

North Dublin – Coast

After the south Dublin coast, property along the north Dublin coast is some of the most sought after in the county. Open spaces, impressive views over Dublin Bay, fishing villages, marinas and accessibility to the Dart suburban rail line are among the key attractions. The area covers Marino, Fairview, Clontarf, Raheny, Sutton, Howth and Malahide. The seaside villages of Howth and Malahide in particular, both boasting marinas, yacht clubs and golf courses as well as cosy restaurants and village atmospheres, are ideal locations – if you can afford the prices.

Best Points
The best points of living along the north Dublin coast are the sea and large parks. Areas like Howth are protected by a special amenity order which limits developments, and the village atmospheres of Howth and Malahide are buzzing with restaurants and bars.

Accommodation

Travelling along the coast north of the city, you'll come to the village of Fairview and behind it, the large residential area of Marino. Both are mature areas with a mix of properties. Marino is home to a large network of former council housing, that is now privately owned. The advantageous location near the city, means that these small three-bed corporation style houses between 750 and 1,100 square feet in area, go for between €500,000 and €600,000. As well as older properties, one-bed apartments in newer developments in the Fairview area start at about €320,000 with two-beds at €420,000 upwards.

The next village, Clontarf, is one of the most sought-after areas in north Dublin – it's not only close to the city, with strong transport links for buses and the Dart, but is beside the sea, with beautiful views and open spaces. Houses are primarily older style but in modern developments. A one-bedroom apartment will cost €400,000 or €450,000 and two-bedroom apartments go for about €500,000 to €600,000. There are some popular roads with attractive Victorian redbrick houses – depending on the size and the size of the garden, these can cost between €900,000 and €2.5 million.

Worst Points
The only disadvantage of living in Howth or Malahide is traffic congestion – if you choose not to take public transport and need to commute to the city centre, it could take an hour to get home during rush hour.

Further along the coast again, sizes – and prices – increase as you near the village of Sutton, where many properties also boast views across the bay. Houses are typically detached, but in estates rather than on their own grounds, and a four-bed can cost anything from €900,000 to €1.5 million. There are also apartments and townhouses in the area, although these tend to be larger and higher spec than in other areas, and with sea views at a premium. Prices are also comparatively higher and a two-bed apartment with sea views will cost between €700,000 and €900,000.

The village of Raheny and surrounding roads, behind Sutton and Clontarf, has more modern semidetached houses, and as they are inland, prices are not as high. An average three-bed or four-bed semi costs around €500,000 to €600,000.

Howth is where prices really rocket – with the panoramic sea views, amenities like a harbour, marina and golf clubs, the one-off detached houses in their own grounds with sea views can cost from €1.5 million up to €10 million. Development is restricted in the area and demand is high, but developments in former hotels and petrol stations might have two-bed apartments with sea views going for around €1 million.

Finally, continuing around the coast, the pretty seaside village of Malahide has a mix of mature estates and newer developments, such as the marina village, where prices for apartments can range between €400,000 and €2 million.

Fresh From The Farm
There is a weekly Farmer's Market in Malahide village.

Shopping & Amenities

Shops in each suburb or coastal village, from Fairview and down through Sutton, Howth and Malahide, are typical of such areas, with convenience stores, bank branches or ATMs, hairdressers, travel agents and cafes being the main outlets. There's a Superquinn supermarket in Sutton and a shopping centre with Tesco at Clarehall on the Malahide Road, and each village has a few ladies boutiques. Raheny village is also well serviced by shops and schools.

Entertainment & Leisure

The sea is one of north Dublin's greatest amenities, with beaches, promenades, sailing clubs at Clontarf, Sutton, Howth and Malahide, fishing and marinas at Howth and Malahide, and spectacular views across the bay, all adding to the attractiveness of the area and making them pleasant places to spend the day in, even if you can't afford to live there.

There are plenty of parks and open spaces – popular ones include Fairview Park, Clontarf Promenade and St Anne's Park, Raheny, a 123 hectare park with sports fields, golf, pitch and putt, a playground, tennis and rose garden. North Bull Island, connected to the mainland by a causeway and wooden bridge, has a large nature reserve, two golf courses and the seemingly endless Dollymount strand (five kilometres long) which is popular for sports like kitesurfing. The Casino (a small house) at Marino is a popular tourist attraction. See Exploring on p.184 for more.

There are golf clubs aplenty along the north Dublin coast, including Donabate (5), Howth (2), Portmarnock (2), Bull Island (2), Clontarf, Malahide and Sutton (see Golf on p.240). Howth village itself is a fishing port with yacht club, marina, piers and summit walks, and the village of Malahide, nine miles from Dublin, also has a yacht club and marina, a tennis club and a Martello tower. See Sailing on p.251 for more.

Find It First Time
Grab the *Dublin Mini Map Explorer* and keep it in your pocket - it has detailed city maps marked with street names, main landmarks, shopping malls, hospitals, hotels and embassies, so that you will always know where you're going.

Healthcare

Beaumont Hospital, on Beaumont Road, is a large acute hospital with 706 beds (01 809 3000, www.beaumont.ie). The Mater Misercordiae University Hospital on Eccles Street, just off Dorset Street Lower, is a large, acute hospital with a number of surgical specialities (01 803 2000, www.mater.ie). Adams Pharmacy in Raheny is open late until 20:00 on Monday, Tuesday and Thursday, and MacNamara's Pharmacy in Raheny opens until 20:00 on weekdays. Costello's pharmacy in Marino Mart (opposite Fairview park) is open until 20:00 Monday to Friday.

Corrigans Pharmacy on the Malahide Road (opposite Griffith Avenue) is open until 22:00 weekdays and McCabe's Pharmacy in Clarehall (Malahide Road) and The Diamond, Malahide, are both open until 21:00 on weekdays. Sutton Cross pharmacy is also open until 21:00 weekdays.

Education

Mixed secondary schools include: The Donahies Community School, Streamville Road (01 847 3522); Malahide Community School (01 846 3244); Marino College (01 833 2100); Portmarnock Community School (01 803 8056); Mount Temple Comprehensive School (01 833 6984); Ardscoil La Salle, Raheny (01 848 0055); Pobalscoil Neasáin, Baldoyle (01 831 6338); Sutton Park School (01 839 9413); Greendale Community School, Kilbarrack (01 832 2735); Belcamp College, Malahide Road (01 846 1275) and St Josephs CBS, Fairview (01 833 6127).

Girls schools include: Manor House School, Raheny (01 831 6782), St Dominic's High School, Santa Sabina, Sutton (01 832 2200); Holy Faith in Clontarf (01 833 1507), St Marys in Killester (01 831 0963) and St Marys primary in Baldoyle (01 832 6782), and for boys, there's St Fintan's National School in Sutton (01 8391067) and St Pauls College, Raheny (01 831 4011, www.stpaulscollege.ie).

Transport

The Dart suburban rail line is the key public transport for the north Dublin coast, travelling through Killester, Raheny and on to either Howth and Sutton or to Malahide and Portmarnock. The 31 bus also serves Howth, via Raheny. Parking in larger residential areas out of town is freely available, though in shopping areas and further in towards the city, parking is pay and display.

Safety & Annoyances

Although prices are high along the coast, as you go inland areas become less well-off and a little more run-down, with local authority flats and housing complexes in areas like Kilbarrack and Killester, each with a few little trouble spots. Both Howth and Malahide can become hectically busy on nice weekend days during summer, with long traffic queues of day-trippers and sightseers forming on the weekends.

Howth

Marino

Malahide

Map p.419, 420
Area ⬤ p.80-81

Best Points

The best points are proximity to the exclusive villages of Blackrock, Monkstown, Dalkey and Killiney along the coast, with most areas well serviced with schools, shops and public transport.

Worst Points

Public transport inland from the N11 dual carriageway and past Sandyford is poor and there are not many local shops within walking distance. Traffic is another nuisance in the area – it can take 20-25 minutes to get through Sandyford Industrial Estate alone during rush-hour and access on and off the M50 is also busy.

South Dublin

Like its neighbouring coastal villages, the inland suburbs and villages of south county Dublin are exclusive and expensive to live in, particularly around Mount Merrion, Foxrock and some areas of Carrickmines, with large houses in their own grounds, expensive cars and sports like rugby, sailing and golf popular among the well-to-do south Dublin set. The area covers Mount Merrion, Stillorgan, Leopardstown, Sandyford, Foxrock, Cabinteely, Carrickmines, Stepaside, Kiltiernan and Dublin 18.

Accommodation

Accommodation varies widely around here. The edges of residential south Dublin suburbs have been extending upwards and outwards in recent years with substantial developments in Sandyford, Stepaside, and Carrickmines at the foot of the Dublin and Wicklow Mountains. New developments of townhouses and apartments allow would-be south county Dublin dwellers to get a foot on the property ladder.

In the well-established residential areas around Mount Merrion, a detached house will cost €3 to €4 million, while in Foxrock, you'll be lucky to get any type of living quarters at all for under €1 million, with prices usually stretching far beyond that into multiple digits. In Sandyford, next to or in the industrial estate, there are a lot of pricey brand new apartment developments. However, if you're going to live in an industrial estate, you can't expect much in the way of aesthetics or amenities. Access to the M50 motorway through Sandyford, and the opening of the Luas light rail line from St Stephens' Green to Sandyford in 2004, has helped keep properties near the Luas in great demand, and work has commenced on an extension which will run further into Sandyford, through Leopardstown and on to Bray in County Wicklow.

Shopping & Amenities

There's a large shopping centre at Stillorgan and in Cornelscourt you'll find a large Dunnes Stores supermarket and homewares shop. The villages of Foxrock, Mount Merrion, Sandyford and Cabinteely have the essentials but there's not much in Sandyford industrial estate apart from a convenience store and some DIY outlets. Nearby shopping centres in the south county area include Dundrum, Dun Laoghaire, Blackrock (see Shopping on p.279) and there's a farmer's market at Leopardstown Racecourse every Friday.

Entertainment & Leisure

A main attraction in this area is Leopardstown Racecourse, which also has a golf club, gym, pool, sports club and a bar (see p.260). Glenalbyn in Stillorgan has a swimming pool open to the public (see p.255).

The main parks in this area are Cabinteely and Deer Park in Mount Merrion. There are golf clubs in Foxrock, Stepaside, Kiltiernan and Leopardstown, with easy access to courses in Bray, Dun Laoghaire and Killiney. Watersports in nearby Dun Laoghaire include sailing, windsurfing, swimming and diving. Dublin has its very own ski-slope at Kiltiernan. Unfortunately, it's artificial, though you can test your downhill skills with south Dublin's finest skiers when the place is packed in December and January in preparation for the obligatory week on Europe's slopes. There are plenty of sports pitches in this area, including rugby clubs at Blackrock, Kiltiernan and Stillorgan. There's no real centre of nightlife, though there are restaurants and a cinema in Stillorgan, as well as a bowling alley and leisure centre, and one or two good restaurants and pubs in Sandyford Village, Foxrock Village and Mount Merrion. The nearest theatres are at the Pavilion, Dun Laoghaire and The Mill, Dundrum (see p.395) and there's also a large cinema at Dun Laoghaire (see p.390). If you're planning on a night on the town though, you'll need to head for Dun Laoghaire, Blackrock or the city centre, see Going Out on p.335.

Healthcare

Beacon Hospital in Sandyford Industrial Estate is a private hospital with a daytime (08:00 to 18:00) A&E department which costs €120 per visit (01 293 6600, www.beaconhospital.ie). Nearest public hospitals include St Michael's Hospital, Dun Laoghaire, an acute hospital with a small accident and emergency department (01 280 6901, www.stmichaels.ie). St Columcille's Hospital Loughlinstown, just off the N11 dual carriageway past Cherrywood, has a number of specialties and an accident and emergency department (01 282 5800), and private clinic Blackrock Clinic has a number of specialties (01 283 2222, www.blackrock-clinic.com). Ballybrack pharmacy is open until 21:00 on weekdays, Hiltons Pharmacy in Cornelscourt village is open until 20:00 on weekdays and McCabe's Pharmacy in Sandyford Hall, D18 (www.mccabespharmacy.com) is open until 21:00 on weekdays.

Education

Large girls schools in South County Dublin include Loreto College Foxrock (01 289 5637), Coláiste Íosagáin, Stillorgan (01 288 4028) and St Raphaela's, Stillorgan (01 288 6878). For boys, there's St Benildus College in Kilmacud (01 298 7836), Coláiste Eoin (01 288 4002) and Oatlands College (01 288 8533). Mixed schools include Cabinteely Community School (01 285 2136) and St Laurence College (01 282 6930). The nearest university is UCD in Belfield, Dublin 4 (see p.150), and the Institute of Art and Design in Dun Laoghaire is nearby (see p.148).

Transport

The Luas light rail line runs from St Stephen's Green through Dundrum, Kilmacud and Stillorgan, finishing in Sandyford, and work has begun on an extension of the line through Leopardstown, Carickmines, Brennanstown and Cherrywood, due to be completed in 2010. The Stillorgan dual carriageway (the N11) is well served by bus routes including the busy 46A route which travels on a QBC – Quality Bus Corridor – direct to the city. There are exits to the M50 motorway at Dundrum/Sandyford and Leopardstown/Carrickmines.

Safety & Annoyances

Most areas in south county Dublin feel safe, though residential roads off main roads can be empty and quiet after dark. One of the biggest annoyances is traffic congestion on the Stillorgan Road/N11 during rush hour and on approaches to the M50 motorway.

Easy access on the Luas

Shopping in nearby Dun Laoghaire

Map p.417, 421
422, 423
Area **M** p.80-81

South Dublin – Coast

With spectacular views over Dublin Bay, beaches, piers, harbours, yacht clubs and pretty villages – the coastal areas of South Dublin are among the most prestigious and exclusive areas to live in the country, but unfortunately with prices to match. From the quiet suburb of Booterstown, through Blackrock village and Dun Laoghaire town, to the even more exclusive Dalkey and Killiney, you'll find period houses in their own grounds with sea views, smartly styled apartment blocks and mature residential estates, home to the well-to-do south Dubliners who can afford the equally exclusive prices. The area includes Booterstown, Blackrock, Monkstown, Dun Laoghaire, Sandycove, Dalkey and Killiney.

Best Points
The best points about living along the coast here have to be the views over Dublin Bay and the easy access to seaside parks, piers, beaches and watersports.

Accommodation

The south Dublin coast has an array of every type of property and you'll pay a premium for seaside locations or sea views. Along the coast, a one-bed apartment in a suburb like Booterstown will set you back at least €450,000 and in 10 year old developments in Blackrock – around Carysfort Avenue – a three-bed mid terrace house will cost €650,000 to €800,000 and a good modern four-bed family home will be around €1 million. Larger period houses can go for anything up to €25 million, but for this you'll get a substantial detached house on its own grounds, most likely on a hill or beside the sea, in Killiney or Dalkey, with views of Dublin Bay.

Worst Points
The traffic is awful. If you're reliant on a car, be prepared to sit in heavy traffic along the Blackrock or Stillorgan Road during rush hour. Parking is comparatively expensive too – you'll be paying €2 an hour up to 20:00 if you park at Dun Laoghaire harbour, and clampers only have a small area to patrol here so clamping is a regular occurrence.

Shopping & Amenities

The village of Blackrock has two shopping centres – Blackrock Shopping Centre and the Frascati Centre, both with supermarkets and there are plenty of hairdressers, travel agents, banks and convenience shops on the main street. Dun Laoghaire town also has all the necessities, as well as two shopping centres, Dun Laoghaire Shopping Centre and Bloomfield, both with car parks and large supermarkets. Other shopping centres nearby include Cornelscourt, Stillorgan and Dundrum. There's a farmer's market every Friday in Dalkey village and every Sunday in People's Park, Dun Laoghaire.

Entertainment & Leisure

Public Pools in the area include Monkstown Health and Fitness Centre (referred to locally as 'Blue Pool'), and Glenalbyn Swimming Pool (see p.255), which is also open to the public. Loughlinstown Leisure Centre has indoor and outdoor soccer, basketball and hockey courts and a gym.

If you choose to live along the south coast, you won't be stuck for things to do. Dun Laoghaire is a busy harbour town with a large ferry port and marina and plenty of water sports, including four yacht clubs, windsurfing, kite surfing, diving and the odd jet ski and water-skier (see Watersports on p.258 and Sailing on p.251). Dalkey, a former maritime port, is a historic village with two harbours, the remains of seven castles, and a 22-acre island, Dalkey Island, 300 yards off shore. Dalkey quarry, behind Killiney Hill, is popular with walking and climbing (see p.241 and p.246). The James Joyce Museum in Sandycove is located in a historical Martello tower and there's the interesting Maritime Museum in an old church in Dun Laoghaire (see Exploring on p.188). There are plenty of sports grounds in the area, and golf courses include Dun Laoghaire and Killiney Golf Clubs with courses in Bray, Stepaside and Foxrock also within reach (see Golf on p.240). For nightlife, Dun Laoghaire, Blackrock and Dalkey have some nice restaurants, cafes and late-night pubs. The Pavilion Theatre is in Dun Laoghaire and in Monkstown, Comhaltas Ceoltóirí Éireann (01 280 0295, http://comhaltas.ie) has traditional music and dance. The Lambert Puppet Theatre is popular with kids. There's also the IMC cinema in Dun Laoghaire and nearby in Stillorgan is The Ormonde Cinema. For more information, see Going Out on p.335.

Brave The Cold

For outdoor sea swimming, the Forty Foot in Sandycove is a popular bathing place, as is the blue-flag beach at Seapoint (see Exploring on p.193).

Healthcare

St Michael's Hospital, Dun Laoghaire, is an acute hospital with an accident and emergency department (01 280 6901, www.stmichaels.ie). St Columcille's Hospital Loughlinstown, just off the N11 dual carriageway past Cherrywood, has a number of specialties and an accident and emergency department, (01 282 5800). The Blackrock Clinic is a private healthcare facility with consultants in many specialties, (01 283 2222, www.blackrock-clinic.com). Beacon Hospital in Sandyford is a private hospital with a walk in accident and emergency service for €120 during the day (01 293 6600, www.beaconhospital.ie). Macken's pharmacy in Blackrock (01 288 9199) is open late weekdays.

Education

Large girls secondary schools in the area include: Loreto Abbey, Dalkey (01 280 3061); St Joseph of Cluny, in Killiney (01 285 5027); Rathdown in Glenageary (01 285 3133); Holy Child in Killiney (01 282 3120); and Dominican College Sion Hill (01 288 6791) and Rockford Manor (01 280 1522), both in Blackrock. Boys' schools include Presentation Brothers, Glasthule (01 280 1338); Blackrock College (01 288 8681); Christian Brothers College, Monkstown Park (01 280 5854); Willow Park in Blackrock (01 288 1651) and Clonkeen College (01 289 2709). Mixed schools include St Andrews College (01 288 2785), Newpark Comprehensive (01 288 3724) and Holy Child Community School in Sallynoggin (01 285 5334). Colleges include Dun Laoghaire Institute of Art and Design (see p.148) and Smurfit Business School, Blackrock (01 716 8934) and the nearest university is UCD in Belfield, Dublin 4 (see p.150).

Transport

The Dart suburban rail line is the best means of transport to the city centre, although Blackrock and Dun Laoghaire are also quite well served by buses. Be warned though, traffic on the Rock Road outside Blackrock is very heavy during morning and evening rush hour.

Safety & Annoyances

Most areas along the coast feel safe, though residential roads off main roads can feel empty and quiet after dark, due to large houses set back off the road. Apart from the high property prices, Dalkey and Killiney can be overrun with 'Sunday drivers' and day-trippers, out to admire the views on weekends.

Sandycove

Dun Laoghaire

Blackrock

Map p.418
Area **N** p.80-81

Southwest Dublin

Tallaght is a large suburb 13km southwest of Dublin, at the foot of the Dublin and Wicklow mountains. Originally a historic village, the area has undergone major growth and development since the 1980s, with many sprawling new housing estates and a new town centre, centring around the main shopping area, The Square.

In the 1980s and 1990s, Tallaght had a reputation for being one of the most deprived areas of the city, and while antisocial behaviour is problematic in some local authority estates, the development boom, kept going by tax incentives and the recent arrival of the Luas, has seen a huge number of new homes and estates.

Older estates in Tallaght, like Springfield and Killinarden, and areas like Jobstown, Firhouse and Knocklyon have a mix of both new and old houses dating from the 1970s and many developments have been built in the last five or six years. Further to the northwest of Tallaght is Clondalkin, which has been built around the old Clondalkin village. This area has also seen a good deal of development. Clondalkin, Tallaght, Firhouse and Knocklyon are all covered in this section.

Best Points

Tallaght has good shopping, schools, parks and access to major transport infrastructures such as the M50 and N7. There is some good value for money property and Clondalkin is handy for access to the Naas Road, M50 and industrial estates around the Naas Road and Nangor Road as well as City West and Park West.

Accommodation

Tallaght and its surrounding areas have a range of properties and prices. Development has slowed somewhat compared to the boom of a few years ago, but there are plenty of new and second-hand properties on the market. In Firhouse, to the east of Tallaght and popular with first-time buyers, a three-bed semi will cost from around €410,000 to €600,000 and upwards. Knocklyon has a mix of apartments – a two-bed might start at €370,000 up to larger homes at around €800,000 or €900,000. In Ellensborough, a six or seven year old two-bed might cost €315,000 or a house around €480,000. Marlfield and Deerpark in the same area, have similar prices. Further out, there has also been a huge amount of housing built around City West. In large developments like The Belfry, which started about four years ago, a three-bed semi might cost around €310,000 or a two-bed apartment around €300,000.

In Clondalkin there is also a good mix of properties from apartments to substantial older houses, mainly around the village. At the lower end of the budget, a three-bed in a former council estate could cost around €290,000 and an apartment in the Green Isle Hotel area starts at €335,000 for a two-bed, or €300,000 for a terraced house. A detached four-bed house in this area might cost around €800,000.

Worst Points

Traffic congestion from the city, towards the M50 and the Naas Road and ongoing construction, with proposed new roads around Watergate Park, the construction of the Metro West line and building developments in central Tallaght, can cause annoyance if you're reliant on a car for transport.

Shopping & Amenities

The Square is the largest shopping centre in the Tallaght area, with Tesco, Dunnes Stores, Debenhams, Easons, and a UCI multiplex cinema. There's plenty of other shopping in the area and a farmers market every Friday on High Street.

In Clondalkin, the main old village has banks and essential services, but not much else in the way of shopping. Off the main street is The Mill Shopping Centre, which has a large Dunnes Stores.

Entertainment & Leisure

Tallaght's sports and arts amenities are spread out over a wide area. There are a number of GAA clubs in the area, 11 astroturf pitches at Bancroft Park, and many football and hockey pitches. Public parks include Watergate Park, Sean Walsh Memorial Park and Tymon Park, a 300-acre area with walks, sports grounds, lakes and a large playground. The National Basketball arena is also in this area, as well as athletics tracks and soccer pitches. There are swimming pools in Jobstown and Balrothery and Dodder Valley Park is on the east side of Tallaght, towards Rathfarnham.

In Clondalkin, there are substantial parklands at Corkagh Park, with fishing lakes, walks and a rose garden. There's also Clondalkin Park, and plenty of sports grounds such as

Clondalkin Sports & Leisure Centre (see p.264), which has a swimming pool. Clondalkin has pay as you play golf at Grange Castle Golf Course and other courses in the area include Citywest Golf Club and Newlands in Clondalkin (see Golf on p.240).

For eating and drinking out, there are plenty of pubs and restaurants in different areas of Tallaght, as well as hotels such as the Plaza Hotel (01 462 4200, www.plazahotel.ie), the Abberley Court (01 459 6000, www.abberley.ie) and the soon to be completed Tower Hotel (01 468 5400, www.towerhotelgroup.com) near Watergate Park.

For eating or drinking out in Clondalkin, hotels include Bewley's Hotel (01 464 0140, www.bewleyshotels.com) at Newland's Cross and The Green Isle Hotel & Spa (01 459 3406, www.lynchotels.com). The Waterside Hotel's Tower Bar & Bistro (01 843 6153) beside the Grand Canal is popular, as is the Red Cow Moran Hotel (01 459 3650, www.redcowhotel.com), home to the Winter Garden Restaurant. The village itself has Indian, Italian and Chinese restaurants, as well as a number of pubs.

Healthcare

The Adelaide and Meath Hospital Dublin, incorporating the National Children's Hospital, in Tallaght, has many specialities and an accident and emergency department (01 414 2000, www.amnch.ie). Meagher's chemist in Castletymon, Tallaght (01 451 1465), is open until 20:00, Monday to Friday; Old Bawn pharmacy in Tallaght (01 452 4312) is open until 21:30 Monday to Thursday and McCabe's Pharmacy in Belgard Square (www.mccabespharmacy.com), Tallaght is open until 21:00 on weekdays.

Education

Mixed community schools in the area include St Marks, Killinarden, Collinstown Park, Jobstown, St Kevin's, Deansrath, Firhouse, Old Bawn, Tallaght and St Aidan's Community Schools; St. Colmcille's Community School in Clondalkin is mixed; Coláiste Chilliain in Clondalkin and Coláiste de hIde in Tallaght are both Irish-speaking mixed schools; Moyle Park College in Clondalkin is a boys school and girls schools include Coláiste Bríde in Clondalkin. The Institute of Technology, Tallaght is in the old village.

Transport

Tallaght and Knocklyon are both well served by buses to the city centre and some services to surrounding areas. In 2004, the Red Line of the Luas light rail opened in Tallaght, with a journey time of 46 minutes from Tallaght to Connolly Station in the city. The intense development in the area has led to increasing traffic congestion, however the proposed Metro West line, due to be completed in 2014, will link Tallaght with Clondalkin and Blanchardstown and also link to the city and airport via the Metro North line. It will also link to the Luas Red Line (which may be extended eastwards), the proposed City West Luas Line, and the existing Kildare and Maynooth suburban rail lines. Clondalkin is beside the Naas Road quality bus corridor, there's a bridge to the Luas at the Monastery end of the village. The Naas Road, the M7, and the M50 are within a short drive, and the area is well served by buses. Clondalkin is on the main Dublin to Kildare railway line and will also be on the Metro West line.

Safety & Annoyances

The areas around Tallaght and Clondalkin have both suffered social deprivation in the past and many estates show the scars of this with well-documented problems such as unemployment, drug-abuse, joyriding and gang feuds earning some areas bad reputations. However the recent economic boom and the intense development of the surrounding area in the last ten years has allowed it to take on the qualities of a small city, with both good and bad areas with differing crime rates. Check out each area thoroughly before you decide to move there.

Map p.406, 414

Best Points
The proximity to Phoenix Park is one of Castleknock's best points; access to the N4 and major roads west are an advantage of Lucan.

Worst Points
Rush-hour traffic congestion, especially coming up to the M50 junction, might influence your decision on whether to live in this area, depending on your transport needs.

West Dublin

West Dublin is one of the areas of the county that has seen major development in the past 10 years, especially around Lucan and northwest towards Clonee, where suburbs of the city and vast, identical housing estates now stretch into what was once rural villages and farmlands, reaching well into counties Kildare and Meath. These are now highly built up areas, where most properties are less than 10 years old.

The area is full of contrasts, from the mature residential areas such as Castleknock to the new urban district of Adamstown beside Lucan, 10 miles west of the city centre and one of the most significant developments in County Dublin. When completed, Adamstown will have 10,000 new homes and shopping, leisure and cultural facilities for an expected population of 25,000 people. The first residents moved in in 2006, and the town is expected to take between 10 and 15 years to complete. The area encompasses Castleknock, Blanchardstown, Lucan, Adamstown and Clonee.

Accommodation

Castleknock is a mature residential area beside Phoenix Park, with an old village centre, and a mix of properties from large detached houses around Park View, Georgian Village, Deerpark and Castleknock Lodge selling for between €2 and €3.5 million; the less expensive properties are further west. A modern three-bed semi-detached house off a road like Auburn Avenue might cost around €800,000. Property prices drop further heading away from Phoenix Park and to the western side of the M50, where a three-bed semi somewhere like Laurel Lodge will be 25% cheaper.

Towards the city, in Chapelizod, Dublin 20, there are plenty of apartments and a one-bed might start at €320,000 or a townhouse at €510,000.

Southwest of Castleknock, in Lucan County Dublin, there have been huge residential developments built in the past 10 to 12 years. There's now a good supply of second-hand properties, mostly three-bed semi-detached houses, ranging from €360,000 to €395,000 for a 1,200 sqaure foot house. Each estate differs, and some properties go up in size to detached five-beds, selling for around €1.25 million.

Out towards Ongar and Clonee (both Dublin 15), a one-bed apartment of around 50 square metres starts at €250,000, a two-bed around €290,000 and a three-bed house from €365,000 to €380,000. In areas such as Blanchardstown or Tyrellstown, one-beds start at around €290,000.

Shopping & Amenities

Lucan village has essentials like banks and convenience stores and, on the other side of the motorway, where most of the housing estates are located, is Superquinn Shopping Centre which also has pharmacies and hairdressers. There's a Tesco at Hillcrest Shopping Centre. The large Liffey Valley Shopping Centre (p.330) has Dunnes Stores, Easons, Marks & Spencer and Top Shop, as well as cafes and a multiplex cinema. There's also a retail park beside the centre.

Blanchardstown Shopping Centre (p.329) is home to a Dunnes Stores, Easons, Marks & Spencer and Boots, as well as banks, cafes, a leisure centre, a cinema multiplex and adjoining retail parks, a library, Draíocht theatre and a drive-through McDonalds.

Entertainment & Leisure

Castleknock Village is a pleasant village with shops, convenience stores, pubs and restaurants, and sports grounds beside Castleknock College and behind the Blanchardstown Centre. Parks in the area include Tolka Valley Park and Corduff Park.

Tee Time In The West
Golf clubs in West Dublin include Lucan Golf Club, Luttrelstown Castle Golf & Country Club in Castleknock, Westmanstown Golf Club in Clonsilla and Elmgreen Golf Centre near Blanchardstown, which also has Pitch and Putt.

There are multiplex cinemas at Liffey Valley Shopping Centre and Blanchardstown Centre, which is also home to the theatre, Draíocht. The National Aquatic Centre is in Blanchardstown (see p.255), with swimming pools, wave machines, water slides and rivers. The old Lucan village is on the river Liffey which is popular for canoeing – the Irish Canoe Union runs courses from its base in Strawberry Beds, further up the river. Lucan has a number of GAA and football grounds and The Dublin Dragons American Football Team are based there. Lucan Sports & Leisure has sports halls, tennis courts and a playground, although there is no swimming pool in Lucan. Parks in Lucan include Griffeen Valley Park which has riverside walks, athletics tracks and an all-weather hockey pitch; some of the area along the River Liffey is also parkland, with walks. There are small parks at Ballyowen Park and Willsbrook Park and many housing estates have public open spaces.

Dublin Doctors
Find out more about healthcare in your area and in Dublin in general in the health section on p.129. It covers doctors, dentists, hospitals, alternative medicine, and much more.

Healthcare

Connolly Hospital Blanchardstown is an acute hospital with an Accident and Emergency department and many other clinics (01 646 5000, www.connollyhospital.ie). Along the M50, in Tallaght, the Adelaide and Meath Hospital Dublin incorporating the National Children's Hospital is an acute hospital, with many specialities and an accident and emergency department (01 414 2000, www.amnch.ie). Chapelizod Late Night Pharmacy is open until 21:00 on weekdays; Lucan Village pharmacy is open until 21:00 every day and McCabe's Pharmacy in The Blanchardstown Centre is open until 21:00 on weekdays.

Education

Boys' secondary schools include Castleknock College (01 821 3051, www.castleknockcollege.ie) and girls' schools include Mount Sackville (01 821 4061, www.mountsackville.ie) in Chapelizod and St Joseph's College, Lucan (01 628 1160, www.stjosephslucan.net). Mixed schools include The Kings Hospital (01 626 5933, www.kingshospital.ie) and Pobalscoil Iosolde (01 626 5991), both in Palmerstown; Riversdale Community College (01 820 1488) and Blakestown Community School (01 821 5522, blakes@iol.ie), both in Blanchardstown, and Castleknock Community College (01 822 1626, www.castleknockcc.ie) . Mixed schools in Lucan include Coláiste Phádraig CBS (01 628 2229) and Lucan Community College (01 628 2077, lucancc@iol.ie) and in Rathcoole there's Holy Family Community School (01 458 0766, hfcstech@iol.ie). There are schools in the Ongar and Clonee area, although with population growth, more are needed.

Transport

Lucan is well placed for access to the M50 and M4/N4 to Galway and Sligo. It is also on a Quality Bus Corridor (QBC) and well served by buses. There is a proposal for a new Luas line to Lucan, but the project details have not been released. Blanchardstown and Castleknock are on the Maynooth and Mullingar to Dublin rail line and also on a QBC, both are also well served by buses. Further west, there are train stations in Ongar and Clonsilla but none in Clonee. Metro West will link Blanchardstown to Clondalkin and Tallaght, and link with Metro North for the city centre and airport, and with the Luas red line. Metro West will not run through Lucan, although it will link to Lucan via the Luas. It is due for completion in 2014. There is also a small private airport, Weston Airport, to the west of Lucan.

Safety & Annoyances

Traffic congestion is a major problem on the N4 heading out towards Lucan, especially at the M50 junction, where tailbacks can stretch for miles during rush hour. Construction, especially around Clonee and further out, can be a nuisance.

Setting up Home

With a roof over your head and maybe even heated floorboards beneath your feet, it would be forgivable to assume that the hard part of moving in is over. Though snagging a great place to live in Dublin is a challenge, setting up your home just the way you want it will probably be just as tiring. Setting up home in Dublin is not necessarily hard, but it will take some effort to locate goods and services and arrange for deliveries and removals, not to mention quite a few fervent prayers to ask that you get what you want when you want it. Moving house in Dublin can be a bit of a laissez-faire business, so maintaining a sense of humour is a must.

Moving Services

Moving services are still relatively new to Ireland but they have caught on fast. High quality services are available, but like most things in Dublin you will probably pay dearly for them. In order to avoid high premiums, many Dubliners choose to go the informal route for moving house and either do it themselves or hire 'a man with a van'. For those renting, this is a logical choice as furnished rentals are the norm, and you'll only be looking at moving your personal possessions. You can also hire a van yourself, but at a few hundred euros per day it's a costly exercise. Hiring someone to help you is a better option and you should be able to find 'a man with a van' for as little as €50. Expect to pay cash only and be warned that there's no insurance, so approach with caution.

To go down the more formal route, the Golden Pages (www.goldenpages.ie) is a great source of information on local removal companies. Make sure that the company you enlist can answer all of your questions, and provide a quote that they'll stick to. Music lovers should take care to ask about the cost of moving a piano, as this is often an additional charge. The cost of packaging materials and packing services is usually extra, and VAT may not be included in quotes, so make sure you know what the final price will be before committing yourself.

Though setting up home in Dublin can be complicated, the Irish have great patience for mistakes and mix-ups so don't stress out about having everything perfectly orchestrated. Gather quotes from moving services and relocation agents, inquire about insurance coverage and ask around; word of mouth is still the best way to get information on standout services and rogue traders (sometimes called 'cowboys' by the Irish). If all else fails, the Consumer Association of Ireland (01 497 8600, www.consumerassociation.ie) sometimes runs information on services in their *Consumer Choice* magazine and may well be able to offer hints to those just settling in.

International Moves

If you are relocating from overseas, contact your local Irish embassy to check on import restrictions for international moves. To avoid paying tax on items you bring in, you'll have to prove that you have owned items for at least 6 months. For this you'll need Transfer of Residence forms, which you can get at your local Irish embassy/consulate. Firearms are outlawed in Ireland, so if you are a lawful gun owner in your home country you will need to dispose of your weapon before your move. Bringing pets into Ireland is also strictly controlled. See p.121.

The total cost of an international move to Dublin will depend not only upon the company you employ but the number of items you bring with you. Hiring out full shipping containers can add up into the thousands, but the cost of furnishing a new home might be the

Smooth Moves

- Contact your local embassy or consulate to find out what household items can be imported free of restrictions or tax duties.
- Contact three or four removal companies for quotes, including packaging materials, packaging services, VAT and insurance.
- Create a thorough household inventory for goods that you are packing, and take pictures of valuable items for insurance purposes.
- Research electricity voltage and outlet design before shipping lamps and electronic goods.
- Consider sending ahead a box or bag of sheets and towels to have with you from the first night.
- Keep family heirlooms, irreplaceable photos and fine jewellery with you.

same. Employing a relocation agent is also an option to help you plan your move and organise your possessions, though this is still a fledgling industry in Ireland and experienced agents are few and far between. For your convenience, Removals Ireland (www.removals-ireland.ie) offers a small comparison of companies operating in Dublin (be sure to look under the Leinster province).

Relocation & Removal Companies

AIM International Moving	1890 668 377	www.aim-moving.com
Allen Removals	01 451 3585	www.allenremovals.ie
Aston Corporate Relocation	051 644 874	www.astoncorporate.com
Budget Mr Mover	087 419 5893	www.budgetmrmover.com
Careline Moving and Storage	01 623 3832	www.careline.ie
Crown Worldwide Removals	01 885 0171	www.crownrelo.com
Enterprise Rent-A-Van	1890 227 999	www.enterprise.ie
Euroteam	1800 771 655	na
Executive Relocations	01 4979 936	www.executiverelocations.com
Home from Home Relocations	086 243 2238	www.hfh.ie
MacDonald Price Relocation	01 295 1478	www.clubi.ie/MacDonald-Price
Murphy's Truck Rental	087 264 0201	www.vanrentals.ie
Relocation Bureau	01 284 5078	www.relocation.com
Upak	1800 668 464	www.upak.ie

Relocating Your Pet

Strict regulations mean that Ireland is not overly welcoming to foreign pets so be prepared for a bit of a drama to get your beloved pet to its new home. If your pet is anything other than a dog or cat, it may need to be rehomed before you come.
If you are coming from the EU, your pet will need an EU pet passport. This is standard throughout the EU and means that your pet has been microchipped, had all its vaccinations, and been tested for tapeworm, ticks and rabies all within the required time limits before travel. You will also need to accompany them on an approved carrier. For UK and Channel Islands residents, including the Isle of Man, there are no passport requirements, and you and your pet can travel freely in and out of the country, so long as they have not travelled outside of this zone. If you are coming from outside of the EU, or if your pet does not yet have an EU pet passport, you will need to get an import license from the Irish government and your pet will have to undergo a six month quarantine period on arrival. For any further queries or for the relevant paperwork, contact your local Irish embassy/consulate or the Department of Agriculture and Food on Klildare Street (01 607 2827, www.agriculture.gov.ie). See p.121 for more information.

Ballymun Flatpack
Be prepared... IKEA, the Swedish furniture giant, is about to land in Dublin, opening a gigantic store in Ballymun. The estimated opening date is 2009, although they have to wait until the roadworks on the M50 are completed.

Furnishing Your Home

While homes for sale in Dublin rarely come all fitted out, fully furnished is the norm for rentals. This means that major appliances and furniture are included in the price of the rental, and extras such as rugs, cookware, cutlery and even household linens may be included as well. In between these two extremes are some semi-furnished offerings. These are rare though but generally include appliances and mattresses, allowing the renter to furnish the rest at will. Televisions and electronic goods are not often included. For those who need to furnish their home, a variety of bargain furniture stores are available in Dublin. Argos (www.argos.ie) is the city's flat pack heaven selling all manner of home furnishings for those with the patience to assemble it. Dunnes (www.dunnesstores.ie) and Marks & Spencer (www.marksandspencer.com) also sell limited furniture ranges at affordable prices, and Bargaintown (www.bargaintown.ie)

117

offers generic furniture at prices that can't be beaten. If you're lucky enough to have a furnishings allowance through your employer, then Habitat (www.habitat.ie), Laura Ashley (www.lauraashley.com) and Pia Bang Home (01 888 3777) might be worth a look, and Harriet's House (01 677 7077) undoubtedly carries just the right throw pillows, mirrors, vases, lamps or prints to finish off your design. When you're ready, Stock (01 679 4316), a funky kitchen supply store, should have you equipped to throw dinner parties before you know it. If you're after something unique and don't mind splashing the cash then bespoke furniture may be more your style. Imbue (www.imbuefurniture.com), Klimmek and Henderson (www.klimmek-henderson.com) and Leo Scarff (www.leoscarffdesign.com) all accept commissions for private pieces, while Kate Fine's original mirrors are the talk of the town (www.finedesign.ie).

Furniture shopping

Second-Hand Furniture

Second-hand furniture is also an option, though most second hand furnishings are passed off as 'antiques' and very well might cost more than a new piece. Local Dublin newspapers such as the *Southside People* and *Northside People* carry ads for used (and free) furniture, and Craigslist Dublin (http://dublin.craigslist.org) carries a few such ads too. Freecycle Dublin (http://groups.yahoo.com/group/freecycleDublin/) has attracted thousands of participants willing to swap items for free, and very often they include delivery. Gumtree (www.gumtree.ie) offers similar classifieds in the 'Stuff for Sale' section. Those who like the buzz of a good flea market will be slightly disappointed by Dublin, but car-boot sales do occur sporadically. Keep an eye on community noticeboards, library noticeboards and church bulletins in particular for news of impending sales. Of course the gift of the gab is a major blessing for most Dubliners, so putting word out there that you are looking for second-hand furniture might just help bring some your way.

Household Insurance

Though Dublin is a still a relatively safe city in terms of violent crime, home burglaries have been on the increase in the past few years and household insurance is advisable. Household insurance in Ireland is made up of two components: building insurance and contents insurance. Building insurance covers the main structures of a home including permanent fixtures and fittings, while contents insurance covers furnishings and household goods (including clothing, jewellery and personal effects). These insurance policies can be arranged separately, so it is possible to apply for contents cover without building cover as well. Buildings and contents insurance cover against a number of risks including theft, fire, smoke, burst pipes, earthquake, lightening, rioting/malicious damage and more. Most insurance policies come with an excess, which means that policy holders must assume responsibilities for losses to a certain value themselves. Individual policies will have other limits and exceptions, and add-ons can be made, so reading

Household Insurance		
AA Ireland	01 617 9950	www.aaireland.ie
Allianz Direct	1850 484 848	www.allianzdirect.ie
AXA Insurance	01 872 6444	www.axa.ie
Eagle Star	1850 447 799	www.eaglestar.ie
FBD	1850 617 617	www.fbd.ie
Hibernian	1890 332 211	www.hibernian.ie
Perlico	1890 252 148	www.perlico.com

and understanding a policy is crucial before signing. You can set one up by visiting your local bank, or one of the private companies who will normally provide quotes via phone or website (see table on p.118). If it's still all too bewildering, the Irish Insurance Federation has a free Insurance Information Service (01 676 1914, iis@iif.ie).

Laundry Services

Most private residences have an all-in-one washer and dryer. Sometimes you'll see in flat ads that a washing machine is 'available' – this means it is somewhere on the premises, most likely shared and often coin or token operated. Otherwise, you'll have one to yourself in your private dwelling. Independent laundrettes can be found across the city, and most operate a wash only service which means you leave your bag of dirty clothes, have them washed and folded, and collect them at will. Unfortunately, this is not cheap. Most service washes are around €10 per bag, though this will obviously depend on the size of the load. Dry cleaners operate separately from laundrettes and they are even more expensive. Dry cleaning just one shirt or pair of trousers can cost up to €10, and suits routinely cost around €15. Very few dry cleaners or laundrettes offer a delivery service.

In practice, reimbursement for lost or ruined items varies and many operators post signs explaining that they have no responsibility for items left in their care. Quite a few companies also sell or dispose of items that are not collected after three months. Be sure to ask about these policies before leaving anything irreplaceable. Also enquire if your employer offers discounted dry cleaning.

Tailors		
Acute Upholstery	Dublin 12	01 456 0581
The Alteration Centre	Dublin 2	01 677 6258
Anne O'Mahoney	Dublin 2	01 672 9369
Blackrock Upholstery Ltd.	Blackrock	01 288 3944
Bogart Tailors	Dublin 1	01 873 0771
Brown Thomas In-House Tailors	Dublin 2	01 617 1161
Des Byrne Tailoring	Dublin 2	01 677 3821
Ideal Upholstery	Dublin 1	086 302 0460

Domestic Help

Domestic help is still a young industry in Ireland as it is only in recent years that the average household has been able to afford it. Some agencies can help place domestic workers, but for the most part you will need to advertise and interview potential candidates yourself. Interestingly, equality legislation does not pertain to hiring domestic help so it is not discriminatory to ask for a particular gender in advertisements. Live-in maids remain extremely rare (and getting a visa for a full time maid is a harrowing task) so most households employ domestic help on a casual/part time basis. Local newspapers, Craiglist Dublin (http://dublin.craigslist.org/) and Gumtree (http://www.gumtree.ie/) often carry ads for domestic help, as do library and supermarket noticeboards.

Many domestic workers in Dublin are migrant workers, often from Eastern Europe, Africa and Asia. Sadly, quite a few of these migrant workers are ridiculously over qualified for these positions – many hold advanced degrees and even medical training. Technically a work permit is required for anyone who originates from outside of the European Economic Area (EEA), though enforcing this has become a government nightmare.

Full time domestic workers are considered employees and as such should have tax and PRSI (Pay Related Social Insurance) deducted directly from their wages and reported by their employer (who must be registered with the Revenue

Domestic Help Agencies		
About Time Home Cleaning	01 894 0444	www.aboutime.ie
Cinderella Works	01 667 2876	www.cinderellaworks.com
Gerry Walsh Domestics	087 673 7607	www.gwdom.com
Liffey Maids	01 836 4052	www.liffeymaids.ie
Maids from Heaven	086 069 8344	www.maidsfromheaven.eu
Proshine Cleaning Services	1890 818 555	www.proshine.ie

119

Commissioners). Revenue (www.revenue.ie) produces a booklet on PAYE/PRSI for Small Employers that is very useful for determining the taxes associated with domestic help. Other types of domestic help include those who work for an agency (agency workers), and those who work part-time for a variety of households (self-employed workers who are responsible for reporting their own income and filing their own taxes).

The going rate for part-time help in Dublin is around €15 per hour and most domestic workers will take two to three hours to clean a family home, though more if they are required to do laundry, look after children or older people or prepare meals. A written contract of employment, payslip and paid public holidays are all rights enjoyed by domestic workers, and the Citizens Information Board (www.citizensinformationboard.ie) and Irish Congress of Trade Unions (www.ictu.ie) can provide further information for prospective employers of domestic help.

Babysitting & Childcare

Childcare is a critical issue in Dublin right now, with the cost of childcare routinely eating up a good portion of one parent's monthly salary and many parents' groups lobbying the government to make childcare more affordable. Many Dublin parents choose to send their young children to creches (day care/nursery facilities) throughout the city, though there are other options. Nannies, au pairs, childminders and babysitters are all available, though their prices – and quality of services – can vary widely.

Babysitting & Childcare		
Belgrave Agency	01 280 9341	www.nanny.ie
Dublin Childcare Recruitment Agency	01 833 2281	www.childcare-recruitment.com
Hynes Childcare Agency	01 872 8170	www.hynesagency.ie
Minder Finders	na	www.minderfinders.ie
Nanny Solutions	01 873 4364	www.nannysolutions.com

Professional nannies are best found through an agency, which vets clients based on references and qualifications. Criminal background checks with the Garda Siochana may be carried out, though this is not always the case so be sure to ask. Salaries tend to range from €450 to €700 per week, though this will depend on how many children are being cared for, if there are any other housekeeping tasks expected, and if they are live in or live out, not to mention their experience and qualifications.

Au pairs tend to be young, female students, often looking to learn the language while earning a little income, as well as a place to live, in exchange for childminding duties. Au pairs require their own room and are usually paid between €100 – €200 per week, depending on the hours of work needed and the tasks expected.

Childminders care for children in their own home, and these self-employed individuals are governed by the Childcare Act 1991, the Childcare (Pre-School Services) Regulations 1996 and their amendments. Among other things, childminders cannot have a criminal background, they must have their premises inspected and approved by the Health Services Executive (www.hse.ie), keep first aid supplies to hand and must never engage in corporal punishment of children.

Babysitters are often the children of neighbourhood friends who agree to mind a child for a few hours in exchange for pay. €10 per hour is the going rate in Dublin. Some teachers moonlight as babysitters in their spare time, though inquiring with school administration about their policies is probably best.

For parents who like to keep their kids close, many hotels throughout Ireland offer a babysitting service either in the family's hotel room or in a dedicated group room.

Modern shopping malls in the suburbs of Dublin also tend to offer pay-per-hour creches so that parents can shop unencumbered. Gyms and restaurants rarely offer childminding facilities, though some family friendly locations may offer entertainment packs or special activities for children. Be sure to call before leaving the books and crayons at home.

Domestic Services

Leaky roofs, leaky pipes and leaky taps seem to be par for the course in Dublin, so keeping your eyes and ears open for little glitches is crucial in avoiding major problems later on. Most landlords are diligent about bringing in specialists for building faults and appliance servicing, though you'll want to read your lease regarding household upkeep and minor repairs to see if you bear any responsibilities. 'Supers' are not common in Dublin apartments and flats, though many modern (purpose built) apartment buildings are under the auspices of a management company that keeps its own plumbers, electricians, etc. on retainer. If you own your home, then bringing in handymen is up to you and you'll want to hope that your disasters occur during working hours because evening, weekend or holiday call-outs can sometimes double the normal fees. Some relief does come from utility services, which generally do not charge extra for home appointments and/or repairs. Pest control, noise

Domestic Services			
A & B Electrical	Dublin 12	01 837 0271	Electricians
BDF Carpentry	Dublin 2	087 684 8022	Carpenters
MD Plumbing	Dublin 22	087 761 0172	Plumbers
Pest Control Ireland	Various Locations	087 755 2504	Pest Control
Pipers Heating and Plumbing	Dublin 6 West	01 460 3692	Plumbers
Rentokil	Various Locations	1890 333 888	Pest Control
Seale Plumbing and Heating	Dublin 9	087 674 0480	Plumbers
Silverdome Electrical	Finglas	01 864 1500	Electricians
W.P. Carpentry	Tallaght	087 790 9658	Carpenters

control, and drinking water issues in Dublin can be taken to the Health Services Executive (www.hse.ie), though the efficiency of their services is widely debated. Finding domestic services is as easy as opening the Golden Pages (www.goldenpages.ie) or asking the neighbours, though more often these services are also advertised on Craigslist Dublin (http://dublin.craigslist.org/) and Gumtree (www.gumtree.ie).

DVD & Video Rental

With the rising cost of night time entertainment, many Dubliners have embraced the concept of a quiet night in. DVD rentals flourish across the city, though few video rentals can still be found. Most DVD rentals are offered by chains such as Xtra-vision (www.xtravision.ie) and Chartbusters (www.chartbusters.ie), though Laser (01 671 1466, 23 South Great George's Street, Dublin 2) is an independent film rental outlet with a huge following. Most of these stores rent new releases for approximately €5 for one night, with a late charge being the same. Older films are often rented for around €3 and sometimes for two or three nights at a time. In order to become a member of a DVD rental store, proof of address and identity are usually required so make sure that you have a household bill handy. Several online DVD rental companies have popped up lately including Screen Click (www.screenclick.com), Moviestar (www.moviestar.ie) and Busy Bee (https://busybeedvd.rentshark.com) which generally offer a monthly subscription fee for receiving DVDs through the post. Return postage is usually free, though since a credit card or debit card (sometimes called a laser card) is kept on file you'll want to read the contract carefully to be sure that you know what will be charged to your account – and how often. Public libraries have also begun to offer DVDs, usually for free and for a borrowing period of one week, but this privilege is only extended to members with a valid library card. See p.244 for a list of Dublin libraries.

Pets

Ireland is an animal loving country, though Dublin itself is not necessarily a city designed for pets. Dogs and cats do well in the city, and 'indoor' pets such as reptiles, fish, turtles, hamsters and guinea pigs flourish, though perhaps more so outside of the city centre This, however, could be because of the high number of rental properties in

121

the city centre, each of which has its own rules about pets in the property. Pet owners new to Dublin should read leases carefully to find out if pets are allowed in particular flats, apartments or houses. In general, flats are the least hospitable to domestic pets and houses are the most.

Ireland is a part of the European Union's Pet Travel Scheme, which means that dogs, cats and ferrets can be transported, without quarantine, throughout the EU as long as they have a Pet Passport which confirms the animal's identity, vaccination record, and tick and tapeworm treatments. A Pet Passport will only be issued to those pets who have been implanted with a microchip (for identity purposes) and passed an antibody titration test to ensure that the rabies vaccinations have worked. Tick and tapeworm treatments must be carried out within 48 hours of travel as well.

Pets Boarding/Sitting		
A1 Cat and Dog Boarding	01 834 4875	Boarding
Active VetCare	01 868 0119	Boarding
Best Kennels and Cattery	087 254 7527	Boarding
Butterfield Boarding Cattery	01 494 3751	Boarding
Creature Comforts	087 136 9242	Sitting
Doggie Day Care	087 761 5520	Sitting and (Home) Boarding
Dublin Doggies	01 833 7597	Sitting
Mutt Ugly	01 475 9449	Sitting/Creche
Pine Forest Boarding Kennels	01 493 2053	Boarding
Safe Hands Pet Care	087 958 0487	Sitting

Those moving from the United States and Canada can also take advantage of this scheme by landing (with their pets) in Britain, having the animal processed through the UK PETS scheme, and then entering Ireland with proof of this processing as well as confirmation that the animal was vaccinated against rabies no longer than six months prior to the entry. For those interested in something a little different, landing in the Isle of Man or the Channel Islands will also net inclusion in the PETS scheme. However, only Dublin Airport is able to process these pets.

Those who do not qualify for these schemes can only import dogs and cats into Ireland. These pet owners will need to ready themselves for leaving their pets in quarantine at the only facility in the country – Lissenhall Quarantine Kennels and Catteries in Swords, County Dublin. This quarantine usually last six months, though some animals are allowed a one month public quarantine followed by a five month private quarantine at the family home, so be sure to ask about options before leaving an animal.

Those leaving Dublin with pets should check with their intended destinations to find out what is required and destinations within the EU should bring easy entry via the Pet Passport. Checking with airlines regarding the requirement of a health certificate for each animal is also recommended. Due to the existence of 'farm diseases' such as Foot & Mouth Disease and Mad Cow Disease, pets which have been in contact with livestock in Ireland will likely require extra attention when transported out of the country. Contacting the Department of Agriculture and Food (www.agriculture.gov.ie) will help new residents confirm what they need to do to both import and export pets. Irish embassies and consulates around the world will also be able to provide up-to-date information, and relocation agents should be able to offer advice as well.

For those who are interested in purchasing or adopting a pet once in Dublin, multiple options exist. Pet shops usually offer an array of supplies and toys as well as animals, and dogs, cats, fish and turtles tend to be in greatest supply. Wackers Pet Shop (Parnell Street, Dublin 1, 01 872 6993) and Petland

Pets Grooming/Training			
A1 Grooming Service	01 834 4875	na	Grooming
Dog Training Ireland	01 864 4922	www.dogtrainingireland.ie	Training
Doggie Style	1890 364 443	www.doggiestyle.ie	Grooming
Dublin Dog Training	086 730 1001	na	Training
The Grooming Pad	01 278 0199	the grooming pad@eircom.net	Grooming
K9 Training Services	087 202 8829	www.k9trainingservices.com	Training
Mutt Ugly	01 475 9449	www.muttugly.com	Grooming/Spa
The Pet Behaviour Centre	01 497 2723	www.petsbehave.com	Training
Tag N Rye Dog Services	01 451 3324	www.tagnrye.com	Training

Veterinary Clinics

Active VetCare Phibsboro	Phibsboro, Dublin 7	01 868 0119
Active Vetcare Sandyford	Sandyford, Dublin 18	01 294 5899
Anicare Vets Blanchardstown	Blanchardstown, Dublin 15	01 640 9010
Anicare Vets Clontarf	Clontarf, Dublin 3	01 833 0744
Anicare Vets Glasnevin	Glasnevin, Dublin 9	01 837 5543
Bairbe O'Malley Veterinary Hospital	Kilmantain Place, Bray	01 272 3857
Irish Blue Cross	Tyrconnell Rd, Inchicore	01 416 3030
Killiney Veterinary Clinic	Killiney	01 285 1542
North County Dublin SPCA Clinic	124a Upper Drumcondra Road, Dublin 9	01 289 4041
Sandymount Pet Hospital	Gilford Road, Sandymount	01 269 5830

(Lower Camden Street, Dublin 2, 01 478 2850) are both great city centre pet shops, while Baumann's Pet Shop (Stillorgan, 01 288 1638) and Breffni House Pets (Windy Arbour, Dundrum, Dublin 14, 01 296 1339) both offer excellent service to those willing to travel to the southern suburbs. Animal rescue organisations are also great sources for adopting pets, including the Irish Society for the Prevention of Cruelty to Animals (www.ispca.ie) and the Dublin Society for the Prevention of Cruelty to Animals (www.dspca.ie). Buying a pet through an advert on Craigslist Dublin (http://dublin.craigslist.org/), Gumtree (www.gumtree.ie), local papers or supermarket noticeboards is also a possibility, though with the number of illegal 'puppy farms' growing in Ireland you will want to investigate the origin of these animals carefully. No matter how you find a pet, make sure that proper documentation and vaccination records are offered with the animal. And, if you would like to help out pets but can't keep one in your own home, consider the DSPCA's 'Sponsor a Pet' programme which starts at as little as €15 per year.

Dog owners will need to arrange for a dog licence as required by the Control of Dogs Act 1986. Fortunately the process is simple and only requires visiting a local An Post (post office) branch and purchasing the licence. Individual licences cost just €12.60 and should be retained in case of future inspections.

Living with pets in Dublin is not hard due to the abundance of parks and beaches for exercise and the ease of finding pet supplies and food in even the smallest corner newsagent. The Phoenix Park is an excellent location to bring pets in need of a little outdoor fun, as are St Stephen's Green and Merrion Square before the crowds hit at lunchtime. Sandymount and Dollymount Strands are also likely to host pet parades on particularly fine days. Public transportation does not usually allow pets other than guide dogs, though an animal loving taxi driver might just come to the rescue when needed. Shops, restaurants and pubs will also ban animals other than guide dogs. If you are interested in taking your pet out in public, be sure to attach an ID tag and bring some pooper-scooper supplies as well. Cleaning up after animals is not just a nicety, it is the law in Dublin and a hefty fine can result for owners unwilling to take responsibility.

Pet owners who work long hours or travel frequently are also in luck, because pet sitting, grooming and training services are just starting to take off in Dublin. Though many Dubliners will still scoff at these posh luxuries, young professionals in particular are more than happy to pay to see to it that their pet gets a little TLC. Prices can vary.

Dog Training Ireland

Eau De Faucet ◀
Bottled water is still popular for those on the go, but at home, most people drink straight from the tap.

Electricity & Water

Like most utilities in Dublin, the government still has involvement in both the electricity and water supplies to the city. The Dublin City Council regulates water supplies, and the Electricity Supply Board (ESB) is still 95% government owned. However, this can't be viewed negatively because there are surprisingly few disruptions to either. Tap water is free for Dublin city residents (though rumours are rife that this can't continue for much longer), and electricity is often included in the price of smaller rentals such as flats or bedsits. For those who must pay for electricity on top of their rent or mortgage, try to rent somewhere with gas fired water heaters or your bills will skyrocket. ESB's NightSaver plan cuts the cost of electricity in half from 23:00 to 08:00 in winter, and from 24:00 to 09:00 in summer, although standing charges will increase.

Electricity

The Electricity Supply Board (ESB) provides electricity in Ireland. Most existing homes in Dublin have electricity connections, so setting up a new account simply requires calling the ESB at 1850 372 372 and giving them the present metre reading. If your house does not have electricity, a reconnection may be necessary and can be arranged through the same number. Newly built homes will need to be connected, call 1850 372 757.

The ESB heavily favours new customers setting up direct debit bill payment, and a €300 deposit is charged to new customers who don't go for this option. Though electricity bills will vary according to usage, a professional couple in a two bed apartment could expect to pay under €100 per month, including standing charges and VAT. If you are interested in the ESB's NightSaver plan, it's worthwhile holding off for a few months before signing up. This way you can work out if the extra standing charges attached to this service are worth the savings.

The main ESB office is located at 27 Lower Fitzwilliam Street, Dublin 2, though most Dubliners will never have set foot in this building in their life. Almost all transactions can be carried out by phone or online. The standard electricity supply in Ireland is 230 volts AC (frequency 50hz). Electrical appliances will need a 13 amp, three-pin (UK style) plug. Most electrical equipment in Ireland is sold with these plugs already attached, though converters and adaptors are readily available.

To close an electricity account, all you need to do is call the ESB with your final meter reading. They will give you further instructions for closing your account or switching to a new location.

Blackouts

Blackouts and brownouts (when there's a drop in voltage and the lights dim) are almost unheard of in Dublin, but keep torches, candles and matches to hand. A more likely scenario you might face is tripping the electricity switches, which will cause certain outlets to go out in your home. Familiarising yourself with your main fuse box will help you to rectify these situations.

Did You Know? ◀
In medieval times, Dubliners used to source their water from the River Poddle, an underground river lying beneath the city. Today, however, city dwellers enjoy their drinking water from reservoirs above ground.

Water

Water is free in Dublin so most houses already have a connection and it requires nothing more than turning on the taps to access clean drinking water. Developers and builders usually deal with new water supply connections, so individuals rarely need to concern themselves with this – although it's a good idea to check that you don't have to pay connection fees. If there are any compromises to local water supplies, nightly newscasts and the morning papers will carry instructions on how to access free replacement water, usually from Dublin City Council's water trucks, though this is incredibly rare. The Water Services Division of Dublin City Council administers the water supplies to the Greater Dublin Area (close to 500 million litres of water per day) and can be contacted via the Council's main switchboard during business hours (01 222 2222).

Gas

Household gas connections in Dublin are administered by Bord Gáis Eireann, usually known simply as Bord Gáis (and pronounced a bit like Board Gosh), which is entirely

What's That Smell?
If you smell gas or think
there may be a leak,
call the Bord Gáis 24
hour emergency service
on 1850 205 050.

government owned. Depending on the power supplies in private homes, gas can be used for both cooking and heating, though some newer apartments have bypassed gas connections all together and run solely on electricity. Those moving into existing houses with gas connections just need to contact the Bord Gáis at 1850 632 632 to change the account to their name. For a natural gas connection, call 1850 427 737. A minimum fee of €220 plus VAT is applied to new connections. Bord Gáis bills are issued every two months and include standing charges and tax as well as a charge for each unit of gas used. Many Dubliners agree that an estimate of €75 per person per month (during the coldest months) is an appropriate bill estimate. To close or move an account, call 1850 632 632 with a final metre reading and forwarding address.

Sewerage

Dublin's underground sewer network is managed by Dublin City Council, free of charge. Serving close to 1.7 million city residents, the network extends over 2,500km and includes 33 pumping stations and multiple storm tanks. The Ringsend Wastewater Treatment Works deals with the city's wastewater by converting waste into Biofert fertiliser and energy valued at €3 million annually. Unfortunately, not all of the city's wastewater is caught by the Works, and some waste still makes its way into Dublin Bay. New homes and businesses may require sewerage connections, which will bring a fee. Further information on Dublin's sewerage system can be obtained from the City Council's Drainage Division. You can contact them via the Council's main switchboard on 01 222 2222 during normal working hours.

Rubbish Disposal & Recycling

Waste services and recycling services are both carried out by Dublin City Council. A 'wheelie bin' system is in place by which private households are given a Council bin (either large or small) and assigned a day of the week on which to leave their rubbish at the curb for collection. A pay per use scheme is also in place such that each bin has a coded sticker that is 'read' by the collection truck and applied to the household's bill. Each bin is assessed using a standing charge (approximately €85 per year) and then a collection charge each time it is used (approximately €5.50 for large bins and €3.50 for small bins). Obviously the less the bin is used the lower the final bill, and many Dubliners have embraced the free recycling services. Green bins are provided for households to deposit their paper, light cardboard, aluminium and steel cans and cartons. For glass, there are bottle banks all over the city. Oxigen Environmental work in conjunction with Dublin City Council for recycling; for more information on recycling, see www.oxigen.ie. For specific locations of the 300+ recycling banks in Dublin, see www.dublinwaste.ie.

Telephone

Eircom, which was a state run company until just a few years ago, is still the major telephone provider in Dublin. Several competitors have cropped up recently, though almost every home in Dublin has an Eircom landline, which must be connected before another provider can take over the line. Eircom itself also supplies a great number of the telephones in Dublin homes, though electronics shops now offer a wide variety as well. Getting a new line installed in newly built houses can take a few weeks, while switching on an existing line for your personal account only takes a few days.

All calls are charged in Dublin, though different local, national and international rates apply. Different rates apply at different times of the day,

Telephone Companies		
British Telecom (BT)	1800 923 924	www.btireland.ie
Eircom	1901	www.eircom.net
NTL	1890 940 624	www.ntl.ie/phone
Perlico	1890 252 148	www.perlico.com
Smart Telecom	01 469 9300	www.smarttelecom.ie

125

Talk Is Cheap ◀
Calling internationally after 18:30 is almost always going to be the cheapest rate, though on holidays such as Christmas some providers offer discounted rates all day.

and daytime, evening and weekend rates will impact the price of a call. Telephone extras such as voicemail, call waiting and call forwarding will bring extra charges and adding a second line with a different phone number will entail a second household bill. Outside of the home, you'll find public phone boxes on almost every corner, though for the most part it's only tourists that use them, as most residents have a mobile phone. Most phone boxes accept calling cards and coins, and some also offer internet access. For new consumers, CallCosts.ie (www.callcosts.ie) provides a price comparison across all mobile phone and fixed line operators.

Mobile Phones

It'll take you no more than 10 minutes in Dublin to notice that the city loves its mobile phones. Most school children carry a mobile phone, and upgrading just for fashion's sake is common. Pay-as-you-go systems (sometimes called 'Ready to Go') are available with 'top ups' in denominations of €10, €15 and €20 increments. You can top up online, at an ATM or at a newsagent or supermarket, although this sometimes incurs a small fee. Monthly bill pay plans are also available, though these are better for people who use their mobile instead of a landline. Some of these plans offer a certain number of free minutes or texts per month, though the numbers may seem laughably low as compared to other countries. No particular residency or identification requirements pertain to buying a mobile phone in Dublin, and the forgetful few should be pleased to hear that they can still retain their number even if they lose their phone.

Mobile Service Providers

3	083 333 3333	www.three.ie
Meteor	1905	www.meteor.ie
O2	1850 601 747	www.o2.ie
Vodaphone	1850 208 787	www.vodafone.ie

Cheap Overseas Calls

Overseas call rates will differ with each telephone provider, but for the most part the rates tend to be within a few cents of each other. Call centres offer access to international phone lines and internet access, but it's best to enquire just how 'cheap' the rates are before you dial. National and international calling cards are also available at most newsagents, though again be sure to ask for the published rates. Dialwise, which can be accessed by dialling 1890 990 505 often offers international access at local rates, though not all countries are accessible. Voice over internet Protocol (VoIP) has only just started to catch on in Dublin, so Skype (www.skype.com) is still the best option for calling through the computer.

Cheap Overseas Calls

Dialwise	www.dialwise.ie
Skype	www.skype.com
World-Link	www.worldlink.ie

Internet

Other options **Websites** p.46, **Internet Cafes** p.367

The internet has become popular in Dublin over the past few years, though not all areas of the city are internet accessible yet and even fewer areas are broadband accessible. Wi-Fi Hotspots are few and far between, and almost all require purchasing internet time. Not even the public libraries can guarantee free Wi-Fi access in Dublin, though they are certainly trying (and they do offer a few computers each with free internet access for library members). With limited options it might seem like internet cafes should flourish in Dublin, but this is not necessarily the case either. Cafes do exist, and many offer rates of just €2 per hour, but printing is almost always extra and the ambience is lacking, to say the least. If you are lucky enough to live in a wired area, both dial-up and broadband access is offered by a variety of internet service providers. Though ISPs routinely offer email addresses, web-based mail such as Yahoo (www.yahoo.co.uk), Gmail (www.gmail.com) and Hotmail (www.hotmail.com) remain popular. Bebo pages (www.bebo.com) also seem to have surpassed personal web pages for the internet

Internet Service Providers

Clearwire	www.clearwire.ie
Eircom	http://home.eircom.net
Irish Broadband	www.irishbroadband.ie
NTL	www.ntl.ie/internet
Perlico	www.perlico.com

savvy. Internet censorship does not exist within Ireland, though frustrated surfers may realise that their Irish IP address limits the sites that they can access. Most broadband deals come at a flat rate, and many providers offer bundles with digital cable television or telephone deals thrown in. For more information on broadband providers in your area, visit www.broadband.gov.ie and be sure to check out the price comparison charts as well.

Bill Payment

Most utility bills in Ireland are issued bi-monthly and almost all can be paid via direct debit, in fact most service providers vastly prefer this option. Online payments and paying public utility bills at An Post offices are usually also acceptable. Missing a payment may result in a late fee, although letting a provider know that a payment will be late often results in these fees being waived (possibly in part) or a hardship payment plan set up. Almost no utilities are shut off immediately if a bill payment is missed (in fact it may take a few payment cycles for this to kick in), if a utility is shut off a reconnection fee may apply. Though bills tend to be sent out weeks before payment is due, checking an account online is also another option for timely payments. Disputed bills are unfortunately not often resolved quickly, so be ready for several weeks of wrangling before they are set right.

Post & Courier Services

Get Your Own Box
Post is delivered daily to your door in Dublin, but you can also get a PO Box if you need one (not many people use them). Application forms can be obtained from the An Post website (www.anpost.ie) and mailed to the Dublin Mails Revenue, An Post, General Post Office, Freepost, Dublin 1.

The Irish government runs An Post, Ireland's national mail service. Branches are located all over the city, and many branches also administer welfare or social services benefit payments, public utilities payments and savings accounts. TV licences can be bought at An Post branches, and passport renewals, travel insurance and mobile phone top-ups can all be conducted at neighbourhood post offices as well. The One4All gift voucher that can be bought from An Post and used in over 600 shops around the country is also a favourite for gift giving opportunities. Unfortunately, many postal workers take their lunch hour at the same time as the rest of the city, so sorting out postal errands can be frustrating for full-time workers.

Post is fairly quick around Dublin with most intra-city mail delivered in just one day. National mail often takes just a few days, and international mail to the USA and within Europe routinely arrives within a week. Post further afield is delivered in a week to 10 days. Of course, at high volume periods such as Christmas it can take longer, so be sure to send out holiday cards early.

Postage prices within Ireland seem to rise frequently, though An Post does offer a handy online postage calculator (http://postage.anpost.ie/) so that no one will be caught short at the counter. Insuring high value items is recommended, though it is rare that something gets lost in the mail. Posting items is very easy. Post boxes stand on most street corners, many newsagents operate postal counters and there are An Post branches all over the city. Stamps can be bought individually or in books, from An Post branches or newsagents. There are stamp machines around the city, but these are not refilled regularly.

Your post is delivered to your door daily in Dublin. However, larger packages tend to be delivered to postal depots rather than left on doorsteps, so the addressee or a designated person (with proof of identity) will need to go to the designated depot to collect them. Mail minding and mail forwarding services are also available Any printed envelopes marked with the word 'Freepost' in the address do not require stamps.

Courier Services

Many Dubliners will tell you that bike messengers are the scourge of the pavements, but businesses would likely be lost without them. Door-to-door couriers tend to operate during normal business hours, and most operate a network of bikes, motorcycles and vans. Nationwide and international deliveries may be offered.

Courier Companies

Coda Couriers	086 828 9328	http://codacouriers.com
Cyclone Couriers	01 475 7000	www.cyclone.ie
DHL	1890 725 725	www.dhl.ie
FedEx	1800 535 800	www.fedex.com/ie
Hurricane Couriers	01 411 4100	www.hurricane.ie
Pony Express	01 661 0101	www.72fm.com/pe
UPS	1800 575 757	www.ups.com

Radio

The Great Irish Phone-In
Dublin radio stations love to answer calls from listeners and to have zany competitions, particularly during drive time, so be sure to tune in for some bizarre conversations.

Radio offerings in Dublin are varied and there is probably something to suit every taste. Radio Telefis Eireann (RTE) (www.rte.ie) is Ireland's state run radio and television broadcaster which offers multiple stations including RTE Radio 1 (88.2 – 90, general entertainment), RTE 2fm (90 – 92, chart music), RTE Lyric FM (96.7 – 99.6, easy listening including classical and jazz) and RTE Raidó na Gaeltachta (92 – 94, all Irish language). Other stations are also licensed to play independently in Dublin, including 98 FM (98.1 – contemporary) Today FM (100 – 101.8, contemporary), FM 104 (104.4 – contemporary), NewsTalk 106 (106 – 108, news and talk), Spin 103.8 (103.8 – chart and dance music) and Q102 (102.2 – easy listening).

Television

All Irish households that have a TV on the premises are required to hold a valid television licence. These licences cost approximately €160 and can be purchased at any An Post branch. Most homes in Dublin are set up to receive at least four basic television stations, RTE 1, RTE 2, TV 3, and TG4, though others come with basic cable, which includes a few more channels such as E4, Channel 4, Sky 1, Sky News, BBC 1 and BBC 2. With the exception of TG4 (also known as TnaG or Telefis na Gailge, an Irish language channel) these stations all broadcast in English. RTE 1, RTE 2, TV 3 and TG4 are all channels broadcast from Ireland, while the others are mainly broadcast from the United Kingdom. This results in a mixture of Irish, British, American and Australian programmes for entertainment. The Irish television stations are predominantly family friendly, though news broadcasts in Ireland may seem gruesome to those who are not used to being shown dead bodies. Those who are offended by television in Ireland can complain to the Broadcasting Complaints Commission (www.bcc.ie).

Satellite TV & Radio

See It All After Nine
There is virtually no censorship of television stations broadcast in Ireland, though particularly racy content is reserved for after the watershed at 21:00.

Extended cable' packages in Dublin are the ones that are beamed in by satellite or delivered via digital wiring. Many Dublin households now enjoy extended cable, though some parts of the city remain unwired for digital cable and many rental properties do not allow satellites. Sky (satellite) and NTL (digital) are the two main extended cable providers. They offer packages starting at approximately €30 per month.

Satellite and digital television stations often have more risque content than terrestrial channels with some stations broadcasting what many consider to be soft porn during the evening hours. Of course with over 100 channels on offer there is much more to watch, including international sports stations

Satellite & Cable Providers

NTL Digital	www.ntl.ie
Sky Television	www.sky.com

such as NASN (North American Sports Network), Eurosport and Sky Sports, and film channels such Film Four and MGM (classic films). The City Channel also caters to pretty much every group in Dublin, with programmes such as 'Oto Polska' and 'Gay OK!' attracting viewers.

These packages often include digital radio stations as part of their line-up, and RTE has rolled out a trial of digital stations for Dublin.

What Are You Entitled To?
For full information on your entitlements and what you're covered for, the Citizen's Information Board is a public service information board with information on the health services, as well as birth, families, law and social welfare. See www.citizens information.ie for more info.

General Medical Care

Healthcare in Ireland is divided into public and private sectors. Individuals and families on low incomes, and those over 70 years of age are entitled to a government medical card, which provides them with free healthcare and medication (see p.130). However, the majority of Irish residents don't fall into these categories, so many choose to take out private health insurance (see p.131). Non-medical card holders are entitled to some free public hospital care (see Main Government Hospitals section on p.132), although this usually only covers essential or basic services and patients can still incur substantial costs for inpatient hospital care.

Your family doctor or general practitioner (GP) will see to most of your healthcare needs and is your first point of call for almost every illness, so it is very important to find someone that you like and trust. Word of mouth is the usual method of finding a good doctor, and as most doctors' surgeries keep regular business hours, it is a good idea to find somewhere convenient to your home or workplace. Unless you have a medical card, you will have to pay for GP visits. Consultations range from €40 to €60 per visit. It's a good idea to check the cost before you make an appointment.

Finding a good dentist is a similar procedure, ask around or keep trying different ones out until you find one you're happy with. Ideally, you should have a check up every six to 12 months. See p.138 for a listing of dentists in your area.

Maternity care in Ireland is free and of relatively good standard. See p.134 for more.

Cosmetic surgery is on the increase and a growing number of clinics are popping up to meet demand, see p.138 for a listing of clinics that cater to both surgical and non-surgical procedures.

Public Hospital Care

The standard of care in state hospitals in Ireland is generally very good, although you can be in for a long wait once you get there. Anyone who is ordinarily resident in Ireland is entitled to free outpatient public hospital services, with the exception of A&E charges which will cost you €60. 'Ordinary residency' is generally understood to mean that you intend living in Ireland for at least a year, and it includes students who are taking a course of a minimum of one year's duration. You may be asked to prove this by producing an employment contract, a lease on rented property or proof of mortgage. If you are referred to the hospital by your GP for outpatient, accident and emergency treatment you will not have to pay a fee.

Inpatient hospital care is charged at €60 per day and this up to a ceiling of €600 in a 12 month period. Medical card holders are covered for both GP visits and for hospital care in a public hospital and are entitled to free pharmacy prescriptions. EU citizens who hold a valid European health insurance card are entitled to the same benefits as Irish medical card holders and can use these cards when they first arrive. Most people choose to take out private health insurance (see p.131).

Government Health Centres & Clinics

Dublin South City Local Health Office	Dublin 2	01 648 6500
Dublin South East Local Health Office	Dublin 6	01 268 0300
Dublin South West Local Health Office	Dublin 12	01 415 4700
Dublin West Local Health Office	Dublin 10	01 620 6300
Dun Laoghaire Local Health Office	Dun Laoghaire	01 284 3579
North Central Dublin Local Health Office	Dublin 3	01 857 5400
North Dublin Local Health Office	Dublin 5	01 816 4200
North West Dublin Local Health Office	Dublin 7	01 882 5000

Private Hospital Care

Most Irish residents who do not qualify for a government medical card have some form of health insurance to cover their medical costs. Policies differ widely and not all private hospitals are covered so do your homework before signing up to one. The main difference between public and private hospitals is the inpatient accommodation. In a private hospital, the wards are smaller and there are more private rooms. With

Well Woman
Women can attend one
of the three Well-
Woman Centres
(www.wellwoman
centre.ie) in Dublin,
situated in Dublin 1,
Ballsbridge and
Coolock. There are no
specialist men's health
clinics in Dublin at
present, but all men's
health services are
available from your GP.

private health insurance you also get to choose your treating physician and it affords you faster access to elective services than in public hospitals, which often have lengthy waiting lists. Some of the more exclusive private hospitals are defined as 'high-tech' by many health insurance companies and are not fully covered under most policies. See p.133 for details of the main private hospitals.

Emergencies

If you find yourself in need of urgent medical care, you can go directly to an accident and emergency (A&E) unit or call an ambulance if you cannot make your own way there. You can also go to your GP for referral to A&E (at which point you will not have to pay when you get there). All of the major government hospitals listed on p.132 have excellent A&E departments. Private hospitals tend not to have them at all and cater more to specialised procedures and elective surgery.

If in doubt in an emergency, always call an ambulance. There are two emergency numbers in Ireland – 999 and 112. 112 works from mobile phones, 999 sometimes does not. You will be asked if you need the police, an ambulance or the fire brigade, and for directions to where you are. Give the most complete address that you can and all details that you are asked for, such as your own name and contact number. Only one person can travel in an ambulance with the patient.

Pharmacies

Certain pain medication is available over the counter without a prescription, but most drugs, including antibiotics, must be prescribed by a doctor. A pharmacist can advise you about which non-prescription drugs are best for you, but they do not have the power to prescribe. If you are asking a pharmacist for advice, ensure that you tell them about any allergies or ulcers that may affect your response to medication. Make sure to tell them if you are on any medication already and always read the leaflet enclosed with the product. There are a number of late night pharmacies in Dublin, and most 24-hour shops will stock ordinary painkillers. Antibiotics are quite commonly used, but doctors are becoming more wary of prescribing them too often.

Private Health Centres & Clinics		
Ballyowen Medical Centre	Southwest Dublin	01 621 4224
Dundrum Medical Centre	Dundrum	01 216 6960
Fitzwilliam Medical Centre	Dublin 2	01 678 5100
Medical Practice – 14 Mountjoy Sq	Dublin 1	01 878 6269
Mercers Medical Centre	Dublin 2	01 402 2300
Temple Bar Medical Centre	Dublin 2	01 670 7255
Tyrrelstown Medical Centre	Dublin 15	01 885 6380
VHI Swiftcare Clinic	Dublin 16	01 799 4188
VHI Swiftcare Clinic	Dublin 9	01 799 4192

Check-Ups

Your GP will take care of most general check-ups. If you do not have a medical card, you will have to pay for this service (usually €40-€60 a visit). If you need a blood test you will be referred to one of the hospitals, as the results can be processed faster if they take the sample directly.

Medical Cards

Medical Cards are are available to individuals and families on low incomes, and anyone over 70 years of age, irrespective of their financial status. They entitle holders to free healthcare and

Dermatologists		
Dr Abdullah Moktar	Dublin 18	01 213 6220
Dr Alan Irvine	Dublin 8	01 474 2408
Dr Brigid O'Connell	Dublin 2	01 644 9696
Dr Paul Collins	Dun Laoghaire	01 280 8521
Dr PJ Walls	Blackrock	01 890 4889

medication. You can apply for one through your local Health Services Executive (www.hse.ie). Approximately 38% of the population has one.

Health Insurance

The state healthcare system entitles anyone who is ordinarily resident in the country to receive free outpatient public hospital services, with the exception of A&E charges (see Public Hospital Care on p.129) and inpatient care. Although these services are not especially expensive, most people take out some form of private health insurance if they are not eligible for a medical card (see p.130). Private health insurance not only means that any expenses incurred are covered, but you will also benefit from faster access to elective services and have a say in who treats you, as well the possibility of having a private room.

Most employers in Ireland offer a health insurance scheme, sometimes at a slightly discounted group rate. The advantage is that your premium is deducted from your salary on payday, spreading the cost across the whole year.

There are three health insurance companies operating in Ireland (see p.130), and packages cover everything from one-off treatments to day-to-day medical costs. The only thing that an insurance policy has to provide is semi-private accommodation for inpatient care in a public hospital, although most consultant and hospital services are covered by standard policies. After this, packages vary widely, in cost and in services covered. You can expect to pay from €330 annually for basic cover for a single person, up to €4,000 plus for comprehensive cover for a family of four. Insurance companies tend to quote prices exclusive of tax relief. All recognised insurance policy holders are entitled to a tax credit on their premium, but this is organised automatically by the insurer. If you find yourself without health insurance on arriving in Dublin, you will still be treated in a government hospital in case of an emergency. See Public Hospital Care on p.129.

Health Insurance Companies		
Quinn Healthcare	1890 700 890	www.quinn-healthcare.com
VHI	1850 444 444	www.vhi.ie
Vivas	1850 717 717	www.vivas.ie

Donor Cards

Donor cards are widely available in Ireland, and can be obtained from your local pharmacy, as well as from some universities and workplaces. Like many countries, Irish driving licences have a box to tick if you wish to become a donor. However, it is important to inform your next-of-kin of your feelings regarding organ donation, as they will be approached for consent even if you are carrying a signed card at the time of death. Organ donations are administered by the National Organ Procurement Service, based in Beaumont Hospital, Dublin 9 (01 809 2759).

Giving Blood

The Irish Blood Transfusion Service is a very visible organisation, running frequent media campaigns and blood drives to raise awareness about blood donation.

Smoking is allowed in designated areas only

Regulations on blood donation in Ireland are quite strict, and it is worth checking online whether you are eligible to donate before making the trip to a clinic. The main blood donation clinics are at D'Olier Street, Dublin 2, James's Street, Dublin 8 and Stillorgan in south county Dublin. Dates and locations for mobile clinics are available on www.ibts.ie. Donors are not paid and a preliminary blood test is carried out beforehand. Each donor is issued with a card that states their donor number and blood group.

Giving Up Smoking

Following the smoking ban that came into effect in 2004, smoking is now illegal in any workplace in Ireland. This includes cafes, pubs and nightclubs. This can be a helpful environment in which to give up smoking since 'trigger' situations are reduced. The Irish Cancer Society has a helpline for smokers hoping to quit, in conjunction with the Department of Health and Children. The National Smokers' Quitline can be reached on 1890 201 203 and calls are charged at CallSave rates. If you require further help, helpline operators can refer you on to the Smoking Cessation Officer attached to your local Health Board.

Main Government Hospitals

Government hospitals provide a range of services such as accident and emergency (A&E), consultancy services and inpatient and outpatient care. In most cases, patients are referred by their GP to hospitals for more specialist care. The exception is in the case of an emergency, when a patient goes directly to A&E. If you don't have a medical card and have not been referred by your GP, a trip to A&E will cost you €60. In cases of hardship, this fee may be waived.

It is also notable that most hospitals in Dublin are not known by their official name, but by their location, which can be confusing – Our Lady's is referred to as Crumlin Hospital, St Colmcille's as Loughlinstown Hospital and The James Connolly Memorial as Blanchardstown Hospital.

Beaumont Rd
Dublin 9
Map 408 E1 **555**

Beaumont Hospital
01 809 3000 | www.beaumont.ie

Beaumont Hospital, located on the north side of the city, is best known as the national referral centre for neurosurgery (including head injuries and brain trauma) and has an excellent reputation in this regard. It is also the national hospital for renal and pancreatic transplantation. Beaumont provides accident and emergency cover for its catchment area and has 54 specialist departments, including cardiology, orthopaedics, gynaecology and ear, nose and throat surgery.

Eccles St
Dublin 7
Map 416 B1 **556**

Mater Misericordiae University Hospital
01 803 2000 | www.mater.ie

The Mater, as it is commonly known, is a teaching hospital affiliated to University College Dublin and to the Royal College of Surgeons in Ireland. As well as providing general hospital services, from accident and emergency to consultancy, it is widely known as a research centre. The hospital provides a range of auxiliary services, including occupational therapy, physiotherapy and dietetics, as well as standard hospital services such as oncology, cardiology, psychiatry and haematology.

James's St
Dublin 8
Map 428 A2 **561**

St James's Hospital
01 410 3000 | www.stjames.ie

St James's Hospital is one of the largest hospitals serving the south city. It is a major centre for the treatment or cancer and cardiac disease, and it also houses a large accident and emergency unit. It is the national centre for bone marrow transplantation and is heavily involved in biochemical research. A full list of services is available online, as well as links to patient support groups and health insurance companies.

Other Government Hospitals

Adelaide & Meath Hospital	Tallaght	Dublin 24	01 414 2000
James Connolly Memorial Hospital	Blanchardstown	Dublin 15	01 288 3144
National Rehabilitation Hospital	Rochestown Avenue	Dun Laoghaire	01 285 4777
Our Lady's Children's Hospital	Crumlin	Dublin 12	01 409 6100
The Royal Victoria Eye and Ear Hospital	Adelaide Road	Dublin 2	01 678 5500
St Colmcille's	Loughlinstown	South Dublin	01 282 5800
St Michael's Hospital	Lower George's St	Dun Laoghaire	01 280 6901

St Vincent's University Hospital

Elm Park
Dublin 4
Map 421 F1 558

01 221 4000 | www.svuh.ie

St Vincent's is one of the main teaching hospitals for nearby UCD. Alongside standard emergency and consultant services, the hospital operates a dedicated breast clinic which provides routine screening and detection as well as cancer care for complex cases of breast cancer. It is also home to the only liver transplant unit in Ireland, as well as over 40 other specialities.

Main Private Hospitals

The hospitals listed below are classified by some insurance companies as 'high-tech' hospitals, which means that you may require a higher level of cover to avail of some of the services offered. It is important to check which hospitals are covered by your chosen policy before signing up.

Blackrock Clinic

Rock Rd
Blackrock
Map 422 B3 554

01 283 2222 | www.blackrock-clinic.ie

The Blackrock Clinic is primarily known as a surgical centre, although they also offer a wide range of advanced diagnostic procedures and outpatient services. Founded in 1984, they are among the longest established and most highly respected providers of cosmetic surgery in Ireland. Their visiting hours are unusually broad – from 10:30 to 21:00 daily – and their accommodation for inpatients is excellent. Some insurance policies classify the Blackrock Clinic as a 'high-tech' hospital and may not cover treatment undertaken here.

Mater Private Hospital

Eccles St
Dublin 7
Map 416 B1 556

01 855 8888 | www.materprivate.ie

Originally owned by the Sisters of Mercy, this hospital has been privately held since 2000, when it was purchased by the board of directors. It is home to the country's only dedicated Chest Pain Clinic, designed to identify cardiac problems in first-time chest pain sufferers and refer them for specialist treatment. They also operate a Sleep Disorders Clinic, the first of its kind in Ireland, as well as a wide range of standard hospital services, including an eye laser surgery clinic.

St Patrick's Hospital

James's Street
Dublin 8
Map 424 A4 560

01 249 3200 | www.stpatrickshosp.com

St Patrick's is a private, non-profit hospital that was founded with funds donated by Jonathan Swift in his estate. The hospital specialises in psychiatric conditions such as mood disorders, substance dependence, depression management and eating disorders, and has built up an excellent reputation in terms of helping not only the patient but also the patient's family to cope with the aftermath of mental illness. The comprehensive information centre within the hospital is open to patients and members of the public who wish to find out more about particular mental or psychiatric illnesses. St Patrick's also has an extensive and successful outpatient facility.

St James's Hospital

Elm Park
Dublin 4
Map 408 C4 599

St Vincent's Private Hospital

01 260 2900 | www.svph.ie

Located close to the public hospital complex, St Vincent's Private Hospital provides both inpatient care and day services. The latter range from a walk-in blood test clinic to diagnostic imaging and cardiology services. At present there are 164 inpatient beds and 36 for day patients. The hospital is hoping to expand and is currently awaiting planning permission.

Other Private Hospitals

Beacon Hospital	Sandyford	Dublin 18	01 293 6600	www.beaconhospital.ie
Bon Secours Private Hospital	Glasnevin	Dublin 9	01 837 5111	www.bonsecoursireland.org
Clontarf Orthopaedic Hospital	Castle Avenue	Dublin 3	01 833 8167	na
Mount Carmel Hospital	Churchtown	Dublin 14	01 406 3400	www.mt-carmel.com

Maternity

Other options **Maternity Items** p.306

Mum & Baby Groups
Without the support of family and friends, a new mum away from home may feel very isolated. It's a good idea to join postnatal classes, sign up for mother and toddler activities such as baby yoga, massage or interactive developmental classes (see p.245) or a parent support group. Check out your local church, supermarket or shop for notices. There are also a number of online forums.

All women ordinarily resident in Ireland are entitled to free maternity care. Up to 1 January, 2005, most expats chose to give birth here because any child born in Ireland was entitled to Irish citizenship. This is no longer the case, but it is still a top choice for many women (see p.61).

While pregnant, and up until the new baby is six weeks old, you are entitled to six free GP visits. Your GP can give you the necessary claim form, which you should return, completed to your local health board.

Maternity care is usually divided between your GP and the hospital where you intend to give birth. As a public patient, antenatal care will be provided by the antenatal clinic in the hospital, and you may or may not deal with the same doctor on each visit. Midwives will deliver the baby (unless there is a complication) and your stay in hospital will be on a public ward. It is essential to book the hospital well in advance but your GP will go through this with you.

Antenatal care for semi-private patients is provided either by a semi-private antenatal clinic or by a consultant. You will deal with the consultant or a member of their team throughout your pregnancy, including during delivery. After the baby is born you will stay in a semi-private ward with three to five others.

Private patients are appointed a consultant, who you will see throughout the pregnancy (although they may not deliver the baby) and, subject to availability; you will be given a private room. Be warned that most health insurance policies only cover maternity care after you've been signed up for a minimum period (often one year) and not all policies will cover the extra costs that come with private care such as ultrasounds and delivery fees.

If you have a gynaecologist and you'd prefer that they oversee your pregnancy, you should discuss this with them and find out how it affects your options for hospital care (see p.136 for a listing of gynaecologists).

Your hospital will also run antenatal classes. Independent classes, such as antenatal yoga and pilates, have recently become popular, and are an excellent way to meet other expectant mums (see Activities on p.274 and p.276 for classes outside of the hospital network).

Epidurals, pethidine, TENS and ethanox masks, as well as natural breathing and relaxation techniques are all common pain relief methods. Elective caesarean sections are rare, but are a possibility. Your antenatal health care provider should discuss all of these options with you.

Most hospitals allow only one person in the delivery room with the expectant mum at any time, so you may not be able to have a doula and the baby's father present together. It is advisable to ask about delivery room procedures as early as possible so you can make your birth plan.

Your baby's birth will be registered by the hospital. After registration you will need to obtain a copy of the baby's birth certificate, which you can do by post. For more on this, see Birth Certificate and Registration on p.61.

After the birth, a paediatrician will examine your baby and several tests will be carried out, including the heel prick test and the Apgar Score to check everything is as it should be. The baby's first follow-up visit is usually with the family doctor, and hospital check-ups are carried out after six weeks, and then 12 weeks. Breastfeeding is very common and is widely accepted.

Postnatal Depression

Many women experience the 'baby blues' after giving birth. Symptoms include feeling weepy, helpless, anxious, afraid or even guilty. Getting your partner, family or friends to help with housework or hiring a babysitter can make a big difference. If the symptoms persist or worsen, it is important to seek help as you may be suffering from post-natal depression. You can speak to your hospital doctor at your six-week check up, or to your family GP. A short course of anti-depressants can help, and your doctor may also offer some practical advice.

Maternity Leave

You are entitled to 26 weeks of maternity leave, and an additional 16 weeks unpaid maternity leave. You must take two weeks of leave prior to the week of the due date and four weeks after. If you have enough PRSI payments (see Work, p.70) you may be entitled to Maternity Benefit. Some employers will continue to pay an employee their usual salary when on maternity leave, minus the Maternity Benefit, but this all depends on your company and the terms of your contract. You must give your employer four weeks written notice of the date you intend to commence maternity leave and the date you intend to return. If you decide not to return to work, your normal notice requirements for resigning apply. Days taken while on maternity leave count towards accruing annual holidays and are considered the same as if you were at work. You are also entitled to public holidays while on leave.

Water Births
Water births are less common in Ireland. You can hire a birthing pool for home births, and some maternity hospitals will allow you to labour in a pool, but not deliver in one.

Alternative Birthing Methods

Most women choose to give birth in one of the country's maternity hospitals, although home births are becoming more common. If you wish to opt for a home birth, you will need to contact your local Health Service Executive Office (see www.hse.ie) and request a list of doctors or midwives. They will help you to arrange it and can advise you further. Another option is to engage a midwife privately – a list of independent practitioners can be obtained from the Homebirth Association of Ireland (www.homebirth.ie). Before you go down this road however, it is a good idea to speak to your GP about the probability of complications, because home births are not recommended for all pregnancies.

Contraception & Sexual Health

The Irish Family Planning Association offers contraception and family planning services, counselling in the event of an unwanted pregnancy, and training for doctors and nurses. Their two medical centres offer well-woman checks, pap smears, treatment for menopause, contraception (including the emergency or 'morning after' pill), testing and treatment for sexually transmitted infections, and vasectomy. The medical centres are in Dublin 1 (Cathal Brugha Street, 01 872 7088) and in Tallaght (The

Maternity Hospitals & Clinics

The Coombe Hospital	Dublin 8	01 408 5200	Both
Mount Carmel Hospital	Dublin 14	01 406 3400	Private
National Maternity Hospital	Dublin 2	01 637 3100	Both
Rotunda Hospital	Dublin 1	01 873 0700	Both

Square, 01 459 7685). IFPA also operates a national pregnancy helpline (1850 495 051). Get more information on your contraceptive requirements and other reproductive issues on the IFPA website (www.ifpa.ie), or call 01 806 9444.

Abortion

Abortions have always been controversial in Ireland, and they remain illegal except in very rare cases where the life of the mother is threatened by carrying the pregnancy to term. Under Irish law, a woman cannot be prevented from leaving the country to have an abortion, and statistics show that a significant number of Irish women choose to do so each year. A number of organisations offer non-directive counselling for women experiencing a crisis pregnancy, and many will offer advice about having a pregnancy terminated overseas, but it is important to research the policies of such organisations as thoroughly as possible to be sure that they are willing to provide the information you need and that they will respect whatever decision you make. Abortion is not available in Northern Ireland.

If you need non-judgemental advice, IFPA (www.ifpa.ie) can offer it to you. If you arrange a face-to-face counselling session, the counsellor can explain your many options and offer information on travelling abroad for an abortion – but this information can only be done in person: it is illegal for IFPA counsellors to provide such information over the phone. The IFPA also offers post-abortion support, including medical checkups and counselling.

Gynaecology & Obstetrics

In Ireland, it is usual to find a gynaecologist by word of mouth – through recommendations from either your friends and colleagues or your GP. It is not necessary to see a gynaecologist to obtain the most common methods of contraception, as your GP can prescribe the contraceptive pill and emergency contraception (the morning-after pill). Condoms can be purchased from any pharmacy and from many supermarkets and corner shops. Your GP may also be able perform a cervical smear test, but many women prefer to see a

Gynaecologists	
Dr Barry Gaughan	01 809 3309
Dr John Murphy	01 221 3057
Dr Mary B Anglim	01 416 2239
Dr Paul Byrne	01 809 3169
Dr Valerie Donnelly	01 296 4807

gynaecologist. Male gynaecologists are very common, so it is important to specify if you wish to see a female. Many gynaecological services are also available through your local Well-Woman centre (see www.wellwomancentre.ie).

Fertility Treatments

Fertility treatments are relatively new in Ireland and in-vitro fertilisation (IVF) is not available through the public health system. There are a number of reputable private clinics offering investigative procedures as well as a variety of assisted reproductive treatments, including IVF. Human Assisted Reproduction Ireland (HARI) is a private clinic based on the Rotunda Hospital campus (01 807 2732, www.hari.ie), and the Merrion Fertility Clinic (01 678 8688, www.merrionfertility.ie) is affiliated with the National Maternity Hospital. Couples can expect to pay up to €5,000 per IVF treatment cycle. The Irish Medical Council have issued a list of ethical guidelines for fertility clinics, but fertility clinics remain largely unregulated, so it is important to seek the advice of a trusted family doctor or gynaecologist.

Get Your Mammies Grammed

Dublin is within a BreastCheck screening catchment area, which means that women over 50 will be invited for a free screening every two years. All women should practice regular self-checks and contact their GP immediately if they notice any lumps, irregularities or changes in appearance. If you have a history of breast cancer in the family, it is important to let your GP know about this. If you find any irregularity in your breasts, contact your GP, who can arrange a mammogram either in your local BreastCheck clinic or your local hospital x-ray department. Results are usually available within a week.

Paediatrics

After your baby is born and has been discharged from hospital, most childhood medical care in Ireland is undertaken by an ordinary family doctor rather than by a paediatrician. If more specialist paediatric care is required, your GP will refer your child to a qualified paediatrician. You are not obliged to see the paediatrician in your maternity hospital. Depending on your health insurance package, a percentage of the cost of GP and consultant visits may be covered.

Paediatrics			
Dr J Murphy	The Children's University Hospital, Temple St	Dublin 1	01 878 4200
Dr Karina Butler	Our Lady's Children's Hospital, Crumlin	Dublin 12	01 409 6338
Dr Rosemary Manning	The National Children's Hospital, Tallaght	Dublin 24	01 414 2925

Children are vaccinated against tuberculosis at birth. At two months old, they receive the first dose of the '5 in 1' vaccination against diphtheria, polio, whooping cough, tetanus and HiB, and also a separate meningitis C vaccine. The MMR (measles, mumps and rubella) vaccine is given between 12 and 15 months after birth, and if a child has not received the HiB vaccine at an earlier age, it will be administered then. It is not possible to receive the MMR vaccine as three separate injections in Ireland or in the UK. Booster vaccines are available free of charge under the School Booster Programme, and they are usually administered by public health nurses in schools. Vaccines are also made available through schools for children who have not already received them, so do not worry if your child has missed vaccinations as a result of moving abroad.

The chickenpox vaccine is not given in Ireland, although most children can expect to come into contact with the disease. Many paediatricians advise that contracting the disease in childhood is less dangerous than risking contracting the adult version later in life. It is not generally a serious condition for a child, although if your child is very young or has a weak immune system, you should contact your GP in the event of exposure. If symptoms persist or are unusually severe, you should seek help. Other common childhood infections such as strep throat can be treated with antibiotics. In general, regular exercise and a good diet with plenty of Vitamin C can help to boost the immune system of a healthy child.

Support Groups

There are many support groups catering to all kinds of parenting issues. The Irish Stillbirth and Neonatal Death Society (01 872 6996, www.isands.ie) provide a range of support services for parents affected by stillbirth and Sudden Infant Death Syndrome. The Miscarriage Association focus on allowing parents to grieve fully and acknowledging their loss (01 873 5702, info@miscarriage.ie). Your GP can direct you to support groups for any illnesses or disabilities that may affect you or your family.

Disabilities & Learning Difficulties

If your child has a physical disability, there are a variety of support groups that can provide help and practical advice for all of the family. Your GP can direct you to groups in your area. Your child may also be entitled to a government medical card to cover disability-related expenses even if your family income would not normally allow you to qualify.

Children with behavioural problems or disabilities such as autism, Aspergers syndrome or ADHD may benefit from some psychological assessment and therapy. For more on this, see Counsellors and Psychologists on p.142. If you suspect your child may have a learning difficulty, discuss it with their teacher as early as possible and contact the National Council for Special Education (www.ncse.ie), who can put you in touch with a Special Educational Needs Officer (SENO) in your area. See p.150 for schools and p.253 for Special Needs Sports.

Dentists & Orthodontists

Most dentistry in Ireland is carried out privately, although government medical card holders and schoolchildren are entitled to free public dental care. For other groups, the cost of some dental procedures can be claimed against PRSI (see Taxation on p.73), although you must have a minimum number of contributions in order to qualify (visit www.welfare.ie/publications for details of the Treatment Benefit Scheme). If you are eligible, you can have dental work carried out as normal by any private dentist who is on the Department of Social and Family Affairs panel, which most dentists are. Your dentist can give you a claim form. The cost of dental care in Dublin can be high – up to €100 for a filling, so it's a good idea to shop around and get quotes before committing yourself to treatment.

For young children, some dentists specialise in paediatric dentistry. Most dentists recommend bringing your child for their first visit at around 3 to 4 years of age. If you're a nervous patient and require sedation during dental procedures, contact the Dental Council (01 676 2069) for a list of practices where this is available.

Cosmetic dentistry is becoming more popular in Dublin, and many dental practices now offer whitening services.

There are also some independent clinics that specialise in whitening treatments. For teeth straightening and other orthodontic treatment, your dentist can refer you to a reputable orthodontist. Orthodontic services are available publicly for school-age children, but the waiting list is quite long.

Dentists & Orthodontists		
Dr Andrew L McDermott	Dublin 1	01 873 0809
Dr Ann Griffin	Dublin 2	01 676 1536
Dr Mark Kelly	Dublin 4	01 665 5900
Dr Michael J Burke	Dublin 8	01 453 1859
Dr Michelle Brady	Dublin 2	01 671 8581
Dr Peter Martin Nitsch	Dublin 5	01 839 9524
Dr Ronan Perry	Dublin 7	01 878 0044
Dr Sinead Fitzgerald	Dublin 1	01 830 5243

Opticians & Ophthalmologists

Opticians are easy to find in Dublin, from small independent practitioners to multi-national franchises, usually situated in shopping areas. Both glasses and contact lenses are widely available, and a number of online retailers specialising in contact lenses are now opening in Dublin. They tend to offer very competitive pricing, although few offer optician services. Regular eye check-ups are a good idea. Eyesight can deteriorate quickly unnoticed, and the eye can also serve as an early-warning system for illnesses. If you are concerned about your eyesight or feel you may need specialist care, the first person you should see is your optician. An optician cannot diagnose an eye disease, but they are trained to recognise warning signs and can refer you to an ophthalmologist (a medical doctor specialising in eye care). If you are concerned about your child's eyesight, the same procedure applies.

Opticians & Ophthalmologists		
Cryan Opticians	Dun Laoghaire	01 280 2816
Dublin Eye Centre	Dublin 6	01 490 5533
Eyewise Opticians	Swords	01 840 4258
Get Lenses	Blackrock	1890 203 043
Insight Opticians	Dublin 1	01 878 1188
JR Manuel	Dublin 7	01 830 5556
MacNally Opticians	Dublin 2	01 676 9452
Specsavers	Dundrum	01 215 6000
Vision Express	Dublin 15	01 822 2066

Laser eye surgery is also growing in popularity, although not everyone who wears glasses or contact lenses is suitable for the procedure. It can cost up to €2,000 per eye, but check the details carefully as some clinics quote prices including aftercare and follow-up visits, so the higher price may represent the best value. The immediate recovery period is a few days, but most clinics advise extra caution for at least a month afterwards. It is also possible to claim tax relief on the cost of laser eye surgery.

Cosmetic Treatment & Surgery

Cosmetic surgery is becoming so popular in Ireland that the industry is reported to be worth €25 million per year. Breast augmentation and reduction, liposuction and facelifts are among the most popular surgical treatments. The number of cosmetic surgery providers in Dublin has grown steadily since the mid-1990s, and most of them are now also moving into non-surgical alternatives like Botox, microdermabrasion, chemical peels and laser therapy. Most beauty salons now offer most of these treatments, and some have visiting nurses who administer Botox injections.

Cosmetic Treatment & Surgery

Advanced Cosmetic Surgery	Mount Merrion	1850 204 090
Ailesbury Clinic	Dublin 4	1850 918 133
Auralia	Dublin 12	1850 909 100
Blackrock Clinic	Blackrock	01 283 2222
Cosmoplastica	Dublin 18	01 213 5630
Derma Laser Clinic	Tallaght	01 414 7781
Easycare	Stillorgan	1890 210 210
Harley Medical Group	Dublin 2	1800 242 442
Venus Medical Beauty	Dundrum	01 296 2747

Alternative Therapies

Alternative or complementary therapies are relatively new in Ireland, although they are growing in popularity. Many people are turning to alternative therapy for relief of muscular injuries, back problems, chronic pain and stress-related disorders.

At present there is no legislation covering complementary therapy practitioners, but there are a number of ways to find a reputable and professional practitioner. Most forms of treatment have a professional association based in Ireland, and these associations generally demand certain recognised qualifications in order to gain membership, which can give you a useful starting point for researching local clinics. Some GPs will suggest complementary therapists, and word of mouth is, as always, one of the best ways to find someone. It is also important to check that your practitioner has a valid insurance certificate. Most Irish health insurance companies are now covering some alternative and complementary therapies, and should be able to supply you with lists of approved practitioners.

Acupressure/Acupuncture

Acupuncture and Chinese Medicine	Swords	01 807 7508
Blackrock Physiotherapy and Acupuncture	Blackrock	01 289 6344
Carmel Bradley	Dublin 3	01 837 0543
Clinic of Holistic Medicine	Dublin 2	01 676 4840
Lucan Acupuncture and Chinese Medicine Clinic	Southwest Dublin	01 621 7057
Malahide Road Acupuncture and TCM Clinic	Malahide	01 832 8491
Michael McCarthy	Harold's Cross	01 497 8958
Raymond Hughes	Dublin 9	01 862 1188
Sue Saunders	Sandycove	01 280 3505

The most popular alternative treatments in Dublin are the longer-established treatments such as acupuncture and chiropractics. Reiki, reflexology and massage therapy are also popular, and most alternative clinics are constantly expanding the range of therapies on offer. Auricular candle therapy is now available in Dublin. This involves the insertion of a specially formulated candle into the ear canal, which provides beneficial suction to treat all sorts of ailments, and can be helpful used as a relaxation and stress relief technique. See the Well-Being section on p.266.

Acupuncture

There is a large Chinese population in Dublin, and traditional Chinese medicine (often called T.C.M.) is now highly visible and easily accessible. The Traditional Chinese Medicine Council of Ireland can provide a list of insured, registered practitioners who are approved by health insurance providers. Many GPs in Ireland are now qualified to administer acupuncture. However, GPs do not usually undergo as intensive or lengthy training as most acupuncturists, and may not always be the best option.

Aromatherapy

Aromatherapy is not that common in Dublin, and you are more likely to find an aromatherapist in a beauty salon than in a specialist practice. However, aromatherapy oils and supplies are widely available. You'll find Bach Rescue Remedy along with lots of similar products in almost any pharmacy and health food store (see Shopping, p.299).

139

Aromatherapy

Aromatherapy Health Care	Tallaght	01 400 0051
Donnybrook Medical Centre	Dublin 4	087 248 7802
Elite Health Studio	Dublin 3	01 658 4619
Nuala Woulfe Beauty Salon	Sandycove	01 230 0244
Shauna's Health Studio	Dublin 2	01 475 5738

Healing Meditation

Harvest Moon	Dublin 2	01 662 7556
Healing.ie	Dublin 9	01 882 8006
Inner Bliss	Dublin 4	087 202 1727

Homeopathy

Declan Hammond	Sandycove	01 202 0018
Dr Brendan Fitzpatrick	Dublin 4	01 269 7768
Dr James A Dolan	Dublin 5	01 833 5962
Michelle Bourke	Dublin 3	01 837 5459
Pauline O'Reilly	Dublin 2	086 629 7708
Ruth Appleby	Harold's Cross	01 491 0387
Sheelagh Behan	North Coast	01 846 1276

Reflexology & Massage Therapy

Ann Hanrahan	Dublin 9	01 804 0688
Beyond Harmony	Dun Laoghaire	01 202 0205
Greenlea Natural Health	Dublin 6	087 774 1852
Kathleen Hollingsworth	Dublin 5	01 848 1590
Magda Batista	Dublin 13	01 832 3777
Melt – Temple Bar	Dublin 2	01 679 8786
Sile Blount	Dublin 1	01 843 6904
Theraputic Bliss	Dublin 6 West	087 281 6068

Healing Meditation

It has been proven that regular meditation helps to relieve stress-related disorders, such as headaches, insomnia, PMS and some fertility issues. Although practiced in some Eastern faiths, the act of meditation itself is not necessarily religious. Meditation is usually practiced at home so it is difficult to say how popular it is, but there are many courses and centres around Dublin that teach the basic principles.

Homeopathy

Homeopathy – the use of minute quantities of active ingredients to stimulate the body's ability to heal itself – remains controversial in Ireland. There are two four-year training courses accredited by the Irish Society of Homeopaths, and a full list of registered and accredited members is available from the Society. There are also several GPs operating in Dublin who are qualified homeopaths.

Reflexology & Massage Therapy

Reflexology has been practised in Ireland since 1985, when the Society of Reflexologists (now the Irish Reflexologists' Institute) was formed. There are a number of reflexology training centres, and the IRI schools adhere to a common curriculum. A wide variety of massage therapies are also available, and include aromatherapy massage, Indian head massage, deep tissue, sports and Swedish massage (see the Well-Being section on p.266 for more). Infant massage has also been shown to be beneficial to babies (see p.245).

Addiction Counselling & Rehabilition

Addiction is a major issue in Irish society, and there are several options for people dealing with addiction problems. A number of conselling and rehabilitation programmes are available, both publicly and privately. If you wish to avail of the public services, your GP can refer you to an addiction counsellor for an assessment, and they will discuss whether in-patient or out-patient care is most suitable for you. In the case of private centres, some of the costs of these are likely to be covered by health insurance, but it is important to research this as aftercare is often excluded from cover. These 'courses' provide excellent care, but many recovering addicts need a more regular support system integrated into their daily lives. A wide range of Twelve-Step groups (AA, Al-Anon, Alateen, Adult Children of Alcoholics, NA, GA and OA particularly) are available in Dublin. Many of them have meetings in the main rehabilitation hospitals, which is especially helpful for former residents who

Addiction Counselling & Rehabilition

Al-Anon/Alateen	01 873 2699	na
Alcoholics Anonymous	01 453 8998	www.alcoholicsanonymous.ie
Gamblers' Anonymous	01 872 1133	www.gamblersanonymous.ie
The Hanly Centre	01 280 9795	www.thehanlycentre.ie
Narcotics Anonymous	01 672 8000	www.na.ireland.org
Obsessive Eaters Anonymous	01 289 1599	www.obsessiveeatersanonymous.org
The Rutland Centre	01 494 6358	www.rutlandcentre.ie
St John of God's Hospital	01 288 1781	www.iol.ie/~stjog/index.htm

140

Rehabilitation & Physiotherapy

Active Physiotherapy and Acupuncture	Dublin 2	01 678 7965
Dublin Physiotherapy Clinic	Dublin 11	01 882 9174
Dublin Spine and Sports Physiotherapy	Dublin 8	01 454 3335
Healing.ie – Glasnevin	Dublin 9	01 882 8006
O'Connell Physiotherapy & Sports Injury Clinic	Dublin 1	01 874 1464
Portobello Physiotherapy Clinic	Dublin 8	01 476 3330
Premier Physiotherapy	Dublin 16	01 296 4964
Riverside Medical Clinic	Dublin 15	01 646 7820
TotalPhysio	Booterstown	01 260 0344

may wish to retain a link with a familiar atmosphere in the early stages of their recovery. Meetings are also held in churches, parish halls, schools and other public spaces. Details about fellowship meetings can be obtained directly from the relevant organisation or by checking local notice-boards. See the table on p.140 for contact details for the various groups.

Rehabilitation & Physiotherapy

Most physiotherapists in Ireland have private practices. If you need physiotherapy as a public patient, you will need a referral from your GP and treatment will usually be as a hospital outpatient. Some of your physiotherapy fees should be covered by your health insurance, but check with your company in advance. You are entitled to claim tax relief on physiotherapy expenses over and above a certain amount. You can get the relevant claim forms from your local tax office.

Back Treatment

Back problems can be extremely debilitating, and Ireland's damp climate can often exacerbate problems, especially muscular ones. Sufferers in Dublin can avail of a variety of treatment options.

Back Treatment

Brenda Bower – Chiropractor	Dublin 9	01 857 3640
Donnybrook Medical Centre	Dublin 4	087 248 7802
Fingal Osteopathic & Sports Injuries Clinic	Malahide	086 400 3089
Fitzwilliam Health Clinic	Dublin 2	01 661 8949
Jean McDonald – CST	Various locations	01 272 2317
Nuala O'Rourke – CST	South Dublin	01 298 2642
Rathmines Chiropractic Clinic	Rathmines	01 491 0448
Stillorgan Chiropractic	Stillorgan	01 205 5550

Acupuncture and massage therapy can be helpful (see p.139 and p.140), particularly for pain relief, and chiropractors and osteopaths are widely available. Chiropractors focus on realigning the bones while osteopaths work on the soft tissue in the back; they sometimes provide massage. Craniosacral therapy (CST) is also available. To find a good practitioner, you can ask around friends and colleagues or obtain a list of practitioners from the relevant professional bodies. Chiropractic care and osteopathy are often covered by health insurance, although CST usually is not.

Nutritionists & Slimming

Losing weight can be very difficult, especially if you live or work in an environment in which convenience food dominates. Having some support can make a huge difference. There are plenty of Weight Watchers groups in Dublin, and you can find your local one at www.weightwatchers.ie. The also run several meetings in the city that are just for men. Exercise is an important aspect of weight loss, and Dublin gyms can be very expensive (see Leisure Facilities on p.263 for listings). Your local YMCA will have gym facilities and these tend to be far cheaper than most gyms. Some personal trainers will come to your home if you don't want to work out in the gym – see the table and listings on p.265 for fitness companies that offer home visits.

The Irish Nutrition and Dietetic Institute (INDI) have a very comprehensive website which allows you to search for nutritionists by both location and speciality (www.indi.ie). Several nutritionists specialise in digestive disorders, and your GP may be able to direct you to one.

Nutritionists & Slimming

Focus Fitness	087 974 2566
Geraldine McGuirk	01 841 2839
Grace Maclean	01 610 6345
Jill Sommerville	086 234 0359
MyPersonalTrainer.ie	087 127 6571
UniSlim	1850 603 020
Weight Watchers	1850 234 123

141

Counselling & Therapy

Mental health issues in Ireland are no longer as stigmatised as they were in the past, and the range of mental health facilities in Dublin is constantly improving. Most of the counselling that takes place in Ireland is in the private sector, although there are public health service psychologists. Some clinics specialise in eating disorders and some of the psychiatric hospitals, such as St John of God, are particularly well regarded for dealing with addiction. Other organisations provide marriage and family counselling, although many of these are church-sponsored so you may find it more beneficial to see a private therapist.

On moving to a foreign country, some people experience depression and culture shock. There are numerous ways to deal with this. You may find it useful to maintain close contact with family and friends at home (see p.126 for internet services and cheap overseas calls) or you may prefer to minimise contact for a short time while you settle in. There are a variety of ways to make friends and meet new people (see Social Groups on p.252, in the Activities chapter), and in Ireland it is not unusual to socialise with work colleagues. If you find that feelings of depression and loneliness persist, you can speak to your GP about the possibility of taking anti-depressants.

Some counsellors specialise in child behavioural issues such as ADHD. Your child's teacher or family doctor may be able to suggest somebody suitable, and if your child is of school-going age, they may be able to get extra academic help in school.

If you suffer from more serious psychiatric problems, consultant psychiatrists are available in all of the major hospitals, although you may need a referral from your GP to get an appointment. There are inpatient wards and outpatient facilities in most of the general hospitals, as well as in the specialist psychiatric hospitals. You can admit yourself to the psychiatric hospital if you feel that you are in urgent need of inpatient care.

Psychiatrists		
Dr Paul Scully	Dublin 8	01 416 2616
Dr Veronica O'Keane	Dublin 9	01 809 3354
Prof Patricia Casey	Dublin 7	01 803 2176
St Vincent's Hospital	Dublin 4	01 221 4884
St Loman's Hospital	Dublin 20	01 620 3401

> **Social Groups**
>
> It can be hard to settle in to a new city when you don't know many people – luckily, Dublin provides lots of opportunities to make friends. There are lots of social groups in the city, as well as sports clubs and evening classes, which are great places to meet people with the same interests as you. For more on this, see Social Groups (p.252) in Activities.

Support Groups

The Irish are famous for emigrating, but in the last 10 to 15 years the pattern has changed and people from all over the world are moving to Ireland to live and work. Expat support groups are not common, but you should be able to find and meet other expats easily. Noticeboards in local shops, churches, specialist grocery shops or restaurants and internet site forums can all provide points of contact and links to support and social groups. Life in Dublin is broadly similar to most other European cities, and culture shock is not usually severe if you are from Europe. For individuals and families affected by illness or disability, there are numerous

Counsellors/Psychologists		
Acacia Counselling Centre	Southwest Dublin	01 628 1012
Beaufield Centre	Blackrock	01 283 0000
Blanchardstown Counselling & Psychotherapy Services	Dublin 15	087 635 5545
Dubh Linn Counselling & Psychotherapy	Dublin 9	01 830 2358
Fitzwilliam Psychotherapy Practice	Dublin 2	01 661 4710
Jung Centre	Dublin 7	01 868 4363
Newlands Institute for Counselling	Dublin 22	01 459 4573

specialised support groups. New mums' groups (see p.134 and p.137), bereavement groups, widowed persons' associations (see table) and 12 Step groups (see Counselling on p.142) are available all across Dublin. You can find details of health-related support groups from your GP or local pharmacy.

Support Groups

Aware – Depression Support Group	1890 303 302
Irish Cancer Society	1800 200 700
Irish Heart Foundation	01 668 5001
Miscarriage Association of Ireland	01 873 5702
National Association of Widowers and Deserted Husbands	01 855 2334
National Association of Widows in Ireland	01 872 8814
Outhouse – GLBT Support Centre	01 873 4932

Government buildings

GPO on O'Connell Street

The Spire

Dublin Castle

Education

Busy At School

Some schools in Dublin run excursions, and parents will be asked to cover the cost of these. Secondary schools occasionally organise overnight trips or trips abroad - usually during Transition Year. Your child may also be required to attend some of the sporting, choir or debating competitions and events that their school is entered into.

The Irish education system is generally very good. Free education is available in state primary and post-primary schools, and all children living in Ireland can avail of this. There are also a number of private, fee-paying schools and some minority religions run specialist schools.

The quality of private schools can vary. Some are still run by religious groups, others are completely non-denominational. Some specialist private schools only cater for students in their final year or two of secondary school, and the focus is solely on exam subjects and achieving good results.

Each school has an enrolment policy drafted by their Board of Management, which is available on request (some schools make them available for downloading on their websites). In order to enrol your child in a school, you must produce a birth or adoption certificate. Although in theory you can enrol your child in the school of your choice, in practice there may be issues with availability, especially in the newer, heavily populated residential areas in which facilities haven't quite caught up with demand. If you need to enrol your child in the middle of a school year, every effort will be made to accommodate them in their local school if possible. It is a good idea to apply to several schools as far in advance as possible to ensure your child has a place in at least one of them. Most schools will give priority to prospective pupils who have a family association with the school (older siblings attending, a parent working there, a parent who was educated there, etc.), and to children living in that area. Class sizes can range from 20 pupils to 30 and over. Many secondary schools have affiliations with primary schools, sometimes sharing a campus or operating under the same name and shared facilities. These secondary schools tend to give priority to children coming from the affiliated primary school, so it is a good idea to research the enrolment policy of your preferred secondary school as early as possible.

Report Thought

If you wish to return to your home country after your child has attended an Irish school, you must get copies of results for any exams taken, and it is a good idea to keep any end-of-term school reports sent out by your child's teachers.

It is compulsory for children to attend school from age 6, but it is more usual for Irish children to start at the age of 4 or 5. They spend eight years in primary education and usually five or six in secondary education, and the normal school-leaving age is 17 or 18. The primary school curriculum focuses on development rather than scholastic achievement, and there is no standard exam taken at the end of primary school.

The secondary school curriculum includes English, Irish and Maths as compulsory subjects, and a variety of optional subjects focusing on foreign languages, science and business and art. Students take the Junior Certificate examination in their third year of secondary school, usually aged 15, and the Leaving Certificate examination at the end of their final year, aged 17 or 18. Copies of subject curricula are available from the Government Publications Office on Molesworth Street, Dublin 2, for about €3 each.

Finding A School

If you would like to get a list of the schools in your locality, the Department of Education's website (www.education.ie) allows you to do a search for all schools, including private schools, in your area. Otherwise, see Residential Areas, from p.80 onwards, for an idea of which schools are in your area.

Most schools will allow you to visit in order to see what facilities are available and many have open days so that new students and parents can get a feel for the school. The quality of teaching is generally consistent in schools in Dublin, but keep your ears peeled and you'll soon find out which ones are the most popular.

At secondary level, the range of subjects available, the teacher to student ratio and the number of teachers per subject are important factors to consider. Another good website with information on schools and listings of schools is www.learn4good.com and www.eirscoil.net has listings and numbers for every school in Ireland, with some website links.

Transition Year

An optional year is offered to secondary school students in Ireland called Transition Year or Fourth Year. This follows the Junior Certificate and allows students to take a break before preparation for the Leaving Certificate begins. No exam study is undertaken and it presents the useful opportunity to take modules in subjects that the student has not taken previously but might like to do for the Leaving Certificate. Some parents whose children started school aged 4 are in favour of Transition Year as it allows them to sit their Leaving Certificate with other pupils of their own age. Some schools offer creative or practical courses, such as cookery, dance or first aid. Transition Year is obligatory in some schools, which is an important thing to check at the enrolment stage. Students who do not take Transition Year go directly from third year to fifth year.

Thinking About The Future
Some state schools, such as Portmarnock Community College (01 846 0927) or Cabinteely Community School (01 284 7145), have especially good reputations as 'feeder' schools to further education.

School Hours & Holidays

The school week runs from Monday to Friday inclusive, and some secondary schools also have a half-day on Saturdays but finish earlier than other schools during the week to compensate. The school day in primary schools usually lasts for a total of five hours and forty minutes, including breaks. Many schools allow children in their first two years of primary school to finish an hour earlier. Schools close for the months of July and August, and for two weeks every Christmas and Easter, with another week off in October, usually incorporating the October bank holiday. There is also a mid-term break of two days' duration in February, but some schools extend this to a full week off. Secondary schools are broadly similar, although the summer break begins in the first week of June to allow the Junior and Leaving Certificate exams to take place later that month.

Nurseries & Pre-Schools

Childcare in Ireland is always a big issue, as there is a shortage of affordable creche places. Many parents of babies and toddlers engage a private childminder to look after their children either in the children's home or in the childminder's. This can be quite expensive if you go through an agency for a registered childminder. You can also find them through The National Child-Minders' Association (01 287 8466) although many childminders are unregistered, so word of mouth is also useful.

Full-time creches are also expensive, although the cost usually drops as the child gets older and requires less care. Some creches will accept babies as soon as statutory maternity leave is finished, but this depends on their resources, as there are strict age-specific adult to child ratios. Normal hours are from 07:00 or 07:30 until 19:00. The National Children's Nurseries Association (01 872 2051) will provide a list of member nurseries in your area and a booklet with advice on choosing a nursery free of charge. Some public facilities like hospitals and shopping malls have drop-in centres for short-term supervision.

There is no statutory qualification that all childcare workers must have, although some first-aid training is expected. When you first visit a creche or a nursery, ask about the qualifications and experience of the staff until you are satisfied.

Montessori creches are available and these keep usual creche opening hours. There are also a number of private schools that use the Montessori system, which usually take children from age 4 until 7 or 8 years old, but these schools adhere to strict hours and do not usually provide after-school care. Be prepared for some contagious childhood illnesses when a child first starts going a creche or pre-

Nurseries & Pre-Schools		
Beginners' World Creche and Pre-School	Dublin 1	01 836 5844
BO Peeps Creche and Montessori	Dublin 1	01 668 6356
Fitzwilliam Nusery and Montessori School	Dublin 2	01 639 8982
Giraffe Childcare and Early Learning Centre	Dublin 1	1850 211 099
Harcourt Creche	Dublin 2	01 478 3361
Laethe Gréine	Dublin 2	01 644 9413
Once Upon A Time	Dublin 2	01 661 9187
YMCA Creche and Montessori	Dublin 2	01 478 2607

145

school, and keep a close eye on them for the first few weeks as they settle in.
The cost of childcare in Ireland is very high, averaging €180 per week for one child, although you will probably get a discount (usually around 10%) for a second child. Prices generally increase by about 10% per year too. Private childminders can be less costly option, especially if you find someone who takes care of a few children in their own home.

Primary & Secondary Schools

If you move to Ireland before your child starts school, enrolling them in a school is relatively easy. Priority is given to children living locally and to children who have a familial link to the school. Primary school children are not required to take an entrance exam, and most schools arrange for incoming pupils to visit the school in June of the year of entry to see what their classroom looks like and to allow the parents to ask any questions they may have.

If your child needs to enrol in the middle of the school year, you may need to go for a family interview and satisfy the school that you are living in their catchment area. The procedure is similar if your child wishes to change schools for any reason, but a child will not usually be allowed to change schools in the final year of primary school for any reason other than moving house.

Most secondary schools will ask all incoming students to sit an entrance exam, but this is usually to assess ability rather than to secure admission. Some schools subdivide years into classes based on ability, others base class divisions on timetabling and subject choice.

The secondary school curriculum includes English, Irish and Maths as compulsory subjects, although it is possible to apply to your child's school principal for a certificate of exemption from Irish if your child has spent a certain number of years abroad, or if English is not their first language. Exemptions can also be obtained for some specific learning disabilities. Other subjects offered include practical ones, such as woodwork, metalwork and home economics; creative subjects such as art and music; human sciences, laboratory sciences and European languages.

Even in the city, most schools have outdoor facilities for break times and for sport, as well as covered sports halls.

Most state and church schools ask parents for a voluntary financial contribution each year, which can range from €50 to €300. While these are voluntary, some schools may put pressure on parents to pay them. Fee-paying schools can range from €2,000 to €7,000 per year for day pupils, and fees for boarders can soar to €15,000 per year, depending on the school. All schools, state or private, will ask for occasional contributions towards excursions, photocopying or facilities, but these are usually only small amounts.

Most Irish schools have uniforms, at both primary and post-primary level. Some of these are purchased directly from the school and some from specialist outlets. They can add on quite a significant cost so make sure to factor this into your fee calculations. Parents also meet the cost of all schoolbooks. Families on lower incomes can apply for allowances.

Milltown
Dublin 6
Map 420 C2 **540**

Alexandra College

01 497 7571 | www.alexandracollege.ie

'Alex' as it is fondly referred to is an all-girls Church of Ireland primary and secondary boarding and day school. Founded in 1866, it has played, and indeed still plays an important role in women's education in Ireland. Students from all over the world and of different religious beliefs are educated in this school, providing a very international mix. A wide range of subjects are offered, and sporting activities such as hockey, tennis and basketball are widely encouraged. A foreign language is part of the curriculum and must be taken by all students up to Leaving Certificate level, options include French, German, Italian, Spanish and Japanese.

79-85 Lower
Leeson St
Dublin 2
Map 430 C4 **540**

The Institute Of Education
01 661 3511 | *www.ioe.ie*
The Institute of Education accepts pupils for their last year or two years of secondary school only. This school focuses entirely on exam preparation and maximising Leaving Certificate results. Indeed, many students who do not get the required points for entry into their chosen university often repeat their Leaving Certificate here and the school has a good reputation. Religion and physical education are not taught and there is no uniform. Supervised study is a major part of the school day and there is a great deal of flexibility in timetabling. Fees for the academic year 2007/2008 were €6,350 per annum.

Kilmashogue La
Whitechurch
Dublin 16

Saint Columba's College
01 490 6791 | *www.stcolumbas.ie*
Saint Columba's College is one of Ireland's oldest private schools and it has an excellent reputation. This secondary school accepts male and female pupils from the ages of 11 to 18. Facilities available on their 140-acre campus include an outdoor swimming pool, five hard tennis courts and a golf course. The school also has a number of extra-curricular societies for drama, music and art. The pupil to teacher ratio averages 10:1 and fees range from €3,000 per term for day pupils to over €5,000 per term for boarders.

Ballinteer Rd
Ballinteer
Dublin 16

Wesley College
01 298 7066 | *www.wesleycollege.ie*
Wesley College is a co-educational day and boarding school. Although it is nominally a Methodist school, they welcome students from all religious backgrounds. Pupils can attend as day pupils or else chose to board for either five or seven nights a week. Fees for students from the EU range from €4,990 for day pupils to €6,800 for five-day boarders and €7,850 for seven-day boarders. Non-EU students can expect to pay from €5,740 for day pupils to €7,820 for five-day boarders or €9,030 for seven-day boarders.

University & Higher Education
Higher education in Ireland is generally very good. All citizens who have been ordinarily resident in an EU member state for five years are eligible for 'Free Fees' for their first undergraduate course. The only cost is the annual registration fee and books; the Irish government covers the rest. The vast majority of recognised courses are eligible for the scheme, but it is always a good idea to check. Registration fees are currently around €900 per year. For this reason, many expats send their children to Irish universities, as it is extremely cost-effective. Students from outside the EU who are not residents can expect to pay fees of up to €15,000 per year. Families on lower incomes can apply for a means-tested grant through their local authority. Several institutions offer scholarships to high-achievers.

University admission is coordinated by the Central Applications Office (CAO) rather than by individual institutions (see p.149). Foreign passport holders or students with learning disabilities may be exempted from the compulsory Leaving Certificate subjects (Irish, English and Maths), or at least be allowed to take exams at Foundation level, and it is vital to make sure that you inform the CAO and the institutions to which you have applied if you are exempt. Irish universities are willing

147

to consider applicants with school leaving exams from other countries with a comparable curriculum, although they may ask for a certain level of proven proficiency in English.

Some courses also demand certain grades in relevant subjects. Engineering and computer science courses will expect a minimum of a C grade on the Higher Level Maths paper, for example. You can contact the admissions office of your chosen university for the entrance requirements for any of their courses.

College life is great fun and is incredibly social. There are regular student nights in Dublin pubs and most universities and colleges organise their own social evenings on campus. Dublin also has a wealth of cultural resources and some excellent public libraries (see p.244), making it a very satisfying place to study.

Adult Education

Whether you are studying simply out of interest or to further your career, there's a night class in Dublin for you. Many universities run adult education programmes, and classes vary between those that are simply undertaken out of interest while others count towards certificates and credits. Your local secondary school or Vocational Education Committee school (VEC) are also good places to start looking. Costs vary widely, depending on the nature of the class and the institution. Nightcourses.com releases a biannual guide to adult education in Dublin, which comes out in the spring and autumn. You can purchase these in any newsagent for about €5. The content gives full details of the duration, times, location, cost and qualifications gained of any listed course. Their website is also very comprehensive, www.nightcourses.com. If you are not a native speaker of English, there are lots of English classes around the city, but be mindful that the most expensive course is not necessarily the best and stick to reputable course providers, see table below.

Just Do It

Make a decision to finally learn that skill you've always wished you'd had. Check out the listings for Music Lessons (p.247), Flower Arranging (p.237), Language Schools (p.242) and Dance Classes (p.233) and discover all your hidden talents.

International Student Visas

If you wish to study in Ireland, you may need to apply for a student visa. In order to do so, you will need to produce proof that you have been offered the course, that you have paid the fees, that you have a sufficient level of English to complete the course and you may have to satisfy the government of your financial stability. Student visas allow you to undertake a certain amount of part-time and holiday work. Not every international student needs to obtain a visa to study here. Full details can be obtained from the Department of Justice (www.justice.ie).

Higher Education

National College of Ireland	Dublin 1	01 4498 500	www.ncirl.ie
Balsbridge College of Further Education	Dublin 4	01 668 4806	www.ballsbridgecollege.com
Dublin Business School	Dublin 2	01 417 7500	www.dbs.ie
Dundrum College	Dublin 14	01 298 2340	www.dundrumcollege.ie
Griffith College	Dublin 8	01 415 04 00	www.gcd.ie
Inchicore College of Further Education	Dublin 8	01 453 5358	www.inchicorecollege.ie
Institute of Art and Design	Dun Laoghaire	01 214 4600	www.iadt.ie
Portobello College	Dublin 2	01 475 5811	www.portobello.ie
Rathmines College	Dublin 6	01 497 5334	www.rathminescollege.ie
Sandford Language Institute	Dublin 6	01 260 1296	www.sandfordlanguages.ie
St Patrick's College Drumcondra (teacher training)	Dublin 9	01 884 2000	www.spd.dcu.ie

Universities

Ballymunn Rd
Dublin 9
Map 408 C2 544

Dublin City University

01 700 5566 | www.dcu.ie

DCU is a relatively new university. Its campus is constantly undergoing development and as a result it boasts extremely modern and up-to-date facilities, including a good sports centre. The humanities faculty is small but both the undergraduate and postgraduate journalism degrees offered are particularly well-regarded, as is the BSc in Computer Applications and the BA in Applied Languages. Degrees in medicine are not offered. The campus is also home to The Helix theatre.

Various Locations
Map 416 B4 539

Dublin Institute of Technology

01 402 3000 | www.dit.ie

DIT is not technically a university, although it has the power to award degrees. It is composed of several individual campuses dotted around the city centre – Mountjoy Square, Rathmines, Cathal Brugha Street, Kevin Street, Bolton Street and Aungier Street are the main ones. DIT's humanities faculty is industry-focused and although wide ranging, does not offer degrees in any pure arts subjects such as philosophy or literature. DIT degrees are highly regarded and their courses are well respected. Part-time courses are also an option.

100 Thomas St
Dublin 8
Map 429 D1 5

National College Of Art and Design (NCAD)

01 636 4200 | www.ncad.ie

The National College of Art and Design is Ireland's most highly regarded and prestigious school of art, with courses ranging from fine arts to fashion design, ceramics, textile design and visual communication. Admission requirements vary depending on the course, and as some courses require submission of a portfolio, it is important to research this as early as possible. They also run taught MA programmes and accept postgraduate students for research degrees at masters and doctoral levels.

College Green
Dublin 2
Map 426 B4 541

Trinity College Dublin

01 896 1000 | www.tcd.ie

Based in the heart of the south city centre, Trinity is the oldest university in the State and one of the most prestigious. It is also a significant tourist attraction, for its grounds, as well as the fact that it is home to the Book of Kells and Ireland's oldest library. The university has roughly 15,000 students and offers a range of degree programmes across all major disciplines. There are a few scholarships for students with exceptional Leaving Certificate results.

CAO

The Central Applications Office, based in Galway, deal with all university admissions. Prospective students must fill out a CAO form prior to February 1 of the proposed year of admission. It is very important to list the courses you are applying for according to preference rather than expected grades.

Admission is then based on the results of the Leaving Certificate exam. Each grade corresponds to a certain number of points. The applicants with the highest total points for a given course will be offered a place, which they can choose to accept or reject. The CAO application system is quite complex and involves a lot of paperwork. Full details are available from your guidance counsellor or your school, and the CAO website, www.cao.ie, is excellent and very comprehensive. If you are unsure about any aspect of the procedure, always ask someone.

Most universities will ask that mature students (over 23), and applicants with school-leaving qualifications from other countries (such as A-levels) apply directly to them as well as to the CAO. Information for non-standard applicants should be requested from the institution. Courses that require the submission of a portfolio (art or graphic design, for instance) or that request an audition (such as music performance or drama) will also expect you to apply directly to them.

Belfield
Dublin 4
Map 421 E2 542

University College Dublin

01 716 0000 | *www.ucd.ie*

UCD is Ireland's largest university, with over 20,000 students from undergraduate to doctoral level. The university offers courses in the fields of arts, life science, social science, engineering, law and business. The newly launched Horizons programme, which began in 2005, allows students to take modules from disciplines other than their own. The campus has some on-site accommodation, a sports centre, recreation facilities and two bars.

Special Needs Education

If your child has special needs, there are a number of options available to you. The majority of children in Ireland with special needs are educated in your average school, some in specialist classes but others in mainstream classrooms. Learning support teachers are available to all schools and can help schools to assess children who may have special needs, as well as providing extra schooling. There are also resource teachers available to children with low-incidence special needs, although the school must make an individual application for such help if the class teacher and learning support teachers feel it is necessary. If your child needs non-teaching assistance in order to attend school, Special Needs Assistants (SNAs) can be engaged to help pupils to eat, use the bathroom or with any other aspect of the school day. Depending on the pupils and the school, they may be hired on a part-time basis or attend to more than one child. The government will help with funding for parents who need to educate their child at home (in case of chronic illness, for instance). If your child is awaiting placement in a suitable school, you can still avail of this service. For Special Needs Sports, see p.252.

Templeogue Rd
Dublin 6 West
Map 419 D4 553

Cheeverstown House

01 490 4681

Cheeverstown House is a charitable voluntary organisation based in Templeogue that provides special needs education and familial support to over 400 people with intellectual disabilities. The organisation specialises in providing services for adults and children with severe or profound disabilities, and offers residential facilities, respite care and support services as well as education. There is also a sister organisation, Cheeverstown Families and Friends, for those affected by a loved one's learning disability.

Obelisk Park
Carysfort Ave
Blackrock
Map 422 B4 551

Saint Augustine's School

01 288 1771 | *staugustines@sjog.ie*

Saint Augustine's is located in Blackrock in south Dublin and offers a five-day residential service for boarders as well as a day-school. They cater for pupils with mild general special educational needs. The school is co-educational and there are a total of 160 places, and children aged between six and 18 are accepted. The school also provides some vocational training and has some recreational facilities.

Grace Park Rd
Drumcondra
Dublin 9
Map 408 C4 549

Saint Joseph's School For The Visually Impaired

01 837 3635 | *www.stjosephsvi.ie*

Saint Joseph's offers a full assessment service for visually impaired children, and complete educational facilities from pre-school to Leaving Certificate. Pobailscoil Rosmini provides fully inclusive secondary education in association with St. Joseph's. Residential facilities are available for pupils from Sunday evening to Friday afternoon. The school also offers a three-year vocational course for those aged 16 or over who are visually impaired and have additional needs.

Saint Josephs School For Deaf Boys

Navan Rd
Drumcondra
Dublin 9
Map 407 E4 **550**

01 838 0058 | *www.stjosephsboys.ie*
Saint Josephs caters for boys with hearing impairments. They accept pupils from primary school until Leaving Certificate level and they cater for both day pupils and boarders. Boarders are accommodated in six houses on the school campus. Facilities include a swimming pool, gymnasium and snooker tables. Transport to the school is provided from major bus terminals and train stations. The school also runs a pre-employment course which includes work experience.

Saint Mary's School For Deaf Girls

Dominican Convent
Cabra
Dublin 7
Map 407 E3 **548**

01 838 5359 | *www.stmarysdeafgirls.ie*
St. Mary's school is actually composed of Marian primary school, for girls aged four to 14, and Rosary school, for post-primary. Both schools welcome severe and profoundly deaf girls of all abilities and prepare students for all state exams. There is a lot of emphasis on extra-curricular activities and facilities for sport and recreation are extremely good. Residential housing for students is available adjacent to the school.

Saint Michael's House

Ballymun Rd
Dublin 9

01 884 0200 | *www.smh.ie*
St. Michael's House is a voluntary organisation running special needs schools. They have schools based on Grosvener Road (Dublin 6), in Hackettstown in Skerries (North County Dublin) and on the Raheny Road in Dublin 5. They specialise in providing services for adults and children with more serious general learning disabilities. They offer education, counselling and clinical care, social and recreational sports, early services, employment aid, respite services, among others. Children's learning needs are outlined in advance with their parents so that they can monitor their development and meet their goals.

Scoil Chiaran

St Canice's Rd
Glasnevin
Dublin 9
Map 408 A2 **552**

01 837 0622
Scoil Chiarain is classified as a school for pupils with mild general learning disabilities. They cater for children aged between five and eighteen. There are just 14 places available each year and as the school has a good reputation, there is a waiting list for applicants. Prospective pupils need to undergo an assessment by the National Educational Psychological Service prior to admission. If your child is currently in school and you wish for them to transfer, you should speak with their present teacher about their needs to find out how to proceed.

Trinity College

Transportation

Other options **Car** p.39, **Getting Around** p.37

Dublin is well serviced by public transport, although unlike many European countries, it is not particularly known for its punctuality or reliability. Trains are usually predictable enough although the odd set of leaves on the track or line-fault can cause disruption. Buses however, which are victims of the city's ever-increasing traffic congestion, can be haphazard – you might wait for one for ages and then four come along at once. However buses can use bus lanes and some routes are on dedicated Quality Bus Corridors (QBCs) so it really depends on the service, how often it runs and how much traffic it has to get through. Busy routes like the 7, 46A and 15 have regular buses whereas routes like the 5 to Sandyford have only five departures per day during the week.

Bus

Bus services in Dublin city and surrounding areas are run by Dublin Bus. Adult fares go from €1.00 to €4.10 and are worked out according to the distance travelled. Children's fares (under 16) are €0.70 or €0.90. Dublin Bus operates an exact fare system – if you don't have change you will have to pay over the ticket price and you'll get a change ticket which you can redeem at the Dublin Bus headquarters on O'Connell Street. It is also possible to buy prepaid daily, weekly and monthly tickets. The Nitelink late-night bus service runs from the city centre to the suburbs, starting at 00:30 and running every hour or so until about 04:30. Tickets are €4 or €6 and the service does not run on Sundays.

Bus Éireann operates intercity coach services from Dublin to cities and major towns in Ireland and Northern Ireland. Fares are reasonable – Dublin to Cork is €10.50 (€18.00 return), Donegal €17.50 (€27), Galway €14 (€18), Sligo €17.50 (€26.50) and Belfast €14 (€20). There are also a number of private bus operators on busy national routes. It is illegal to smoke on Dublin Bus and Bus Éireann services. For more information on routes and timetables, see www.dublinbus.ie or www.buseireann.ie.

Dart

The Dart suburban rail service runs from Malahide and Howth in north county Dublin, around Dublin Bay and southwards to Greystones in County Wicklow. Adult fares go from €1.20 to €3.70, depending on the distance travelled and the age of the commuter, and weekly and monthly tickets are available. See www.irishrail.ie.

Luas

There are two Luas light rail lines. The Green Line runs from St Stephen's Green to Sandyford with a total journey time of 22 minutes, and the Red Line runs from Busáras bus station to Tallaght in southwest Dublin, taking approximately 46 minutes. Adult fares go from €1.25 to €2.20, depending on the number of zones travelled. Prepaid tickets are also available. See www.luas.ie.

Rail

There are various suburban rail options from Dublin – the Arrow commuter rail service runs from Heuston Station to Kildare; the Northern Suburban rail runs from Connolly Station to Dundalk, the southeastern suburban service runs to Arklow, and the Western suburban service runs to Sligo. It is possible to connect with some of the suburban services from the Dart line – for example the Maynooth train stops at Lansdowne Road. Many commuter rail routes, particularly those to Kildare and Meath, become particularly crowded during morning and evening rush hour with standing room only.

Iarnród Éireann's intercity trains are convenient but expensive – a direct train to Cork takes 2 hours and 45 minutes, however a single one-way ticket costs €56.50 and a return is €61. Galway (just under 3 hours) costs either €30 or €42, Sligo is €25.50 or €36 and Belfast is €34.50. For more information see www.irishrail.ie.

Driving

Driving around the city is not too bad; if you can deal with the traffic congestion and one-way systems in the city centre. Parking in the city is difficult though. It's expensive and convenient spaces are scarce during busy periods. In most suburbs especially near the city, parking is pay and display, although residents can apply for a residents parking permit for an annual fee. If you park illegally or don't pay for parking, you risk being clamped and will receive an €80 fine. There are a number of city centre car parks that offer hourly or daily rates, although these are expensive, and some companies and apartments rent spaces by the month or year. If you do park in a pay and display area for the day during business hours, you will need to make sure you keep the payments topped up to avoid being clamped.

Cycling

There are a number of cycle lanes throughout the city, although cycling is a bit of a dice with cars, trucks, buses and other obstacles blocking up the lanes, pulling in and out without indicating and generally not leaving enough room. Cycling is a convenient way to get around – as it avoids traffic congestion – but you need to have your wits about you to avoid injury. Helmets are not compulsory but lights at night are.

Taxis

Taxis, although expensive are subject to fare control and a new fare structure, which came into effect in September 2006. This consists of an initial charge of €3.80 (€4.10 between 20:00 and 08:00 on Sundays and public holidays) plus a charge for the distance travelled or time taken, and extra charges, such as booking fees or extra passengers, where applicable. Taxis can use bus lanes during business hours, which is an advantage if you're in a hurry.

You can hail a taxi on the street (if the roof light is on it means the taxi is available); at a taxi rank or else book one by telephone, although punctuality is not always guaranteed, especially during busy periods when the company might tell you they 'don't have a driver in the area'. Booking through your company's taxi account is a good way to avoid this, especially if you need taxis for work.

Driving In Dublin

The main challenge with driving in Dublin is traffic congestion, especially during morning and evening rush hour. Driving in Dublin is not cheap – the cost of cars plus motor tax, motor insurance, driving licence, NCT test, parking and petrol are all expensive compared with many other countries, and once you factor in servicing and repairs, it can add up to a considerable sum. In 2007, the AA estimated that the cost of motoring for a vehicle up to 1000cc costs 59 cents per kilometre to run, with a vehicle of over 3,000cc costing €1.35 per kilometre to run. Over the past year, petrol prices have been creeping up, with costs hitting an average of €1.17 per litre during May, June and July of 2007. Also, as a result of the housing boom, many petrol stations around the city have been closing to make way for development.

Although car tax, insurance and petrol are not cheap, with the Irish economy boom which started in the 1990s, car sales went through the roof and there seemed no shortage of cash to spend on motoring. Although the city is relatively small, a lot of Dubliners like to own a car, even if they use public transport for work. This enables

Car Security

Car thefts and car break-ins are a problem throughout the city – don't leave anything visible in your car and try not to leave anything valuable at all. If you must leave a bag or container, put it in the boot, making sure nobody sees you, and keep car doors and boots locked while driving and when the car is unattended. Many cars are fitted with immobilisers and alarms.

them to drive in and out of the suburbs for socialising, shopping, hobbies and sports activities, school runs and various errands, as well as getting out of the city at the weekend, and many households own more than one car.

To drive in Dublin, you must have a valid driving licence, which should be carried at all times, plus valid motor insurance and motor tax (see p.157) and the vehicle must have an up to date NCT certificate. Car pooling hasn't really taken off in Dublin although people do work out informal arrangements and pool school runs. The website www.dublintraffic.ie provides a platform for people to set pooling schemes up.

There are no free parking spaces in the city Monday to Saturday. Parking in the city until 19:00 is either pay and display, which can cost from €1.00 an hour up to €2.70, or public car parks which are around €5 per hour. In larger suburbs and those near the city centre, street parking is also pay and display. Residents can apply to their local authority for a parking permit. For the Dublin City Council area, a permit costs €70 for one year and €130 for two years, and for a permit, you will need to show evidence of residency at the address, such as utility bills and a motor insurance policy in your name. If you fail to pay for parking you can be clamped, and clamping vans go around regularly to check. It costs €80 to remove a clamp and if you don't pay the fine, after 24 hours your vehicle will be taken to a pound.

Driving Habits

Congestion and traffic jams keep traffic moving at snail's pace within the city centre, but once out on the main raods outside the city limits it's a different story. Accidents and road deaths are frequent on Irish roads and the Road Safety Authority, gardai and other organisations run high visibility campaigns to counteract problems such as speeding and drink driving.

Non-Drivers

Footpaths and pavements run alongside most Dublin roads, keeping pedestrians away from traffic. There are pedestrian crossings at most traffic lights. Some roads and streets have cycle lanes, although many take up part of a vehicle lane so cars and buses must overtake the cyclist by changing lane. As in many cities, there is a healthy disrespect between car drivers and cyclists, with car drivers complaining that cyclists weave in and out of traffic, and cyclists complaining that cars leave them no room.

Traffic Rules & Regulations

The Rules Of The Road booklet is published by the Road Safety Authority. It can be purchased for €4 in shops, and in late 2007, the authority started sending a copy of the booklet to all households in the country.

Driving in Ireland is on the left-hand side of the road and vehicles overtake on the right. Seatbelts are compulsory for all passengers and using a mobile phone while driving is an offence. If you are changing lanes, give way to traffic already in that lane. You must stop at a stop sign, even if the way seems clear and traffic must keep to the left of single or double white lines in the centre of the road at all times. You can cross a broken line, if safe to do so.

Bus lanes are reserved for buses, taxis and bicycles during certain hours of the day, usually from 07:00 until 19:00, and driving in a bus lane during these times can incur penalty points. You must not enter a yellow box junction unless you can leave it without stopping. A double yellow line on the side of a road means no parking at any time, while a single yellow line means no parking during certain hours.

There are different speed limits for different roads. The main speed limits are 50 kmph for roads in built up areas, cities and towns; 80 kmph for non-national roads; 100kmph for national roads and 120kmph for motorways. There are speed cameras on some roads and Gardai also use equipment to spot check if vehicles are within the speed limit.

If you park illegally, especially in the city centre, expect to get clamped or worse, towed away to the vehicle pound. The clamp removal fee is €80 and impound fees are charged per day. If you are parked dangerously, you can also be prosecuted and incur penalty points.

Ireland operates a penalty points system for traffic offences – see Traffic Fines & Offences on p.158.

Drink Driving ◀

Drink Driving
The legal blood/alcohol limit in Ireland is 80 milligrams of alcohol per 100 millilitres of blood. Gardaí carry out random breath tests and drivers convicted of drink driving are disqualified from driving from between one and six years. You may also be fined up to €5,000, sentenced to prison and will have penalty points added to your licence.

Petrol Stations

The main petrol station chains in Dublin are Esso, Maxol, Shell and Statoil, with smaller chains including Texaco and Applegreen, as well as many independently owned stations. Stations sell both petrol and diesel. Due to high property prices and the construction boom, filling stations in the city centre are few and far between and many stations in the suburbs have also started disappearing to make way for development. Most petrol stations are self-service and will contain water/air services and convenience shops, and some have car washes.

Petrol in Ireland, along with the rest of the Euro Zone, is expensive. In July 2007, a litre of unleaded petrol costs on average 117.8 cents and diesel was 109 cents per litre – this compares with 1.06 cents in Greece and 1.41 cents in Belgium during the same period. In the USA, the equivalent cost in euro for petrol was 62 cents per litre and for diesel 58 cents, while in the UK it was 1.44 cents and 1.45 cents respectively.

Driving Habits

With traffic congestion, delays and everybody rushing about, Dublin drivers have become increasingly aggressive and road rage is abundant – it's not uncommon to witness horn-honking and rude hand gestures. One of the worst habits of Dublin drivers, and the cause of many of these angry exchanges, is pulling in or out without looking, or failure to signal, especially on roundabouts. Some drivers seem oblivious to other drivers and fail to signal or inform those behind of their intentions, which often leads to nasty accidents. When approaching a roundabout, you should signal appropriately to indicate where you intend to exit.

Vehicle Leasing

The vehicle leasing market in Dublin is mostly for corporate and company cars, although this is changing, with the emergence of a small market for private leasing of cars for individuals, influenced by similar systems in the US. You can lease a vehicle for a number of months up to a number of years, and you will need to have an Irish bank account. If you're a foreign national, a copy of your passport may be required.

If it is a corporate or company lease, the company arranges all documentation and paperwork. If your employer provides you with a company car, you will be liable for 'Benefit In Kind' tax on the car. Rates vary, so contact your local tax office for more information or see ww.revenue.ie.

Buying A Vehicle

It is possible to buy a car for practically any budget, although since the National Car Test (NCT) came into effect in 2000, a mandatory test for vehicles every two years, the more unroadworthy wrecks have disappeared off the roads.

As well as many new and second-hand car dealers around the city, there are popular car websites and you'll see classified ads in newspapers, where both dealers and private sellers can advertise and cars can also be bought at auction. Weekly car magazines include *Car Buyer's Guide* and *Auto Trader*, with websites www.carzone.ie, www.cbg.ie, and www.autotrader.ie all having large amounts of motor listings.

If you are buying through a dealer, it's better to use one that is registered with the Society of Motor Industry (SIMI). You have more legal and consumer rights buying a car from a dealer than buying privately.

Car Rental Agents		
Avis Fleet Services	01 866 0520	www.avisfleetservices.ie
Caroll & Kinsella	01 460 6070	www.carrollkinsella.com
Fleet First Contract Hire	1850 353 383	www.fleetfirst.ie
Gowan Leasing	01 617 4100	www.gowanleasing.com
Leaseplan Fleet Management	01 240 7600	www.leaseplan.ie
Murphy & Gunn Leasing	01 406 8600	www.murphygunn.com
Premier Fleet	01 405 0505	www.premierfleet.ie
Walden Leasing	01 864 9300	www.waldenleasing.ie
Westland Motor Group	1850 605 511	www.westland.ie

Vehicles are registered by year so a '04' vehicle will be four years old in 2008. Shop around and get to know the prices for different models and years – there's a good guide to new car prices under 'new cars' at www.carzone.ie.

Buying Privately

Buying a car privately will almost certainly guarantee a cheaper price than from a dealer, although you will have to take the seller's word for the car's history and whether it has been involved in an accident, and you will have no come-back if there are faults found after the purchase. For this reason, it is a good idea to have the vehicle inspected by a mechanic, and the AA (Automobile Association) offers a range of vehicle inspection services, including quick checks from €225 and full, in-depth inspections from €336.

You can check that there is no hire purchase owed on a vehicle by contacting the Hire Purchase Information Centre at 01 260 0905. If there are payments outstanding, the car is still legally the property of the hire purchase company. The search fee is €15. Buying a car privately is straightforward enough – make sure you get the vehicle registration certificate or log book and details for the change of ownership form, which should be sent in to the local motor tax office. You can download the relevant forms and information at www.motortax.ie.

Importing A Car

If you're importing a car, you will need to register it with the Revenue Commissioners and pay Vehicle Registration Tax (VRT), based on the open market selling price, at your local Vehicle Registration Office (VRO). In Dublin, there are two VRO's, at St John's

New Car Dealers

Alfa Romeo, Fiat	J Donohoe Dublin Ltd	01 621 5000	na
Alfa, Chevrolet , Fiat, Opel, Ssangyong Audi, Mazda, Mercedes Benz,	Airton Motor Centre Ltd	01 463 2622	www.airton.ie
Porsche, Volkswagen	Belgard Motors	01 404 9999	www.belgard.ie
Audi, Volkswagen	Foster Motor Company Limited	01 288 4333	www.fostermotorco.ie
BMW	Murphy & Gunn Milltown Ltd	01 283 0580	www.mgunn.ie
BMW, Mini	Maxwell Motors Ltd	01 288 5085	www.maxwellmotorsbmw.ie
Chevrolet, Ssangyong	Airside Chevrolet (Fangar Ltd)	01 813 2066	www.airsidechevrolet.com
Chevrolet, Ssangyong	Kylemore Chevrolet	01 439 5500	www.kylemorechevrolet.ie
Chrysler Jeep, Dodge	Alasta Auto Engineers Ltd	01 660 3982	www.alastaautos.com
Citroen, Subaru	Bursey – Peppard Ltd	01 456 1022	www.burseypeppardltd.ie
Ford	Airside Ford	01 870 8900	www.airsideford.ie
Honda, Volvo	Tom Canavan Motors	01 836 4433	www.tomcanavanmotors.ie
Hyundai	Kingstown Motors Ltd	01 278 2000	www.kingstownmotors.ie
Land Rover, Volvo	H B Dennis Airside	01 870 1400	www.dennis.ie
Lexus, Toyota	Carroll & Kinsella Motors Ltd	01 288 8624	www.ckb.ie
Lexus, Toyota	Denis Mahony Limited	01 832 2701	www.denismahony.ie
Mercedes Benz, Volkswagen	Ballsbridge Motors	01 665 6600	www.ballsbridgemotors.ie
Mitsubishi, Kia	Michael Tynan Motors	01 403 6700	www.tynanmotors.ie
Nissan	Windsor Airside	01 870 8700	www.windsor.ie
Opel	Crosson Cars Ltd	01 890 1122	www.crossoncars.ie
Peugeot	Westland Motor Group Limited	01 605 5111	www.westland.ie
Renault	Citygate Renault	01 883 0500	www.renault.ie
Renault, Mazda	Sandyford Motor Centre	01 206 9200	www.sandyfordmotorcentre.com
Saab	Faichney Ringwood Ltd	01 293 0055	www.faichneyringwood.ie
Seat	Bill Sheehan & Sons	01 497 0123	www.billsheehan.webzone.ie
Skoda	Phoenix Motorcar Company Ltd	01 838 0799	www.phoenixmotors.ie
Subaru	Carroll & Roche Cars	01 464 2444	www.carrollrochesubaru.com
VW, Audi, Mercedes, Skoda, Smart	Motor Services Ltd	01 409 4444	www.msl.ie

156

House, High Street, Tallaght, (01 414 9700) or Unit H, Furry Park Industrial Estate in Santry (01 414 9700). The registration must be done within a day of the vehicle arriving in Ireland. The VRO will inspect the car to work out the VRT due. Second-hand cars will also need a foreign registration document.

You will then receive the car's registration number. Those who can get reliefs and exemptions from VRT are people who have owned their car abroad for over six months and are moving here either temporarily or permanently, or diplomats.

To drive the car, you will also need motor insurance and motor tax (see separate sections, below). A car dealer who has imported the car has to register the car and pay the tax, which will then be included in the price, and it should have its registration plates already fitted.

Vehicle Finance

Getting car finance is pretty easy as long as you have a good credit record. When buying a new or used car, the dealership can usually arrange the finance for you, and this will often work out to be the cheapest option thanks to special partnerships they may have with finance companies. It is also the easiest option, since the dealer will take care of all the paperwork – the most you usually need to do is provide proof of salary and sign on the dotted line. You can also shop around for better deals though – check first with your bank (see a list of banks on p.71), since as an existing customer you may have some negotiating power.

Vehicle Finance		
AIB	1850 724 724	www.aib.ie
Car Finance Ireland	1850 320 920	www.carfinance.ie
Permanent TSB	1890 500 168	www.permanettsb.ie

Motor Insurance

You have to be insured to drive in Ireland, and will need proof of insurance to tax a vehicle. Insurance disks have to be displayed in the windscreen of the car, and uninsured driving is a major offence. Insurance costs depend on the value and size of the vehicle, and policies range from fully comprehensive to third party, fire and theft. It is possible to have named drivers on your policy if the car is used by more than one person. If you have had no accidents, you are entitled to a 'no claims bonus' on second and subsequent years of your policy – the value of the bonus increases with the number of accident-free driving years you accumulate. You can arrange insurance either through a broker or direct with an insurer and it's worthwhile shopping around for insurance – prices vary, some companies offer lady-driver or age discounts, and some offer discounts for applying direct or through the internet. If you are dealing with a broker, ask them to get you the cheapest quote and then compare it with a direct quote from an insurance company.

Registering a Vehicle

New vehicles need to be registered with the Revenue Commissioners and vehicle registration tax (VRT) applies to imported vehicles. You need to apply to the Vehicle Registration Office (see Importing A Car on p.156). Once the VRT is paid, you will then receive the car's registration number. Cars from dealers and second-hand cars will already be registered. Registration numbers go by year and county, so a car registered in Dublin in 2007, will start with '07 D' followed by the unique registration number. This registration number applies for the lifetime of the vehicle. The registration number is used to trace the owner for any traffic fines, speeding charges or offences, so

Car Insurance Companies		
123.ie	1850 221 123	www.123.ie
AA Ireland	01 617 9950	www.aaireland.ie
Allianz Direct	1850 484 848	www.allianzdirect.ie
Axa Insurance	1890 282 820	www.pmpa.ie
FBD Insurance	1890 617 617	www.fbd.ie
InsureMe.ie	01 279 9850	www.insureme.ie

157

See You In Court
The following charges require a
court appearance and court fine:

Offence	Points
Driving when unfit	3
Parking dangerously	5
Breach of duties at crash	5
Driving without insurance	5
Careless driving	5

if you sell or pass on the car, you need to register a change of ownership with the Motor Tax Office.

Vehicle registration plates must conform to legal guidelines and the law sets out exactly what they must look like, with black numbers on a plain white background. A leaflet on vehicle plates in on the Revenue website (www.revenue.ie).

When a car reaches the end of its life, it can be brought to a scrapyard, although scrap is currently not valuable and you will need to pay a charge, usually about €50, to have the battery removed and the vehicle scrapped. Depending on the model, it's worth calling around dealers and scrapyards first to see if anyone is interested in the car for parts, as this will save you the scrap charge. You will need the Vehicle Licensing Certificate or Registration/log book for the vehicle and once you hand the vehicle over to the scrapyard, the ownership will be transferred out of your name. Make sure the scrapyard is bona fide.

Ecocabs
*Ecocabs have been
cruising the streets of
Dublin since 2007,
offering free rides for
inner-city travel
between 10:00 and
20:00. See
www.ecocabs.ie for
more info.*

Traffic Fines & Offences

Ireland operates a penalty points system where offences are recorded on your driving licence record. For minor offences, the offence is a fine (a fixed charge) and penalty points on your licence. For more serious offences, you might be charged in court. If you collect 12 points over 36 months, you will be banned from driving.

There are two ways for offences to be detected – you will either be stopped by a garda or be detected by a speed camera. If you are stopped by a garda, you must show your driving licence and give your name and address. You will receive notice of the fine by post and the penalty points will be applied to your licence record. If a camera records you breaking the speed limit, you'll receive the fine by post. For a complete list of offences and penalty points, see www.penaltypoints.ie.

Breakdowns

If your car breaks down, switch your hazard lights on and try to move the vehicle off the road or if on a motorway, on to the hard shoulder. If you need rescue, try to move your car to a well-lit area and call for assistance either from your mobile phone or a phone box nearby. Stay in the car (unless you are on a motorway, which can be dangerous) and keep all doors and windows locked. Ask any rescue patrols or tow services for proof of identity.

The AA provides a rescue assistance service – annual AA membership is €126 and the service can rectify minor problems like a flat battery, puncture or lost key on the spot. The RAC also offers roadside assistance. It's a good idea to carry a mobile phone, especially when undertaking long journeys or when going to a remote area.

Penalty Points		
Offence	Points	Fine
Speeding	2	€80
Not wearing front seatbelt	2	€60
Using mobile phone while driving	2	€60
Dangerous overtaking	1	€80
Failure to stop at a stop sign	2	€80
Failure to yield at a yield sign	2	€80
Failure to obey traffic lights	5	€80
Driving on footpath or cycle track	1	€60
Driving without reasonable consideration	2	€80
Note: Points increase for each of the above on conviction. Fines increase if not paid within 28 days.		

Recovery Services/Towing (24 hour)	
Ailesbury Auto Services	01 668 3446
AMK Auto Recovery	087 645 5482
BRS Ltd	01 286 0771
CAS Breakdown Assistance	086 880 2212
DMS Towing	087 223 0395
DW Motors	087 990 2417
Eyre Motors	087 257 9041
M50 Motors	086 259 9674
N2 Autocare	1850 918 197
Pat Keogh Towing Services	087 256 0597
Tom Kane Motors Ltd	01 833 8143

Traffic Accidents

If you are unlucky enough to be involved in an accident, there are a number of things you should do and some things you must do by law. You must stop your vehicle and remain at the scene for a reasonable time. If appropriate, secure the scene and warn oncoming traffic to prevent further accidents by using hazard lights and a reflective emergency triangle. You must give your name and address (plus those of the vehicle owner), the vehicle's registration number and insurance details either to a garda or to the other driver. You should also ask them for their details (the name and address of their insurance company – their insurance number will be on the insurance disk on their windscreen) and also get the names and contact details of any witnesses. If anyone is injured or property is damaged, the accident must be reported to the gardaí.

You should write down the exact details of the accident, including date and time, road conditions, vehicle speeds, injuries and vehicle damage and other relevant details such as road signs, markings and whether seat belts were worn. If the gardaí or any other services are present, record their name or number. You could even go as far as keeping a disposable camera in your car and take photos of the scene and any damage.

Vehicle Repairs

There are plenty of service and repair garages throughout Dublin. Some operate express services for tyres and exhausts and have branches all over the city, such as Fast Fit Tyres (1890 489 737, www.fastfit.ie) and Advance Pitstop (01 408 0900, www.advancepitstop.com), while others need advance booking. Most cars come with warranties lasting three or four years and repairs will be organised through the dealer as many large dealers have their own service and repair sections. There are also numerous smaller garages that deal with service and sales, and prices will vary so it's worth shopping around for repair quotes.

If you claim on your insurance, there will usually be an 'excess' – an initial amount that you have to pay before the policy kicks in. This could be €50 or €100. Also, if you are claiming, make sure the repair is worth losing your insurance 'no claims' bonus for. You will need to give a quote to your insurance company so find out beforehand if they prefer you to deal with a specific garage or are happy for you to find your own. Also, check whether they will pay the garage direct or reimburse you afterwards. Some insurance companies or garages will provide a replacement vehicle while repairs are being undertaken.

Ecocab on O'Connell Street

The Dart

159

Therapeutic Feeding

Essential Medicines

Surgery

MEDECINS SANS FRONTIERES
أطبــاء بــلا حــدود

Providing emergency medical
relief in over 70 countries.

help us help the helpless

Exploring

Exploring

Easy Exploration ◀

Exploring the city is easy due to its compact size. It's ideal for walking, weather permitting, as most of the major sights can be reached on foot, allowing you to savour the sights and sounds and unexpected treasures of the side streets, squares and curiosity shops, especially in the Temple Bar area.

Exploring

Dublin, from the time of the Vikings to the present, has always attracted visitors. Be it the warm Irish welcome, the compact size of the city or the wide range of attractions, there is much to offer people living in and visiting the capital.

With a population of just over one million, Dublin is a relatively small city. It has increased in size massively over the last decade, mainly due to the influx of people either returning to live in Ireland or those seeking employment in the 'Celtic Tiger' economy. This has led to a more multicultural city and one that has a lot more to offer than it did in the 1980s and early 1990s.

While the recent, and indeed continuing, economic boom has enriched the city's atmosphere, with prosperity seen in the many new designer shops, outdoor cafes and general joie de vivre of the Dubliners themselves, the overall landscape has remained much the same, with little obstructing the skyline apart from the statuesque millennium spire on O'Connell Street. Architecturally speaking, this new affluence has encouraged more freedom, as seen in the newly constructed Millennium Boardwalk and numerous bridges crossing the River Liffey such as the James Joyce and the Sean O'Casey.

The river divides the city into north and south, and there is a continuing debate over whether the south side is more attractive then the north. While the city centre is greatly populated, it is the suburbs on both sides that are home to the many students and families that make up the capital. In fact, due to such a large number of students, Dublin is regarded as one of the youngest cities in Europe in terms of the age of the population. Over the years, Dublin has become increasingly popular as a weekend city break because of its rich cultural heritage and lively nightlife. Indeed the city's extensive array of pubs – many offering live music, pub grub and a variety of beers and wines – has made the city famous.

Dublin's tram system, the Luas, is the city's newest and most reliable means of transport, and plans are in motion to extend its network. The Dart is the city's light rail network and runs along the coast from Howth to Bray. Being by the sea, the city has the added advantages of great seafood, sailing, watersports and unspoiled beaches.

To kickstart your exploration, see the 21 must-do ideas starting on p.163. Each area is also covered in more detail (see p.168), highlighting its hidden gems and offering helpful insights. Finally, this chapter guides you through Dublin's museums, parks, beaches and other attractions, and suggests some great daytrips and weekend breaks.

O'Connell Street

Guinness Storehouse p.199

This is an obvious one but it's often forgotten by residents and should be a must, if for the Gravity Bar alone. Once inside you can explore over seven floors and even try your hand at pulling a perfect pint. On the top floor, the Gravity Bar offers you a breathtaking 360 degree view of Dublin, something you won't find anywhere else in the city. Plus you get a free pint with your entry ticket, so bottoms up!

Grafton Street p.321

This is Dublin's high-end pedestrianised shopping thoroughfare. Lined with some excellent shops, including the mother of all department stores, Brown Thomas, it's the place to be when you want to splash some cash. It's best avoided at midday on a Saturday if you're in a hurry as there's always a buzz on the street. Long after the shops have shut, buskers play music into the night.

St Stephen's Green p.194

This is one of the most popular parks in the city centre, and on a sunny day it's the ultimate place to munch on your lunch-time sandwiches and enjoy the weather. It's inevitably jam-packed during summer, and you'll have to hunt for a spare patch of lawn. It is the location for many summer concerts in the pavilion on Sundays.

Cathedrals p.186

Not short on churches and cathedrals, Dublin's landscape is peppered with spires and grand stone edifices. Ireland has a history in which religion features prominently, and a visit to any of Dublin's cathedrals is a good way to find out more about its fascinating past. Among the most impressive are St Patrick's, St Mary's Pro and Christchurch cathedral. Try and get a ticket to the festive and extremely popular Christmas Carol service at St Patrick's.

Phoenix Park p.194

The big mamma of Dublin parks, this one covers over 700 hectares and offers a real break from the city. As well as endless types of flora and fauna (a herd of deer roams freely through the grounds), the park also hosts concerts and festivals throughout the year. Áras an Uachtaráin (the official residence of the President of Ireland) is situated on the park grounds and can be visited on Saturdays.

Temple Bar p.170

Temple Bar is Dublin's cultural quarter. Its cobbled streets bring you a selection of markets, the Irish Film Institute (see p.390), eclectic art galleries and a host of festivals, and of course its legendary bars and restaurants. Some Dubliners will tell you to avoid it on the weekends, but with a colourful collection of stags and hens, it's often the best time for a laugh! Find out more at the Temple Bar Cultural Information Centre (p.171).

Dart Along The Coast p.41

If for no other reason than to avoid the traffic, take the Dart from Pearse Street station to Bray and enjoy the beautiful coastal views. Keep your eyes peeled especially between Dalkey and Killiney (p.176), easily the most picturesque part of the journey.

Dublin Castle & The Chester Beatty Library p.183

Sadly little remains of the original 18th century structure of the Dublin Castle, apart from the record tower, but taking a tour around the majestic rooms still gives you a sense of Ireland's history. The adjoining, award-winning Chester Beatty Library (see p.188) is full of treasures from the near and far east, and is well worth a visit. Once you're all cultured up, find a spot in the gardens and enjoy the sunshine.

Famine Memorial p.169

Wander past Custom House on the north side and you'll come across the Famine Memorial – like figures trapped in time, these figures are a moving sight as they seem to struggle along the boardwalk of the river. They form a poignant tribute to those who suffered during the famine years, and perhaps a rather brutal reminder to those who turned a blind eye.

Irish Museum of Modern Art (IMMA) p.181

IMMA is located in the 17th century Royal Hospital Kilmainham, a beautiful building reminiscent of Les Invalides in Paris. The manicured grounds are perfect for a Sunday stroll and the Museum has showcased travelling works from artists such as Martin Puryear, Francesco Clemente, Juan Uslé, Vik Muniz, Margherita Manzelli and Marc Quinn. It's a good venue to combine with a visit to the nearby Kilmainham Gaol.

O'Connell Street p.168

O'Connell Street, with its bridge as wide as it is long, has cleaned up its image over the last 10 years. Apart from being home to some great shops and restaurants, it also features a great history lesson with its many statues, original buildings. Many of the original edifices were destroyed in the early 20th century but a few still remain, like the Royal Dublin Hotel and the GPO.

Trinity College p.170

Perhaps one of the most famous of all tourist attractions in the city, Trinity College is grandiose as soon as you walk through its arched entrance. The main attractions of the college are the Book of Kells and the Old Library, but just walking around its grounds gives you a sense of the longevity of this teaching institution. During the summer, students and visitors lounge outside the Pavilion Bar to watch cricket.

Merrion Square p.194

Merrion Square, one of the largest Georgian squares in Dublin, is surrounded by houses of venerable heritage. Past owners include Daniel O'Connell, WB Yeats and Oscar Wilde. The manicured park is a pleasure to walk around and is a favourite with office workers. On the west side of the square, you'll find the National Gallery of Ireland (see p.182) and the Natural History Museum (see p.190).

Coastal Boat Tour p.199

Everyone should take advantage of the opportunity to see Dublin from the sea. Offering a truly different aspect of the city to the resident, with nuggets of local information thrown in by the crew, it's a particularly enjoyable way to spend an hour or two, especially during the summer months.

Markets p.328

Markets are experiencing somewhat of a rebirth, and can be found all over Dublin. The covered market off South Great George's Street is great for second-hand clothes, while the Powerscourt Townhouse Sunday market sees up and coming designers displaying their wares. Cow's Lane Fashion Market, the food market and book market in Temple bar are also extremely popular, not to forget the most famous of them all, Moore Street market, for an undiluted, traditional Dublin experience.

Catch A Game – Croke Park p.261

The shouts, cries and recriminations are all part of a day at a hurling or Gaelic football match in Croke Park. During the game the atmosphere is electric while the after-match excitement is perhaps the best part, as fans stream into the surrounding pubs. For those who prefer a more sedate introduction to the GAA (p.239), visit the museum on the grounds of Croke Park (p.175).

GPO p.168

The GPO remains an important reminder of the 1916 Easter Rising, when the Irish Citizen Army fought the British Army for a week before being forced out. Visitors can still see marks from the bullets on the grand columns outside the building. Once inside, its immense size lends a magnitude to the statue of the mythical Irish warrior Cuchulainn (see p.5), dedicated to those who died in the Rising.

Malahide Castle p.183

Malahide is a past winner of the Tidy Towns competition, and is a very pleasant place to spend the day. Be sure to visit this restored castle, set on 250 acres of land, alongside the botanical gardens and complete with five ghosts, allegedly. Also situated in the grounds of the castle is The Fry Model Railway, a collection of hand-made miniature trains with an impressive working railway of over 2500 square feet.

Kilmainham Gaol p.187

Unused now for over 80 years, this prison held many who fought for Irish independence, such as Charles Stuart Parnell, Robert Emmett, Joseph Plunkett and James Connolly. The last prisoner was Eamonn De Valera, who was released in 1924. The tour takes in the original cramped cells, and includes some insight into what conditions were like for prisoners there. A morbid, yet fascinating and highly recommended, glimpse into the past.

Dublin Mountains p.215

The Dublin Mountains offer a superb daytrip away from the hustle and bustle of the city – many hikes are available, so breathe in the brisk air and enjoy a bit of exercise. And if that sounds too much like hard work, then pay a visit to Johnnie Fox's pub in Glencullen (01 295 5647, www.jfp.ie), one of the oldest and most traditional pubs in Dublin, famous for its live music sessions.

Collins Barracks – National Museum of Ireland: Decorative Arts & History p.190

The original buildings in Collins Barracks date back to the 1700s and more were built in the next two centuries. The Museum of Decorative Arts & History holds a wide range of artefacts such as weapons, furniture, silver, ceramics, and costume.

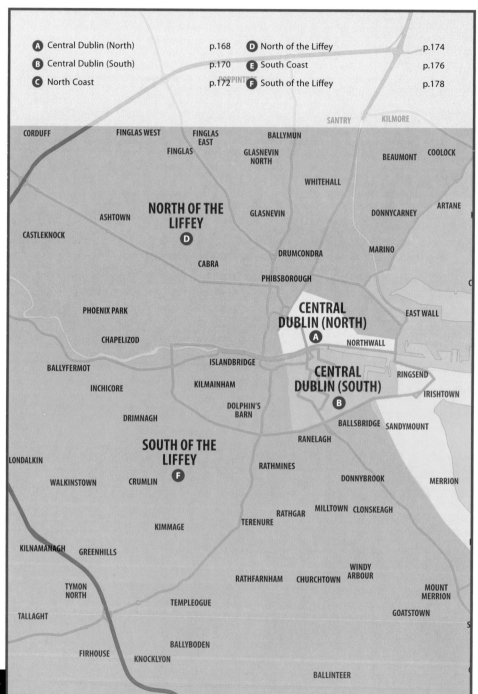

A Central Dublin (North)   p.168   D North of the Liffey   p.174
B Central Dublin (South)   p.170   E South Coast   p.176
C North Coast   p.172   F South of the Liffey   p.178

SANTRY   KILMORE

CORDUFF   FINGLAS WEST   FINGLAS EAST   BALLYMUN
FINGLAS   GLASNEVIN NORTH   BEAUMONT   COOLOCK
WHITEHALL
NORTH OF THE LIFFEY   GLASNEVIN   DONNYCARNEY   ARTANE
ASHTOWN   D
CASTLEKNOCK   MARINO
DRUMCONDRA
CABRA
PHIBSBOROUGH
PHOENIX PARK   CENTRAL DUBLIN (NORTH)   EAST WALL
CHAPELIZOD   A
NORTHWALL
ISLANDBRIDGE
BALLYFERMOT   CENTRAL DUBLIN (SOUTH)   RINGSEND
KILMAINHAM
INCHICORE   B   IRISHTOWN
DOLPHIN'S BARN
DRIMNAGH   BALLSBRIDGE   SANDYMOUNT
RANELAGH
SOUTH OF THE LIFFEY
LONDALKIN   RATHMINES
WALKINSTOWN   CRUMLIN   F   DONNYBROOK   MERRION
MILLTOWN   CLONSKEAGH
RATHGAR
KIMMAGE   TERENURE
KILNAMANAGH   GREENHILLS
WINDY ARBOUR
RATHFARNHAM   CHURCHTOWN   MOUNT MERRION
TYMON NORTH
TEMPLEOGUE   GOATSTOWN
TALLAGHT
BALLYBODEN
FIRHOUSE   KNOCKLYON
BALLINTEER

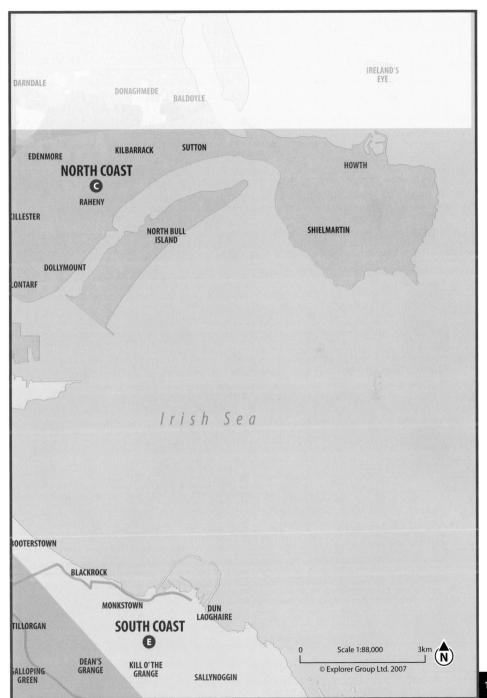

IRELAND'S
EYE

DARNDALE

DONAGHMEDE

BALDOYLE

EDENMORE

KILBARRACK

SUTTON

NORTH COAST
C

HOWTH

RAHENY

KILLESTER

NORTH BULL
ISLAND

SHIELMARTIN

DOLLYMOUNT

LONTARF

Irish Sea

BOOTERSTOWN

BLACKROCK

MONKSTOWN

DUN
LAOGHAIRE

TILLORGAN

SOUTH COAST
E

GALLOPING
GREEN

DEAN'S
GRANGE

KILL O' THE
GRANGE

SALLYNOGGIN

0   Scale 1:88,000   3km

© Explorer Group Ltd. 2007

N

The Complete **Residents'** Guide

Map p.426, 427
Area **A** p.166-167

Central Dublin (North)

Often portrayed as the ugly sister to its counterpart south central Dublin, north central Dublin has had a reputation of decline and neglect for many years. However, O'Connell Street, officially the centre of Dublin geographically speaking, has an air of optimism about it these days.

The Good

The Luas tram system passes through O'Connell Street, linking the city centre to Heuston Station, Connolly station, Busáras, James's Hospital, the National Museum of Decorative Arts and History and the Four Courts.

O'Connell Street was once the main thoroughfare of the city and it was scene of many dates in Ireland's struggle for independence. Grandiose in structure, the last 40 years have seen arcades and fast-food joints taking up residence in nearly all its commercial premises. However, with new planning strategies now in place the area is set to regain some of its former glory. The street has already benefited from the restoration of some of its monuments, the creation of a central pedestrian island, and the planting of trees and addition of new street furnishings.

At the centre of O'Connell Street is the Spire, 140 metres of stainless steel, and the GPO (01 705 7000), one of the most historically important buildings in Dublin. It was the epicentre for many a battle fought for Irish independence and still functions as the General Post Office, its historical past undiminished due to intensive restoration and glorious original features. Today it's a very nice place to buy stamps or pay for your TV licence.

The Bad

Despite recent years and the general clean up of O'Connell street, it is still not the safest area to walk around late at night. Take a taxi when possible.

Also near the GPO is Eason's Bookshop (p.288), one of Dublin's biggest bookshops, providing a wide selection of books and stationery supplies.

Walking the length and breadth of O'Connell Street, despite some areas of decay, it is easy to imagine how it was in its glory days, and what a great venue it is for the St Patrick Day celebrations (www.stpatricksday.ie), when the street is closed off to traffic and filled with music, floats and dancers (see p.47).

At the top of the street is Parnell Square, complete with Georgian houses, galleries, gardens and renowned restaurant Chapter One. As the restoration of O'Connell Street comes to an end, Parnell Square is next in line. At the centre of the square is the Rotunda Maternity Hospital (see p.135), once the biggest in Europe, and the Garden of Remembrance (see p.193), a poignant reminder of the sadness of war. On the north side of the square, the Hugh Lane Gallery (see p.180), formerly Charlemont House, is a splendidly spacious and airy gallery devoted to modern and contemporary art. Artists such as Manet, Monet, Renoir and Degas are exhibited here as well as works by leading national and international contemporary artists. The Hugh Lane also acquired the contents of Francis Bacon's studio on his death and has recreated it in the gallery.

The Lowdown

Erected in 2003, the Spire (or its official name The Monument of Light) stands on the spot of Nelson's Pillar, which was bombed and destroyed in 1966. This spot is traditionally supposed to mark the centre of the city.

A few doors down from the Hugh Lane is the Dublin Writers Museum (see p.190) where you can view the lives and works of Irish writers such as Swift, Sheridan, Wilde, Shaw, Yeats, Joyce and Beckett.

Just below the Dublin Writers Museum is Chapter One Restaurant (see p.352), a superb eatery which combines Irish and French cuisine in a beautiful setting, and which should be on your dining 'must-do' list.

Must-Do

Visit Moore Street. Not only is there a wide selection of fresh produce but the overall atmosphere of the place is unique in modern Dublin, with traditional markets such as this a rarity.

The James Joyce Centre (p.188) is a must for anyone interested in the famous Irish writer, with walking tours, exhibitions, lectures, a cafe and a bookshop run by the centre. It is the primary setting for the Bloomsday festival every year in June (p.48).

Moving back down towards O'Connell Street is the Gate Theatre (see p.394), one of Dublin's oldest theatres and where Orson Welles and James Mason began their acting careers. Nearby, the Ambassador Theatre (Upper O'Connell Street, 1890 92510), a relic of the not-so-distant past, opens occasionally for concerts and plays, and is worth a visit if just to see its unusual circular interior. The Abbey Theatre (p.394), founded by W.B. Yeats in 1904, has always nurtured new talent and is set to continue, welcoming new and creative writing to its stage.

Streets branching off O'Connell Street such as Henry Street, Abbey Street and Talbot Street are all prominent in the area and full of Dublin character. Henry Street is the busiest of the shopping streets and has a good portion of the high street chain stores, as well as large department stores such as Arnotts (p.322), Jervis and the Ilac Centre (see p.330). Just off Henry Street is Moore Street, famous for its lively market atmosphere, with stalls of fruit, veg and clothes lining the street. Capel Street, on the other hand, has many DIY, sofa and interior shops (see Shopping on p.279).

Although there are numerous hotels in the area, The Gresham (p.31) is the most prestigious and one of the few remaining buildings on O'Connell Street with its original facade, apart from perhaps Clery's department store (p.323), and the GPO.

At the south end of O'Connell Street lies the bridge of the same name, made famous due to the fact that it is as wide as it is long, and the quays, where you will feel the breeze coming in off the sea: pleasant in the summer and bitterly cold in the winter. Walking up Eden quay will bring you to Busáras Station (p.39) the central bus station, and past that again is the Financial services centre, a neighbourhood built around the IFSC building and the many financial institutions operating there. This is a nice place to wander around in the summer as the Docklands (01 818 3300, www.ddda.ie) hosts many events and open-air markets which lend a buzz to an area that was deserted 20 years ago.

On Bachelors Walk, the other quay, there's a selection of budget-friendly hostels and of course the Hapenny Bridge, a famous symbol of the Dublin of yesteryear. Opened in 1816, it got its name from the amount charged for crossing it: half a penny. Opposite this Bridge is Liffey Street, packed with cafes and small shops selling bargain items from clothes to suitcases.

Dublin's Italian Quarter (Lower Ormond Quay) is located further down the quay. Go to Bloom's Lane where you will find Enoteca delle Langhe (see p.373), a cosy wine bar, perfect for a romantic rendezvous on a cold winter evening. You'll also get to see 'Dublin's Last Supper', an artwork by John Byrne, in which he recreates the last supper using every-day Irish people (including a tattoo artist and a Trinity student).

Boardwalk along the north quays

O'Connell Street

Moore Street market

Map p.426, 427
430, 431
Area **B** p.166-167

Central Dublin (South)

South Central Dublin is a very popular part of Dublin and is full of shops, restaurants and bars. The main artery is Grafton Street, which runs up to St Stephen's Green, from which most other major streets (such as Dawson Street, Nassau Street, Kildare Street and Wicklow Street) are linked by a succession of side streets. The best part of this area is the myriad of cafes and boutiques that you'll stumble upon by chance when wandering around.

The Good

There are so many shops in this area of Dublin it is hard to know where to start. Keep in mind though that many close at 18:00 on weekdays, while late opening until 21:00 is on a Thursday. Most shops are closed on Sundays, apart from the larger stores.

There is a lot crammed into this relatively small space. Perhaps the most striking, and indeed synonymous with Dublin, is Trinity College (see p.170), which covers nearly 40 acres and is situated right in the heart of the city. Dating from the 15th century it is the oldest college in Ireland and walking around the Old Library and the Book of Kells, you're likely to be struck with a sense of quiet awe. Famous scholars include Ussher, Marsh, Dodwell, and Stearne.

Walking from Trinity towards Grafton Street, you'll pass the statute of Molly Malone. Famous for selling cockles and mussels and, if her costume and folklore are anything to go by, catching the eye of the local men. She is as famous to Dublin as Guinness is to Ireland.

The Bad

It is near impossible to get a taxi on a Thursday, Friday and Saturday night after 01:00. If you are planning a late one, book a taxi in advance.

Grafton Street is like a shot of vodka to cure a hangover; it will either kill you or cure you. This usually depends on your shopping threshold. Permanently busy, and even more so during the summer with tourists, it remains the most popular shopping street in Dublin. Brown Thomas (see p.323) leads the way as far as kudos and breaking the bank go, followed by the less expensive BT2 (01 605 6666, www.brownthomas.com), A/wear (see p.292), and a legion of other high street stores. Top Shop (see p.292) has its flagship store at the top, on Stephen's Green.

The Powerscourt Centre (01 671 7000, www.powerscourtcentre.com) at 59 South William Street, an elegant 18th century Georgian town house, is a beautiful place to have a cup of coffee accompanied by live piano music. Upstairs, the Design Centre offers an array of new designers. The Bistro restaurant (4/5 Castlemarket Street, 01 671 5430), across the road, is a lovely place to eat Sunday brunch washed down by a nice glass of wine, and on a sunny day, you can nab a table outside. Costume (see p.292), a trendy designer shop, is opposite and the covered market arcade (between Drury Street and South Great George's Street) offers quirky shops and stalls selling wine, cheese and tea.

The Lowdown

Rush hour in Dublin is particularly bleak on a Friday evening and if you have to get across the city centre in time for a train or bus, leave plenty of time for delays. Traffic along the quays grinds to a halt between 16:30 and 18:30.

Clarendon Street and South William Street have flourished in the last few years, with cafes and restaurants growing like mushrooms, and yet they have retained a kind of charm that invites you to return. The Tourist Office on Suffolk Street (01 605 770, www.visitdublin.com) is situated in an old church, and is within walking distance of Grafton Street. It has maps and information on local sights and music venues, as well as the Dublin Pass, which gives free entry to numerous attractions. On the same street, is Rhinestones (see p.304) an antique jewellery shop that heralds many a rare find.

St Stephens Green is a hotspot during the summer, with 22 acres providing space for people to relax and enjoy the sun, while also providing a backdrop to some events throughout the year. One of the most famous buildings on the square is The Shelbourne hotel (01 663 4500, www.theshelbourne.ie); it's a must for a sophisticated sip of champagne.

Must-Do

Go see a brass band playing in St Stephen's Green on a sunny, Sunday afternoon. It's worth the wait for the summer months when they finally arrive.

Although impressive architecturally, St Stephen's Green doesn't have the same wow factor as Fitzwilliam Square and Merrion Square which are very beautiful in their Georgian perfection. In June, Merrion Square hosts the Street Performance World Championships (see p.48) an event that is as entertaining as it is bizarre.

Temple Bar, situated along the south banks of the River Liffey, is the hub of Dublin's nightlife for tourists and visitors. Many Dubliners don't frequent these pubs although Sunday afternoon is a good time to find the odd local listening to the live music sessions that are held in many of the pubs. The cobbled streets give it a bit of old world charm, while the markets, especially Cow's Lane and the food market in Meeting House Square are a definite Saturday morning activity. The Dublin Film Festival (Filmbase, Curved St, Temple Bar, 01 672 8861, www.dubliniff.com) hosts many of its activities in Temple Bar and for a retrospective look at the city, the National Photographic Archive is brilliant (see p.182).

For general information about Temple Bar and on all events, visit the Temple Bar Cultural Information Centre (01 677 2255, www.temple-bar.ie).

The National Concert Hall (01 417 0077, www.nch.ie) situated off St Stephen's Green, holds many musical and opera performances throughout the year. As does the Gaiety Theatre (see p.394) which also runs a pantomime season and operates a nightclub open until 04:00 (late by Dublin standards). The Olympia Theatre on Dame Street (01 679 3323) offers a wide range of entertainment.

Other streets leading off St Stephen's Green are Harcourt Street, Leeson Street and Merrion Row, all of which have many offices, bars and nightclubs. Leading on to Baggot Street, here you'll find many restaurants, pubs and wine bars.

The four-day Taste of Dublin event (see Annual Events on p.48) held in the Iveagh Gardens (which are very pleasant to visit at any time of the year, see p.194) just off Harcourt Street and behind the National Concert Hall (01 417 0077, www.nch.ie), brings together many major restaurants in Dublin, with gourmet food and wine tasting sessions. If you go for the VIP ticket, you will get entry to the VIP enclosure and to Lillie's Bordello nightclub (see p.386) a Dublin institution.

Finally, if you fancy a peep at the Taoiseach (Ireland's Prime Minister), his offices are located in the 18th century Leinster House (see p.185). This is where all the action happens, politically speaking, and you may even see the odd protest outside. If you're more interested in seeing where the taxpayer's money goes, you can opt for a guided tour.

Molly Mallone statue

Georgian Doors in Merrion Square

Temple Bar

Map p.410-413
Area **C** p.166-167

North Coast

Howth, the northern-most tip of Dublin Bay, is the north side's equivalent of affluent Killiney, minus the international celebrities. What it lacks in celebrity kudos it makes up for in award winning golf courses, long unspoilt beaches and a fun nightlife. The town itself has a charming seaside atmosphere, which is particularly enjoyable during the summer months.

Dublin city centre, only nine miles away, is easily reached by both road and rail, yet is far enough away to feel you've escaped from the rat race. Dublin airport (www.dublinairport.com) is also within a stones throw, ideal for any spontaneous holidays. Howth harbour is the heart of the village, both aesthetically and economically. Here you'll hear the gentle clink of fishing boats and find the modern Howth Yacht Club (see p.251) the largest in Ireland with over 2,000 members and one of the most important racing clubs on the east coast. You can learn to sail or hire a boat from the yacht club or from Sutton Dinghy Club (01 839 3135, see p.251). Along the West Pier you'll sniff out the fish warehouses of companies such as Beshoff's (01 839 0766, www.beshoffs.ie), who also have a fish and chip shop in the village, Doran's (01 839 2419) and Wrights (01 816 7347, www.wrightsofhowth.com). You can get fresh fish here almost every day. From the harbour, you can take a boat trip to Ireland's Eye and the bird sanctuary (see p.196), a pleasant place to spend an afternoon.

For sports fans, there are extensive sports facilities in the area, with cliff and rock climbing, watersports, and golf courses. One of the most famous golf courses in the area is the Portmarnock Golf and Country Club (01 846 2968, www.portmarnockgolfclub.ie), while Deer Park public golf course (Deer Park Hotel and Golf Course, 01 832 2624, www.deerpark-hotel.ie) is within walking distance of the harbour. Others include Howth Golf Club (see p.240) and Sutton Golf Club (see p.240). Indeed, golfing in Ireland in general is taken very seriously and in the private clubs, membership is strict and sometimes hard to obtain. The courses around Howth are especially attractive due to the scenic routes and exceptional facilities. The aforementioned Portmarnock Golf and Country Club is regularly voted Ireland's best golf course.

Howth's nightlife is highly recommended. Two places worth a visit are Wrights Findlater's (Harbour Road, 01 832 4488) and Abbey Tavern (01 839 0307, www.abbeytavern.ie). The latter has been around for 40 years and still entertains the punters with Traditional music. The Howth Peninsula Festival (www.howthpeninsula.com) in June runs a variety of family-friendly events.

Howth's National Transport Museum is a quirky little museum and the collection of old vehicles is worth a peek (01 848 0831, www.nationaltransportmuseum.org). Beside the museum is Howth Castle, which can be viewed from the exterior but the interior is closed to visitors.

Malahide Castle (01 846 1284, www.malahidecastle.com), just a short distance from Howth, is an attractive fortification situated on extensive parkland, including a botanical garden and a model railway track. This castle has been around since the 12th century and in recent years has been restored to its former glory. Tours take you around the many reception rooms and bedrooms, and if you're lucky you might spot one of the many ghosts who are said to walk the castle's corridors.

Malahide itself, winner of the Tidy Towns Competition, is a pretty village with a port and a good range of sporting, recreational and community activities, making it very appealing to young families. Sutton is another charming seafront village with plenty of shops and good restaurants. The long sandy beaches around these areas are great for Sunday walks. Examples include Portmarnock, Claremont and Burrow beaches, with others in Malahide and Sutton.

When out exploring, Ardgillan Castle and Demesne Regional Park in Balbriggan (01 849 2212) is beautiful. Although a little out of the way, between Skerries and Balbriggan,

The Good
The coastal walks around Howth Head offer breathtaking views of the bay and the chance to enjoy this very scenic area.

The Bad
Much of this area has suffered from overdevelopment with properties springing up everywhere. Many otherwise picturesque locations have been ruined because of this.

The Lowdown
The Golfing Union of Ireland (01 505 4000, www.gui.ie) has information on all golf courses in Ireland and is helpful for anyone searching for a golf course and facilities to suit them.

Must-Do
Visit the gardens at Malahide Castle during May and June, the flowers are in full bloom and they are at their most beautiful.

due to its high position it has fantastic views of the coast and surrounding countryside. The ground floor and kitchen of the castle (although it looks more like a country house) are open to guests, with tours operating throughout the day. Must-sees here are the Rose Garden, the Victorian Conservatory and the 200 acres of parkland with woodland walks and picnic areas. In the summer, a second cafe opens near the walled garden, so you can enjoy your tea alfresco.

Fingal county council (01 890 5000, www.fingalcoco.ie) has invested a lot in walks around Howth and its environs, which is evident in the various trails they have created. Itineraries include the coastal walks from Howth through Sutton and Baldoyle; Portmarnock to Malahide passing the Martello Towers; Malahide to Swords through Broadmeadow Estuary; and Donabate to Portrane. These routes are signposted at Balscaddan carpark, Bailey carpark, Balkill Park, sea front near Howth Dart Station, Tower View carpark Portrane and the beach carpark in Donabate. The cliff paths around Howth Head are especially scenic, affording walkers stunning views of Dublin Bay and the Wicklow mountains.

Newbridge House (01 843 6530), a period estate situated in 370 acres of parkland designed by Charles Fritzell, has been restored to a very high level and has a replica of a traditional 18th century farm along with children's playground and orienteering course.

For something out of the ordinary and a little further a field (40 miles from Howth), visit the megalithic passage tomb at Newgrange (Donore, County Meath, 041 988 0300). It dates back to 5000BC, pre-dating the pyramids by a few thousand years. Inside are a number of burial chambers and during the winter solstice light passes through a box shaped opening above the entrance and travels down the passage to the centre of the mound. It's a fascinating visit, just not for the claustrophobic.

Howth Village

Wrights of Howth

Tourist attractions in Malahide

173

Map p.406-409
424, 425
Area **D** p.166-167

The Good
The Botanical Gardens are a great amenity and are especially useful for information on how to plan a garden, what plants to use and general advice on plant and tree maintenance.

The Bad
Some areas of North Dublin are a bit rough (such as Ballyfermot, Ballymun and some parts of Phibsborough) and care should be taken, especially at night.

The Lowdown
Tickets for any sporting event, GAA or otherwise, and indeed entertainment such as concerts and comedy nights, are available through Ticket Master (www.ticketmaster.ie).

Must-Do
A game in Croke Park. This is something anyone who lives in Dublin must do as it is unique to Ireland and usually a very enjoyable day, and night, out.

North Of The Liffey

Home to many students, spiritual home of GAA fans and near enough to the Four Courts to keep you on your toes, this section of Dublin holds a wide variety of attractions for the resident.

Perhaps the greenest part of the city, Phoenix Park (main entrance at Parkgate) has a circumference of 11km and is the biggest city park in Europe (see p.194). A great place to stretch your legs or go for a cycle, it offers the possibility to get away from the city without having to go too far. There's an array of activities on offer, from tours and talks on wildlife and botany to visiting the deer park (even though it's not open

Deer in Phoenix Park

to the public, you will be able to see them), Áras an Uachtaráin (presidential building) and Dublin Zoo (see p.197). The Phoenix Park Visitor Centre organises all tours and is a mine of information on the park, and can tell you what events are on during the summer months and over Heritage week (www.heritageireland.ie) in August.

With the Luas tram system (www.luas.ie, 1800 300 604) running through a good section of Dublin's north side, parallel to the River Liffey, one can easily reach Smithfield and the Four Courts. Indeed with its proximity to the Four Courts, this is a convenient place for any prospective legal eagle. The Four Courts, at 15/24 Phoenix Street North in Smithfield (01 888 6000, www.courts.ie), gets its name from the divisions of law in Ireland: Chancery, King's Bench, Exchequer, and Common Pleas. The most arresting features of this building are the dome and main portico, which make a very grandiose statement.

Smithfield was in a somewhat rundown state a few years ago but with urban regeneration it has upgraded its image. Now there are plenty of apartments, a fruit, and veg market and at least two very good pubs, namely The Dice Bar (Queen Street, Smithfield, 01 872 8622), for the trendsetters, and The Cobblestone (77 North King Street, Smithfield, 01 872 1799), the owner of which guarantees traditional and folk music every night. Also, an outdoor ice rink is erected during the Christmas period in December and January.

The Old Jameson Distillery (see p.200) is around the corner from Smithfield and offers a chance to taste a range of whiskeys and learn about the distillation process. If this isn't your cup of tea (or whiskey as the case may be), hop on the Luas and head down towards Collins Barracks and the National Museum of Decorative Arts and Crafts on Benburb Street (see p.190) which has a wide range of interesting artefacts and often has touring exhibitions. Otherwise, if wanderlust has taken hold, take the Luas to Heuston Station (www.irishrail.ie, 1850 366 222) and head off into the big wide yonder. The Point Theatre (01 836 3633, www.thepoint.ie), one of the largest purpose built venues in Dublin, has a capacity of 8,500 people and hosts a whole range of national and international acts from Ballet to rock and boy bands to opera.

Moving northward on the light rail Dart system (see Transportation on p.152) is Clontarf, a picturesque seaside area with village atmosphere. Only one stop from the city centre, it is a popular place from which to commute. St Anne's Park in Raheny (see p.194), former home of the Guinness family and with an award winning rose garden, is especially charming, while the Blue flag Dollymount strand (see p.35) is popular for walking and sunbathing. Also, Bull Island is within easy reach by boat and makes an interesting daytrip. Clontarf Castle (Castle Avenue, Clontarf , 01 833 2321, www.clontarfcastle.ie), now a luxurious hotel, is a lovely place to have Sunday lunch, cloistered in the warmth of old walls and open fireplaces.

For any avid gardeners or simply those with an interest in plants and flowers, the National Botanical Gardens (see p.195) are a great asset. Situated in Glasnevin, they were established in 1795 and still have the beautiful cast iron Palm House and Curvilinear glasshouses. Not only are they beautiful, the aim of the Gardens are to educate visitors on the importance of plants and increase awareness through conservation, education and the general helpfulness of the staff; a definite for anyone needing advice on planning a garden.

Croke Park stadium (01 819 2300, www.crokepark.ie), home of the Gaelic Athletic Association (GAA), has far less virtuous but nonetheless genuine ambitions. Its aim is to entertain the masses with fast paced, highly exciting Irish sport. What county will win the next hurling championship? Will the Kilkenny Cats claw their way to the top for yet another year? All is to play for, and whether your team wins or loses, the high spirits promise to last well after the game has ended and on into the night. As well as hosting matches, Croke Park also stages concerts and is home to the GAA museum (http://museum.gaa.ie), which was established to celebrate the involvement of the GAA in Irish sport and gives a history of its achievements. Fagan's (Drumcondra Road Lower, 01 8369491) near Croke Park is a popular pub and a favourite of the present Taoiseach, Bertie Ahern.

Finally, DCU, Dublin City University (see p.149), one of Dublin's foremost universities, is situated in the area and often holds conferences and other events on campus. Non-students are also free to make use of their impressive sports facilities (including pool, sauna, fitness centre, squash courts, climbing wall, five-a-side soccer pitches, and more) once they join as a member.

Four Courts

Viewing chimney in Smithfield

Park on Wolfe Tone Quay

Map p.422, 423
Area **E** p.166-167

South Coast

Often said to rival the Bay of Naples, Killiney bay is certainly breathtaking and this perhaps may explain its popularity with the showbiz elite of Ireland. Home to Bono and The Edge from U2, it has more stars per mile than anywhere else in the country. One of the best ways to enjoy the view of the bay, believe it or not, is to travel on the Dart rail network (www.iarnrodeireann.ie/dart). Not very glamorous perhaps but it will take you all the way down the coast from the city centre to Bray.

Killiney boasts a long attractive beach (see p.193), which usually becomes packed quickly in the summer but at all other times of the year is more or less deserted. It makes for a beautiful walk, especially in the early morning on a clear day, and can invigorate even the most tired soul. White Road has another popular beach.

There are many walks in the area, from Dalkey to Killiney, which take you along the rugged coast. Walk along Dalkey Hill, Sorrento Park, and Vico Road or Dillons Park to Coliemore Road. Most of these walks are signposted and can be followed with ease, although some are quite steep.

Killiney's neighbouring town, Dalkey, is larger (Killiney is more of an area rather than a village) but no less full of names with Meave Binchy, Neil Jordan, Van Morrison and Lisa Stansfield residents here. It was also the former home of George Bernard Shaw and the town of seven castles, although only two survive today. Dalkey has remained largely unspoilt, and has many high quality art galleries, restaurants, and shops. Queens (12 Castle Street, 01 285 4569) is an especially popular pub along with Ragazzi's Italian restaurant (109 Coliemore Road, 01 284 7280). Tramyard Art (14 Castle Street Dalkey, 01 235 1346) and Dalkey Arts (19 Railway Road, 01 284 9663) are two prominent art galleries in the town.

Dalkey Island is about 300 metres off the coast and is popular for picnics and outdoor pursuits. Goats wonder the hills and you can visit the Martello Tower and ruins of a seventh century church among other things. The island is also good for fishing and spotting the seals play in shallow water. If you're lucky you may also see a porpoise. To get there, you can hire a boat or get a lift on a fishing boat from Coliemore harbour, which was the main harbour before Dun Laoghaire took over due to its greater size and depth.

Dun Laoghaire, midway between Dublin and Killiney, is a large town with amenities to

The Good

The pure beauty and charm of Killiney, and wonderful landscape of this area can almost make you forget that you are in Dublin, and sometimes this can be a good thing.

The Bad

The astronomical property prices make this a very unaffordable location for the majority of people and snobbery is rife.

Must-Do

The view from Killiney Hill Park, off Victoria Road, is well worth the steep climb. From there, you will see Howth Head, Bray Head and the Wicklow Mountains beyond.

Dalkey

Mountain walk from Dalkey to Killiney

Dublin – Main Areas

The Lowdown

Being on the Dart line makes all the towns along the coast easily accessible and gives an alternative to long queues in traffic.

suit all age groups, from the large harbour to its Maritime museum (Haigh Terrace, 01 280 0969), abundant sailing facilities and many shops and restaurants. For information on the wide range of events and sailing courses on offer, contact Dun Laoghaire Harbour (www.dlharbour.ie). The harbour itself has two piers, West and East Pier, with the various yacht clubs in between, the best known of which is The National Yacht Club (www.nyc.ie). For those looking for wind, the West Pier proves very popular with windsurfers and other speed junkies. Ferries leave the harbour travelling to Holyhead (www.directferries.ie) providing an alternative to flying.

Also in and around Dun Laoghaire, there are various walks (www.dun-laoghaire.com/walks) that will enable you to see the best of the coast and scenery. Many are signposted, making it very easy to find your way around. For more information, contact the Dun Laoghaire Tourist Information Office at Avoca House, 8 Marine Road (01 205 4855, www.dlrtourism.com).

To see the coast by boat, take a Dublin Sea Tour (01 492 5919, www.dublinseatours.ie) from either Poolbeg marina in Dublin city centre to Dun Laoghaire, Dalkey and around the Killiney area. The crew will show you the natural and historical sights as well as throwing in a bit of local gossip (including where the celebrities live).

The 40 Foot in Dun Laoghaire is a famous bathing location. Originally only for male (nude) bathing, it is now open to everyone. People swim off this point every day, even in the depths of winter and every Christmas there is a morning swim that is watched by onlookers with a mixture of disbelief and head shaking, it's certainly only for the brave!

Sandycove (Glasthule stop on the Dart) is an upwardly mobile town and area, with a lot of great shops and pubs. Cavistons at 58/59 Glasthule Road (www.cavistons.com, 2809120), a delicatessen and fish shop, is especially popular and is famous for its lunches and great seafood. Be warned though that queues snake around the corner for their Christmas turkeys. That said, they do try and make it as painless as possible by offering customers hot whiskey and nibbles.

Staying in this area, Fitzgeralds at 11 Sandycove Road (01 280 4469) is a great traditional pub, especially on Bloomsday (www.jamesjoyce.ie), while clothing and shoe shops Rococo at 20 Glasthule Road (01 230 0686) and Soul at 4A Glasthule Road (01 280 8895) are also worth a visit.

The Dublin Mountains, about 20 minutes away by car, are a beautiful natural resource and are especially popular with walkers and hikers. The Wicklow Mountains are also very scenic, but a good bit further away.

For something out of the ordinary, visit the old gambling emporium, the Hell Fire Club, on Mount Pelier Hill in South County Dublin. Although it was abandoned hundreds of years ago, it still remains a talking point as rumours abound as to what really went on up there. It was built as a hunting lodge but urban myth says that it was a site used for satanic practices, and that the devil himself appeared there. Ruins and rumours aside, its position affords one of the best views of Dublin.

Dun Laoghaire

Map p.414-421
428, 429
Area **F** p.166-167

South Of The Liffey

South of the Liffey, past the city centre zone, is a place of affluent neighbourhoods dotted with cathedrals and embassies, and one of the biggest universities in Ireland. It is where the young professionals live, or strive to if they can afford the rent, especially Ballsbridge, Sandymount, Rathmines, Rathgar and Ranelagh.

The Good

With both the Luas and the Dart running though much of this area, it's a very convenient place to live and work. No more being stuck in traffic.

Definite must-sees in the Kilmainham area are the Museum of Modern Art in Kilmainham Royal Hospital on Military Road (01 612 9900, www.imma.ie) and Kilmainham Gaol on Inchicore Road (01 493 5984). The former merits a visit for its interesting exhibition schedule and beautiful building and surrounding gardens, the latter for the lesson in Irish history, its empty corridors relating more than any book could ever hope to. St James's hospital (James's Street, 01 410 3000, www.stjames.ie) is behind the Kilmainham Gaol (the Luas stops next to it).

The Bad

The traffic in Ballsbridge is particularly bad in the morning and at any other rush hour time, as is parking, so travelling by car can be more hassle than it's worth. Try to avail of public transport or just walk when possible.

Moving towards Christchurch, St Patrick's Cathedral (Saint Patrick's Close, 01 453 9472, www.stpatrickscathedral.ie) and Christchurch Cathedral (Christchurch Place, 01 677 8099, www.cccdub.ie) fill the horizon with buttresses and spires. Both are impressive cathedrals but the history of St Patrick's is especially intriguing. It is said to have been built beside the well where St Patrick baptised converts in the fifth century. Today's building dates back to the 13th century and inside you can see the coats of arms of the prominent families in Ireland throughout the ages. An interesting object to see here is an old door with a hole in it. This door is said to have been the only obstacle remaining between two warring families in the late 15th century, headed by Lord Kildare and Lord Ormond (who was hiding in the chapter room of the cathedral at the time). In a bid to form a truce, Lord Kildare made a hole in the door and stuck his hand through it as a sign of peace, whereupon they shook hands and the war ended. This is where it is said that the expression 'chancing your arm' comes from.

The Lowdown

Francis Street is an up-and-coming art quarter with many artists opening private galleries and studios there.

Dublinia (St Micheal's Hill, Christchurch, 01 679 4611, www.dublinia.ie), located in a Victorian building designed by the same architect who restored Christchurch cathedral in the 19th century, is an exhibition that covers Anglo-Norman history in Ireland from the 12th century to the 16th.

Once seen as student areas, Rathmines and Ranelagh have become more popular with young professionals since the renovation in recent years of many Georgian houses here. This of course has resulted in rocketing rents. They are however very desirable areas to live in (along with Portobello and Rathgar) as the Green Line of the Luas (1800 300 604, www.luas.ie) runs straight through this area connecting them with St Stephens' Green, Dundrum and Sandyford. The Dundrum shopping Centre (see p.329) and Cineplex (01 291 6802, www.movies-at.ie) have opened recently – Here you'll find Harvey Nichols and House of Fraser (see p.325) and an array of other enticing shops and restaurants including Dunne & Crescenzi's (01 216 6764).

Must-Do

The Christmas Carol service in St Patrick's cathedral is one of the most festive events in Dublin. To attend, you must have a ticket (which is free of charge). Contact the Cathedral for information.

For a cosy dinner in Rathgar, a short distance from Rathmines, visit Bijou Restaurant (47 Highfield Road, 01 496 1518), where the fish cakes are renowned.

Ballsbridge, on the other hand (an area close to Baggot Street), has many of the main embassies, as well as some financial institutions. You will also find the RDS (01 668 0866, www.rds.ie), a popular venue for fairs, property shows and concerts. Next to it is the Four Seasons Hotel (see p.33), which is home to the ICE bar and some of the best cocktails in town, albeit with a Four Seasons price tag.

Lansdowne Road, although currently undergoing intensive renovation, (see p.261) is traditionally where rugby and football matches are held, along with the odd concert. Post Leinster rugby match drinks for games played in Old Wesley in Donnybrook are usually held in Kiely's bar (22 Donnybrook Road, 01 283 0209), while those held in Lansdowne Road are traditionally followed by drinks in Paddy Cullen's (14 Merrion Road, 01 669 4492). While Lansdowne Road is closed for renovation, matches will be held in either Croke Park or Donnybrook. For dog racing, go to Shelbourne Park (see p.262).

Blackrock, situated on the coast and on the Dart light rail line (see p.41) boasts a cosmopolitan atmosphere and is home to the famous Blackrock College (01 288 8681, www.blackrockcollege.ie), past pupils of which include Eamonn de Valera and Bob Geldof. The area has a good selection of bars, a park with a children's playground, a weekend market (www.blackrockmarket.com) and unique shops such as Khan boutique at 15 Rock Hill, Main Street (01 278 1646). There isn't a beach in Blackrock, but there is a long strand from Sandymount to Booterstown that is ideal for walking. Moving away from the coast, and towards Stillorgan, is Leopardstown Racecourse (see p.260), where you can enjoy a day at the races and a bit of a gamble at the bookies. It has private suites, restaurants, bars and the famous, if very cheesy, Club 92 (see p.385). University City Dublin (see p.150) or UCD as it is known, is one of Ireland's biggest universities and has been teaching students for the last 150 years. As well as its broad range of degree and postgraduate courses, its campus offers an endless range of sports facilities and a gym (see p.265), which is open to the general public (01 716 2185). The Office of Public Works (01 647 6000, www.opw.ie) and the Heritage Council of Ireland (01 777 0777, www.heritagecouncil.ie) operate closely with national and private museums, ensuring that treasures are preserved and can be enjoyed by the public. National museums are free of charge and offer a range of tours, events and literature, encouraging participation in and discussion about the exhibits. Irelands chequered past ensures an interesting choice as far as museums go. From decorative artefacts and literature to the Vikings and Guinness; there's something to please every age and interest.

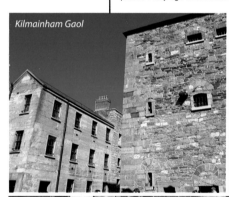
Kilmainham Gaol

Irish Museum of Modern Art

St Patrick's Cathedral

Guinness Storehouse

Art Galleries

Other options **Art** p.227, **Art & Craft Supplies** p.285

Dublin, when compared to the likes of Paris or New York, may not have the same size and abundance of galleries but with the wealth of emerging contemporary Irish talent and the renewed interest in art collection due to a health economy, galleries are steadily growing in number. One positive aspect of the majority of Dublin's art galleries is that they don't have an admission charge, so exposure to art is accessible to everybody.

There is not really an arts quarter in Dublin, although many galleries and studios are located in city centre areas like Temple Bar, Stephen's Green and, more recently, Francis Street. This street and the surrounding area an increasingly popular destination for antique shops, art galleries and studios. A few notable galleries to visit on Francis Street include the Bad Art Gallery at number 79 (01 453 7588, www.thebadartgallery.ie), Kevin Sharkey at number 80 (01 453 6282, www.kevinsharkey.com) and the Cross Gallery at number 59 (01 473 8978, www.thecrossgallery.ie). Entrance to all of these is free of charge.

During summer weekends, the railings around Merrion Square double as an art gallery as local artists exhibit their work while the weather is good. Not only can you find some interesting pieces created by young talent, but it makes an already pretty square even more charming.

Many of the larger galleries also run lectures, concerts, children's programmes and drawing classes, which are an enjoyable ways to learn about art and art appreciation. For more information on galleries in Dublin (and in Ireland as a whole) Arts Listings (www.arts.ie) has a helpful database. Irish Art (www.irishart.com) is a useful website for anyone wishing to buy art in Ireland.

Trinity College
Dublin 2
Map 820 B4 **543**

Douglas Hyde Gallery

01 608 1116 | www.douglashydegallery.com

The Douglas Hyde Gallery, part of Trinity College, hosts a wide range of contemporary art exhibitions that are usually not too mainstream. Tours and discussions encourage the public to contemplate the work. The gallery is open from 11:00 to 18:00 Mondays to Fridays (except for Thursdays, when it remains open until 19:00), and from 11:00 to 16:45 on Saturdays. Entrance is free of charge, and there is a bookshop.

Farmleigh
Castleknock
Dublin 15
Map 800 A4 **45**

Farmleigh Gallery

01 815 5900 | www.farmleighgallery.ie

The Farmleigh Gallery was opened in 2005 and the works exhibited are drawn from the OPW Government Art Collection, the Guinness family, and loans from other art galleries such as the National Gallery of Ireland. The gallery is open from 10:00 to 17:30, Thursday to Sunday and on Bank Holidays. As well as the gallery, visitors can enjoy the house and grounds. Entrance is free of charge.

Charlemont House
Parnell Sq Nth
Dublin 1
Map 820 A2 **14**

Hugh Lane Gallery

01 222 5550 | www.hughlane.ie

The Hugh Lane gallery houses a huge range of modern and contemporary art, arguably one of the biggest in Ireland, and runs classes and workshops encouraging art appreciation for both adults and children. The paintings bequeathed by Sir Hugh Lane to the gallery are from Courbet, Degas, Manet, Vuillard and Monet, and are shared with the National Gallery of London. The Hugh Lane also boasts a large collection of contemporary Irish art in different media, by the likes of Barry Flanagan, Neil Jordan, Tony O'Malley and Sean Scully. The sculpture hall has works from Rodin and others. The gallery is open from 10:00 to 18:00 Tuesday to Thursday, from 10:00 to 17:00 on Friday and Saturday, and from 11:00 to 17:00 on Sunday. It is closed on Mondays. Entrance is free of charge.

Royal Hospital
Military Rd
Kilmainham
Dublin 8
Map 809 E2 **198**

Irish Museum Of Modern Art (IMMA)
01 612 9900 | *www.modernart.ie*
The venue alone is reason to visit IMMA, and if it is a sunny day, a picnic in its grounds makes for a very pleasant and relaxing afternoon. The beautiful former Kilmainham hospital offers the perfect stage for the various forms of contemporary and modern art exhibited here from its own collection or from its Education and Community programme. The large square courtyard displays various sculptures. IMMA is open from 10:00 to 17:30 Tuesdays to Saturdays (except on Wednesdays, when it opens at 10:30), and from 12:00 to 17:30 on Sundays and holidays. It is closed on Mondays. Entrance is free of charge.

Anne's La
South Anne St
Dublin 2
Map 824 B1 **184**

Kerlin Gallery
01 670 9096 | *www.kerlin.ie*
Kerlin Gallery is a leading gallery featuring contemporary Irish and international art. Founded in 1988, the gallery covers 3,600 square feet and has exhibited artists such as Sean Scully, Willie Doherty and Chung Eun-Mo. It is open from 10:00 to 17:45 Mondays to Fridays, and from 11:00 to 16:30 on Saturdays. Entrance is free of charge.

41/43 Watling St
Usher's Island
Dublin 8
Map 818 C4 **183**

Mother's Tankstation
01 671 7654 | *www.motherstankstation.com*
This gallery prides itself on having an innovative way of exhibiting visual art and holds exhibitions from very character-driven artists. It is not a commercially focused gallery and exhibits unfamiliar and often complex projects to the Irish market. So, in other words, it's home to all that is weird and wonderful in the art world. The gallery is open from 12:00 to 18:00, Thursday to Saturday, but remains closed for the months of July and August.

Enjoying the gardens at the IMMA

The Hugh Lane Gallery

100 Thomas St
Dublin 8
Map 823 D1 **5**

National College Of Art & Design (NCAD)

01 636 4200 | *www.ncad.ie*

NCAD is Ireland's premier school for art and design education. Every year in June the graduates exhibit their final year projects offering the public a chance to see the new generation of Irish talent in the fields of design (ceramics, metals, fashion, textiles) and fine art (print, media, painting, sculpture). Check the website for upcoming events.

Merrion Sq West
Dublin 2
Map 824 C1 **197**

National Gallery Of Ireland

01 661 5133 | *www.nationalgallery.ie*

As the name suggests, this is the leader of the pack, the forerunner of galleries in Dublin. Built in 1864, it houses many important Irish and European artists such as Jack B Yeats, Orpen, Turner, Caravaggio, Mantegna, Goya, Vermeer, Pierrot and Monet. Entrance is free, as are guided tours that operate at various times throughout the day. There are also many lectures about specific artists in the gallery or eras and styles, as well as children's playtimes most weekends. Opening hours are from 09:30 to 17:30, Monday to Saturday (although the gallery is open until 20:30 on Thursdays), and from 12:00 to 17:30 on Sunday. Photography is not permitted, although sketching is, with prior permission.

Meeting House Sq
Temple Bar
Dublin 2
Map 820 A4 **20**

National Photographic Archive

01 677 7451 | *www.nli.ie*

This gallery houses the photographic collection of around 600,000 photos from the National Gallery. Although most of the photographs are historical, there are some modern collections, such as portraits, political occasions and more, with exhibitions changing throughout the year. There is a shop and reading room on site. This archive will be of great interest to anyone interested in photography and Irish history. The gallery is open from 10:00 to 17:00, Monday to Friday. On Saturdays, it is open from 10:00 to 14:00. Entry is free.

15 Ely Place
Dublin 2
Map 824 C3 **178**

Royal Hibernian Academy

01 661 2558 | *www.royalhibernianacademy.ie*

This is one of the largest exhibitions buildings in Dublin and is dedicated to developing the public's perception of the various art forms. It hosts many visiting exhibitions and shows, featuring paintings, sculpture and other forms of art from the best of Irish and international art, and indeed new and emerging artists. The gallery is open from 11:00 to 17:00, Tuesday to Saturday (with a late closing time of 20:00 on Thursdays), and from 14:00 to 17:00 on Sunday. It is closed on Mondays. Entrance is free of charge.

Powerscourt
Townhouse Centre
59 South William St
Dublin 2
Map 824 A1 **567**

Solomon Gallery

01 679 4237 | *www.solomongallery.com*

The Solomon Gallery opened in 1981 in the drawing room of the Powerscourt Townhouse and plays host to over 30 Irish and international contemporary artists whose work is mainly representational or figurative. The gallery holds around 13 exhibitions per year. Opening hours are from 10:00 to 17:30, Monday to Friday, and from 11:00 to 16:00 on Saturdays. Entrance is free of charge.

Forts & Castles

Castles featured strongly in the Irish countryside hundreds of years ago but many have been destroyed due to war or neglect. In the Dublin area, there are slim pickings but the few that do still exist have been well preserved and make interesting

Good Things Come To Those Who Wait...

Dublin is home to many annual events that are arts-based, such as the Dublin Film Festival, the Diversions Festival, Culture Night and the Dublin Theatre Festival. See Annual Events on p.49 for more information.

trips. They also provide a history of the city and a way to get to know how Dublin was created and under what conditions people lived, albeit the very wealthy. In most castles or buildings of this kind, there is an entrance fee, although this usually goes towards preservation.

Off Dame St
Dublin 2
Map 823 F1 **189**

Dublin Castle
01 645 8831 | *www.dublincastle.ie*
The Dublin Castle you see today is a mere shadow of its former glory. Much of it was destroyed hundreds of years ago in more turbulent times but it is still an impressive building in terms of history and the legacy it brings to viewers through its restored halls and beautiful interiors. A guided tour is especially beneficial and sheds light on Ireland's struggle for independence, and indeed the Ireland of today. There are numerous interesting venues within the castle grounds, such as the Chester Beatty Library (p.30) and the Garda Museum, which is located in the Norman Record Tower.

Malahide
North Coast

Malahide Castle
01 846 2184 | *www.malahidecastle.com*
In terms of being able to imagine yourself in period costume, this an impressive castle. Out of the rat race of city centre Dublin, this 14th century castle on 250 acres lies comfortably in the surrounding countryside. Guided tours (€7 for adults, €20 for families) take you around the various halls complete with 18th century furniture. On the grounds there is also the Fry Model Railway, Talbot Botanical Gardens and, if legend is to be believed, a number of curious ghosts.

Various Locations
Map 815 E1 **177**

Martello Towers
The Martello Towers were built by the British during the Napoleonic war as lookout posts in the event of invasion. If any foreign approaching ships were sighted, the guard would light a fire on its flat roof. The next tower along would see this and do the same until the warning reached all of the towers along the coast. These small round defensive towers can be found dotted along the east coast in numerous places such as Sandycove (01 280 9265, www.dun-laoghaire.com/dir/jjtower.html), Dalkey Island, Howth, and Sutton.

Rathfarnham
South Dublin
Map 813 A3 **201**

Rathfarnham Castle
01 493 4962 | *rathfarnhamcastle@opw.ie*
Open from May to September, Rathfarnham Castle plays host to a number of events such as art exhibitions, concerts and tours. The castle has a colourful history, and one

Dublin Castle

Malahide Castle

of the most famous stories is the one about the skeleton of a woman that was found in one of the castle's secret wall compartments. Legend has it that two men were competing for her affections so they locked the woman away and agreed to a duel, with the winner being the one to free her. Sadly for the woman, both men died and she stayed in the secret compartment until her remains were found over a century later. Restoration work is ongoing at the castle.

Historic Houses

Many of the historic houses in Dublin have been restored and converted into government offices, galleries, museums, hotels or residential use. The restoration and continued care of these houses is guided by the Office of Public Works (01 647 6000, www.opw.ie) and the Heritage Council (056 777 0777, www.heritagecouncil.ie) and must adhere to specific restoration guidelines and planning. This safeguards against mistakes being made and precious historical features being ruined, which was a regular occurrence in the 1960s and 1970s. Most historic house interiors are open to the public, although a few can only be viewed externally. Many Georgian terraces in Dublin have been damaged over time but some fine examples still remain in Fitzwilliam Square, Merrion Square, Leeson Street, Harcourt Street, and St Stephen's Green.

29 Fitzwilliam Sq
Dublin 2
Map 824 C3 **181**

29 Fitzwilliam Square

01 702 6165 | *www.esb.ienumbertwentynine*

29 Fitzwilliam Square provides a realistic look at what life was like in the 19th century for a middle class family in Dublin. Complete with furniture, plasterwork, paintings and decorations of the era, you really do feel like you've travelled back to the Georgian period. The house is open from 10:00 to 17:00, Tuesday to Saturday, and from 13:00 to 17:00 on Sundays. It is closed on Mondays. Admission costs €5, but children under 16 can go in for free.

Phoenix Park
Dublin 8
Map 808 C1 **222**

Áras an Uachtaráin

01 617 1000 | *www.president.ie*

Who wouldn't want a nosey around the home of the President of Ireland? Guided tours offer a glimpse of its beautiful interior and although it is only open on a Saturday, it could be incorporated in a visit to the Phoenix Park (see p.194) or Dublin Zoo (see p.197). Guided tours take place (Saturdays only) from 10:15 to 16:30 in summer and from 10:15 to 15:30 in winter. Meet at the Phoenix Park Visitors Centre.

Fairview Park
Dublin 5
Map 803 D4 **357**

Casino Marino

01 833 1618 | *casinomarino@opw.ie*

Its urban setting lies somewhat at odds with the beautiful lines of this summer villa, built for Lord Charlemont in the 18th century. It is an excellent example of Palladian architecture in Ireland and architecturally speaking, a gem of a house with innovative designs for its time. Its name means 'small house', which is quite ironic as it has 16 rooms. Entrance is by guided tour only. Admission costs €2.90 for adults, €2.10 for senior citizens and groups, €1.30 for students and children and €7.40 for families.

Custom House Quay
Dublin 1
Map 820 C3 **188**

Custom House

01 888 2538

Now used as government offices, this building has an interesting past, having faced near destruction in the 1920s, after which it was not restored completely until 1991. For the best view of its facade and to get an idea of its size, go to the south side of the Liffey. It's an iconic building that is one of the most familiar sights of the Dublin skyline. Entrance is free of charge.

Castleknock
Dublin 15
Map 800 A4 **45**

Farmleigh House
01 815 5900 | www.farmleigh.ie
Originally the home of the Guinness family, Farmleigh was bought by the Irish State and renovated by the Office of Public Works in 1999. It has hosted many events on behalf of the state and has entertained many political visitors. The 18th century house and 78 acre estate are also immensely popular with the public due to a lively events programme aimed at all the family (see the website for details). The house is open from 10:30 to 17:00, and guided tours are available on Thursdays and Fridays (by appointment only). There is a cafe and restaurant on site.

Kildare St
Dublin 2
Map 824 C1 **194**

Leinster House
01 618 3000 | www.irlgov.ie
Home to the Dáil and the Seanad (Houses of Parliament), this magnificent building is where all the important decisions regarding the government are made. Guided tours can be arranged in advance and they will show you around the main rooms where all the action takes place.

Dawson St
Dublin 2
Map 824 B2 **190**

Mansion House
www.dublincity.ie
The official residence of the Lord Major of Dublin, Mansion House is a beautiful example of a Queen Anne style building. Built in the early 18th century, it was first home to Joshua Dawson whose name was taken for Dawson Street. Set back from the street, it has a cobbled courtyard in front of it and a restaurant to its side. It is not open to the public.

33 Synge St
Dublin 8
Map 824 B2 **190**

Shaw's Birthplace
01 475 0854
As the name suggests, this is the birthplace of George Bernard Shaw. The playwright and Nobel Prize winner was born in 1856 and lived here, before later moving to London. In the house you can visit his bedroom and kitchen, where he spent much of his time. It also gives a good idea of what life was like in a Victorian middle-class family. There is a bookshop on site, and guided tours are available. Open May to October from 10:00 to 17:00, Monday to Saturday and on Sundays and Public Holidays from 11:00 to 17:00. Entrance costs €6 for adults, €5 for senior citizens and students, €3.50 for children and €17 for families. You can also get a discounted combination ticket with the Dublin Writers Museum and James Joyce Museum.

Custom House

Religious Sites

Dublin, indeed Ireland in general, is predominantly Roman Catholic. However, in the last 10 years, it has become more multicultural due to the booming economy and quality of life in Dublin. At present, the Roman Catholic faith represents nearly 90% of the population, while Protestant religions make up 3.5%, Muslim 0.5%, Orthodox Christians 0.2% and Jewish communities 0.05%.

A useful website for finding a Christian church in Dublin is www.dublinchurches.com, while www.ireland.anglican.org and www.dublindiocese.ie provide information about Church of Ireland and Roman Catholic communities respectively.

For information on the Jewish community in Dublin, contact the Jewish Community Centre located at Herzog House, 1 Zion Road in Rathgar (01 492 3751, irishcom@iol.ie). The Islamic Cultural Centre Ireland (ICCI) at 19 Roebuck Road in Clonskeagh (01 208 0000, www.islamireland.ie) is based in Clonskeagh and has information on Islamic practices in Ireland. Irrespective of your beliefs though, the many beautiful buildings that bear witness to the different faiths are well worth a visit, and it is always interesting to discover the intricacies of other religions.

Christchurch Pl
Dublin 8
Map 823 F1 `185`

Christchurch Cathedral

01 677 8099 | www.cccdub.ie

Opposite Jury's Inn Christchurch, and next to Dublinia Museum, Christchurch Cathedral (Anglican) was originally a Norman church dating back to the 12th century, but today only parts of it remain from this time. Daily services are open to everyone. A donation is requested for the upkeep of the church. On sunny days, Dubliners stroll into the grounds to picnic or just chill out on the grass in front of this magnificent cathedral.

163 South Circular Rd
Dublin 8
Map 810 A4 `179`

Dublin Mosque

01 453 3242 | www.islaminireland.com

The Dublin Mosque and Islamic foundation was built in 1976 from funds raised from relations of Muslims in Dublin as previously there had been no mosque In Ireland. Non-Muslims are welcome to go and visit the mosque. The mosque also forms the headquarters of the Islamic Foundation of Ireland, which takes care of the religious, educational and social needs of Ireland's Islamic population.

Marlborough St
Dublin 1
Map 820 B3 `196`

St Mary's Pro Cathedral

01 874 5441 | www.procathedral.ie

Built in Greek Doric style in the 19th century, St Mary's Pro Cathedral (Roman Catholic) is right in the centre of Dublin, near O'Connell Street. The cathedral choir sings a Latin mass every Sunday at 11:00 and the Parish Office sells Mass cards and catholic literature. The Saturday Vigil Mass at 18:00 is served by Cantors and visiting choirs throughout the year. Visitors are asked to avoid moving around the church while services are in progress and to turn off mobile phones before entering the church.

Christchurch Cathedral

Patrick's Cl
Dublin 8
Map 823 E2 `200`

St Patrick's Cathedral

01 485 4817 | www.stpatrickscathedral.ie

A beautiful Anglican cathedral dating back to St Patrick which is currently being renovated, hence the entrance fee to visitors outside of times of worship. The choir is one of the best in Ireland. Historically this is a fascinating cathedral – it is where Jonathan Swift is buried alongside his great love Esther Johnson (who he always called 'Stella'). After paying the €5 entrance fee, you are free to wander around the cathedral at will, exploring the many stone carvings, stained glass windows and interesting architecture. Staff are on hand to answer any questions you may have. There is a small gift shop near the entrance.

Clarendon St
Dublin 2
Map 824 A1 186

St Teresa's Church

01 671 8466 | www.clarendonstreet.com

St Teresa's Carmelite Church just off Grafton Street (also known as Clarendon Street Church) is an oasis of calm in the busy city centre. It is worth a visit to see the beautiful stained glass windows and the Resource Centre where parishioners can borrow books, CDs and videos. The church also holds art exhibitions and has displayed icons by some of Ireland's leading iconographers.

Rathfarnham Rd
Terenure
Dublin 6
Map 814 A2 202

Terenure Hebrew Congregation

01 492 3751 | www.jewishgen.org/JCR-UK

Founded in the 1900s, Dublin's main synagogue is based in Terenure in south County Dublin and provides daily Scharit and Mincha/Maariv services. Visitors are welcome to attend the Shabbat and Yom Tov services. The website has information on the Irish Jewish Museum, and provides a directory of numbers for other synagogues, places to stay, schools and a list of kosher suppliers.

Heritage Sites

There are a limited number of official heritage sites in Dublin, as many are listed under houses (see p.184) or museums (see p.188). The heritage council of Ireland is very strict in its rules and regulations and if you are looking for a more in-depth list of all heritage sites in Dublin and indeed Ireland, contact their head office in County Kilkenny (056 777 0777, www.heritagecouncil.ie or www.heritageireland.ie). Most of them charge a nominal entrance fee, which is usually put towards the upkeep of the site.

Dame St
Dublin 2
Map 819 F4 30

City Hall

01 222 2222 | www.dublincity.ie

This impressive building, designed by Thomas Cooley, was built in the 18th century to be used as the Royal Exchange. Today it functions as a meeting place for the council and as the venue for many a launch party and film premiere. The history of the building can be viewed on the ground floor. There is no entrance fee.

Inichore Rd
Kilmainham
Dublin 8
Map 809 E3 193

Kilmainham Gaol

01 453 5984 | www.heritageireland.ie

Although now no longer used as a prison, Kilmainham Gaol was open for business for nearly 130 years up until the 1920s. A guided tour will show you around its immense structure and paint a picture of the many famous former prisoners, their deaths and how the history of this building and Ireland often intertwined. You can explore certain parts of the prison on your own, but the guided tour takes you to some areas that are not otherwise accessible. It also includes a fascinating audiovisual show on the history of the uprisings, with authentic footage of some of the jail's most famous occupants.

Lusk
North-west Dublin

Lusk Heritage Centre

01 647 2461 | www.heritageireland.ie

Lusk Heritage centre has information and an exhibition on North Dublin's medieval churches and the 16th century effigy tomb of Sir Christopher Barnewall. Also by the centre are a 19th century church, a round tower and a medieval belfry. Entry costs €1.60 for adults, €1.10 for children, €1.00 for students and €4.50 for families.

Phoenix Park
Dublin 8
Map 808 C1 222

Phoenix Park Visitor Centre

01 677 0095 | www.heritageireland.ie

Here the visitor can see an audiovisual exhibition showing the history of the park and its wildlife. There is a restaurant on the grounds and beside the Visitor Centre is the restored Ashtown Castle dating back to the 17th century. Guided tours are available and last 30 minutes. Entry costs €2.75 for adults, €2 for groups and senior citizens, €1.25 for children and students and €7 for families.

Museums

The Office of Public Works (01 647 6000, www.opw.ie) and the Heritage Council of Ireland (056 777 0777, www.heritagecouncil.ie) operate closely with national and private museums, ensuring that treasures are preserved and can be enjoyed by the public. National museums are free of charge and offer a range of tours, events and literature, encouraging participation in and discussion about the exhibits.

Clock Tower Bld
Dublin Castle
Dublin 2
Map 823 F1 529

Chester Beatty Library

01 407 0750 | www.cbl.ie

A unique and interesting insight into Far Eastern art; the gallery exhibits Chinese Jade Books, and Burmese and Siamese art dating from the 18th and19th centuries, which illustrate folktales through colourful drawings. There are also illustrations by Buddhist monks. The library won the European Museum of the Year award in 2002. Open from 10:00 to 17:00 Monday to Friday, 11:00 to 17:00 on Saturdays and 13:00 to 17:00 on Sundays. Closed public holidays and Mondays from October to April. Entrance is free.

St Michael's Hill
Christchurch
Dublin 8
Map 823 E1 204

Dublinia

01 679 4611 | www.dublinia.ie

Here you can step back in time to Medieval Ireland and experience life as it was then. Dublinia presents history in a fun and memorable way. Many of the exhibits are interactive, presenting a fascinating insight into Dublin's early days. You should be able to get round the whole museum in less than two hours, so this is a good venue to combine with a visit to Christchurch Cathedral, which you can access via a pedestrian overpass. During high season (April to September), Dublinia is open daily from 10:00 to 17:00. From October to March, it is open from 11:00 to 16:00 Mondays to Fridays, and from 10:00 to 16:00 on Saturdays, Sundays and bank holidays. Admission costs €6.25 per adult and €3.75 per child. Family and group rates are available.

35 North Great
George's St
Dublin 1
Map 820 B2 10

James Joyce Centre

01 878 8547 | www.jamesjoyce.ie

Filled with information about James Joyce, this is definitely the place to come to brush up on Joyce's literature and life through a series of tours, exhibitions, lectures and events. Whether or not you've read Ulysses (and whether or not you understood it), a highlight of the calendar for Joyce enthusiasts is of course Bloomsday on June16 (see Annual Events on p.47). The centre is open from 10:00 to 17:00, Tuesday to Saturday. Admission is €5 for adults and €4 for students.

Haigh Terrace
Dun Laoghaire
Map 817 F4 192

The Maritime Museum

01 280 0969 | maritime@ireland.com

The Maritime Museum, located in the former Mariner's Church out in Dun Laoghaire, is only open at the weekend (from 13:00 to 18:00). Exhibits include the Bantry Longboat (which was captured by the failed French invasion in the 18th century), a cannon from the Spanish Armada and the Opica from Bailey Lighthouse in Howth. Admission is free.

Chester Beatty Library

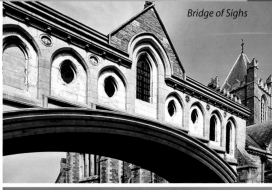

Bridge of Sighs

Dublinia

City Hall

Kilmainham Gaol

James Joyce Centre

St Patrick's Cl
Dublin 8
Map 823 F2 205

Marsh's Library

01 454 3511 | www.marshlibrary.ie

Marsh's Library was the first public Library in Ireland and was built in 1701, celebrating 300 years in 2001. Books date from the 16th to the 18th century and cover a wide range of topics, from medicine to travel. The interior is beautiful with dark oak bookcases and cages in which patrons can be locked if they wish to view rare books. It's not a place to bring children (although entry is free for them) but is a must for any bookworm. Entry is €2.50 for adults and €1.25 for students and senior citizens. The library hosts many events throughout the year – check the website for details.

Collins Barracks
Benburb Rd
Dublin 7
Map 809 F2 42

Museum of Decorative Arts & History – Collins Barracks

01 677 7444 | www.museum.ie

The Museum of Decorative Arts and History exhibits a wide range of objects from ceramics to clothing. The building dates from the 1700s but the interior is modern and spacious with multimedia points to aid in education and enjoyment. There are guided tours as well as annual events and temporary exhibitions. The museum is open from Tuesdays to Saturdays between 10:00 and 17:00, and on Sundays from 14:00 to 17:00. It is closed on Mondays. Entry is free of charge.

Kildare St
Dublin 2
Map 824 C2 42

National Museum Of Ireland – Archeology & History

01 677 7444 | www.museum.ie

Officially opened in 1890, this striking Palladian building houses over two million artefacts dating from 7000BC to the medieval period. The regular temporary exhibitions and events make for interesting viewing and facilities include a shop, cafe, and education resource room. The museum is child friendly with tours and events aimed at education through fun. It is open from 10:00 to 17:00 Tuesday to Saturday, and from 14:00 to 17:00 on Sundays.

Merrion St
Dublin 2
Map 824 C2 254

Natural History Museum

01 677 7444 | www.museum.ie

The National History Museum has thousands of creatures on display, some of which are now extinct. Sunday and weekend programmes offer children the possibility to learn about animals and wildlife both in Ireland and abroad, not that the majestic stuffed animals won't appeal to the inner child in everyone. There is a shop, and the museum offers guided tours for a small charge. Opening hours are from 10:00 to 17:00, Tuesday to Saturday, and from 14:00 to 17:00 on Sundays.

18 Parnell Sq
Dublin 1
Map 819 F2 180

Writer's Museum

01 872 2077 | www.writersmuseum.com

Have you ever wondered why figures like James Joyce, Patrick Kavanagh or WB Yeats are such important figures in Irish history, despite being mere writers? The Writer's Museum will tell you just that, and lots more, allowing you to discover Dublin's literary heritage through books, letters, art and memorabilia. The museum covers the last 300 years and often has visiting exhibitions, lunchtime events and lectures. It is open from 10:00 to 17:00 daily, except for Sundays and bank holidays when it only opens at 11:00. Adults must pay an entry fee of €7.

Dublin Writer's Museum

When you're lost what will you find in your pocket?

Item 71. The half-eaten chewing gum

When you reach into your pocket make sure you have one of these minature marvels to hand... far more use than a half-eaten stick of chewing gum when you're lost.

Explorer Mini Maps
Putting the city in your pocket

Parks & Beaches

Dublin is one of the greenest cities in Europe and the city's main public parks are well maintained. Phoenix Park is a great example, with its huge circumference and range of amenities. These open spaces are very popular during the summer when they are the setting for festivals and concerts, as seen in St Stephen's Green and Merrion Square. Many of the parks don't actually have designated sports facilities (except for Herbert park which has excellent facilities) but this doesn't stop impromptu games of Frisbee, football and the like, especially in the bigger spaces. Cycling is also popular, with tours to begin in the Phoenix Park. Rollerblading however is usually not tolerated, even if in some places it is technically permitted. Dogs are allowed in parks while on a leash but remember that any waste your four legged friend leaves on the footpath is your business too – what is pooped must be scooped (it's the law, so tidy up after your dog!). Beaches in Dublin are quite scenic if you are brave enough to bare the chilly temperatures of the Irish Sea. They vary in quality and size, from lovely long stretches to pea-sized coves but for the most part they are clean and have parking facilities. Due to the windy nature of the Irish coast, watersports such as windsurfing and sailing are popular. For information on specific beaches, contact the relative county council: Dun Laoghaire (south Dublin, 01 205 4700, www.dlrcoco.ie) or Fingal (north Dublin, 01 890 6758, www.fingalcoco.ie). The quality of the water is monitored regularly to make sure it adheres to EU regulations and lifeguard facilities are provided by the county council in the summer months, from June to August.

Beaches

Other options **Parks** p.193, **Swimming** p.254

Sandycove
South Coast
Map 817 F4 **225**

40 Foot

This is a historical bathing area, originally for men only but now open to everyone. The water is extremities-shrinking cold and only for the very brave, but it's probably worth a dip once in a lifetime at the very least. And you won't be alone, as a good crowd of hardcore swimmers come here every day to brave the frosty temperatures. A brisk swim on Christmas Day is a favourite tradition. Brrrr.

Balbriggan
North Coast

Balbriggan Beach

Balbriggan is home to three beautiful sandy beaches that are very popular when the weather is fair. Lifeguards are on duty during summer to ensure that swimmers are safe. Keep your eyes peeled for the nearby seal colony – you may be lucky enough to see a troupe of whiskered friends enjoying a swim near the harbour. The town of Balbriggan is located just past Skerries on the north coast.

Sutton
North Coast
Map 806 B1 **229**

Burrow Beach

This long sandy beach is great for a brisk seaside walk, as it's about 1.2km long. The water quality on this beach is carefully monitored and meets the standards set by the European Union, so it's great for swimming too – lifeguards are on duty during the summer to make sure everybody is safe. Getting there is easy – just hop on the Dart and hop off at Sutton (alternatively you could get the 31 bus). On a clear day you have a great view of Ireland's Eye from this beach.

Howth
North Coast
Map 806 C1 **218**

Claremont Beach

Claremont beach is a small sandy stretch near Howth Harbour. Due to its scenic location, there are many restaurants and cafes along Harbour Road, so this is an area that has a great buzz when the weather is lovely. The Dart stops nearby and there are lifeguards on duty during the summer months.

Dollymount
North Coast
Map 805 D4 **215**

Dollymount Strand

Dollymount was the first beach in Dublin's city centre to be awarded Blue Flag status, which means that it meets a list of conditions laid out by the European Union relating to cleanliness, water quality and dog control, among others. It's just a short trip north of Dublin, and is usually fairly quiet – you'll see a few locals, plenty of dog walkers, joggers and even the occasional kitesurfer. The beach is a Unesco Biosphere Reserve.

Killiney
South Coast

Killiney Beach

Killiney Beach is 800 metres long and, although it is a pebbly beach, it is very scenic. The sea gets deeper very gradually, so it's a great beach for paddling. Lifeguards are on duty during summer. It's a popular spot for swimming and sunbathing because it is fairly sheltered. And who knows, you may even spot one of Killiney's many celebrity residents taking their pooch for a stroll. It's easy to get there – the Dart (see p.41) stops right in front of the beach.

Portmarnock
North Coast

Portmarnock Beach

Near Portmarnock, this beach has views of Howth Head and Ireland's Eye. It is suitable for both sunbathing (weather permitting, unless you're really desperate for a tan!) and swimming and becomes packed in the summer. People often play football or other beach games, and due to its length it is also ideal for walking. Lifeguards are on duty in the summer.

Sandymount
South Coast
Map 811 F4 **226**

Sandymount Strand

While it's a great beach to walk along, it's not so popular for swimming due to the unpredictable tide. Sandymount's claim to fame is its mention as the beach in *Ulysses* by James Joyce. It is also a good starting point if you want to do some exploring and check out one of the Martello Towers (see p.183).

Dun Laoghaire
South Coast
Map 816 C3 **216**

Seapoint Beach

Seapoint beach (awarded the Blue Flag) is shallow and suitable for swimming at high tide, when it still remains fairly shallow. Surfers and canoeists enjoy the southern part of the beach while swimmers stick to the north. There are lifeguards on duty throughout the summer.

Parks

Other options **Beaches** p.192

Parnell Square
Dublin 1
Map 820 A2 **221**

Garden Of Remembrance

01 874 3074

Perhaps a bit more sombre than other parks, but no less beautiful, is the Garden of Remembrance, which commemorates the thousands of Irish lives lost during the struggle for freedom in Ireland. A poignant statue is the highlight of the gardens. It is based on the Irish legend of the Children of Lir, who were turned into swans for a period of 900 years. This is a park designed for quiet reflection rather than for ball games.

Ballsbridge
Dublin 4
Map 811 D4 **214**

Herbert Park

Situated in Ballsbridge, this park of 32 acres is very popular with the after-work crowd and offers great sports facilities such as football, tennis, boules, croquet and a children's playground. The circumference of the park is about one mile, and forms a popular route for joggers and walkers. There is a GAA sports field maintained by Dublin City Council. There is also a lovely duck pond so don't forget to take along those bags of stale bread.

Iveagh Gardens

Harcourt St
Dublin 2
Map 824 A3 **217**

This place is an oasis in the centre of Dublin. Situated directly behind St Stephen's Green, this shy little garden is reached through a hidden gate off Harcourt Street. Designed in 1863 by Ninian Niven, features include a cascade waterfall, fountains, rose garden and archery grounds.

Merrion Square

Merrion Sq
Dublin 2
Map 825 D2 **220**

The grandest location in town, Merrion Square has a beautiful setting framed by Georgian buildings on three sides and by Leinster House on the fourth. Inside the square are colourful flowerbeds and a statue of a very relaxed looking Oscar Wilde lounging on a rock – this is the only coloured statue in Dublin and is a popular

A pint in the park

tourist spot. Perhaps more interesting are the columns in front of the Oscar statue, in which some of his more famous quotes are inscribed. Entrance is free of charge.

Phoenix Park

Phoenix Park
Dublin 8
Map 808 C1 **222**

Situated in the west of the city, Phoenix Park is the largest enclosed park in Europe and gives Dubliners the benefit of its manicured gardens, wildlife areas and nature trails, along with many varieties of trees and plants. It is home to Dublin Zoo (p.197) and the president's residence (p.184). You'll find the Wellington monument, the Papal Cross and numerous sports fields. Entry is free of charge. The Phoenix Park Visitor Centre (01 677 0095, phoenixparkvisitorcentre@duchas.ie) has information on tours and upcoming events, such as Heritage week (www.heritageireland.ie) in August.

St Anne's Park

Raheny
Dublin 5
Map 804 B3 **224**

Situated on Dublin's north side, this park is one of the largest parks in the city, measuring some 250 acres. It's ideal for a family Sunday walk or the panic-driven, get-in-shape-quick biannual jog you do just after Christmas or before your summer holidays. The best time of year to visit is from June to September when the rose garden is in full bloom. There are recreational facilities and entrance is free of charge.

St Stephen's Green

St Stephen's Green
Dublin 2
Map 824 B2 **228**

Not the biggest of green spaces, but definitely one of the most popular, St Stephen's Green boasts the best location in town, right smack in the centre. The bandstand, dating from the late 19th century still belts out live music in the form of show tunes and jazz during the summer months. When the weather is good you'll struggle to find a spare patch of lawn at lunchtime, when people come to enjoy lunch alfresco.

War Memorial Gardens

South Circular Rd
Islandbridge
Dublin 8
Map 809 D2 **227**

01 677 0236 | *www.heritageireland.ie*

These famous memorial guardians commemorate the deaths of nearly 50,000 Irish soldiers who died in the first world war. Their names are inscribed in the book rooms. It's a beautiful garden in terms of landscaping and if you get chance to visit in summer you'll see the rose gardens at their very best.

194

Amusement Centres

There aren't that many amusement centres in Dublin, with only the occasional arcade on O'Connell Street, and even these are slowly being closed down. The main attraction for any thrill seekers in Dublin is Funderland (www.funfair.ie), a touring amusement fair. It comes to Dublin in December each year, and is held in the RDS (see p.50). A huge variety of rides and games are offered for people of all ages, from the teacups to the white knuckle, stomach-churning thrillers.

Botanical Gardens

The Irish are, in general, very keen gardeners. Garden centres specialising in 'mine-is-bigger-than-yours' water features have sprung up everywhere, landscaped gardens are the norm and numerous gardening programmes offer advice on what plant to put where. However, for many people having a beautifully kept private garden is not a possibility, so it is a breath of fresh air to have botanical gardens in the city, a place to go to for uncomplicated botanical advice and inspiration. As well as the thousands of different species of leafy lusciousness, they are in themselves a beautiful place to walk around and gather your thoughts. The two botanical gardens in Dublin are both on the north side, in Glasnevin and Malahide, with perhaps Glasnevin National Botanical Gardens the bigger and more influential of the two.

Botanic Av
Glasnevin
Dublin 7
Map 802 A3 **207**

National Botanical Gardens

01 837 4388 | *www.botanicgardens.ie*

As soon as you walk into the gardens and see the cast iron glasshouses, an old world feeling gathers you and brings you back to the era of rose gardens and Victorian carpet bedding. Apart from this antiqued charm, the gardens provide a very practical function of advising visitors on ecological and botanical matters, as well as having over 20,000 species of plants spread over 49 acres. The park is open from 09:00 to 18:00 in summer and from 09:00 to 16:30 in winter. It is only about three kilometres from the city centre, and entrance is free. There is plenty of parking, at a flat fee of €2.

Malahide
North Coast

Talbot Gardens

01 846 2184 | *www.malahidecastle.com*

Although not as big as the National Botanical Gardens in Glasnevin, the Talbot Gardens are still an inspirational place to walk around. The Gardens were designed by Lord Milo Talbot between the 1940s and 1970s. They contain over 5,000 species of plants, with the majority from the southern hemisphere and pretty walled gardens within gardens. There's a restaurant at the Castle if you fancy stopping for lunch.

National Botanical
Gardens

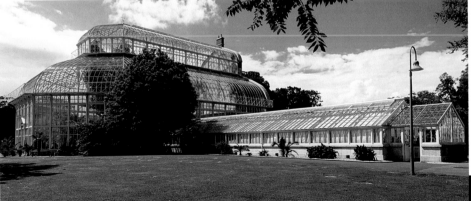

Nature Reserves

Dublin in recent times has become more ecologically aware. Sanctuaries have been set up with an astute awareness of the importance to preserve and protect endangered species. Although not a nature reserve, Phoenix Park is very involved in educating and bringing awareness to the public about the park's flora and fauna, and the importance of striving for balance in nature. Also worth a visit are the National Botanical Gardens (see p.195), whose staff are dedicated to the conservation of rare plants and ecological education. For further information on nature reserves and Ireland's policy on ecological issues, contact the Department of the Environment, Heritage and Local Government (01 888 2000, www.environ.ie).

Dalkey
South Coast

Dalkey Island

Sat about 300 metres offshore from Dalkey village lies the rocky Dalkey Island. It's a bird sanctuary, is home to seals and porpoise, and is generally an enjoyable place to walk around or spend an afternoon. To get there, head for Coliemore Harbour where you should find plenty of local fishermen willing to take you over in their boat – the trip only takes about five minutes.

Off Howth Head
North Coast

Ireland's Eye

Ireland's eye is an islet just off Howth. It is also a bird sanctuary where you can see colonies of puffins, guillemots and razorbills, among others. You can get to the islet by boat from Howth. For more information on wildlife on the island, check out www.birdweb.net/irelandseye.html and for information on Birdwatching, see p.229.

Dollymount
North Coast
Map 805 E3 209

North Bull Island

North Bull Island is a nature reserve and bird sanctuary. It is listed by Unesco as a Biosphere Reserve. Expect to find oystercatchers, pale-bellied brent goose, kestrals and grey plovers as well as other birds and mammals. There is a visitor centre which is open seven days a week. For more information on Birdwatching, see p.229.

Zoos & Wildlife Parks

Being a city, Dublin doesn't have a lot of space for wildlife parks and open farms, although it does have a national zoo. However, you will find bird sanctuaries, traditional farms and parks just a short distance from the city centre. Agriculture is of great importance in Ireland, so by going further afield you can enjoy more rural and traditional settings.

The parks and farms listed below will be of special interest to children, especially those who may have been raised in an urban environment. By visiting these places, kids can watch and learn all about the animals, and sometimes play a more interactive role in their care. Dublin Zoo, for example, features a great 'meet the keeper' programme where kids can chat to a zookeeper and watch the animals being fed.

Upper Kilmacud Rd
Dundrum
Map 815 D4 212

Airfield

01 294 4301 | *www.airfield.ie*

Situated only a few minutes from Dundrum shopping centre, Airfield is an urban farm in the true sense of the word. It has a wide range of animals such as cows, sheep, goats and pigs, as well as a beautiful garden and restaurant. For anyone interested in cars, there is also a small car museum with automobiles from the 1920s and 30s. Airfield is open from 10:00 to 17:00, Tuesday to Saturday, and from 11:00 to 17:00 on Sundays and public holidays. The admission fee is €6 per adult and €3 per child (concessions available). You can get to Airfield on the Luas green line – just hop off at Balally station.

Phoenix Park
Dublin 8
Map 808 C1 222

Dublin Zoo

01 474 8900 | www.dublinzoo.ie

Dublin zoo is the third oldest zoo in the world and is an old favourite with school tours. It has had great success breeding lions, one of which appears (and roars) at the beginning of MGM films. They have recently had their first elephant birth and also have a wide range of animals from the African plains. Some of the other animals that you can see in this zoo include giraffes, hippos, rhinos, chimpanzees, tigers, a range of monkeys and many more. The zoo's opening times vary according to the time of year, so check the website for updated information. Adult admission costs €14; a family ticket (two adults, two children) costs €40.

Newbridge
Northwest Dublin

Traditional Farm Newbridge

01 843 6534 | parks@fingalcoco.ie

Part of Newbridge House, this traditional farm gives you an insight into the workings of a traditional farm in the 19th century, complete with machinery, animals and historical tours. The opening times of the farm vary, but in general, it is open from 10:00 to 17:00 on weekdays (except Mondays, when it is closed), and from 14:00 to 18:00 on weekends. During winter (October to March), the farm is only open on weekends from 14:00 to 17:00. Admission is €3.80 per adult and €2.50 per child. If the kids get tired of exploring the farm, they can let off some steam on the children's playground. The farm has a coffee shop, toilets and a picnic area.

Garden of Remembrance

Phoenix Park

St Stephen's Green

197

Tours & Sightseeing

A guided tour can often inspire school trip nostalgia. This can be a good thing or a bad thing, depending on the person, but Dublin has a collection of guided tours that will appeal to many tastes. A good place to start is the Dublin Tourism Office on Suffolk Street (01 605 7700, www.visitdublin.com) which has information on all the tours available in Dublin, with brochures, leaflets and staff who will be able to suggest a tour that meets your requirements. Many of the city's guided tours take place on the ubiquitous open top buses, showing off the city's many different sights, with the option of hopping on or off at various points. Walking tours are also extremely popular. Dublin is a great city to walk around and you can cover a surprising amount of ground in a short time. A walking tour lets you appreciate the city's sights at a slower pace, and you have the chance to ask the tour guide plenty of questions (see p.206).
For further information on tour guides in Dublin and Ireland, consult the AATGI – Association of Approved Tourist Guides of Ireland (01 278 1626, www.tourguides.ie).

> **It's On The Map!**
> If you're not sure what's where and how to get there, feet can swell and tempers can flare. Avoid the upset and turn to p.402 for an overview of the city and make sure your sightseeing days are a breeze.

Bicycle Tours

Bicycle tours, faster than walking but more leisurely than bus or car, are a pleasant way to see Dublin and get a bit of exercise at the same time, which is never a bad thing. With new and improved cycling lanes in the city, hopping on your bike is becoming more popular as the risk of being squashed by a speeding double-decker is reduced. A limited number of tour operators offer tours around the city centre, with many more preferring the arguably better idea of touring the lush countryside. These tours are especially enjoyable due to the scenic landscape.

Belfield Bike Shop
UCD, Belfield
Dublin 4
Map 421 E3 **542**

Irish Cycling Safaris

01 260 0749 | *www.cyclingsafaris.com*
Irish Cycling Safaris offer a wide range of Bicycle tours both in Dublin and around the country, guided and self guided. Those in Dublin range from a self-guided tour from Dun Laoghaire to Killiney (lasting around three hours) to a guided three-day trip around the Dublin and Wicklow mountains. You can even do a seven-day self-guided tour around various counties in Ireland. Other tours are available but depend on demand. Equipment is provided, and a luggage van makes sure your bags are delivered to your next overnight stop – saving you (and your legs) the trouble!

9a Capel St
Dublin 1
Map 819 F4 **244**

Neills Wheels Rent a Bike & Bicycle Tours

085 153 0648 | *www.rentabikedublin.com*
Neills Wheels run a bicycle tour around the city centre with a born and bred Dubliner showing you the sights along the way. They usually begin at 18:30, leaving from Essex Bridge, and last for about two and a half hours. All equipment is provided. See their website or call for more details.

Phoenix Park
Dublin 8
Map 808 C1 **222**

Phoenix Park Bicycle Tours

01 888 3213
The OPW (The Office of Public Works) introduced bicycle tours around Phoenix Park in June 2007, which are guided by the park rangers. This makes for a very interesting tour for anyone interested in flora and fauna as the rangers' in-depth knowledge is second to none. You need to bring your own bicycle though! For more information, contact the park directly.

Boat Tours

There are a couple of boat tours offered around Dublin Bay, which extend up or down the coast, with a variety of different boats, speeds and itineraries. It all depends on what kind of tour you'd like, be it high speed and exciting or more sedate and scenic. These tours can be a good idea for groups as you can hire the boat itself and have a private tour. They are also popular as corporate or team building events.

All companies should be licensed and abide by safety standards as issued by The Department of Communications, Marine and Natural Resources.

Dublin Sea Tours

Various Locations ◀ Dublin Sea Tours
01 492 5919 | *www.dublinseatours.ie*
This tour shows you the highlights of Dublin Bay, starting from either Poolbeg Marina or Dun Laoghaire Harbour, moving up or down the coast as desired on their Redbay Stormforce, 11 metre RIBs (rigid inflatable boats). You can choose your own itinerary or leave it to the crew. Highly recommended for a clear day but avoid when rainy, as visibility will be poor. The tour generally lasts just over an hour and cost €35 per person.

The Boardwalk ◀ Liffey River Cruises
Bachelors Walk
Dublin 1
Map 820 B4 **251**
01 473 4082 | *www.liffeyvoyage.ie*
Suitable for both the young and old, these tours take you up and down the River Liffey giving insights into Dublin's history and folklore. Tours last 45 minutes and leave from Bachelors Walk. A tour costs €12 for an adult and €7 for a child, with kids under 4 years going free. There are no cruises in December, January or February.

Dublin City Moorings ◀ Safari Tours
IFSC
Dublin 1
Map 821 E3 **247**
01 855 7600 | *www.seasafari.ie*
Safari Tours are for the brave at heart, with high speed spills and thrills the name of the game. The tour takes you around the coastline and provides a mixture of local lore with exciting turns and twists on the RIBs (rigid inflatable boats). Again, weather is an important factor and the tour usually lasts about an hour. The cost is €30 per person. Safari Tours also operate from Malahide Marina.

Brewery & Vineyard Tours

Rumours that the Liffey is made up of 10% Guinness are totally unfounded, but there's no getting away from the 'black stuff' in Dublin. It's hard to explain the importance of Guinness to Ireland's national pride, but it's right up there with shamrocks and leprechauns. Both the Guinness Storehouse and the Jameson Distillery provide fascinating insights into the production of two famous Irish brands. The tours focus on the brewing or distilling processes and the history of both companies in Dublin. And both tours include a free tipple at the end (but only for people over 18).

St James's Gate ◀ Guinness Storehouse
Dublin 8
Map 809 F2 **249**
01 408 4800 | *www.guinness-storehouse.com*
This seven-floor shrine to Ireland's most famous import is situated in St James's Gate brewery, and is undoubtedly Dublin's most popular visitor attraction. A virtual

199

brewer demonstrates the brewing process along with other interactive exhibits telling you all you'll ever need to know about Guinness. The tour culminates in a free, well-deserved pint in the Gravity Bar over looking the city. While you wait for your pint to settle you can muse over the view, which stretches for miles on a clear day. It's easy to get there: it's easily walkable from the city centre (it should take about 20 minutes from the Hapenny Bridge), or you can take bus 123 from Dame Street or O'Connell Street, or the Luas to James's Street. The Storehouse is open daily from 09:30 to 17:00, except for during July and August when it stays open until 19:00. Adult admission is €14, children under 12 pay €5, and children under 6 go free. You get a 10% discount if you book online.

Jameson Distillery

Bow St
Smithfield
Dublin 7
Map 819 E3 **245**

01 807 2355 | *www.jamesonwhiskey.ie*

A trip to the Jameson Distillery begins with a video giving an introduction to the whiskey making process, followed by a tour and then whiskey tasting in the Jameson Bar. If you do go on the tour, be sure to volunteer to be a taster – at the end of the tour you get to sample four different types of whiskey to see if you can tell which is Jameson's! Even if you are not one of the volunteers, you still get a complimentary glass of Jameson's at the end of the tour. There is also a restaurant and gift shop. To get to the distillery, you can take the Luas red line, or various buses from the city centre. The distillery is also a stop on most of the hop-on, hop-off bus tours. Tours are on seven days a week, from 09:00 to 18:00. The distillery is closed on Good Friday and during the Christmas Holidays, but is open on bank holidays.

Bus Tours

Other options **Walking Tours** p.206

Dublin Bus City Tour

59 Upper
O'Connell St
Dublin 1
Map 820 A2 **12**

01 873 4222 | *www.dublinsightseeing.ie*

The fleet of City Tour buses trundle around Dublin all day, stopping at the major attractions such as Trinity College, Christchurch Cathedral, the Guinness Storehouse, Kilmainham Gaol, the National Museum, Phoenix Park, Grafton Street and many more – in fact there are 21 stops in total. A one-day ticket (valid for 24 hours) costs €14 per adult and €6 for children under 14. Buses go from 09:30 to 15:00 daily, with buses passing every 10 minutes. From 15:00 to 17:00 they pass by every 15 minutes. The last bus stops at 18:30 at the Writers Museum in Parnell Square. There is a live commentary

Jameson Distillery

Liffey River Cruises

on every bus, and if you're lucky you'll get a jovial bus driver who knows all the words to 'Molly Malone' and has a great jokes catalogue. Highly recommended.

Gray Line Day & Half Day Tours

Dublin Tourism Centre
Dublin 2
Map 824 A2 **250**

01 605 7705 | *www.irishcitytours.com*
Take a Gray Line tour to various locations in and around Dublin, such as Dublin Bay, Malahide Castle, the Wicklow Mountains, the Tomb at Newgrange and Glendalough – all beautiful places to visit, especially if you want to get away from the city for a while. A seven-hour tour to Wicklow costs just €30 per adult, €25 for students and senior citizens and €15 for children. Prices to Newgrange are in and around the same mark, while tours of Dublin Bay and areas closer to the city are a bit cheaper.

Gray Line Dublin Tour

14 Upper O'Connell St
Dublin Tourism
Dublin 1
Map 820 B2 **241**

01 458 0054 | *www.irishcitytours.com*
This hop-on, hop-off, bright yellow bus follows a set route around 20 different stops, each one near a major Dublin attraction. You can either stay on the bus for the entire route (this would take around 90 minutes) or hop off whenever you want to explore further, and hop on to the next one that comes along. An adult ticket costs €15 (€6 for children) and is valid for 24 hours. Buses depart daily at 09:30, and operate until 17:30 in summer and 16:30 in winter.

North Dublin & Castle Tour

59 Upper O'Connell St
Dublin 1
Map 820 A2 **12**

01 703 3028 | *www.dublinsightseeing.ie*
Starting out at the Dublin Sightseeing stand at Dublin Bus headquarters on O'Connell Street, this tour brings you along the north Dublin coastline. Taking in historic houses such as Casino Marino, Malahide Castle and the pretty seaside town of Howth, you'll come back via Dollymount Strand and the North Bull Island bird sanctuary. The tour lasts around three hours. Tours cost €22 for adults and €12 for children and includes entry to Malahide Castle. You can get a discount by booking online.

South Coast & Garden Tour

59 Upper O'Connell St
Dublin 1
Map 820 A2 **12**

01 703 3028 | *www.dublinsightseeing.ie*
Starting out from Dublin Sightseeing tours at Dublin Bus, your double-decker bus you will pass by Dun Laoghaire, Sandycove and many beautiful coastal views, followed by the Wicklow Mountains, Enniskerry and the Powerscourt estate. This is truly a scenic route and if the weather is fair you should get some great snaps. The duration of the tour is four and a half hours, and costs €25 for adults and €12 for children. The tour fee includes admission to Powerscourt Gardens.

Wild Wicklow Tours

14 Lower Albert Rd
Sandycove
South Coast

01 280 1899 | *www.wildwicklow.ie*
As the name suggests (although Wicklow is perhaps not that wild), these tours offer a glimpse of Dublin's neighbouring county Wicklow. Called the Garden of Ireland, it is no surprise that so many people visit it while living in Dublin – it is home to some of the most beautiful countryside in Ireland. Tours take in a coastal drive, a visit to Avoca Handweavers

Gray Line Dublin Tour

(see p.365), Glendalough and the Sally Gap. The Wild Wicklow Tour costs €28 for adults and €25 for children. The bus stops at various pick-up points in the city centre, including Dublin Tourism on Suffolk Street, the Gresham Hotel on O'Connell Street, and the Jury's Hotel in Ballsbridge. Check the website for further details.

Helicopter & Plane Tours
Other options **Hot Air Ballooning** p.202, **Flying** p.238

For a bird's eye view of the city there is nothing better than a helicopter ride. Although only for the generous of wallet, it really does make for a memorable experience, or, for the imaginative, a romantic date.

Prices vary as most trips are tailor-made but expect to pay at least €150 for about 20 minutes. Weather conditions are also a factor so it is best to ring the company on the day of (or the day before) the flight to confirm the booking. Some helicopter hire companies also do limousine hire so you could combine the two if you're really feeling flush. Private jet hire is available from a limited number of companies.

Various Locations ◄

Limo-co
01 843 9055 | *www.limo-co.ie*
For €850 (two or four people), you will be picked up in a limousine and taken to your helicopter for a 30 minute joyride over Dublin city. Limo-co also offers a range of tour options that you can enjoy from the comfort of a limousine. The Liffey Tour, for example, lasts for 90 minutes and costs €240 for two passengers in an American super stretch limo (there are cheaper options). Your driver will take you up the north and south quays, past all the major attractions and interesting buildings. For €270 you can take a five-hour tour of Glendalough.

The Drive ◄
Orlynn Pk
Lusk
North County Dublin

The Limousine Company
01 843 9169 | *www.limousine.ie*
The Limousine Company offers tours combining limousine hire and helicopter tours. A sample package would include collection by the limousine and journey to the helicopter pad, followed by a 100 mile scenic flight over the Dublin Mountains, the city centre, or the River Liffey to name but a few. On return, the limousine will take you to your destination of choice. The cost for two people is €995.

Cargo Terminal 1 ◄
Dublin Airport

Swiftair Aviation
01 808 0088 | *www.swiftair.ie*
With offices based on the second floor of the Cargo Terminal in Dublin Airport, Swiftair Aviation is ready to jet you off. Swiftair offers helicopter tours of Dublin city, flying over Phoenix Park, the Guinness Storehouse, The Four Courts, Trinity College, Lansdowne Road, the RDS and Dun Laoghaire Harbour. Prices for the helicopter tours start at €160 for 20 minutes. They also offer a charter service for private jets. Prices are available on request.

Hot Air Ballooning
Other options **Flying** p.238

14 Newtown Close ◄
Abbeyview, Trim
County Meath

Irish Balloon Flights
046 948 3436 | *www.balloons.ie*
Treat yourself to a romantic trip in a hot air balloon to see some of Ireland's most beautiful scenery from above. Up to 11 passengers can fit into one balloon (plus the pilot, of course), and costs start at €240 per person (but the price drops for larger groups). Flights typically take off in the early morning and early evening

when the wind is lower, and last about an hour – however, once you land you are given a glass of champagne to celebrate the flight, so you should allow three to four hours for this, the flight and the instructions.

Novelty Tours

You'd imagine Dublin would have plenty of novelty tours given the Irish disposition and readiness for a laugh but in fact there are only a few, most of which take place

Horse & carriage near St Stephen's Green

on a bus, but some of which are conducted on foot. A date to highlight if you seek people dressed in costume is June 16th. The Bloomsday festival (www.jamesjoyce.ie) offers tours and events in costume to celebrate the writings of James Joyce.

For further information on tours contact the Dublin Tourist Office on Suffolk Street (01 605 7700, www.visitdublin.ie).

The Brazen Head
20 Bridge St
Dublin 8
Map 819 E4 **379**

An Evening Of Food, Folk & Fairies

01 493 2543 | *www.irishfolktours.com*

This is an evening with a theme that is truly away with the fairies. Located in the Brazen Head pub (the oldest in Dublin), your guide will entertain you with stories of how Irish people lived in centuries past, their superstitions, and tales of legends of magic and the otherworld. The price per person is €40, which includes a traditional Irish meal.

59 Upper
O'Connell St
Dublin 1
Map 820 A2 **12**

Ghost Bus

01 874 4222 | *www.dublinbus.ie*

If you like the sensation of a chill running down your spine then this is the tour for you. They will guide you through two hours of ghost stories of Dublin past and present, and you'll even learn the legend of Dracula. Finally, what tour wouldn't be complete with a course in body snatching? Dress warmly as the tour takes place in the evening and you will be outdoors for some of it.

64-65 Patrick St
Dublin 8
Map 823 E1 **243**

Viking Splash Tour

01 707 6000 | *www.vikingsplash.ie*

This loud and exciting tour will teach you about the Vikings and how they came to Dublin over a thousand years ago, as well as many other interesting facts about the city. The 'Viking Captains' wear Viking costumes and if you're one of the lucky ones, you'll get to wear your very own Viking helmet, complete with horns. At first you may think this is just a bus tour, but towards the end the bus drives into the Grand Canal Basin for a water-based tour. Never fear though – the tour bus is actually an amphibious truck dating back to the second world war. Phew, that was a close one! Tours last around 75 minutes (20 minutes of which is on the water). Tickets cost €20 for adults, €10 for children, €18 for senior citizens and students and €60 for families (two adults and three children).

Private Tours

Private tours offer the chance to have the tour guide all to yourself and ask all those questions you daren't utter in front of strangers. There are various types of companies who specialise in this service, and others that can facilitate both public and private tours. As with anything tailor-made, you can expect to pay more, with prices depending on the size of the group and their needs. These made-to-measure tours are especially popular for corporate events and special occasions.

Another option for a private tour is to take a horse-drawn carriage ride around the Georgian areas of Dublin – you'll see the carriages waiting at the entrance to St Stephen's Green park. Opt for a quick spin around the park, or go for a full tour of the surrounding area.

Discover Dublin
20 Lower Stephens St
Dublin 2
Map 824 A1 **15**

The Cube
01 475 3313 | *www.discoverdublin.ie*
The Cube is a moving venue – a bus, complete with bar, band and seating so that you can take your party anywhere you want. There is space for up to 40 people, and it is ideal if you are celebrating a big birthday or any other special occasion. You can decide where the bus drops you off and picks you up again; in fact you can tailor-make your whole trip. Now that's quite a party.

Various Locations

Paola Pohli
01 851 2269 | *ppohli@ireland.com*
Paula Pohli offers personalised tours of Dublin in both English and German. She is an approved Dublin City Tour Guide and organises walking tours, bus tours and tailor-made historical tours, including literary tours, covering of course James Joyce and more. Transport can be arranged on request.

65 Heathervue
Greystones
Wicklow

Vagabond Adventure Tours
01 660 7399 | *www.vagabond-ireland.com*
This award-winning company runs adventure tours for small groups all over Ireland, with the focus being on tours outside of Dublin. Trips can be tailor made to your specific needs and the choices really are endless. You can tour Northern Ireland, the west of Ireland taking in the Ring of Kerry and Connemara, go horseback riding, walking or surfing, and much more. Tours can last for three to seven days and prices vary. Ideal for families, private groups or corporate tours.

Pub Crawl Tours
As the name suggests, the pub crawl often involves crawling (stumbling) from pub to pub on a tour that is bound to be as memorable as you may want it to be forgettable – yes, you really did dance a jig on a table in front of the whole tour group while singing Molly Malone! The *craic* is mighty and it's worth doing at least once. They usually run from April to November and cost around €12. Private tours are also available.

1 Suffolk St
Dublin 2
Map 824 B1 **237**

Dublin Literary Pub Crawl
01 670 5602 | *www.dublinpubcrawl.com*
If you like your pub crawl to be a little more high brow, yet still hugely entertaining, then this is the tour for you. This award winning pub crawl involves professional actors performing extracts from the writings of Joyce, Beckett, Oscar Wilde and more. The actors are hilarious and really inject some colour into Dublin's history. It's highly recommended. The tour starts daily during summer at 19:30 from The Duke Pub.

Discover Dublin
20 Lower Stephen's St
Dublin 2
Map 824 A1 **15**

Traditional Irish Musical Pub Crawl
01 475 3313 | *info@discoverireland.com*
Starting at the Oliver St John Gogarty's Pub in Temple Bar, your tour guides are two professional musicians who take you on a tour of some of Dublin's traditional pubs. Along the way you'll learn about Dublin's musical history, right up to current Irish bands. A highlight of the tour is when participants are invited to share their own musical talents. The tour does cover a fair bit of ground, so be kind to your feet and wear comfy shoes. Tours start at 19:30 every evening and costs €12 per adult.

Babywear p.98
Bank Loans p.22

Written by residents, these unique guidebooks are packed with insider info, from arriving in a new destination to making it your home and everything in between.

Explorer Residents' Guides
We Know Where You Live

Walking Tours

A popular choice of tour, despite being weather dependent much of the time, walking tours are a great way to see Dublin due to its fairly small dimensions. You'll find a range of themed walks, from historical to novelty, which generally manage to appeal to just about everyone, and the specialised guides are able to answer even the most unusual of questions. There are different schedules for the winter and summer with a designated meeting point for both, so it is worth checking with the Dublin Tourism Centre on Suffolk Street (01 605 7700, www.visitdublin.com) before setting out. It has maps for four tourist trails (Old City, Georgian Heritage, Cultural Heritage and Rock 'n Stroll) which you can do on your own.

International Bar
Dublin 2
Map 824 A1 `445`

1916 Rebellion Walking Tour
086 858 3847 | www.1916rising.com
This tour tells the tale of how Dublin changed after the 1916 Easter Rising and covers the events leading up to it. Led by a local historian, this is an informative tour and gives a good insight into the development of the city, which was turbulent, messy, but always interesting. It starts at the International Bar (01 677 9250) at varying times throughout the day, depending on the season.

23a Cowper
Footsteps
Rathmines
Dublin 6
Map 814 B1 `242`

Dublin Footsteps Walking Tours
01 496 0641
These tours run from June to September and are literary, historical and architecturally themed. Starting at 10:30, they last about two hours and leave from Bewley's Café in Grafton Street. Various themed walks are available, so give them a call to get more information.

Trinity College
Dublin 2
Map 820 B4 `543`

Historical Walking Tours
01 878 0227 | www.historicalinsights.ie
The historical walking tour runs over two hours and takes in the main historical landmarks of the city. It is led by history graduates of Trinity College, and they will fill you in on some of Dublin's most interesting historical showdowns, lowdowns and secrets. Tours depart from Trinity College twice a day in summer (May to September, 11:00 and 15:00), once a day in April and October (11:00), and on weekends only during winter (November to March, 11:00). They're highly recommended.

Various Locations
Dublin 2

Legend Tours
087 778 2887 | www.legendtours.ie
Legend Tours offers a series of tours that cover all the myth and legend of Dublin's history, and if Irish lore is anything to go by, there's plenty of it! You can choose from the Historic Sites tour, the Secret Societies tour, or the tour of Dublin's Crypts and Vaults – an intriguing glimpse into the past lives of the tombs and mummies inhabiting St Michan's Church and Christchurch Cathedral. Tours run every day except Saturdays in the summer, and in winter they are run by request.

101 Queens Ct
Queens Park
Monkstown
South Coast
Map 816 C4 `238`

Walk Macabre
087 271 1346
This 90 minute tour run by the Trapeze Theatre Company depicts in full gory glory dark and macabre events of old Dublin, and includes re-enacted scenes

A Brilliant i-Dea
You can download walking tours for your iPod at www.visitdublin.com. These audio walking tours are narrated by well-known Dublin tour guides, and provide a fascinating insight into various aspects of Dublin. Tours available include Georgian Dublin, The Historic north side, Viking and Medieval Dublin and In the Steps of Ulysses.

from the writings of Bram Stoker, Yeats, Joyce and Oscar Wilde. It's not for the faint of heart, and definitely not for children. Tours leave from St Stephen's Green at 19:30. Advance booking is necessary. The tour costs €12 per adult.

Tour Operators

As Dublin is the capital city, Dublin-based tour operators usually operate excursions in the city and all over the country. This is very handy for anyone new to the city as it is a great way to get your bearings and discover how beautiful Ireland is. Fáilte Ireland, the National Tourist Development Authority (Amiens Street, 1890 525 525 or 884 7700, www.ireland.ie), supports and develops Irish tourism and if a tour operator is recognised or approved by Fáilte it is a good indication that it will be well organised, informative and value for money. Tours are a good option especially if you want to travel out of Dublin and see a

Tour Operators		
CIE Tours	na	www.cietours.ie
Dublin Bus	01 703 3028	www.dublinsightseeing.ie
Dublin Sea Tours	01 492 5919	www.dublinseatours.ie
Rail Tours Ireland	01 856 0045	www.railtours.ie
Vagabond Adventure Tours	01 660 7399	www.vagabond-ireland.com
Walking Cycling Ireland	na	www.irelandwalkingcycling.com

good few places in a limited amount of time, as trying to organise all the accommodation and itinerary would be time consuming and often more expensive in the long run. Booking online has also become ever more popular and convenient, and often there is a discount for doing so.

Tours Outside Of Dublin

There are an innumerable amount of tours departing from Dublin, either for daytrips or longer sojourns that will take you to anywhere you wish to go. They are mainly bus tours with a set schedule for the day, fitting in as many sights as possible but the advantage is that they are stress-free and everything is taken care of. Or, you can also set your own itinerary with more specialised tours. Again, it is worth checking out the Tourism Centre (Suffolk Street, 605 7700, www.visitdublin.com) for an extensive list of tours but here are just a few to whet your appetite.

Causey Experience

Causey Farm
Girley, Fordstown,
Navan, County Meath

046 943 4135 | www.causeyexperience.com

If ever you dreamed of what it would be like on a 'real' Irish farm, here's your chance. Learn to Ceili dance (an important ability of all Irish farmers), cut turf, play the bodhran as well as have a hurling introduction and sheepdog demonstration. An enjoyable day out.

Bus Eireann Tours

Travel Centre
Busaras, Store St
Map 426 C3 408

01 836 6111 | www.buseireann.ie

Bus Eireann, the national bus company, offer a wide range of tours in the surrounding counties which provide a great sight-seeing opportunity. Tours include Wicklow, Newgrange and the Boyne Valley, Kilkenny City, Clonmacnoise and Locke's Distillery Museum, and Waterford.

Discover Wicklow

1 Fairway Green
Griffith Rd
Dublin 11
Map 407 F2 171

01 834 0941 | www.discoverwicklow.com

This company offers daytrips around Wicklow to smaller groups, ensuring a more unique and personalised trip. Tours includes Glendalough and lunch in a traditional Irish pub.

61 Rathlyon Grove ◄
Firhouse
South Dublin

Extreme Ireland

086 407 6985 | www.extremeireland.ie

Extreme Ireland specialises in active and adventure tours, such as walking, hiking and other out door pursuits. They offer tours throughout Ireland.

12 St Catheryn's Ct ◄
South Coast

Newgrange Tours

01 283 9973 | www.newgrangetours.com

May Gibbons runs historical tours to Newgrange and the Hill of Tara (which includes the River Boyne and Hill of Slane). Newgrange is a fascinating monument that you should definitely make the time to see.

Dun Laoghaire ◄
Map 423 F4 700

Railway Preservation Society Of Ireland Tour

01 280 9147 | www.steamtrainireland.com

A definite for the trainspotters among us, the Railway Preservation society of Ireland runs trips on steam locomotives along the Wicklow Coast, Vale of Avoca and into Wexford. Check out their website for full details. Guinness and Heineken are served on board.

9 Tramway Tce ◄
Douglas, County Cork

Discover Ireland Tours

021 4892687 | www.discoverirelandtours.com

Discover Ireland Tours offer Choral, Garden, Golf and Agricultural Tours as well as specialised and private tours. They also provide a wide range of unusual tours to all parts of Ireland.

Monastic Ruins, Glendalough

Round Tower, Glendalough

Daytrips From Dublin

There's lots to see and do in Dublin city, but one of the city's great advantages is that with its ideal location between the sea on one side and mountains on the other, it's easy to get out of the city either for the day, or just for a few hours, to relax, take in some fresh air, and explore some of the culture and history of the surrounding countryside.

The county of Dublin is bordered by three other counties: Meath to the north, Kildare to the west and Wicklow to the south, and each has its own social, historical and cultural attractions and is worth a visit.

Spend the afternoon exploring Neolithic passage graves at Newgrange in County Meath; go for a hike and a picnic by the lake at Glendalough, County Wicklow; or admire the beautiful race horses at The National Stud in County Kildare, before seeing how Newbridge Silverware is made. You'll find Palladian mansions, Japanese gardens, man-made lakes; sweeping boglands full of gorse and heather and fifth century monastic ruins. You can go canoeing on a mountain lake or indulge in a cooking class. Whether you fancy walking on a long, sandy beach, admiring the interior of a stately home or enjoying tea and scones at a country-style cafe, it's all within reach of the city and the best thing is that you don't need to spend weeks organising your trip – if it's a sunny day, then load up the car and off you go.

The best way to explore the surrounding counties is by car – you're free to stop off at a pub for lunch, a forest park for a walk or a petrol station for icecreams. However, there are bus services to most of the popular daytrip destinations, as well as organised coach tours (see each section to follow for details), with various pick-up points and times around the city.

Wicklow Wonders
Head off to Wicklow armed with plenty of useful info and tourist tips. Check out Wicklow county's tourism website: www.wicklow.ie

Glendalough & Wicklow

One of the loveliest daytrips out of the city has to be to the county of Wicklow, known as the 'Garden of Ireland' for its lush green scenery, picturesque mountains and sweeping valleys. If you drive from Dublin for just half an hour along the N11 or the M50 motorway, you'll notice the scenery becoming greener and more hilly as you enter the county. The best way to explore Wicklow is by car, but there are also many day tours by bus and coach, such as the Glendalough, Powerscourt and Wicklow Panorama Tour with Bus Éireann, which departs town at 10:00 and returns at 17:45, every day from March to October and three days a week from October to December (www.buseireann.ie). Wicklow is a popular daytrip destination so there are many other tours, such as the Wild Wicklow Tour (www.wildwicklow.ie) or those run by Irish City Tours (www.irishcitytours.com), Coach Tours of Ireland (www.coachtoursofireland.com), Day Tours Unplugged (www.daytoursunplugged.ie), Over The Top Tours (www.overthetoptours.com) and a rail tour by Railtours Ireland (www.railtours.ie), which includes travel by rail and coach.

The highlight of most Wicklow tours and daytrips is a visit to Glendalough – from the Irish Gleann Dá Lough meaning 'valley of two lakes' – a beautiful, isolated area set in a

Glendalough & Wicklow

Avoca	Enniskerry	01 204 6066	www.avoca.ie
Bray Seafront Market	Bray	086 683 9156	na
Courtyard Restaurant	Enniskerry	01 286 7928	www.summerhillhousehotel.com
Glencree Visitor Centre	Glencree	01 282 9711	www.glencree.ie
Glendalough Hotel	Glendalough	0404 45135	www.glendaloughhotel.com
Glendalough Visitors' Centre	Glendalough	0404 45325	na
Lynhams' Of Laragh Hotel	Laragh	0404 45345	www.lynhamsoflaragh.ie
Powerscourt Estate & Waterfall	Enniskerry	01 286 7676	www.powerscourt.ie
The Hungry Monk Restaurant	Greystones	01 287 5759	hungrymonk@eircom.net
Wicklow Mountains National Park	Glendalough	0404 45656	www.wicklownationalpark.ie

209

valley which contains lakes, forests, mountains and some well-known monastic remains. You can see a round tower, a decorated cross and stone churches, dating back to the sixth century, when St Kevin took refuge in the area and founded a monastery. Glendalough is ideal for a lakeside or forest walk, and you can explore the churchyard and graveyard, though you might not be able to reach up to the entrance to the 33m tall round tower, as the doorway is four metres from the ground. The Visitor Centre is good for finding out about the area's monastic history and the whole area is a great place to spend a day or half a day away from the city – it can get busy in good weather but if you walk for a bit you'll find a peaceful spot to enjoy the tranquility. It's also an extremely popular area for hiking.

Many people bring picnics for the day – the village is small and there are few places to eat, although the Glendalough Hotel (www.glendaloughhotel.com) is pleasant enough. During summer, there are takeaway and icecream vans beside the car park.

To get to Glendalough, you can either follow the N11 all the way to Ashford and turn off there, or turn off earlier on the N11 for Enniskerry (just beyond Bray), and you'll pass through Roundwood, Ireland's highest village. There's not much there for tourists, but the 18th century Roundwood Inn (01 281 8107) is a popular stop off for post-hike refreshments.

On the way back to Dublin, take the road through the Sally Gap, where you'll pass the stunning lakes of Lough Dan (you'll need to walk a little to see it) and Lough Tay on the Luggala estate – a moody, black lake deep in a valley and surrounded by sheer, rocky cliffs. Further on, the trees melt away and you'll be driving through the wild, desolate and remote expanses of the Sally Gap, a bleak area of bog, often inaccessible in winter. Parts of the film *Braveheart* were filmed in this area.

You'll also pass through the tiny village of Glencree with a small graveyard dedicated to military casualties from the first and second world wars, and the Glencree Reconciliation Centre (www.glencree.ie), in an old military barracks. From here you can return to Enniskerry and on to the N11.

Lake in Glendalough

Drive Safe
The roads around the mountains are narrow and winding in many places – make sure you take your time and go slow. Apart from your own safety and that of others, you won't be immune to speeding tickets just because you've made it to the countryside.

Powerscourt Estate & Enniskerry

Powerscourt Estate and Gardens forms another lovely Wicklow daytrip. Powerscourt is set in the foothills of the Wicklow mountains, just 20km from Dublin, so it can be done in half a day if time is limited.

If you are driving, head south out of the city on the N11 and take the turnoff for Enniskerry, a pretty village you'll pass on the way. You could also take bus 44 to Enniskerry from Dublin city centre, or take the Dart to Bray and then bus 145 to Enniskerry. Powerscourt is also a stop on many guided tours of Wicklow, so you may be able to combine several Wicklow attractions in one go.

The gardens at Powerscourt House were first planned and created in the 1740s. The 47 acres of formal gardens are home to several ornamental lakes, walled gardens, secret hollows and rambling walks, and have one of the most dramatic settings you'll find – looking out onto the Wicklow mountains with the Great Sugar Loaf mountain in the background.

The house itself (yet another 18th century Palladian mansion) was occupied by the same family for nearly 400 years. Sadly, on completion of a long restoration project, the house was gutted by fire in 1974, on the eve of its reopening. It has since been restored and now has shops, an exhibition, a garden centre (just outside), and a lovely terraced cafe from where you can enjoy the spectacular view while munching on home-style cooking.

While you are here, you can also visit Powerscourt Waterfall – you can either walk through the estate or drive by road (it's around six kilometres away). It is the highest waterfall in Ireland at 398 feet, and if you have a few hours to spare there are some beautiful forested mountain walks that will take you up to the back of the waterfall. For more information on the Powerscourt Estate and Gardens, and the waterfall, visit the website www.powerscourt.ie or call 01 204 6000. Admission to the estate and gardens is €9 per adult and €5 per child. Admission to the waterfall is €5 for adults and €3.50 for children.

Driving south along the R760 from Enniskerry, turn off for the N11 and Kilmacanogue and here, between the Little Sugar Loaf and Great Sugar Loaf mountains, you'll find a village which is divided by the busy N11 dual carriageway, but boasts the popular haven of Avoca Handweavers – many people drive out from the city for the day just to experience the mouthwatering home cooking, salads, scones and at the cafe which also has an outdoor terrace, opening onto small gardens. Apart from the cafe, the main attraction is the craft shop – the Avoca Handweavers operation has grown from a hand-weaving mill which was started in the 1720s and now sells a range of carefully selected items from woven fashions to homewares and gourmet gifts and treats.

Blessington Lakes & Russborough House

The Blessington Lakes, situated high up between the rolling, rugged hills of Wicklow and its low sweeping valleys with sandy shores, are so picturesque that it's hard to believe they were man-made. They are actually part of the Poulaphouca Reservoir, created in the 1940s by flooding valleys in the area to supply Dublin with water. The lakes are popular for walks, fishing, boating and more adventurous watersports such as sailing and waterskiing. At Avon Rí Activity Centre, you can do canoeing, kayaking, windsurfing and sailing or if you don't feel like getting wet, try archery, orienteering or clay pigeon shooting. Blessington Sailing Club (www.blsc.ie) is a great family sailing club, although you need to be a member to use the facilities.

Blessington is 35km south-west of Dublin – by car take the N81 and you'll be there in about 45 minutes or there's the number 65 bus from Eden Quay, which takes about an hour and a half – make sure you check bus times as the service is infrequent – only one bus every hour or more.

Russborough House (045 865 239) is one of Ireland's most spectacular stately homes. Like Castletown House (p.214), Russborough is also built in the Palladian style which was extremely popular in Ireland in the 1700s. It has an impressive facade and interior, with many fine examples of stucco decoration and Rococo plasterwork.

While it is certainly famous for historical reasons – the house was captured by Irish forces during the 1798 rising and only handed back in 1801 – Russborough House is probably more well known for a string of unfortunate art theft. When Sir Alfred Beit bought the house in 1952, he filled it with a collection of renowned artworks. In 1974, the IRA stole 16 paintings, which were later recovered. In 1986, the house was robbed again and while some paintings were recovered, some had been damaged. In 2001, paintings worth €4 million were taken, and in 2002, five more paintings were stolen, although both sets were recovered.

Don't leave Blessington without having lunch or afternoon tea at the Grangecon Café in the village (Kilbride Road, 045 857 892). Situated in a pretty converted schoolhouse, everything is cooked or baked on the premises and the delicious salads, pies, cakes and breads are created from a selection of Wicklow's finest and freshest produce. Everything is organic too, right down to the flour and sugar. You can also buy breads, chutneys and preserves to bring home.

Megalithic Art
Newgrange displays many fine examples of megalithic art. The famous triple spiral design and lozenges feature prominently throughout. Among the treasures found at the site were Roman coins, an iron wedge and a stone phallus.

Newgrange, Boyne Valley & Hill Of Tara

The beautiful Boyne Valley in County Meath makes another ideal daytrip – less than one hour from Dublin by car, it's full of prehistoric sites and monuments, stories of mythical Ireland and picturesque, sweeping vistas over hills, rivers and valleys.

The best way to travel is by car, heading up the M1 motorway from Dublin, or the N2 if you'd like to see the pretty village of Slane with its bridge and Slane Castle. There are also bus tours organised by Bus Éireann, leaving Dublin at 10:00 and returning at 17:45, taking in the Boyne Valley and Newgrange as well as other attractions in the area, or the Mary Gibbons Tour which leaves town between 09:30 and 10:30 (various pick-up points) and returns at 16:15. The Newgrange Shuttlebus is a bus service to the site only – it leaves the city at between 08:45 and 09:00 or 11:15 and 11:30 (depending on pick-up location) and takes 45 minutes to get to Newgrange.

Newgrange is an important archaeological site – at over 5,000 years old, the megalithic passage grave at Newgrange is older than even the Pyramids or Stonehenge. Archaeologists believe that it was built around 3200BC and the large grassy mound of stone and earth contains a long, narrow passage which leads to a burial chamber. It is surrounded by 97 kerbstones, many containing impressive examples of megalithic art – the triple spiral on the entrance stone and in the chamber is one of the best-known motifs.

Newgrange is part of the Brú na Bóinne complex in County Meath, which includes a series of other passage tombs, graves and monuments. In 1993, Unesco designated Newgrange, and its sister sites Knowth and Dowth, a World Heritage Site.

Admission to Newgrange is by guided tour only, from the Brú na Bóinne Visitor Centre at Donore (041 988 0300). It takes about one hour to visit the Visitor Centre, two hours

County Meath

Ardboyne Hotel	Navan	046 902 3119	info@ardboynehotel.com
Beacon Restaurant	Trim	046 943 1237	www.brogans.ie
Bellinter House Hotel	Navan	01 677 4845	www.bellinterhouse.com
Boyne Valley Tourism	Boyne Valley	na	www.theboynevalley.com
Ryan's Bar	Navan	046 902 1154	www.ryansbar.ie
Trim Castle Hotel	Trim	046 948 3000	www.trimcastlehotel.com
Trim Visitor Centre	Trim	046 943 7227	trimvisitorcenter@eircom.net

to visit the Centre and Newgrange, and three hours if you visit both plus Knowth. Newgrange gets very busy in summer and access is not guaranteed – so arrive early and book ahead. Admission charges vary from €2.90 to €10.30 per adult and from €1.60 to €4.50 per child, depending on how many of the sites you will be visiting. Every year during sunrise at the time of the Winter Solstice – 19th to 23rd December, sunlight enters Newgrange through a specially designed roof box opening directly above the entrance, and travels along the passage to light up the inner chamber. The chamber is usually illuminated for 17 minutes. Admission to the chamber of the tomb at Newgrange for the Winter Solstice sunrise is by lottery – for each of the five mornings that the chamber is illuminated, there are 20 places. You can apply for the draw at the Brú na Bóinne Visitor Centre. In 2006, over 25,000 people applied for the places.

The nearby Hill of Tara (046 902 5903) is the ancient seat of the Irish High Kings, and it is said that you can see 23 of Ireland's 32 counties from the top on a clear day – however if you can't see that far, the views over the Boyne Valley alone are worth the trip. The Hill of Tara is 12km south of Navan, along the N3.

For food and refreshments, you can either take advantage of the cafes at Brú na Bóinne or the Hill of Tara visitor centres, take a picnic if the weather is nice, or check out the pubs and restaurants in surrounding villages or in the large town of Drogheda, County Louth, which is around 11 kilometres from Newgrange.

Kildare

Kildare town is around 50km west of Dublin. Take the M/N7 if you're driving, but there is also a train or bus service from Dublin. Kildare has many places to explore on a daytrip, and some of the highlights are the Irish National Stud, the Japanese Gardens, Newbridge Silver and the Kildare Village outlet shopping centre.

Ireland is renowned worldwide for its excellent horse racing and equine breeding programmes, and the Irish National Stud, just outside Kildare town in Tully, is a source of national pride. Each year the stud provides the services of some of the world's top stallions to breeders around the world. You can take a walk around the stud and go on a guided tour to learn about the world of horse racing and breeding – some of the money that changes hands for the services of a good stallion will surprise you! You can also explore the ruins of the Black Abbey, enjoy a picnic in the picnic area, have lunch at the on-site cafe, browse the craft shop or go on a woodland walk. Admission is €10 per adult and €25 per family, which includes admission to the Japanese Gardens. For more information see www.irish-national-stud.ie or call 045 522963.

Japanese Gardens

The Japanese Gardens, situated in the grounds of the National Stud, were created in the early 1900s and symbolise the life of man, from birth to death. The gardens contain rare plants and some beautiful tranquil spots where you may find yourself reflecting on the trials and tribulations of your own life. A new garden, dedicated to St Fiachra (the patron saint of gardeners), was created at the stud in 1999.

Newbridge Silverware has been around since the 1930s, when its carefully crafted cutlery sets were used for special occasions in many Irish dining rooms. In the 1990s, Newbridge expanded its range to include beautiful giftware, tableware and jewellery. Visit the Newbridge Silverware Visitor Centre (045 431 301) on Cutlery Road to

213

browse their big showroom and learn about the history of Newbridge. There is also a good restaurant – Ross Morgan's – on site.

Kildare Village, just beside Kildare town, is an outlet shopping village with over 30 outlets offering discounts of 30% to 60% on last season's collections. Brands include Karen Millen, Molton Brown, Villeroy & Boch, Nike, Pepe Jeans, Levis, Petit Bateau, Coast, Radley and Monsoon, so it's well worth a visit when you've got the time to browse. There is a restaurant and cafe within the village, and a shuttle bus runs to and from Kildare Town at regular intervals (www.kildarevillage.com).

Kildare

Carton House Hotel	Maynooth	01 505 2000	www.cartonhouse.com
Courtyard Hotel	Leixlip	01 629 5100	www.courtyard.ie
Irish National Stud	Tully	045 522 963	www.irish-national-stud.ie
K Club Golf & Spa Resort	Straffan	01 601 7200	www.kclub.com
Killashee House Hotel	Naas	045 879 277	www.killasheehouse.com
Straffan Butterfly Farm	Straffan	01 627 1109	www.straffanbutterflyfarm.com

Castletown House, Kildare

Castletown House (01 628 8252) in Celbridge, County Kildare, is the largest Palladian style country house in Ireland and a lovely place to spend an hour or two, learning about life in the 18th century or just taking in the magnificent architecture. Built in 1722, the house was designed by the Italian architect Alessandro Galilei for the Speaker of the Irish House of Commons, William Conolly (1662-1729), and it was continued by Edward Lovett Pearce (who also designed the Bank of Ireland building on College Green). Conolly was the wealthiest man in Ireland at that time, having made his fortune through land transactions, and the house is a great showcase for the lavish furnishings of the period. The Long Gallery contains Venetian chandeliers, decorated walls and ceilings and delicate furniture, and the house also has a Print Room, its walls decorated with prints and borders according to the fashion of the time. The Print Room, designed by Lady Louisa Lennox, who lived there until 1759, is the only intact example in Ireland. The house and grounds were in the same family until 1965 when they were sold to property speculators, and in 1967, Desmond Guinness purchased the property and set up the Irish Georgian Society there, also setting up the Castletown Foundation which maintained and restored the house and opened it to the public. The state took it over in 1994.

Castletown House is in the village of Celbridge, just 20km from Dublin on the N4/R403, or take a 67 or 67A bus from Wellington Quay. A guided tour of the house takes about 45 minutes. Admission is €3.70 per adult and €8.70 per family.

Mountains & Beaches

Unlike many busy capital cities around the world, Dublin is ideally located with the sea on one side and mountains on the other, meaning that planning an afternoon getaway to either doesn't actually take too much organising – you can head off to either on a whim, for a great day or afternoon out and a breather from the city.

When the weather is good, Dubliners flock south in their hundreds to Wicklow's sandy gem, Brittas Bay (just in case you wonder why there's rush-hour traffic heading south on a Saturday lunchtime), its long beach and sand dunes popular with holidaymakers and daytrippers. The long bay stretches between the towns of Arklow and Wicklow and is about one hour's drive from Dublin. Take the N11 south and you'll pass through the tree-filled Glen of the Downs on the way. See www.brittasbay.org for more information. Mount Usher Gardens (near Ashford), 20 acres of gardens designed by Edward Walpole in the 1860s, is a nice place to spend an hour or two if you're in the area

Pack A Picnic
*Enjoy a picnic
watching crashing
waves on sandy
shores, or with
cracking views from
mountaineous
lookouts; you'll find all
you need in Dublin's
finest delicatessans in
the city centre (see
p.297), or at one of the
city's bustling markets
(see p.328).*

(www.mountushergardens.ie), or further south in Rathdrum, you'll find Avondale House and Forest Park (0404 46111), a Georgian House built in 1777 which has great scenic spots for picnics. Also in Ashford, you'll find Ballyknocken House and Cookery School (0404 44627, www.ballyknocken.com), a 19th century Victorian house which runs popular weekend cookery courses (see the Activities chapter on p.231) and also has guest accommodation.

Further south again is the beautiful Vale of Avoca, with the picturesque Meeting of the Waters and Avoca village, made popular by the 1990s BBC TV series Ballykissangel. The original Avoca Handweavers Mill is also in Avoca (0402 35105, www.avoca.ie).

Another popular getaway is to the Dublin Mountains or Wicklow Mountains – within an hour's drive of the city, you could be exploring a forest park or hilly trail. There are many forest parks dotted throughout the mountains, and the Wicklow Way is also a popular walking trail – over 130km long, it starts at Dublin's Marlay Park and ends at Clonegal in County Carlow. It takes about a week to walk the entire length, along picturesque walking trails through the county's gorse-filled hills, valleys and boglands, so a lot of people do it in various stages.

A good stop-off on the way back from the mountains is Johnnie Fox's pub in Glencullen (01 295 5647, www.jfp.ie), the highest pub in Ireland. Established in 1798, the pub has a stone floor strewn with sawdust and with nightly live music and ancient bric-a-brac hanging from the walls, its lively atmosphere keeps it busy every night of the week. There's also a selection of wholesome food – including a great seafood menu.

Johnnie Fox's Pub

Upper lake, Glendalough

Weekend Breaks

Ireland has endless choices for weekend getaways. From villages and castles to deserted beaches and cliffs, and from islands and ruins to mountains, forests and lakes, you'll encounter breathtaking scenery within just a few hours' drive of the city. Thanks to its location in the middle of the east coast, Dublin is ideally located for weekend breaks, north or south.

The Road Is Long

These are long drives from Dublin so make sure you have plenty of time to make the trip and enjoy what you find along the roads of Ireland's largest county.

The cities of Galway to the west and Cork to the south are two of the most popular destinations for weekend breaks from Dublin – the main roads are good for driving, and there are also direct trains and plenty of bus services. Driving to Cork (around 250km from Dublin) takes about three hours and the train takes just under three hours, so you can take off on a Friday after work, return on Sunday and still have a great break. For Galway (around 200km), the journey by either car or rail takes around three hours or less. If you have a little more time, the mystical county of Kerry in the south-west, and the rugged, bleak landscapes of Donegal in the north west are great places to explore, especially by car, with wild dramatic scenery, stunning mountains, lakes and deserted beaches. Each part of the country is quite different from the next, and quite easily accessible.

If you're looking for adventure rather than just scenery, there's plenty on offer. There are golf courses around the country and sports like surfing have become hugely popular along the west coast in recent years. Horse riding, mountain climbing, fishing, cycling, river cruising and relaxing in spas and resorts are also popular activities for weekend breaks and short holidays.

For accommodation, hotels and B&Bs are the most popular places to stay and there are plenty of each in every destination around the country. In addition, most hotels have special weekend offers with two nights bed and breakfast and one dinner included, which can work out to be great value, especially off season. It's a good idea to travel by car if you plan to do lots of sightseeing, but for a two-day city break in Cork or Galway, you can travel by train and get by without a car.

Cork

If you'd like to kiss the Blarney Stone, see some wildlife on Fota Island, visit the Titanic's last port of call in Cobh or relax, enjoy the sea air and eat gourmet seafood in the pretty fishing village of Kinsale, then Cork is for you. Cork city and county, on the south coast of the country, are fun places to explore. The city itself is small but there's lots to do as well as good shopping, dining and pubs. The Cork International Jazz Festival

Cork				
Blarney Castle	Blarney	021 438 5252	www.blarneycastle.ie	Visitor Attraction
Blarney Woollen Mills	Blarney	021 451 6111	www.blarney.ie	Mill & Crafts Shop
Cork Tourist Office	Grand Parade, Cork city	021 425 5100	www.corkkerry.ie	Tourist Office
English Market	Grand Parade, Cork city	na	na	Indoor Food Market
Fota Wildlife Park	Carrigtwohill	021 481 2678	www.fotawildlife.ie	Visitor Attraction
Greene's Restaurant at Isaacs Hotel	48 MacCurtain Street	021 455 2279	www.isaacs.ie	Restaurant
Imperial Hotel with Escape Salon & Spa	South Mall	021 427 4040	www.flynnhotels.ie	Hotel & Spa
Max's Wine Bar	48 Main Street, Kinsale	021 477 2443	www.kinsale.ie	Wine Bar & Restaurant
Merchant's Quay Shopping Centre	Patrick Street	021 427 5466	www.merchantsquaycork.com	Shopping Centre
Pier House	Pier Road, Kinsale	021 477 4475	www.pierhousekinsale.com	Guest House
The Queenstown Story	Cobh Heritage Centre, Cobh	021 481 3591	www.cobhheritage.com	Visitor Attraction

(www.corkjazzfestival.com), on the October bank holiday weekend each year, is extremely popular, with formal and informal jazz gigs in venues around the city. Note that accommodation gets booked up weeks ahead of the festival, so it's something you should plan well in advance.

One of the things Irish people are most famous for is having the 'gift of the gab' and to kiss the Blarney Stone at Blarney Castle, eight kilometres from the city, is supposed to give you this quality. The castle dates back to the 10th century, and in its grounds is a mystical rock garden with wishing steps and a fairy glade, making it a fun place to explore on an afternoon out.

It was from the town of Cobh, once the south-east's main port, in Cork's large harbour, that millions of Irish people emigrated, especially during the famine years from 1844 to 1848, and also from where the Titanic set sail on the last leg of its ill-fated cruise in 1912. The Queenstown Story in the heritage centre, in a restored railway station, tells the story of the port's tragic history. Just a short drive away from Cobh is Fota Island where you'll find Fota Wildlife Park, a 78 acre park with many different species of animals in their natural habitats, including giraffes and zebras.

West Cork is an extremely popular tourist destination with its rugged coastline, steep mountains and pretty, coastal villages. The village of Kinsale, about 40 minutes' drive south west of Cork city, is popular for its gourmet dining – this and its picturesque scenery keep it busy with tourists, especially in summer. Further along, the drive through Clonakilty and Skibbereen past Cape Clear, Mizen Head and Sheep's Head and finishing in Bantry, is rewarding, with plenty of beaches and coves, hills and harbours to discover – these are long drives from Dublin so make sure you have plenty of time to make the trip and enjoy what you find along the roads of Ireland's largest county.

Oops

Have we missed out your favourite daytrip or neglected your award-winning weekend break B&B? Tell us! Visit our website and fill in our Reader Response Form (www.explorer publishing.com).

Kerry

Beautiful and mystical, with mountains, beaches and lakes, County Kerry is one of the most visited destinations in the country and it's not hard to see why. The Ring of Kerry, with its beautiful sea and mountain views, the moody Dingle Peninsula, the expanses of Killarney National Park and the deserted Blasket Islands make the southwest magnetic and memorable. Parts of Kerry are quite a drive from Dublin (five hours at least to Dingle) and you'll need your energy for sightseeing around the

Kerry

Blasket Islands Visitors Centre	Dún Chaoin, Tralee	066 915 6444	www.heritageireland.ie	Visitor Attraction
Bricín	26 High Street, Killarney	064 34902	www.discoverireland.com	Craft Shop & Restaurant
Castle Ross Hotel & Golf Resort	Lakes of Killarney	064 31144	www.castleross.com	Hotel
Funghi Boats	Unit 2, The Pier, Dingle	066 915 0768	www.discoverireland.com	Visitor Attraction
Killarney National Park	Muckross, Killarney	064 31440	http://homepage.eircom.net/~knp/	Visitor Attraction
Killarney Outlet Centre	Fair Hill, Killarney	064 36744	www.killarney.ie	Outlet Shops
Lord Baker's Restaurant & Bar	Main Street, Dingle	066 915 1277	na	Pub and Restaurant
Muckross Park Hotel	Lakes of Killarney	064 23400	www.muckrosspark.com	Hotel
Park Hotel Kenmare	Kenmare	064 41200	www.parkkenmare.com	Luxury Hotel
The Lime Tree Restaurant	Shelburne Street, Kenmare	064 41225	www.limetreerestaurant.com	Restaurant
The Malton Hotel	Killarney	064 38000	www.greatsouthernhotelkillarney.com	Hotel & Spa
Tourist Office	Beech Road, Killarney	064 31633	www.corkkerry.ie	Tourist Office

county, so this type of trip would suit a longer break, perhaps a long weekend, to really appreciate and discover some of the county. A car is ideal for exploring, although there are coach tours if you decide to take a train from Dublin to Killarney (three and a half hours, with one change).

The town of Killarney is a good base for exploring the county. From here you can drive around the Iveragh Peninsula, taking the traditional Ring of Kerry drive (180km), stopping off at pretty villages, bays, inlets and coves and admiring the majestic mountains of Macgillacuddy's Reeks. Or stay near to Killarney for the day and discover the lakes, forests and mountains of Killarney National Park, with the elegant Muckross House and its landscaped gardens. The Gap of Dunloe is a stunning scenic walk that goes around Muckross Lake, measuring around 13km in total. If walking such a distance is not for you, you can hire a pony and trap to transport you in style!

To the south, Kenmare is a pretty village right between the Iveragh and Beara Peninsulas, with good pubs and restaurants. Further north is the Dingle Peninsula, the most westerly part of the country and another great place to explore. The town itself is colourful and becomes busy in summer and one of the most popular attractions is the local resident dolphin Funghi, who has been amusing visitors for over 20 years. Take a boat trip from the pier to see if you can spot the friendly mammal, or try taking a swim with him on an organised tour.

The bleak-looking Blasket Islands, uninhabited since 1953, were once home to a population of fishermen and storytellers, made famous in a series of traditional Irish stories. It's possible to spend a day on the islands, to get a taste of island life or just enjoy total tranquility. There's a Visitors Centre in Dunquin which is interesting to visit, even if you don't make it over to the islands.

The Shannon Region

Another great place to explore on a weekend break is County Clare and the Shannon Region, home to the spectacular limestone landscape of The Burren, the ancient Aillwee Cave and the breathtaking Cliffs of Moher. Shannon airport is the nearest airport to the region, or drive to Clare from Dublin, taking the main road for Limerick City, a historic city where the River Shannon meets the Atlantic Ocean. The 200km drive takes about two and a half hours and there are also trains and buses, which take around the same time.

There are some interesting sights in Limerick city, such as King John's Castle, but if it's your first visit to the area, you'll want to head out of the city towards Ennis, making

Mini Map

There may be plenty to see outside of the city, but Dublin's bustling centre has a whole lot to offer too. Make the Dublin Mini Map your perfect companion. It's teeny, it's tiny, but unfold it and you will hold the entire city in your hands. Pinpoint the main streets and areas, shops and heritage sites; fit the city in your pocket.

Shannon

Aillwee Cave	Ballyvaughan, Clare	065 707 7036	www.aillweecave.ie	Caves
Arthur's Quay Shopping Centre	Arthur's Quay, Limerick	061 419 888	www.visitlimerick.com	Shopping Centre
Ballyvaughan Lodge	Ballyvaughan, Clare	065 707 7292	www.ballyvaughanlodge.com	Guesthouse
Barrtra Seafood Restaurant	Lahinch, Clare	065 708 1280	www.barrtra.com	Restaurant
Bunratty Castle and Folk Park	Bunratty, Clare	061 360 788	www.shannonheritage.com	Visitor Attraction
Bunratty Village Mills	Bunratty, Clare	061 364 321	na-	Shopping
Cliffs of Moher Visitor Experience	Doolin, Clare	065 708 1171	www.cliffsofmoher.ie	Visitor Attraction
Sancta Maria Hotel	Lahinch, Clare	065 708 1041	www.sancta-maria.ie	Hotel
The Burren Centre	Kilfenora, Clare	065 708 8030	www.theburrencentre.ie	Visitor Attraction
Tourist Information Office	Arthur's Quay, Limerick	061 317 522	www.shannonregiontourism.ie	Tourist Office

sure to visit The Burren and the Cliffs of Moher. You'll first come to Bunratty Castle, which has been there in some form since 1250. Bunratty holds medieval feasts and banquets with music for visitors at night, and the adjacent Bunratty Folk Park with a reconstruction of a 19th century Irish village is an interesting place to visit. At night, Durty Nelly's pub (www.durtynellys.ie) is a lively spot.

The Burren National Park covers much of the north of County Clare and its desolate limestone landscape, full of cracks and fissures, makes a big change from the lush green scenery of the surrounding counties. Although soil is scarce, there are plenty of wildflowers between the cracks and many animals live in the area also.

Nearby, on the road to the village of Ballyvaughan, is Aillwee Cave, with 3,400 feet of caves and underground passages, some with waterfalls. Carved out from limestone, the caves are two million years old, and there are regular guided tours of the caves which take about 30 minutes.

The dramatic Cliffs of Moher, which run for five miles along the coast near The Burren, have sheer vertical drops of 700 feet into the sea and are really breathtaking to see. There's a visitors centre for tourists (of which there are many, especially in summer) and you can go along walking paths, although it's advisable to stay away from the edge.

County Clare is said to be the home of traditional music, and great villages in the area to stay in include Lahinch, where surfing has become very popular in recent years and where there are surf schools for lessons, and Doolin further north, where traditional music in the tiny village's pubs always makes for a fun night.

Galway, Connemara & Mayo

Galway, Connemara, the Aran Islands and the scenery of Mayo are some of the jewels of the West of Ireland. For a weekend break, Galway city is a great destination. A compact, vibrant city with a buzzing arts and music scene and colourful, cobbled streets, Galway is a hive of culture and atmosphere. Salthill is a short drive – or walk – from the city centre and here you'll find a beach, amusements, pubs and B&Bs. If you continue west along the coast, you can take a day's drive around Connemara, passing through the Gaeltacht (Irish-speaking) region and through the boglands, mountains and villages of this pretty area. The town of Clifden is a nice place to stop for lunch or tea and a good halfway point on the drive, if you are taking the main road back to Galway via the pretty village of Oughterard and along Lough Corrib.

Galway, Connemara, Mayo

Aran Islands Tourist Office	Kilronan, Inis Mór, Galway	091 61263	www.visitaranislands.com	Visitor Attraction
Druid Lane Restaurant & Wine Bar	3 Quay Street, Galway	091 563 015	na	Restaurant & Wine Bar
Foxford Woollen Mills Visitor Centre	Foxford, Mayo	094 925 6756	www.foxford.mayo-ireland.ie	Visitor Attraction
G Hotel	Wellpark, Galway	091 865 200	www.monogramhotels.ie	Luxury Hotel
Ireland West Tourism	Forster Street, Galway	091 537 700	www.irelandwest.ie	Tourist Office
Kylemore Abbey	Kylemore, Connemara, Galway	095 41146	www.kylemoreabbey.com	Visitor Attraction
Spiddal Craft and Design Studios	Spiddal, Galway	091 553 376	www.spiddalcraftvillage.com	Crafts Shopping
The Céide Fields Interpretive Centre	Ballycastle, Mayo	096 43325	www.heritageireland.ie	Visitor Attraction
The Harbour Mill	Westport, Mayo	098 28555	www.theharbourmill.com	Holiday Apartments
The Lemon Peel	The Octagon, Westport, Mayo	098 26929	www.lemonpeel.ie	Restaurant

219

One of Galway's main attractions is the Aran Islands. These famous islands are rich in culture and heritage and as Gaeltacht or Irish speaking areas, they tell a lot about Irish language and traditions. There are three islands, with Inis Mór the largest. You can either fly to the islands or take one of the popular ferries from Galway city or from Rossaveal in Connemara (there are also ferries from Doolin in County Clare). If you continue north from Clifden, you'll come to Connemara National Park

Inis Meáin, Aran Islands

and nearby, Kylemore Abbey, a romantic, lakeside castle that is definitely worth seeing. If you travel north towards Leenane, you'll encounter dramatic slopes sweeping down to Killary Harbour, a long inlet shaped like a Norwegian fjord. Further north again is the town of Westport, situated between Clew Bay and its drumlins, and the dramatic Croagh Patrick, a mountain and important pilgrimage site (climb up barefoot if you really want to walk in the footsteps of St Patrick). Westport is another good place to stay, with a thriving atmosphere, and a great base for exploring the surrounding scenery. Beside the town itself, Westport House and its adjacent beach make a fine half-day out, and there are plenty of activities in the area like walking, cycling, horse riding, golf and adventure sports.

Further north in Mayo, Achill Island joined to the mainland by a bridge, is Ireland's largest offshore island and worth a visit for its dramatic cliffs and abundant wildflowers. The Céide Fields, a Stone Age site of great archaeological significance, was only discovered in the 1930s and gives a great insight into the past. To the east of County Mayo is Our Lady's Shrine at Knock, and Knock Airport, where there are flights to Dublin. Like Galway, parts of County Mayo are in the Gaeltacht and are Irish speaking areas.

Sligo

Sligo, in the north-west of Ireland, is a fascinating place to visit, with a vivid archaeological and historical heritage as well as beautiful beaches and mountains. Much of the county is dominated by the moody and majestic Ben Bulben mountain

Sligo

Breeogue Pottery	Knocknahur, Carrowmore	071 916 8929	www.calleryceramics.com	Crafts Shopping
Celtic Seaweed Baths	Strandhill	071 916 8686	www.celticseaweedbaths.com	Visitor Attraction
North-west Regional Tourist Office	Temple Street, Sligo Town	071 916 1201	www.irelandnorthwest.ie	Tourist Office
Pepper Alley	Rockwood Parade, Sligo Town	071 917 0720	na	Restaurant
Quayside	Sligo Town	071 915 1599	www.quayside.ie	Fashion Shopping
Radisson SAS Hotel	Ballincar, Rosses Point Road	071 914 0008	www.sligo.radissonsas.com	Hotel
Sligo Folk Park	Millview House, Riverstown	071 916 5001	www.sligofolkpark.com	Visitor Attraction
Sligo International Tourist Hostel	Finisklin Road, Sligo Town	071 917 1547	www.harbourhousehostel.com	Hotel
Triskell	The Strand Bar, Strandhill	071 912 8402	na	Restaurant

and the mountains around it, which change appearance by the hour, depending on the weather and light conditions. The county also has a rich literary heritage, having been favoured by the poet WB Yeats, who is buried there. The county's coastal towns, such as Strandhill and Enniscrone, are popular for watersports like surfing, sailing and windsurfing.

Sligo town is small but colourful, with many interesting restaurants and cafes, particularly along the Garavogue River. There are two cathedrals, a theatre and the Sligo County Museum, and the Quayside Centre (www.quayside.ie) is popular for shopping. However if you have a car, you'll find lots of exploring to the east with Knocknarea Mountain and the coastal village of Strandhill, and further south to Enniscrone. To the north of Sligo town is Yeats Country, with lots of good drives including a scenic drive around Lough Gill. Everywhere you go in this area, you'll see different views of Ben Bulben and Knocknarea in the distance, and you'll come across attractions like Parkes Castle, the Glencar Waterfall and heritage house Lissadell House (www.lissadellhouse.com). WB Yeats is buried in Drumcliffe graveyard, also north of Sligo Town.

To the west of Sligo town is Rosses Point, a small village with long, golden beaches, fishing, a golf course and a sailing club. Surfing has become very popular in the area in recent years and there are surf schools in the villages of Enniscrone, Strandhill and Bundoran (20 minutes drive, in County Donegal) and plenty of other surf clubs around the coast. Seaweed baths are also a popular way to relax, and you'll find them at both Enniscrone and Strandhill.

Donegal

The scenery in Donegal in the north-west of Ireland is a mix of lush green fields, golden beaches and bubbling streams contrasting with bleak and desolate cliffs, barren rocky mountains and rugged coastlines, constantly bashed by the wild Atlantic Ocean. One of the county's highlights is Glenveagh National Park and Donegal also has a huge Gaeltacht (Irish-speaking area), especially around Gweedore.

Starting in the south of the county, just north of Sligo, the town of Bundoran is popular for its golden beaches and surfing. It also has amusements and seaweed baths and gets busy in summer with visitors from Northern Ireland. Surfing on the huge, long beach at Rossnowlagh, further north, is also popular, although there's not much else in the small village.

Donegal				
Ostan Gweedore	Bunbeg, Donegal	074 953 1177	www.ostangweedore.com	Hotel
The Clock Tower Bar & Bistro	Fintra Bay, Killybegs, Donegal	074 974 1922	www.theclocktower.ie	Restaurant
Donegal Adventure Centre	Bayview Avenue, Bundoran	071 984 2418	www.donegaladventurecentre.com	Visitor Attraction
Downings Bay Hotel	Downings, Letterkenny, Donegal	074 915 5586	www.downingsbayhotel.com	Hotel
Glenveagh National Park	Churchill, Donegal	074 913 7090	www.npws.ie	Visitor Attraction
Letterkenny Shopping Centre	Port Road, Letterkenny	074 912 3094	na	Shopping Centre
The Lobster Pot	Burtonport, Donegal	074 954 2012	na	Restaurant
The Craft Shop, Glencolmcille Folk Village	Glencolmcille, Donegal	074 973 0017	www.glenfolkvillage.com	Shopping
Tourist Office	The Quay, Donegal Town, Donegal	071 984 1350	www.irelandnorthwest.ie	Tourist Office

Continuing northwards, past Donegal town, there are scenic views around the south-west of the county along by Mountcharles and Killybegs, a busy fishing port. There's an interesting folk village museum at Glencolumbcille, on the southwest coast of County Donegal.

Further north in the county, the scenery becomes more wild and desolate, with rocky, hilly fields full of sheep – the only thing you can see for miles along some of the winding roads. Mount Errigal is an interesting mountain which can be viewed from many villages along the coast, such as the popular seaside village Bunbeg. Gleneagh National Park covers an area of 14,000 hectares, with lakes, mountains and nature trails to explore and wild deer and eagles just some of the wildlife. There's a visitor centre and Glenveagh Castle, which you can do a tour of, is also in the park. To the east of the county, The Inishowen Peninsula has lots of interesting drives and sweeping coastal views. Donegal also has one or two islands which are possible to visit and stay on – Tory Island to the north and Aranmore to the West, although you should factor in a few days either side of your visit in case you get stuck due to weather.

It's possible to fly to Donegal, though it's best to travel by car so that you can explore and appreciate the scenery. Parts of Donegal are quite a drive from Dublin so might be more suited for a longer break, however Bundoran is just 20 minutes north of Sligo town (three hours from Dublin), so is easily accessible for a surfing or seaside weekend.

Northern Ireland

Largely due to its troubled history, Northern Ireland hasn't been a hugely popular holiday destination in the past. However, with the success of the peace process in recent times, there's no reason not to visit the region. Like the rest of the island, the north has some spectacular scenery and visitor attractions, and with Belfast just two hours drive from Dublin on the M1 motorway, it is ideal for a weekend break.

Northern Ireland is part of Great Britain and the United Kingdom and the currency is pounds (sterling), so prices are often different than those in the Republic, due to different tax and import duties. The main city in the north is Belfast and many people from the Republic go to Belfast for a shopping weekend as prices are often cheaper (people near border counties and in north Dublin often drive up to go grocery shopping in the north when prices are also cheaper).

Further north, at the very top of Ireland, you'll find some spectacular coastal scenery, including the Giants Causeway (www.giantscausewayofficialguide.com) in County Antrim, a World Heritage Site of bizarre column rock formations forming part of the shore. Nearby is the Old Bushmills Distillery, the world's oldest distillery, in the small town of Bushmills. To the east is the village of Portstewart, a popular seaside holiday destination for northerners.

Northern Ireland

Benedict's Hotel	7-21 Bradbury Place, Belfast	048 9059 1999	www.benedictshotel.co.uk	Hotel
Castlecourt Shopping Centre	Royal Avenue, Belfast	048 9023 4591	http://westfield.com	Shopping Centre
Craftworks	Bedford House, 16-22 Bedford St, Belfast	048 9024 4465	na	Crafts Shop
Giants Causeway Visitor Centre	44 Causeway Road, Bushmills, Antrim	028 2073 1855	www.giantscausewaycentre.com	Visitor Attraction
Old Bushmills Distillery	Main Street, Bushmills, Antrim	028 2073 1521	www.bushmills.com	Visitor Attraction
Royal Court Hotel	233 Ballybogey Road, Portrush, Antrim	048 708 2236	www.royalcourthotel.co.uk	Hotel

Other highlights of Northern Ireland include Belleek Pottery (www.belleek.ie) and the Marble Arch Caves (www.marblearchcaves.net) in County Fermanagh, and the Ulster American Folk Park (www.folkpark.com) in County Tyrone, all to the west of the province, Glenariff Forest Park, also to the west and Lough Neagh, County Armagh, towards the centre. One of the province's most picturesque locations is the Mountains of Mourne to the south, with beautiful long drives along the coast and through inland valleys, passing castles, forest parks and sandy beaches. The start of the 85km Mountains of Mourne drive at Newcastle, is just a two-hour drive from Dublin. Carlingford nearby is another popular town for a weekend break from Dublin, set on Carlingford Lough and overshadowed by the Cooley Peninsula's mountains. It hosts many summer events, including a popular Oyster Festival every August.

Lakes of Killarney

Gap of Dunloe

Waterfall in Muckross Park

Dingle, County Kerry

Dingle Peninsula

Jump over the daily grind.

Fly over nagging thoughts.

Glide into your own space.

Cut through monotony.

Ski Dubai. Leave it all behind.

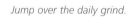

ESCAPE EVERY DAY

SKI DU

an unforgettable snow expe

Activities

Student Life

For students, Dublin's colleges and universities offer a range of activities (see p.97 for a list of colleges and universities). A list of women's clubs can be found at www.womeninsport.ie.

Sports & Activities

Be it indoors or out, there's plenty to keep you occupied in and around Dublin. Joining a sports or social club can be the easiest way to meet people and make new friends, especially if you are new to the city. Despite unforgiving weather, especially in the winter, true enthusiasts don't let a bit of rain or cold put them off. Armed with the right clothing, Ireland never really gets too cold or too miserable to keep you indoors and Dublin's prime coastal location, surrounded by rugged mountains and sprawling green fields, provides the perfect setting for getting a breath of fresh air. However, if you really can't face another muddy hike or washed out game, there are plenty of indoor venues for soccer, badminton, basketball, and a host of other sports.

Sailing (p.251) and other watersports are popular, as is fishing (p.237). Traditional sports such as hockey (p.241), tennis (p.256) and rugby (p.250) are widely played, and you can't beat playing in a gaelic game (p.239), or even just watching from the stands (p.261). No matter what sport you are interested in, you should find an enthusiastic club looking for members, right in your neighbourhood. Have a look at www.getactive.ie for listings of clubs and activities near you.

Find a list of sports facilities, including gyms, health clubs and recreation centres, on p.265. This chapter also features a range of non-sport activities, from art classes and music lessons to libraries and photography, as well as a section on pampering yourself in Dublin's top spas, beauty salons, hairdressers and yoga studios.

Aerobics & Fitness Classes

You won't have any trouble finding a gym or fitness centre near you that offers some sort of class, with activities like aerobics, pilates, circuit training and step. Prices vary but average around €15 for non-members (members usually get a reduced rate). In general, places in central Dublin tend to be pricier than those further out. All of the following offer a wide variety of classes with varying price ranges, although some are only open to club members.

Aqua Aerobics

Aqua aerobics is an effective workout that doesn't put a strain on the body, and is particularly good for people with knee or lower back injuries, osteoporosis sufferers and pregnant women. Try one of the bigger hotels such as the Rochestown Lodge Hotel (www.rochestownlodge.com), or swimming pools such as Rathmines Swimming Pool (01 496 1275) which also offer weekly classes. See Swimming on p.254 for more.

Aerobics & Fitness Classes

Name	Phone	Web	Type of Class
ALSAA	01 886 3332	www.alsaa.ie	Step, circuit training, body sculpting
DCU Sports Complex	01 704 5810	www.dcu.ie	Aerobics, spinning, boxercise, circuit training
Dundrum Family Recreation Centre	01 298 4654	www.dlrcoco.ie	Aerobics, aqua aerobics
The Fitness Dock	01 405 3777	www.coralleisure.ie/ fitnessdock	Fitball, khai-Bo, pump & sculpt, spinning, step
Irishtown Stadium	01 669 7211	www.dublincity.ie	Running, aerobics, gym
Jackie Skelly Fitness	01 677 0040	www.jackieskellyfitness.com	Pole dancing, rebounding, spinning, tae-bo, step
Markievicz Leisure Centre	01 672 9121	www.dublincity.ie	Aerobics, circuit training, pilates
Newpark School Sports Centre	01 283 3037	www.newparksportscentre.ie	Circuit training, yoga, pilates, swimming
Studio 32	087 055 7166	www.studio32.ie	Pilates
Westwood	01 853 0353	www.westwood.ie	Spin, body pump, body balance, body combat
YMCA	01 478 2607	www.ymca.ie	Aerobics, cardio funk, khai bo, pilates

Art Classes

Other options **Art Galleries** p.180, **Art & Craft Supplies** p.285

Ireland has a great appreciation for the arts and this is evident throughout Dublin and the rest of the country. There are courses for all ages and abilities; it's just a case of finding the one to suit you. The National Gallery of Ireland puts on Art for all Ages and Gallery Drawing Days, and you can check out their website for more information (www.nationalgallery.ie). They also provide a service for people with vision impairments to appreciate paintings through touch. An Access guide, Braille guide and Picture sets are available from the information desk. Tours are free of charge but must be pre-booked (with two weeks' notice for group bookings). Also check out your local library, as many offer children's art classes and some offer classes for adults too (see www.dublincity.ie for a list of libraries).
The Charleville Mall Branch Library (01 874 9619, North Strand, Dublin 1) holds ladies' classes every Monday from 10:30 to 12:30 and an adult group class on Fridays; they also offer children's art classes every Monday at 15:00. The Coolock Branch Library (01 847 7781, Barryscourt Rd, Dublin 17) holds adult art classes every Monday and Friday from 11:30 to 13:00; children's art classes take place on Saturdays from 11:30 to 13:00 during the school term. The Walkinstown Branch Library (01 455 8159, Percy French

227

Road, Dublin 12) offers children's art classes every Saturday from 11:30 to 12:30 and on Tuesday mornings at 10:30 there's a Ladies Art Group.

Dublin City Gallery, The Hugh Lane

Charlemont House
Parnell Sq North
Dublin 1
Map 426 A2 **14**

01 222 5558 | *www.hughlane.ie*

This gallery offers short courses for adults with a prior knowledge of drawing, as well as a programme to encourage the younger generation to gain an appreciation for the arts. Kids' classes are also available, including Sunday Sketching for 7 year olds and upwards. These classes are free (no prior booking necessary) and parents can also participate. The Saturday workshops run along the same lines but the theme varies each week. You can buy tickets for the Saturday workshop from the gallery bookshop (01 222 5576). Sign up for the Kid's Club online for information on upcoming events.

Dun Laoghaire Institute of Art, Design Technology

Kill Av
Dun Laoghaire

01 214 4600 | *www.iadt.ie*

This Institute of Technology offers full-time and part-time courses in a range of disciplines. The School of Creative Arts offers everything from degree programmes and certificates to special interest classes and workshops covering various disciplines, including watercolour and oil painting, still life drawing, portfolio preparation, film and media studies, creative writing, and more.

INTROART

Abbey House
15-17 Abbey St Upper
Dublin 1
Map 426 A3 **104**

01 872 7930 | *www.youth.ie*

INTROART works towards helping young people with disabilities integrate into the community and gain access to youth services through the arts. They regularly organise workshops and training courses.

National College of Art and Design

100 Thomas St
Dublin 8
Map 429 D1 **5**

01 636 4200 | *www.ncad.ie*

Without a doubt the most prestigious art college in the country, NCAD offers a variety of courses at various levels. Widely recognised for its excellent standard of teaching, courses offered include certificates in various disciplines, teacher training courses and postgraduate studies, as well as evening classes that run from March to October. Summer classes (lasting one to four weeks) are run in July and there are short courses commencing at Easter and in the autumn too. The college also has an extensive library.

Pine Forest Art Classes

Glencullen
Kilternan
Dublin 18

01 294 1220 | *www.pineforestartcentre.com*

Pine Forest offers classes for kids aged between 5 and 19 years. Set in the scenic surroundings of the Dublin Mountains, full supervision is provided, although the emphasis for the junior courses is on being creative in a fun environment. Senior classes include a portfolio preparation course. Classes in sculpture, drawing, painting, pottery and enamel work, among other crafts, are available for all levels.

Astronomy

Astronomy Ireland

Various Locations

01 847 0777 | *www.astronomy.ie*

This is Ireland's national astronomy club, and also the largest in the world (in relation to population). They focus on promoting education about astronomy and space through lectures, talks, observing sessions and the press. In addition to a shop selling all the best star gazing gear (Unit 75, Butterly Business Park, Kilmore Road, Artane, Dublin 5),

228

they also have a phone news line that you can call for weekly updates (1550 111 442). The website also has information on evening classes and links to useful sites.

Badminton

Widely practised in schools and colleges, from primary upwards, badminton is a fun, competitive sport and a great way to keep fit, no matter what your level. Most clubs also host social evenings. See the table for a list of clubs in your area or check out the Badminton Union of Ireland website for dates of fixtures, events and club listings (www.badmintonireland.com).

Basketball

If you're keen to shoot a few hoops, you'll be pleased to hear that basketball is popular in the city, with tournaments and leagues held regularly each season and many indoor and

Badminton		
Aer Lingus Badminton Club	Dublin 9	01 886 3332
Ailesbury Badminton Club	Blackrock	087 905 5426
Mount Pleasant	Dublin 6	01 497 3733
St Judes	Dublin 6 West	087 294 5522
Terenure Badminton Centre	Dublin 6 West	01 450 5966
YMCA	Dublin 2	01 635 9905

outdoor courts. All the major colleges have teams and clubs and compete regularly. The National Basketball Arena holds Easter, summer and Halloween camps for juniors and adults, as well as hosting many events. See www.nationalbasketballarena.ie. Dublin Indoor Sports (see p.264) is very sociable and is open to anyone to join. They have several centres dotted around the city and are open to both teams and individuals to join. Basketball Ireland (01 459 0211, www.basketballireland.ie) have information on a range of camps and professional coaching on offer in the Dublin area and further out (see Eastern region on their website).

Feathered Friends
Bird enthusiasts will find plenty of interesting news and facts on www.fatbirder.com.

Birdwatching

While many species have upped and flown the coop, Ireland is still home to some rare species not commonly found in Europe. This combined with stunning natural scenery and a whole range of birdlife, common or not, make birdwatching in Ireland an attractive pastime. The Birds of Ireland News Service (1550 111 700) offers birding tours for individuals and small groups. To book tours or to report sightings, contact Eric Dempsey at 01 830 7364 or email birdsireland@eircom.net or irishbirdnews@eircom.net.

Find The Birdies
Cities rarely have abundant bird life, but Dublin is slightly different. Sure, you might not see a 'lifer' walking down O'Connell Street, but just a short drive outside the city centre you'll be in beautiful Irish countryside and prime birdwatching territory. Check out the Exploring chapter on p.51 for information on great daytrips out of the city.

Various Locations

BirdWatch Ireland
01 281 9878 | www.birdwatchireland.ie

Set up in 1968, BirdWatch Ireland is Ireland's largest and most active voluntary conservation organisation. They focus on the conservation of wild birds and their habitats. Annual membership for individuals is €40, family €50, concession €25. Members receive a copy of *Wings*, a quarterly magazine, as well as a free DVD on spotting common birds, and invitations to events and guided tours. Wildlife courses covering topics on photography, field tours, and birdwatching, as well as lectures and workshops are available. Fees vary.

229

Bowling

Various Locations

Leisureplex
01 288 1656 | www.leisureplex.ie

There are branches of Leisureplex dotted around Dublin, and they are well worth a visit. They offer bowling, Q-zar, pool tables, video games, and a children's play adventureland called Zoo. A diner serving fast food sorts out any tummy rumblings so that you can concentrate on your game. Bowling prices vary according to peak and off-peak times but a game starts at €4.70. One hour of bowling (for up to six people) starts at €24 per hour. The Coolock branch also has a synthetic ice-skating rink. A whip round will cost you €13.25 from Mondays to Thursdays and €15 on weekends and bank holidays. See the table for other centres. Leisureplex is open seven days a week; for further information, please log on to www.leisureplex.ie.

Bowling			
Dundrum Bowl	Ballinteer Rd, Dundrum	Dublin 14	01 298 0400
Leisureplex	Malahide Rd, Coolock	Dublin 5	01 848 5722
Leisureplex	Blanchardstown	Dublin 15	01 822 3030
Leisureplex Tallaght	Village Green Ctr, Old Bawn Rd	Dublin 24	01 459 9411
XL Bowl Ten Pin Bowling	Palmerstown Shopping Ctr	Dublin 20	01 626 0700

Boxing

When it's done right, boxing is no thug's sport. You don't have to be interested in competing to join a club – boxing is a great way to keep fit. On the other hand, if you are keen to compete then there are plenty of local, national and European competitions to motivate you to train that bit harder. Not all clubs are open to females, so phone around to find a club that is – try contacting Baldoyle Boxing Club in Dublin 13 (01 839 1132). The Irish Amateur Boxing Association (www.iaba.ie, 01 453 3371) has full listings of affiliated clubs around the county. For some general history and interesting articles and updates on current events, see www.irish-boxing.com and www.womenboxing.com.

Canoeing
Other options **Outdoor Goods** p.310

Taking to the open waters is a year-round activity, and canoeing conditions are often better in the colder months. It may be a bit chillier but for the sheer excitement factor, the fast-flowing rapids in fuller and flooded rivers are unbeatable. The paddler scene in Ireland is incredibly popular and social and it is a great way to meet a fun, easygoing crowd. You can aspire to compete in the Liffey Descent (www.liffeydescent.com), an annual race open to all grades, which attracts both national and international competitors, or you can just enjoy it as a hobby on weekends, taking your successive grade exams as you go. Most clubs provide all the gear so all you'll need is the appropriate clothing – wetsuits and some type of closed shoe are a must. Some clubs have fixed bases while others just transport the gear to a meeting point each week and you go from there. Different

Oops!
Have we missed out your club? If you run a sports club, a social group or any kind of activity in Dublin, we want to give you a free listing in our next edition. Visit us at www.explorerpublishing.com and give yourselves a shout-out.

types of canoeing include sea kayaking, wild water and flat water racing, slalom and open canoeing. The Irish Canoe Union has information on everything to do with the sport, as well as training, races and contact details for the multitude of clubs around the country (see www.canoe.ie for more details). Fingal Sailing School (see table, p.251) also arranges classes and trips.

Cookery Classes

71 Waterloo Rd
Ballsbridge
Map 431 E4 102

Alix Gardner's Cookery

01 668 1553 | www.dublincookery.com

Can't cook? No worries! Alix and her team will teach you the secret of the culinary arts in fun practical classes. With a maximun of eight students to a class, you will learn to cook a two-course dinner for two in the big kitchen of a Georgian house. The classes can be taken in blocks of either five or 10 evenings, one day a week. There are also occasional classes on Saturdays. Alix has been teaching people how to cook for over 20 years, as well as catering for dinners, parties and receptions. She is recommended by *The Dubliner and The Best of Bridgestone.*

Glenealy
Co Wicklow

Ballyknocken Country House & Cookery School

01 40 444 627 | www.ballyknocken.com

Run by Catherine Fulvio, this cookery school offers a selection of day, weekend and evening courses with themes such as Gourmet Cooking on a Budget, BBQ, Southern Italian Cuisine and Baker's Delight. Only local or homegrown ingredients are used. Cookery classes for children from age 7 upwards are available and tour groups are also catered for. Packages include a Brown Bread Making Demonstration and morning coffee stop, Irish Stew Making and Lunch. The school has adequate facilities for people with special needs. Courses cost from €55 per person, special packages for coaches start at €10 per person. Group rates are available upon request.

2 Charlemont Tce
Crofton Rd
Dun Laoghaire
Map 423 E4 90

Cooks Academy

01 214 5002 | www.cooksacademy.com

This school runs cookery classes on an 'as per bookings' basis, and they're busy most of the year round. Temperamental chefs aside, you should learn plenty about the business of cooking great Thai, Italian, Seafood, Asian and other cuisines for you, your friends and family, through the different classes on offer. Prices vary depending on the course. Individual classes start at €50 and Essential Cookery Courses cost €590 for five full days of intensive classes. See the website for details of the many options on offer. If it's your dream to cater to a wider audience, professional certificate courses for a block of 20 classes over five, full-day weeks are available for €2,950. Gift vouchers are available if you're keen to get someone else to do the cooking for you! For €65 a bit of dating is thrown into the mix with the Friday Singles Supper Clubs. Courses in wine and spirits appreciation, cocktail making and food and wine matching are also available. Last but not least, keep an eye out for the celebrity chefs that come to join in the fun on a regular basis, giving out precious pearls of kitchen wisdom – for a limited duration only of course!

2 Brookfield Tce
Blackrock
Map 422 B4 89

Dublin Cookery School

01 210 0555 | www.dublincookeryschool.ie

Courses and classes ranging from professional certificates for serious chefs to fun (and improved!) home cooking, and from learning how to make tapas to cooking a Christmas feast, all feature at the Dublin Cookery School, plus many more. Friday's cooking parties are a social occasion outside the pub when you and your family and

231

friends can come and cook dinner, learn a few new tricks and recipes and then sit down to enjoy it with a glass of wine. For men who are not afraid to enter the kitchen and well aware that the way to any heart is through the stomach, there are week-long 'men only' courses on offer. For those just needing a little hint and some encouragement, gift vouchers are available. Times and prices vary making learning to cook accessible to all – so leave the excuses at home and get to it. All classes are taught by trained professionals and experienced chefs.

Cricket

Cricket in Ireland has taken on a new life after the 2007 World Cup, in which the Irish team stormed past the mighty Pakistan to qualify for the Super 8 round – a surprise to everyone, considering it was Ireland's first ever World Cup tournament in cricket. For anyone who can understand this complex game, and then have the patience to actually go on to play it, there are plenty of clubs in the Dublin area for cricket enthusiasts. The Leinster Cricket Union is based in Malahide (01 845 0710) and will help you to locate clubs in your area, or see www.cricketeurope4.net.

Dublin Rd
Malahide

Malahide Cricket Club
01 845 0607 | www.malahidecc.org

This friendly club organises many social events for its members, from summer barbecues to marquee parties with dinner and drinks. Anyone can become a member, all skill levels and ages are welcome. Bitesize Cricket for boys and girls aged between 6 and 10 years is held on Sunday mornings (just turn up!) between 10:00 and 11:00. Interclub competitions are played regularly. Family membership is also available.

Phoenix Park
Dublin 8
Map 414 C1 222

Phoenix Park Cricket Club
01 677 0121 | www.phoenixcricketclub.com

Located in Phoenix Park, Phoenix Cricket Club was established in 1830 and is today one of Ireland's most successful clubs. Five men's teams, two ladies teams, three schoolboy teams and a very successful Taverners squad form the club. Many members are from overseas, so you can expect to play alongside players from some of the best cricket playing nations in the world – South Africa, New Zealand, Australia and even Pakistan (just don't mention the world cup). There's plenty of Irish players too, so it's sure to be good *craic*. Players of all levels are welcome to join. See the website for further details.

Cricket in Phoenix Park

Cycling

Other options **Cycling** p.233, **Sports Goods** p.315

Despite the constant bad weather, you'll see many a cyclist in Dublin – much of the city has dedicated cycle lanes to encourage cycling as a viable alternative mode of transport to driving. If you are keen to join a club, remember to arrive in appropriate clothing, especially waterproof gear if rain is forecast. It's also a good idea to bring your own repair kit, enough water, and some money in case of any stop offs.
A few companies offer tours and safaris (see p.198 for more information), and you can get a list of local cycling clubs from Cycling Ireland (www.cyclingireland.ie) or Irish Cycling (www.irishcycling.com).
If it's the thrills and saddle sores of mountain biking you're after, joining a club is probably the best way to enjoy the sport as they'll organise trips, show you the best trails and routes, offer advice and support and provide a good social network. Mountain Biking Ireland is a mountain biking information website set up by keen mountain bikers and welcomes members (individual membership is free). Their website has a list of affiliated clubs which you can join (www.mtbireland.com), as well as news on Irish mountain biking and a mountain biking forum.

70 Priory East
Navan Rd
Dublin 7
Map 407 D3 **101**

Dublin Wheelers Cycling Club

086 405 6653 | www.dublinwheelers.com

This club is open to boys and girls from late teens and upwards. Terrain covered ranges from flat to hilly but beginners and newcomers are welcome – just make sure you're reasonably fit so you can do your best to keep up. The Wheelers meet every Saturday (and some Sundays) at 09:30 at Santry traffic lights, beside the Morton Stadium, and head off in groups of anything from 10 to 20 people. Only cyclists wearing helmets can join the rides. Distances covered vary between 45 and 50 miles, stopping for a tea break after about 30 miles. Members are notified by text message of any trips planned. An experienced member will show you the ropes and give some pointers on cycling etiquette and riding in groups. For more information, contact the club secretary, Wes Murphy (wesley.murphy@helaba.de).

Yellow House Pub
Rathfarnham
Dublin 16
Map 419 F4 **149**

The MAD Club

087 792 7730 | www.madmtb.com

The best way to keep up with the antics of this mountain biking crowd is to keep a regular eye on the website and sign up to their mailing list. The group enters into official competitions, does weekend trips to Glendalough and around Wicklow and Dublin's more rugged outcrops. Muddy, tree-lined trails with steep slopes and set routes have been set up for training purposes, as well as for fun, and are open to expereinced riders and beginners alike. Introductory courses are run for beginners, including tips on bike maintenance. The website also has a helpful section on how to start mountain biking and plenty of useful and sensible tips on getting into the sport. Membership costs €20 per year and in order to become a member you must also join Cycling Ireland (www.cyclingireland.ie) for €35.

Dance Classes

Other options **Music Lessons** p.247

From the time of the weekly dances held at country crossroads to the present day, the Irish have always loved to dance. These days there's far more than a festive jig on offer: Dublin is home to numerous dance schools and clubs catering to all tastes. Fancy a bit of oriental bellydancing? Try Litton Lane Dance Studios. Or do you long to tango across the

233

dancefloor with a Latino hearthrob? Learn how with the Dublin Argentine Tango Society or Campadtrito Tango. Ballet Ireland caters to more classical tastes, and Dance World covers the more contemporary approach. Enjoy some Irish *craic* at a traditional Ceili (an evening of Irish dancing), but take some lessons first – Churchtown Irish Dancing offers classes and so does the Catherine Smith School of Dancing. Broaden your horizons with Irish Set Dancing, where you'll learn to dance as a foursome rather than as a couple, or go really broad minded and take some pole dancing classes with Polestars. You can find a list of dance classes and schools on the Dance Ireland website, and they also have an online shop so you can get yourself all kitted out before you start.

Dance Ireland
Foley St
Dublin 1
Map 426 C2 118

Biodanza

086 121 1909 | *www.biodanzaireland.com*
Biodanza is a dance form that was created in Chile by psychologist Rolando Toro, who used music and movement in healing. Biodanza means 'dance of life', and can help with numerous health problems like depression and stress, as well as helping people improve their non-verbal communication skills. A class is held every week in Dance Ireland on Foley Street (near Connolly Station). Classes are from 19:00 to 21:00 on Wednesdays, and each class costs €20. Wear loose clothing and bring a bottle of water.

14 Sackville Place
Dublin 1
Map 426 B3 88

Cois Ceim

01 878 4063 | *www.coisceim.com*
Cois Ceim has been up and running for nine years and is one of the country's most respected schools and dance companies. Try ballet, jazz or contemporary dance from beginner level to intermediate. A course of classes over eight weeks for adults costs €100. Young people aged 14 to 24 years can enrol in term classes in which they will choreograph a piece and then perform it at the end of the 10 week training session. These classes cost €100 (€75 concession).

Bloomfields
Shopping Centre
Lwr George's St
Dun Laoghaire
Map 423 E4 111

Dance Theatre of Ireland

01 280 3455 | *www.dancetheatreireland.com*
Live the dancer's dream at this dance studio – bright, airy, with mirrors and a barre – it's the perfect place to learn under the instruction of qualified, professional staff. Single classes vary in price depending on the class being taught, but reductions are offered for block bookings. Learn ballet, jazz, hip hop, pop, capoeira and modern dance, among others. Classes are also available for professional dancers, and the school offers summer courses for adults and young people from 8 to 17 years.

Liberty Cnr
Foley St
Dublin 1
Map 426 C2 133

DanceHouse

01 855 8800 | *www.prodanceireland.com*
DanceHouse is a non-profit organisation under the umbrella of the National Association of Professional Dancers in Ireland (APDI), set up with the primary objective of supporting and promoting dance in Ireland. It's accessible to all ages and groups, from beginners to professionals, and class fees are very reasonable for both members and non-members. Disciplines studied include ballet, including professional ballet classes with Ballet Ireland, contemporary dance using the Gyrokinesis dancer-specific training methodology, jazz, flamenco and Biodanza. Facilities at the centre include a cafe, wireless internet, relaxation areas, changing rooms with hot showers and lockers.

Various Locations

Fiona Kinsella School of Ballet

01 845 4242 | *kinsellaballet@eircom.net*
This school offers ballet classes for children, aged 3 and upwards and Ballet Fit classes for adults. Royal Academy of Dance exams can be taken here and are optional. Classes

take place in Portmarnock Sports & Leisure Centre and in Scoil Aine, Raheny. Contact Fiona Kinsella personally on 087 828 9342, or the school, for more information.

Various Locations

Flora Millar Dance Ireland
01 288 8455 | www.floramillar.com

Flora Millar is one of Ireland's top professional dance schools, and this is evident in the fact that Flora herself has been awarded the Carl Alan award, one of the industry's most prestigious awards. The school offers a range of classes for children aged 4 and upwards and adults. Four, six and ten-week courses are run throughout the summer and autumn, starting at €60. Private tuition is also available. Dances covered include beginner and advanced classes in foxtrot, waltz, quick step, cha cha and swing.

Various Locations

Just Dance
01 827 3040 | www.justdance.ie

Just Dance offers weekly dance classes taught by professionals throughout the city in everything from salsa, tango and merengue, to hip-hop and waltz. They offer instruction in pre-wedding dances, an agency service for registered dancers to find work on stage or TV, and also the opportunity to enter competitions for all levels and styles. They offer kids' classes for children and teenagers from 6 to 16 years, starting at just €8 per hour. A six-week course of adult clases starts at €70. Private lessons are also available.

Dance Classes		
Ballet Ireland	046 955 7585	www.balletireland.com
Catherine Smith School of Dancing	01 204 1736	na
Churchtown Irish Dancing	01 298 8816	na
Compadrito Tango	086 374 7958	www.tangofever.net
Dance World	01 497 6128	www.dance.ie
Dublin Argentine Tango Society	na	www.dublintango.com
Irish Set Dancing	na	www.setdancingnews.net
Litton Lane Dance Studios	01 872 8044	na
Polestars	1890 882 324	www.polestars.ie

Diving

20 Terenure Pk
Dublin 6W
Map 419 F2 92

Discover Scuba
01 492 7392 | www.discoverscuba.net

This is an internationally recognised PADI dive school located in south-west Dublin, running all levels of courses from total beginners up to dive master level. All instructors are fully qualified and are a friendly bunch, making it an enjoyable diving experience. From a trial dive in a swimming pool costing around €70 (redeemable if you then go on to do a dive course) to refresher courses for €75, and courses for every level costing from €395 upwards, including speciality dive courses for AWARE, boat, drift and drysuit diving, among others, this place has it covered. Enthusiasts will be pleased to hear that there are weekends away, open water diving, new Nitrox courses and Emergency First Response courses. Prices are competitive. Prospective divers must be aged 10 years and over.

Boat Yard
Coal Harbour
Dun Laoghaire
Map 423 E4 112

Oceandivers
01 280 1083 | www.oceandivers.ie

Dublin Bay offers many interesting places to dive such as Maiden Rock, Dalkey Island, the Muglins and the Dublin Bay wrecks, with the season running from April to October. Oceandivers offers both tours and lessons, while Dive Ireland (www.tempoweb.com/diveireland) has general information about diving in Ireland.

Dog Training

Other options **Pets** p.312

Dunsoghly La
St Margarets
Dublin Airport
Dublin 9

Dog Training Ireland

01 864 4922 | *www.dogtrainingireland.ie*

Dog Training Ireland is staffed by qualified (HNC CBT), certified (MAPDT, CAP 1&2) and insured trainers. They have an indoor heated training centre with rubber flooring, and they offer courses in puppy socialisation, obedience (all levels), agility training, gundog, and aggression management. DTI also hosts regular weekend workshops and seminars. Check their website for more information and also for their online shop.

Wendon Mt Versus Rd
Rockbrook
Rathfarnham
Dublin 16

The Pet Behaviour Centre

01 497 2723 | *www.petsbehave.com*

This centre specialises in solving behavioural issues with your pet, no matter what the age or species. All training methods are rewards based, and clicker training is used to accelerate learning for pet and owner. You can take your dog to the centre in Rathfarnham or a behaviour specialist can come to your home. The PBC can help with aggression, separation anxiety and noise phobias in dogs, and spraying, scratching and excessive grooming in cats, among many other behavioural problems.

Church Grove
Aylesbury Estate
Tallaght

Tag N Rye Dog Services

01 451 3324 | *www.tagnrye.com*

Julie Holmes can teach you how to train your family dog, irrespective of age, breed or behavioural problem. She can give you an insight into why your dog behaves the way it does, and offer solutions based on specific behaviours. Julie has over 25 years of experience of working, training and competing with dogs, and her own dogs are available for film or television work. Distance is no problem and she will gladly come to you to solve your pet problems!

Drama Groups

Dalkey

The Dalkey Players

www.dalkeyplayers.ie

Founded in 1976, Dalkey Players is one of Ireland's best-known amateur drama groups. They rehearse every Tuesday and Sunday from September to May, and perform regularly in the Pavilion Theatre, Dun Laoghaire and in the Dalkey Town Hall. The group runs regular workshops on acting, directing, movement and voice for its members. Recent productions have included works by Friel, Wilde, Miller, Shakespeare, Chekov, Behan and Churchill. Dalkey Players has won numerous awards on the festival circuit. They are always looking for new members, either to be on stage or behind the scenes.

Bad Actor?
If you just can't find your inner thespian, but you love the theatre nonetheless, check out the listings for theatre in the Going Out section (p.393). It features all of Dublin's prominent theatres, so that you can leave the board-treading to the professionals.

The Mill Theatre
Dundrum Town Centre
Dundrum
Map 421 D4 24

Drama League of Ireland

01 296 9343 | *www.dli.ie*

The Drama League of Ireland represents local drama groups and individual actors, directors and stagehands. They put on various workshops and courses, they hold an extensive library of scripts, and they provide assistance with securing performing rights. Annual membership costs €35 for an individual and just €100 for a group.

Environmental Groups

Other options **Voluntary & Charity Work** p.69

Environmental Groups		
Citizen's Information	01 605 9000	www.citizensinformation.ie
Cultivate Living & Learning Centre	01 674 5773	www.cultivate.ie
ENFO Information on the Environment	01 888 3910	www.enfo.ie
Kids Against Waste	na	www.kidsagainstwaste.ie
Race Against Waste	01 284 6317	www.raceagainstwaste.com
Sustainable Energy Ireland	01 836 9080	www.sei.ie

Ireland has had to take some pretty drastic measures to fall in line with EU regulations on waste management and environmental awareness. There are several organisations that work to educate the public on these important issues and help the recycling effort. You can help in the war on global warming by making some surprisingly small changes in your own home, and these organisations publish leaflets and list some good ideas on their websites.

Fishing

As an island with massive rainfall, Ireland is a top fishing destination simply because it has water – and lots of it. You'll find a wide variety of species in Ireland's coastal and inland waters, such as carp, salmon, trout, bass and even shark (if big game fishing is more your thing). There are various tagging and protection schemes in place to protect the marine population – the Central Fisheries Board can point you in the right direction (01 8842 600, www.cfb.ie).

Fishing	
Dublin Telesport Sea Angling Club	www.dublintelesport.com
Federation of Irish Salmon & Sea Trout Anglers	http://fissta.com
Howth Sea Angling Club	www.howthsac.com
Irish Federation of Sea Anglers	www.ifsa.ie
Marine Times Newspaper	www.marinetimes.ie
Portobello Angling Club	www.portobelloangling.com

Flower Arranging

Other options **Gardens** p.297, **Flowers** p.295

465 South Circular Rd
Dublin 8
Map 428 A1 97

Kay's School of Floristry
01 453 8649 | www.kaysschool.ie

You can study various aspects of flower arranging at Kay's – commercial, bridal, sympathy and hand-tied bouquets to name a few. Each module can be done in four days, and you can choose whether you want to do that during the week, or over weekends. Each module costs €600, but book all three in one go (€1,800), and you'll get a pair of florist's scissors and a professional florist's table. Places on each module are limited and you need to book in advance – check the website for module dates.

A beautiful environment is worth protecting

Flying

Other options **Hot Air Ballooning** p.202

Dublin Airport is relatively small (for a capital city airport), and therefore it is easy for various flying clubs to use their facilities. Some flying clubs offer pilot training, and some offer aircraft rentals.

Flying	
Airport Flying Club	www.airportflyingclub.com
Dublin Gliding Club	www.dublinglidingclub.ie
National Aero Club of Ireland	admin@aeroclub.ie

Swords
Dublin 9

PC Pilots Ireland

087 257 0020 | www.pcpilotsireland.com

While there may not be any real planes involved, PC Pilots Ireland is a club for users of Microsoft Flight Simulator. They have 220 members, not just from Ireland but from around the world. The club meets twice a year in Dublin for a day of virtual flying, and they have an active forum where members can communicate with each other. Their quarterly magazine *PC Flight* features product reviews and articles on flight simulation and real aviation.

Football

Dalymount Park ◀
Phibsborough
Dublin 7
Map 408 A4 117

Bohemian Football Club

01 868 0923 | www.bohemians.ie

Founded in 1980, BFC plays in the Premier Division of the Eircom League of Ireland – so it may not be the club for you if you fancy a casual kickabout after work. However, it is a community-based club and fields schoolboy teams from under 7s to under 17s, and it also runs Easter and summer soccer camps for children. Home games are played on Friday nights, and fixtures are listed on the website.

Various Locations ◀

Netball Dublin

087 667 7737 | www.netballdublin.com

Don't be fooled by the name: apart from a netball league, this organisation also runs a popular indoor football league. You can join as an individual or you can get a whole team together, and the registration fee per person is €20. A match fee also applies. Football is played at two venues, one on the north side and one on the south. Both venues are within walking distance of the city centre.

Tolka Park ◀
Richmond Rd
Drumcondra
Dublin 9
Map 408 C4 28

Shamrock Rovers Football Club

01 460 5948 | www.shamrockrovers.ie

Shamrock Rovers Football Club is the most successful football club in Ireland, having won the League of Ireland Trophy on 15 occasions and the FAI cup a record 24 times. The Hoops are arguably the most famous sporting club in Ireland, and have produced some of Ireland's greatest ever footballers. You can become a member for just €10 a week, see the website for details.

Tolka Park ◀
Richmond Rd
Drumcondra
Dublin 9
Map 408 C4 28

Shelbourne Football Club

01 837 5536 | www.shelbournefc.ie

Shelbourne was a founder member of the Football League of Ireland in 1921, and to date they have 13 league titles to their name. The club colours are red and white, with home jerseys being predominantly red (hence their nickname, the Reds). Shelbourne has a vibrant 'Young Reds' youth academy, with teams from under 7s to under 18s. These teams are coached to UEFA standards and play their home games at the AUL complex in Clonshaugh.

Richmond Pk ◀
Inchicore
Dublin 8
Map 415 D3 **139**

St Patrick's Athletic Football Club

01 454 6332 | *www.stpatsfc.com*
St Patrick's Athletic are currently one of the leading clubs in the Eircom League of Ireland, which is the top division in Irish Football. Based in Inchicore, the 'Super Saints' are a very strong, community-based club, which always ensures a great atmosphere at Richmond Park on match night.

Belfield Pk ◀
UCD, Belfield
Dublin 4
Map 421 E2 **542**

University College Dublin Football Club

01 716 2142 | *www.ucdsoccer.com*
Based in Ireland's largest university, UCD FC is currently playing in the Eircom League of Ireland Premier Division. Although the club is based in the university, it is not a student club. Indeed, the club boasts some of the brightest young football talent in Ireland.

Gaelic Games

Founded in 1884, the Gaelic Athletic Association (GAA) is the governing body for Gaelic football and hurling in Ireland. There are over 2,500 clubs in the country and most clubs play both sports, with leagues, cups and championships organised on a local level. The winners will then go on, from provincial level, representing not only their county but also their province, all the way up to national level competitions and a chance to win the All Ireland final. All finals are played in Croke Park stadium (www.crokepark.ie) where there is also a GAA museum. See p.261.

Hurling is played with a stick (*camán* in Irish) and a ball (*sliothar* in Irish). It's a serious goal scoring game – one of the fastest on land – where players can either slap the ball into the goal (similar to hockey), or over the bar, as in a rugby conversion. Players can run bouncing the ball on their hurley, pass it down the field, or hold it in their hand (for a limited number of steps) and it's a fiercely competitive and often bloody sport as opponents will swipe their stick wildly to try and retrieve possession of the ball, and are not shy to tackle and disable a would-be point scorer!

Gaelic football on the other hand is played with a ball that is slightly smaller than a soccer ball. You can kick, carry (for four steps), hand pass or bounce the ball and scoring is the same as for hurling, either below or above the bar, each one notching up different points.

Both games are fiercely competitive, wild and fast, and bring out a strong national pride in supporters, with many teams having long-standing rivals. For Dublin

Camogie in Phoenix Park

239

Gaelic Games

Castleknock Hurling & Football Club	Dublin 15	www.castleknock.net
Dublin Camogie County Board	Swords	www.dublincamogie.ie
Hill 16	Dublin 5	www.hill16.ie
Na Fianna	Dublin 9	www.clgnafianna.ie
Portobello GAA & Social Club	Rathmines	portobellogaa1@eircom.net
Whitehall Colcille	Dublin 9	www.whitehallcolmcille.ie

teams, see www.hill16.ie. or the Leinster website (the Province to which Dublin belongs, see. p.4 for more on this) at www.leinster.gaa.ie. Hill 16 is the official site for Dublin with information on clubs, games, results and coaching. There is a full listing of clubs on the website as well as the latest news on results and upcoming events. Tickets to matches can be brought online at www.gaa.ie and for matches at local level, you can just go along and see what it's all about for free, the players will surely be glad of the support. For camogie (the female version of hurling – be warned, it's not for the meek and mild!), see www.camogie.ie. Similarly, for ladies Gaelic football, see www.ladiesgaelic.ie.

Golf

When the sun is shining, there can be few things better than a walk round 18 holes on one of Ireland's beautiful greens. But even in driving rain, freezing temperatures or blustery winds, golfers will still tee off. In 2006, the Ryder Cup was played at the K Club in County Kildare (www.kclub.ie), undoubtedly one of the top courses in Europe, and situated just a short drive out of Dublin. However, Dublin has its own collection of wonderful courses – over 50, in fact. Most insist on soft spikes (but this is becoming more common everywhere these days), and most have golf carts for hire.

Newlands Cross
Clondalkin
Dublin 22

Newlands Golf Club
01 459 3157 | www.newlandsgolfclub.com
Just minutes away from the hectic frenzy of the M50 lies this tranquil golf course designed by James Braid. The par 71 course measures 5,947 metres over 18 holes, and non-members can tee off on weekdays for just €75 (and for only €20 if accompanied by a member). A club and cart hire service is available.

Balheary Ave
Swords
Dublin 9

Swords Open Golf Course
01 840 9819 | www.swordsopengolfcourse.com
It's always tee-time at this friendly golf course, which is easily accessible thanks to its reasonable green fees (€20 midweek and €25 on weekends). Its location on the picturesque banks of the Broadmeadow River is just five minutes from Swords, and 10 minutes from Dublin Airport. The course offers a rental service on clubs and golf carts.

Golf

Name	Area	Phone	Web	Length	Par
Castle Golf Club	Dublin 14	01 490 4207	www.castlegc.ie	6246m	70
Clontarf Golf Club	Dublin 3	01 833 1892	www.clontarfgolfclub.ie	5317m	69
Dun Laoghaire Golf Club	Dun Laoghaire	01 280 3916	www.dunlaoghairegolfclub.ie	5313m	71
Elm Park Sports & Golf Club	Dublin 4	01 269 3438	www.elmparkgolfclub.ie	5942yds	69
Forrest Little Golf Club	Cloghran	01 840 1763	www.forrestlittle.ie	5900m	71
Grange Golf Club	Dublin 16	01 493 2889	www.grangegolfclub.ie	5396m	68
Howth Golf Club	Sutton	01 832 3055	www.howthgolfclub.ie	5479m	72
Malahide Golf Club	Malahide	01 846 1611	www.malahidegolfclub.ie	6066m	71
Milltown Golf Club	Dublin 14	01 497 6090	www.milltowngolfclub.ie	5638m	71
Portmarnock Golf Club	North Coast	01 846 2968	www.portmarnockgolfclub.ie	6826yds	71
The Royal Dublin Golf Club	Dublin 3	01 833 6346	www.theroyaldublingolfclub.com	7250yds	72
St Anne's Golf Club	Dublin 5	01 833 6471	www.stanneslinksgolf.com	6643yds	71
Stackstown Golf Club	Dublin 16	01 494 1993	www.stackstowngolfclub.com	6152yds	72
Sutton Golf Club	Sutton	01 832 2965	www.suttongolfclub.org	2889yds	35

Hiking

Other options **Mountaineering** p.246,
Outdoor Goods p.310

61 Mountjoy St
Dublin 7
Map 425 F1 98

An Oige Hillwalking Club

01 882 2562 | www.anoige.ie

An Oige offers hikes for all levels of
experience – their moderately hard
programme is best for those who have done
some hillwalking before but have not
reached the level of hardcore hikers. There's
an introductory hard hike every month, in
case you want to test your mettle before
signing up. Club activities include various
social expeditions, weekends away and

Hiking trail in Glendalough

holidays in Ireland and abroad. Membership costs €20 per year, which includes a
monthly magazine and third party insurance.

Various Locations
South Dublin

Countryside Hillwalkers Association

www.cha.ie

There are numerous trails and hiking paths on the Dublin and Wicklow mountains,
with Sundays the day of choice for most people. For more information on trails, events
and tours, contact the Countrywide Hillwalkers Association or the Tourism Centre on
Suffolk Street (01 605 7700, vwww.visitdublin.com).

Hockey

Hockey is popular in Ireland and Dublin has no shortage of clubs you can join, from
beginner to semi-professional level, with both men's and women's leagues. Many of
the leisure facilites have outdoor and indoor hockey pitches (see p.263 for more), and
most of the universities have teams – check out the websites for Dublin City University
(www.dcu.ie), University College Dublin (www.ucd.ie) and Trinity College (www.tcd.ie).
Like most sports in Ireland, hockey is accompanied by a lively social scene. League
games bring out the competitive side in most players, especially when there's a trophy
at stake, and most teams have bitter rivals somewhere or other that they've previously
lost out to, but that's all part of the fun. For a listing of teams in the Dublin area and
information on the sport itself, see www.hockey.ie. Some popular clubs include St
James's Gate (www.gatehockey.com), Old Alexandra Ladies Hockey Club
(www.oldalexhc.ie) and Corinthian Hockey Club (www.chc.ie).

Horse Riding

Equestrian sports are very popular in Ireland and Kildare is the capital of horse
breeding. The Association of Riding Establishments (www.aire.ie) offers a list of riding
schools in Ireland, with some schools offering trails in Wicklow. If you're not quite
ready to hop on and gallop away yourself, the Dublin Horse Show held in the RDS
every summer might inspire you (see p.49 for more).

Carrickmines
South Dublin

Carrickmines Equestrian Centre

01 295 5990 | www.carrickminesequestrian.ie

Carrickmines Equestrian Centre offers trekking for all levels on their 80 acres of
farmland. It has the largest all weather equestrian arena in Ireland and offers activities
such as show jumping, polocrosse and dressage. Group lessons are held Tuesdays to
Sundays (private lessons are available by arrangement). A one-hour group lesson costs

241

€32 per adult and €23 per child, although you can save a substantial amount by getting a 'term card' (paying for a number of lessons in advance). CEC also runs pony camps during the summer, for children aged 6 to 14 years.

Karting

Old Airport Rd
Santry
Dublin 9

Kartcity
01 842 6322 | www.kartcity.net

Karting enthusiasts can take a tour of Dublin's largest tracks at speed from €20 per person for 15 minutes. Corporate packages are available. Mini Grand Prix, Full Grand Prix and Team Building and Mini Enduro events are also on offer. Children under 16 must be accompanied by an adult and can use the intermediate track from €15 in the 'Arrive & Drive' sessions. You can book online, see the website for details, by phone, email or by fax. Trophies and medals and a bottle of bubbly will be awarded to the winning teams or people at the end of the races. Now, who said you didn't have a competitive streak? Open Monday to Friday from 14:00 to 22:00 and from 12:00 until 22:00 on Saturdays and Sundays.

Kids' Activities

11a Eustace St
Temple Bar
Dublin 2
Map 426 A4 86

The Ark
01 670 7788 | www.ark.ie

The Ark is a children's cultural centre that hosts programmes and promotes cultural art by children. A range of Irish and international artists collaborate with The Ark to create programmes that children will find amusing, inspirational and educational. There are programmes designed for children between the ages of 3 to 14. Check the website for updated information on current programmes.

The Stables
Strand Rd
Portmarnock

Artworks Cafe
01 828 4000 | www.artworkscafe.ie

Artworks provides pottery painting fun seven days a week. It is aimed at adults and children who can drop in, select a 'naked' piece of pottery, paint it and then take it home. Prices start at €12 per person, and their range of pottery includes dinnerware, vases, souvenirs and animals. Artworks specialises in tailor-made adult and youth workshops and runs a programme of camps, clubs and special events. The cafe is open every day between 11:00 and 19:00 and there is no need to book (unless you are in a group of six or more people).

Blessington
Co Wicklow

Eve Studio Pottery
045 865 850 | evestudiopottery@gmail.com

Eve's offers classes for children aged 4 and upwards. Children get to paint on pottery while learning about pottery making or can take part in their own pottery making class. Summer camps are run from the beginning of June to the end of August, Monday to Wednesday and include, in addition to the above, designing their own pillowcase and learning the art of batik.

Language Schools

1 Kildare St
Dublin 2
Map 430 C1 84

Alliance Française
01 676 1732 | www.alliance-francaise.ie

Going to the Alliance Française in the heart of Dublin's city centre is less a chore than a pleasant cultural experience. Staff are friendly and efficient, and most importantly they are all native French speakers. Courses in French language and culture, translation and interpreting for companies and other legal and business French courses are covered, as well as primary school level French, and all their courses have a good success rate. Your level will be decided by a test taken before class semesters begin to ensure you are not in over your head or bored because you're not learning anything new. Cultural events such as gigs, book signings and artists' exhibitions take place in Café des Amis on the ground floor – open to everyone for lunch, snacks or just a chat and a coffee. Open Monday to Friday from 09:00 to 19:30, and Saturday from 09:00 to 13:00. The French library is the largest of its kind in Ireland and has over 20,000 books and publications. Videos, DVDS and CDS are also available for rent.

1 Clarinda Pk North
Dun Laoghaire

Annalivia School
01 230 1100 | www.annaliviaschool.com
Annalivia teaches English to foreign students, focusing on core grammar and vocabulary use, both in written work and when speaking. Bi-weekly social events are also organised whereby students get to put what they've learned into practice. Long and short courses are available for all levels with a maximum of 12 to a class in peak periods. Evening adult courses are available. They also offer the TEFL course here.

Filmbase Bld
Curved St
Temple Bar
Dublin 2
Map 426 A4 123

Gaelchultúr Teoranta
01 675 3658 | www.gaelchultur.com
Gaelchultúr Teoranta was established in 2004 with the aim of promoting the Irish language and various aspects of Irish culture, including music, song and dance, in Dublin city and other parts of the country. Since 2005, Gaelchultúr has provided Irish language training to a wide range of public sector bodies, as well as general Irish language courses to the public at six levels, three times a year. Other activities on offer include concerts, plays, a lunchtime discussion group, workshops in sean-nós singing and dancing, and a book club.

Ballast House
Westmoreland St
Dublin 2
Map 426 B4 107

GEOS English Academy
01 679 2997 | www.geosdublin.com
GEOS Dublin is part of an international group of approximately 500 schools worldwide. The Dublin branch can be found right in the centre of town, overlooking the Liffey and O'Connell Bridge. All GEOS teachers are qualified native speakers with university degrees and TEFL qualifications, as well as many years of experience teaching English as a second language both here and abroad. The school is recognised by the Department of Education. They offer full-time and part-time courses, and there are evening classes too.

37 Merrion Sq
Dublin 2
Map 431 D2 94

Goethe-Institut
01 661 1155 | www.goethe.de
This is where German language and culture enthusiasts flock to soak up some German culture and learn or improve their linguistic skills. It's also an excellent place to meet fellow countrymen if you're German and moving to Dublin for the first time. All levels of classes are offered, from one-to-one classes to corporate and extensive courses. Culture nights and film screenings are put on regularly and distance learning classes are also offered. The library has a broad range of CD-ROMS, DVDs, CDs and books to help you perfect your knowledge. The school closes for much of August but is open the rest of the year round.

Oops!
Have we missed out your club? If you run a sports club, a social group or any kind of activity in Dublin, we want to give you a free listing in our next edition. Visit us at www.explorerpublishing.com and give yourselves a shout-out.

243

45 Kildare St
Dublin 2
Map 430 C1 96

The Language Centre of Ireland

01 671 6266 | www.lci.ie

This friendly, welcoming school teaches English classes in the heart of Dublin. Courses on offer include internationally recognised English examinations such as the Cambridge exams, the TOEIC exam, and the IELTS exam. On arrival you will do a placement test and have an interview to ensure you're studying the correct level. Afternoon (14:30 to 16:30) and evening classes (18:30 to 20:30) are available, as well as 20 hour (standard course) and 26 hour (intensive) weekly courses. Teaching English as a foreign language can be studied through the CELTA and TEFL courses. Student accomodation options are also available. Fees vary per course – see the website for more details. LCI is recognised by the Irish Department of Education.

Libraries

Other options **Second-Hand Items** p.313, **Books** p.287

From basic book lending to art classes, research opportunities, poetry and book readings and storytelling for children, libraries offer an invaluable service to their members. There are numerous public libraries throughout Dublin, so to find the one closest to you, see www.library.ie. Membership is free.

For foreign languages, the Italian Cultural Institute has a good range, the Alliance Française (p.242) also has an excellent library for francophones, and the Goethe Institute caters to German langauge enthusiasts (p.243).

138–144 Pearse St
Dublin 2
Map 431 D1 87

Dublin City Library and Archive

01 674 4999 | www.dublincity.ie

Anyone who holds a current research card can access this library. Cards are issued through the Dublin City Public Libraries (open to everyone). It is also home to Dublin City Archives, which follows the history and development of the civic government of Dublin over eight centuries (1171 up to the late 20th century) through records, land deeds, maps, drawings, account books, correspondence, and much more. It also houses private collections on the history of the city of Dublin and Ireland up until the 21st century. There is a reading room on the first floor. It is best to request required reading material in advance, especially for early printed books and manuscripts. If you're keen to trace your family history and Irish roots, this is a good place to start. Open Monday to Thursday from 10:00 to 20:00 and Friday and Saturday from 10:00 to 17:00. Closed Sundays. Wheelchair access.

11 Fitzwilliam Sq
Dublin 2
Map 430 C3 85

Italian Cultural Institute

01 662 0509 | www.iicdublino.esteri.it/IIC_Dublino

This extensive library contains mainly Italian material, so it's a great resource if you're studying the language. However, it also has a selection of Italian novels that have been translated into English, so even if you don't speak Italian it's a good way to broaden your horizons. The institute often exhibits works from Italian artists and hosts a variety of events with an Italian flavour.

Kildare St
Dublin 2
Map 430 C1 129

National Library of Ireland

01 603 0200 | www.nli.ie

This library, located in the centre of Dublin, is home to the world's largest collection of Irish documentation, including manuscripts, books, newspapers, periodicals, photographs and maps. Access is free but you will need to get a reader's ticket to be able to use it. You can apply for one of these at the information desk. Just bring two passport photographs and some valid ID. You can download the application form

Libraries

Name	Address	Area	Phone
Central Library	Ilac Centre, Henry St	Dublin 1	01 873 4333
Charleville Mall Library	North Strand	Dublin 1	01 874 9619
Kevin Street Library	18 Lower Kevin St	Dublin 8	01 475 3794
Music Library	Ilac Centre, Henry St	Dublin 1	01 873 4333
Pearse Street Library	138-144 Pearse St	Dublin 2	01 674 4888
Pembroke Library	Anglesea Rd	Dublin 4	01 668 9575
Phibsboro Library	Blackquire Bridge	Dublin 7	01 830 4341
Raheny Library	Howth Rd, Raheny	Dublin 5	01 831 5521
Rathmines Library	157 Lower Rathmines Rd	Dublin 6	01 497 3539

online to save time filling it out once there. The library does not have a book lending facility but you can consult any of the collections in the reading rooms. You can also get photocopies, photographs, slides, or microfilm of most items. Other gems on offer are the various ongoing exhibitions, and a library shop. The library is open from 09:30 Monday to Saturday. Different rooms open and close at different times so check the website for details.

Martial Arts

Martial arts is not just about fighting – it's also about discipline of the mind and body. It's an excellent way to get fit too. Dublin has a great selection of classes and workshops available in many different martial arts forms, from aikido and kickboxing to karate and taekwondo. Below is a list of organisations that regulate each form, and you will find a list of clubs on their website. One club that is particularly worth a mention is the Clever Little Monkeys Martial Arts Academy in Tallaght – they specialise in teaching various martial arts to children (phone 086 815 1092 or 087 121 2768, or email info@cleverlittlemonkeys.com).

Martial Arts

Allstyles Kickboxing Association of Ireland	www.kickboxing.ie
Clever Little Monkeys	www.cleverlittlemonkeys.com
Irish Aikido Association	www.aikidoireland.ie
Irish Karate Advisory Board	www.irishkarate.ie
Irish Martial Arts Commission	www.martialarts.ie
Irish Taekwon-Do Association	www.taekwondo.ie

Mother & Toddler Activities

If you're looking for baby swimming classes, check out your local pool (see p.254). Alternatively, some of the schools and colleges with swimming pools also offer classes, such as The Marian College in Ballsbridge (01 668 4036, www.mariancollege.ie). The National Aquatic Centre also offers swimming classes for little fish aged between six months and two years (p.255).

Various Locations

BabyMassage.ie

01 821 2958 | www.babymassage.ie

Infant massage is an ancient, beautiful and enjoyable art, which encourages learning about you, your baby and his or her needs. It encourages bonding, it can help new parents gain confidence in handling their baby, and it can also be helpful in alleviating postnatal depression. Benefits of baby massage include improvement of colic and constipation, wind relief, better sleeping patterns, weight gain and growth in premature babies, better digestion and circulation, improved skin condition and better muscle tone. Plus is is relaxing for both the parent and the baby, which is always a welcome side effect in the first few whirlwind months after the birth! Group Classes are available in Castleknock and Lucan or you can book private sessions anywhere in Dublin.

Various Locations

Gymboree Play & Music

www.playandmusic.ie

Gymboree is an American franchise that can now be found around the world, across Ireland, and even in Dublin. They offer music and activity sessions for kids of all ages in a safe environment. Activities are age appropriate, and even newborns are engaged in a way that they can enjoy and respond to. The emphasis is on early child development, but sessions are lots of fun too. They also do birthday parties. The first class costs €12, after which you can sign up for a three-month membership (€145) or a six-month membership (€220). If you're not interested in the classes but you'd like to take your child to use the facilities, open gym costs €7 per hour for non-members (free for members). They have locations all over Dublin, and you can find the one nearest to you by checking their website or emailing info@playandmusic.ie.

Various Locations

Jo Jingles
01 869 0344 | www.jojingles.ie

Jo Jingles classes offer a fun introduction to music for babies and toddlers through lively and interactive classes. The session gives an introduction to music through the use of various activities, such as percussion instruments, singing, music, and sound and rhythm games. The classes are structured and educational so over a term you will see your child develop a real love and understanding of music. In addition, children will learn about the world around them – space, the farm, colours and so on. Mothers are asked to stay with their children in order to reinforce the lessons learned and encourage participation. Classes are small and age specific, which keeps the group informal and friendly. Check the website for details on classes around Dublin, including north Dublin, south-east and south-west Dublin.

Various Locations

Kindermusik
086 840 1475 | www.kindermusikwithcynthia.com

Kindermusik is all about music and movement classes for babies and young children, from newborns to 3 years. Each class is full of energy, imagination, music and dancing. In every class, you'll see your child's developmental evolution in language skills, literacy, listening, problem solving, social skills, self esteem and musical appreciation. Small class sizes allow for individual attention as well as a chance to get to know other parents and children. Cynthia's classes take place in Mount Merrion Community Centre and Blackrock, but for other locations in Dublin, see www.kindermusik.co.uk.

Mountaineering

There are hundreds of clubs in Ireland that cater to mountaineering, hillwalking, climbing and rambling. Many of these use the beautiful Wicklow Mountains as their primary base for walks. Clubs set their own membership fees and in general these vary between €25 and €60 for annual membership. The Mountaineering Council of Ireland (www.mountaineering.ie, 01 625 1115) is Ireland's representative body for the sport. You can join the MCI for €42 a year. This includes insurance and your subscription to the quarterly magazine, the *Irish Mountain Log*. To get involved in regular outings though, it's best to join a club. See their website for a list of affiliated clubs.

Various Locations

Irish Mountaineering Club
086 402 7652 | www.irishmountaineeringclub.org

This club's main activities are rock climbing, alpine mountaineering and hillwalking. It's a fun, social club and if you don't have a climbing partner you can come along and find one through them. Membership is open to everyone. They offer a beginners course in April/May, which is a good introduction to the club, summer meets on Thursday evenings in Dalkey Quarry (including night hikes for the more experienced!), regular trips in Ireland and abroad, and training courses. During the winter, members meet at Teachers' Club, Parnell Square. They also have a hut in the Wicklow mountains that you can rent out for a small fee, and which they use for club weekend getaways.

Mountaineering Council of Ireland

Sport HQ
13 Joyce Way
Park West Business Pk
Dublin 12

01 625 1115 | *www.mountaineering.ie*
The Mountaineering Council of Ireland (MCI) is the national governing body for the sport of mountaineering in Ireland. They cover bouldering, hillwalking, rambling, rock climbing, alpinism and indoor climbing. They provide safety training to walkers and climbers and encourage responsible use of the mountain environment. You can find a comprehensive list of clubs on their website.

Wayfarers Association

61 Westgate
St Augustine St
Dublin 8
Map 416 A2 99

www.wayfarersassociation.com
The Wayfarers Hillwalking Cub is one of the largest Dublin based hillwalking clubs with over 200 members. On a weekly basis they organise two hikes with a short and a long hike option. Most of their hiking is in the Wicklow Mountains, but they also have regular trips away where they visit other mountain ranges both in Ireland and abroad. Anyone over 18 is welcome to join.

Music Lessons

Other options **Dance Classes** p.233, **Musical Instruments** p.309

Dublin School of Music

22 Dodder Rd Lwr
Rathfarnham
Dublin 14
Map 420 A3 93

01 492 9998 | *www.dublinschoolofmusic.com*
This established music school teaches individual and group lessons in a variety of instruments, including guitar, drums, singing, piano, violin and flute. They also offer various behind-the-scenes courses, including band management and studio engineering. A 12 week course costs €180 for groups and €280 for one-to-one tuition. The school has branches in Castleknock, Tyrrelstown, Rathfarnham and Rathgar.

Kay's Piano Studio

Various Locations

www.pianolessonsdublin.com
Kay is an experienced piano player and teacher, and has a real passion for her craft. She has seen countless students grow from beginners to gifted recital performers, thanks to her teaching which incorporates techniques, ear tests and performances. She will work with students of all levels and has an excellent exam success rate.

Walton's New School of Music

**69 South Great
George's St**
Dublin 2
Map 430 A1 100

01 478 1884 | *www.newschool.ie*
Over a thousand students complete music lessons at this school each term. Walton's teaches individual and group lessons in singing, guitar, piano, violin, harmonica and percussion, as well as theoretical courses like song writing and music reading. Perhaps most interestingly, they offer a range of courses in Irish traditional music, with lessons on instruments such as the fiddle and the bodhran.

Netball

Dublin Indoor Sports

Fairbrook Mews
Ballyboden Rd
Rathfarnham
Dublin 14
Map 419 F4 122

087 904 8810 | *www.dublinindoorsports.ie*
You can play social or competitive netball at Dublin Indoor Sports, as well as football, basketball and touch rugby. You don't need to have a team lined up before you join: they can put you in a team if you join on your own. To play, each player must pay a one-off registration fee of €20, and a game fee of €8 per player per game.

iPod Broken?

Make your own music instead, and impress your friends with your nimble fingers on the guitar or piano, or even on a traditional Irish instrument. Once you've decided on music lessons, find out where you can buy your instrument in the Shopping chapter (p.309).

247

Various Locations

Netball Dublin

087 667 7737 | www.netballdublin.com

Netball Dublin oversees 34 adult teams, some of which are six-a-side, and some of which are seven-a-side. They accept memberships from individuals or entire teams – individuals will be slotted in to existing teams where required. There's a €20 registration fee per person, which includes a T-shirt and a backpack. To play in the league, a game fee of around €56 applies, depending on the location. Netball Dublin games take place in two main locations, one on the north side and one on the south. Both venues are within walking distance from the city centre.

Netball	
Anzac Netball Club	086 197 6818
Leinster Netball Club	087 919 0640
St Annes Netball Club	086 858 5880

Orchestras & Bands

Other options **Music Lessons** p.247

There are many orchestras in Dublin, both professional and amateur, many of which are run on a volunteer basis. Classical music lovers will delight in the many wonderful performances, be they modern or traditional, held in Dublin throughout the year at venues such as the National Concert Hall (ww.nch.ie) and The National Gallery (see p.182), while the musicians themselves benefit from a group within which they can rehearse and perform and enjoy their talent.

The Dublin Symphony Orchestra (www.dublinsymphony.org) was established more than 40 years ago and is a non-professional orchestra with rehearsals throughout the year. Interested parties should contact them at admin@dublinsymphony.org. The Hibernian Orchestra performs concerts regularly and is always looking for new members and players. See their website for more details on events and audition contact information (www.thehibernianorchestra.ie). For the younger generation the Dublin Youth Orchestra runs courses, rehearsals, and performs concerts. See www.dublinyouthorchestras.ie for more information.

Mount Anville School
Goatstown
Dublin 14
Map 421 E4 **134**

Dublin Orchestral Players

www.dublinorchestralplayers.com

The Dublin Orchestral Players is a voluntary group that gets together to practise and play on a weekly basis. The group first played before an audience in 1940, and are still going strong today, performing at various venues throughout Dublin. Rehearsals take place on Tuesday nights in the Mount Anville secondary school in Goatstown. Amateur players wishing to join should fill in the online application form.

Suite 33, 2nd Floor
32 Nassau St
Dublin 2
Map 430 B1 **144**

National Youth Orchestra of Ireland (NYOI)

01 616 9638 | www.nyoi.ie

The National Youth Orchestra of Ireland is made up of players aged 13 to 18 years, from all over the country. Audition centres are listed on the website but the Dublin one is in Alexandra College in Milltown. Auditions close on 1 October each year. It is a wonderful experience to grow and improve as a musician for those lucky enough to be accepted; additionally, workshops are held each year (only open to those who have already applied to audition at the NYOI), as are summer training courses to help players who have not yet reached the standard of the NYOI audition.

Admin Building, RTE
Dublin 4
Map 421 E2 **105**

RTE National Symphony Orchestra

01 208 2617 | www.rte.ie

The RTE National Symphony Orchestra is the resident orchestra of The National Concert Hall and holds weekly performances, and is broadcast on the radio and television. Tickets to live concerts can be purchased online or by calling 01 408 6793, and cost from €10 for a standard ticket, with attractive deals for students, members and senior citizens. Otherwise you can tune into Lyric FM to listen to live performances. For aspiring musicians, vacancies are listed on their site.

Rowing on Blessington Lake

Paintballing

Old Airport Rd
Santry
Dublin 9

Kart City
01 842 6322 | www.kartcity.net
Kart City provides both urban paintball and karting facilities (see p.242). Twenty acres of paintball battlefield are at your disposal, as you head out, fully equipped with goggles, protective suit, mask and semi-automatic weapon. Games cost €30 per adult, and you can buy extra ammo for €10 per 100 'bullets'. A maximum of 40 people can play at any one time. You can book online (see their website for details), by phone, email (info@kartcity.net) or by fax (01 842 6185).

Photography

Photography is perhaps one of the most accessible art forms available today. Even if you were never a great artist at school, it's hard not to get excited when you get lucky and snap an amazing picture, even when it is only on your point-and-shoot camera. However, once you start learning more about photography, you quickly realise just how much there is to learn, which is what makes photography a rewarding, if frustrating, hobby. One of the best ways to accelerate your knowledge of photography is to join a photography club - apart from being able to tap into the knowledge of fellow members, you'll get the opportunity to go out on photo shoots as a group.

Photography	
Bray Camera Club	www.braycameraclub.com
Dublin Camera Club	www.dublincameraclub.ie
Malahide Camera Club	www.malahidecameraclub.com
National Photographic Archive	www.nli.ie
Tallaght Photographic Society	www.tallaghtphotographicsociety.com

Photography Ireland (www.photographyireland.net) is an active discussion forum offering help for beginners, advice for experts, and a platform where you can submit your photos and receive comments from other board members. The National Photographic Archive in Temple Bar, Dublin 2, regularly holds exhibitions and offers competitively priced photography courses for all levels.

Rowing

The Irish Amatuer Rowing Union is the governing body for rowing in Ireland. Rowing is pretty much a year-round sport, and winter weather does little to deter keen enthusiasts. Competitive races such as Heads of the River Races are generally held from October to March while regatta season runs from April to September. Popular among the universities, many former college rowers go on to set up clubs such as the Old Collegians BC after they've graduated. The IARU also promotes para olympic adaptive rowing. The boats used vary, and rowers can either use one oar (sweep oar rowing) or two (known as sculling), depending on the class of boat being used (there are eight classes in total). For full details about the sport and for listings of events and affiliated clubs, see the IARU's website (www.iaru.ie) or contact them directly (01 625 1130).

Rowing	
Commercial RC	085 730 5929
D.I.T. RC	087 293 3442
Dublin Municipal RC	086 815 0968
Dublin University BC	085 723 3266
Dublin University Ladies BC	087 954 8419
King's Hospital BC	01 643 6518
Lady Elizabeth BC	086 171 7146
Neptune RC	087 908 1173
Old Collegians BC	01 260 8992
UCD BC	086 312 0806

249

Rugby

Rugby is popular in Dublin, with strong local, provincial, and national teams making more and more of an impact each year. Many schools have teams and organised training sessions as do clubs, offering the opportunity to compete in local and international competitions. Rugby League teams in the Dublin area include the Dublin Blues (www.dublinblues.com), Dublin City Exiles (www.rli.ie/exiles/), and the North Dublin Eagles (www.eastcoasteagles.com). For more information on all Rugby League teams and fixtures, news and events, see www.rli.ie.

Dublin 4 is a real rugby homeground with senior and junior teams playing for the Bective Rangers (01 283 8254; www.bectiverangers.com), Old Wesley (01 660 9893; www.oldwesley.ie) and Old Belvedere (01 660 3378; www.oldbelvedere.ie) all in Donnybrook, and Monkstown Rugby Club (01 269 1794) at Sydney Parade and Wanderers (01 269 5272; www.wanderersfcrugby.com) in Ballsbridge.

62 Lansdowne Rd
Dublin 4
Map 417 E3 **13**

Irish Rugby Football Union

01 647 3800 | www.irishrugby.ie

The IRFU is the governing body for Rugby Union in Ireland. The IRFU comprises four branches based on the four provinces of Ireland: Connacht, Leinster, Munster and Ulster. The IRFU supports rugby at all levels in Ireland from amateur to professional in both clubs and schools. For more details or to find a club in your area log on to www.irishrugby.ie. The Irish Rugby Supporters Club (see the website) has frequent competitions to win tickets away and at home, hosts members' events and produces newsletters. If you're hoping to get tickets to a home game, your chances are massively increased if you're a member of a rugby club, or of the Supporter's Club or similar organisation.

Running

Despite the rain and the cold, runners bravely pound Dublin's pavements throughout the year. Whether you choose to run through the streets of the city centre, or further out in the suburbs, you can enjoy some of the most scenic running in the world. Train hard enough and you'll be able to compete in the Dublin Marathon (www.adidasdublinmarathon.ie).

Morton Stadium
Santry
Dublin 9

Clonliffe Harriers

01 837 0278

This club is suitable for all ages – they have divisions for everybody from veterans and seniors, to juniors and juveniles. Clonliffe has coaches in the disciplines of road running, cross country running, and track and field events. Apart from world-class athletics facilities in the Morton stadium, Clonliffe also has a very social clubhouse that includes a members' bar. New members are always welcome.

Irishtown Stadium
Irishtown
Dublin 4
Map 417 E3 **128**

Crusaders Athletic Club

087 782 8053 | www.crusadersac.org

The Crusaders are based in Irishtown Stadium, which has excellent all-round facilities including a gym and an indoor soccer pitch. The club has had many successful athletes in track and field events and in marathons. Annual membership is €85 for adults, €40 for juniors, and €140 for family membership.

Chapelizod Rd
Dublin 20
Map 414 C2 **114**

Donore Harriers

www.donoreharriers.com

With a great location near the city centre, and Phoenix Park virtually next door, this is a great club if you fancy training in scenic surroundings. The club is active in road and cross country running, as well as 20 track and field events. Anyone over the age of 11 is welcome to join this friendly club: annual membership is €120 per adult, €30 per child, and €135 per family.

Dundrum South Dublin Athletic Club

Dundrum
Dublin 16

www.dsdac.com

This all-round, friendly club is active in many athletics disciplines, and they are always on the lookout for new members. If you are interested in joining the club, you can check out the training schedule on their website (the club trains on Tuesdays, Wednesdays, Thursdays and Saturdays), and just join in on a training session.

Sailing

Howth Yacht Club

Harbour Rd
Howth
Map 413 D1 127

01 832 2141 | www.hyc.ie

This is the largest sailing club in Ireland, with over 2,000 members. With a 300 berth marina and a large dinghy fleet, the club is active at all levels. HYC members have won championships at home and abroad, and the club itself has hosted several national and international championships. Each year the club provides training for new members and a highly successful junior sailing course in the summer. The stylish clubhouse is a notable landmark in Howth, and includes facilities such as a bar and restaurant, changing rooms, offices and meeting rooms.

Sailing		
Fingal Sailing School	01 845 1979	www.fingalsailingschool.com
Glenans Irish Sailing Club	01 661 1481	www.glenans-ireland.com
Malahide Yacht Club	01 845 3372	www.myc.ie
Royal Irish Yacht Club	01 280 9452	www.riyc.ie
Sutton Dinghy Club	01 839 3135	www.sdc.ie

Howth Yacht Club

251

National Yacht Club

01 280 5725 | www.nyc.ie

The National Yacht Club enjoys a unique position on the Dun Laoghaire harbour waterfront, adjacent to the east pier, and it is noted for its particularly friendly ethos and world-class sailing. The club is an ISA-recognised centre for all forms of sailing and powerboat training, and provides a full range of courses for children and adults. The club is active throughout the year and has full dining and bar facilities. It hosts a number of winter activities including bridge, snooker, quiz nights, wine tasting and special events.

Scouts & Guides

Scouting Ireland is a nationwide organisation that promotes scouting in Ireland and oversees various scouting groups. Beavers, Cub Scouts and Scouts are hugely popular in Ireland, and Scouting Ireland has around 40,000 members. Find out more information, as well as a list of troops in your area, by visiting their website: www.scouts.ie. For girl guides, contact the Catholic Guides of Ireland (01 661 9566, www.girlguidesireland.ie) or Irish Girl Guides (01 6683898, www.igg.ie).

Scouts & Guides		
13th Dublin Scouts	Rathfarnham	dublin13th@yahoo.co.uk
17th Dalkey Scouts	Dalkey	www.dalkeyscouts.ie
Johnstown/Killiney Scouts	Killiney	59-dublin@gmail.com

Skiing & Snowboarding

Ireland's rainy climate and lack of substantial annual snowfall pretty much dashes any dreams of wooden ski lodges and wild apres ski parties. The dry slopes at Kilternan (see below) make sure that before you hop on a plane to do the real thing you can learn the basics and have some jolly good fun. Snowboarding enthusiasts may be interested in joining the free online Irish Snowboarding Club (www.irishsnowboarder.com).

Ski Club Of Ireland

01 295 5658 | www.skiclub.ie

Kilternan is the only skiing facility in Ireland. The dry slopes are a good place to learn the basics or improve your technique before heading off on a skiing holiday abroad. The Ski Club provides the skis, boots and poles, so all you need to do is to come kitted out in appropriate winter woolies! Season membership offers reduced rates, otherwise a course of four skiing classes (each lasting an hour and a half) costs €140 for adults, €120 for students and €95 for children (aged 7 and upwards and accompanied by an adult). Practice rates are €30, €25 and €22 respectively. For teeny tots aged between 4 and 7 years, there's Kindergarten on weekends from 13:00 to 14:00.

Social Groups

Other options **Support Groups** p.142

Bright Lights Dublin City

086 266 1040 | www.brightlightsdublincity.com

This social club has over 200 members, from different backgrounds and nationalities, and ranging in age from 20s to mid 40s. The purpose of the club is to provide interesting events where members can enjoy themselves while getting to know other people. In general, two events are organised every month – events vary from hiking, museum visits and concerts to dinners out, makeup nights and even weekends away. You are welcome to attend an introductory event for free – a committee member will meet you first to break the ice. Thereafter membership costs €80 a year.

24 Elmcastle Green
Tallaght

The Corporate Club
01 461 0935 | www.corporateclub.ie

Since 1997, the Corporate Club has been encouraging members to mingle and widen their social horizons. They organise a host of exciting events, such as wine tasting evenings, Theatre nights, weekends away, sports events and regular socials. Anyone over 18 is welcome to join, and all you need to do is fill out the membership form and pay a fee of €295 (membership costs €150 for each subsequent year). They also offer a trial membership of three months, for a fee of €120, which is then refundable against your annual membership if you decide to join. If you're new in town it's well worth it to improve your social network.

24 Elmcastle Green
Tallaght

The Network Club
01 451 5512 | www.networkclub.ie

This sports and social club is for people over the age of 18 and provides plenty of opportunities to meet new people. It currently has over 200 members. If you fancy making new friends while enjoying quiz nights, hill walks, tennis, sailing, horse riding or even weekends away, then you should join this club. A year's membership is €170 (renewal for each subsequent year is only €100).

Special Needs Activities

Ireland hosted the Special Olympics in 2003 and there has since been increased awareness and great support for mentally and physically challenged people in Ireland, as well as improved integration into local communities. Many clubs and associations are actively working to offer recreational and competitive sport in a fun, supportive and enthusiastic environment. Volunteers are always welcome to help out in all areas so if you think you can spare some time, contact one of the organisations listed to find out what you can do.

Sport HQ, Joyce Way
Parkwest Business Park
Dublin 12

Cerebral Palsy Sport Ireland
01 625 1160

Soccer, boccia, lawn bowls, swimming and athletics are all offered through this group. Athletes of all abilities are encouraged to work as a team and the group regularly participates in the Paralympic Games and other competitions.

Special Olympics Monument

National Council
For The Blind
115 Lower George's St
Dun Laoghaire

Irish Blind Sports
01 202 0118 | www.ncbi.ie

This group helps the blind or visually impaired to enjoy recreational and sporting activities. No prior experience is necessary to join in and full training is provided. Angling, athletics, chess, equestrian, football, goalball, golf, judo, swimming, tandem cycling, tenpin bowling and waterskiing are offered. They also put on social evenings and offer art and culture classes, as well as many other activities.

40 Lwr
Drumcondra Rd
Dublin 9
Map 408 C3 95

Irish Deaf Sports Association
01 830 0522 | idsa@eircom.net

Founded in 1968, the IDSA provides sporting activities such as football, bowling, swimming, ladies basketball and waterpolo.

Irish Wheelchair Association

01 818 6400 | *www.iwasport.com*

IWA Sport in Clontarf promotes sport through its centres, schools and clubs. Participants are encouraged to try out all the sports on offer until they find the one they like, no matter what their level, and some even go on to compete at national and international level. Sports such as track, field, basketball, rugby, swimming, archery, boccia and table tennis, among others, are offered.

Special Olympics Ireland

01 882 3972 | *www.specialolympics.ie*

Set up in 1978, the Special Olympics network continues growing and is working towards setting up clubs in communities where they do not already exist. The club offers year-round training and competitions for adults and children with learning disabilities in Olympic type sports such as basketball, alpine skiing, football, gymnastics, and golf, irrespective of the individual's ability. They are also working towards getting more sports recognised in the International Special Olympics.

Squash

Other options **Leisure Facilities** p.263

Racketball sports are popular in Dublin. Some of the tennis clubs also have squash courts on site, such as Mountpleasant LTC (01 497 3733, www.mountpleasantltc.ie) in Ranelagh, and Sutton LTC (01 832 3035, www.suttonltc.com). Sports and Recreation Centres (see p.263) also often have courts that can be rented on an hourly basis. Some clubs will rent out rackets and balls, although you will probably prefer to get your own. See www.irishsquash.com for more details, including rules of the game, and links to useful sites. Total Fitness sports clubs (www.totalfitness.org), in various locations around the city, also have courts, although you will may need to be a member to be able to use them. In general, you can expect to pay anything up to €10 for 45 minutes of playing time.

Squash		
Aer Lingus Squash Club	01 886 3332	http://indigo.ie/~alsc
Bayside Squash & Tennis Club	01 832 2498	na
Irish Squash	01 450 1633	www.irishsquash.com
Old Belvedere Squash Club	01 268 9748	na
RTE Sports & Social Club	01 208 2042	na
Sandycove Tennis & Squash Club	01 280 8769	www.sandycovetsc.ie
Westwood Leisure Centre	01 289 5665	http://westwood.hosting365.ie

Swimming

Other options **Leisure Facilities** p.263, **Beaches** p.34

Dublin has quite a collection of public swimming pools, which are run on a pay-per-visit basis (as opposed to membership). You can usually expect to pay around €5 per person per session. Your local health club (p.263) or sports club (p.263) may also have a swimming pool, which may be available for use by non-members for a small session fee. All pools are manned by lifeguards, and most offer swimming lessons at an additional cost. At certain times of day you may find that the pool is reserved for lane swimming only, and

Open Water Swimming

Every year big swimming events take place in open waters in Dublin and around the rest of the country. Two of the biggest ones are the Dun Laoghaire Harbour Swim, held in August, and the Dublin Liffey Swim, taking place in September. Numerous fun swims for charity and competitions are also held annually. See www.swimleinster.com for details.

Swimming

Belvedere College	Sth Great Denmark St	Dublin 1	01 858 6608
Dundrum Family Pool	Meadowbrook	Dublin 14	01 698 0183
Glenalbyn Swimming Pool	Glenalbyn Rd	Stillorgan	01 288 1502
Markievicz Centre	Townsend St	Dublin 1	01 677 0503
Mespil Swimming Pool	Sussex Rd	Dublin 4	01 668 4626
Monkstown Health & Fitness Centre	Monkstwon Ave	Monkstown	01 230 1458
Rathmines Public Swimming Pool	Rathmines Rd Lower	Dublin 6	01 496 1275
Riverview Sports & Leisure Centre	Clonskeagh	Dublin 14	01 283 0322
Tallaght Leisure Centre	Fortunestown Way	Dublin 24	01 452 3300
Westwood Health Club	Clontarf Rd	Dublin 3	01 853 0353
Willie Pearse Park	Crumlin	Dublin 12	01 455 5792

at other times there might be a dedicated children's section in the shallow end.

You will need to wear a swimming cap, but most pools sell them if you forget yours. You will also need to bring your own towels and goggles. Brave swimmers should head out to the coast and take a dip in the icy Atlantic waters. The famous 40 Foot swimming spot in Dun Laoghaire should be tried at least once in your lifetime – this once nudist spot for male swimmers only now has a die-hard cluster of men and women who swim there every day, good weather or not (see p.177 for more information).

Swim Ireland, the governing body of the sport of swimming in Ireland, has a listing of pools, both indoor and outdoor, as well as links to water polo, special needs swimming, diving and competitive swimming (www.swimireland.ie).

Snugborough Rd
Blanchardstown

National Aquatic Centre
01 646 4300 | www.nationalaquaticcentre.ie

Located on the outskirts of the city, just off the M50, this centre is accessible to everyone. There's a massive range of activities on offer, from pleasure rides including flumes, a pirate ship and a flow rider, to lane swimming, swimming lessons (including mothers and babies), diving lessons and aquafit classes. Facilities include a 50m pool, a 5m diving pool, a competition pool with moveable floor and diving boards, a leisure pool and health club, showers, changing rooms with lockers, toilets and a cafe. The centre is open seven days a week, between 06:00 and 22:00 on weekdays and closing a bit earlier on weekends. The centre has adequate wheelchair access and lifts.

Swimming in The Liffey

40 Foot Swimming Pool

Team Building

Collinstown
Business Park
Airport Rd, Cloghran

Ireland Xtreme
01 862 2000 | www.irelandxtreme.ie
This group will custom design a team building day in line with your company needs, be it to unwind or challenge. Activites include *Survivor Challenge*, clay pigeon shooting, off-road driving and blind-fold driving, treasure hunts and cookery classes. The focus is on motivating groups and on working together, in a fun, relaxed atmosphere.

Kippure Estate
Manor Kilbride
Blessington
Co Wicklow

Kippure Corporate
01 458 2889 | www.teambuildingireland.com
Based less than an hour outside Dublin, this group offers both indoor and outdoor events. Set in the scenic Wicklow Mountains, activities range from adrenaline infused tightrope walks and map and compass treks, to scavenger hunts, archery and tribal dance! There are competitive and non-competitive options, but all activities are about maintaining a sense of fun and promoting group work. Evening entertainment is also provided to round off the day.

Tennis
Other options **Leisure Facilities** p.263

In Dublin, tennis is often more about the socialising than the sport, so don't feel you have to play a perfect game to join one of the tennis clubs. It's a great way to meet new people and become a better player at the same time.
You can rent a public court for around €5 per person, but entry is on a first-come, first-served basis. If you want to play on a more serious level, or on a frequent basis, you may be better off joining one of the clubs where you will also have access to coaching, organised tournaments, and the many social events taking place at your club. Men, women and children of all ages can join. Membership rates vary from club to club, but many clubs allow non-members to 'pay and play'. There are courts for hire in the National Tennis Centre (01 884 4010) inside Dublin City University (www.dcu.ie).

Make A Racquet
There are numerous public and private tennis courts around Dublin, and you can find a complete list on the website www.tennisireland.ie, or on your local county council website.

Mt Pleasant Sq
Ranelagh
Dublin 6
Map 416 B4 135

Mount Pleasant Lawn Tennis Club
01 497 3733 | www.mountpleasantltc.ie
Founded in 1893, Mountpleasant is one of Dublin's most popular clubs. Boasting over a thousand members, the club provides tennis (11 all-weather courts) squash and badminton courts, as well as table tennis facilities. Circuit training and a gym ensure players keep up their fitness levels while personal coaching makes sure those backhands and drop shots are perfect. Saunas and changing room facilities are provided

Tennis

Aer Lingus Tennis Club	ALSAA Complex	Dublin 9	www.aerlingustennis.net
Bective Lawn Tennis Club	Main St, Donnybrook	Dublin 4	www.bective-tennis.com
Castleknock Lawn Tennis Club	Navan Rd, Castleknock	Dublin 15	www.cltc.ie
Elm Park Golf & Sports Club	Nutley Lane, Donnybrook	Dublin 4	www.elmparkgolfclub.ie
Malahide Lawn Tennis Club	The Square	Malahide	www.mltcc.com
Portmarnock Tennis Club	Blackwood Ln	North Coast	www.geocities.com/pslctennis
Sutton Lawn Tennis Club	176 Howth Rd, Sutton	Dublin 13	www.suttonltc.com
Swords Lawn Tennis Club	Swords Town Park	Swords	www.swordstennisclub.net

for all members. The club actively participates in, and hosts, tournaments and leagues, including the annual summer Tennis Open Week. New members are always welcome and are free to come and view the club on open days before signing up. A club bar and numerous social events ensure that this club remains one of Dublin's favourites.

Various Locations

Parks Tennis
01 833 8711 | www.parkstennis.com

Parks Tennis is a non-profit organisation set up by a group of volunteers who represent various local bodies such as Tennis Ireland. Coaching is offered to young people from 6 to 17 years of age, as well as for adults, for a low fee. They focus on introducing the game to the greater public, in particular people from disadvantaged social backgrounds, and encourage community integration. They have access to courts all over the city so you can choose the one that is most convenient for you. See their website for details. The fee for five weeks of one-hour lessons is around €30.

Triathlon

Various Locations

Piranha Triathlon Club
www.piranhatri.com

Piranha is Dublin's leading triathlon club. The club welcomes people of all abilities and experience, from those who just wish to use the facilities or enjoy the atmosphere, to those who want to compete at the highest levels of the sport in Ireland and internationally. The club's size means that it has several bases throughout the city. Regular training for all levels includes swim coaching, running technique and group sessions, bike technique and group rides. The club also organises a warm-weather training week in Italy each year, and it hosts the annual Dublin City Triathlon. New members are always welcome at this friendly and vibrant club, which has a great training programme and a good social scene. See the website for more details.

Triathletes getting ready for the swim

Triathlon Ireland

98 Charlesland Ct
The Glen, Greystones
Co Wicklow

www.triathlonireland.com

Triathlon Ireland (TI) is the national governing body for the sport of Triathlon, Duathlon and Aquathlon in Ireland, affiliated to the International Triathlon Union (ITU) and the European Triathlon Union (ETU). Their job is to promote and sanction triathlon events in Ireland and help the sport grow. Annual membership costs €50, and allows you to race in all TI events, and provides you with third party insurance. You will also receive the monthly newsletter with results and news about upcoming fixtures.

Watersports

From sailing (p.254), surfing and windsurfing, to kitesurfing and canoeing (p.230), there are plenty of options on offer in Dublin's coastal waters and a multitude of schools ready to teach you a new sport. For those already adept at their chosen sport, many clubs and groups organise weekends away, taking you to the best spots around the country. Useful websites include the Irish Surf Assocation (www.isasurf.ie), UCD surf club (www.ucd.ie/surf) and www.beachwizard.com – a site providing info on surfing and coastal waters in Europe.

East Coast Surf Club

2 Eaglewood Hse
Rochestown Av
Dun Laoghaire

086 852 2030 | www.eastcoastsurfclub.com

The East Coast Surf Club represents the Dublin area (contact Charlotte O'Kelly by email at eastcoastsurfclub@gmail.com). In the quest for serious waves, the club organises trips to the north and west of Ireland where the Atlantic offers some great surfing. Members are a social bunch and the club holds monthly club meetings and weekly social evenings. The website has details on buying wetsuits and boards and other helpful information. Membership includes third party insurance cover, affiliation to the Irish Surf Association and club events, trips away, and the use of club boards.

Fingal Sailing School

Upper Strand
Malahide

01 845 1979 | www.fingalsailingschool.com

This Malahide school covers windsurfing, kayaking, sailing and powerboating. Little ones can learn watersports at an early age with the kids' club, and week-long certified courses cover various activities in the summer. All equipment and wetsuits are provided for these courses. Weekend and evening courses are available for everyone from land-loving beginners to advanced watersports junkies, as is basic equipment rental. All gear is supplied and instructors are fully qualified with plenty of experience and courses are all certified. Comprehensive insurance cover is also provided.

Golden Falls Waterski Club

Ballymore Eustace
Blessington
Co Kildare

087 668 6225 | www.goldenfallswaterski.com

The Golden Falls Waterski Club is based 42km from Dublin city centre and offers full-day or half-day waterskiing sessions for those who want to improve their skills, or for those who just want to learn how to stay upright. Group and individual sessions are available; check website for details.

SurfDock Windsurfing

Grand Canal
Dockyard
Dublin 4
Map 417 D2 **126**

01 668 3945 | www.surfdock.ie

Surfdock offers windsurfing, kitesurfing, surfing, kids' courses and summer camps and the emphasis is on learning in a safe, freshwater environment. Surfdock Safaris are organised regularly for intermediate and advanced levels, with the aim of getting people out there to meet like-minded enthusiasts, discover the best locations around the country, and generally have a great time.

Spectator Sports

Sports enthusiasts don't have to be fighting fit and out training every night of the week to be recognised assets to any team, event or association. Indeed, many an enthusiast is quite the opposite! The spectator plays a pivotal role, and can be thanked for their contribution to the all-important electric atmosphere and a show of deafening encouragement. Irish supporters are known for being good sports too, win or lose, which makes such occasions all that bit more enjoyable.

Ireland's favourite spectator sports, especially if a little bit of money is to be made, include greyhound racing, horse racing and equestrian events such as the ever-popular annual Dublin Horse Show. Ball sports on the other hand, such as hurling, rugby and soccer, are top of the list on the Irish sporting calendar and are always accompanied by serious, loyal supporters. All the major games and events usually receive both radio and television broadcasts, so you can watch from home or your local pub, so you don't have to miss out even though you've not managed to get your hands on a ticket to a live game (which are like gold dust, by the way). And just in case you do miss the game, you'll be able to catch the results in the papers the next day. *Craic* (good fun), probably some *ceol* (music) and a good few beverages to crank up the merriment are par for the course with every spectator sport in Ireland, so go with it and have some fun.

Equestrian Sports

Equestrian sports are big in Ireland, and some of the top trainers and best bloodstock come from Irish soil. Race days, big or small, are incredibly popular and provide a fun day or evening out. Those who fancy a bit of a flutter can happily do so – indeed, it seems to add to the sometimes electric atmosphere, and there are plenty of bars and eateries set up to make sure you can stay till the end. Whether you choose to wait it out in one of the tents and see it all on TV or stand up by the railings and cheer them on, you're sure to enjoy racing, showjumping and every other horsey event on offer. For a trip further afield, the Irish Grand National is held at Fairyhouse Racecourse (www.fairyhouse.com) in County Meath. Traditionally held on Easter Monday every year, it's a biggie for the betting offices and is always televised. Located about 25km north of Dublin, you can drive there or use the bus service put on by Dublin Bus, leaving from Busaras (see www.dublinbus.ie for details).

Exit 12 off the M7
(southbound)
Co Kildare

Curragh Racecourse

045 441 205 | www.curragh.ie

The first race to take place here was in 1791, and the 'sport of kings' is just as popular here today. Less than an hour from Dublin, the name appropriately means 'place of the running horse', and that they do. Many of the top trainers keep their horses here, and it offers some of the best training grounds in the world. The last season race takes place in October. The big event is The Irish Derby, which takes place annually. Much like the Dublin Horseshow, it's a popular day out. As with top race days around the world, fashion, food and liquid refreshment make the horses almost second billing! On race days, Bus Eireann puts on a series of special buses leaving from Busaras. You can also take the train directly to the Curragh, from Heuston Station in Dublin.

RDS, Merrion Rd
Ballsbridge
Map 417 E4 23

Dublin Horse Show

01 668 0866 | www.dublinhorseshow.com

The Dublin Horse Show is a popular annual event, when Ireland's horsey set turn out to watch some of the world's best international showjumpers strut their stuff and battle it out to win the Nation's Cup and the Aga Khan Challenge Trophy. Held each summer, it attracts specators from around the world and is one of Dublin's biggest events, and with crafts and antiques stands, multiple eateries and bars, it makes for a fun day out for the whole family. Ladies' Day offers a chance to win prizes up to €10,000, and to dress up in your finest – hats are a must! Tickets can be purchased online. Getting to the RDS is easy: if you're driving from the city centre, just head along Merrion Road (but good luck with parking if you get there too late). The RDS is on all main bus routes, and if you're taking the Dart, you can walk to the show grounds from the Lansdowne Road or Sandymount stations.

Leopardstown Racecourse

Leopardstown Rd
Leopardstown
Dublin 18

01 289 0500 | www.leopardstown.com

Leopardstown is the only racecourse within Dublin county. Originally built in 1888, it was bought by the Racing Board in 1967, and extensively refurbished. It's biggest annual racing fixture is the Champion Stakes, with prize money of €1 million. This event is a great day out, with fashion, restaurants, plenty of bars, live bands, and of course the horses and the frenzied betting all adding to the lively atmosphere. General admission is €15, Miller Party tickets cost €28 and the Silken Gilder Pavilion package costs €65 and includes a seated buffet and other perks. The racecourse is also home to the longstanding Club 92 nightclub so if you're still there into the wee hours you can pop in. The racecourse is just a short walk from the Sandyford stop on the Luas green line, but Busaras also operates a special service on race days.

Punchestown Racecourse

Woolpack Rd
Punchestown, Naas
Co Kildare

045 897 704 | www.punchestown.com

Punchestown Racecourse, the home of Irish National Hunt racing for over 150 years, hosts a total of 17 race meetings throughout the year. The highlight of the racing and social calendar is the four-day Irish National Hunt festival which takes place each April and attracts crowds in excess of 90,000. Facilities include a panoramic restuarant (packages are available with tickets – see the website for details) bars (including a champagne and seafood bar and other food outlets) and a self-service restaurant. A shopping village with over 60 units adds a little extra to the occasion of the Hunt Festival. With over €2.5 million in prize money over these four days, it's one of the highlights of the equestrian year. Busaras runs a special bus service on race days.

Punchestown Racecourse

Spectator Sports

Lansdowne Road

First opened in 1872, Lansdowne Road has long been home to rugby and soccer in Ireland. Located in Ballsbridge, Dublin 4, the venue had become increasingly rundown over the years and is currently closed for refurbishment (for more details see www.lrsdc.ie). It's due to reopen in 2009 with a seating capacity of 50,000. All games and matches are currently being played in Croke Park.

Football

Although Ireland has many football enthusiasts, going to see a match is nothing in comparison to the neighbouring UK. Big European and international level games are played on Irish turf, namely in Landsdowne Road and, more recently, in Croke Park (due to the refurbishment of the former), but these opportunites arise only a few times a year. If you're keen to see some action anyway, and not just on the telly, see the Football Association of Ireland's website at www.fai.ie for more details.

Gaelic Games

Come September, tensions are at their sporting highest as hurling and Gaelic football fans hustle for tickets to an All Ireland Final (see p.239 for more on these sports). If you manage to get one, count yourself lucky as they're like gold dust and fans will turn out in hail, rain or snow to cheer on their team in the hope that they will be bringing home the coveted cup. It's an exciting time and the atmosphere is electric and often nail-biting as at this level it's usually very evenly matched, with points scored practically by the second. If you don't manage to get a ticket, don't worry. While it may not be quite the same as the deafening roars you'll hear in the stadium, you'll find plenty of pubs showing the game. Alternatively, you can catch it on TV or the radio as coverage is wide – just pay attention though, because the commentary is often as fast as the game!

Croke Park Stadium
Dublin 3
Map 408 C4 59

Croke Park

01 819 2300 | www.crokepark.ie

Croke Park is where it's at come county finals season and there's no better venue for it. The recently renovated, state of the art stadium can hold a whopping 82,000 crazed fans so you can only imagine the electric atmosphere at a live game. For tickets, go to www.gaa.ie or www.ticketmaster.ie. Purchased in 1913 by the GAA, it has been home to Irish sport ever since; the Constitution of the GAA having banned the playing of rugby and football on its grounds, citing that they were in direct competition with the Irish sports and therefore should not be allowed. In 2007, rugby and football were allowed to be played on the grounds for the first time. The decision was brought about by the closing of the Landsdowne Road stadium for renovation. Parking is available for 600 vehicles (including special needs parking), which is not many considering how many people can fit into the stadium! Police often clamp illegally parked vehicles in the area, so it really is worth using public transport. Croke Park is served by numerous bus routes, and it is a short walk from Busaras and Connolly Station (about 15 minutes). You can download a handy public transport guide from the website.

Croke Park

Golf

The Irish golfing season runs from April to October, with tournaments and championships taking place all over the country. The biggest golf tournaments in Ireland generally take place outside of Dublin, many being hosted by the popular and swanky K Club in Straffan, Co Kildare (01 601 7300, www.kclub.ie), which is easily accessible for Dublin residents. Ireland is a small country, so it is not out of the question to travel to the opposite side to catch a sporting event, and even if you can't make it in person, all major golfing events, such as the Irish Open and the Ryder Cup, are televised. In 2011, Ireland will be hosting the Solheim Cup at Killeen Castle, County Meath, when international women's golf takes centre stage. For more information on upcoming tournaments and events and tour operators, see www.golf.ireland.ie. For a list of golf courses in Dublin, see p.240.

Greyhound Racing

Harold's Cross Rd
Harold's Cross
Dublin 6 West
Map 420 A1 51

Harold's Cross Stadium
01 497 1081 | www.igb.ie
Monday, Tuesday and Friday nights are the regular race nights in this Dublin institution. A little wager on the dogs makes for an exciting, alternative evening out, and many people count it as one of Dublin's must-do experiences. Dobbins At The Park will take care of any hungry bods, while totes and bars take care of the rest – although it's probably best to place your bets before taking a tipple! Races kick off at 20:00. Admission fees are adult €10, students and OAPs €5. Limited car parking is available, but the track is also served by public transport.

Shelbourne Park
Dublin 4
Map 417 E3 52

Shelbourne Greyhound Stadium
01 668 3502 | www.igb.ie
A bit of a flutter on your favourite hound is a favourite past time of many a Dubliner. And even if you're not a regular at the tracks, it's a fun and inexpensive day out and worth a visit at least once in a lifetime. Races take place every 15 minutes, the biggest one of the year being the Derby Final Night when six dogs battle it out for prize money of €280,000. Races take place every Wednesday, Thursday and Saturday night – as you may well know if you live in the vicinity (the roars of the excited crowd are infamous!). Plenty of restaurants and dining options, including the infamous Dobbins At The Park will keep you full and entertained during the evening. Entry is adult €10, students and OAPs €5. Car parking is available for around 250 cars, so consider using public transport on busy race nights.

Rugby

55 Main St
Donnybrook
Dublin 4
Map 421 D1 58

Leinster Rugby
01 269 3224 | www.leinsterrugby.ie
The Leinster club embodies pride, flair and passion. Leinster Rugby competes in the Magners League and Heineken Cup competitions. The province returned to the RDS in September 2007, and will hope to build on an impressive campaign again under Head Coach Michael Cheika. The squad boasts many Ireland international stars including Gordon D'Arcy, Girvan Dempsey, Jamie Heaslip, Denis Hickie, Shane Horgan, Malcolm O'Kelly and skipper Brian O'Driscoll. Australian World Cup winner Chris Whitaker moved to the province in 2006, while Argentina out-half Felipe Contepomi has been the club's top points scorer in recent years. Tickets are available through the website.

Various Locations

Rugby League Ireland
www.rli.ie
Rugby League Ireland governs the game of Rugby League in Ireland. All club details and match fixtures and contacts can be found on their website, so if you're planning to catch a live game, that's where you can get more information. Any activity related to the game, such as coaching, refereeing and playing is handled through the RLI committee which you can contact through the website or by emailing info@rli.ie.

Health Clubs

Castleknock Hotel
& Country Club
Porterstown Rd
Dublin 15

Club Tonic
01 6406 300 | www.castleknockhotel.com

Attached to a four-star hotel, your expectations of this country club are bound to be high, and luckily it doesn't disappoint. The club overlooks landscaped gardens, man-made lakes and the hotel's golf course. Inside, an 18 metre heated swimming pool, with a separate children's pool, sauna, steam room, spa and Jacuzzi are all on offer. For more action, a spacious gym has the full range of the usual high-tech equipment to whip you into shape. Day and evening classes are free for members, and cover such activities as khai-Bo, Pilates, body conditioning and aqua aerobics. The Lavendar Lane health and beauty centre takes care of everything else. Open Monday to Friday from 07:00 to 22:00, and on Saturdays, Sundays and bank holidays from 08:00 to 20:00.

Aston Quay
Temple Bar
Dublin 2
Map 426 B4 50

Crunch Fitness Premier
01 675 9984 | www.crunchfitness.ie

A boutique, luxury fitness club, this health haven is a joy to visit. Right in Dublin's city centre, 25,000 square feet await you, combining a massive sauna, 18 metre deck level pool, poolside power showers and lounging areas, steamroom, solarium and locker and shower area. The gym boats 40 treadmills, as well as an extensive range of weights and strength training equipment. Classes on offer include ab attack, yoga, Pilates, salsa, spinning, khai bo, fat burner and fitball, among others. To join, all you have to do is call in, take a tour or call or email them (templebar@crunchfitness.ie) for more information. Spectacular finishings put this on the A-list of Dublin's health clubs. Other outlets are in Dun Laoghaire and UCD.

Leopardstown
Racecourse
Leopardstown
Dublin 18

Westwood
01 289 3208 | www.westwood.ie

This chain of body-beautiful centres has just about everything you need to get in shape and stay that way. From yoga and aerobics, to classes such as body attack and body balance, a swimming pool, a range of weight machines, five-a-side football, tennis and squash courts, it's all here. Childcare facilites are also offered. If that was not enough, there's a Day Spa called re:fresh at each branch which is open to both men and women and also to non-members. re:fresh offers the usual body beautifying treatments, along with a sauna, plunge pool, steam room, Jacuzzi, Thalassotherapy Pool, Turkish Bath and Caladrium. Different massage types are also available from Swedish and Sports massage to aromatherapy and reflexology. The Clontarf branch also has a climbing wall, and the Little Monkey's Kids Club provides climbing activities for children aged 7 to 13. For a bite to eat after a hard workout, there's an O'Brien's sandwich bar located in each branch. Other branches can be found in Clontarf (01 853 0353) and Sandymount (01 269 5250).

Sports & Recreation Centres

There are many sports and recreation centres in Dublin. These tend to offer cheaper membership and rates than Health Clubs and include sports grounds, swimming pools, gyms and sometimes other entertainment facilities such as pool, darts, etc. Many are council-run initiatives such as the Irishtown Stadium, the Markievicz Leisure Centre (01 672 9121), and the Finglas Leisure Centre (01 864 2584). All of the above have received the White Flag Award, which measures quality and high standards of excellence, and has been awarded to sports facilities throughout the country. Alternatively, for something a little less sporty and more fun orientated, the Leisureplex centres (www.leisureplex.ie for a list of centres in Dublin) are open 24

263

hours and feature bowling alleys (see p.230), ice rinks (synthetic), children's play areas, painting groups, Q-zar and indoor soccer. Teenage social evenings such as discos and karaoke nights (see www.teenkicks.bebo.com) are also organised as well as corporate events and private parties. Finally, Astropark (www.astropark.ie) provides great football facilities in Coolock (01 806 0088) and Tallaght (01 459 9822).

Toberbunny
Dublin Airport
North Dublin

ALSAA

01 886 3332 | www.alsaa.ie

From ten-pin bowling and cross-country training tracks to rugby and hockey pitches, swimming pool and darts room, ALSAA offers a monumental range of activities. A huge gym has all the best get-fit paraphernalia and there's a range of classes on offer, as well as indoor basketball, squash and badminton courts. Facilities include a creche so you can bring the little ones along, sunbeds, saunas and Jacuzzi, hair salon and massage and beauty treatments and a bar and restaurant. All-inclusive membership (including access to the gym and pool) is €360 for singles or €600 for families.

Nangor Rd
Clondalkin
Dublin 22

Clondalkin Sports & Leisure Centre

01 457 4858 | www.clondalkinsports.com

This mega club has a whole series of action-packed activities on offer. There's a swimming pool, sports hall (including basketball, indoor football, netball, badminton, volleyball courts), an indoor climbing wall and archery and gynastics facilities. Aerobic classes cost €5.50 per hour and cover step, khai bo, aqua fit and body blast. For €44 per hour, groups can hire out the hall year round. Swimming classes are available, along with lane swimming, adult sessions, senior sessions and mother and toddler sessions. Pool parties can be arranged for children's birthdays. Other facilities include a cafe, Footprints Montessori school, Kyphi Natural Healing aromatherapy and massage and First Physio physiotherapists. Golf lessons can also be arranged, as well as canoeing, kayaking and gorge walking – contact the club for details.

Fairbrook Mews
Rathfarnham
Dublin 14
Map 419 F4 122

Dublin Indoor Sports

087 907 8814 | www.dublinindoorsports.ie

Dublin Indoor Sports organises leagues and tournaments in basketball, touch rugby, netball and football throughout the year, with centres on both the north and south sides of the city. They hope to include cricket, badminton and volleyball in the near future. Men and women from age 12 upwards are invited to get active. Registration fees per person are €20 a year. You can register as an individual or as a team. If you don't have a team already, they will organise it all for you. On top of this, you will have to pay a contribution to the team game fees for the season and each team must put down a refundable deposit (which varies from sport to sport). See their website for more details and for venues. Office hours are from 18:00 to 23:00 Monday to Thursday and from 12:00 to 18:00 on Sunday.

Irishtown
Dublin 4
Map 417 E3 128

Irishtown Stadium

01 669 7211 | www.dublincity.ie

Set around the perimeters of an eight-lane athletics running track, this is another council-managed sports facilities centre, complete with outdoor all-weather pitches and a soccer pitch. The club offers aerobics and pilates classes, has a fully equipped gymnasium, with floor to ceiling windows that give it a spacious, bright and airy feel. Changingrooms are available. Wheelchair access. Open Monday to Thursday from 10:00 to 22:00.The centre closes at 21:00 on Fridays, at 17:00 on Saturday, and 16:00 on Sundays. Use of the gym costs just €5.50 per hour (call for monthly and annual rates). Pitch-hire costs from €50 at peak times to €40 at off-peak times, and €25 on weekends.

Santry
Dublin 9

Morton Stadium

01 837 0278 | www.worldstadia.com

Morton Stadium is Dublin's National Athletics Stadium. Located in Santry, it is often referred to as 'Santry Stadium'. All major athletics events are held here and it is also the home base for the Clonliffe Harriers Athletic Club, Ireland's oldest athletics club (01 837 0278, www.clonliffeharriers.com). The 2003 Special Olympics World Games were held here. The stadium has both indoor and outdoor athletics training facilities.

Gyms

There's a fine line between Health Clubs and Gyms and Sports Centres, but gyms tend to focus on using equipment such as treadmills, weights and exercise bikes to get wobbly bodies into shape. Many gyms offer additional classes in aerobics, step, body sculpting or stationary cycling (sometimes called spinning or rpm). Facilities are usually well maintained, and offer a great workout experience.

Personal Trainers

If you're tired of the gym or find it hard to motivate yourself to go, KB Fitness are a group of personal trainers that will give you all the attention you need to focus on getting your body into serious shape. A one-to-one training session also means that you've little choice but to get stuck in! See their website or call for details (01 662 9723, www.kbfitness.ie).

1-4 Lwr Camden St
Dublin 2
Map 430 A3 49

The Fitness Dock

01 405 3777 | www.coralleisure.ie

The Fitness Dock offers top of the range cardio (stepping machines, treadmills) and weightlifting equipment, as well as classes in step, fit-ball, martial arts, khai-bo, spinning, box circuits and pump and sculpt, among others. Other perks include a relaxation suite complete with sauna, steamroom and tylarium to soothe those muscles after a serious workout. Open Monday to Thursday from 06:30 to 22:00, Friday from 06:30 to 21:00, and on weekends from 10:00 to 18:00. Contact them for rates as there are often promotions on membership. The Fitness Dock has adequate wheelchair access.

Clarendon St
Dublin 2
Map 430 A1 52

Jackie Skelly Fitness

01 677 0040 | www.jackieskellyfitness.com

Jackie Skelly gyms are dotted all over Dublin so you're sure to find one close and convenient to you, no matter where you are. Serious equipment is at hand to help you get in shape and stay that way, from treadmills, rowers and bikes to weights, steppers and arc climbers. Gym miles can be collected, which you can exchange for vouchers and prizes (an incentive that should hopefully make you keep going). A swimming pool, a relaxation room and a range of beauty treatments are also available. Classes on offer include over 60 Fit for Life, children's classes, aerobics and swimming lessons. The Park West centre also offers physiotherapy. Centres in the Dublin area include: Ballsbridge (01 678 1490), Clarendon Street (01 677 0040), Park West (01 630 1456), Swords (01 807 5620) and Rathfarnham (1850 543 210).

Gyms

DCU Sports Complex	DCU Dublin	Dublin 9	01 700 5797
LA Fitness	31 Palmerston Gdns	Dublin 4	01 491 1675
Perfect Fit	4 Brookcourt	Monkstown	01 280 5458
Sanovitae Health & Life	Excise Walk	Dublin 1	01 433 8877
UCD Gym	Belfield	Dublin 4	01 260 3155
World Gym	8/9 Talbot St	Dublin 1	01 874 6099

265

Well-Being

Well-being is uppermost in the priorities of the modern Dubliner. Ireland is gaining an international reputation for its high-end, destination spas and Dublin is spearheading this trend. Beauty salons are increasingly taking a holistic approach, using natural ingredients and incorporating ancient rituals into their treatments. Massage, especially La Stone Therapy and Swedish massage, are ideal to ease away the stresses of modern day living. The flipside of the holistic coin is the popularity of more medicalised treatments, such as Chemical Fillers, Microdermabrasion and Laser Hair Removal. These results-driven treatments hold a huge appeal. Irish people tend to be well travelled and many salons offer treatments that are indicative of this. The influx of people from all over the world to Dublin has also brought fresh ideas to the field. With the increasingly frenzied pace of modern-day Dublin, both men and women are turning to alternative therapies. Acupuncture, reiki and herbalism are used to combat physical and mental aliments. Yoga studios have cropped up all over town with a bewildering array of classes for all levels. Destination spas are perfect for a couple of hours of pure indulgence. Weekends away at spa hotels are great for a romantic getaway and there are many within an hour's radius of Dublin.

Beauty Salons

Other options **Perfumes & Cosmetics** p.311, **Health Spas** p.271

Beauty Salons			
Name	Address	Area	Phone
Benefit Brow Bar	Benefit Counter, Brown Thomas Cosmetics Hall, Grafton St	Dublin 2	01 679 5666
Bliss	BT2, Sandyford Rd	Dublin 16	01 296 8400
Blue Moon	8 St James Tce	Malahide	01 845 2349
Derma Laser	53 Rock Rd, Blackrock	Dublin 4	01 278 8211
Derma Laser Clinic	14 Village Green Shopping Ctr, Tallaght	Dublin 24	01 414 7781
High Maintenance	17 The Mall, Donnybrook	Dublin 4	01 260 3803
Institute of Beauty Science	47 Lower Leeson St	Dublin 2	01 661 1078
Urbana	9 Wicklow St	Dublin 2	01 635 1616

Aim to have some me-time every month and take advantage of all the cutting-edge treatments and products that Dublin has to offer. You do not have to be incredibly rich to treat yourself either. For beauty on a budget, contact the Institute of Beauty Science on Leeson Street (www.beautyschool.ie). Their Student Salon offers Dermalogica Facials for €30, pedicures for €12 and full leg and bikini wax for €12. High Maintenance in Donnybrook (www.highmaintenance.ie) manages to provide a top-quality service at an affordable price (brow shaping €8, bikini wax €10 and spray tanning €25). Remember the beauty counters in the main department stores offer treatments redeemable against purchase. In Brown Thomas on Grafton St, MAC offer make-up lessons (€50), while Estée Lauder offer Brow Shaping (€20) and Sisley periodically offer facials (€50) – all redeemable against purchase. Check out www.ivenus.com or www.beaut.ie for an unbiased take on the latest treatments and beauty salons.

23 Terenure Pl
Terenure
Dublin 6 West
Map 420 A2 **157**

The Beauty Parlour

01 492 9977 | www.beautyparlour.ie

The Beauty Parlour is a closely guarded secret of the Dublin glossy posse. Proprietor Yvonne Laird has won several Beauty Therapist awards and her Guinot facials are legendary. Try the famous Guinot Hydradermie Facial (€75), which can be customised for all skin types. After deep cleansing, the Hydraderm machine employs mild electrotherapy to open pores and allow Hydradermie gels to thoroughly permeate the skin. The face is then massaged with essential oils to reveal a radiant, younger-looking

266

Is getting lost your usual excuse?

Whether you're a map person or not, this pocket-sized marvel will help you get to know the city like the back of your hand – so you won't feel the back of someone else's.

Dublin Mini Map
Fit the city in your pocket

complexion. For optimum results, book a course of three treatments over a five to six week period. Another star treatment is Eyelash Extensions (€90), which negate the need for mascara for up to two months and are a godsend for fair-haired ladies.

The Bodyclinic

24a Wicklow St
Dublin 2
Map 430 B1 159

01 633 9900 | www.thebodyclinic.ie

The bodyclinic specialises in laser hair removal, skin rejuvenation, hair restoration, thread vein removal, cellulite reduction and dental treatments in a medicalised setting. All staff are highly trained and well placed to advise on which treatments will work best for you. Finance is available for treatments over €1,000, so that they can be paid in instalments. There are special offers each month and discounts are available to students. The products on sale reflect the results-driven ethos of The Bodyclinic and include Rodial, MD Formulations and Dermalogica. Centrally located and open seven days a week, The Bodyclinic is ideal for busy professionals, both male and female. A sister company City Dental provides a full range of dentistry services, including teeth whitening and veneers, under the same roof. All treatments bring lasting results and leave you more than ready for your close-up.

Brazilia

50 South William St
Dublin 2
Map 430 A1 11

01 675 0000 | www.brazilia.ie

Brazilia is dedicated to hair removal and caters for both men and women. The therapists are highly experienced and immediately put nervous clients at ease. Spacious treatment rooms guarantee a high level of privacy. Waxing treatments are available for every conceivable part of the body and prices are reasonable with a leg and bikini wax costing €40. Brazilia are the exclusive Irish distributors for the Lycon Wax System, an Australian hot wax range, and run training courses for beauticians in its use. Lycon waxes are infused with aromatherapy oils to lessen irritation and are especially good for shorter hairs. Tendskin, the famous ingrown hair treatment, is for sale here (€22). Check out www.brazilia.ie for a full menu of services and an online booking facility.

Carter Beauty

46a Patrick St
Dun Laoghaire
Map 423 E4 164

01 280 8880 | www.carterbeauty.com

Carter Beauty offers advanced skincare in chic, girly surroundings. Marissa Cater, Irish Beauty Professional's Association 2007 Facial Therapist of the year, specialises in two distinct kinds of treatments: anti-acne and anti-ageing. The anti-acne treatments can control symptoms, reduce scarring, greatly improve the appearance of the skin and are suitable for both men and women. The anti-ageing treatments act as non-surgical facelifts, improving the skin's muscle and tone. These treatments are results driven and employ high-end products such as Dr de Paoli (exclusive to Carter Beauty), Dr Danné Montague King, Dr Murad and the recently launched Carter Beauty Skincare. Another star treatment is the Dr Danne King Medi-Pedi, which leaves feet baby soft with no unpleasant scraping. Instead, an alkaline solution is massaged onto feet to dissolve hard skin. The Carter Beauty website (www.carterbeauty.com) is extremely informative and features monthly special offers, as well as an online booking facility. Carter Beauty offers a full range of beauty treatments in addition to its paramedical treatments. Closed on Mondays.

Brazilia

Nue Blue Eriu

01 672 5776 | www.nueblueriu.com

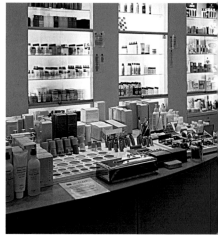

Nue Blue Eriu

Since opening in 2002, Nue Blue Eriu has become synonymous with luxury, service and exclusivity. This lifestyle store offers a lush range of high-end treatments but the vibe remains easygoing and friendly. Try an Ishi facial – this Italian brand uses caviar, truffles and chocolate to give skin a youthful glow. The Pink Pamper Massage is one of Nue Blue Eriu's signature treatments – an hour-long massage with Moroccan Rose Oil whilst lying on a bed of rose petals. Also noteworthy is the J-Sisters waxing services. Nue Blue Eriu brought the famous J-Sisters to Dublin to train the Nue Blue Eriu therapists in waxing the Brazilian way. Finally, there is the Nue Blue Eriu Store, which offers an extensive range of cosmetics, skin, hair, therapy, scent and lifestyle products, including Diptyque, Phyto, Chantecaille, La Prairie, Aqua di Parma among others. Check out the Nue Blue Eriu website (www.nueblueriu.com) to shop the extensive product line, book appointments, purchase gift vouchers, browse the treatment menu and pick up a beauty tip or two. Closed Sundays.

Therapie

01 472 1222 | www.therapie.ie

Therapie effortlessly blends the holistic (massage, seaweed body wraps) with modern miracles of science (laser hair removal, crystal clear microdermabrasion). Facial therapies are of a particularly high standard. There are five ranges of treatments to choose from: Eve Lom, Anne Semonin, Dermalogica, Murad and Elemis. Particularly recommended is the Murad Environmental Shield Vitamin C Facial, which infuses the skin with powerful anti-oxidants and sloughs away dull skin to reveal a fresh, flawless complexion that lasts long after you step out the door. Eve Lom facials are a well-known tool in the modern girl's armour against less than perfect skin. Therapie's retail store is well stocked with the latest beauty must-haves including products from the above-mentioned ranges, as well as Freeze 2407, Caudalie and Pu-erh Tea. Check out the Therapie website (www.therapie.ie) for online booking, a full menu of services and special offers. Open seven days a week.

Hairdressers

There's nothing like a new hairstyle to put a spring in your step. Equally a bad cut can plunge you into the pits of despair. Shop around and be assertive about what you want – remember it's your hair! If you are on a budget check out student classes, especially for colour. Students get a 25% discount in most salons from Monday to Thursday. Peter Mark (www.petermark.ie) and Toni & Guy (www.toniandguy.ie) are Dublin's biggest hairdressing chains. Peter Mark's flagship salon on Grafton Street is good for an impromptu blow-dry and is open on Sundays. Student classes are available in the Peter Mark Academy in the Stephen's Green Shopping Centre (01 475 1126). Toni & Guy offer extensive student classes in their training academy on South William Street (01 670 8749). The newly opened Toni & Guy branch on Clarendon Street (01 671 4401) offers a full beauty service (www.metrospa.ie). For men, the Regent Barber in Temple Bar is a good choice. This family run business has been going strong for over 50 years and is great value with a cut costing just €12. For children, Kiddies Kuts has several branches around the city and plenty to distract fidgety little ones. For extensions and help with hair loss conditions, such as alopecia, trichotillomania and thinning hair, contact the Hair Extension Studios on Baggot Street. For afro hair check out the Charity Hair Studio in the Moore Street Mall.

Brown Sugar

50 South William St
Dublin 2
Map 430 A1 **11**

01 616 9967 | *www.brownsugar.ie*

Husband and wife team, makeup artist Paula and hairstylist Mark, have pooled their resources to create this one-stop shop for all your hair and make-up needs. A fashion forward look has made Brown Sugar a firm favourite of celebrities, including Amanda Byram, Samantha Mumba and Nadine Coyle. Brown Sugar is all about attention to detail – massages are given as hair is being washed. Separate therapy rooms are available for make-up consultations. Nail treatments and tanning can be arranged. There is an extensive food menu, including wine, if you are feeling peckish. Luxury treatments for private wedding parties include champagne for the bride. The salon has an excellent selection of hair and beauty products for sale, including Paula's own brand of make-up, Kohl, and HiShi tan and L'Oreal Kerastase products.

Dylan Bradshaw

5 Johnsons Pl
Dublin 2
Map 430 A1 **165**

01 671 9353

This salon is one of Ireland's best, with more industry awards than you can shake a stick at. A favourite among local celebrities, including U2 and The Corrs, Dylan Bradshaw's work regularly appears in Vogue, Marie Claire and Irish Tatler. The keywords here are 'high-end, creative haircare' in a sleek, minimalist setting. An hour is devoted to each appointment, including a complimentary shiatsu massage. Try the three-part Tanagra Repair System to restore seriously frazzled hair to its former glory. Colour is another strong point with three L'Oreal Colour Trophies to the salon's credit; ideal for an image overhaul. Depending on the stylist, there is a three to four week waiting list; so book early. There is an eight-week waiting list for an appointment with Dylan Bradshaw himself. Prices: haircut from €100; half-head highlights €130; full-head highlights €200; conditioning treatment €30 – 40; Tanagra Repair System €150; full colour tint €80.

Origin Hair Company

41 Ranelagh Village
Dublin 6
Map 416 B4 **162**

01 497 1209

In the heart of trendy Ranelagh, Origins is an unpretentious and easygoing salon with a long list of regular customers. Owner Martin Corbett was formerly a top stylist for Peter Mark. A walk-in service is available but it is better to book as this is a popular spot. The architecturally designed space is small but perfectly formed with a cute terrace and minimalist decor. Origins is particularly good for colour, with a colour correction service available. A full range of L'Oreal Kerastase products are on sale – try the divine Masquintense deep conditioning treatment. Prices: blow-dry €25 - €30; haircut €55 - €70; gent's haircut €35; upstyle from €50; highlights €50 - €110; conditioning treatment from €20; full colour tint €45.

Hairdressers

Charity Hair Studio	Dublin 1	01 874 6681
Ciaran Nevin Hair & Beauty Salon	Dublin 6W	01 405 5256
Hair Extension Studios	Dublin 2	01 667 4180
Hession Hairdressing	Dublin 9	01 837 6265
House of Colour	Dublin 2	01 679 9044
Jaz Hair Company	Sandymount	01 668 0843
Kazumi Hair Salon	Dublin 2	01 678 5004
Kiddies Kuts	Dublin 1	01 873 3679
Noel Higgins Hairdressing	Blackrock	01 278 9135
Regent Barber	Dublin 1	01 677 8719
Toni & Guy Essensuals	Dublin 2	01 633 7712

21 Dawson St
Dublin 2
Map 430 B2 **156**

Reds

01 678 8211 | www.redshairgroup.com

In the business for over 20 years, Reds is one of Dublin's most well established salons with some of Ireland's top stylists. The antithesis of the bigger super salons, this is an intimate, friendly space. Exclusive to Reds is the Philip Kingsley range – a favourite of Jerry Hall – try the Elasticiser treatment for silky, shiny hair. Classic cuts and even classier colour make Reds a firm favourite of ladies who like to lunch and some of Ireland's top politicians. A call-out service can be arranged for bridal parties etc. If you are on a budget there are Student classes on Tuesday and Wednesday evenings, a haircut is €20 and highlights cost just €35. Contact the salon for further information. Prices: blow-dry from €40; haircut from €90; half-head highlights €120 full-head highlights €170; conditioning treatment €25; full colour tint €70.

24 South Anne St
Dublin 2
Map 430 B1 **158**

Whetstone

01 672 4727 | www.whetstone.ie

Aveda's flagship Lifestyle Salon and Spa – Whetstone – is an oasis of calm just off bustling Grafton Street. Aveda is well-known for its environmentally friendly, chemical free ethos and this is reflected in The Whetstone's natural tones, walnut flooring and grass cloth wallpaper. All hair treatments, even a blow-dry, include complementary hand and arm massage, Aveda relaxing tea, use of stress relief massage chairs and a make-up retouch. There is no bleach used in any of the colorants and all products down to the nail varnish are 100% natural. Famous clients include Riverdance star Jean Butler. In terms of beauty treatments, the Natural Plant Waxing service comes highly recommended for super-speedy service and excellent results. An extensive range of Aveda products are for sale in-store. Prices: haircut €55 - €105; blow-dry from €35, colour tint €85 - €95, half-head highlights €110 - €125; full head highlights €170 - €200; conditioning treatment €20; Hair Spa €75.

Health Spas

Other options **Leisure Facilities** p.263, **Massage** p.272

Treating yourself to a couple of hours of complete relaxation is the perfect antidote to the miserable Irish weather. City spas are popping up all over Dublin and are especially popular for hen parties and baby showers. Most spas allow you to stay as long as you like, so take advantage of their on-site facilities (pool, sauna, steam room, relaxation room). A great way to kick-start a girly night out is to have treatments and catch-up with friends at the same time. Within an easy drive of Dublin, there are some fab health spas in atmospheric country house hotels. Bellinter House (046 903 0900; www.bellinterhouse.com) in County Meath is comparable to Babington House in the UK. Its spa offers seaweed therapy, Uspa treatments and extra relaxing massages. Temple Spa (057 933 5118; www.templespa.ie) is relatively small but offers over 80 treatments, gym, pool, hair salon, nail bar and that's not all! Yon-ka addicts take note – their divine facials are available here. Perfect for a weekend away and guaranteed to bring a smile to your face.

Health Spas

Bellinter House	Navan, Co Meath	046 903 0900
Serenity Day Spa	55 Glasthule Rd, Sandycove	01 230 0255
Temple Spa	Moate, Co Westmeath	057 933 5118
Tethra Spa	Upper Merrion St, Dublin 2	01 603 0600

52 South King St
Dublin 2
Map 430 A2 **166**

The Buff Day Spa

01 677 4624 | www.thebuffdayspa.com

The Buff Day Spa takes up the first and second floor of a Georgian building, beside the Gaiety Theatre. The first floor, which acts as a chill-out zone and

271

manicure/pedicure station, is bright and spacious with mosaic tiles and wooden floors. The second floor is where you will find the steam room, sauna and treatment rooms. The Buff Day Spa takes a holistic approach to beauty; thus no medicalised treatments are available. Therapists are well trained, particularly in La Stone Massage and reflexology. The atmosphere is relaxed and friendly. All-day use of the sauna and steam room is included in all treatments over €30. The most popular package is the Half Day Indulgence (€190), which includes a Spa Custom Facial, Swedish Massage, Pedicure and Manicure. Open seven days a week; reasonably priced for the level of service and slap bang in the middle of town, the Buff Day Spa is perfect for some well-deserved pampering.

La Stampa Hotel
35 Dawson St
Dublin 2
Map 430 B1 **17**

Mandala Spa

01 671 7099 | www.mandala.ie

Mandala is an eastern retreat in the heart of the city, and wins the title of Dublin's most luxurious spa hands-down. Step through the doors and be transported to a faraway land. Low lights, polished teak, carrera marble, spacious treatment rooms and expert therapists seal the deal. Chose from treatments inspired by India, China, Thailand, Bali and Japan. Massages are particularly good; try the Mandala Synchronised Four Handed Massage (€150) for ultimate relaxation with two therapists to ease your stress. After your treatment you are free to sip green tea in the relaxation room for as long as you like. Products used in the treatments are on sale. Check out Sundari an organic range created by Christy Turlington and Ytsara an ayurvedic-inspired range, which is exclusive to Mandala.

Westwood Gym
1a St Johns Rd
Sandymount
Dublin 4
Map 421 F1 **174**

re:fresh

01 269 5764 | www.westwood.hosting365.ie

Part of the Westwood Gym, re:fresh offers a range of day spa packages (€65 - €350) using USPA products. Unlimited access to the thalassotherapy area and gym is included with the day spa packages. The gym is lovely but the main attraction here is the thalassotherapy area with its saltwater pool, hydrotherapy baths, sauna and steam room. Under 18's are not allowed, so you can chill out to your hearts content without getting splashed by excitable, little ones. Due to the pool's unique filtration system, there is no need to wear a swimming cap. The pool is always heated to 33°C, the body's optimum temperature. This Spa is particularly relaxing and is ideally suited to mums-to-be or new mums.

Massage

Other options **Leisure Facilities** p.263, **Health Spas** p.271

Massage is the ideal way to ease away the stress of modern day living. Believe it or not you should get a massage every six weeks and not when your muscles start to ache. Massage is available in most beauty salons but health spas, holistic centres or a recommended independent practitioner are usually a better bet. The Pregnancy Store (01 671 8111; www.thepregnancystore.com) on Dawson Street offers a great range of pregnancy massages (€36 - €71) and have a special massage table with an opening in the centre to ensure both bump and mum-to-be are comfortable. Infant Massage has been shown to relieve colic and improve bonding. Saffron Kirwan (087 991 2945; www.bumpbabyandbeyond.com) provides group and individual instruction in infant massage. If you have Vivas Health Insurance (1850 717 717; www.vivashealth.ie), they will cover a proportion of the cost of a massage with a certified practitioner. The

Massage		
Michael Cantwell	Dublin 2	01 661 6195
Olive Kelly	Various locations	086 337 6244
The Pregnancy Store	Dublin 2	01 671 8111
Rosemary Khilafia	Various locations	01 883 0656
Saffron Kirwan	Various locations	087 991 2945

272

Irish Massage Therapists Association (086 377 3801; www.massageireland.org) is a mine of information with details of practitioners, as well as training courses.

Bodytime

120 Baggot La
Ballsbridge
Dublin 4
Map 431 F4 **154**

01 660 1741 | www.bodytime.ie

Bodytime is a well-established massage studio in leafy Dublin 4. A wide range of massages, including deep tissue, sports, Indian head, sports and hot stone, are on offer, with prices averaging €60. Bodytime also offers Reiki, Aromatherapy and physical therapy. Mobile services can be arranged. The website has an online booking facility and a full menu of the services provided.

Meditation

Meditation targets mind, body and soul. Spiritually, meditation opens our minds to greater spiritual awareness, which helps us develop as human beings. Physically, meditation calms the body down reducing blood pressure, cholesterol, chronic pain and stress. Mentally, meditation improves concentration levels and helps us focus on what is truly important in our lives. Meditation is increasingly popular and elements of it have been incorporated into many alternative therapies. The best-known meditation centre in Dublin is the Dublin Buddhist Centre at 42 Lower Leeson Street (01 661 5934; www.dublinbuddhistcentre.org). You do not have to be a Buddhist or even be interested in Buddhism to attend. A five-week course costs €150 and €95 for students and the unemployed. Courses in yoga and Buddhism are also available.

Nail Bars

Finger Point

Unit 11
Westbury Mall
Dublin 2
Map 430 B1 **43**

01 679 6088

In the business for over 20 years, Finger Point is Dublin's longest running nail bar. Manicures are priced at €32.95 and mini-manicures at €22. They're experts in acrylic and gel nails (€65). Gel toes (€40) are popular for summer lasting for four to six weeks without chipping and no filing or buffing is required. A special gel is applied to toes and after being hardened under ultraviolet lights, they can then be customised. Special wedding packages are available. Call-out service can be arranged. Open six days a week and late night opening on Thursdays.

Ger Walsh

Various Locations

086 847 6170 | www.thinknblink.ie

Ger Walsh is a mobile nail technician whose celebrity clients include Louise Kennedy and Caroline Morahan. After several years managing a city-centre nail bar, Ger started this call-out nail service five years ago. She now has a team of mobile nail technicians working for her, as well as her own events company, which provides manicures and pedicures for product launches and nail parties. Products used include Unique Gel Nails from the Netherlands, the French Nailtheque brand and Clarins hand creams. If you wish to have an appointment with the lady herself, specify when booking as she gets booked up fast.

Mink Hand and Foot Spa

45 Main St
Donnybrook
Dublin 4
Map 421 D1 **163**

01 260 3076 | www.mink.ie

Mink is every bit as upmarket and chic as its location. Customer service is excellent with the owner very much present, unlike the bigger chains. The massage chairs are ideal to drift away on while receiving your treatment. Prices start at €25 for a Mini Manicure and €30 for a Mini Pedicure. Other treatments vary in cost from €35 for a

273

Solar Manicure to €95 for a Jurlique De Luxe Foot and Leg Treatment. Nail extensions (or nail enhancements as they are referred to in Mink) cost €90. Mink also has specific treatments for men and even for 'little princesses' (up to 13 years old). Perfect for an indulgent afternoon or pre-holiday blitz. Do remember to wear sandals if you are getting a pedicure, as you don't want to smudge those tootsies after all that hard work. You can book online. Open Monday to Wednesday from 10:00 to 20:00; Thursday and Friday from 10:00 to 21:00; Saturday from 10:00 to 18:00.

Donaghmede
Shopping Ctr
Dublin 13
Map 411 D1 **16**

Nail & Beauty Bar
01 847 4344 | www.nailandbeautybar.ie

Here you will find Ireland's top nail technician, Ms Louise Flannagan. Louise won this accolade at the 2007 Irish Beauty Professionals Association (IBPA) awards. This is one of the best places in Dublin to get nail extensions and at €60 for a full set they are competitively priced. Manicures range in price from €15 for a file and polish to €32 for a Paraffin Wax Treatment. Pedicures start at €18 for a Toe Polish to €50 for a Spa Deluxe Pedicure. Check out their website for discount vouchers and an online booking faculty. There are also Nail & Beauty Bar branches in the Clare Hall, Blanchardstown and the Northside Shopping centres.

Nail Bars		
Associate Nails	Arnott's	01 805 0400
Nail Angel	Various locations	087 136 0166
Nails Inc	Brown Thomas	01 605 6795

Pilates
Other options **Yoga** p.276

Pilates tones and lengthens specific muscles to produce a lean, lithe body. Pilates can be practised either on a mat or using a special pilates machine known as a Reformer. Core muscles in the stomach and lower back are particularly targeted and regular practice leads to enviably toned abs. Pilates is, therefore, especially good for getting back into shape after having a baby. If you do not have time to get to classes, consider hiring a personal trainer. Fitness4u in Ballsbridge, Dublin 4 (01 462 6764) offer personal training for €70 an hour, as well as more affordable group classes. This gentle, non-impact workout is suitable for a wide range of people, both men and women of varying fitness levels. See Sports & Leisure Facilities on p.263 for other listings and Dance Classes on p.233.

Park Shopping Ctr
North Circular Rd
Dublin 7
Map 818 C1 **172**

Bodyfirm
01 868 4600 | www.bodyfirmpilates.com

Dublin's longest-running Pilates centre offers an extensive range of classes including group classes, personal training, intensive bootcamp courses, sports training, pregnancy and post-natal pilates. Drop-in classes cost €18 and a month's course costs €136. A number of physical therapies are also available, including various types of massage and Bowen Therapy (a holistic healing technique).

8 Cumberland St
Dun Laoghaire
Map 423 E4 **168**

Pilates Plus
01 280 6120 | www.pilatesplusdublin.com

Direct from LA and exclusive to Pilates Plus is the Systeme Dynamique technique, a favourite of celebrities such as Jennifer Anniston and Courtney Cox. Classes utilise a ProFormer machine (an advanced version of a pilates Reformer machine) with traditional circuit training exercises. Systeme Dynamique specifically targets certain muscles in the hips, thighs and stomach to achieve a toned body in record time. Classes are tough but the results speak for themselves.

Reiki

Reiki is a form of Japanese energy healing, which means 'spiritually guided life force energy'. Reiki is not a religion but it is a spiritual practice, which involves a 'laying of the hands' to promote healing of physical or emotional pain. Reiki is said to accelerate the healing of bone, muscle and tissue, to alleviate the symptoms of many diseases including arthritis and cancer, as well as emotional problems and stress. You can teach yourself Reiki as the technique is relatively simple. In fact even children can learn it. Angela Gorman (01 087 274 9701; www.thehealingpages.com) runs a range of courses in Reiki. Reiki can be used to treat animals, Vivien Ni Duinn (04 589 0984; 085 724 5578; ansionnach@eircom.net) is a reiki master who practises a number of holistic therapies, including animal reiki to heal traumatised animals. Check out the Reiki Ireland website (www.reiki.ie) for a list of reiki practitioners and teachers throughout Ireland.

Killiney

Jane Hill
086 312 4151 | janemhill@gmail.com

Jane Hill is a qualified herbalist and Reiki Master who aims to treat the mind, body and soul with a range of holistic therapies including iridology and reflexology. As a Reiki Master, Jane is also qualified to teach Reiki. One session of Reiki with Jane costs €45. During a typical session, Jane has a general chat with the client and they then lie down on the plinth, where Jane lays hands on them and prays. Energy levels are balanced leaving the client revitalised and relaxed.

Stress Management

Other options **Support Groups** p.142

A certain level of stress is normal and indeed necessary. However, due to our hectic and often unpredictable lives, stress levels can rise to unhealthy levels. Stress causes an increase of the hormone cortisol in the bloodstream. Increasingly, people live in a state of constant stress meaning their levels of cortisol are always too high. This in turn has consequences on emotional and physical health including high blood pressure, hyperglycaemia, lowered immunity and weight gain. To combat high stress levels we need to learn techniques to control our stress. Creating and maintaining a stress free life is not easy and involves making difficult life changes, such as putting our own needs first and learning to say no to others. Cognitive Behaviour Therapy and hypnosis are both useful tools in this. LifeHandle in County Meath (www.lifehandle.com) offers Stress Management Courses as well Cognitive Behavioural Therapy (CBT). Relaxing our bodies through yoga, meditation, physical exercise or flotation also helps to reduce stress levels. The Harvest Moon Centre on Baggot Street (www.harvestmoon.ie) manages stress holistically and offers flotation tank sessions, which will leave you blissfully stress-free and relaxed. Acupuncture is a useful tool in restoring our natural balance. Melt in Temple Bar (www.meltonline.com) offers acupuncture session with a massage for €60.

Tai Chi

Tai Chi is an ancient Chinese Martial Art and is often described as the subtlest form of acupuncture. Tai Chi consists of slow movements combined with deep breathing to focus on building up powerful, open, loose muscles and bones performing at their optimum with the absolute minimum of contraction, which in turn leads to the smooth, graceful flow

Stress Management

Harvest Moon Centre	24 Lower Baggot St	Dublin 2	01 662 7556
LifeHandle	5 Greenfield Grove	Co Meath	087 618 1992
Melt	2 Temple Lane South	Dublin 2	01 679 8786

people recognise as Tai Chi. With an emphasis on awareness and mental presence, tension and thus stress levels are reduced, balance, co-ordination and muscular control are heightened, and the immune system is bolstered; every system in our body benefits. Tai Chi is suitable for all ages and levels of fitness. In China, 100 million people practice Tai Chi on a daily basis. For optimum results, Tai Chi should be part of an overall balanced lifestyle but daily practise of Tai Chi is a great way to encourage you to make those all-important changes.

Various Locations ◄

Tai Chi Ireland
087 979 5042 | www.taichi-ireland.com

Jan Golden is Ireland's foremost Tai Chi instructor and gives classes in three locations: in his Harrington Street studio, in Scoil Bride in Ranelagh and in St Michael's House in Rathmines. Beginners study a Wu short form in four modules of seven weeks duration each, which cost €130 to €150 per module with discounts for students and OAP's. Classes are limited to 10 participants to ensure plenty of individual attention. Weekend Tai Chi Workshops (€150), Chi Gung classes and one-to-one training (€50 per hour) are also available. Check out the Tai Chi Ireland website for further information (www.taichi-ireland.com).

Yoga
Other options **Pilates** p274

Yoga is a 5000-year old Indian system of philosophy that aims to unite body and mind through a series of poses and breathing techniques. The benefits are well documented and include improved flexibility, stamina, balance, concentration, weight loss and stress relief. There are many different types of yoga with Hatha, Iyengar, Ashtanga and Bikram being the most common in Dublin. You are also far less likely to injure yourself as yoga is gentle and non-impact. Yoga is not just for women either – in fact many top rugby players practise yoga. Sunrise Yoga in Dun Laoghaire (01 289 8391) offer men-only classes. Yoga can be practised by people of all ages including children. Many yoga studios run pregnancy yoga classes and active birth workshops – the breathing techniques employed in yoga are said to help during labour. There is a certain etiquette for yoga classes – arrive on time, bring a clean mat, shower beforehand and do not eat a heavy meal in the two hours before a class. Yoga can be a spiritual experience and is thus far more interesting than step aerobics at an overcrowded, expensive gym. Check out www.yoga-ireland.com for up-to-date listings of classes. Before you start a course of yoga classes, your studio should give you some guidelines on the correct yoga etiquette. Each studio will have its own set of rules, although there are some issues that are universal. One of the most important rules of yoga etiquette is to stick to the times of the class. Rushing in five minutes after the class has started is not only disrespectful to the instructor, it won't win you any points with your classmates who are trying hard to concentrate. Similarly, leaving before the end of the class is also frowned upon, not just because of the disruption, but because you will miss out on your Savasana – an essential part of the class.

29 Avenue Rd ◄
Portobello
Dublin 8
Map 429 F4 **161**

Bikram Yoga Studio
01 657 0061 | www.bikramyoga.ie

Bikram yoga is definitely not for wimps, this extreme yoga workout consists of 90 minutes of poses and stretches carried out in a room heated to 44°C. This is how the likes of Madonna and Gwyneth Paltrow keep so svelte. Apparently after 60 days of daily practise you too can have a new body. Bikram yoga combines all the well-known benefits of yoga with a cardiovascular workout. This group has an introductory offer of €25 for 10 days unlimited classes. Otherwise a single class costs €18 and monthly unlimited access costs €185. It's hardcore but it achieves the all-important, red carpet results.

15 Wicklow St
Dublin 2
Map 430 B1 155

Lotus Yoga

087 207 1530 | www.lotusyoga.ie

Find inner peace at this tranquil studio located on Wicklow Street (between Nourish health food shop and L'Occitane). There are classes in various disciplines, including hatha, kundalini, satyananda and viniyoga. Prenatal and children's classes are also available. A six-week course costs €90 and an eight-week course costs €120. If you want to just try one class, it costs €18 for a 90 minute class, but you will only be allowed in if there is space. Lotus Yoga also offers meditation classes.

Various Locations

Orla Punch Yoga

087 934 0839 | www.orlapunchyoga.com

To gain a deeper knowledge of Yoga and ensure you are doing the poses and breathing correctly, personal classes are a good option. Indeed, it is only in recent years that yoga has been practised in larger groups. Orla Punch is a highly experienced yoga teacher with over 10 years experience and specialises in Iyengar yoga. She also teaches group classes in the Westwood Gym, Leopardstown and at No.15 Street, Stephen's Green - check her website for up-to-date listings.

Dartmouth Pl
Off Grand Parade
Ranelagh
Map 416 C4 170

Yoga Dublin Studios

01 498 2284 | www.yogadublin.com

Yoga Dublin offers classes in everything from pilates to Vinyassa, Ashtanga and Hatha and Mysore yoga and various types of massage in spacious studios with professional, friendly teachers. Mums-to-be can partake in prenatal yoga and pregnancy massage and reflexology. Postnatal classes, baby massage and Mums and Babies postnatal classes are all offered. Class times vary and there are options all day long. Treatments on offer include somatic movement education, physiotherapy, osteopathy and shiatsu and holistic massage. There's a second centre at 17 Dame Court, Dublin, 2 (01 675 9860). Drop in classes range in price between €16 -18, depending on the duration, and eight-week courses cost €125. Various package are available. An onsite shop will help out with yoga mats and clothing needs. Showers and changing rooms are available on the premises. The website has comprehensive details on both studios, including timetables and bios on the teachers so you can see what's what before you sign up.

262 Merrion Rd
Dublin 4
Map 421 F1 160

The Yoga Room

01 219 6666 | www.yoga.ie

The Yoga Room offers a wide range of yoga classes and is open seven days a week. The Yoga Room also organises a range of yoga workshops and even yoga holidays. Good for beginners, they have a special offer of a four-week Introduction to Yoga course and three weeks unlimited access pass for €95. Otherwise, a single class costs €16 and monthly-unlimited access costs €180.

Yoga			
Name	Address	Area	Phone
Ashtanga Yoga Dublin	Sion Hill Continuing Education Ctr, off Mount Merrion Ave	Blackrock	087 237 6383
The Elbow Room	32 North Brunswick St, Stoneybatter	Dublin 7	01 677 9859
Sunrise Yoga	48a Rogan's Court, Patrick St	Dun Laoghaire	01 289 8391
Yoga Ireland	6 Lower Merrion St	Dublin 2	087 681 1240

277

CROSS BORDERS WITHOUT BARRIERS.

Whether you're connecting with family and friends or sending goods for business, you'll find all the help you need to cross borders without barriers at one of our many offices around the world.

www.dhl.com

Shopping

Clothing Sizes ◀

Figuring out your size isn't rocket science, just a bit of a pain. Firstly, check the label – international sizes are often printed on them. Secondly, check the store – they will often have a helpful conversion chart on display. Otherwise, a UK size is always two higher than a US size (so a UK 10 is actually a US 6. To convert European sizes into US sizes, just subtract 32 (so a European 38 is actually a US 6). To convert European sizes into UK sizes, a 38 is roughly a 10, but some countries size smaller so you'll have to try clothes on to be sure. Italian sizing is different again.

Shopping

Dublin is fast becoming a European capital with a flair for fashion. Irish designers like Orla Kiely, Ciaran Sweeney, John Rocha, Paul Costelloe, Louise Kennedy and milliner Philip Treacy have already taken the world by storm, and if the National College of Art and Design has anything to say about it, the next generation will produce even more sartorial superstars. Dublin Fashion Week (see p.393) is also an up and coming phenomenon and while many of the events are limited to industry insiders and journalists, the series of public talks attracts crowds from far and wide.

Unfortunately, as much as Dubliners have come to enjoy fashion and shopping, prices on almost everything remain high in the city. A 21% government value added tax (VAT) is added onto most price tags, so it can be a bit demoralising to see the euro prices in Ireland listed as much higher than those for other EU countries. Thankfully Dublin remains a literary city and tax is not added to books, and with the current baby boom parents are very happy that children's clothes and shoes are exempt also. Prices are steep for traditional Irish woollen goods; the quality of these items generally makes up for the sticker shock though. Dublin is catching on to the fact that deep discounts will attract consumers more than any window display. The sales in late December and late June offer up to 50% (and in some cases 70%) off most items in most stores, so big ticket purchases such as electronics, home appliances and furniture are worth the wait. The sales are advertised for several weeks in advance in print, on public transport and even in a few sneaky television adverts, so there's little chance of missing these events.

Like most of Dublin, shopping can be divided into two distinct areas: north of the River Liffey and south of the River Liffey. On the north side, Henry Street and O'Connell Street are firm favourites for chain stores, discount stores and the occasional outdoor market stall. On the south side, Grafton Street and Nassau Street offer more designer gear and ambience for ladies who lunch.

If you're looking to escape the crowds, you should consider visiting the shopping centres that have sprung up in the suburbs (though only weekday mornings will truly minimise the numbers). Blanchardstown (see p.329), Liffey Valley (see p.330) and Dundrum (see p.329) are all modern malls that were designed for maximum shopping with minimum effort. The city's only Borders Books is found in Blanchardstown, while House of Fraser, LK Bennett, Hobbes and Harvey Nichols can be found exclusively at Dundrum. Dedicated followers of fashion may want to leave the city to drop into Kildare Village (www.kildarevillage.com) for some chic outlet shopping, and crafty shoppers should take a daytrip to follow the Kilkenny Crafts Trail to find one of a kind pottery, jewellery, glass items and leather goods (http://kilkennytourism.kilkenny.ie/eng/Crafts/Craft_Trail/)

Of course, even the most passionate shopper may have trouble spending money in Dublin and not because they haven't brought enough cash. Irish shop assistants can be stereotyped as a particularly disinterested breed, so searching a store to find a checkout that is open can often take a while; on the flip side though, no one could claim that Dublin shop assistants badger anyone into a sale.

Clothing Sizes

Ireland follows the British model for clothing and footwear sizes. This means that the marked sizes can be converted to both American and European sizes with some simple arithmetic. For women, labels will usually show both the British/Irish and American sizes, but for the most part subtracting four from the marked size will offer the American equivalent (for example, an Irish size 8 is an American size 4), and adding 28 to the marked size will give the European size (for example, an Irish size 8 is a 36). For men, Irish sizes are generally the same as American ones, but adding 10 will offer the European size (for example, an Irish size 32 is a European size 42).

Importing Goods
Further information on imports into Ireland can be obtained from Revenue's Notice No. 1882 – Ordering Goods over the Internet or from Mail Order Catalogues. You can find this online at the Revenue's website (www.revenue.ie).

For footwear, women will need to subtract 2.5 from an American size to find the equivalent Irish size, but men will only need to subtract a half size (just to make it complicated!). Once the American sizes are found, adding 30 to these numbers will result in the European size for women. Of course using a calculator such as www.onlineconversion.com and keeping one's measurements safely stored on a scrap of paper will negate the need for mental maths every time you turn around.

Online Shopping

Online shopping has become popular with Dubliners as they search the web for brands and bargains that can't be purchased in the city. Fashion and beauty products are probably the most sought-after online, followed by shoes, books, DVDs, and even flat pack furniture. Delivery charges from the US and UK can be steep with fees of up to €50 or more for large or expensive orders, but for the most part this is made up for in the savings against the weak dollar. Firearms, ammunition, explosives, illegal drugs, indecent or obscene publications, meat and meat products, and quantities of alcohol and cigarettes are prohibited from being shipped into Ireland so Dubliners don't even bother with such purchases. Items that are shipped to Ireland are subject to customs duty, excise duty and value added tax (VAT), though in practice a shipment actually being examined and charged at customs is quite rare.

Surf & Shop
Online shopping tied to stores that are in Dublin is rare, and most shoppers only bother if they want a particular item that can't be found elsewhere. Even more rare is shopping online at Irish owned, internet-only sites, though a few do exist, and this sector is set to expand.

Online Shopping

www.amazon.co.uk	Books, CDs, DVDs, home & garden, toys and more
www.beorganic.ie	Nationwide organic delivery service
www.cdwow.ie	CDs, DVDs and video games
www.clothing.ie	Reviews and links to clothes stores supplying Ireland
www.ebay.ie	Ireland's eBay auction site
www.econatural.com	Natural, organic, eco-friendly and Fair Trade products
www.gumtree.ie	Natural, organic, eco-friendly and Fair Trade products
www.hairybaby.com	Funky tshirts for men, women and children
www.ikea.com/gb/en/	IKEA flat pack furniture
www.landsend.co.uk	Family clothing and home goods
www.littleshopofbeauty.ie	International health and beauty products
www.moviestar.ie	Online DVD rental
www.murphyofireland.com	Twee – and tweedy – traditional Irish goods
www.oxfamirelandshop.com	Oxfam Ireland online shop
www.play.com	Books, CDs, DVDs, electronics, clothing and more
www.shoponlineireland.com	Online directory of shops that ship to Ireland
www.tesco.ie	Supermarket site and online grocery shopping
www.ticketmaster.ie	Tickets for music, theatre, sports events and more
www.yoox.com	Discount designer clothing

Refunds & Exchanges

The rights of Irish consumers are guaranteed under the Sale of Goods and Supply of Services Act 1980. Under this act, consumers are entitled to a refund, replacement or the repair of an item if it was not as described, fit for purchase or of sellable quality. Unfortunately these terms are vague and some merchants may try to take advantage of this to deny a refund or exchange, but for the most part it's easy to obtain either of these in Dublin. Most stores post their refund or return policies in writing near checkout points but remember to ask about time limits. Usually stores accept an item for refund or exchange within 30 days of purchase, but some operate on a tighter timescale. Many shops print their policies on receipts, and these receipts are key to obtaining a refund or exchange as most shops will require them as proof of purchase. Some stores will also request that you have not removed any sales tags. In addition to refunds and exchanges, many stores offer store credit for an item, and many stores attempt to enforce an 'all sales are final' policy during the sales. Consumers who do not feel that they are receiving fair treatment should enlist the aid of the Consumers Association of Ireland (www.consumerassociation.ie).

Consumer Rights

The CAI
Consumers who do not feel that they are receiving fair treatment should enlist the aid of the Consumers Association of Ireland (www.consumer association.ie).

The rights of Irish consumers are mainly safeguarded by the Sale of Goods and Supply of Services Act 1980. Multiple organisations exist to help Irish consumers, including the Consumer's Association of Ireland (www.consumerassociation.ie) and the National Consumer Agency (www.consumerconnect.ie) which operates a consumer helpline at 1890 432 432. Complaints can be made to either organisation as well as the Advertising Standards Authority (www.asai.ie), which will investigate complaints (confidentially) about advertising. Citizens Information (www.citizensinformation.ie) can also advise consumers about their rights, and Citizens Information Centres (www.comhairle.ie/citizens/citizens_centres.html) offer further legal and financial advice. The European Consumer Centre (www.eccdublin.ie) is also on standby to provide information about consumer rights in the European Union.

Shopping in Temple Bar

Designer goods on Grafton Street

Moore Street Market

Shipping

Consumers are always advised to ask about shipping charges before making any big purchases. Rarely is home delivery free or included in the price of items, but having items shipped to a shop in order to be collected might not cost anything extra. An Post offers a variety of shipping options for private individuals (http://postage.anpost.ie) and several international shipping companies also operate in Dublin including DHL (www.dhli.ie), FedEx (www.fedex.com/ie) and UPS (www.ups.com). Regardless of the company, shipping rates are usually determined by the weight of the item, desired speed of shipping and overall destination. Optional extras such as insurance may bump up the cost of shipping.

How To Pay

Hey Big Spender
If a money exchange (or wealthy relative) hands you a €500 note, you may find it difficult to actually use it, since most shops don't tend to keep large amounts of cash accessible in-store (for security reasons). Try to get smaller notes instead.

The bad news is that Dublin is expensive; the good news is that it accepts a variety of payment types. Cash is always accepted and can be accessed at the ATMs found on most street corners, in all major bank branches and even in a few city pubs (affectionately known as the 'drinklink'). ATMs generally dispense only €20 and €50 notes, so don't be embarrassed about using larger notes for small purchases. Major credit cards such as Visa, MasterCard, Maestro and Eurocard are accepted in most establishments, though American Express, Diners Club and the Discover card are not nearly as common or commonly accepted. Debit cards drawn on Irish banks and the European Debit Card are commonly accepted, and ATMs generally accept MasterCard/Cirrus and Plus cards. Cheques and travellers cheques often require photo identification and are not as commonly accepted as cash or credit cards. Though some city centre pubs will accept British pounds as well as euros, this is rare in any other kind of establishment so make sure to use one of the many bureaux de change that can be found throughout the city if you have foreign currency.

Bargaining

Dublin is a 'what you see is what you get' kind of city and this certainly holds true for its price tags. Bargaining is all but unheard of in city shops, and outdoor artisan and organic markets are not the place to try out your bargaining skills either. A few of the city's flea markets may accept a small bit of barter banter as it draws nearer to closing time, though it's not guaranteed. Though some independent shops may respond when a competitor's (cheaper) price is brought to their attention, this tactic will likely produce an outraged result. In general the best way to bag a bargain in Dublin is to wait for the sales or take your custom somewhere else.

What & Where to Buy – Quick Reference

283

Alcohol

Other options **On the Town** p.368, **Drinks** p.338

Liquor stores are known locally as off licences or 'offies', and can be independent, a branch of a chain or even attached to a supermarket. The legal age to purchase alcohol in Dublin is 18, and those who stand outside off licences have usually been banned for a reason so its best to avoid buying alcohol for anyone you don't know. A six-pack of beer goes for around €9, though special offers can sometimes see a case go for under €20. European and Asian beers are particularly popular, and go on special more often than other types.

The price of wine varies greatly in Dublin depending on the vintage, but bargain bottles can be as low as €6. Most well-known brands of spirits can be found in Dublin, though again prices vary. A decent bottle of vodka will cost €25. Those passing by Duty Free during their travels should take advantage, as prices are almost always lower.

Alcohol

Berry Brothers & Rudd	4 Harry Street	Dublin 2	01 677 2444	www.bbr.com
Celtic Whiskey Shop	27-28 Dawson Street	Dublin 2	01 675 9744	www.celticwhiskeyshop.com
Dunnes Off Licence	Stephen's Green Centre	Dublin 2	01 478 0188	www.dunnesstores.ie
Enowine	Custom House Square, IFSC	Dublin 1	01 636 0616	www.enowine.ie
Mitchell & Son	21 Kildare Street	Dublin 2	01 676 0766	www.mitchellandson.com
Molloys Liquor Stores	Village Green	Tallaght	01 451 4857	www.molloys.ie
O'Briens Off Licence	169 St Mobhi Road, Glasnevin	Dublin 9	01 837 3220	www.obrienswine.ie
Oddbins	17 Baggot Street Upper	Dublin 4	01 667 3033	www.oddbins.com

Art

Other options **Art Galleries** p.180, **Art & Craft Supplies** p.285, **Art Classes** p.227

Dublin may not be an artist's mecca, but it does hold fine art in high regard. Jim Fitzpatrick's Irish folk art, Guggi's minimalist paintings, Louis Le Brocquy's landscapes and Roisin O'Shea's watercolours have all graced the city and inspired countless art students who may just become tomorrow's masters. The Irish Art Fair (www.irishartfair.com) takes place twice a year, in the spring and the autumn, while the National College of Art and Design (see p.149) offers end of year exhibitions every June. A host of art galleries across the city delight art lovers and serious collectors alike, and the Sunday art exhibitions at Merrion Square as well as occasional painting and photography exhibits at St Stephen's Green (see Exploring on p.180) offer interested parties the chance to buy artwork for prices as low as €20.

> **Say Cheese**
> If you're looking for a portrait photographer, visit the Irish Photographers' website (www.irishphotographers.ie) for links to leading Dublin photographers. See also p.249.

Stephen's
Green Centre
Dublin 2
Map 430 A2 26

The Green Gallery

01 478 3122 | www.greengallery.com

The Green Gallery is open seven days a week and displays contemporary works from over 50 artists. Portraits, still lifes, landscapes and seascapes make up the majority of the Green Gallery's offerings, though portraits for commission are available as well. A bespoke framing service is available at the gallery. Online shopping is available.

26 St Stephen's Green
Dublin 2
Map 430 A2 26

James Adam & Sons

01 676 0261 | www.adams.ie
Adam's offers expertise in the sale of Irish art, fine period furniture, silver, contemporary and modern art and much more. In addition to sales, they also offer a valuation service for insurance and probate needs. First time buyers can read Adam's terms and conditions at any time on the company's website.

29 Molesworth St
Dublin 2
Map 430 B1 594

Jorgenson Fine Art Gallery

01 661 9758 | www.jorgensenfineart.com
Jorgenson's regularly shows a variety of Irish, English and European art, specialising in 19th and early 20th century Irish art. They also showcase new artists through changing exhibitions each month. This gallery focuses on paintings for the serious art lover. Open Monday to Friday from 09:00 to 17:30 and from 09:30 to 14:00 on Saturdays.

Art for sale

44 Westland Row
Dublin 2
Map 431 D1 601

The Oisin Gallery

01 661 1315 | www.oisingallery.com
The Oisin Gallery specialises in traditional and contemporary art with new exhibitions mounted at least every six weeks. The Gallery also offers free advice on starting, or adding to, a private or corporate art collection and can source art from other dealers or galleries as requested. Shipping is available worldwide. Open Monday to Friday from 09:00 to 17:30 and from 10:00 to 17:30 on Saturdays.

10 St Stephen's Green
Dublin 2
Map 430 B2 581

The Rubicon Gallery

01 670 8055 | www.rubicongallery.ie
The Rubicon Gallery strives to offer contemporary artists, both Irish and international, a space to display their works in all forms of media. The Gallery presents 10 exhibitions per year, and produces approximately five publications annually. Private appointments may be arranged.

Blackrock
Shopping Ctr
Blackrock
Map 422 B3 613

The Waldock Gallery

01 278 1861 | www.irishpaintings.com
The Waldock Gallery is open seven days a week and offers new paintings weekly. Art can be purchased in the gallery or online, and international shipping is available. Sculptures, ceramics, art glass, limited edition prints, frames and gift vouchers are all available. The staff are knowledgeable about what they sell and can advise you on investing in art – don't let the suburban location put you off. Open Monday to Wednesday and Fridays and Saturdays from 10:00 to 18:00, and until 19:00 on Thursdays. Sunday opening is by appointment only.

Art & Craft Supplies

Other options Art p.284, **Art Galleries** p.180, **Art Classes** p.227

Arts and crafts is sometimes referred to as 'make and do' in Dublin and is usually well enjoyed throughout the city. Art and hobby shops can be found across the city as well as online (www.artnhobby.ie or www.irishartonline.com). Hickeys

285

(www.hickeysfabrics.ie) are fabulous fabric shops that also offer an array of craft materials. Stores in the city centre include one in Stephen's Green Centre and one at 5 Henry Street, but there are many all over Dublin. Artzone (www.artzone.ie) offers art classes and parties for children in which all equipment is supplied. Craft Supplies (www.craftsupplies.ie) is an online shop offering an array of materials with shipping for just €3 across Ireland. M Kennedy & Sons (www.kennedyart.com) is Ireland's oldest artist supply shop and operates a respected loyalty card scheme. It has also opened an online shop. Demonstrations and occasional classes are carried out at the shop at 12 Harcourt Street (01 475 1749).

Supermarket Babies

Generic baby items – nappies, bottles, dummies (pacifiers) – are available in most major supermarkets and nationwide Dunnes Stores.

Baby Items

Expectant parents all over the country flock to Dublin for fun and funky supplies. Aptamil, Cow and Gate, Baby Organix, Heinz and Milupa baby foods and formulas are available in most supermarkets, though posh parents may opt for Chill Baby organic baby food. You can buy this in various locations throughout the city: see their website for details (www.chillbaby.ie). Baby clothes and toys are available for bargain prices at Dunnes, Penneys and Marks & Spencer, although Benetton, Avoca, and Mamas & Papas offer wide ranges as well. Baby necessities like prams, cots and cribs can be found at Mothercare, Murphy's Prams and Eurobaby. Second-hand nursery goods and baby toys can also be found on Gumtree (www.gumtree.ie). Mums-to-be delight in the maternity clothes at the MomSoon personal shopping service, which will come to you, and at the Nelo, Formes, Mama Mondo, and Bella Mamma boutiques, and the wide variety of fashion and beauty finds at The Pregnancy Store.

Baby Items

Avoca	11 Suffolk Street	01 677 4215	www.avoca.ie
Bella Mamma	The Triangle, Ranelagh	01 496 8598	na
Benetton	Stephen's Green Shopping Centre	01 478 1799	www.benetton.com
Chill Baby	Butternut House, 50 Coolmine Ind Est, Clonsilla	01 823 8395	www.chillbaby.ie
Dunnes Stores	Stephen's Green Shopping Centre	01 478 0188	www.dunnesstores.com
Eurobaby	Unit 1 Finches Park, Longmile Road	01 419 7090	www.eurocycles.ie
Formes	15 South Anne Street	01 671 9054	www.formes-ie.com
Mama Mondo	51 Clontarf Road	01 833 4334	www.mamamondo.com
Mamas & Papas	Blanchardstown Centre	1890 882 363	www.mamasandpapas.com
Marks & Spencer	15-20 Grafton Street	01 679 7855	www.marksandspencer.com
MomSoon	90 Ashton Avenue, Knocklyon	087 204 6917	www.momsoon.ie
Mothercare	Stephen's Green Shopping Centre	01 478 4755	www.mothercare.com
Murphys Prams	Main Street, Rathcoole	01 405 5711	www.murphysprams.ie
Nelo	39 Clarendon Street	01 679 1336	www.nelomaternity.com
Penneys	47 Mary Street	01 872 7788	www.primark.co.uk
The Pregnancy Store	53 Dawson Street	01 671 8111	www.thepregnancystore.com

Beachwear

Beachwear remains scarce in Dublin during the off season, so stocking up during the spring and summer is essential. Most department stores stock swimsuits and beach accessories, including Dunnes, Marks & Spencer, Debenhams, Clerys, Arnotts and Brown Thomas. Sports stores such as Champion Sports and Lifestyle Sports stock a good selection of workout suits, goggles and swim caps year round, and Boots is the place to go for sunscreen and skin creams. For women, swimwear is often sold with lingerie such as at MeMe Lingerie, and in fashion shops such as TopShop and H&M.

Beachwear

Arnotts	12 Henry Street	01 805 0400	www.arnotts.ie
Boots	12 Grafton Street	01 478 4368	www.boots.com
Brown Thomas	88-95 Grafton Street	01 605 6666	www.brownthomas.com
Champion Sports	Ilac Centre	01 872 7274	www.champion.ie
Clerys	18-27 Lower O'Connell Street	01 878 6000	www.clerys.com
Debenhams	Jervis Centre	01 878 1222	www.debenhams.com
Dunnes	Stephen's Green Shopping Centre	01 478 0188	www.dunnesstores.ie
H&M	Dundrum Town Centre	01 299 1502	www.hm.com/ie
Lifestyle Sports	Stephen's Green Shopping Centre	01 478 3366	www.lifestylesports.com
Marks & Spencer	15-20 Grafton Street	01 679 7855	www.marksandspencer.com
MeMe Lingerie	6 Town Centre Mall	01 890 3225	www.memelingerie.com
TopShop	St Stephen's Green	01 672 5009	www.topshop.com

Bicycles

A variety of bike shops can be found in Dublin, including the Artane Bike Centre, Belfield Bike Shop in UCD, The Bike Rack, Commuting Solutions and Cycleways, as well as the Eurocycle superstore (see table). Most shops offer a repair service or the recommendation of a repair service, which comes in handy with the number of bikes that are vandalised in the city centre. With prices for bikes starting at around €150, many Dubliners choose to buy second-hand bikes that they find on Gumtree (www.gumtree.ie) or in the local papers, and invest in a sturdy lock instead. Those looking for a bike on a once-off occasion should visit Rent A Bike or Neills Wheels Rent A Bike where prices start at about €20 a day.

Bicycles

Artane Bike Centre	5 Grace Court Mask Road	01 831 2444	na
Belfield Bike Shop	UCD, Belfield	01 260 0749	www.ucd.ie
The Bike Rack	Johnstown Road, Cabinteely	01 284 0609	www.thebikerack.ie
Commuting Solutions	138 Lwr Rathmines Road	01 496 5314	na
Cycleways	185-186 Parnell Street	01 873 4748	www.cycleways.com
Eurocycles	Unit 1, Finches Park, Long Mile Rd	01 419 7090	na
Neills Wheels Rent A Bike	9a Capel Street	085 153 0648	http://rentabikedublin.com
Rent A Bike	58 Gardiner Street Lower	01 872 5399	na

Books

Other options **Second-Hand Items** p.313, **Libraries** p.244

Books remain exempt from the 21% VAT applied to most consumer items, although book sales and even 'three for two' offers appear only occasionally throughout the year. Almost all Dublin bookshops sell books in English only, and occasionally in Irish, with the exception of some tourist guides of the city that are available in other languages. Some of the smaller bookshops may be willing to order special items. In general, bookshop staff know their business and 'staff picks' are usually worthwhile. Books that are in print but are not on shelves can generally be ordered (free of shipping) from most major outlets. Ordering books online through Amazon (www.amazon.co.uk) is also popular.

36 College Green
Dublin 2
Map 426 B4 598

Books Upstairs

01 679 6807 | *www.booksupstairs.com*
Probably Ireland's foremost independent bookseller, Books Upstairs is known in the city as a heavily academic bookshop. In addition to books, cultural magazines and journals are also on offer and prices are truly as good as advertised. Teachers and

287

lecturers are also in for a treat as Books Upstairs specialises in bulk buys for classes, which means that students reap the rewards as well. Browsers should keep a tight hold on the purse strings, however, as every visit seems to unearth a treasure that shouldn't be left behind. Open from 10:00 to 19:00 Monday to Friday, Saturdays from 10:00 to 18:00, and Sundays from 13:00 to 18:00.

Borders Books

Blanchardstown Centre
Dublin 15

01 823 5888 | *www.bordersstores.co.uk*

Borders not only sells a wide variety of books, but is said to have the biggest magazine rack in Dublin – which is not hard to believe once it is seen. In addition to literary offerings, Borders also stocks Paperchase stationery and shelters a Starbucks cafe, which provides a meeting place for book groups. They also organise children's events throughout the year. Unfortunately it is rumoured that Borders will be franchising out this location in the future, but with the loyal following it has gained investors would do well to keep the environment the same.

Cathach Rare Books

10 Duke St
Dublin 2
Map 430 B1 **580**

01 671 8676 | *www.rarebooks.ie*

For 20th century Irish literature lovers, Cathach Books will become their headquarters. In addition to general stock, first editions of Joyce and Yeats can be found in the shop, as well as a wide variety of antiquarian maps and topographical treatises. For those not intrigued by Cathach's shelves (there might be one or two out there), an online search facility is available on the website.

Chapters Books

108/109 Middle Abbey St
Dublin 1
Map 426 A3 **582**

01 872 3297

Voracious readers take note – Chapters buys back used books. This service is incredibly rare in Dublin, and while the prices are not much (€2 is common), dropping in a large number will result in either enough cash to purchase something new or enough store credit to take home a number of used books. The basement is reserved for the adventurous only as the hodge-podge of stacks would drive those in need of order right up the (heaving) walls, but the potential for an out-of-print find is half the fun. If you're looking for something that is in print but out of stock, they'll gladly order it for you. Open Monday to Wednesday from 09:30 to 18:30, Thursdays, Fridays and Saturdays from 09:30 until 20:00, and Sundays from 12:00 to 18:30.

Dubray Books

36 Grafton St
Dublin 2
Map 430 B1 **599**

01 677 5568

Dubray Books has a premier, multi-storey shop on Grafton Street that lures customers in through eye-catching displays. Once inside, the shop doesn't disappoint. A wide variety of fiction titles cover the ground floor and non-fiction is shelved both by subject and alphabetically on the upper floors. Some cute stationery is on offer, as are a few bookmarks and other accessories, but nothing takes away from the books themselves. Even magazines and newspapers are banished, so bibliophiles are in for a treat. Be sure to check out the display windows for notices of visiting authors, as Dubray's is often a welcoming stop for book tours. Open Monday to Friday from 09:00 to 22:00, until 18:00 on Saturdays and open from 11:00 until 18:00 on Sundays.

Eason Books

40 Lower O'Connell St
Dublin 1
Map 426 B3 **600**

01 858 3800 | *www.buy4now.ie/eason*

Easons is probably Ireland's premier bookseller and its flagship store, on O'Connell Street, spans four floors with its offerings of books, magazines, newspapers, stationery, DVDs, CDs, toys and more. The magazine selection is large with many foreign languages represented, and Tower Records has a smaller concession upstairs. The Muse Café offers browsers a nice rest area, and those that don't want to leave the comfort of their own homes can shop online. Pre-releases can also be ordered online. Open from 08:30 to 18:45 Monday to Wednesday, on Fridays until 19:45, and on Saturdays and Thursdays until 20:45. It also opens between 12:00 and 18:00 on Sundays.

Hodges Figgis

56-58 Dawson St
Dublin 2
Map 430 B1 604

01 677 4754 | *www.hodgesfiggis.com*
Made famous by a mention in James Joyce's Ulysses, Hodges Figgis has an old-world feel that often delights browsers, as does the open and airy floor layouts. The shop is well stocked, and carries an array of Irish interest titles, as well as stationery upstairs. Comfortable chairs are scattered throughout the upper floors, making the wide front windows an excellent place to sit on a rainy day. If something is not in stock, the knowledgeable shop assistants will place a special order. If you can hold out for the sales you'll be richly rewarded with a good deal of stock reduced to as little as €5. Loyalty cards also bring frequent customers savings throughout the year. Open from 09:00 daily. Late night opening on Thursdays until 20:00. Open Sundays from 12:00 until 18:00.

Hughes & Hughes

Stephen's Green
Centre
Dublin 2
Map 430 A2 26

01 478 3060 | *www.hughesbooks.com*
Having just completed a major renovation, Hughes & Hughes is back in fine form with a spacious store that stocks just enough to keep the tourists happy, making it slightly heavy on Irish interest coffee table books and biographies. Unfortunately this branch is too small to compete with other city centre giants, but the Irish interest sections are well stocked and its children's section is particularly inviting. Some comfy chairs are scattered throughout, and the staff are not known to hustle so browsing or killing time here is a joy.

Murder Ink

15 Dawson St
Dublin 2
Map 430 B1 585

01 677 7570 | *murderbk@iol.ie*
As you might guess from the name, Murder Ink specialises in murder, mystery and suspense novels and is even a bit dark and mysterious. The staff are knowledgeable about the stock and more than willing to make suggestions for new customers, which is helpful given that there are literally hundreds of titles in stock. Quite a few American imports are available here, and a few atmospheric accessories such as busts and prints are for sale as well. A must see for any serious murder or mystery fan. Call ahead for opening hours.

Reads Of Nassau Street

24-25 Nassau St
Dublin 2
Map 430 C1 589

01 679 6011 | *www.readsbooks.ie*
More like an over-stuffed newsagent than a bookshop, Reads attracts customers with not only its willingness to order books and magazines, but also with its cut-price stationery. All books and magazines (including a wide selection in foreign languages) are subject to a 10% discount on the already discounted prices, and the basement stationery shop offers bargain basement prices that attract students. A comparatively large cookery book section offers some of the best deals in Dublin, and Richard & Judy Book Club selections are almost always on the shelf. Some items are also available for purchase online. Opens at 08:30 daily. There's late night shopping on the weekend until 19:30 and it's also open from 11:00 to 18:00 on Sundays.

289

7 Dawson St
Dublin 2
Map 430 B1 **611**

Waterstone's

01 679 1415 | *www.waterstones.co.uk*

Located directly across the street from Hodges Figgis, Waterstone's does not suffer for its location. In fact, most consumers bounce between the two to fulfil their reading needs. Like any branch of the Waterstone's chain, this shop features slick displays, good stock and some great 'three for two' deals during the sales. Its main distinguishing features are the delicious Readers Café upstairs and the Irish interest shelves holding pride of place on the ground floor. Open daily from 09:00. There's late night opening until 20:00 on Thursdays and the store opens from 11:00 to 18:00 on Sundays.

Camera Equipment

Other options **Electronics & Home Appliances** p.293, **Photography** p.249

Picture It
For those who don't
have the eye
themselves, the
National Photographic
Archive in Temple Bar
(01 671 0073) regularly
stages exhibitions and
also offers
competitively priced
courses for beginners
or advanced
photographers (see
p.249 for more on
photography classes).

With so much going on in the city, you'll want to capture your Dublin memories from the very beginning so don't leave home without your camera. Unfortunately prices in Ireland are steep for even a run-of-the-mill digital camera so if you have the chance to shop at Duty Free while outside the country you should take it. Waiting for the sales will also likely net you big savings with outdated cameras descending to prices as low as €100, while still carrying the standard 90 day warranty as well. If you are stranded in Dublin without a camera, try one of the branches of Camera Centre Dublin (01 677 5594, www.cameracentre.ie), Pixels (01 878 6166, www.pixels.ie), or Conn's Cameras at 54 Clarendon Street (01 677 7179, www.connscameras.ie). There are plenty of camera shops that offer second-hand gear and will repair your camera if anything should go wrong. For those who haven't gone digital, all the usual films (and some of the more unusual ones) are available in the city and there is a good choice of facilities for developing your masterpieces, from professional labs to chemists. The latter are not only the most economical option, but will surprise you with their mostly excellent quality. Those looking for more professional supplies should check out the Society of Wedding Portrait Photographers' (SWPP) list of photographic suppliers for useful contacts, links and news of photographic events taking place in the nearby UK (www.swpp.co.uk). The Irish Photographer's Website (www.irishphotographers.ie) also contains useful information for Dublin shutterbugs.

Carpets

Other options **Bargaining** p.283, **Souvenirs** p.314

Whether you're simply covering your floor or attempting to make an investment, Dublin has a number of carpet outlets that should suit your purpose. The Carpet Showrooms (www.thecarpetshowrooms.com) have branches all over the city and Clerys department store (www.clerys.com) has a useful section that offers remainders at bargain prices. Those looking for a more upscale purchase should visit Kashan Oriental Carpets (www.kashancarpets.ie), Pars Gallery (www.parsgallery.com) or Myles Quirke (http://mylesquirke.com), who also does valuations and leasing. For other stockists, check out the Golden Pages (www.goldenpages.ie).

Clothes

Other options **Beachwear** p.286, **Lingerie** p.305, **Sports Goods** p.315, **Shoes** p.313

You'll see every kind of fashion on the streets of Dublin which means there's never the 'But I have no place to wear it!' excuse when checking out new threads. Though it can be a costly hobby, clothes shopping in the city is practically mandatory since all of the Yummy Mummies, Daddy's Girls and Mammy's Boys need to be right on trend. And don't think that the Pretty/Preppy/Sporty Boys get away without clothes shopping either. Most Dubliners buy their clothes in the large department stores or high-street chain stores that populate the city street corners, though some independent boutiques still hold their own and luxury designers are taking up concessions as well. To find a list of stores in the city, just go to the Shopping section that interests you for an idea of what's out there.

A Stitch In Time

For those looking for a unique look, making friends with a smart tailor is a good idea, see p.119 for more.

Unusual Sizes

Unusual sizes can be hard to find in Dublin as both 'big and tall' and petite collections are scarce. Principles do a solid petite line for women, and Simply Be (www.simplybe.ie) has just entered the online market supplying fashion finds for women with curves. Mr. Big 'n' Tall (www.mrbigmenswear.com) also operates an online store as well as a shop in the suburbs.

Accessories

Whether it's a punchy umbrella to hold off the rain, a cosy scarf to keep away the chill or a giant plastic necklace to distract from an otherwise mundane outfit, accessories are de rigueur in Dublin. Urban Outfitters is a haven for the tragically hip as are high-street favourites Accessorize and Claire's Accessories, which provide budget versions of catwalk trimmings. All kinds of jewellery, scarves, belts and bags can be found at the Kilkenny Design Centre, and the Designyard incorporating Whichcraft supplies accessories for both the body and home. The Temple Bar Fashion and Design Market provides appreciative audiences with the best up-and-coming designers' bags, belts, gloves, hats, jewellery, broaches and more, and Oshun can tempt even the most over-accessorised with new ways to part with their cash. Those looking for sumptuous leather goods should head to Chesneau (though waiting for the half price sales in January and June will get you double your money). For something a little more upmarket, add a little sparkle to an outfit at Rhinestones, a jewellery maiden's haven of vintage costume jewellery. Otherwise, you can invest in the real thing at Appleby's or Boodles. Department stores like Arnotts and Clerys also stock a wide range of accessories while Harvey Nichols and Brown Thomas provide that certain something for a fanciful evening, including Chanel and Louis Vuitton bags.

Summer dresses

Designer Clothing

Designer clothing is relatively new to Dublin but it's catching on fast. Brown Thomas stocks Armani Collezioni, Balenciaga, Burberry, Chanel, Christian Dior, Derek Lam, Edun (hometown hero Bono and wife's new line), Hermès and much more. Harvey Nichols isn't falling far behind with its collections including Marc Jacobs, Pucci, Diane von Furstenberg and Missoni (to name a few), plus accessories from Cherry Chau, Alexander McQueen and what seems like endless Paul Smith. Both department stores also feature the creme de la creme of international footwear in their respective showrooms, so a quick ogle at Repetto flats at Harvey Nichols or the scarlet soles of Christian Louboutin at Brown Thomas won't hurt anyone.

Clothes

A Star Is Born	50 Drury Street	01 677 0406
A-Wear	26 Grafton Street	01 872 4644
Accessorize	38 Grafton Street	01 671 7005
Appleby's	Johnson's Court, Grafton Street	01 679 9572
Arnotts	12 Henry Street	01 805 0400
Boodles	71 Grafton Street	01 679 0203
Brown Thomas	88-95 Grafton Street	01 605 6666
Chesneau	37 Wicklow Street	01 672 9199
Chica	Westbury Mall, Harry Street	01 671 9836
Claire's Accessories	Blanchardstown Centre	01 824 3938
Clerys	18-27 Lower O'Connell Street	01 8786 000
Costume	10 Castle Market Street	01 679 4188
Debenhams	Jervis Centre	01 878 1222
Designyard	12 East Essex Street	01 474 1011
Dolls	32 Clarendon Street	01 672 9004
Dunnes	Stephen's Green Shopping Centre	01 478 0188
Enable Ireland Shop	25 Capel Street	01 873 3867
Fran & Jane	Clarendon Street	01 672 9176
H&M	Dundrum Town Centre	01 299 1505
Harlequin	13 Castle Market	01 671 0202
Harvey Nichols	Dundrum Town Centre	01 291 0488
Jenny Vander	50 Drury Street	01 677 0406
Kennedy & McSharry	39 Nassau Street	01 677 8770
Lara	1 Dame Lane	01 6707 951
Laura Ashley	60-61 Grafton Street	01 679 5433
LifeBoat Shop	168 Lower Rathmines Road	01 497 4870
Louis Copeland & Sons	18-19 Wicklow Street	01 872 1600
Marks & Spencer	15-20 Grafton Street	01 478 4755
Monsoon	38 Grafton Street	01 671 7322
Mr. Big 'n' Tall	Goatstown Road	01 288 0164
Next	67 Grafton Street	01 679 3300
Oasis	3 North Street, Stephen's Green	01 671 4477
Oshun	Castlegate, Lord Edward Street	01 677 8539
Penneys	37-39 Lower O'connell Street	01 872 0466
Principles	72 Grafton Street	01 296 2926
Rhinestones	18 Street Andrew Street	01 679 0759
Rococo	Westbury Mall	01 670 4007
Susan Hunter Lingerie	Westbury Mall	01 679 1271
Temple Bar Fashion and Design Market	Cows Lane, Temple Bar	01 677 2255
Top Man	Jervis Centre	01 822 2194
TopShop	Jervis Street	01 672 5009
Urban Outfitters	7 1/2 Fownes Street, Templebar	01 670 6202
WaWa	3 Wynnefield Road	01 496 1766
Whichcraft	Saul's Court, Cows lane	01 474 1011
Zara	Roches Stores, Henry Street	01 291 0700

Vintage Clothing

Vintage fashion remains a firm favourite with Dublin fashionistas and revolutionary students alike. Jenny Vander is the pinnacle of vintage shopping in Dublin, with its stock of fashion and accessories dating as far back as the 18th century (and no pieces on offer that were produced later than 1950). Legend has it that supermodels and actresses can be found prowling the nooks and crannies of this store, and some stock has been sold at auction to collectors and sourced for film costumes around the world. Right around the corner from Jenny Vander, literally, is Harlequin, which is chock-a-block with shirts, shoes, jackets, dresses and bags – most from the 20th century. The Eager Beaver is often described as a retro or thrift shop and while it used to be known for great bargains, it has become slightly pricey of late. The collection of coloured leather jackets (powder blue, anyone?) is not to be missed, and anyone interested in old school T-shirts will want to make a beeline for the Eager Beaver's racks. Some great vintage deals can also be found at A Star is Born, though this garage-like shop opens randomly (it's part of Jenny Vander) and the staff are not always the most knowledgeable about the stock. Finally, charity shops such as the WaWa (Women's Aid), Lifeboat and Enable Ireland can be a great source of vintage gear, though if something catches your eye in the window you'll want to ask what day the display goes on sale because it's first come, first served in these urban jungles.

Boutique Shopping

Boutique shopping is alive and well in Dublin with many independent clothes stores still thriving. Louis Copeland & Sons remains the premiere men's suit establishment in the city, though the lads who favour Kennedy and McSharry (including the entire Irish rugby team) might disagree. Costume stocks a wide selection of elegant women's apparel, but girly girls will be in heaven at the Westbury Mall (see table above) which is home to Rococo, Chica, Dolls, and Fran & Jane – all indie shops selling quirky, sparkly, and frilly women's clothing and accessories. And for those who need a little confidence underneath their new outfits, Susan Hunter Lingerie is in the mall as well. Lara on Dame Lane is worth a visit for casual clothing, and a quick stroll down the road to Suffolk Street brings boutique shoppers to Avoca Handweavers, the mothership of all things bright and beautiful (see p.365). Women's clothing and accessories, bath products, books, kitchenware, children's wear and toys all compete for space in this five-floor store.

High-Street Shopping

The bread and butter of Dublin clothing is the myriad of high-street brands selling in the city. Dunnes Stores, Penneys, Marks & Spencer and Debenhams all offer hard-wearing clothes for the whole family at reasonable prices, and department stores like Clerys and Arnotts offer a number of different brands all under one roof including Gap, Tommy Hilfiger, Old Navy, FCUK, Liz Claiborne, Wallis, East, Timberland, Esprit and more. Next offers both men and women great work clothes at value conscious prices and both Laura Ashley and Monsoon offer women good wardrobe basics for both the working week and the weekend. TopShop and TopMan both stock trendy pieces at affordable prices, as do H&M and Zara. Women are especially lucky as A-Wear and Oasis seem to make it their mission to supply an ever-changing array of cheap and cheerful outfits. high-street shopping has never been so easy.

Beth Friends

Clever fashionistas will want to keep in touch with Boulevard Beth in Cork city (021 427 4300) for updates on when owner Beth Haughton will once again bring her designer wares to the Merrion Hotel for an open evening.

Babelicious

If you can't bear the thought of paying designer prices but can never seem to leave the designer pieces behind, log on to Billion Dollar Babes (www.billiondollarbabes.ie) immediately for more information on when this travelling designer sale will next hit Dublin (generally twice a year, but get on the mailing list quick).

Computers

Other options **Electronics & Home Appliances** p.293

Only about 50% of Irish households own a home computer, but Dubliners tend to lead the pack. Unfortunately for technophiles the latest technology tends to take a little while to get to Dublin, but once here there is a wide selection of gadgets, hardware and software available in the city. Dell (www.dell.ie) will custom make and ship a computer to your specifications, while Hewlett Packard (www.hp.com/ie) also offers custom service. The Sony Centre (www.sony.ie) has branches throughout the city that sell the coveted Sony Viao laptops, and Apple Macs can be bought online (www.apple.com/ireland_store) or from 3G outlets around the city (www.buy4now.ie/3G). Peats World of Electronics (www.peats.com) and Dixons at the Jervis Centre (01 878 1515) both sell a wide variety of computers and electronics, but those looking for truly affordable prices might want to keep an eye out for Dunnes Stores (www.dunnesstores.ie) specials – as long as brands you're unfamiliar with aren't a problem. No matter where you buy your computer, a short warranty is standard and buying the extended warranty is a good idea as computer repairs, especially for laptops, are often completed outside of the city or even the country, so shipping costs alone can sky-rocket.

Electronics & Home Appliances

Other options **Camera Equipment** p.290, **Computers** p.293

Due to Ireland's quirky standard voltage of 220V AC at 50Hz, it's best to buy electronics and home appliances when you arrive, and forget about trying to take them with you when you go. A great selection of second-hand goods is often advertised via expat groups such as the American Women's Club of Dublin (www.awcd.net), online via sites such as Freecycle Dublin (http://groups.yahoo.com/group/freecycleDublin/) and

293

Gumtree (www.gumtree.ie), as well as in local papers and on supermarket noticeboards. Department stores also carry a wide selection of electronics and home appliances, as do dedicated electronics stores across the city.

Argos

Stephen's Green
Centre
Dublin 2
Map 430 A2 **26**

01 478 0095 | *www.argos.ie*

Argos offers a good range of reasonably priced electronics and home appliances. Brands like Cookworks, Kenwood and Morphy Richards are all available and when the weather turns warmer, the selection of standing and desk fans come in handy. Home entertainment goods from Sony, Panasonic and Philips are also available. You won't be able to get any big-ticket items like fridges and freezers here, but you should be able to cover the basic smaller ones such as toasters and kettles. Home delivery is available for some purchases. You can view their catalogue online and reserve items you want to buy – this should save some time queuing in the shop. Other outlets in the city centre include those in the Jervis Centre and Ilac Centre, but you'll also find stores further out in Swords, Tallaght, Dun Laoghaire, Rathfarnham and Dundrum. See the website for a store locator.

Arnotts

12 Henry St
Dublin 1
Map 426 A3 **6**

01 805 0400 | *www.arnotts.ie*

The basement in Arnotts contains a vast selection of electronics and home appliances including steamers, rice cookers, microwaves, bread makers and more. Those who can't wake up without a mug of something hot should also check out the extensive electric kettle and coffee, espresso, cappuccino maker selections, as well as grinders and teapots. There is also a wedding list service. Limited online shopping is available.

B&Q

Liffey Valley
Retail Park
Clondalkin
Dublin 22

01 629 9499 | *www.diy.com*

The mother of all DIY stores, B&Q stocks a huge range of home appliances including refrigerators, freezers, washers, dryers, dishwashers and more. They also do a lighting range and heating and cooling systems. Delivery is available, though it may take a few weeks, but installation is generally left up to you and your trusty toolbox, unless you're prepared to pay them extra to do it for you. Other stores can be found in Swords (01 870 8599) and in Tallaght (01 6804 600).

Dixons

Jervis Centre
Dublin 1
Map 426 A3 **572**

01 878 1515 | *www.dixons.co.uk*

This trusty UK retailer provides electronics and home appliances at reasonable prices, though the Dublin branch is fairly limited. You can talk to the salespeople about ordering in items seen on the website though, and they usually oblige. You'll find audio equipment, small electrical appliances like vacuum cleaners and irons, and bigger household appliances. Ask about home delivery too. There are also outlets in Blanchardstown (01 452 2855) Quarryvale (01 626 9008) and Swords (01 890 4531).

Kitchenworld

28 Finglas
Business Centre
Jamestown Rd
Finglas

01 864 6028 | *www.kitchenworld.ie*

Stocking Bosch, Hotpoint and Powerpoint appliances, as well as kitchen accessories such as door handles and rails, Kitchenworld is well worth the trip out of the city to Finglas. Warranties are as standard by manufacturer, and staff are both knowledgeable and pleasant. Nationwide delivery is available, though complete kitchen fit-outs from design to installation are the norm here.

25 Parnell St
Dublin 1
Map 425 F3 `590`

Peats World of Electronics

01 872 7799 | www.peats.com

Peats World of Electronics stocks an excellent range of home entertainment electronics including computers and laptops, DVD players, televisions, and digital radio components. The store also carries a great variety of cables and adaptors, tools and even books on electronics. Bose and Yamaha fans should head here for a good selection of their favourite products. There is another store at 12 College Green (01 672 5555) and in Blanchardstown Shopping Centre (01 826 2222).

Eyewear

Other options **Sports Goods** p.315

Since you're no one in Dublin without a pair of designer shades (dahling), it's a good thing that quality eyewear outlets abound – with the backing of a qualified optician in most. Specsavers is a trusty nationwide chain that offers eye tests for a reasonable €27 and this can often be covered by insurance or qualify for tax back (ask in store for details). Specsavers is also the home of truly affordable glasses and contact lenses, with some complete pairs starting for as little as €50 and designer 'two for one' offers appearing regularly. Insight Opticians is another trusty chain, while McGivneys offers great service and styles. MacNally Opticians offers luxury frames and shades (with a luxury price tag), as do Optica and Dixon Hempenstall. Most opticians are able to take a reading from existing glasses if you're stuck without your original prescription, and most also offer daily and monthly contact lenses. Prescription glasses and sunglasses can be made in just a few hours if everything is in stock, but usually take no more than a week to prepare if something needs to be ordered. Those looking for non-prescription sunglasses should check out Boots (with stores all over the city, www.boots.com) for value accessories or the Sunglass Hut for name brands.

Eyewear		
Boots	Stephen's Green Shopping Centre	01 478 4368
Dixon Hempenstall	14 Suffolk Street	01 677 1334
Insight Opticians	5 Cows Lane	01 677 2070
MacNally Opticians	Nutgrove Shopping Centre	01 494 1066
McGivneys	41 Henry Street	01 873 0544
Optica	Royal Hibernian Way, Dawson Street	01 677 4705
Sunglass Hut	Liffey Valley Shopping Centre	01 822 0150

Flowers

Other options **Gardens** p.297

For a pretty bouquet that will last a few days and won't put a dent in your wallet, you can't beat the flower stalls on Grafton Street. Likewise Marks & Spencer offers pre-made bouquets of roses and tulips that are guaranteed for at least a week and cost about €5 each. If you're looking for something with a little more pizzazz, take a quick detour to Blooming Amazing in Ranelagh or just ring up to ask about their city-wide flower and plant delivery. A1 Rosary Florist online florist takes your delivery options a little wider with guaranteed deliveries worldwide from their Irish Florist website (1800 490 490, www.irishflorist.com), and Interflora associates like Flowers in Dublin make sure you have plenty of delivery options as well. Brides to be will want to check out the aptly named Mad Flowers – a gold medal winner at the 2007 Bloom! flower show – and Sheila's Flower Shops which, though they are Bray based, deliver across the world and are an Irish Flower Council 'Bridal Florist of the Year' winner.

Grafton Street Flowers

Bespoke services for special events are the norm with Dublin florists, though those looking for a cheap and cheerful arrangement to take home can be satisfied just as easily. Plant enthusiasts should check out Garden.ie (www.garden.ie) for more information on plant centres across Ireland.

Flowers

Annuna Flower Design	Smithfield Village	01 873 5168	na
Blooming Amazing	38 Ranelagh Village	01 491 0233	www.bloomingamazing.ie
Branching Out	75b Morehampton Road	01 660 2588	na
The Flower Box	67 Mespil Road	01 660 9470	na
Flowers in Dublin	Main Street, Blanchardstown	01 820 4466	www.flowersindublin.com
Marks & Spencer	15-20 Grafton Street	01 478 4755	www.marksandspencer.com
Sheila's Flower Shops	31 Southern Cross Business Park, Boghall Road, Bray	01 276 2255	www.buy4now.ie/Sheilasflower

Food

Other options **Health Food** p.299, **Markets** p.328

Dublin has never been known for its gastronomic delights, but the food scene in the city is rapidly changing. Everyday groceries and a range of pre-prepared dinners can be bought at supermarkets like Dunnes, Tesco and Superquinn, or smaller chain stores like Londis, Spar and Centra. A weekly budget of about €80 for two people is probably average for basic items, but bargain emporiums like Aldi and Lidl have also moved into Dublin recently, bringing with them cut-price fruit, vegetables and a variety of lesser-known brands. Smaller delicatessens and speciality food shops offer more gourmet delights such as home-made conserves, excellent cheeses and organic sausages, while for bread and pastries to rival the French, La Maison des Gourmets, Queen of Tarts and La Boulangerie should satisfy. Marks & Spencer offers tasty own-brand foods, but be careful about visiting during the city's lunch hour or

Food

Blazing Salads	42 Drury Street	01 671 9552	www.blazingsalads.com
Butlers Chocolate Café	Various locations	01 671 0599	www.butlerschocolates.com
Centra	136 Capel Street	01 878 2297	www.centra.ie
Donnybrook Fair	91 Morehampton Road	01 668 3556	www.donnybrookfair.ie
Dunnes	South Great George's Street	01 611 1600	www.dunnesstores.ie
Fallon & Byrne	11-17 Exchequer Street	01 472 1010	www.fallonandbyrne.com
La Boulangerie	47a-47b Bulfin Road	01 476 3818	na
La Maison des Gourmets	15 Castle Market	01 672 7258	na
Listons	25 Lower Camden Street	01 405 4779	na
Londis	32 Wexford Street	01 475 4622	www.londis.ie
Marks & Spencer	Jervis Centre	01 872 8833	www.marksandspencer.com
Mortons	15-17 Dunville Avenue	01 497 1254	www.mortons.ie
Olio & Farina	17 Camden Street	01 475 9641	www.olioefarina.com
Oriental Emporium	25 South Great George's Street	01 677 8985	na
Queen of Tarts	4 Cork Hill Dame Street	01 670 7499	na
Sheridan Cheesemongers	11 South Anne Street	01 679 3143	www.sheridanscheesemongers.com
Silk Road Café	Chester Beatty Library, Dublin Castle Grounds	01 407 0770	www.silkroadcafe.ie
Spar	6 Smithfield Village	01 874 7710	www.spar.ie
Superquinn	Northside Shopping Centre, Coolock	01 847 7111	www.superquinn.ie
Supersam Polish Food Express	15 Dorset Street	01 873 4130	na
Temple Bar Food Market	Meeting House Square	01 677 2255	na
Tesco	15 Lower Baggot Street	01 676 1253	www.tesco.ie

Organic food market in Temple Bar

after-work rush hour as crazed professionals ruthlessly fight over the take home meals.

Another food shopping option in Dublin is to wait for the weekend food markets. Temple Bar puts on a great Saturday organic farmers market in Meeting House Square, and Howth has a similar deal on Sundays in the harbour.

Speciality Food Stores

On the more specialised side, oriental emporiums have sprung up across the city offering packaged and frozen foods direct from Asia (as well as a great selection of woks and steaming baskets) and Camden Street leads the way for halal butchers and Middle Eastern markets. Supersam is a Polish food shop, and a variety of African markets flourish near Moore Street. Listons is a fantastic Italian speciality store, as is the internationally known Olio & Farino. For those with a little more money to spend, Fallon & Byrne, Donnybrook Fair and Mortons are all renowned for their delectable selections of meats and cheeses, as well as imported wines, biscuits and other nibbles. Sheridan's Cheesemongers can be smelled from several paces, but hold your nose and indulge in some of the best cheeses in Ireland. The Temple Bar Food Market also offers a wide array of speciality items and fresh fruit and vegetables.

A Gourmet Palate

For those looking for gourmet delights while out and about, Butlers Chocolate Cafes offer the some of the best sugar highs in the city with their traditional Irish chocolates, although the Queen of Tarts is definitely a close runner up due to its sweet and savoury baked goods. La Maison des Gourmets quite possibly offers the best bread in Dublin, and their breakfast pastries are out of this world. Blazing Salads is the place to go for vegetarian options, while those with a sweet tooth will want to check out La Boulangerie for both traditional French and Middle Eastern treats (including their gorgeous gingerbread). The baklava at the Silk Road Café (p.351) will having you coming back again and again but don't miss the generous helpings of fresh salads, quiches, hummus or baba ghanoush either. The cafe even shares some of its recipes online (www.silkroadcafe.ie), although it's probably nicer just to let them spoil you.

Gardens

Other options **Flowers** p.295, **Hardware & DIY** p.299

Though the Irish love their gardens, few Dubliners are lucky enough to have the space to develop their own. Instead, visiting the Phoenix Park, St Stephen's Green, Merrion Square and the Iveagh Gardens (see p.194) provide enough greenery to make up for the lack of privacy. Die-hard gardeners do have some options, however, for advice, support and everyday garden needs such as Oasis Florist and Garden Centre in Terenure, Blackbanks Garden Centre on the Howth Road, and Forest Flame on Lower Kimmage Road (see table). For all the basics, Mr Middleton Garden Shop in the city centre will see to it that you have all your seeds, bulbs, pots, electronic dog and cat scarers and shrubs to make the best garden you can.

Gardens

Gardens			
B&Q	Liffey Valley Retail Park East, Coldcut Road, Clondalkin	01 629 9499	www.diy.com
Blackbanks Garden Centre	754 Howth Road, Blackbanks, Raheny	01 832 7047	na
Forest Flame	173 Lower Kimmage Road	01 406 4831	na
Mr Middleton Garden Shop	58 Mary Street	01 873 1118	www.mrmiddleton.com
Oasis Florist & Garden Centre	90 Terenure Road North	01 490 0112	na

Those with more exotic yearnings should also register at Garden.ie (www.garden.ie) where the 'For Sale' board allows specific requests to be placed and offers made from across the country. B&Q also stocks garden equipment and furniture. They also have stores in Swords (01 8708 599) and in Tallaght (01 6804 600), as well as Liffey Valley (see table). See the website for further details (www.diy.com).

Gifts

Unfortunately most of the specialised gift shops in Dublin lean towards items covered in pictures of pint glasses, leprechauns and shamrocks, which verge ever so slightly on the tacky side. Someone must enjoy these creations, however, as Carolls Gift Shops have spread throughout the city at an alarming rate. Those interested in Irish gifts of a

Gifts			
Arnotts	12 Henry Street	01 805 0400	www.arnotts.ie
Blarney Woollen Mills	21-23 Nassau Street	01 451 6111	www.blarney.com
Brown Thomas	88-95 Grafton Street	01 605 6666	www.brownthomas.com
Carrolls Gift Shops	2-5 Westmoreland Street	01 677 5088	na
Clerys	18-27 Lower O'Connell St	01 878 6000	www.clerys.com
Dublin Tourism Centre	Suffolk Street	01 605 7700	www.visitdublin.com
Hallmark	31 Grafton Street	01 679 4958	na
Kilkenny Design Centre	5/6 Nassau Street	01 677 7075	www.kilkennyshop.com
Trinity Sweater Shop	30 Nassau Street	01 671 9543	www.sweatershop.ie
Weir & Sons	96-99 Grafton Street	01 677 9678	www.weirandsons.ie

slightly higher standard should head to the Dublin Tourism Gift Shop and the Kilkenny Design Centre for moderately priced arts, crafts, crystal, china, jewellery and leather goods. The Blarney Woollen Mills and the Trinity Sweater Shop offer traditional woollen and linen items.

Blarney Woollen Mills

Gifts for special occasions are much easier to find, with Arnotts, Clerys and Brown Thomas all offering wedding registries for everything from kitchen equipment to bed linens. Weir & Sons is a jeweller that also offers a wide variety of collectibles to mark Baptisms, Holy Communions and Confirmations, while Hallmark stores provide similarly sentimental items for those on a tighter budget. Of course special events can also be marked with gift cards or even cash or cheques, and a variety of 'money cards' can now be found at stationery stores and newsagents and are increasingly popular.

Hardware & DIY

Other options **Outdoor Goods** p.310

Dedicated DIY enthusiasts will need to head beyond the city limits to the homecare warehouses that have sprung up in the suburbs. B&Q offers a vast selection of tools, lighting, flooring, building, electrical and plumbing supplies and much, much more. Dedicated and knowledgeable sales staff makes it a pleasure for even hardware novices and citywide delivery as well as 'how to' guides make home installation relatively simple. Atlantic Homecare offers similar products and services with a great range of paints and painting supplies as well as outdoor storage, garden tools and power tools. Woodie's DIY offers solutions for flooring, shelving, heating and storage needs and the barbecue and patio heating ranges can't be beat for making the cool climate amenable to outdoor entertaining.

Within Dublin itself, few supermarkets carry DIY supplies so head to Northside Tool & Hardware for a mix of just about everything including pots and pans, plants and shrubs, paints and rollers and nuts and bolts. On the south side, Weirs of Baggot Street offers much the same as well as a while-you-wait key cutting service. Mulveys of Ranelagh is known for flooring, decking, hardware and paint supplies and though the store itself is crammed full of items – making it somewhat risky for those suffering from claustrophobia – the Cedar Decking line of woods and accessories has a loyal following. It is linked to Canadia Distributors so it's also the perfect place to inquire about hot tubs – if you're lucky enough to have the room for one.

Hardware & DIY

Atlantic Homecare	Liffey Valley Retail Park, Clondalkin	01 605 5088	www.buy4now.ie/atlantic
B&Q	Liffey Valley Retail Park, Clondalkin	01 629 9499	www.diy.com
Canadia Distributors	32/33 Second Av, Cookstown Ind Est	01 461 0997	na
Mulveys of Ranelagh	113-115 Ranelagh	01 496 4000	www.mulveys.com
Northside Tool & Hardware	Northside Shopping Centre, Coolock	01 848 1880	na
Weirs of Baggot Street	21 Baggot Street	01 668 5229	na
Woodie's	Arena, Whitestown Way, Tallaght	01 459 6944	www.woodiesdiy.com

Health Food

Other options **Food** p.296, **Health Clubs** p.263

Though mainstream grocery stores today carry an array of products to appeal to those with dairy and wheat allergies, celiac disease and a yen for vitamin and mineral supplements, health food stores are still the one-stop shops for those in search of healthy living. Holland and Barrett, Nourish, Health Matters, The Health Store and Tony Quinn (www.tonyquinn.com) are all health food chain stores with locations around the city selling vitamin and mineral supplements, organic and natural toiletries, aromatherapy oils, and a wide selection of healthy snacks and ingredients like soy, spelt and sprouts. The Hopsack, Down to Earth and the Nature Store are all independent shops

Health Food

Absolutely Organic	Walkinstown	01 460 0467
Be Organic	3 Dalymount, Phibsborough, rear Mews	01 838 5552
Down to Earth	73 South Great George's Street	01 671 9702
Dublin Food Co-Op	12 Newmarket	01 873 0451
Health Matters	8 Grafton Street	01 671 0166
The Health Store	Frascati Shopping Centre, Blackrock	087 329 4256
Holland & Barrett	Ilac Centre	01 872 8391
The Hopsack	Swan Centre, Lower Rathmines Road	01 496 0399
Nature Store	324a NCR, Phibsborough	01 830 4904
Nourish	Liffey Street	01 873 4098
Temple Bar Food Market	Meeting House Square	01 677 2255
Tony Quinn	66 Eccles Street	01 830 5859

299

Fresh Delivery
*For those with more
money than time,
Absolutely Organic and
Be Organic (see table
on p.299) operate box
schemes that deliver
fresh fruit and
vegetables right to
your door.*

offering chilled drinks and meals, family friendly beauty products, natural and
organic baby food and environmentally friendly cleaning supplies. Unfortunately,
prices are usually higher in health food stores than major supermarkets and retailers,
but a clear conscience is often more valuable to loyal shoppers than what's left in
their purses. See the table for contact details. A trip to the Saturday Dublin Food Co-
Op (www.dublinfood.coop) or Temple Bar Food Market will let you praise your local
suppliers face to face.

Home Furnishings & Accessories
Other options **Hardware & DIY** p.299

Since staying in is the new going out in Dublin, you'll want to make sure that your home
is comfortable and well equipped for entertaining. Montana, Classic Furniture and
Bargaintown are all dedicated furniture stores with prices to suit any budget, while
chain stores like Dunnes, Argos and Marks & Spencer are super suppliers of value
furniture and accessories. Department stores such as Clerys and Arnotts offer some
home furnishings, though furniture selections are often limited. Those looking for
something a bit different should check out Avoca, Habitat, Inreda, Laura Ashley, Pia
Bang Home and Urban Outfitters, or wander up Camden Street and Richmond Street
(Dublin 2) or Capel Street (Dublin 1) to browse antique shops like Christy Bird and quirky
independent shops selling one of a kind items. Still can't find what you're looking for?
Consider commissioning a bespoke design from John Doolin of Imbue Furniture Design
and no doubt you'll get exactly what you've been picturing in your mind.

Home Furnishings & Accessories

Argos	Stephen's Green Shopping Centre	01 478 0095	www.argos.ie
Arnotts	12 Henry Street	01 805 0400	www.arnotts.ie
Clerys	18-27 Lower O'Connell Street	01 878 6000	www.clerys.com
Dunnes Stores	Stephen's Green Shopping Centre	01 478 0188	www.dunnesstores.com

*11 Suffolk St
Dublin 2
Map 430 B1 41*

Avoca
01 677 4215 | www.avoca.ie
Avoca's range of glittery, girly home furnishings tends to delight females of all ages.
Candles, mirrors, tea sets, tea lights, decorative boxes, ingenious baskets and lush wool
blankets all fight for space in the quirky city centre store while upstairs in the children's
section a variety of hand-painted toys and nursery accessories tempt young visitors. A
limited selection of furniture – mainly just stools and the occasional chair – is on offer
and obviously made for more decorative purposes. Bring your credit cards though,
because Avoca's prices are not for the faint of heart.

*Queen St Bridge
Dublin 1
Map 425 D4 615*

Bargaintown
01 677 4015 | www.bargaintown.ie
If money is in short supply, Bargaintown is the perfect place to outfit a home from
scratch. Rugs, desks, tables, as well as full bedroom and dining sets can all be bought
either off the floor or from the catalogue, and delivery costs just €19 citywide,
regardless of the number of items in the order. Just don't expect innovative design or
exotic fabrics – Bargaintown is strictly good, solid basics.

*32 South Richmond St
Dublin 2
Map 430 A4 597*

Christy Bird
01 475 4049 | www.christybird.com
Christy Bird's South Richmond Street shop is now run by the third generation and is
apparently bigger and better than ever. Antique, second-hand and new furniture are all

Life in the fast lane?

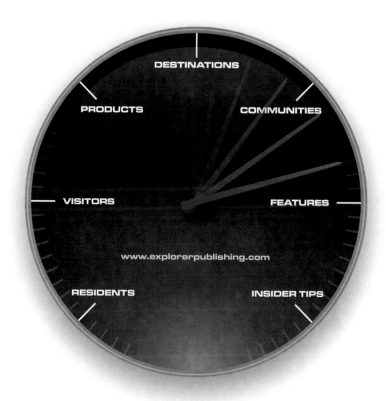

Life can move pretty quickly so make sure you keep in the know with regular updates from **www.explorerpublishing.com**

Or better still, share your knowledge and advice with others, find answers to your questions, or just make new friends in our community area

www.explorerpublishing.com – for life in real time

www.explorerpublishing.com

sold on the premises but be sure to ask a knowledgeable member of staff for advice as reproductions are often thrown into the mix as well. Prices are surprisingly affordable for many items, and new stock is introduced constantly.

3 Westend Retail Park
Blanchardstown
Dublin 15

Classic Furniture
01 822 2822 | *www.buy4now.ie/classic*

Classic furniture specialises in pieces for the bedroom, dining room and living room. Solid furniture for solid prices can be found in the showroom or ordered online, though the advertised 'international designs' may not be all that striking. A free five year warranty is offered with every piece and free home installation is also offered. Expedited delivery is available at a cost, so with the 'buy now, pay later' offers you just might have some leftover cash to splash.

6-9 Suffolk St
Dublin 2
Map 430 B1 609

Habitat
01 677 1433 | *www.habitat.ie*

Only one branch of this British chain store exists in Dublin, but since it's crammed full of contemporary chairs, tables, rugs and beds, just the one branch is probably enough. Think sleek designs and simple looks. Prices are steep at Habitat, so signing up to the mailing list is a good idea for information on 'members only' sales and discounts. Catalogues are for sale, though visiting online generally yields the same results and the interactive room planner can be a lot of fun. If you don't find exactly what you want, talk to the sales staff about special orders and deliveries.

60 Dawson St
Dublin 2
Map 430 B1 605

Harriet's House
01 677 7077

Harriet's House looks like the kind of shop that men wait outside of while their wives browse, and probably with good reason. Though everything inside the shop is of exceptional quality, Harriet's House is positively crammed with frilly, busy home accessories. Lamps, mirrors, ornate picture frames, cut glass paper weights, intricate armoires and a variety of other knick-knacks encroach on the floor space, meaning that customers must step over some stock to continue their investigations. Professional interior designers swear by Harriet's House, and it has been featured in *House and Home* magazine more than once. Bring your credit cards, and ring ahead for opening hours.

27 Redleaf
Business Park
Turvey, Donabate

Imbue Furniture Design
086 832 1922 | *www.imbuefurniture.com*

Imbue designs and manufactures contemporary furniture, though clients' pre-drawn designs are welcome also. 2D and 3D designs will be drawn up, and you will be shown sample materials, and given an indication of cost. Once the design has been finalised you will be asked to pay a deposit. Contact John Doolin via the website contact form for further information about private commissions. Delivery in the greater Dublin area is offered free of charge.

71 Lower Camden St
Dublin 2
Map 430 A3 612

Inreda
01 476 0362 | *www.inreda.ie*

Offering cool Scandinavian designs, Inreda is a favourite with the young and trendy. Accessories like candle holders, lamps, vases and futuristic rubbish bins are big sellers, as are the mod sofas and chairs. They also do a lighting range. A wedding list service is available, and the website features a 'top 10 gifts' section. Though the store itself is small, staff have big personalities and grand design dreams that can easily fill up a room – or an entire home.

60/61 Grafton St
Dublin 2
Map 430 B1 606

Laura Ashley

01 633 0050 | www.lauraashley.com

Though it has a reputation for being a grandmother's favourite, the home furnishings offered at Laura Ashley are making a comeback as shabby chic has nudged its way back into style. Stripes, florals and polka dots are a regular feature on Laura Ashley designs, but the wallpaper and bed linen prices can't be beat during the semi-annual sales. Decidedly feminine cups, glasses, candles and mirrors abound, though some leather boxes and frames might appeal to more masculine palates.

T11 Maple Av
Stillorgan
Industrial Park
Stillorgan

Montana

01 293 7000 | www.montana.ie

Montana offers modern bedroom, living room and dining room furniture from Italy, Denmark, Spain and North America. An online room planner allows shoppers to refine their thoughts at home before making the trek to the Sandyford showroom, and the home entertainment units are well known for being good value. Sales clerks are particularly helpful with tricky design decisions, and ordering special items from suppliers' catalogues is not a problem.

2 South Anne St
Dublin 2
Map 430 B1 587

Pia Bang Home

01 888 3777

Danish-born Pia Bang used to offer trendy women's fashions on Grafton Street, but recently she has moved to South Anne Street to concentrate on a country-kitchen style homewares shop. Most of the furniture is imported from across Europe and the selection leans heavily on goods from Belgium, Holland and France. Cosy accessories like mirrors, candlesticks and traditional toys are favourites here. Furniture in Pia Bang isn't cheap, but a housewarming present can be picked up for under €20. Be sure to visit often as new stock arrives monthly.

7 1/2 Fownes St
Temple Bar
Dublin 2
Map 426 A4 610

Urban Outfitters

01 670 6202 | www.urbanoutfitters.com

If you're yearning for the perfect plastic ashtray, a bobble-head doll for your dashboard or a cutting board so funky it'll make you see stars, then look no further than Urban Outfitters. It's doubtful that anyone would want to accessorise their entire home from Urban Outfitters – or could afford to, given the prices – but for unique conversation pieces it can't be beat. Be prepared for loud music, and don't bother to look at the card selection if you're easily offended.

Homeware at Dunnes

303

Jewellery, Watches & Gold

For all of its love of luxury, modern Ireland is still only just beginning to explore the lure of high quality jewellery and watches. Cheap accessories can be bought by the dozen at Accessorize and Claire's Accessories, with branches all over the city, and vintage pieces can be examined at Jenny Vander, Harlequinn and Rhinestones. A great source of silver jewellery is New Moon Silver, and just around the corner The Crown Jewels offers customers the chance to string their own beads into earrings, necklaces and bracelets. Sparkling crystal accessories can be found in Swarovski's various stores. Vivien Walsh does great feminine jewellery with a bygone era feel. For traditional Irish designs, go to the Kilkenny Design Centre, which carries collections from Newbridge Silver, Alan Ardiff and many more. Fine jewellery and gems are on offer at Appleby's, Boodles and Links of London, though the price tags are enough to send anyone into a state of shock. Similarly, the antique and estate jewellery at Windsor Antiques and Delphi Antiques is often worth saving up for. Appleby and Weir & Sons are the places to go for most brands of luxury watches, though sports watches are a great bargain at sports stores like Champion and Lifestyle Sports.

Jewellery, Watches & Gold

Accessorize	38 Grafton Street	01 671 7005	www.monsoon.co.uk
Appleby's	5/6 Johnson's Court, Grafton Street	01 679 9572	www.buy4now.ie/appleby
Boodles	71 Grafton Street	01 679 0203	www.boodles.co.uk
Champion Sports	Ilac Centre	01 872 7274	www.champion.ie
Claire's Accessories	Blanchardstown Centre	01 824 3938	www.claires.com
Crown Jewels	12 Castle Market	01 671 3452	na
Delphi Antiques	Powerscourt Townhouse Centre, Clarendon Street	01 679 0331	na
Harlequinn	13 Castle Market	01 671 0202	na
Jenny Vander	50 Druiry Street	01 677 0406	na
Kilkenny Design Centre	5/6 Nassau Street	01 677 7075	www.kilkennyshop.com
Links of London	25-26 South Anne Street	01 633 4818	www.linksoflondon.com
New Moon	28 Drury Street	01 671 1154	na
Rhinestones	18 St Andrew Street	01 679 0759	na
Swarovski	5 Grafton Street	01 633 4033	www.swarovski.com
Vivien Walsh	24 Lower Stephens Green	01 475 5031	na
Weir & Sons	96-99 Grafton Street	01 677 9678	www.weirandsons.ie
Windsor Antiques	Powerscourt Townhouse Centre, Clarendon Street	01 670 3001	na

Kids' Clothes

There are few places in Dublin where children aren't welcome, as the number of babies doing Sunday brunch duly proves, and clothing shops have responded with wardrobe options to boggle the mind. Dunnes and Penneys provide cheap and cheerful play clothes for kids, as well as inexpensive beachwear right in time for the holidays. Marks & Spencer and Benetton have casual baby and children's ranges, as do some branches of Debenhams and TK Maxx. Parents of young children will also delight in the baby and toddler ranges at Mothercare, and to a lesser extent Avoca where the few clothes available are cute but the selection is limited and prices are high. Jacadi is the place to go when children up to the age of 12 need to look smart, unless of course you take a detour and head to Jenny Wren for a dressy outfit for young children instead. If party shoes are needed to complete a look, head to The Clarks Shop, Buckle My Shoe at BT2 or Barratts Shoes. When an occasion calls for it, fancy dress costumes are readily available from Marks & Spencer, Wigwam and Clown Around. Further information on retailers specialising in children's clothing can also be found online at Clothing.ie (www.clothing.ie). Du Pareil au Meme (DPAM for those in the know) is a French label that does very affordable gorgeous and bright children's and baby clothes. They have a store in the Dundrum Centre but you can also order online at www.dupareilaumeme.com. Further information on retailers specialising in children's clothing can also be found online at Clothing.ie (www.clothing.ie).

Kids' Clothing

Avoca	Dublin 2	01 677 4215
Barratts	Dublin 2	01 8724 033
Benetton	Dublin 2	01 478 1799
Buckle My Shoe	Dublin 2	01 605 6666
The Clarks Shop	Dublin 1	01 873 2592
Clown Around	Dublin 2	01 677 5040
Debenhams	Dublin 1	01 878 1222
Du Pareil au Même	Dublin 14	01 298 6938
Dunnes Stores	Dublin 2	01 478 0188
Jacadi	Dublin 2	01 671 1418
Jenny Wren	Dublin 6	01 497 1771
Marks & Spencer	Dublin 2	01 679 7855
Mothercare	Dublin 2	01 478 4755
Penneys	Dublin 1	01 872 7788
TK Maxx	Dublin 2	01 475 7080
Wigwam	Dublin 2	01 478 1290

Lingerie
Other options **Clothes** p.290

Bloomers
If you're searching for lingerie in Dublin, get ready to use the thesaurus. 'Knickers', 'pants', 'underpants', and 'underwear' are all used to describe good old undies, though 'panties' may cause a few snickers here and there.

Packs of cotton underwear are available in most Dunnes and Penneys stores, though Marks & Spencer is renowned for its affordable, basic lingerie as well as enthusiastic sales assistants just dying to get a hold of you with their tape measures. La Senza offers an array of affordable bras, a variety of underwear options (boy shorts and low cut options seem to fly right out the door). Slinky pyjamas and nightdresses, and special occasion lingerie, can be found at Susan Hunter Lingerie and from Agent Provocateur and La Perla, both at Brown Thomas. Fetish fans should traipse down to Miss Fantasia's Exotic Adult Boutique (or one of the other adult shops on South William Street), though Anne Summers might suffice for those just dipping their toes into this saucy scene.

Lingerie

Anne Summers	30-31 Lower O'Connell Street	01 878 1385	www.annesummers.com
Brown Thomas	88-95 Grafton Street	01 605 6666	www.brownthomas.com
Dunnes Stores	Stephen's Green Centre	01 478 0188	www.dunnesstores.com
La Senza	Dundrum Town Centre	01 623 2210	www.lasenza.com
Marks & Spencer	Jervis Centre	01 872 8833	www.marksandspencer.com
Miss Fantasia's Exotic Adult Boutique	25 South William Street	01 671 3734	www.missfantasia.ie
Penneys	47 Mary Street	01 872 7788	www.primark.co.uk
Susan Hunter Lingerie	Westbury Mall, Grafton Street	01 679 1271	www.susanhunterlingerie.ie

Luggage & Leather
Other options **Shipping** p.283

The Irish love to travel, so luggage and leather goods are widely available. The Bag Shop (www.thebagshop.ie) offers a range of cheaper luggage, including Jansport backpacks and bags, and Dunnes' (www.dunnes.ie) own-brand luggage usually performs well on short trips. Benetton's (www.benetton.ie) bright, hard-backed cases are both durable and easy to spot, and with the one-off pieces at TK Maxx (www.tkmaxx.com), you can often pick up a brand name on the cheap (but steer clear if you like matched sets). A variety of international brands like Delsey, Antler and Samsonite can also be found at Adamson Luggage (www.adamsonluggage.com), and their range of small leather goods including wallets, pencil cases, passport covers and glasses cases can't be beaten – except when they drop their own prices at the semi-annual sales. Chesneau's

305

(www.chesneaudesign.com) executive and travel ranges will delight first class travellers, as will the luxury luggage at Louis Vuitton and Prada at Brown Thomas (www.brownthomas.com), both of which also offer an array of small leather goods.

Maternity Items

The past few years have seen an explosion of maternity shops in Dublin. Beautiful Shapes specialises in formal, black tie maternity wear for hire, while Nelo and Mama Mondo offer beautiful, though pricey, smart and trendy clothes. Bella Mama stocks both clothing and gorgeous maternity lingerie, while Marks & Spencer also does a maternity line that matches the clothing offered in their women's collections. Mothercare is a source of almost everything you'll need for a successful pregnancy and birth, as is The Pregnancy Store. Here you'll find clothing and underwear for expectant mothers, and a host of treats such as morning sickness oil, Preggie Pops (to combat nausea) and belly belts and baby belts to help support bumps. The Pregnancy Store also offers a spa menu for pregnant women and new mothers, including an option for hospital visit make-up application, and a dedicated yoga and Pilates studio for evening classes. Bump and Beyond offers similar services in their private treatment room, as well as a host of beautiful clothes from Ireland and Europe, including the sought after maternity jeans. Finally, if you're too tired to face the crowds, call MomSoon and revel in their personal maternity shopping service in the comfort of your own home, or log on to Gumtree (www.gumtree.ie) and search for second-hand maternity and nursing items at affordable prices.

Maternity Items		
Beautiful Shapes	15 Main Street	01 601 0824
Bella Mama	The Triangle, Ranelagh	01 496 8598
Bump & Beyond	Cooldriona Court, Main Street	01 807 9943
Mama Mondo	51 Clontarf Road, City Centre	01 833 4334
Marks & Spencer	15-20 Grafton Street	01 679 7855
MomSoon	90 Ashton Avenue, Knocklyon	087 204 6917
Mothercare	Stephen's Green Centre	01 478 4755
Nelo	39 Clarendon Street	01 679 1336
The Pregnancy Store	53 Dawson Street	01 671 8111

Medicine

Other options **General Medical Care** p.129

Small Print ◀
Not all medications are dispensed with detailed instructions or information on interactions, so feel free to ask pharmacists for further information at any time.

Pharmacies are also known as chemists in Dublin, and they are usually either independent shops or part of larger drug store chains. Rarely are chemists open 24 hours, though the few who are will generally advertise this fact aggressively in neon lights. Not all chemists' staff are qualified, though pharmacists will always display their diplomas in plain sight. Pharmacists are able to give over-the-counter pharmaceutical advice, but GPs should still be consulted for medical mysteries and in order to get prescriptions. General pain relievers like Anadin, Panadol and aspirin are all available over the counter, though many cough and cold medicines, as well as athlete's foot and thrush medications are kept behind the till and will require asking a member of staff for access.

Pharmacies		
Boots	12 Grafton Street	01 478 4368
Hickey's Pharmacies	21 Grafton Street	01 679 0467
McCabe's Pharmacies	Blanchardstown Centre	01 822 2171
Nelson's Homeopathic Dispensary	15 Duke Street	01 679 0451
St Jame's Late Night Pharmacy Chemist	The Concourse, St James Hospital	01 473 4022
Unicare Pharmacy	Ashleaf Centre, Crumlin Cross	01 455 0974

Mobile Telephones

Other options **Telephone** p.125

There are only a few mobile phone providers in Dublin, and purchasing mobile phones and accessories from their official branches is imperative. Further information on mobile phone stores can be found from the service providers, 3 (www.three.ie), Meteor (www.meteor.ie), 02 (www.02.ie) and Vodafone (www.vodafone.ie). You'll find shops for these providers all over the city – check their websites for exact locations and see also p.125 in the Resident's chapter. Independent shops selling unlocked or repaired phones should be avoided, as there is no way of knowing if a phone was stolen before being displayed in these windows. That said, buying 'pay as you go' phones is probably a safe bet as you'll be able to tell if the package has been opened already or not.

Music, DVDs & Videos

Any city that has launched the likes of U2, Sinead O'Connor, The Corrs, Thin Lizzy and (though it may not want to admit it) Westlife and Boyzone, is a city that loves its music. Dublin attracts a huge number of international stars to perform at venues like The Point Depot, The Village and Vicar Street (see p.392), but for those who don't want to put on their dancing shoes a number of music stores offer CDs from approximately €9.99 through to about €30 for some imports. Independent and chain stores both still flourish on the Dublin music scene, though downloading music online is slowly but surely catching on. DVDs are also available from both independent and chain stores, and generally ring up at the same prices, though there are some steals available during the sales. Videos are rarely sold in Dublin these days, though if you don't want your VCR to go to waste you could always try a charity shop in the hopes that some Good Samaritan has donated his old copy of Beetlejuice to a good cause.

> ### Irish Tunes
> The ubiquitous iTunes is available in a dedicated iTunes Ireland store, though you'll need a credit card with an Irish mailing address to be able to register. Songs go for about 99 cents on iTunes, and most albums for €9.99. Free podcasts, on everything from language lessons to yoga classes to grammar guides, can be downloaded from the store, and some videos are available as well. See www.apple.com.

Abbey Discs

21 Lower Liffey St
Dublin 1
Map 426 A4 588

01 873 3733 | www.abbeydiscs.ie

Abbey Discs carries stock for most musical styles, though it is rather top-heavy with techno, progressive, hard house and trance. New and second-hand CDs and LPs are available with most prices bringing you change from a €20 note. Turntables are available for customer use, and the staff takes a keen interest in your selection and offers good recommendations. Check in regularly as stock turnover can be quick.

Celtic Note

14/15 Nassau St
Dublin 2
Map 430 B1 584

01 670 4157 | www.celticnote.com

Celtic Note may be packed to the rafters with tourists, but anyone with Irish interests will appreciate their stock of CDs, DVDs, books and Ts. In their own words, Celtic Note features 'Irish and Roots' music, including works by Dolores O'Riordan, Christy Moore, Celtic Woman and Andrea Corr. There is a good selection of world music also offered, and the Irish Dance section is sure to delight those who need to practise. The DVD section is decidedly Irish focused, though it does include films, documentaries and even sports shows. If you're looking for another copy of Angela's Ashes or a hard to find Michael Flatley performance, then Celtic Note is the place to go. There's also an online shop (see their website for details).

307

5 Cope St
Dublin 2
Map 426 A4 603

Freebird Records

01 675 9856 | *www.freebird.ie*

Freebird is Ireland's second oldest independent music store, though it has had a variety of locations before its new Cope Street home. Freebird purports to offer the largest vinyl selection in Dublin and new imports arrive weekly from both the US and Jamaica. Avid amateurs and professional DJs alike shop at Freebird, where hip hop, soul and dance music are all given equal attention. Vinyl goes for about €7 at Freebird, and most CDs for about €20. A few music-related DVDs are also available though prices vary. Online orders are also taken.

65 Grafton St
Dublin 2
Map 430 B1 607

HMV

01 679 5334 | *www.hmv.co.uk*

HMV covers three storeys in a prime Grafton Street location. Books, video games, vinyl, posters, T-shirts, CDs and DVDs clog the shelves, and the aisles are usually just as crowded. HMV carries both mainstream and lesser known CDs and DVDs, although prices can be a bit steep at up to €30 a pop, or upwards of €100 for some DVD box sets. Fortunately HMV puts on great three for €30 sales throughout the year, and their semi-annual blowouts can reduce prices to as little as €4.99. If you're looking for anything, entertainment wise, then stop in HMV – even if they don't have it, they might be able to get it. There are also stores on Henry Street (01 872 2095), in Blanchardstown Shopping Centre (01 822 1775), in Swords (01 890 2433) and at The Square in Tallaght (01 452 5844).

13 St Andrews St
Dublin 2
Map 430 A1 583

Laser Video

01 670 5183

Laser Video sells DVDs, but you can't fault a shop for not changing its name when it already has a loyal customer base. Laser is known for its wide selection of art house, world cinema and foreign language films, and its sales often drop DVD prices to around €10. Laser Video is connected to the Laser Specialist Video Libraries (Dublin 2 – 01 671 1466 and Dublin 6 – 01 497 3893), though they do not share a main computer so you'll need to visit each branch to find out what is in stock.

16b Fade St
Dublin 2
Map 430 A1 586

Road Records

01 671 7340 | *www.roadrecs.com*

Road Records continues to be a standout independent music shop featuring 'real music' like indie, alternative underground rock, electronica, country, folk, and more. Owners Dave and Julie not only know their stock but also keep up to date with developments on the independent music scene and are all but guaranteed to have an answer to your pressing music questions. Weekly lists of New Releases helps shoppers stay current, while staff picks for favourite singles and albums might just introduce a curious listener to something new. MP3 samples and an online shop feature on the shop's website, though postage does differ for CD and LP orders.

47 Nassau St
Dublin 2
Map 430 C1 589

Sound Cellar

01 677 1940

The Sound Cellar is literally a cellar, hidden away underneath the Subway outlet on Nassau Street, but don't let the location fool you. This shop offers a wide selection of CDs, with an emphasis very clearly on rock, hard rock and heavy metal. The Sound Cellar is also a great place to buy tickets to gigs, so check the chalkboard outside the door for information on what's happening in and around the city. Call ahead to verify opening hours, however, as there is no formal schedule when the shop gets short staffed.

32 George's
St Arcade
Dublin 2
Map 430 A1 **596**

Spindizzy

01 671 1711 | *www.myspace.com/spindizzyrecords*

This hole-in-the-wall offers new and used CDs and vinyl as well as a few turntables for customer use. Spindizzy stocks most musical styles, though there does seem to be an emphasis on dub, electronica and techno. €13-€15 is the normal price range for CDs, though vinyl can go for as little as €5. A large quantity of as yet unreleased music is also available as promotional copies, so pop in regularly to keep up with the latest and greatest unsigned DJs.

6-8 Wicklow St
Dublin 2
Map 430 B1 **608**

Tower Records

01 671 3250 | *www.towerrecords.ie*

Tower Records remains dedicated to offering customers a wide selection of music, books, DVDs and games, not to mention T-shirts, headphones, electronic music software and magazines. For those so inclined, Tower is one of the only outlets in Dublin to sell US magazines like *People* and *US Weekly*, as well as the *Sunday New York Times* (though its usually about a week late). Tower also retains a small selection of VHS videos, and adult DVDs. It regularly has acts performing in store, and online shopping is available with delivery services via An Post.

Dundrum Town Centre
Dublin 16
Map 421 D4 **24**

Virgin Megastore

01 296 3130 | *www.virginmegastores.co.uk*

Virgin Megastore is making its presence known once again in Dublin by infiltrating the giant suburban shopping centres springing up around the city, and the Dundrum Town Centre site is one of the largest entertainment stores in the region. CDs, DVDs, games and books can all be found in the store, and the separate section for TV series box sets was a stroke of genius. Most chart music and films are available at Virgin, though a good selection of alternative and world music is also on offer. The book selection is fairly small, but interesting nonetheless with an emphasis on biographies of some of the world's more colourful characters.

Musical Instruments

Other options **Music, DVDs & Videos** p.307, **Music Lessons** p.247

It probably won't take you longer than one pub sing-along to realise that Dublin is a musical city. If you want to join in the fun and purchase your own instrument, a variety of options exist. The McCullough Pigott Music Shop is Ireland's oldest music shop and offers string instruments, woodwinds, guitars, keyboards, percussion instruments and more. All instruments come with a one-year warranty and Joe Lynch, the proprietor, has worked in the music industry for over 40 years. Accessories such as music stands, tuners and metronomes can also be picked up here, as well as traditional Irish instruments such as bodhrans and tin whistles. Some second-hand

Musical Instruments		
James Beatley	83 Manor St, Stoneybatter	01 671 1721
McCullough Pigott	11 South William Street	01 670 6702
Music Maker	29 Exchequer Street	01 677 9004
Opus II	24 South Great George's Street	01 677 8571
Perfect Pitch	35 Exchequer Street	01 677 1553
Thornton Pianos	7 Berkely Road	01 830 5223

instruments may be stocked at McCullough Pigott, but usually only when the school year starts in the autumn. Gumtree (www.gumtree.ie) also offers second-hand instruments, sheet music and affordable tuition offers.

Music Maker is a rocker's paradise stocking Fender, Boss and Marshall guitars as well as Pearl and Sabian drums and a variety of amplifiers. Music software is also available,

309

including Ableton and Digidesign, and the staff are helpful and knowledgeable. Just down the street at Perfect Pitch, the range of acoustic and electric guitars is amazing, including brands such as Gibson, Martin and Epiphone, and studio gear such as microphones, stands and mixers.

Thornton Pianos specialises in – you guessed it – pianos, as well as digital keyboards, and all of their pianos come with a five-year warranty. The shop also offers rentals, rent to buy arrangements, and piano tuning, moving and valuations. For a custom-made piece, James Beatley creates violins from just €150 and cellos for as little as €450. He also does custom restoration and repairs. When you're ready to learn a few songs, head to Opus II for sheet music.

Outdoor Goods
Other options **Hardware & DIY** p.299, **Sports Goods** p.315

Outdoor enthusiasts are in luck because a variety of stores stocking outdoor goods are located within Dublin's city limits. The Outdoor Adventure Store (www.outdooradventurestore.ie) sells a wide range of skiing, sailing, diving, camping, climbing and kiting clothing and accessories, and if you get on the store's mailing list you will be notified of new collections and in-store promotions. Staff themselves tend to be hardened outdoor adventurers and can give you first-hand reviews of many of the items for sale. The Great Outdoors (www.greatoutdoors.ie) is another store catering for outdoor fitness pursuits, climbing, camping and adventure travel, and their range of socks and footwear include brand names such as Teva, Reef, Brasher and Meindl. Their tent range is extensive, suitable for both outdoor adventures and festival weekends, and their range of North Face clothing and accessories is sought after as much for its fashion cache as its outdoor appeal. In addition, K2, Capel Camping and Millets Camping are all city centre stores stocking a comprehensive range of tents, sleeping bags

Mini Marvels
If you get bored with the Dublin shopping scene, take your fistful of credit cards to one of shopping capitals of the world: Dubai, where gold shops line the streets; London, where quality always comes before quantity; or New York, where you can buy anything your heart desires, no matter what time of day it is. Just don't forget to take your Mini Explorer guide – Explorer has packed a wealth of shopping and travel tips into handy little books on these shopping hotspots and many more.

Outdoor Goods		
Capel Camping	132 Capel Street	01 873 4292
The Great Outdoors	Chatham House, Chatham Street	01 679 4293
The Great Outdoors Watersports Centre	Chatham House, Chatham Street	01 672 7154
K2	101 Talbot Street	01 874 1717
Millets Camping	61-62 Mary Street	01 873 3571
Onboard	Unit 28, Creation Arcade, Duke Lane	01 672 8767
The Outdoor Adventure Store	34-35 Upper Liffey Street	01 872 5177
Patagonia Outlet	24-26 Exchequer Street	01 670 5748

and rucksacks for both novices and advanced campers. The Great Outdoors Watersports Centre is ground zero for kayaks, canoes and surfboards, and Onboard (www.onboard.ie) stocks all the sailing, surfing and extreme temperature clothing and equipment that you could want. Those just looking for some waterproof clothing to make it through the wet Irish weather should also visit the Patagonia outlet store where these superior outdoor clothes and accessories are offered at discounted prices. Up to date information on outdoor goods can also be obtained from *Outsider Magazine* (www.outsider.ie), Ireland's outdoor magazine. See table for company listings.

Party Accessories
Other options **Parties at Home** p.389

Parties have reached lofty heights in Dublin, with many a First Communion now celebrated by booking a room at a local restaurant or hotel. But it is parties at home that really have the edge.

Hallmark, Marks & Spencer and Dunnes all do basic invitations, accessories such as hats and balloons, and gift wrap, tissue paper and cards. For kids' parties, little items for goody bags can be collected at Toymaster or Smyth's Toy Superstore.

Although home-made cakes tend to be that bit nicer, popular spots for shop-bought versions include Marks & Spencer (think soccer pitches and princess cakes), while Cafe Leon, La Boulangerie, La Maison des Gourmets and Queen of Tarts offer a more upmarket selection. Catering services such as Amitan, Berman & Wallace and Unique Dining can all sweep in and take care of everything too (see Catering on p.389 for more). For parties with a little more pizzazz, costume hire is available from A1 Costumes and Clown Around. You can get some beats going thanks to Star DJs and bouncy castles from Adventure Play & Design will entertain for hours. Face painting, jugglers and even custom quizzes can also be provided for parties in Dublin, so visit Party.ie (www.party.ie) for a comprehensive list of party services in the city. Paddy Magic (www.paddymagic.com) and Loopy Lenny's Balloons (www.loopylennysballons.com) should also help to make any occasion extra special. See p.389 for Caterers and Parties at Home.

Party Accessories

A1 Costumes	16a Eastmoreland Lane	01 668 5200	na
Adventure Play & Design	4 Racecourse Common	01 843 0830	www.adventureplayanddesign.com
Amitan	Kildare	01 272 2623	www.amitan.ie
Berman & Wallace	Belfield Office Park, Clonskeagh	01 219 6252	www.bermanandwallace.com
Cafe Leon	14-15 Trinity Street	01 671 7331	na
Clown Around	Clarendon Market	01 677 5040	na
Dunnes Stores	46-50 South Great George's Street	01 61 1600	www.dunnesstores.com
Hallmark	31 Grafton Street	01 679 4958	www.hallmarkuk.com
La Boulangerie	Camden Street	01 476 3818	na
La Maison des Gourmets	15 Castle Market	01 672 7258	na
Marks & Spencer	15-20 Grafton Street	01 679 7855	www.marksandspencer.com
Queen of Tarts	4 Cork Hill Dame Street	01 670 7499	na
Smyth's Toy Superstore	Jervis Centre	01 878 2852	www.toys.ie
Star DJs	9 Willow Business Park, Knockmitten Lane	1800 782 735	www.stardjs.ie
Toymaster	48 Mary Street	01 872 7100	na
Unique Dining	Cookstown Business Centre, Belgard	01 427 1011	www.uniquedining.ie

Duty Free Deals

Stocking up at duty free counters is a good idea, particularly because special travel kits are often available at airports or on flights that aren't sold elsewhere – Dublin Airport Duty Free is also one of the best-value cosmetic shops around.

Perfumes & Cosmetics

In Dublin, perfumes and cosmetics are generally bought from either department stores or chemists. Clerys has recently given its cosmetics department an extreme makeover and now houses concessions for Clinique, Estee Lauder, Origins, Benefit and Smashbox, among other brands. Arnotts offers these and more, including Nina Ricci and Elizabeth Arden. But it is Brown Thomas that is the mother of all perfumes and cosmetics halls with concessions for Molton Brown, Jo Malone, Chanel, Yves St Laurent, Stila, MAC and more. House of Fraser and Debenhams also offer cosmetics and perfumes sections, and Harvey Nichols' beauty bars and perfumery now offer Tom Ford, Vera Wang, Cheeky Girls, Fake Bake, Mario Badescu and some Bliss products (of London spa fame), as well as an array of other brands. At the local chemist you'll likely find Rimmel, No. 7, Max Factor, Revlon, Bourjois, L'Oreal, Ruby & Millie, Clarins and Lancome. Lush, the fragrant brand of natural cosmetics and beauty products that you'll smell before you reach the door, and The Body Shop also have stores in Dublin. Waiting for special offers is a smart idea, particularly as department stores give out free gifts with purchases every few weeks, but always have a look around because what is offered at one store may not be duplicated at another. Many salons and spas will also sell beauty products, though prices are generally higher that at other retail venues. You can check Irish beauty blog Beaut.ie (www.beaut.ie) for news and reviews before going off on a hunt.

Perfumes & Cosmetics			
Arnotts	12 Henry Street	01 805 0400	www.arnotts.ie
The Body Shop	82 Grafton Street	01 671 3725	www.thebodyshop.com
Brown Thomas	88-95 Grafton Street	01 605 6666	www.brownthomas.com
Clerys	18-27 Lower O'Connell Street	01 878 6000	www.clerys.com
Debenhams	Jervis Centre	01 878 1222	www.debenhams.com
Harvey Nichols	Dundrum Town Centre	01 291 0488	www.harveynichols.com
House of Fraser	Dundrum Town Centre	01 299 1400	www.houseoffraser.co.uk
Lush	116 Grafton Street	01 677 0392	www.lush.com

Pets

Other options **Pets** (Residents, p.121)

Pet shops in Dublin offer an array of supplies and toys, though animals are often limited to dogs, cats, fish, turtles and occasionally birds, hamsters and other small animals. Pedigree pets are not the norm here and you will most likely have to go through a private owner. See the classifieds section of one of the major newspapers (see p.45 for more). Back to pet shops though; for a good selection and helpful staff, visit Wackers Pet Shop or Petland in the city centre or Baumann's Pet Shop or Breffni House Pets in the southern suburbs. Instead of buying, pets can also be adopted from animal rescue organisations such as the Irish Society for the Prevention of Cruelty to Animals (www.ispca.ie) and the Dublin Society for the Prevention of Cruelty to Animals (www.dspca.ie). Buying a pet through an advert on Craigslist Dublin (http://dublin.craigslist.org), Gumtree (www.gumtree.ie), local papers such as the *Southside People* and *Northside People*, or supermarket, school or church noticeboards are also possibilities. Unfortunately, a growing number of illegal puppy farms have developed in Ireland so you will want to investigate the origin of animals offered privately to make sure that you are not funding these inhumane ventures.
No matter how you find a pet, proper documentation and vaccination records should be offered with the animal. You should also be informed of registration and vaccination requirements that you must see to, so be sure to ask about these administrative details. Before leaving Ireland with a pet, check in with the embassy or consulate of the country to which you are headed to make sure that you have all of your animal immigration documents in order, and try to do this several months ahead of time as transporting animals internationally is often complex and time consuming.

Pets				
Baumann's Pet Shop	4 Old Dublin Road	Stillorgan	01 288 4021	www.baumanns.ie
Breffni House Pets	Breffni House, Dundrum Road	Dublin 14	01 296 1339	na
Petland	61 Lower Camden Street	Dublin 2	01 478 2850	na
Wackers Pet Shop	177 Parnell Street	Dublin 1	01 872 6993	na

Portrait Photographers & Artists

Few Dublin households indulge in private portrait photography, though there are a few experts to turn to if you are so inclined. Cliona O'Flaherty Photography (087 958 1048), Photogenic Photographers (01 284 5697) and Circus Photography (01 406 6547) are all well known for their portraiture and all offer portfolios to view, and quotes on pricing, that you should take into account before making your final decision. Portrait artists are much harder to find, so you will need to spread your net to encompass the entire country. Kerry based Jenny McCarthy (087 929 3823), Donegal based Stephen Bennett (07 495 1652) and Galway based Vincent Ryan (087 642 4453) are three artists who show portraits regularly. Call ahead for information on commissions and rates.

Second-Hand Items

Other options **Books** p.287

Find It Online
Take advantage of the web to hock second-hand goods. Bargains abound on Craigslist Dublin (http://dublin.craigslist.org), Gumtree (www.gumtree.ie) and Freecycle (http://groups.yahoo.com/group/freecycleDublin), as well as through many expatriate community email lists.

The high cost of living in Dublin makes scouting for second-hand items a good, and economical, idea. Outdoor markets such as Liberty Market (01 280 8683) and Blackrock Market (01 283 3522) offer an abundance of second-hand clothing, accessories, books, CDs, home accessories and even some types of furniture (see p.328). Charity shops are another great source of second-hand clothing and knick-knacks, so visit the WaWa Shop (01 296 0284), Mrs Greene's (01 492 48867) or Enable Ireland (01 478 0647) to browse their displays, racks and shelves. When the time comes to purge your own home, don't forget that you can donate to these shops as well. Second-hand items including bikes, cars, furniture, musical instruments and baby accessories are also frequently advertised on supermarket noticeboards, in school or church newsletters, at public libraries and community centres and in each issue of local newspapers such as the *Southside People* and the *Northside People*.

Shoes

Other options **Beachwear** p.286, **Sports Goods** p.315, **Clothes** p.290

A Lighter Step
For those looking to spend their money in an unquestionably ethic way, check out the Terra Plana range at Arnotts or The Natural Shoe Store.

If you don't feel like waiting for the Dart, Luas or a Dublin Bus, or indeed if the city centre traffic is more than you can bear, walking is always a viable alternative in Dublin. Of course commuting on foot will require you to have comfortable shoes, so find the best fit for your feet by correctly calculating your Irish size. Women will need to subtract 2.5 from an American size but men will only need to subtract .5 to find their Irish equivalent. For European women, subtracting 28.5 will result in the Irish size. Many different qualities of shoes are available in Dublin, though experts agree that the better the quality of a shoe the more comfortable the fit. For casual shoes for the whole family, head to Clark's, the Birkenstock shop or department stores such as Arnotts and Clerys. Children's shoes are also available from Buckle My Shoe at BT2 and Barratts. For something a little more luxurious, handcrafted men's shoes are available from Louis Copeland and Brown Thomas, which also houses a women's shoe showroom filled with Pied a Terre, Christian Louboutin, Jimmy Choo and more. Also feeding the luxury women's market is the shoe boutique at Harvey Nichols which offers Chloe, Marc Jacobs, Lanvin and a host of

Shoe shopping

Shoes

Arnotts	12 Henry Street	01 805 0400
Barratts	GPO Buildings, 1 Henry Street	01 8724 033
Birkenstock	Wicklow Street	01 675 3766
Brown Thomas	88-95 Grafton Street	01 605 6666
Buckle My Shoe	BT2, 28 Grafton Street	01 605 6666
Champion Sports	Ilac Centre	01 872 7274
Cherche Midi	23 Drury Street	01 675 3975
The Clarks Shop	25 Henry Street	01 873 2592
Clerys	18-27 Lower O'Connell Street	01 8786 000
Great Outdoors	Chatham House, Chatham Street	01 679 4293
Korky's	GPO Buildings, 4 Henry Street	01 8731 359
Lifestyle Sports	Jervis Centre	01 873 1037
Louis Copeland & Sons	18-19 Wicklow Street	01 872 1600
The Natural Shoe Store	25 Drury Street	01 671 4978
Nine West	83 Grafton Street	01 677 0445
Office	6 Henry Street	01 874 8250
Onboard	Unit 28, Creation Arcade, Duke Lane	01 672 8767
Schuh	47-48 Lower O'connell Street	01 804 9420
Zerep	31A Henry Street	01 873 1644

other brands. Cherche Midi boutique on Drury Street also offers a range of lovely shoes.

More casual women's shoes can be found at Schuh, Office and Nine West, and casual shoes for both genders are available at Zerep and Korkys. Sports footwear can be found in any of the chain sports stores like Champion or Lifestyle Sports, though more sturdy shoes for both summer and winter outdoor pursuits can be found at Great Outdoors and Onboard.

Souvenirs

Traditional souvenirs of Dublin, including shamrock printed tea towels, Guinness pint glasses, leprechaun playing cards and much more can be found in the Carrolls Gift Shops that have sprung up all around the city, including at Dublin Airport. The Dublin Tourism Centre also offers some bargain souvenirs, though undoubtedly more authentic souvenirs such as Waterford Crystal, Newbridge Silver and the handcrafted woollen goods that can be found at the Kilkenny Design Centre,

Souvenirs

Arnotts	12 Henry Street	01 805 0400
Blarney Woollen Mills	21-23 Nassau Street	01 451 6111
Carrolls Gift Shops	2-5 Westmoreland Street	01 677 5088
Dublin Tourism Centre	Suffolk Street	01 605 7700
Elverys Sports	24 Dawson Street	01 679 1141
Kilkenny Design Centre	5/6 Nassau Street	01 677 7075
McCullough Piggot	11 South William Street	01 670 6702
Trinity Sweater Shop	30 Nassau Street	01 671 9543

Blarney Woollen Mills and the Trinity Sweater Shop are better quality and most likely, more popular on the receiving end. Sporty acquaintances might enjoy Irish rugby jerseys or Gaelic Athletic Association jerseys that can be found at Arnotts and Elverys Sports, while musical mates might prefer a bodhran (a type of hand-held Celtic drum) or a tin whistle (similar to a recorder) from Ireland's oldest music shop, McCullough Pigott. For fashion forward friends, have a look at Chesneau leather goods or the Alan Ardiff jewellery line at the Kilkenny Design Centre.

Typical Irish souvenirs

Sports Goods

Other options **Outdoor Goods** p.310

Soccer, rugby, hockey, hurling and Gaelic football are all popular sports in Dublin, and a number of sports stores in the city supply footwear and sportswear for fanatic fans and athletes alike. Champion Sports and Lifestyle Sports supply general gym wear, bags and accessories such as water bottles and sweat bands, and they both do a decent range of swimsuits, swim caps and goggles as well. Elvery Sports has a decidedly masculine edge with an emphasis on soccer, rugby and GAA (Gaelic Athletic Association) items including soccer and rugby balls, shin guards, gum shields, and jerseys. The Nike outlet opening soon on Grafton Street will offer only Nike goods. Foot Locker is a great place to find basketball shoes and gear. TK Maxx is a bargain bin for finding odd bits such as yoga mats, Pilates videos and hand weights, and both Onboard and The Great Outdoors have an extensive range of gear and equipment for outdoor pursuits including camping, climbing, sailing and surfing. Arnotts has a sports section that offers a little of everything including golf clubs and golf clothing, as well as some fitness equipment for home gyms. Argos also has a range of basic treadmills and weights for the home but VJ's World of Home Fitness is the place to go to outfit an entire gym (whether private or commercial), right down to a portable hot tub to soothe aching muscles.

Sports Goods

Argos	Stephen's Green Centre	01 478 0095	www.argos.ie
Arnotts	12 Henry Street	01 805 0400	www.arnotts.ie
Champion Sports	Ilac Centre	01 872 7274	www.champion.ie
Elverys Sports	24 Dawson Street	01 679 1141	www.buy4now.ie/elvery
Foot Locker	44 Grafton Street	01 671 0021	www.footlocker.com
Lifestyle Sports	Jervis Centre	01873 1037	www.lifestylesports.com
Onboard	Unit 28, Creation Arcade, Duke Lane	01 672 8767	www.onboard.ie
The Great Outdoors	Chatham Street	01 679 4293	www.greatoutdoors.ie
TK Maxx	Stephen's Green Centre	01 475 7080	www.tkmaxx.com
VJ's World of Fitness	Coolmine Industrial Estate, Coolmine	01 820 2757	www.vjhomefitness.com

Stationery

From the quirky to the mundane, a huge range of stationery is available in Dublin. At Reads of Nassau Street all stationery, including school supplies, business diaries and everyday greeting cards are offered at discount prices, while Book Station and Easons offer economic options as well. Hallmark is an old standby for stationery, including cards for every milestone and a variety of sentimental gifts, and Swalk is an undeniably girly stationery shop that is crammed with patterned notebooks, emblazoned address books, sparkly cards and even candles and eye masks. Daintree offers pretty papers, envelopes and ribbons, though the prices reflect the superior quality. The Pen Corner also stocks higher quality papers such as boxed sets of Crane stationery, as well as

Stationery

The Bookstation	Nutgrove Shopping Centre	01 496 9287	na
Daintree Paper	64 Pleasants Place	01 475 7500	www.daintree.ie
Easons	40 Lower O'Connell Street	01 873 3811	www.buy4now.ie/Eason
Hallmark	31 Grafton Street	01 679 4958	www.hallmarkuk.com
House of Fraser	Dundrum Town Centre	01 299 1400	www.houseoffraser.co.uk
Lantz	2 Charlemont Street	01 478 0733	www.lantz.ie
Pen Corner	12 College Green	01 679 3641	na
Reads of Nassau Street	24-25 Nassau Street	01 679 6011	www.readsbooks.ie
Swalk	Royal Hibernian Way, Dawson Street	01 671 1155	na

315

moleskin notebooks and a variety of individual greeting cards. House of Fraser has an up-and-coming stationery section as well. Wedding stationery including seals, stickers and do it yourself sets is available at Lantz, though certainly no one will chase you out of the shop if you aren't on your way to a wedding anytime soon.

Tailoring

Other options **Clothes** p.290, **Souvenirs** p.314, **Textiles** p.316, **Tailors** p.119

Custom-made clothes remain relatively rare in Dublin, though some bespoke services are available since tailors' shops still thrive on minor alterations. A 'turn up' will cost you around €10, and more if taking in or letting out is involved. Those who are flush enough to afford custom clothing should call Anne O'Mahony for one of a kind women's wear or Brown Thomas's in-house tailor Alessandro DeMatte whose menswear is reported to be exceptional. On occasion the *Irish Times* will also carry announcements from out of town tailors who are setting up for a day in a city centre hotel and offer dress shirts and suits at affordable prices. Most dry cleaners also offer some form of alteration service too,

Oops!
Have we missed out your best bookshop or your favourite factory store? Tell us about it! Log on to www.explorer publishing.com, fill out the Reader Response Form, and give your friendly local retailer a big shout-out.

Tailoring		
Alteration Centre	28 South Anne Street	01 677 6258
Anne O'Mahoney	Dublin 2	01 672 9369
Bogart Tailors	17 Capel Street	01 873 0771
Brown Thomas In-House Tailors	88-95 Grafton Street	01 617 1161
Des Byrne Tailoring	5 Grafton Street	01 677 3821
Des Leech	3 Cavendish Row	01 874 6330

though those that send out do strictly that – send garments to an off-site tailor so you'll have no say in what they do once its gone. Customers for these tailors will need to have their garments pre-marked for how high to hem, so these services should only be used if you are confident in your own judgement.

If you're heading to a fancy dress party or really want to look original over Halloween, try Des Leech, who specialises in theatrical costumes, as well as horse-riding wear for men and women.

Textiles

Other options **Tailoring** p.316

If custom-made clothes are rare in Dublin then home-made clothes are downright exceptional. Those who do like to run up a little something of their own should head to Universal Fabrics, a wholesale distributor on the outskirts of the city that offers prints, plains, velvets and even curtain liners. Hickeys stocks a wide variety of fabrics, trimmings and patterns, and smaller 'leisure sections' offer craft patterns, kits and even fabric paints. Murphy Sheehy Fabrics is another great source of textiles in Dublin, with sales offering some fabric from as low as €10 per metre and stock changes with the seasons meaning that a wide variety of tweeds are on offer in the autumn and multiple linens in the summer. Faux fur, silks and organzas are also usually in stock, so a formal ball gown can

Textiles		
Hickeys	5 Henry Street	01 873 0714
Murphy Sheehy Fabrics	14 Castle Market	01 677 0316
Universal Fabrics	Blanchardstown	01 861 2160

be organised just as easily as some new striped curtains. And if you like the idea of textile projects but have no idea how to get started, ring up the Marino College of Further Education (011 8557116, www.marinocollege.ie) or Ringsend Technical Institute (01 668 4498) for more information on their dressmaking courses, or check out the National College of Art and Design's textile programmes (see p.149 for more).

Work Visas p.54
Weekend Breaks p.155

Written by residents, the Barcelona Explorer is packed with insider info, from arriving in the city to making it your home and everything in between.

Barcelona Explorer Residents' Guide
We Know Where You Live

EXPLORER

www.explorerpublishing.com

Toys & Games

While there are no landmark toyshops in Dublin, there are certainly enough to keep kids of all ages happy. Toymaster and Smyth's Toy Superstore carry mainstream toys and board games, from marbles to Guess Who and from baby doll brands like Baby Born and Chou Chou. On the more alternative side, Wood You Like stocks old fashioned wooden puzzles for children and Rainbow Crafts sells wooden toys, games and a variety of stamps, figurines and dolls for younger kids. The Early Learning Centre and The Toy Store both offer entertaining and educational toys, books and games as well. T Bear & Co is a premier soft toy store in Dublin, though The Bear Factory actually allows children to select the components for their new friends, right down to name, voice and clothing styles, and carry them home in a personalised carrier. If favourite soft friends are loved a little too much, a trip to the Dolls Hospital and Teddy Bear's Clinic might be in order. Computer and video game fans should head to HMV for new and popular games, or Gamestop to for a variety of new and used games or to turn in their beaten games to get credit for new ones. And if you need a new toy fast, log on to Toystore.ie (www.toystore.ie) or Imaginarium.ie (www.imaginarium.ie) for a full selection of toys and games, all with speedy home delivery.

Toys, Games & Gifts		
The Bear Factory	Liffey Valley Shopping Centre	01 874 5724
Dolls Hospital & Teddy Bear Clinic	62 South Great George's Street	01 478 3403
The Early Learning Centre	3 Henry Street	01 873 1945
Gamestop	7 Upper Georges Street	01 872 5488
HMV	65 Grafton Street	01 679 5334
Rainbow Crafts	Westbury Mall	01 677 7632
Smyth's Toy Superstore	Jervis Centre	01 878 2852
T Bear & Co	Stephen's Green Shopping Centre	01 478 1139
The Toy Store	Sun Alliance House, 13/17 Dawson Street	01 677 4420
Toymaster	48 Mary Street	01 872 7100
Wood You Like	Powerscourt Centre	01 679 4666

Market Arcade

Grafton Street Busker

Wedding Items

Dublin may not be a world-renowned location for wedding shopping, but it can hold it's own in the glamour stakes. Bridal Heaven is a one-stop shop for wedding gowns, bridesmaid's dresses and flower girl dresses, not to mention tiaras, veils and shoes. For those looking for designer labels, The Bridal Corner is an exclusive Irish stockist of four major European designers, and Butterfly Bride carries a few designer frocks as well. Marian Gale is arguably the most well known bridal boutique in Dublin with gowns to suit every budget, though Brown Thomas's Vera Wang Salon is the place to go to really splash the cash. On the opposite end of the spectrum, Marks & Spencer have just introduced a wedding line that includes budget gowns and tuxes for males young enough to view the ceremony from their prams. For friends and relatives, Personal Touch and Pronuptia both offer bridesmaid's dresses and evening wear suitable for mothers of the bride and groom and guests ready to kick up their heels can rent suits and tuxes from Bond Bros or Black Tie. Dresses from Monsoon and Coast are almost always in attendance at Irish weddings as well.

In addition to sartorial standouts, Dublin also offers a number of sources for wedding supplies. Daintree and Lantz are both highly regarded outlets for wedding stationery, while Cakes & Co and Cakebox offer designs that taste even better than they look. Gift giving is also a snap for Dublin weddings as most couples register at Department stores such as Clerys, Arnotts or Brown Thomas. Of course with the number of international weddings growing, arranging for gift delivery straight to the married couple's new home is always a good idea, and no new couple would sneeze at cash, a cheque or a gift voucher to wish them well either. No matter what type of gift you choose, just remember that weddings are usually huge in Ireland, and they're always great *craic*.

Tiny Dub

If you've got far-flung relatives heading to Dublin to help you celebrate your wedding, get them a copy of the *Mini Dublin Explorer*. It's a teeny, tiny tome of useful information on the city, meaning they'll be out and about discovering the city, leaving you more time to concentrate on your last minute wedding plans!

Wedding Items

Arnotts	12 Henry St	01 805 0400	www.arnotts.ie
Black Tie	Westmoreland Street	01 679 1444	www.blactie.ie
Bond Bros	8 Willowfield Park, Goatstown	01 296 7744	www.bondbros.ie
The Bridal Corner	Harts Corner, 1 Prospect Avenue, Glasnevin	01 860 0140	www.bridalcorner.ie
Bridal Heaven	Carnegie Court, North Street	01 810 7907	www.bridalheavenonline.com
Brown Thomas	88-95 Grafton Street	01 605 6666	www.brownthomas.com
Brown Thomas Vera Wang Salon	88-95 Grafton Street	01 617 1133	www.brownthomas.com
Butterfly Bride	67 Main Street	01 275 5784	na
Cakebox	64a George's Street	01 280 1870	www.cakebox.ie
Cakes & Co	Jane Cottage, Newtownpark Avenue	01 283 6544	www.cakesandco.com
Clerys	18-27 Lower O'Connell Street	01 878 6000	www.clerys.com
Coast	Dundrum Town Centre	01 299 1400	www.coast-stores.com
Daintree Paper	64 Pleasants Place	01 475 7500	www.daintree.ie
Debenhams	Jervis Centre	01 878 1222	www.debenhams.com
Lantz	2 Charlemont Street	01 478 0733	www.lantz.ie
Marian Gale	The Mall, Donnybrook	01 269 7460	www.mariangale.ie
Marks & Spencer	15-20 Grafton Street	01 679 7855	www2.marksandspencer.com
Monsoon	38 Grafton Street	01 671 7322	www.monsoon.co.uk
Personal Touch	Sutton Cross Centre, Howth Road, Sutton	01 8322 234	na
Pronuptia	24 Strand Street	01 874 6200	na

Places To Shop

Made For Walking

No matter what you're searching for, be sure to put on your walking shoes before venturing out into the Dublin shopping scene as there's plenty of ground to be covered and you'll have to do most of it on foot.

Dublin is a compact city, but it certainly conforms to the shopper's maxim that 'good things come in small packages'. Two main shopping areas are available in Dublin, both of which are largely pedestrianised though cyclists, delivery vans and garda cars routinely drive through the crowds. On the south side of the city, Grafton Street and its surroundings provide an upscale climate while Henry Street and O'Connell Street attract bargain hunters on the north side. Though they may sound worlds apart, in reality the regions are only separated by the River Liffey and multiple pedestrian bridges link the two. The proliferation of chain stores in recent years now means that almost anything to be found can be found in the city centre, but a wide variety of modern shopping malls in the suburbs have brought in a whole new range of stores including Borders, House of Fraser and Harvey Nichols (all located in the Dundrum Centre, see p.329). These malls provide a warm and dry environment in the (frequent) event of bad weather, but many Dubliners still prefer to shop in the independent stores in the city centre.

Streets & Areas To Shop

Heading North

All buses bound for the city centre will allow passengers to jump out close enough to walk to the Henry Street and O'Connell Street area, and the Jervis and Abbey Street stops on the Luas red line will take you right into the middle of this district.

Dublin city centre has two distinct shopping areas, one either side of the River Liffey. On the south side, Grafton Street and its surrounding streets offer more luxurious shopping while O'Connell Street and Henry Street on the north side offer more bargains – or so the stereotype goes. In reality, prices across Dublin are much the same because stores tend to be similar branches of the same major chains. Due to Dublin's rich history, both areas are full of tiny lanes and even a few dodgy alleys that can hold wonderful treats and treasures, and since Dublin is a fairly safe city there's usually no harm in following directions to 'yer man's shop down the lane'.

Henry Street & O'Connell Street

Henry Street and O'Connell Street have had a long tradition of outdoor markets and discounted prices, but both seem to have diminished somewhat in the face of the Celtic Tiger. In their place chain stores, the occasional outdoor stall and any number of ethnic food stores have cropped up and now attract a wide and varied crowd. Generic brands, tracksuits and jeans do tend to proliferate in this area, and dressing up in designer duds is definitely not required.

Department store giants Clerys (p.323) and Arnotts (p.322) are both in the area, and the Ilac Centre and Jervis Centre (p.330) are just a short walk from one another. Discount stores Lidl and Aldi are both in this region as well, so it's probably very true that there is

Henry Street

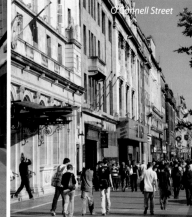

O'Connell Street

something to suit everyone in this city centre locale. At the moment there are few eateries unattached to the shopping centres on Henry Street or O'Connell Street, but an Italian Quarter is blossoming near Blooms Lane just a few blocks to the west. A massive cineplex is also situated on Parnell Street, so it's fair to say that this entire section of the city is experiencing a bit of a revamp. Perhaps the strongest sign of regeneration was celebrity chef Garry Rhode's selection of the corner of Mary's Abbey and Capel Street as the site of his D7 restaurant (p.345), which has brought a more upscale vibe to the area. That said, it's still an area where you'll find an interesting selection of porn shops and pawn shops too!

Grafton Street

All buses bound for the city centre will allow passengers to jump out close enough to walk to the Henry Street and O'Connell Street area, and the Jervis and Abbey Street stops on the Luas red line end smack in the middle of this district.

Heading South
Grafton Street and its surrounding area can be reached by taking the Luas green line to the Stephen's Green terminus, which discharges passengers at the top of Grafton Street. All buses bound for the city centre terminate within walking distance.

Grafton Street

If you're looking for Dublin's equivalent of Fifth Avenue, Miracle Mile or New Bond Street, head for Grafton Street on the south side. You might not find the same proliferation of designer emporiums as you would in other shopping capitals, but you will find huge branches of some great high-street brands like Marks & Spencer, Laura Ashley, HMV, and of course the big daddy of department stores: Brown Thomas (p.323). It is closed to vehicular traffic, but think again if you are expecting a stress-free stroll down the cobbled walkway – you'd have to get up pretty early in the morning to see Grafton Street when it's not packed with shoppers, tourists and buskers. It is close to Trinity College, Dame Street, the Molly Malone Statue and St Stephen's Green, so it sees a lot of action. On weekends the coffee shops and cafes are full to bursting with Dubliners people watching and checking out the papers over a latte.

Once you've walked up and down Grafton Street, be sure to explore the surrounding streets too. You'll find a variety of unique boutiques and funky little shops that could become part of your essential shopping list. Nassau Street is a tourist favourite (many a passing tour bus has a guffaw at the shop with the funniest name in Dublin: Knobs & Knockers). Drury Street is becoming known as a great area for hair and beauty outlets, and George's Street Arcade retains its arty edge.

Temple Bar

A lot of people will tell you that Temple Bar is nothing more than a destination for tacky stag and hen parties but don't believe them: this diverse area is chock-a-block with some fascinating independent stores and galleries and should not be avoided by any serious shopper. Fashionistas can shop for shoes at China Blue (01 671 8785, www.chinabluestore.ie) or ethnic fashions at En Route (087 940 1464), both in Merchant's Arch, or for vintage bags and jewellery and some quirky fashions at SeSi on Fownes Street (01 677 4779). Combine your shopping with helping a good cause at

321

the Cultivate Centre on Essex Street West (01 674 5773, www.cultivate.ie), which sells a range of environmentally friendly products, or at the Amnesty International shop on Fleet Street (01 677 6361), which only sells products that comply with free trade guidelines. Kit out your home with some funky decor purchased from 2cooldesign on Cow's Lane (01 672 5402, www.2cooldesign.ie), or browse an eclectic music collection at Mojo Records in Merchant's Arch (01 672 7905). The best part about shopping in Temple Bar is that as soon as you feel the fatigue, there are many lovely little cafes, or pubs if you need a stronger form of refreshment, in which to take a breather.

Department Stores

Department stores have been embraced by Irish consumers to the point that it often seems like you can't walk a city block without running into one. All Irish shopping centres have at least one department store as their anchor and thank goodness, because city centre shopping is made much easier when one store offers most necessities. Brown Thomas is the most elegant of Irish department stores offering exclusive labels and designer goods including fashions, shoes and homewares though Arnotts and Clerys are both historic favourites, particularly at sales times. Dunnes and Roches stores are uniquely Irish department stores that could easily be equated to an American Walmart or Target, though Dunnes only sells its own label, St Bernard's, and often hosts a full grocery store as one of its departments. Penneys, Marks & Spencer and Debenhams are all British high-street favourites that have crossed the water and made a big splash, and Harvey Nichols and House of Fraser are fairly new additions to the Irish market. These two currently enjoy exclusive status at the Dundrum Town Centre but many are hoping that this will change in the next few years. Many Dubliners still use 'Roches' (an Irish department store chain that was taken over in 2006) at the Ilac Centre as a landmark, but this is now a Debenhams. Any stores still trading as Roches will be rebranded shortly.

12 Henry St
Dublin 1
Map 426 A3 [6]

Arnotts
01 805 0400 | *www.arnotts.ie*

Opened in 1843, Arnotts announces itself as Ireland's oldest department store though you'd never know it from browsing this multi-storey monster. As the largest department store in Ireland it certainly is well stocked and well spaced, making it easy to navigate from the extensive homewares and electronics sections in the basement, to the cosmetics and shoe halls on the ground floor to the uniforms (both school and professional) above at loftier heights. There is something for every budget at Arnotts and serious cooks will love the extensive ranges of Le Creuset and Jamie Oliver cookware, while sports fans will rejoice in the number of Dublin GAA jerseys and Leinster rugby jerseys to be had as well as the year round stock of swimsuits (not an easy find in Dublin). A vast giftwares section also makes Arnotts a great stop when looking for something to bring back to family and friends if you wish to avoid the shamrock covered tat sold at most tourist traps. Waterford Crystal, Stephen Pearse Pottery and Newbridge Silver are all stocked at Arnotts. Those setting up new homes will also want to take note of their top floor bed and bath department and their interior design service, and if you've got your wedding around the corner, you may want to consider the extensive wedding registry service. Though riddled with stairs and escalators, and therefore not particularly wheelchair or pram friendly, Arnotts does offer a clean bank of elevators, a nail bar and gents barber shop, a few bright though not particularly memorable cafes and relatively clean toilets. Arnotts is open from 09:00 to 18:30 daily except on Tuesdays when it does not open until 09:30 and Thursdays when it stays opens late until 21:00. Shortened hours are in operation on Sunday when the store opens from 12:00 to 18:00. Online shopping is also available through the website.

88 – 95 Grafton St
Dublin 2
Map 430 B1 **569**

Brown Thomas

01 605 6666 | *www.brownthomas.com*

Brown Thomas is where the moneyed and manic head when they want to go on a spending spree. Daring window displays advertise the luxury goods inside and most of the designer concessions in the city – Prada, Gucci, Louis Vuitton, Hermes, and Chanel, to name a few – are located in this sophisticated department store. The first floor women's shoe boutique is a great draw, while those in need of a little pick-me-up can often be found getting spritzed and sprayed in the cosmetics hall below. In-store tailoring services and a nail bar help make sure that everything bought at BTs is just right. Those with a serious style craving can even apply for a Brown Thomas MasterCard to rack up rewards points. Brides also flock to Brown Thomas for the Vera Wang Salon and Wren Press stationery, not to mention to get their names on the Brown Thomas gift registry list. Unfortunately the homewares department is rather small and expensive, so Brown Thomas truly makes it mark as a fashion forum. Though Aya Sushi is often linked to the Brown Thomas name, this restaurant is actually located behind the store, but there are a few small cafes perfect for people watching inside. Though wheelchair and pram accessible, the walkways inside Brown Thomas can be slightly cramped, particularly when shoppers are fighting to the death for sale items in the aisles. The store's bathrooms are lovely and clean, and while a few of the shopgirls may have a reputation for surliness overall the staff are friendly and helpful. Brown Thomas stays open late each evening (remember that this is by Dublin standards), with opening hours from 09:00 to 20:00 each weekday except Tuesday when it does not open until 09:30. On Saturdays the store is open from 09:00 to 19:00 and from 10:00 to 19:00 on Sundays.

18-27 Lower
O'Connell St
Dublin 1
Map 426 B3 **565**

Clerys

01 878 6000 | *www.clerys.com*

Winner of the 2006 Best Independent Department Store of Britain and Ireland award from Drapers magazine, Clerys certainly does excel at its value for money philosophy. Though it is housed in a listed (protected) building dating back to 1853, Clerys went through a complete refurbishment in 2004 and while there are still a few remnants of construction going on, for the most part it has emerged bigger and better than ever. Mid-range prices and bargain steals abound, and the summer and winter sales are not to be missed. Whether you are on the hunt for a blender, a carpet, a hat or some perfume, Clerys likely stocks it. Karen Millen, Sisley, Noa Noa, Ben Sherman, Top Man

Brown Thomas

Clerys

323

and Van Heusen can all be found in Clerys hallowed halls, and a raft of young men can often be found buyng their Calvin Klein underwear here too. Landlords and renters particularly love Clerys 'Apartment Pack' offer which aims to completely kit out one and two bedroom apartments with minimal fuss. The giant clock suspended above the store's main entrance is something of a landmark for Dubliners with many a date being arranged to 'meet under the clock,' and the crowds often do make their way inside so try to keep your patience during the busy lunchtime and post-work hours. Clerys offers clean toilets for anyone caught short in the city centre, but since this seems to be just about everyone the wait can be long. The 'Something Blue' gift registry is also a favourite for Dublin brides. Clerys is open from 09:00 to 19:00 each weekday with late openings until 21:00 on Thursdays and 20:00 on Fridays, from 09:00 to 18:30 on Saturdays and 12:00 to 18:00 on Sundays. Online shopping is also available through the website.

Jervis Centre
125 Upper Abbey St
Dublin 1
Map 426 A3 **572**

Debenhams

01 878 1222 | *www.debenhams.com*
British retailer Debenhams has made quite an impact on the Dublin shopping market, and there are now five Debenhams branches in Dublin. All branches sell similar fashions, including brands like Jasper Conran, John Rocha and Betty Jackson, although the branch on Henry Street (which used to be Roches Stores) does include concessions among its departments including The Pier (for home furnishings). In general, all branches are great for fashion, accessories and decorative items for the home. The mid-range collections at Debenhams usually offer shoppers good value for money though fashionistas are still waiting for a large selection of Frost French and Melissa Odabash pieces to make their way over. If something can't be found at a Debenhams branch in Ireland, the staff are helpful in directing shoppers to the company website on which you can shop online. Not all items can be shipped to Ireland, although a quick call to the helpline will clear up any confusion. The Debenhams gift list can also be accessed in both the UK and Ireland, so cross-border gifts are no longer a headache. Whether or not gift vouchers can be used in both the UK and Ireland remains a mystery. Branches include Blackrock (01 200 1700), Blanchardstown (01 829 5500), Henry Street (01 814 7200) and Tallaght (01 468 5700).

Stephen's Green
Centre
Dublin 2
Map 430 A2 **26**

Dunnes

01 478 0188 | *www.dunnesstores.ie*
More formally known as Dunnes Stores, Dunnes is a catch-all of products for anyone with even a few euros in their pocket. Selling only their own label – St Bernard's – Dunnes has branched out recently to include several different collections for men and women including Savida for the female fashionplate and New Have Fashions for the preppy pretty boy. A staple across Ireland, Dunnes is known for providing a wide variety of fashions, accessories, toys, linens and even suitcases at relatively bargain basement prices. Kids clothes are especially good value from Dunnes as they are cheap and cheerful, not to mention easily replaced. Paul Costelloe Living and Twiggy Town and Country have brought an air of sophistication to Dunnes' homewares and their kitchen and bathroom selections can't be beat, though their home entertainment offerings do remain a bit bare. Dunnes also offers grocery stores with a wide selection of items, most recently new 'Polskie Producty' racks serving the large Polish community in the city. Wine, beer and spirits are also usually on offer in the off licences adjacent to the grocery stores. Frequent shoppers should sign up immediately for a Value Club Card as it can be used in every department and frequently brings special coupons and offers in the post. Dunnes is open in the Stephens Green Centre on weekdays from 08:30 to 20:00, except for a late opening until 21:00 on Thursdays, Saturdays from 08:30 to 19:00 and Sundays

Harvey Nics

from 10:00 to 19:00. Some of the other Dublin branches include Dun Laoghaire (01 280 1823), Georges Street (01 611 1600), Grafton Street (01 671 4629), Ilac Centre (01 873 0211), Liffey Valley (01 621 5955), Rathmines (01 496 4266), Tallaght (01 452 6566) and Henry Street (01 872 3911).

83 Talbot St
Dublin 1
Map 426 B3 **568**

Guineys

01 874 7211 | www.michaelguiney.com
Guineys advertises 'always discount prices' but unfortunately what you gain in savings you may lose in service and quality. That said, there is a wide selection of family fashions and household linens, and their homeware department sells things like drying racks, bar stools, mugs, plates and curtains at really low prices. A maternity wear section is coming soon too, which might just be the answer to many expectant mothers' prayers for cheap and cheerful fashion for the warmer weather. Guineys tends to be cramped, disorganised and products are not always clean (certainly not the towels that end up on the floors, anyway). Some online shopping is available. Guineys on Talbot Street is open from 09:30 to 18:00 on Mondays through Saturdays and closed on Sundays. Other Dublin branches can be found on North Earl Street (01 872 4377) and at 93 Talbot Street (01 878 6788).

Dundrum
Town Centre
Sandyford Rd
Dublin 16
Map 421 D4 **24**

Harvey Nichols

01 291 0488 | www.harveynichols.com
Harvey Nics, as it's known to those who frequent this small department store, has become a firm favourite of the Dublin jet set. Selling only luxury fashions, accessories, food and wine, you would be forgiven for thinking that a quick trip in and out is all it takes to see the extent of the stock but this is not the case. A dazzling array of items are elegantly displayed inside, meaning that anyone willing to break their budget will certainly find something worthy of their savings. For those who prefer not to browse the racks of Diane von Furstenberg, Pucci or Armani, or try on coveted Jimmy Choo heels, Chloe boots or Lanvin flats, a personal shopping service does exist. An electronic newsletter also keeps those on the cutting edge on the, well, cutting edge. The First Floor Restaurant and Bar (p.350) and ground floor Espresso Bar are both delicious venues for a coffee break or meal, and the see and be seen potential is unprecedented. Opening hours for the Town Centre are 09:00 to 21:00 on weekdays, 09:00 to 19:00 on Saturdays and 10:00 to 19:00 on Sundays, though the eateries have their own hours.

Dundrum
Town Centre
Sandyford Rd
Dublin 16
Map 421 D4 **24**

House of Fraser

01 299 1400 | www.houseoffraser.co.uk
While it tries to live up to the luxury of its neighbour Harvey Nichols, House of Fraser has one important benefit – you don't need to default on your mortgage to shop here. It stocks everything from flowers to fashion to flatware, but a noticeable gap is their lack of furniture. There is a great cosmetics hall, with Chanel, Clinique, Aveda, Origins and more, and the stationery department is well worth a browse. High-end stock means some expensive prices, but for the most part House of Fraser conforms to the 'you get what you pay for' school of thought. Those in the know will join the Members

325

Club and sign up for a Rewards Card to make the most of their purchases, no matter how infrequent they may be. Ladies will also do well to remember that there is a bank of fitting rooms in the middle of the women's fashion department. These rooms usually go unnoticed while the rooms at concessions such as Hobbes and Coast can have long queues. Unfortunately online shopping can only be delivered to mainland UK addresses at present, but gift vouchers can be purchased and delivered to Ireland. Opening hours for the Dundrum Town Centre are 09:00 to 21:00 on weekdays, 09:00 to 19:00 on Saturdays and 10:00 to 19:00 on Sundays.

15–20 Grafton St
Dublin 2
Map 430 B1 **564**

Marks & Spencer

01 679 7855 | *www.marksandspencer.com*

Marks & Spencer has worked its retail magic just as efficiently in Ireland as it has in the United Kingdom. Its flagship Dublin store on Grafton Street, has a sleek yet charming exterior that practically begs shoppers to come inside and brave the grand staircase to explore its four floors. Variously referred to as Marks and Sparks, M&S and even Magic & Sparkle at Christmas (due to its unrelenting holiday advertising campaign), this department store offers smart clothes for middle of the road prices as well as a wonderful foodhall in the basement. A Café Revive has just been added on the ground floor and though prices can seem slightly high for M&S brand food, the airy environment and comfortable leather chairs go a long way towards justifying the extra expense. Selling only its in-house St Michael's brand, Marks & Spencer has recently added a number of new fashion collections including Per Una and a Limited label for women. 'Marks' knickers' are ubiquitous in the city as they represent some of the only true value in women's undergarments, and special occasion cards and gift wrap may be hidden down in the grocery department but are usually worth the hunt. Though the Grafton Street branch does not carry homeware and furniture, both the Mary Street and Dundrum Town Centre branches do. Returns purchased at any branch can be returned to any branch, so it's easy to buy something, try it on at home, and then return it to any of their stores if you don't like it. Marks & Spencer on Grafton Street is open from 09:00 to 20:00 on weekdays with a late opening until 21:00 on Thursdays, from 20:30 to 19:00 on Saturdays and 12:00 to 18:30 on Sundays. Other Dublin branches include Liffey Valley (01 616 1800), Mary Street (01 872 8833), and Dundrum Town Centre (01 299 1300).

47 Mary St
Dublin 1
Map 425 F3 **566**

Penneys

01 872 7788 | *www.primark.co.uk*

Though Penneys opened first in Ireland, it is now known as a branch of the British retail chain Primark and should not be confused with American retail chain JC Penneys. Penneys is known for budget clothes and accessories as well as bigger sizing in men's, women's and children's fashion. Everything sold in the store is an in-house brand, including Cedarwood State men's casual wear, Rebel Active for young men and Secret Possessions undergarments. Trendy young things often frequent Penneys to pick up whatever is in fashion at the moment and have no qualms about disposing of these items at the end of the season. Beach holiday items, particularly bathing suits and sarongs, beach bags and plastic sunglasses, are popular, as are inexpensive seasonal items at Christmas. Penneys stores are usually crowded and in the city centre branches you are bound to find jumbled heaps of clothing rather than displays, but a good rummage is all part of the experience. Penneys on Mary Street is open from 09:00 to 18:30 every day except for late opening on Thursdays until 21:00 and Fridays until 19:00, and reduced hours on Sundays from 12:00 to 18:00. Other Dublin branches include Blanchardstown Centre (01 820 8408), O'Connell Street (01 656 6666), Dundrum Town Centre (01 215 7202), Dun Laoghaire (01 280 1946), Rathfarnham (01 493 3382) and Swords (01 807 4484).

Independent Shops

With so many chain stores jostling for space on Dublin's shopping scene it's easy to forget that there is still a plethora of independent shops providing unique and distinctive goods at affordable prices. Independent stores tend to cluster on the south side of the city, though this is probably in direct proportion to the fact that there are more true shopping streets on that side of the Liffey.

Independent fashion boutiques are experiencing a resurgence in Dublin right now as those with money to burn no longer want to look just like everyone else. Chica and Roccoco are both gorgeous boutiques stocking eclectic women's fashion while Cherche-Midi and China Blue provide shoes to match all budgets. Jenny Vander offers vintage vixens antique clothing and accessories that are often perused by stylists and professional costumers, and Rhinestones can provide that perfect piece of costume jewellery to top off any outfit. For those with more modern tastes, Whichcraft sells contemporary jewellery, crafts and art work and Nue Blue Eiru (p.269) provides not only brand name beauty products, but also a wide selection of spa treatments to put the finishing touches on any look.

The Dublin entertainment scene still has a few independent outposts as well. Books Upstairs offers a range of quality books as does the Winding Stair, which closed recently but has reopened under new management. Reads and Chapters both offer cut-price books and stationery, and Reads even offers a standard 10% discount off of its entire range of international magazines while Chapters buys back some books for cash or store credit. Cathach Books is an internationally recognised rare books shop and is worthy of a quick browse at the very least. On the music front, Road Records remains staunchly independent as does The Celtic Note.

A few independent home furnishing stores can be found in Dublin, including Pia Bang Home, Stock and the hilariously, yet accurately, named Knobs and Knockers. Fallon & Byrne is an independent, luxury foodhall that will provide tasty treats to bring back to any well furnished home. But before you write your grocery list, be sure to visit The Pen Corner for beautiful stationary and quality writing implements.

Of course no discussion of independent stores in Dublin would be complete without mentioning Avoca, even though it has expanded itself to a few branches and even has a Maryland, USA location now. Avoca is a girly haven with a proliferation of colourful, cute products that you don't yet know that you need. Bath products, books, tableware and women's and children's fashions and accessories are all stocked at Avoca, and the small basement foodhall regularly competes with the larger top floor cafe for customers. Even when the two fill up you needn't go hungry as the takeaway pantry is always well stocked.

Live Like A Shopaholic

It's all very well knowing about all the great shops in the city centre, but what if you need to shop in your own neighbourhood? Turn to the guide to Residential Areas, starting on p.80, to find out where's hot and where's not if you love to shop.

Independent Shops

Avoca	11-13 Suffolk Street	01 677 4215
Books Upstairs	36 College Green	01 679 6687
Cathach Books	10 Duke Street	01 671 5120
The Celtic Note	12 Nassau Street	01 670 4157
Chapters	108/109 Middle Abbey Street	01 872 3297
Cherche-Midi	23 Drury Street	01 675 3974
Chica	Westbury Mall	01 671 9836
China Blue	14 Merchant's Arch	01 671 8785
Fallon & Byrne	11-17 Exchequer Street	01 472 1010
Jenny Vander	50 Drury Street	01 677 0406
Knobs & Knockers	19 Nassau Street	01 671 0288
Neu Blue Eiru	7 South William Street	01 672 5776
The Pen Corner	12 College Green	01 679 3641
Pia Bang Home	2 South Anne Street	01 888 3777
Reads	24/25 Nassau Street	01 679 6011
Rhinestones	18 Andrews Street	01 679 0759
Road Records	16b Fade Street	01 671 7340
Roccocco	Westbury Mall	01 670 4007
Stock	33-34 South King Street	01 679 4316
Whichcraft	Cow's Lane, Temple Bar	01 474 1011
Winding Stair	40 Lower Ormond Quay	01 872 7320

327

Markets

Historically Dublin has been a city with a rich tradition of outdoor markets, but with the recent 'Celtic Tiger' prosperity these gems have been almost completely pushed out in the rush to modernise. Of the few that do remain, most host stalls staffed by incredibly friendly (and chatty) salesmen. Bargaining is not generally accepted, but you could always 'chance your arm' as the Dubliners say.

Farmers' markets are making a bit of a comeback now that organic and whole food is once again in vogue, and locally produced items such as fruit, vegetables, breads, cheeses, chocolates and more are almost always on offer. Notable city centre food markets include St Mary's Church (Anglesea Road, Ballsbridge) every Thursday from 11:00 to 19:00, IFSC/Docklands (National College of Ireland Street, IFSC) every Wednesday from 11:00 to 16:00, St Andrew's Centre (Pearse Street, Dublin 2) every Saturday from 09:00 to 15:00, Ranelagh (Ranelagh Multidenominational School, Ranelagh, Dublin 6) every Sunday from 10:00 to 16:00, and the Temple Bar Market (Meeting House Square, Temple Bar) every Saturday from 10:00 to 17:30.

Temple Bar also offers a range of other speciality markets, including a book market every Saturday and Sunday from 10:00 to 17:30 and a Fashion and Design Market (Cow's Lane, Temple Bar) every Saturday from 10:00 to 17:30. Other fashion discoveries can be found at the new Fashion Market at Powerscourt Centre (p.331) which is open in the top floor Loft every Saturday. Those looking for funky finds should also check out the Blackrock Market (19a Main Street, Blackrock, County Dublin) which is just a short trip outside of the city and best reached by taking the Dart (see p.41) to the Blackrock Station. The Blackrock Market hosts over 50 stalls each weekend so shoppers can browse pieces of art, decorative items for the home, books, food and more. The Blackrock Market is open on Saturdays from 11:00-17:30 and Sundays and Bank Holidays from 12:00 to 17:30.

The George's Street Arcade (South Great George's Street, Dublin 2) should probably be included in any discussion of Dublin markets, though whether or not it is truly a market is debatable. More like one large Victorian building, the arcade hosts an array of shops with multiple market stalls in the middle and has a distinctly student feel. Slogan T-shirts, earthy jewellery, used book stalls and independent coffee shops abound. Opening hours vary. Another market well worth visiting, particularly if you're hungry, is the Sunday market in Howth Harbour. The main commodity here is food, and lots of lovely delicacies that will make your mouth water.

In addition to these fantastic markets there are a few duds in modern Dublin. Blackberry Fair (Blackberry Lane and Rathmines Road) is still advertised on many websites and guides as being a treasure trove, but unfortunately this market has closed down so don't

Howth Market

be fooled if you still see advertisements. Moore Street Market is also often discussed as a huge market and while there are still some fruit, vegetable and flower stalls in the area this small market has been squeezed between mega shopping centres and has attracted a variety of stalls selling shoddy knock-off fashions. However, it has to be said that if you want fruit, veg or fresh flowers, it's still worth a wander. Similarly, the well-known Liberty Market (71 Meath Street, 280 8683) is open on Fridays and Saturdays and offers an array of discounted clothes, shoes and homewares but it has been looking fairly shabby lately and seems to be making a big advertising push to attract new customers. Finally, while the Iveagh Markets in the Liberties and the Markets Area near Smithfield sound

328

promising, these are historical market areas that are only just being refurbished and finding their feet once again. But keep an eye out, because rumour has it they are going to be 'born again' into market hubs for the city.

Shopping Malls – Main

Shopping malls are only in their infancy in Dublin, and the biggest and best sit solidly in suburbs rather than in the city centre, where street shopping is popular. The northern suburbs are home to the Liffey Valley Shopping Centre in Clondalkin and the Blanchardstown Centre in Blanchardstown, while the south side is home to The Square in Tallaght, the Dundrum Town Centre in Dundrum and the Nutgrove Shopping Centre in Rathfarnham. In the city centre the Ilac Centre, the Jervis Centre, the Powerscourt Centre, the Westbury Mall and Stephen's Green Centre attract huge crowds, particularly on rainy days. In general, all Dublin shopping centres offer similar chain stores selling everything from clothes to furniture to electronics, but the more suburban centres, being only recently opened, offer great amenities for families and shoppers with disabilities. These suburban malls also tend to offer more parking (which is often free), foodcourts, cinemas, medical clinics, financial services and customer discounts on their websites. If you can visit these malls during daytime hours you should, since early evenings can get pretty crowded.

Navan Rd/N3
Blanchardstown
Dublin 15

Blanchardstown Centre

01 822 1356 | *www.blanchardstowncentre.com*
Mid-range clothes shops, furniture stores, sporting emporiums, nail bars, hairdressers, dry cleaners, opticians, bookmakers and more all jostle for space in this bright and airy mall, and even the variety of supermarkets and bakeries is a good showing for one area. Borders also has it first Irish store here with what is advertised as Ireland's largest magazine rack. Over 20 restaurants and fastfood outlets are available for the hungry (including TGI Fridays, a Starbucks and a Bon Expresso). An oratory run by the Capuchin monks caters to those with a different kind of hunger and a purpose-built public library, nine-screen cinema and Draiocht Arts Centre with a theatre and two exhibition galleries rounds out the extraordinary extracurricular offerings. Banks, a Bureau de Change, credit unions and multiple ATMs make spending money at Blanchardstown very easy, while the Braille lifts and disabled friendly telephones, toilet stalls, entrances and parking spaces won the Centre a 2004 award from the Centre for Independent Living in recognition of its facilities. 6,500 free parking spaces make driving to Blanchardstown a viable option, though there are over 600 Dublin Buses serving the Centre everyday on routes 39, 70, 76a, 220, 237, 238, 239 and 270. Blanchardstown Centre is open from 09:00 to 21:00 on Mondays through Fridays, 09:00 to 19:00 on Saturdays and 11:00 to 18:00 on Sundays and Bank Holidays. Draiocht theatre, the cinema and some restaurants open later each evening.

Sandyford Rd
Dundrum
Dublin 16
Map 421 D4 **24**

Dundrum Town Centre

01 299 1700 | *www.dundrum.ie*
House of Fraser, LK Bennett and Harvey Nichols have all made their Irish debut at Dundrum, though Marks & Spencer and bargain buddy Penneys also have huge units as well. There are no banks available in the Centre, but there is a Bureau de Change and many ATMs as well as mobile phone re-charger for those who need to call home for more money. RTE radio also has a studio at Dundrum, making the outdoor area fairly jolly in good weather. A medical centre, several hairdressers including an upscale Toni and Guy, Parker Browns Nightclub, a creche and the Mill Theatre all round out the amenities offered at Dundrum. While it is easy to become overwhelmed by the almost ostentatious offerings at Dundrum it is worth remembering that this is mainly a

329

fashion haven so those looking for electronics and homewares probably won't have much luck. In the event of true frustration, a snack break at the Harvey Nichols Espresso Bar is recommended for people watching, and a meal at Dante Italian Bistro or Dunne & Crescenzi tends to leave even the most exhausted shoppers recharged. The Dundrum Town Centre is served by five bus routes – Dublin Bus 17, 44/C, 48A, 75 and the 48 Nightlink – as well as the Luas green line via the Ballaly stop. Currently car parking costs approximately €2 for a three-hour visit, though between 11:00 and 07:00 parking is free for those taking advantage of the 24 hour Tesco grocery store. The rest of the Dundrum Town Centre is open from 09:00 to 21:00 Mondays through Fridays, 09:00 to 19:00 on Saturdays and 10:00 to 19:00 on Sundays.

Henry St
Dublin 1
Map 426 A3 **571**

Ilac Centre

01 704 1460

Built in the 1980s, the Ilac Centre could do with a makeover – low ceilings and dark and dingy feel make this centre possibly one of the least inviting in the city, although a massive refurbishment is under way. A variety of independent boutiques, bargain fashion marts, the ubiquitous Dunnes Stores and a number of international fastfood outlets make up most of this multi-storey mall, though there is a chapel and public library located here as well. International chains Zara, H&M and Debenhams have now also moved in, so it could be that the centre is moving towards more chains in its line-up. The Central Library is perhaps the most comprehensive of the Dublin City public libraries offering members a business library, music library and language library in addition to the general collections, and a variety of community groups also use the premises for meetings. The Ilac Centre is just a short walk from most city centre bus stops, and the Jervis stop on the LUAS Red line also serves the centre. The Jervis Car Park is closest to the centre, but with only 750 parking spaces this pay-per-hour lot fills up quickly. Opening hours are 09:00 to 18:30 every day except Thursday when there is late opening until 21:00 and on Sundays when the centre is open from 12:00 to 18:00.

Henry St
125 Upper Abbey St
Dublin 1
Map 426 A3 **572**

Jervis Centre

01 878 1323 | *www.jervis.ie*

The Jervis Centre attracts shoppers of all ages and budgets with its eclectic mix of stores. Department stores Marks & Spencer and Debenhams, along with electronics giant Dixons, firmly anchor this shopping centre, which also offers an Argos catalogue shop, an Art & Hobby shop, a Sony Centre, a few mobile phone stores and several sports shops and clothes stores. A multi-level Waterstones bookshop also tempts shoppers, as does the foodcourt with its offerings of KFC, Burger King and less recognisable pastry and potato outlets. The shopping centre is wheelchair and pram accessible. The Jervis Centre is within easy reach of all city centre bus stops, and if you are driving, its own car park has 750 pay-per-hour spaces available. The Jervis stop on the Luas red line also serves the centre. Opening hours are 09:00 to 18:00 every weekday except for a late opening until 21:00 on Thursdays, 09:00 to 18:30 on Saturdays and 12:00 to 18:00 on Sundays and bank holidays.

Fonthill Rd
Clondalkin
Dublin 22

Liffey Valley Shopping Centre

01 616 0200 | *www.liffeyvalley.ie*

Liffey Valley has over 90 retail units as well as a multiplex cinema, a foodcourt and a creche for children called Kids R Us. Marks & Spencer and Dunnes will appeal to those looking for wide variety and good value for money, and for the most part all of the stores could be described as bargain or mid-range, though there is no specific grocery store in the centre, so you just have to stock up on all the delicious goodies available in the M&S foodhall. Liffey Valley is wheelchair accessible and offers around 3,500 free parking spaces. A variety of buses serve the centre, including Dublin Bus routes 78, 78A, 210 and 239, while Bus Eireann route 120 and Morton's Circle Line routes CL1 and CL2 stop on the main road right near the bridge to the centre. Opening hours are from 10:00 to 19:00 on Mondays and Tuesdays, 10:00 to 21:00 on Wednesdays, Thursdays and Fridays, 09:30 to 19:00 on Saturdays and 11:00 to 19:00 on Sundays and bank holidays.

Nutgrove Shopping Centre

Nutgrove Av
Rathfarnham
Dublin 14

01 493 3289 | *www.nutgroveshoppingcentre.ie*

Nutgrove Shopping Centre has had something of a revamp lately, perhaps to compete with the award winning Dundrum Town Centre that has opened up nearby. Whatever the reason, Nutgrove has a tremendous selection of shops including banks, chemists, an FX Buckley butchers, a 24 hour Tesco, an X-tra Vision film rental as well as a Social Welfare Local Office, a Motor Tax Office and even a filling station. Bargain department store Penneys also has a huge outlet at Nutgrove. Unless you're a fastfood lover be sure to eat before heading to Nutgrove as there are few other options for a quick meal or snack, but nice extras include 950 free parking spaces, multiple ATMs, a serviced recycling bank, a post office and even a car start-up facility that can be requested from the security office. Nutgrove Shopping Centre is only serviced by a few Dublin Bus routes – 161, 16A, 17 and 75 – and Morton's Circle Line buses CL1, CL2 and CL3. The Nutgrove Shopping Centre is open from 09:00 to 18:00 on Mondays and Tuesdays with late openings until 21:00 on Wednesdays, Thursdays and Fridays, from 09:00 to 18:00 on Saturdays and 12:00 to 18:00 on Sundays.

Powerscourt Centre

59 South William St
Dublin 2
Map 430 A1 567

01 671 7000 | *www.powerscourtcentre.com*

Powerscourt Centre has a unique collection of shops now housed in a refurbished historical building. FCUK is about the only chain store found in the centre, with the rest of the building dominated by a wing of antique stores, several wedding stores, both vintage and modern jewellers, a children's shop or two, several art galleries and now a bustling Saturday fashion market. Though its wares could probably be considered more decorative than functional, Powerscourt Centre is always a great place to pop into just to see what is being sold that day. Ba Mizu, a bar and eatery, also attracts a young professional crowd, although they are usually balanced out by the droves of more staid women visiting Buttercups beauty salon. A variety of restaurants are also available to suit any budget, including a Quiznos sandwich shop preferred by penny pinching students. The centre can be accessed by a quick walk from most city centre bus stops, and there are five pay-per-hour car parks nearby: Brown Thomas (right next to the centre), Drury Street, Royal Surgeons, Trinity Street and Stephens Green. Be sure to check the signs throughout the city during your ride in though, as car parks fill up quickly and may be closed to new visitors if you get there too late. Walking from the Luas green line's Stephens Green terminus is also an option. The Powerscourt Centre is open from 10:00 to 18:00 on weekdays with late opening until 20:00 on Thursdays, 09:00 to 18:00 on Saturdays and 12:00 to 18:00 on Sundays.

The Square

Tallaght
Dublin 24

01 452 5944 | *www.thesquaretallaght.com*

With over 150 stores, 10 restaurants and a multiplex cinema it's not likely that you could go in search of something and come up short at The Square. If in doubt, just check in at the customer service centre on the second floor where lost property and a community noticeboard facility support the advice of friendly staff. Debenhams, Heatons, and Dunnes department stores can all be found at The Square, as can a 24 hour Tesco and a Boots chemist, among a variety of other shops. The Square is fully serviced by the Luas red line's Tallaght stop and Dublin Bus routes 49, 50, 54A, 65/B, 69/X, 75, 76/A/B, 77/A/X and 201. The Square is open from 09:00 to 18:00 on Mondays, Tuesdays and Saturdays, 09:00 to 21:00 on Wednesdays through Fridays and 12:00 to 18:00 on Sundays. The cinema, Dunnes and Tesco run longer individual opening hours.

St Stephen's Green
Dublin 2
Map 430 A2 **26**

Stephen's Green Shopping Centre

01 478 0888 | *www.stephensgreen.com*

This centre is in the ideal location to catch plenty of tourist traffic, so it's always busy, even on weekdays. A huge Dunnes, complete with large grocery department, anchors the centre, and a TK Maxx offers discounts on everything from fashion to free weights. A variety of hairdressers have branches in the centre, and a newly refurbished Hughes & Hughes bookshop offers some comfortable leather chairs for perusing your selections. Benetton, Mothercare, an Argos catalogue shop, a Hickeys fabric store and a tiny Sony outlet round out the truly useful units in the centre. Flanking the centre is a branch of TGI Fridays (01 478 1233) and the city's only Wagamama restaurant (p.356), but inside there is little in the way of tasty food. The centre is not particularly friendly for wheelchair users or children in prams as its three vast floors are served by one old elevator, but it is easily accessible to city centre traffic with both the Stephen's Green and Royal Surgeons pay-per-hour carparks nearby, the pedestrian Grafton Street allowing visitors to walk from city centre bus stops, and the Luas green line terminating just outside its front entrance. Stephens Green Centre is open from 09:00 to 19:00 each day except for late night shopping on Thursdays when it is open from 09:00 to 20:00 and Sundays when it is open from 11:00 to 18:00. Individual retailer hours may vary.

Powerscourt Centre

Dundrum Town Centre

We Know Where You'll Live

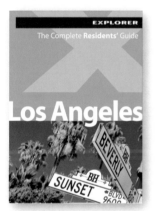
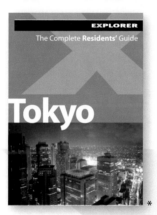

The world has much to offer.
It's just knowing where to find it.

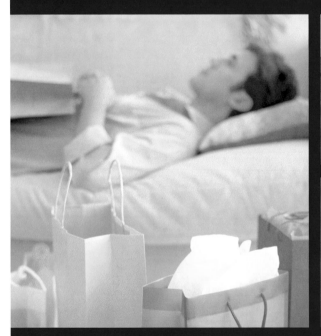

If you're an American Express® Cardmember, simply visit **americanexpress.com/selects** or visit your local homepage, and click on 'offers'. You'll find great offers wherever you are today, all in one place.

selects

THE WORLD OFFERS. WE SELECT. YOU ENJOY

Going Out

Going Out

A To Z
The restaurants in this chapter are listed by cuisine, but if you're looking for a particular restaurant by name, flip to the index at the back of the book and search for it alphabetically.

Going Out

Dublin has a lively social scene. Although largely centred around 'the drink', there are plenty of other options to keep you out of the house and entertained. Pubs start filling up anytime from 18:00 on weeknights when many Dubliners head out for a quiet drink after work. At weekends people start filling tables between 20:00 and 22:00; no matter what time you go out, you will usually find a good crowd somewhere. Dubliners are very stubborn and resistant to change when it comes to their pubs and clubs and many establishments have been going for decades –so don't be surprised if you hear somewhere being referred to by its old name long after it has changed hands. In recent years, eating out has become an integral part of a night on the town. Since the mid 1990s there has been an explosion of restaurants and cheap eateries, and these days the greasy burger is losing face to the cut-price Korean barbecue and the plate of tapas. Tourists tend to concentrate on Temple Bar, which has an international reputation as Dublin's party quarter and it is a hugely popular destination for stag and hen parties. It's not the spot for a quiet drink and a chat (although there are some hidden gems), but it is home to some interesting venues, such as the Temple Bar Music Centre (see p.392), the Project Arts Theatre (see p.395) and numerous good restaurants. The Irish Film Institute (see p.390) shows an interesting range of off-the-beaten-track films and has an onsite cafe, shop and a bar, which has less of the in-your-face, party-hard atmosphere that is so prevalent in the rest of the area.

The best multi-screen cinemas are found north of the Liffey, with Cineworld on Parnell Street and the Savoy on O'Connell Street, although more and more suburban shopping centres are now boasting large cinema complexes (see Cinemas on p.390 for more). Theatres, long-established and experimental, tend to cluster in the city centre, but the smaller suburban theatres are good places to look for more unusual productions and cheaper tickets prices (see p.393). For new ideas, or just to be in the know, there are several free magazines distributed around the city with extensive entertainment listings.

> ### Restaurant Timings
> Restaurants usually open around 17:00 or 18:00 and close between 23:00 and 00:00 (often closing earlier on Sundays). Many places are open for lunch between 12:00 and 15:00. Most restaurants don't open on Christmas Day or St Stephens' Day (December 26), so a Christmas dinner package in one of the hotels might be a better option. No alcohol is served on Good Friday, and many outlets remain closed on this day.

Eating Out

Eating out in Dublin has become a far more diverse experience since the Celtic Tiger economy of the mid 1990s transformed the city. The variety of restaurants has improved and the quality, which has always been quite high, has been invigorated by

Cuisine List

American	p.340	International	p.349	Mediterranean	p.358
Asian Subcontinent	p.340	Irish	p.352	Middle Eastern	p.359
Chinese	p.341	Italian	p.353	Seafood	p.360
European	p.842	Japanese	p.356	Spanish	p.361
French	p.346	Korean	p.356	Thai	p.361
Indian	p.348	Latin American	p.357	Vegetarian	p.363

increased competition. There is a range of cuisines available, from traditional Irish pub grub to authentic international tastes.

Most restaurants open in the early evening, between 17:00 and 19:00, and closing time is usually between 23:00 and midnight. If you're willing to dine early, you can find a bargain 'Early Bird' menu in most places before 19:30; bookings usually start from 20:00. On week nights it is easier to get a table on short notice, although for more than four people it is always worth booking in advance. Weekends, bank holidays, Valentine's Day, Mother's Day and Father's Day tend to be especially busy.

Restaurants in Ireland are not as family-friendly as in most European countries, but you should still be able to enjoy a meal out with children. Special seats will be provided if necessary and staff will be happy to heat a bottle or baby food. Theme restaurants like Captain America's (01 671 5266, www.captainamericas.com) and Eddie Rockets (p.340) are particularly child-friendly, and almost every establishment will make you feel welcome. Some more upmarket restaurants may be less welcoming, so if you think your children will require any special attention, such as modified dishes or special seats, ask about this at the time of booking. Some pubs will display notices barring children or under 18s after a certain time, but these are rarely enforced unless there is a threat to their safety or if they're unsupervised or extremely disruptive.

The variety of restaurants in all areas of the city is good, although some areas are a little more specialist. For authentic Korean and Chinese food, Parnell Street and its surroundings in Dublin 1 is the place to go, and nearby Moore Street boasts some authentic African eateries.

Delivery

When up against the famous Irish rain, it's no surprise that many people like to have food delivered to their door. There are plenty of outlets that deliver pizza, fish and chips, Chinese and curries, and the food quality in the latter two can be excellent if they're attached to a restaurant. Restaurant Express (www.restaurantexpress.ie) provides delivery from a number of well-regarded Dublin restaurants.

The mighty pint

The Great Outdoors
With Ireland's climate, it's not often you'll be enjoying your lunch or dinner alfresco. So when the sun does shine, be prepared by knowing some of the best alfresco restaurants off by heart: Lemon Jelly (p.384), Rhodes D7 (p.345), Chez Max (p.346), Bar Italia (p.353) and Cafe Mao (p.361) all have wonderful outdoor seating areas.

Drinks

Other options **Alcohol** p.284, **Food & Drink** p.20

Alcohol is widely available and sold for 363 days of the year (the exceptions are Christmas Day and Good Friday, when pubs are closed). The legal drinking age is 18, and if you're under 23 you're legally obliged to carry proof of age. Although alcohol prices are controlled in Ireland, they're pretty high, and you can expect to pay more in city centre venues, hotel bars or anywhere that has table service. A pint of beer can cost up to €4.75 and a pint of cider up to €5. A spirit and mixer can cost up to €7. A quarter bottle of wine starts from €4.50 and a full bottle averages between €20 and €30. Cocktails also tend to be expensive as you will be charged per shot, but you'll find them in every club. There are several good wine bars in the city centre, notably Ely CHQ (see p.343) and La Cave on South Anne Street (01 679 4409, www.lacavewinebar.com). Most restaurants will have a wine list, although some are better than others. Soft drinks are available everywhere – including the uniquely Irish red lemonade – and most places that serve cocktails will offer a few non-alcoholic mocktails too.

> **Drinking & Driving**
> The legal blood alcohol limit for driving in Ireland is 80mg/100ml. If you are caught driving over the limit and are convicted, you will be disqualified from driving for anything from one to six years. Taxi queues can be horrendous in the city centre on a weekend night so beat the possy and head to a rank well before closing time.

Hygiene

All food service outlets in Ireland must conform to the Hazard Analysis and Critical Control Point (HACCP) food management system. The Health Service Executive carries out inspections of premises, although the Food Safety Authority is the overseeing body for food standards. Most premises will display their HACCP certification. As a rule, most establishments are very hygienic, but always apply some common sense – never eat somewhere that you feel uncomfortable and be a little wary of mobile food service outlets. For more on food hygiene, visit the Food Safety Authority website at www.fsai.ie.

> **Door Policy**
> Door policies are quite relaxed, but tend to be stricter for men than women. If you're being loud or visibly drunk you'll be turned away, especially in a large group. Some nightclubs are fussy about dress code - sports clothes are a definite no (did you hear that, chavs?). Very few bars are members-only, although some have members' areas. Membership costs and criteria are available from individual bars.

Special Deals & Theme Nights

Many venues run drinks promotions year round, when a particular drink will be offered for free or sold at a discount price. These are especially prevalent on the biggest nights of the social calendar, notably New Years' Eve, St Patrick's Day, Halloween and practically every night in the weeks running up to Christmas as old friends meet and catch up. On Halloween, you can expect a lot of fancy dress nights with prizes and promotions, and most venues will advertise these ahead of time. Bank holidays also tend to be heavy on drinks promotions as more Dubliners hit the town.

> **Hidden Charges**
> Tips tend to be at the discretion of the customer, but for parties of six or more a service charge is usual. Some restaurants have a standard service charge, but this should be clearly stated on your menu. Prices include VAT.

Tax & Service Charges

Some restaurants will add a service charge, which can range from 10% to 25%. The service charge should be stated at the end of the bill, with the percentage clearly marked, and it will be included in the total. Restaurants usually price inclusive of

VAT (which is higher for eating in than for take away). You are not expected to tip if there's a service charge, although many people like to leave some change to ensure that their particular server gets something.

Room With A View
Unfortunately, not many of Dublin's restaurants come with what you'd call 'classic views'. You'll find pleasing views at Restaurant Patrick Gilbaud (p.348) and The Winding Stair (p.353), but apart from that, you'll have to rely on people-watching for your visual entertainment. Fortunately, that is definitely one of Dublin's most interesting views!

Tipping

It is considered usual to tip in any establishment, pubs included, where the servers come to your table to take your order. In a restaurant, 10% of the bill is the normal amount and most diners leave cash tips so that their server will be more likely to receive it. In cafes and bars, however, things can be a bit more complicated. If you go to the bar or counter to place your order but it is brought to your table, a smaller tip is fine, and most people simply round the bill up to the nearest euro or two and leave the remainder. In self-service outlets, there will usually be a tip jar on display but don't feel obliged – it will be appreciated, but not really expected.

Independent Reviews

All of the outlets in this book have been independently reviewed by a team of food and nightlife experts who are based in Dublin. Their aim is to give clear, realistic and, as far as possible, unbiased reviews of each venue, without back-handers, hand-me-downs or underhandedness on the part of any restaurant owner, nightclub promoter, crafty PR guru or persuasive barista!

Restaurant Listing Structure

There are so many places offering varied cuisine in Dublin that choosing the perfect place to eat out can be an arduous task. Reviewing every single restaurant, bar, nightclub and coffee shop would fill an entire book in itself, so this section of the *Dublin Explorer* features just under 200 outlets that have been carefully selected by a team of food and nightlife experts who live and breathe the social scene.

Each review attempts to give an idea of the food, service, decor and ambience, while those venues that are particularly brilliant earn the coveted 'Explorer Recommended' big yellow star.

Primarily the restaurants have been categorised according to cuisine (in alphabetical order), but if you want to go out for a special occasion, such as to watch the match, eat outdoors, impress a date, get sozzled on cocktails or eat on a budget, see 'The Great Outdoors' on p.337, 'Sports Bars' on p.374, 'Always Ace That First Date' on p.364, 'Tummies & Pockets Full' on p.366 and 'Late Date' on p.371.

The Yellow Star
Keep your eyes peeled throughout this chapter for this bright yellow star - it marks those restaurants which are really special. It may be because they're fancy, it may be because they're cheap and cheerful, or it may even be because it's impossible to go there and not have a great time. Whatever the reason, the outlets with the star should be on your to-do list.

Vegetarian Food

Vegetarianism is relatively common in Ireland and almost every restaurant will serve a vegetarian option or two. There are a few specialist vegetarian restaurants in Dublin, such as Cornucopia on Wicklow Street (see p.363) and Govinda's on Aungier Street (see p.364), both in Dublin 2. If you're eating out with a group and want something to suit everyone, Indian restaurants are among the best for vegetarians, and many Chinese, Japanese and Thai restaurants will use tofu as a meat substitute in some dishes. Italian food can also be very veggie-friendly, especially if you opt for pizza.

American

7 South Anne St
Dublin 2
Map 430 B1 **517**

Eddie Rocket's

01 679 7340 | www.eddierockets.ie

Eddie Rocket's is an overpriced chain of 1950s style diners but heck, the milkshakes are tasty. A bit like something from the film *Grease*, from its seated booths with red leather upholstery to the bar stools at the chrome counter, this burger bar is American retro, loud and proud. Plates are perplexingly too small for the burgers and salads are more expensive than the burgers, but there is a veggie burger option for herbivores. The cheesy fries are a tad extortionate at €4.45, while breakfast add-ons – tomato, mushrooms and fried egg – start at 55 cents each. It's a shame the mini-jukeboxes are just for show but the stereo gaily plays the likes of *Blue Moon*, *Lollipop* and *Will You Still Love Me Tomorrow?* anyway. Not quite happy days, but a novelty nonetheless.

18 Temple Bar
Dublin 2
Map 425 A4 **485**

Elephant & Castle

01 679 3121 | www.elephantandcastle.ie

The fact that Colin Farrell once endorsed this informal restaurant in a travel feature for *American Way* magazine doesn't necessarily say much – a few paragraphs later, he also revered national shawarma chain Abrakebabra. Still, thanks to its prime location in Temple Bar, chargrilled gourmet burgers and a convivial and laidback atmosphere, Elephant & Castle is a hit with Dubliners and tourists alike. The fact that it's an offshoot of the Elephant & Castle in Greenwich Village, NYC, helps seal the deal. Staple dishes include caesar salad and baskets of chicken wings; portions bountiful. There's not a great deal of choice for vegetarians though. Due to E&C's popularity, it's often hard to get a seat – especially on a Sunday for brunch – but it is arguably worth the wait.

Asian Subcontinent

46 Upper Baggot St
Dublin 2
Map 431 E4 **508**

Langkawi

01 668 2760

This restaurant offers authentic Malaysian cuisine at fair prices. The space itself is small, which makes for a good atmosphere when busy – which it commonly is during business lunches and after work noshes – and the staff bid a warm welcome that is maintained throughout. Langkawi offers a variety of meat and seafood mains, from chicken devil curry to stuffed dried fish, although vegetarians might feel short changed by fairly uninspiring veg stir-fries and herbivorous side dishes. There have been some whinges about portion size, but since when was waste and 'waistful' super-sizing a good thing? Besides, the dishes are so bountiful with herbs and spices, you don't need a mound the size of the Petronas Towers.

Elephant & Castle

28 Eustace St
Temple Bar
Dublin 2
Map 426 A4 **497**

Monty's Of Kathmandu

01 670 4911 | www.montys.ie

It's all about the momo at Monty's. The signature dish at this delightful Nepalese restaurant should be ordered 24 hours in advance but as the adage goes, the best things come to those who wait and these spice-stuffed dumplings will not disappoint. A respite from run-of-the-mill curry houses, Monty's has won a plethora of restaurant awards throughout the noughties, and celebrity diners include Bono, Quentin Tarantino and John McKenna. And if it's good enough for them… True, the dining space is so small you could barely swing a goat (although there is an upstairs) but this makes for a lively atmosphere when busy – which it is often. The no-frills decor perhaps keeps prices down – main courses average at €15 – but service is efficient and friendly, particularly if you're a virgin to Nepalese cuisine: they will likely recommend sister signature dish, the kachela; raw minced lamb with garlic, herbs and spices washed down with a shot of whisky. The tandoori and yogurt-based dishes are also a boon, while vegetarians will go neither hungry nor dissatisfied. The wine list has a decent mix of old and new world. Book that momo now.

Chinese

139 Parnell St
Dublin 1
Map 425 A2 **475**

China House

086 340 8340

The words 'popular', 'cheap' and 'cheerful' sum up this place. And as you would expect from such praise, the decor is basic (formica tables, cruel lighting), the service efficient (no dramatic pauses between courses) and dishes uncomplicated. The sweet and sour options are highly recommended, ditto the ribs, and the crab stir-fry so fresh it even comes with claws. Incredibly, mains are less than €10 each and portions border on colossal, so go easy on the mid-afternoon grazing beforehand. Also, its proximity to the cinema makes it a smart option for anyone wanting to curb their overpriced popcorn and hotdog habits. Despite the somewhat shabby interior, it has been billed by many as the best Chinese restaurant in town, so if you can't beat 'em…

18 South Great
George's St
Dublin 2
Map 430 A1 **484**

Good World

01 677 5373

Got a dim sum craving in the dead of night? Then Good World it is. This late night haunt is a gem for late eaters and anyone not wanting to spend through the nose for a King Do. Overall, the quality may well depend on the state you're in when visiting, but

Good World

341

it's a popular place during daylight hours also and is commended by the Chinese community. There are duck, chow mein, curry and seafood options galore making it a good choice for large groups to each chip in and share each other's nibbles. Prices middle at €12 for mains so it's not bad value at all.

New Millenium Chinese Restaurant

51 South King St
Dublin 2
Map 430 A1 530

01 635 1525

This wood-cladded Chinese eatery is as easy on the pocket as the tastebuds. Main dishes average at €14 with seafood plates slightly higher, while the gamut of diners from the Chinese community is a heartening sight. Curiously, though, this restaurant has two menus – one authentically Cantonese and one adapted to the Western palate (or rather, what is generally believed to please, even in this culinary climate where Indian and Thai dishes are at their peak). Ask for the Dim Sum one and you'll be decently sated. Eeney-meeney-miney-mo the fairly extensive range from soups to seafood, chow mein to chicken dishes and, of course, dim sum to duckling. Alternatively dabble in the generous pre-theatre menu, such is its proximity to the Gaiety: three courses for €20 between 15:00 and 20:00.

European

Other options **Spanish** p.361, **French** p.346, **Italian** p.353, **Mediterranean** p.358

Brasserie Sixty6

66-67 South
Great George's St
Dublin 2
Map 430 A1 513

01 400 5878 | www.brasseriesixty6.com

Perpetually busy despite its competitive location, Brasserie is as cacophonous as it is hip, trendy, clever, oh, and so tasty. Ticking most of those all-important boxes, the fresh produce is imported locally and there's a deli next door for those on the hoof. The decorative plates on one wall, though, remain a whimsical mystery in an otherwise super modern interior. For lunch, there are starters and mains plus gourmet sandwiches and salads for lighter stomachs. For dinner, the same again plus meat platters and a rather fine vegetarian menu. Forward planners may be interested to know that a roast suckling pig can be ordered at least a fortnight in advance for optimum rubs and marinades (with a deposit of €150), while beef is hung for 21 days for optimum flavour. There's also a long brunch every Saturday and Sunday from 10.00 to 17.00.

The Cellar Restaurant

Upper Merrion St
The Merrion Dublin
Dublin 2
Map 430 C2 29

01 603 0600 | www.merrionhotel.com

As with most swish hotel restaurants, The Cellar doesn't cut corners when it comes to design, its white up-lit vaulted ceiling making for a soothing ambience. Indeed, the colour palette is composed almost entirely of creams and beiges, which are at once relaxing and reviving. The dishes themselves are also aesthetically pleasing, and comprise patriotic Irish ingredients. Typical options include roast breast of duck and baked figs and seared chicken with truffled polenta and white asparagus. But have no fear, The Cellar's raison d'etre is far from pretentious with good old-fashioned fish'n'chips and mint mushy peas, steaks and even calf liver with bacon. There's a two course lunch menu at €21.95, three courses at €24.95, and Sunday brunch (plus children's corner) at €29.50 for two courses and €35 for three a la carte.

Eden

Meeting House Sq
Temple Bar
Dublin 2
Map 426 A4 20

01 670 5372 | www.edenrestaurant.ie

This Mediterranean-style brasserie with an Irish bent has enjoyed a sound reputation since its opening in 1997, and rightly so. True, on closer inspection at the time of writing, the mosaic-tiled space (swimming pool chic?) is starting to look a little shabby.

But its dishes are enough to redeem any scuffed chair, with the menus changing every season to help keep diners on their toes and drooling at the mouth. Downstairs, the open kitchen provides a focus point, while the mezzanine boasts a large semi-private table. There's also a covered and heated terrace open May to September for those, er, hot summer days and nights. The lunch menu offers two courses for €22 and three at €26 while there's a pre-theatre Menu every Sunday to Thursday from 18:00 to 19:00 at €27. Saturday and Sunday proffer brunch a la carte.

Wellington Quay
Temple Bar
Dublin 2
Map 426 A4 492

Eliza Blues
01 671 9114 | *www.elizablues.com*

This family-run restaurant opened its panoramic glass doors in 1999. The blue and gold mosaic interior may be reminiscent of a Roman bath, but the menu is less bacchanalian and more contemporary European fusion. Pasta dishes nestle alongside burgers, paninis and salads. But Ms Blues's trump card is seafood, with produce sourced from the Irish coasts. The chowder is pleasingly riddled with mussels, smoked and fresh fish, and the good old-fashioned fish and chips don't disappoint. Its quayside location in bustling Temple Bar makes it a particular hit with visitors. There's an early bird Sunday to Friday between 16:00 and 20:00 at €18 for two courses and €22 for three.

Custom House Quay
Dublin 1
Map 427 D3 527

Ely CHQ
01 672 0010 | *www.elywinebar.ie*

As the Celtic Tiger grows, so does Ely Wine Bar. Now a trilogy of branches, Ely's growth is a reflection not just of Dublin's booming culinary scene but also the brand's solid reputation for fuss-free nutritious food in stylish surroundings. Ely CHQ is its most recent addition; a cavernous contemporary basement with low arched ceilings, subdued lighting and exposed brickwork. All lamb, pork and beef produce is sourced from an organic family-run farm in Carron, County Clare, while cheeses, seafood and vegetables are sourced from local suppliers. The menus also helpfully suggest a wine per dish so you don't end up having – heaven forbid – a sauvignon blanc with your organic beef carpaccio. All branches are highly recommended, and given their canny locations, prime bait for business luncheons. Other branches: 22 Ely Place, Dublin 2 (01 676 8986), Ely HQ, Hanover Quay, Dublin 1 (01 633 9986).

The Mansion House
Dawson St
Dublin 2
Map 430 B2 536

Fire
01 676 7200 | *www.mansionhouse.ie*

Lovely building, lovely staff, lovely food. Large groups are – pardon the pun - like moths to a flame at Fire. And with its efficient service, super amiable staff and heated outdoor terrace overlooking the Lord Mayor's garden, it's easy to see the attraction. Built in 1710

Eliza Blues

Fire

343

by property developer and merchant John Dawson – hence the name Dawson Street – the Mansion House is an easy draw. The creamy Bantry Bay mussels starter is worth a trip alone (served with chunky chips), while its signature prime Irish beef fillet gets the thumbs up. All three courses plus sides and wine works out expensive, but given the plush surroundings and quality ingredients, you don't mind. There's an early bird menu between 17:30 and 18:30, Monday to Thursday, and 17:00 to 18:00 on Friday and Saturday. The measly two salads come in two sizes – starter or main course, and the desserts are worth leaving room for – chocolate polenta pudding anyone?

Local Cuisine

Traditional Irish food tends to be carb-heavy, warming and comforting. Roast dinners, potatoes, vegetables, pies and soups are the most obvious examples of traditional Irish meals. Guinness beef pies and the side dish champ are worth trying. Along the coast, the fresh seafood is excellent; in particular the Dublin Bay prawns. As for beverages, apart from the obvious Guinness choice, a tall glass of milk or some red lemonade will complete the Irish dining experience.

Ormond Quay
Morrison Hotel
Dublin 1
Map 425 F4 **533**

Halo

01 887 2400 | www.morrisonhotel.ie

Design-wise, The Morrison hotel is exactly what you would expect from fashion designer John Rocha – stylish, sophisticated and sleek. Its restaurant Halo is exactly that: all clean lines, ambient lighting and an impossibly high ceiling. Indeed, its split-level loftiness is a blessing and a curse, emanating a rather distinct lobby lounge vibe, especially if you have the misfortune of being seated alongside the defunct bar area. But don't let that put you off – the food is exquisite and the service impeccable. The quality-over-quantity menu boasts obligatory posh nosh terms like 'jus' and 'compote', and meat and fish dishes (avoid the sea bass at your peril) tend to be 'topped with a foam of…' There are also platters for groups of six people and over. Meanwhile, its list of famous diners is enough to give any velvet rope a run for its money: Beyonce and Jay-Z, Christina Aguilera and The Arctic Monkeys. Heavenly.

1 Windsor Tce
Portobello
Dublin 8
Map 416 A4 **467**

Locks Restaurant

01 454 3391

Chef of the moment Troy Maguire of L'Gueuleton fame gave this understated eatery a style injection and change of staff in June 2007. The new space is light, bright and reminiscent of a New England bistro, all wooden floors, Daz-white linen and groovy lamps. It's all so darned aesthetically pleasing, it doesn't even have front door signage outside, only an Art Deco-like emblem. Food-wise, dishes are simple but with a quirky twist such as rib-eye steak with the option of a bearnaise or snail and roquefort sauce or Dublin Bay Prawns with pigeon biscuit (pronounced 'biscay' but still involving pigeon and another feathered friend/foe, foie gras). Meanwhile, the saddle of lamb, and seafood stew, deserve a round of applause, although veggies will lament for a main dish other than the risotto. Desserts are equally lacklustre. Such is the restaurant's buzz at the time of writing though, that booking a table can be tricky – only time will tell if the best things come to those who wait.

69/70 Dame St
Dublin 2
Map 426 A4 **515**

The Mermaid Café

01 670 8236 | www.mermaid.ie

The brainchild of chef Ben Gorman and artist Mark Harrell, The Mermaid Café is stylish but unpretentious and has the air of a bistro, thanks to the simple blonde wood furniture and flooring and large windows overlooking busy Dame Lane. Contrary to its fishy name, the eatery doesn't just serve seafood, taking in also oriental duck, calves' liver with horseradish mash and roast lamb with a Moroccan bent to name but a few. Vegetarians fair worse, though, with just one main dish at the time of writing. Despite the geographically diverse

344

assortment of platters, they keep it short but sweet opting for quality over quantity of dishes and with inventive combinations of ingredients. Don't be fooled by the low-key decor though – main dishes clock in at around €26. That said, the lunch menus are good value at two courses for €21.95 and three for €25.95, and Sunday brunch a la carte is a delight – enhanced by the jugs of bellinis, sangria and mimosa at €24.

The Capel Bld
Mary's Abbey
Dublin 7
Map 425 F4 **535**

Rhodes D7

01 804 4444 | www.rhodesd7.com

Whether or not you mind paintings of the cattle you're eating adorning the walls of a restaurant may dictate your feelings towards D7. Otherwise, though, celebrity chef Gary Rhodes is difficult to fault, barely challenging the man's five Michelin stars. Dishes are hearty and unpretentious, despite their aesthetically pleasing production; the roasted chicken with buttered asparagus and almond and tarragon tagliatelle giving a particularly stellar performance, ditto the braised shank of lamb with ragout and champ mashed potato. Salads can be ordered 'starter size' or as a main, and desserts are to die for; even the egg custard, which seldom features on fine dining menus. The layout is also tasty, with a modern mezzanine level and a heated outdoor area perfect for Dublin's tumultuous weather. The scant of pocket, meanwhile, can avail of the Business Lunch Menu between 12:00 and 15:00, which changes daily.

7 Ballsbridge Tce
Dublin 4
Map 417 D4 **516**

Roly's Bistro

01 668 2611 | www.rolysbistro.ie

By the time you read this, Roly's may well have taken a slight tumble since a local magazine gave it a scathing review, notably criticising its service, or lack thereof – dirty plates were not cleared until waiting staff were prompted to do so, and one waiter even wiped a used fork on his apron and moved on… Likely, though, Roly's will live, learn and return to its former glory as one of Ballsbridge's busiest and best restaurants. As it should; its dishes hark back to good, honest recipes, which are so popular with Dublin's foodies these days. There are set menus for lunch and dinner as well as a pricey a la carte, but one hopes that it stops living up to its reputation – enhanced by the Pied Piper of Hamlin-esque aromas wafting outside – and starts surpassing it after the recent fall from grace.

Westbury Hotel
Grafton St
Dublin 2
Map 430 B1 **43**

Sandbank Bistro Cafe

01 679 1122 | www.jurys-dublin-hotels.com

Restaurants in excellent hotels seldom disappoint, Sandbank being a case in point. Top notch food in casually salubrious surroundings doesn't come cheap of course – main courses are around €25 – and this isn't even the hotel's fine dining option (that honour goes to the Russell Room). But for a special occasion or business lunch to impress the head honcho, this bistro/cafe is worth pushing the boat out for. The menu is succinct, with two vegetarian dishes at the time of writing (one being – quelle surprise – risotto), and boasts a prime beef fillet and a super seared halibut in an intriguing minestrone style sauce with crispy Parmesan. As always, the side dishes of mash et al bump up the price but do leave room for dessert if you have particularly sweet tooth – many of the dishes are combinations, the creme brulee comes with chocolate cake icecream and caramelised pears, and the chocolate fondant is accompanied by a raspberry confection and Baileys sorbet.

Four Seasons Dublin
Simmonscourt Rd
Dublin 4
Map 417 E4 **25**

Seasons Restaurant

01 665 4000 | www.fourseasons.com/dublin

This Four Season's signature restaurant is rumoured to be the favourite of Louis Walsh, but don't let that put you off – there's nothing as dire as One True Voice here. Rare does any Four Seasons eatery anywhere in the world let you down, and this dining room is no exception. It's expensive, naturally, but that is to be expected from such a welcomingly fancy brand – starters, er, start at €14 and mains are generally in the €40 bracket. Located overlooking a pretty gardened courtyard, Seasons – funnily enough – boasts seasonal produce, and focuses as much as possible on Irish-grown ingredients. They also occasionally have special promotional menus oriented around one particular ingredient such as asparagus or mushrooms. The only downside is a minimal choice for vegetarians; however, meat-eaters can rejoice in loin of spiced Irish lamb, butter-soft Dover Sole stuffed with fennel and a cheese ravioli with plump Dublin Bay prawns among other magnificent morsels. There is also an extensive menu for kids, resplendent with age brackets, and without a whiff of eggs and chips.

Dylan Hotel
Eastmoreland Pl
Dublin 4
Map 431 E4 16

Still Restaurant

01 660 3000 | www.dylan.ie

Modern dining means stylish designs at the Dylan hotel's restaurant. The tablecloths are Persil-white, the mirrored wall cubes shiny and the cream leather seats comfier than being sat in a pot of creme brulee. There's an outdoor terrace too, boasting black wicker chairs and less formal tables than inside. A la carte lunch and dinner menus start with a choice of – among others – oysters, chicken liver parfait and the somewhat less illustrious pea soup, followed by a succinct list of meat and seafood (vegetarians lose out somewhat: a 'Tasting of Asparagus' my dear?). There are as many desserts as starters and mains. Naturally the presentation is almost as handsome as the space, and it's no surprise that this restaurant is quietly becoming a staple on Baggot Street's culinary scene.

French

1 Palace St
Dublin 2
Map 430 A1 465

Chez Max

01 633 7215

Oh happy days when you can eat delicious, unpretentious French fare in welcoming surroundings, including a glass of quality wine, at a very reasonable price. Chez Max, situated right at the pedestrian entrance to Dublin Castle, is a real culinary find – you can just stroll in at lunchtime for a light meal, or linger over a romantic meal in the evening. The menu is simple yet completely adequate, as is the wine list. And if the weather permits you can eat out in the pretty little garden at the back. There are additional alfresco tables outside the front door, although being so near one of Dublin's most popular visitor attractions may make you feel a little bit exposed to passing tourist traffic. Otherwise, this French charmer is highly recommended.

109a Lower Baggot St
Dublin 2
Map 431 D3 35

L'Ecrivain

01 661 1919

Established in 1989, L'Ecrivain has managed not to be edged off the culinary map thanks to being an excellent all-rounder – the French-styled brasserie has won a variety of major food awards during the noughties alone. The decor is light and airy – warm creams and red – with a mezzanine level nestling into the tall, pointed ceiling. There are also some jaunty booth-style couches spooning into decorative banisters, and – better yet – an outdoor terrace. Menu-wise, take your pick; there's one for lunch, three for dinner – a Tasting Menu, an a la carte, and a Prix Fixe – and remarkably for

Chez Max

a Gallic establishment, a vegetarian menu. And as you'd expect, there's an extensive wine list of old and new grapes. Also, as you'd expect, a trip to L'Ecrivain doesn't come cheap but you get what you pay for, and quality here is guaranteed.

La Mère Zou

22 St Stephen's Green
Dublin 2
Map 430 B2 490

01 661 6669 | *www.lamerezou.ie*

Experienced and knowledgeable staff, coupled with fine cuisine, put La Mère Zou high on the list of places to dine. Such acclaim comes at a price, naturally, but if you're looking for somewhere to celebrate a special occasion, this is it. Located in the basement of a Georgian house, the bistro is intimate and cosy, and provides an ideal backdrop to live jazz every Saturday night. Contrary to the stereotype of Gallic cuisine – stuffy, spartan and pretentious – La Mère Zou is anything but, thanks to its friendly service. Yes it serves snails, yes, some dishes include garlic, but there are many more fresh flavours beside, including a bounty of seafood. There's also an early bird menu at €24.50 between 18:00 and 19:00 every Monday to Saturday, and all night Sunday. The wine menu, meanwhile, is appropriately extensive and exclusively *française*.

La Stampa Balzac Restaurant

La Stampa Hotel
35 Dawson St
Dublin 2
Map 430 B1 17

01 677 8611 | *www.lastampa.ie*

This lovely, lofty brassiere-style restaurant is simply and elegantly designed with high ceilings, large mirrors and Victorian accents. To echo the faintly Parisian surroundings, Balzac has a predominantly French menu, which is limited in range but certainly top quality. The mussels mariniere are suitably plump and creamily piquant while the steak is sublime. As with many a Gallic restaurant, vegetarians are scarcely catered for here but carnivores and pescatarians will absolutely rejoice in the fleshy fare. Main courses start at €18 with side dishes at €4.50. Add the vino, and you've an expensive night out but one that will ensure a repeat visit, especially for lovers' trysts.

Les Frères Jacques

74 Dame St
Nxt to Olympia Theatre
Dublin 2
Map 425 A4 520

01 679 4555 | *www.lesfreresjacques.com*

This much-loved French restaurant combines Irish-produced ingredients with Gallic recipes and a certain 'je ne sais quoi'. Spending an evening here is such a treat, the restaurant even offers gift vouchers – a perfect present for a gourmand if ever there was one. Main courses are around €34 and include fresh vegetables at no extra price. Naturally, snails feature – as a ravioli starter – and the cheeseboard is magnifique. As one would expect from a French restaurant, the a la carte menu is short but sweet and includes a refined selection of meat and seafood dishes. Vegetarians need not apply, though – at the time of writing, there's not one flesh-free option. How very French. Those wishing for a piece of the action but can't afford veal medallions at €36 should try the Table d'Hote at €17.50 for two courses and €22.50 for three (lunch) and four courses at €36 (dinner), some dishes of which are priced 'extra', such is their poshness – steamed blue lobster thermidor has a set menu 'add-on' of €24. Also, at the time of writing there's a 50% discount off bottles of wine every Monday and Tuesday.

Pearl Brasserie

20 Merrion St Upper
Dublin 2
Map 430 62 488

01 661 3572 | *www.pearl-brasserie.com*

What's this – a French restaurant with a vegetarian menu?! Dix points for Pearl Brasserie! No wonder Pearl has garnered a plethora of foodie awards since it opened in late 2000, and that's just the cherry on top – there's also an Oyster Bar to prop up should you not fancy a full-on feast. Exposed brickwork juxtaposed with white walls and bright blue and yellow soft furnishings make for a contemporary setting not least with the beautifully crafted dishes – themselves works of art. Like it or loathe it, the baked loin of rabbit consistently gets a resounding thumbs-up, while the panfried sea bass and crab meat tortellini deserves an encore. As well as a la carte, there are two set menus in addition to the aforementioned veggie one, priced at €45 and €55 respectively for three courses including tea or coffee. There's also a lunch menu with starters at €8 and mains at €16, Monday to Friday from noon.

Restaurant Patrick Guilbaud

21 Upper Merrion St
The Merrion Dublin
Dublin 2
Map 430 C2 **29**

01 676 4192 | www.merrionhotel.com

Overlooking the grounds of the splendid Merrion Hotel, Restaurant Patrick Guilbaud is a sight for sore eyes. And unsurprisingly, the food ain't bad either what with French masterchef Guilbaud directing its French-Gaelic fusion of seasonal Irish ingredients. There's a two-course lunch priced at €33 and a three-course at €45, with main dishes at the time of writing including panfried skate wing and roast fillet of lamb with spiced jam, while the a la carte dinner menu boasts lobster ravioli, veal sweetbread and liquorice and wild seabass fillet. The wine list is extensive and includes a wide variety of champagne. Unsurprisingly, such esteemed morsels don't come cheap with mains averaging at €45, but if you want a dinner to remember then this is it.

Indian

Diwali

Castle House
South Great George's St
Dublin 2
Map 430 A1 **525**

01 475 0091

A bustling restaurant, and quite rightly too. To describe Diwali as 'no-frills' would be a slight since it suggests lackadaisical service and nasty decor – not so. However, this informal eatery is back-to-basics in terms of good honest food at good honest prices – you'll pay approximately €15 per main. Unlike many Indian restaurants where you get an unnecessary feast and end up finishing the night off with a box of Rennies, Diwali serves proper sized portions; that is, ones that don't include waste, or indigestion. On offer are delicately seasoned meats, fish and veg – authentic mid-Asian cuisine, although the menu does boast a feisty prawn vindaloo. Typically, there are vegetarian dishes for herbivores, and four biryani dishes. Tables fill up quick but seldom do you have to wait long. Furthermore, the central location and late opening hours make it an ideal spot for a big night out.

Jaipur

41 South Great
George's St
Dublin 2
Map 430 A1 **507**

01 677 0999 | www.jaipur.ie

As the modern interior suggests, Jaipur's selling point is Indian classics with a contemporary slant. A staple on Dublin's culinary scene, Jaipur has spawned outlets in Dalkey and Malahide thanks to the success of its city centre homestead. Contrary to the ubiquitous Indian takeouts, this cuisine is relatively light on the tastebuds and thus more reflective of the region's culinary diversity. Unless that is you want your dish super spicy – the charming staff will be more than happy to accommodate. Dishes are based on the harmonious principles of Ayurveda, with mains averaging at €20, which isn't cheap when including add-ons such as naan and rice. However, you do get what you pay for here – quality ingredients, great service and a cosmopolitan crowd guaranteed.

Monsoon

306-308 Lower
Rathmines Rd
Dublin 6
Map 814 B1 **500**

01 491 1666 | www.monsoon.ie

This popular contemporary restaurant takes a snapshot of different cuisines from the four corners of India – and executes them beautifully. Firstly, the modern interior – sleek tented ceiling, low lampshades, majestic purple velour seating – is a far cry from the flocked wallpaper of your local takeout curry house and far more suited to a posh

348

hotel in Mumbai. The food tastes fresh and flavoursome, the dhal tarka is a particular highlight, followed by a kastoori kebab main – chicken pieces fried in herbs and spices. But take care to leave a space for the mango kulfi dessert – you won't regret it. Furthermore the service is impeccable, and – cop this – there's even a takeout menu.

16 Harcourt St
Dublin 2
Map 430 A3 `480`

Saagar

01 475 5060 | www.saagarindianrestaurants.com

Sleepy Mullingar might not seem like the most likely Irish town to spawn an Indian restaurant back in 1992, but the charming Indian restaurant came on in such leaps and bounds that it spread to Dublin and Athlone. The former branch is located in the basement of a building which was a former home of Dracula author Bram Stoker, and is surprisingly light and airy, with fuss-free contemporary soft furnishings, wooden floors and a nifty bar. Dishes on the extensive menu are ranked with a spice rating and originate from the length and breadth of India, from Goan prawn curry to Kashmiri rogan josh, and are excellent value for money with main courses rarely exceeding €15. Portions are huge, there's naan aplenty and the kulfi is comely. Vegetarians are also suitably sated with a variety of meat-free options.

International

9-11 Crown Alley
Temple Bar
Dublin 2
Map 426 A4 `523`

Bad Ass Café

01 671 2596 | www.badasscafe.com

Ignoring the novelty factor of your order being shot across the room on an overhead pulley and Sinead O'Connor having once worked here as a waitress, Bad Ass Café is essentially a mediocre eatery popular with tourists and teenagers whose tastebuds have yet to mature. Certainly, it looks the business, with its multi-windowed facade and 1950s flourishes, but if your rule of thumb is to never trust a bar or restaurant which sells its own merchandise, you might want to give this a wide berth. You would miss, though, an extensive burger selection and pizzas with silly names such as 'Nicoise Work If You Can Get It' and 'Chilli Willy' in medium and large sizes. There are excellent lunch specials though at €8 including a glass of wine, Heineken, Murphys or a soft drink, and a dinner counterpart at €18.15 for two courses and €21.50 for three.

Jaipur

The Bad Ass Café

349

Bang Cafe

01 676 0898 | www.bangrestaurant.com

11 Merrion Row
Dublin 2
Map 430 C2 471

This place boasts a great location off St Stephen's Green, and great food to boot. The service is less consistently on the ball but not downright lousy enough to forever shirk the mouthwatering morsels on offer: pan roasted scallops, bangers'n'mash, succulent Thai-baked sea bass. Even pigeon gets a makeover – roasted and served with sherried leeks and smothered in chocolate sauce. Alas, vegetarians may not be too thrilled with the dual choices of mains – a vegetable salad and the ubiquitous risotto, nor indeed the inclusion of 'cruel meats' foie gras and veal. However, carnivores and seafood lovers will be more than happy with the short but sweet selection in a bustling and contemporary setting.

Street Food

On weekend nights, you will usually find a few vans parked on the main streets in the city centre dishing out burgers and chips. Most of these mobile units stay open until after the nightclubs have closed. During the day, Lemon, a creperie with outlets on South William Street and Dawson Street, is quick and filling, and every convenience shop does custom-made sandwiches. The Epicurean Food Hall on Liffey Street has a good range of outlets where you can eat-in or takeaway. For a taste of New York, It's a Bagel has branches around the city (see p.366). Irish-owned coffee shop chain Insomnia is good for soup and paninis.

Boulevard Café

27 Exchequer St
Dublin 2
Map 430 A1 496

01 679 2131

This small, informal eatery is largely popular for its lively atmosphere and central location. The menu is many things for many people, taking in Asian (crab cakes, chicken satay) and American (Surf 'n' Turf, Barbery duck) dishes, but mostly with an Italian bent such is the dominance of pasta, pizza and dishes with Caesar sauces. Given the casual setting though, such dishes are a tad overpriced for what they are, and the service can be erratic. Still, it's busy all the same and atmosphere goes a long way.

Darwins

16 Aungier St
Dublin 2
Map 429 A2 479

01 475 7511

Don't let the bizarre interior design decision to name and theme a restaurant after the man who developed a theory of evolution which has been lambasted by practically every religious denomination to put you off. In fact, shirk at your peril because both the food and service are superb. Proprietor Michael Smith also owns a butcher's shop, which speaks volumes about the quality of organic meat here, and surprisingly vegetarians are also well catered for with a fully-fledged flesh-free menu. Dishes across the board are interesting yet unpretentious – rack of lamb, fresh oysters, stuffed roast quail, couscous cake, risotto, steaks a-go-go – and there's a pre-theatre menu at €19.50 and €23.50 from 17:30 to 18:50 every Monday to Thursday. Now that's evolution.

First Floor

Dundrum Town Centre
Dublin 16
Map 421 D4 24

01 291 0488 | www.harveynichols.com

Commonly named after whichever storey it's on, Harvey Nic's Dublin First Floor restaurant is housed in Dundrum's shopping mall and makes a classy alternative to your usual 'Golden Arches'. The excellent Sunday brunch menu encompasses all that you could wish for on the sleepy Sabbath – American-style pancakes, bagels, and omelettes. Take or leave the Tandoori chicken skewers, mind, unless you've got a particularly stealthy hangover to chide. But during the rest of the week, First Floor also pleases in so far as almost being able to forget you're eating in a shopping mall – certainly the prices will remind you – not least for the blood red bar which begs to be propped up along with your bulging bags.

Millstone Restaurant

39 Dame St
Dublin 2
Map 429 F4 `503`

01 679 9931 | www.millstonerestaurant.com

In its former life, the Millstone Restaurant was a rather shabby cafe. Thankfully, the premises cleaned up its act in June 2007 and morphed into a quaint split-level eatery with one of the loveliest facades on Dame Street (and that's saying a lot). Inside, the whimsical antique theme continues with a splendid chandelier, convex mirrors with grand gilded frames and a green-tiled counter. Even the tunes are reassuringly bygone, from Nina Simone to the Buena Vista Social Club. But for all of this understated chic, the food can border on the exuberant – the pizzas certainly. While they're quickly becoming popular, Millstone's speciality pizzas are so encrusted with ingredients that you might wish you'd ordered a plain and simple margherita. From fajita to jalfrezi, Thai to wild boar pizza, it's all going on. You may not need to order a starter or dessert – making it a great spot for a cheap date!

Peploe's

16 St Stephen's Green
Dublin 2
Map 430 B2 `481`

01 676 3144 | www.peploes.com

This stylish basement bistro has been a stalwart on Dublin's culinary scene. Restaurants on St Stephen's Green don't come cheap, and Peploe's falls under that same category, but boy does it look the bee's knees. If you're dining to impress, then Peploe's ticks the aesthetically pleasing box every time. From the Cubist-influenced wall murals to the vaulted ceiling at the bar, the bistro is evocative of a Manhattan Upper East Side restaurant circa the 1950s. It also has a similar formal sensibility, aided by an unwritten dress code – dress to the nines to fit in. Menu-wise, there's some serious meat action for the mains, from steak to magret of duck to loin of venison, plus seafood gems including brochette of monkfish and prawns and a pan-seared tuna. Vegetarians, naturally, get risotto. Mains at both lunch and dinner nudge €30, and there are group menus for parties of eight persons or more. Fans of the grape, meanwhile, will be in rapture with the 200 strong wine list.

The Saddle Room

The Shelbourne
Dublin 2
Map 430 B2 `9`

01 663 4500 | www.marriott.co.uk

The colossally revamped Shelbourne Hotel dates back to 1824, and while it may be a Dublin institution, you'd be forgiven for thinking you were in a Manhattan steakhouse while dining at its stupendously swish Saddle Room. It oozes elegance; labyrinthine rooms, clandestine alcoves, high-backed leather chairs, flocked wallpaper and the height of class – an oyster bar. But then you'd expect such sophistication from a hotel that had a multi-million euro makeover before throwing open its expensive doors in March 2007. But for all the pomp, the atmosphere is most welcoming and chilled out. Service is attentive of course but not suffocating. There are steaks galore, and an intriguing gin and tonic grilled salmon. Desserts are appropriately decadent too, with the chocolate millefeuille a must for anyone with a sweet teeth.

Silk Road Café

Chester Beatty Library
Dublin Castle Grounds
Dublin 2
Map 429 F1 `529`

01 407 0770 | www.silkroadcafe.ie

The Silk Road is more than your average cafe (and serves wine). It has a stellar reputation thanks to its niche cuisine inspired by, you guessed it, the Silk Road – the Middle East and Mediterranean purveyed in the stylish, skylit setting of the Chester Beatty Museum (admission to both the museum and the cafe is free). Typical dishes on offer include moussaka, lasagne, falafel, tabouleh, baklava – a mixture, then, of mezze and mains all served halal and kosher. There are even gluten and dairy-free options for the health-aware diner. Silk Road also does outside catering and banquets, and there's a takeaway menu for those on the hoof.

351

3 St Andrew St
Dublin 2
Map 430 B1 499

Trocadero Restaurant

01 677 5545 | www.trocadero.ie

A stalwart on the pre and post-theatre dinner scene, Trocadero is to thespians like face-paint, upward inflections and understudies. Since its opening in 1957 – making it one of the oldest Italian restaurants in Dublin – the 'Troc' has retained its decadent, bygone charm flaunting red velvet drapes, mood lighting and gleaming mirrors, and has played host to many a jobbing actor as illustrated by the photos aplenty of showbiz types on its walls. Food is likewise theatrical but not showy. On the somewhat overpriced a la carte menu, starters include deep-fried brie and chicken liver pate and for mains, panfried sticky monkfish, steaks, beef cannelloni and poached breast of chicken in a creamed coconut sauce. It's fairly 'middle of the road' stuff, but if you're looking for a dining experience rather than a value meal, this is it. Naturally, there's a pre-theatre menu at €25 for two courses between 17:00 and 19:00 including tea or coffee.

Irish

18/19 Parnell Sq
Dublin 1
Map 425 F2 486

Chapter One Restaurant

01 873 2266 | www.chapteronerestaurant.com

With tables more covetable than a four-leaf clover, this multi-award winning restaurant has enjoyed a consistently brilliant reputation since it first opened its doors in 1992. Located in the basement of the Dublin Writer's Museum, Chapter One has excelled thanks to its patriotic dishes given a cosmopolitan edge by Irish-born and bred proprietors Ross Lewis and Martin Corbett. All ingredients are organic and locally produced, and by sheer word of mouth, one can expect to wait six months for a table… You have been warned. But as the adage goes, the best things come to those who wait, such as the best rack of lamb this side of New Zealand and desserts to die for. You get what you pay for but given its proximity to the Gate Theatre, the three-course pre-theatre menu at €35 is worth a look in – if you can get a seat.

14 Merrion Row
Dublin 2
Map 430 C2 477

Kitty's Bistro

01 662 3350

Have you ever designed your own burger? Go on. A novel spin on the pervasive dish, at Kitty's you can request whatever tickles your fancy between your buns than risk a rogue gherkin or dollop of mayo. But then this is a unique establishment in that it successfully straddles the fine line between rustic and urbane in an area highly

Chapter One

The Tea Rooms

populated by eateries and bars. This is what sets Kitty's Bistro apart from the competition; its laidback cafe-style atmosphere split across two floors married with formal execution. Pasta and specials approximate at €15 per dish making for very good value indeed; ditto the lush salads at less than €10 a pop. A smart choice for group outings, too, who will appreciate the chirpy atmosphere.

The Tea Rooms

The Clarence
Temple Bar
Dublin 2
Map 425 F4 **3**

01 670 7766 | www.theclarence.ie

Co-owned by U2's Bono and The Edge, The Clarence hotel is the very height of art deco sophistication with a contemporary, er, edge. And naturally, given its superstar pedigree, neither The Tea Rooms's food or knowledgeable service staff disappoint. Nor is it as cheap as chips, but then you'd hope not in such salubrious and ice-cool surroundings. Nevertheless, the daily changing market menus for lunch (two courses at €26) and dinner (Sunday to Thursday 19:00 to 20:00, three courses for €39) are a veritable bargain, each dish comprising top-notch ingredients presented on a plate so nicely that's it's almost sacrilegious to sully them with a fork. Almost. Those strapped for time will be pleased to know about its 45-minute 'In-N-Out' policy for market lunchers (of up to four people), making it an ideal haunt for brisk business liaisons.

The Winding Stair

40 Lower
Ormond Quay
Dublin 1
Map 425 A4 **506**

01 872 7320 | www.winding-stair.com

Once a cafe above a locally revered bookshop, its reincarnation in 2007 as a fully-fledged restaurant (still above a bookshop) was met with rapturous applause. It still retains its ye olde cafe characteristics, however, which is part of its informal charm: wooden floorboards, rustic furniture, chalkboards featuring daily specials and a smorgasbord of fine wines, and large windows offering excellent views of the Liffey's Hapenny Bridge. The space itself is small and can get rather hot when busy (which it is, frequently). But fret not – the apple crumble with cinnamon icecream alone is worth dabbing one's brow for. The Stair reflects the current trend for 'simple but effective' cuisine – traditional, unpretentious, hearty and comforting food, such as locally caught seafood, meats from neighbouring counties and delicious Irish cheeses. Highly recommended, and if your companion proves to be a bore, then you can always grab one of the books off the shelf and read until your heart's – and stomach's – content.

Italian

Other options **Mediterranean** p.358

Bar Italia

26 Lower
Ormond Quay
Dublin 1
Map 425 A4 **494**

01 874 1000 | www.baritalia.ie

More trattoria-style cafe than fully-fledged restaurant, this bustling chain draws crowds largely due to its informal atmosphere and prime locations. Alfresco seating in 'summer' only adds to the continental vibe. The menu boasts antipasti, salads, pasta and meat dishes, with starters around the same price as mains. The vino isn't cheap either, given the casual but stylish setting, but dish ingredients taste fresh and the cheese board is a perfect accompaniment to a shared bottle of pinot grigio. A good spot for after-work gossip and light bites, as long as you can get a table during 'rush hour' of course.

Boccaccio

18 Dame St
Dublin 2
Map 425 A4 **483**

01 679 7049

If you like delicious, authentic Italian food, reasonable prices and exotic waiters, Boccaccio may just have what it takes to lure you in off Dame Street for a meal. Something about the decor lets it down (it could be the yellowish lighting or the plastic

353

flowers), but only very slightly, and you'd be a fool to pass this place by for a few style sins. The menu is extensive and is crammed with Italian classics. The meat and poultry dishes are certainly worth a look, but if you've come to an Italian restaurant with pizza or pasta on your mind, you'll be in tastebud heaven – pizzas are thin, crispy, and filled with some delectable and innovative toppings, while pasta dishes are flavoursome and never overpowering (although they do arrive at your table in man-sized portions).

24-25 Parliament St
Dublin 2
Map 425 F4 493

Ciao Bella Roma
01 677 0004

Good value food usually means scrimping on ambience, but this Italian eatery has it in droves thanks to a constant flow of diners including many Italians – always a good sign. Dishes are basic but hearty, and the early bird menu – two courses at €12.50 – even includes a glass of wine, although connoisseurs of the grape may choose to pay extra for a more superior glass a la carte. Service is hit and miss depending on what time of day you go and who serves you and which side of the bed they got out of, but by and large this is a hotspot for anyone on a budget and with a penchant for authentically thin 'n' crispy pizza or bella pasta al dente.

8 South Anne St
Dublin 2
Map 430 B1 521

Gotham Cafe
01 679 5266

This popular cafe-style restaurant is many things to many people – not always a good thing when pizzas are nestling next to Louisiana crab cakes next to tiger prawns in chilli and coconut sauce, but in this instance, it really works. Prices are fair, and the demographic mainly twenty and thirtysomethings, which makes for a good *craic*. Gourmet pizzas are Gotham's speciality resplendent with Manhattan namesakes such as the TriBeCa (Thai prawns), Bowery (Italian sausage) and Flaitron (barbecued chicken). The bustling eatery may not mean anything to Batman, though, since the name has absolutely nothing to do with the Caped Crusader. Which is probably just as well, since too much of the tasty tagliatelle would have him bursting out of his bat suit. Kapow!

10 South William St
Dublin 2
Map 430 A1 468

Il Pomo D'oro
01 671 8767

Sicilian chefs lend an authentic edge to this utter gem of an Italian restaurant. Diners are being steadily coaxed inside by a growing (and glowing) word of mouth – or perhaps it's the, er, comely sculpture of a very naked lady outside? Sex sells; even pizzas it seems. Lovely thin and crispy ones to boot, exactly as a pizza should be, none of this 'crusts loaded with cheese' malarkey. At the time of writing, the crab and mussel starters were mini marvels, and the fresh tomato pasta sauce piquant enough to have any Soprano salivating. Prices are all super reasonable. Decor-wise, think minimalist Baroque; a contradiction in terms but a pleasing polygamous marriage of sleek dark wood, large crystal chandeliers and big Louis XVII mirrors, which lends it a clandestine and romantic air once the table candles have been lit.

D'Olier Chambers
16a D'Olier St
Dublin 2
Map 426 B4 528

Mona Lisa Restaurant
01 677 0499 | www.monalisabistro.com

Located in the lovely yellow-bricked D'Olier Chambers corner building, the Mona Lisa is more about atmosphere than fabulous food. Service is generally friendly if not necessarily always proficient, but anybody counting their euros will appreciate the value menu of three courses for €19.95 available all day and the 'buy one pizza/pasta get one free' between 12:00 and 18:30. There's also a student night every Sunday to Tuesday at €9.99 for one pizza or pasta and a pint of Stella or soft drink. On the a la carte is a gamut of pizza and pasta dishes, and meat dishes include pork medallions in

354

various Italian sauces plus steak, and two Mediterranean influenced fish plates. There's also a grills section, purveying lamb shank, bangers and mash and, curiously, beer battered cod – grilled, really?

Nico's

53 Dame St
Temple Bar
Dublin 2
Map 426 A4 **511**

01 677 3062
This old school Italian restaurant hits the spot in terms of simple trattoria-style food and old world ambience. Barely has Nico's changed since it opened thirtysomething years ago – it still has a pianist that tinkles the ivories nightly and flocked wallpaper – and that's exactly part of its charm. Unpretentious and quietly confident, the dark red velveteen stalwart appeals across the board for those very reasons. Starters are back to basics and kitsch (prawn cocktail, parma ham and melon, egg mayonnaise) – even the mains include Steak Diane, scampi and a side order of cauliflower cheese – retro a-go-go! Of course there is also a short but sincere array of pasta, the spag bol being a particular highlight. Ditto the calamari with home-made chips. Tony Soprano would be here in a heartbeat…

Steps Of Rome

1 Chatham St
Dublin 2
Map 430 A1 **464**

01 670 5630
A one-room eatery fronting Chatham Court with floor to ceiling windows, the small but perfectly formed Steps specialises in authentic pizza and is usually full to the brim with repeat customers. And Italians – always a good sign. You can choose from pizza by the slice or by the full-on whole: three calzones, ones with egg, four cheeses and the spicy salami'd Lucifero are to name but a tasty few at around €12. The fresh tomato sauce base that is often sadly lacking in many a supposedly authentic pizza is here daubed nice and thick, and the bruschetta – all four different versions of them – are well worth making a prelude to the main meal. The pasta is equally splendid at the same price, from rich Spaghetti al Pomodoro to creamy lasagne. There are also omelette and meat and seafood dishes, with which sides come at no extra charge. Who needs Pizza Hut?

Town Bar & Grill

21 Kildare St
Dublin 2
Map 430 B2 **489**

01 662 4800 | *www.townbarandgrill.com*
In a nutshell: amazing food, surly service, expensive wine. Located in the old cellars of Mitchell's Wine Merchants on Kildare Street, this contemporary Italian trattoria – billed as 'The Irish Ivy' – wouldn't look out of place in Manhattan, and by that we don't mean the cheap and chintz of Little Italy – Uptown more like. A perfect backdrop for celebrating a birthday, anniversary or even just-for-the-hell-of-it indulgence, Town Bar & Grill, if nothing else, is a must for the discerning steak eater – eat the Hereford rib eye and weep. Starters are around €13 and include hot and cold oysters, salads and antipasti, while mains are, simply, outrageously divine at approximately €28. There are three excellent value lunch menus: one course at €18.95, two at €22.95 and three at €27.95 (the same prices apply for Sunday lunch), plus a three-course pre-theatre menu at €29.95 between 18:00 and 19:15. The children's menu is also excellent and chicken nugget free. Given the quality of ingredients and the plush surroundings, it's no wonder Town Bar & Grill has won a succession of culinary awards since it opened in 2000, and has launched a South Bar & Grill in Sandyford (01 293 4050, www.south.ie).

Unicorn

12b Merrion Ct
Merrion Row
Dublin 2
Map 430 C2 **473**

01 662 4757
A Dublin institution, all hell almost broke loose among foodies when the Sidoli family sold the restaurant to new owners. Since then, there have been a few falls from grace – mainly rude staff – although the food has largely maintained its greatness. Typical starters include poached veal with tuna, capers and olive oil, chicken Caesar salad with

355

a pancetta twist and, bizarrely, the distinctly un-Italian Clonakilty black pudding. The Dublin Bay Prawns and Lemongrass Chowder is fabulous. Mains range widely from €12.80 to €46.50 for New York Cut Beef Sirloin (which just can't compete with Chapter One). Set in a lovely secluded location near St Stephen's Green, Unicorn really comes into its own in summer when doors open out on to a terrace. There's also a split-level Piano Bar called Number Five featuring live music, and a Unicorn deli emporium around the corner full of tasty but expensive morsels.

Japanese

49-52 Clarendon St
Dublin 2
Map 430 A1 526

AYA

01 677 1544 | www.aya.ie

Dublin's first conveyor belt sushi bar, Aya has had consistent bums on seats since its opening in 1999. Brainchild of the Hoashi family who launched the city's first ever Japanese restaurant 16 years earlier (Ayumi-Ya), this informal contemporary sushi bar and boothed restaurant is great for a quick, healthy bite. Choose between the conveyor belt plates, a la carte or set menus comprising sushi, tempura, teriyaki and teppanyaki dishes. There's an excellent 'Last Call Sushi' concept every Thursday from 22:00: pay €2 to sit at the conveyor belt and all dishes are €1.25. Meanwhile, greedy guts' will love the daily 'Sushi 55' – all you can eat including a drink and miso soup in 55 minutes for €31 including seating charge. Superb value.

South King St
Dublin 2
Map 430 A2 534

Wagamama

01 478 2152 | www.wagamama.ie

You know exactly what you're going to get with this Japanese noodle house – cantina seating, quick and freshly cooked food that may or may not arrive at exactly the same time as your fellow diner but that's ok because the yasai yaki soba and side dish of endamame washed down with a Tiger beer are so good you won't care. Arguably one of few international franchises that actually produces nutritious and freshly cooked food, Wagamama is a staple for Grafton Street shoppers. Located in a basement at the side of St Stephen's Green Shopping Centre, it's a perfect pitstop for those on the hoof before or after another round of retail therapy. Some folk don't like the communal long benches, but each to their own. The staff are always amiable.

71 South Great George's St
Dublin 2
Map 430 A1 519

Yamamori Noodles

01 475 5001 | www.yamamorinoodles.ie

Yamamori on George's Street has been such a hit on Dublin's eating out scene since launching in 1995 that it recently opened a new, sushi-oriented outlet on the Quays. Depending on which dish you plump for explains if or not the flagship Yamamori deserves such an esteemed reputation – general consensus: sizzling dishes good; soba not so good. That said, all the food is fresh and zippy and the staff friendly. Pretty flower petal fairy lights illuminate the long street-fronting windows, while the Quays' branch has an even more understated facade. The wine list in both venues is extensive, although mostly of old world grapes.

Korean

102 Parnell St
Dublin 1
Map 426 B2 469

Alilang Korean Restaurant

01 874 6766

This cheap but not always cheerful restaurant is ever popular for its exceptionally good value meals and novelty 'barbecue' hobs on each table. Alilang is rough around the edges – the service is appallingly inefficient – but there's little disputing the superbly tasty food which includes Korean classics such as mung bean pancakes, wok-fried meat and veg, and spicy seafood. In fact, the menu is so extensive that the most conservative to the most adventurous tastes can be catered for. You can choose from the a la carte menu or from a variety of sets, and the table hobs allow you to cook or heat your own dishes. The biggest endorsement though has to be the plethora of diners from the Asian community.

Latin American

11 Ballsbridge Tce
Ballsbridge
Dublin 4
Map 417 D4 **470**

Bella Cuba
01 660 5539 | www.bella-cuba.com
The bijou Bella Cuba warmly evokes the Latin spirit with vibrant wall murals and authentic Cuban dishes embracing rich slow-cooked Spanish, Caribbean and South American elements: black bean soup, Caribbean jerk of lamb and seafood enchiladas. What results is an adequate execution of cuisine enhanced by its cosy setting and excellent mojitos. Given the Lilliputian dimensions, it's a crime to see the space when deserted. But when busy, the atmosphere positively buzzes, making it a top choice for large groups, which can almost literally have the place to themselves. The fairly extensive menu is bilingual and informative, and there's a two-course 'early bird' menu at €20 between 17:00 and 19:00. Bargain.

17 Upper Stephens St
Dublin 2
Map 430 A1 **482**

Brasil Brazilian Grill
01 405 3854
If you fancy a break from your local Chinese or Italian, then check out this casual but expensive niche restaurant. The jolly white, yellow and green exterior continues inside with fairly basic furniture, evoking an authentic Bahia vibe. Typical dishes include juicy steak, crab and beef stews – vegetarianism is not exactly rife in Brazil, so expect feasts of barbecued and slow-cooked meat and seafood, plus an overpriced and mediocre salad bar. The cocktails fair better – snub the Caipirinha at your peril.

Millenium Walkway
Middle Abbey St
Dublin 1
Map 426 A3 **532**

Cactus Jacks
01 874 6198 | www.cactusjacks.ie
Casual and cosy Mexico-themed restaurant resplendent with rustic wooden tables and chairs and portions bigger than a sombrero. All the usual suspects are here from tacos to nachos to enchiladas, plus four flesh-free dishes that constitute a 'vegetarian menu'. It's the thought that counts, right? The staple house specialities are big on traditional accompaniments such as refried beans and rice, and the beefburgers and parrillada (grilled steaks) are tastier than a Gael Garcia Bernal and Salma Hayek sandwich. The kids' menu though is more Montana less Mexico City: burger, baked beans, chicken nuggets and chips.

Irish Life Mall
Abbey St
Dublin 1
Map 426 B3 **531**

Floridita
01 878 1032 | www.floridita.co.uk/dublin
Incongruous location aside – Floridita is nestled in the not-at-all-attractive Irish Life Mall behind scruffy Talbot Street – this Cuban chain and travel agency has a lot going for it. Offering contemporary interpretations of Latin American cuisine, their emphasis is on quality not quantity – hence the short but sweet a la carte menu. There are canapes and tapas for smaller stomachs, plus a lunchtime set menu (Monday to Friday, 12:00 to 15:00) the same price as the pre-theatre menu (Tuesday to Saturday 17:30 to 19:00): €25.50 for two courses and €28.50 for three. The stylish split-level venue has its trademark 13 metre long bar downstairs which you can prop up while chuffing on a

357

cigar, supping a Daiquiri No.5 and shimmying to live Cuban music. Speaking of which, it also occasionally hosts the odd South American music superstar – such as cuatro virtuoso Eliades Ochoa of Buena Vista Social Club fame.

Mediterranean
Other options **Spanish** p.361, **Italian** p.353

13 South Great
George's St
Dublin 2
Map 430 A1 **474**

Café Bar Deli
01 677 1646 | www.cafebardeli.ie
If you've not been to Café Bar Deli, you haven't lived. A stalwart on the city's eating scene, CBD ticks all the boxes in terms of quality, value for money and ambience. The decor is reminiscent of a simple Victorian conservatory – dark wooden chairs, dark velveteen booths, fireplaces and potted plants – but the menu is quintessentially cosmopolitan and easy on the purse. Portions are plentiful and include daisy-fresh ingredients, as clearly illustrated by the juicy smorgasbord of salads from Mediterranean to Moroccan. The spaghetti with tomato rocket pesto, roasted aubergines and toasted hazelnuts are a party for the palate while the creamy rigatone with sage, spinach, mascarpone and chopped walnuts is another firm favourite. Pizzas are just as sublime, their thin crispy bases a perfect foundation for a plethora of pine nuts, chorizo, cheeses and grilled greens. Note also that CBD opens for breakfast, and you should definitely try the sin-in-a-bowl porridge with brown sugar and fresh clotted cream. Other branches can be found inside Bewley's on Grafton Street (01 672 7720) and in Ranelagh (01 496 1886).

50 Dawson St
Dublin 2
Map 430 B1 **509**

Fitzers Restaurant
01 677 1155 | www.fitzers.ie
A slightly over-rated but well-established trio nonetheless: Dawson Street is the cherry on top, with the outlet in the National Gallery of Ireland a good option for cafe-style food on the hoof. The Temple Bar branch however is distinctly lacklustre in terms of both service and quality. Dishes by and large are well presented and 'homely' – cue steaks, salmon fillets, pork loins, chorizo spaghetti and fish'n'chips – and the staff friendly despite the standard throngs. The Dawson Street outlet has a streetside terrace conducive to boozy summer lunches, and given its informal atmosphere, is a safe bet for large groups of diners. Other branches: Temple Bar Square (01) 679 0440, National Gallery (01 670 6577).

Fitzers on Dawson Street

14 Dame Ct
Dublin 2
Map 430 A1 **476**

Odessa
01 670 7634 | www.odessa.ie
This trendy but unpretentious restaurant boasts a stellar Sunday brunch. It's play Spot the Hangover every Sabbath, when there's nothing like a fried egg, sunny-side up and plump couches downstairs to chide away the ghosts of the night before. During the rest of the week, it's business as usual, i.e. equally buzzing and packed with the city's young and restless. The menu hasn't changed much since it opened in 1994, bar the use of seasonal ingredients, but if it ain't broke don't fix it, and the seafood is catch of the day fresh. Main courses on the dinner menu range from the awesome roasted red

snapper with braised fennel, mash and shellfish butter to the signature Odessa burger, taking in honey and cumin glazed lamb. Vegetarians rejoice though, Quorn Quesadillas and other abundant veggie options are available. There are mirror image lunch and brunch a la carte menus, plus an early bird one at €18.50 for two courses including tea/coffee every Sunday to Friday.

Middle Eastern

The best fish and chips in Dublin

11a St Andrews St
Dublin 2
Map 430 B1 **472**

The Cedar Tree
01 677 2121
This is one of Dublin's most established restaurants, serving diners Lebanese food for the past 20 years. Spacious and decorated with traditional Arabic furniture, The Cedar Tree purveys a variety of mezze typical to the Middle East such as hummus, baba ghanoush, tabouleh, shawarma, and kebabs – nothing remotely like the dubious ones picked up on the way home at 04:00 and instantly regretted. In proper Middle Eastern fashion, the emphasis is on picking as many mezze as you fancy and sharing it with your fellow diners- and you'll need to since the portions are abundant. It's also a hit with vegans and vegetarians, serving a range of pulse-based dishes, including the choice of meals cooked in oil or butter if you just pipe up to the waiting staff. The early bird menu is worth noting because, thanks to the 'pick me!' assortment mezze, The Cedar Tree can turn into an expensive night out.

37 Wicklow St
Dublin 2
Map 430 A1 **502**

El Bahia
01 677 0213 | *www.elbahia.com*
One could call this a hidden gem, since its entrance is indicated by a wee door on Wicklow Street. The service though is infamous; many reports of staff rudeness and table trouble – either from having to wait a long time for one despite pre-booking (parties of more than four persons only) or effectively having to share one to accommodate other diners. Thankfully the food's reputation is more reliable, though somewhat overpriced nudging €20 per dish. The tagines are well regarded, with vegetarian options available plus a selection of starters that can be eaten mezze style. The 'exotic' decor is also a draw with Moroccan furniture, lamps and all, and an obligatory bellydancer. But whether the temperamental staff can ameliorate such details is arguable.

31-32 Lower Pembroke St
Dublin 2
Map 431 F3 **501**

Layla Turkish Restaurant
01 662 2566
To those in the know, Layla is an oasis southeast of St Stephen's Green. Diners fluent in karniyariks will be happy with their lot, while anyone not knowing their adana from their baklava will be suitably sated. There's an abundance of mezze on offer here from vine leaves to poached anchovies, plus a variety of main dishes typical to the region such as charcoal-cooked meats and sizzling meatballs with rice, and for dessert, filo pastry drizzled in honey and chopped walnuts (kadayif). Is a Turkish restaurant incomplete without a resident bellydancer and flavoured shisha? Not this one. The wine list is succinct, but staff couldn't be more helpful.

359

Seafood

14 Westmoreland St
Dublin 1
Map 426 B4 **478**

Beshoff's

01 677 8026 | www.beshoffrestaurants.ie

A Dublin institution, Beshoff's is arguably second to Leo Burdock's as best fish'n'chipper. Named after its original owner, Ivan Beshoff, who survived the mutiny on the battleship Potemkin and opened a fish shop in Howth (still there and always busy), the family-run chippy is a fully-fledged sit-down cafe unlike take-out Burdock's. The O'Connell Street branch is split-level and has great streetside views upstairs, and catch of the day keeps things interesting for regular punters. Portion sizes are just right – not too much, not too little – and all the seafood is caught locally.

2 Werburgh St
Nr Christchurch
Cathedral
Dublin 8
Map 429 F1 **487**

Leo Burdock's

01 454 0306 | www.leoburdock.com

The fish and chips from Leo Burdocks is well worth spending a few hours in the gym for, and the long queues are testament to the tastiness and freshness of their consistently good offerings. If you're after the traditional fish and chips experience, go for the cod and chips which come wrapped up in paper (they don't use newspaper anymore). But if you fancy a new twist on this classic dish, try the lemon sole goujons – they are absolutely lip-smacking. Portions are huge so you might need to share with a friend. The guys behind the counter are friendly and will engage in a bit of cheeky banter while you're waiting for your order. Leo Burdocks counts as a definite 'must-do' at least once while you are in Dublin (if not once a week!).

9 Ballsbridge Tce
Ballsbridge
Dublin 4
Map 417 D4 **522**

The Lobster Pot

01 668 0025 | www.thelobsterpot.ie

Established in 1980, this quaint first floor restaurant in a Ballsbridge terrace is one of a clutch beside Bella Cuba and Roly's Bistro. As the name suggests, emphasis is on seafood, and excellent seafood at that; simply cooked, seasoned and sauced just so. Check out the moules mariniere starter or smoked mackerel on a leafy knoll, and also the prawn bisque with Cognac, which is a tango for the tastebuds. There are two lobster main courses priced per weight and plenty of other fishy delights in the twentysomething euro region – salmon in a Hollandaise sauce is an oldie but a goodie, and the poached blacksole bon femme is a melt in the mouther. The Maitre D will big up the daily specials, and you're guaranteed a prescriptive service. The small setting also makes for an intimate and charming evening.

23 Christchurch Pl
Dublin 8
Map 429 F1 **491**

Lord Edward Pub & Restaurant

01 454 2420

No wonder the Lord Edward is Dublin's oldest seafood restaurant – it's astonishingly good. Something of a Dublin institution, the Lord Edward's 'dad pub' downstairs belies the veritable bounty of cuisine der mer upstairs and seldom disappoints. Covering three floors in total, the colossal Lord reigns over possibly the best seafood in town served by friendly, mature and knowledgeable staff. Decor-wise, you'd be forgiven for walking into a time-warp – think Edwardian dining room – aided by many retro dishes such as seafood cocktail, melon Oporo, avocado with pear. But it's all part of the charm. The prawn bisque and seafood chowder meanwhile are wow, and a fitting prelude for what's to come. The seafood section reads like a fish market inventory, with a smorgasbord of platters cooked in a variety of different ways – simply but effectively, plus a table d'hote and specials menu. There are a few non-fishy dishes on offer also, but alas nothing for vegetarians. Pricey but well, well worth it.

Spanish

Other options **Mediterranean** p.358

3 Camden Market
Grantham St
Dublin 8
Map 429 F3 498

Havana

01 476 0046 | *www.havana.ie*

This popular tapas bar with decently priced dishes was/is so bustling that it also opened a sister restaurant on South George's Street. For merely the peckish, there's a yummy starter plate with a confusing Moorish/Italian/TexMex bent – hummus, olives, pesto, nachos and Bretzel baked breads. Bigger hunger pangs will be sated by the cockle-warming chorizo and lentil stew, pork and beef meatballs in a rich tomato sauce and fat tiger prawns cooked with chickpeas in a white wine sauce. Set menus are also available. Slow service, meanwhile, doesn't usually stop those bums on seats but then both Havanas boast prime locations, the South George's Street premise shimmying with salsa every Friday and Saturday.

1 St Andrew's St
Dublin 2
Map 430 A1 466

Salamanca

01 670 8628

This is a pricey but infinitely tasty tapas restaurant. More often than not, this little haven is ram-packed with light-biters stocking up on mini morsels to share over a bottle of wine and while Spaniards or anyone else with a vested interest in Spain and Spanish cuisine may initially balk at the prices and artistic licence with staple dishes, an overall positive experience is guaranteed. The spicy-sauced patatas bravas are arguably inauthentic but a perfect accompaniment nonetheless to any of the meat or seafood dishes that include squid in chilli butter, a cassolet of chorizo sausage, paella, lobster and whisky terrine and anchovies on bruschetta. Vegetarians won't feel left out either, with a gamut of flesh-free offerings. There are also sherries on hand – a traditional accompaniment to tapas, as well as a fair wine list.

Thai

Dundrum Town Centre
Dundrum
Dublin 16
Map 421 D4 24

Café Mao

01 296 2802 | *www.cafemao.com*

If the weather is good, you could hardly be in a better place than on the Mao terrace in front of the dancing fountains at the Dundrum Centre. The food is almost a happy bonus, although even if bad weather makes indoor seating the only option, it is so delicious that you'll still have a great dining experience. The Asian menu, with a strong Thai influence, includes yummy dishes like coconut lamb korma, chilli mango duck, nasi goreng, tempura of lemon sole and five spice chicken. Main dishes all come in at under €20, with starters under €10. An interesting menu of daily specials is also worth a look.

55 Pembroke La
Dublin 2
Map 430 C3 512

Diep Le Shaker

01 661 1829 | *www.diep.net*

Despite the name and live jazz band every Tuesday and Wednesday, this really is a Thai restaurant. And a very good one at that, as illustrated by its many awards over the years including most recently The Mark of Quality for Excellence in Service and Cuisine from the Royal Thai Government. Its sunny yellow contemporary interior, plethora of

Café Mao

long/short/champagne/fruit/dessert cocktails designed by head bar tender Colin Hutton (ex-Mint Bar, Westin Hotel) who was trained under the authority of all things shaken and stirred, Angus Winchester, and choice of dishes make this a winning combination for Thaiphiles. The food is excellent and plentiful with the most exquisite seafood options, and the service impeccable. There's also an extensive old and new world wine list. What's not to like?

Siam Thai

26-28 Clarendon St
Dublin 2
Map 430 A1 **495**

Saba

01 679 2000 | *www.sabadublin.com*

Atmosphere: tick. Friendly staff: tick. Stylish decor: tick. Cocktails: tick. So the food's really bad, right? Wrong – Saba is one gem of a south-east Asian eatery ticking those all-important boxes since it launched in 2006 by Paul Cadden of Diep le Shaker fame. Combining Thai and Vietnamese cuisine, Saba (Thai for 'happy meeting place') is almost always busy and thus a great option for a big night out with friends. The menu is vast with a profusion of fried, noodle, curry, salads and seafood dishes given spice ratings ('BOOM!!!' means hot – no confusion there) accompanied by sublime coconut rice – or perhaps you'd prefer brown and red rice, or how about steamed fragrant rice? There are healthy options, including vegetarian. Signature dishes include green monkfish curry and Cua Lot, a soft-shell crab with red hot chillis, galangal root and Kaffir lime leaves, both of which are taste sensations. Sealing the deal are two set menus – the Sanook and Sawasdee at €29.50 and €38.50 respectively.

15 Andrew St
Dublin 2
Map 430 A1 **524**

Siam Thai

01 677 3363

This is the third restaurant in a countywide chain, its flagship eatery in Malahide and an older sibling up in Ballsbridge. Opened in 2003, Siam Thai has an extensive choice of dishes, with the choice of set menus or a la carte at lunch and dinner. The fare is traditional – no fussy fusion here, although the ubiquitous side order of french fries lurks on the menu – and involves the usual suspects such as staples pad thai, tom yam goong, satays, yellow, red and Penang curries – all strictly sans monosodium glutamate as its website emphatically states in a red and underlined font. Meanwhile, the fairly formal decor makes it a popular option for business lunches and after-hours soirees and the staff are friendly to boot. Other branches: Malahide (01 845 4698), Ballsbridge (01 660 1722).

7 Westmoreland St
Temple Bar
Dublin 2
Map 426 B4 **518**

Thai Orchid

01 671 9969

This is a traditional Thai restaurant that's fairly pedestrian in terms of decor and menu – even the front signage resembles the Thai Airways logo. However, it may hit the spot for anyone looking to sate a pad thai or green curry craving. Certainly its central location is not to be sniffed at. Friendly staff lead you gently into the three-floor venue which is filled with the usual knickknacks from Buddha statues to fairly crammed wooden furniture. There are curries aplenty, noodle dishes, soups and salads at approximately €18 a piece excluding rice sides. If you like your Thai particularly spicy then do ask; the dishes seem 'watered down' for supposedly western tastes. Annoyingly, two European dishes crept on to the menu – sirloin steak and a salmon steak. Who visits a Thai restaurant to eat Euro food?

3a Talbot Place
Dublin 1
Map 426 C2 504

Thai Spice

01 855 0226

A diamond in the rough (the Talbot Street area is not great for decent places to eat out), the self-proclaimed vegetarian and seafood specialists wins muchos kudos thanks to its sea bass dishes, particularly the deep-fried version bathed in a garlic and chilli sauce – paradise on a plate. The geaw nam soup also hits the spot, especially if you ask for it extra spicy, indeed, such requests are very welcome since their standard dishes are fairly mild otherwise. The interior design is nothing to write home about but the space is intimate, the service swift. And although the take-out menu parps 'Home of Singha Beer' it doesn't actually sell it – raise your glass to the Chang instead.

La Stampa Hotel
35 Dawson St
Dublin 2
Map 430 B1 17

Tiger Becs

01 677 4444 | www.lastampa.ie

Anywhere that serves 'dessert cocktails' deserves an award. But then Tiger Becs is not your usual Thai restaurant – its interior has a Moroccan theme. Quite what Parisian designer Miguel Cancio Martins was playing at when creating this aesthetically schizophrenic space is anyone's guess (perhaps he couldn't decide?), however, the overall ambience is opulent, enticing and has the bonus of being downstairs from SamSara Café Bar – also Moorish. The Tiger Becs' menu is confident in its 'Thai-ness', though, with an array of meat, seafood, noodle and rice dishes appropriate to any self-respecting south-east Asian palate. The fresh fish dishes are sublime, and the prawns plump and delicious in a variety of aromatic sauces. And as for those dessert cocktails? They're a happy, coronary-inducing halfway house between pudding and nightcap. Try a Mudslide for size and watch the waistband expand.

Vegetarian

19 Wicklow St
Dublin 2
Map 430 B1 7

Cornucopia

01 677 7583

One can only imagine what Dublin residents first made of this vegetarian wholesalers when it opened in the mid 1980s. 'It wouldn't last', probably. Back then there was a small cafe in the back, but as the city's demographic shifted so too did the customers, and by 1993 Cornucopia was a fully-fledged restaurant. Now, the premise is set to expand into the downstairs space of the neighbouring Georgian terrace. More room means more food, and if you like tagines, daily changing salads, quiche, curries, soup and Mediterranean-inspired bakes, you'll be laughing. Desserts are appropriately naughty but nice, and many dishes – both sweet and savoury – have yeast-free, dairy-free, gluten-free and wheat-free options. There's also a Cornucopia cookery book so you can try your hand at home.

Cornucopia

Fresh

Powerscourt Centre
Dublin 2
Map 430 A1 **567**

01 671 9669 | www.cafe-fresh.com

Nestled on the top floor of the handsome Powerscourt Centre, Fresh stands by its name with a profusion of newly-plucked and produced ingredients. The canteen-style concept is not for everyone, but what you can expect are hearty portions at low prices. The diverse menu covers pretty much all the bases you need for either a healthy lunchtime snack or after-office supper, from paninis to frittatas, baked potatoes to lentil lasagne. Food comes out quick and staff are super friendly. It's no wonder then that the eatery continues to expand its portfolio, with a Café Fresh Cookbook by chef and owner Mary Farrell for sale, and vegetarian cookery classes for anyone requiring extra kitchen aid.

Always Ace That First Date

So you've found someone decent enough to go on a date with – don't blow it by going to a rubbish restaurant. The following romantic settings should guarantee you at least a second outing; after that you're on your own!

L'Ecrivain	p.346
The Cellar	p.342
Chez Max	p.346
La Mère Zou	p.347
La Stampa Balzac	p.347
Pearl Brasserie	p.347
The Saddle Room	p.351
Il Pomo D'oro	p.354
Unicorn	p.355
The Lobster Pot	p.360

Govinda's

4 Aungier St
Dublin 2
Map 429 A1 **505**

01 475 0309 | www.govindas.ie

The words ridiculously budget and ridiculously tasty aren't regular bedfellows, but just because Govinda's is cheap, it doesn't mean it's nasty. Govinda's rocks. Run by Hare Krishna's, there's the sort of chilled-out vibe you'd expect from such an establishment although do expect canteen-style service. Such is Govinda's popularity, there is also an outlet on Middle Abbey Street with all three venues offering different menus. Getting your chops around the Govinda Special – a feast of vegetables or subji cooked in a variety of different ways and served with basmati rice – is never a bad thing and comes in regular and small sizes at €6.15 and €9.30 respectively. There are also fellow dishes of the day, such as tagliatelle, lasagne and Shepherd's Pie. Vegan options are also available, and don't leave without sampling the homemade cheesecake.

Juice Vegetarian Restaurant

South Great Saint
George's St
Dublin 2
Map 430 A1 **31**

01 475 7856

Vegan-friendly, Octo-friendly, Lacto-friendly... But is it any good? The consensus is mixed. Billed as Dublin's only vegetarian restaurant – Juice still looks like a cafe no thanks to the white garden furniture-style functional seating. But judge a book by its

Stop for a light bite

cover and you might miss a hidden gem, and while Juice isn't likely to win a Michelin star, its range alone hits the spot. Every Monday to Friday from 12:00 to 17:00, is a lunch deal comprising soup or a fresh juice and a warm pita pocket with choice of two pates. There's also an abundance of breakfast-type dishes, such as french toast, organic muesli pancakes and eggs on toast in addition to heartier fare. Early birds will like the three-course menu – a steal at €14.95 between 17:00 and 19:00, and thereafter is a hefty dinner menu. Furthermore, a blackboard of specials changes daily, and there's brunch every Sunday. All in all, great value, despite the cafe trappings.

Cafes & Coffee Shops

Avoca

11-13 Suffolk St
Dublin 2
Map 430 B1 **41**

01 677 4215 | *www.avoca.ie*

Avoca cafe is probably one of the nicest breakfasts or lunches you'll get in Dublin. Fresh, home-baked breads, scones, tarts and quiches, crispy salads and tasty dishes-of-the-day and you can't go too far wrong. Drinks on offer range from homemade lemonade and the usual coffee and tea selection to a decent wine list. The Dublin city centre cafe off Grafton Street, like all other branches, has floors of lovely goodies to buy, from fashion and foodstuff to toys and kitchenware. If you've ever tasted the deserts you'd have to have iron resolve not to be tempted a second time – they're scrumptious. Outside catering is available, or you could just buy the cookbook and impress your friends all by yourself! Other branches include Rathcoole on the Naas Road and several outlets in the Wicklow area.

Bagel Haven

5a Cow's La
Temple Bar
Dublin 2
Map 425 F4 **412**

01 675 9900 | *www.bagelhaven.ie*

You probably wouldn't go here for the decor (bland) or the atmosphere (muted). But what you should go for (and what will keep you coming back) is the chocolate-spreaded bagels, a totally delectable way to start your day. There are plenty of other yummy bagel fillings, from the virtuous Mauritian Chicken Salsa to the hard-core Music Hall (bacon, melted brie and mayonnaise), and they also do a good lunch menu in case you're all bagelled out. The best time to go? Definitely on a sunny Saturday afternoon when you can sit outside and watch beautiful vintage fashion flapping in the breeze at the Cow's Lane Fashion Market.

Butlers Chocolate Café

24 Wicklow St
Dublin 2
Map 430 B1 **410**

01 671 0591 | *www.butlerschocolates.com*

Chocolate lovers of the world unite! This cafe combines fine chocolate with fine coffee in a lovely setting, creating the perfect place to rest your feet. The world-famous Butler's hot chocolate is undoubtedly one of Dublin's most sublime pleasures. Take the chocolatey bliss up a notch by adding a shot of flavour (try irish cream, mint chocolate or raspberry), and then once you've licked your cup clean, prolong the experience by picking up a box of Butler's finest choccies on your way out. If you need a chocolate fix but you're nowhere near Wicklow Street, never fear, because there are Butler's branches on Grafton Street (01 616 7004), Chatham Street (01 672 6333), Nassau Street (01 671 0772), Henry Street (01 874 7419), as well as in Dundrum Town Centre (01 296 3180), Heuston Station (01 672 8780) and Dublin Airport (01 814 1480).

Bewleys Chocolate Cafe

Cafe Ulysses

James Joyce Centre
Dublin 1
Map 426 B2 **10**

01 878 8547 | *www.jamesjoyce.ie*

You may have noticed by now that James Joyce is a pretty big deal in Dublin, and this cafe is yet another homage to the Ulysses author. Situated in the Maginni room of the James Joyce Centre, the French-themed cafe has been designed to bring a little bit of Paris to Dublin. Open from 10:00 to 17:00, Thursday to Saturday, Ulysses is a pleasant place to enjoy a cuppa and a pastry while you try to unravel the plot mysteries of the book of the same name.

Epicurean Food Hall
Lower Liffey St
Dublin 1
Map 425 A3 **414**

Itsa Bagel
01 874 0486

This walk-in, eat-in or take-away bagel haven is a stalwart with the lunchtime crowd. Just like you'd find in downtown Manhattan, there's every type of bagel imaginable – plain, poppy seeded, raisin, wholewheat – and the fillings are equally as tempting with salmon, cream cheese, honey mustard mayo, homemade relishes and deli meats. The fussier client can opt for the 'Create your Own' bagel, while others should not pass up the Bagelini – a panini made with a bagel. They also serve homemade soups and a wide choice of drinks, from smoothies to organic health drinks and the usual coffee and tea selection, with fair-trade options for an extra 25 cents.

5/6 Nassau St
Dublin 2
Map 430 B1 **441**

Kilkenny Restaurant & Cafe
01 677 7075 | *www.kilkennyshop.com*

This pleasant cafe above the Kilkenny shop on Nassau Street is a great place to meet up for a quiet breakfast or a mid-morning coffee – as long as you get there early enough. Kilkenny is right by one of the stops on the various open bus tours of Dublin, so come midday it's packed full of tourists, which may make for good people watching, but not for a quiet cup of tea! Once you're in, just pick up a tray and select what you want from the delicious selection of scones, pastries, sandwiches and hot meals, and then bag yourself a table near the windows for a beautiful view over the campus gardens of Trinity College. The food is super fresh and the prices are fair, leaving you some spare cash to spend in the shop downstairs.

8 Parliment St
Dublin 2
Map 425 F4 **413**

The Larder
01 633 3581

Whether you're the type who likes to grab a smoothie and run, or you prefer to linger for hours over scones and coffee, the Larder will suit you. The decor is tranquil, with a cool facebrick interior dotted with cream, avocado and tangerine fittings, and soft natural lighting that encourages lengthy sit-downs with a good book or a good friend. But the service is efficient too, so it's also great for a quick coffee of the 'get-in, get-out' variety. The Larder serves a surprisingly good range of food options for such a smallish cafe, so if you're after a relaxing lunch or an early dinner, pop in for a while.

21 Suffolk St
Dublin 2
Map 430 B1 **409**

Nude
01 676 1367

If you're hoping that the name correctly reflects what you'll find inside this cafe (in terms of food, not of dress code), you won't be disappointed. Food is focused on the more health conscious patron, with low fat, tasty wraps, homemade soups, salads and juices on offer. It's a popular lunch hangout and given its location, just off heaving Grafton Street and surrounded by numerous retail outlets and banks, it's always busy so don't expect to find a seat easily. Think clean lines and green and white hues, and good eat in or take out, guilt-free munching – at least that's the idea!

Full Tummies & Pockets

Don't spend a fortune feeding yourself - Dublin is home to some great little places where you'll get a slap-up meal at a price that won't give you indigestion afterwards.

Internet Cafes

You'll find plenty of internet cafes around Dublin, although those in the high-tourist-traffic areas are going to be more expensive (so that's O'Connell Street and Grafton Street out then). Instead, try to find ones that are in quieter streets, and you'll get more surfing for your money. An hour online could cost you as little as €1, although this can go up to €3 in touristy areas.

Internet Cafes		
Central Cyber Cafe	Dublin 2	01677 8298
Global Internet Cafe	Dublin 1	01878 0295
Net House Internet Cafe	Various locations	01496 0261
Planet	Dublin 2	01670 5183
Right-Click	Dublin 2	01475 9681

Brunch

Brunch in Dublin is heavily dominated by the all-day breakfast. Most cafes that serve breakfasts will serve them all day on Saturday and Sunday, and the range normally includes the traditional Irish fried breakfast, continental breakfasts, French toast, pastries, bagels and eggs benedict. Prices will often include tea or plain black coffee, although there may be a supplement for herbal teas and gourmet coffees. Juices and smoothies are often served too but are rarely included in the price. Overall, you can expect to pay about €10-€15 per person.

Brunch		
Harry's Cafe Bar	21 George's Street, Dun Laoghaire	01 280 8337
The Epicurean Food Hall	Liffey Street, Dublin 1	na
South Street Restaurant	South Great George's Street, Dublin 2	01 475 2312
Heavenly Café	84-87 Camden Street, Dublin 2	01 405 3990
Lemonjelly Creperie	Millenium Walk, Dublin 1	01 873 5161

As the weekend brunch scene tends to revolve around cafes and some hotels, you will find that most outlets are informal and relatively child-friendly. Entertainment for children is rare in Irish eateries, although some places will provide colouring books and crayons. If you're unsure, bring something small from home for them to play with.

Internet Cafe

Nude

Safe Drinking

*If you routinely find
yourself drinking so
much that you black
out, throw up or
embarrass yourself,
maybe it's time to learn
more about your limits.
Log on to
www.drinkaware.com
for some really useful
(and non-judgmental)
tips on safe drinking.*

On The Town

There's no doubt that there's great *craic* to be had in the capital of *craic* itself, Dublin. Not only are the locals fond of a big night out, but people fly in from other countries to enjoy the trappings of Temple Bar on many a stag or hen night (it's not hard to spot them: just keep your eyes peeled for pink tiaras, customised T-shirts, and polystyrene balls and chains). While many born-and-bred Dubliners will steer clear of Temple Bar, you shouldn't – it has a great mix of pubs, clubs and restaurants that are well worth visiting. Of course there are plenty of touristy hotspots that sell the 'paddy' experience in one convenient

The Bank on College Green

package (traditional music, pints of the black stuff, Irish tat on the walls, and the obligatory painting of James Joyce), and these are fun to visit now and then, but should really be avoided in favour of some of the more authentic venues that can be found in the area. And if watching a bride-to-be vomit into her feathered stetson at the end of an evening offends you, then perhaps it could be argued that you should definitely avoid Temple Bar on a Saturday night, when it's hen night central. As for the rest of Dublin, what you'll notice is the absence of any real 'superclubs'. Dubliners are happy to find their own way in terms of nightlife, and they don't need multi-storey, double dancefloor venues to do it. They are just as happy sat round a table in the back of a pub as they are dancing to cheesy tunes in their favourite nightclub.

Door Policy

There are a couple of clubs where a strict door policy is in force, so you need to make sure you get glammed up before you go. Improve your chances of getting in by looking cool and acting cool (no begging). If that fails, head off to one of the less pretentious venues in Dublin (of which there are many) – they're usually more fun anyway!

Dress Code

Dublin is a lot more casual than other major cities and if you're heading out for a night in the pub you can get away with a bit of a shabby appearance. If you're off out for a big night that will involve clubbing, it's worth dressing up as some venues have strict door policies. To make sure you don't make a dress faux pas, always check the venue's website for guidelines – most will have some clues as to what's acceptable.

Smoke In The Water, Pong In The Pub

Even if it's pouring with rain outside, that's where you'll be smoking - the Ireland smoking ban was introduced in 2004, amid much grumbling from smokers who felt that a night out just wouldn't be the same. Three years on, the ban is going strong. People still go out, but instead of having to sit in a fog of nicotine, the air inside is clear and the smokers huddle outside in smoking areas. The only downside? Some people say that the smell of smoke inside has been replaced by a rather more unpleasant pong emanating from a 'southern' part of the body and said to be a common side effect of drinking guinness. Ewww.

Small but indispensable…

Perfectly proportioned to fit in your pocket, these marvellous mini guidebooks make sure you don't just get the holiday you paid for, but rather the one that you dreamed of.

Explorer Mini Visitors' Guides
Maximising your holiday, minimising your hand luggage

Bars & Pubs

Other options **Nightclubs** p.385

4 Dame Lane ◀
Dublin 2
Map 426 A4 388

4 Dame Lane

01 679 0291 | www.damelane.com

This super stylish double-floor venue has different DJs upstairs and down, and the upper level boasts a dancefloor that you couldn't swing a cat around on weekends. The decor is delightfully dusky. On a Wednesday, grooves upstairs include jazz and funk; every Thursday is Clampdown which comprises electronica and punk and a smidgen of indie, while Friday and Saturdays embody all those and more. Downstairs, the bar area also doubles as a showcase for local artists, and the booth seating is great for group nights out. Of course style comes at a price so expect to pay a bit more for your pint here than elsewhere. That said, a good night out is practically guaranteed at this almost always packed nightspot.

Duke St ◀
Dublin 2
Map 430 B1 402

The Bailey

01 670 4939 | www.baileybar.ie

Laidback yet plush, The Bailey is a magnet for anyone around Grafton Street looking for a side order of people-watching with their bottle of wine. With large street-fronted windows and outdoor seating (heated in the chillier months), this popular bar is perfect for kicking back and watching the world go by. A succession of large lampshades dominate a long communal table, while those less sociable may prefer the wee tables and square comfy cushion seating. The Bailey also serves brunch, lunch and dinner with dishes ranging from hot pies to chicken Caesar salad. There are also function rooms for anyone wanting to host a private or corporate party.

20-22 College Green ◀
Dublin 2
Map 426 B4 380

The Bank on College Green

01 677 0677 | www.bankoncollegegreen.com

Built between 1893 and 1895 and designed by William Henry Lynn, the former Belfast Bank is a prime example of Victorian commercial architecture. Split level, peppered in mosaic tiles and with a lofty stained glass ceiling, it was originally commissioned for £8,000 and in 1927 sold to the Royal Bank of Ireland for £125,000 – that's inflation for you, and a precursor to the Celtic Tiger era. Open all day for breakfast, lunch and dinner, suited and booted after-workers tend to congregate here for its edible fare at fair prices. Often it's difficult to get a seat, but the full house makes for a big atmosphere.

Powerscourt Centre ◀
Dublin 2
Map 430 A1 567

Bar Mizu

01 674 6712

This cavernous basement bar located in the Powerscourt Centre is usually full to the brim with trendy types. The staff though could do with a 'How To Be Friendly' workshop – they're not the most helpful, and will absolutely not go out of their way to bring you a pint from the main bar if a certain beer runs out. Shame. Otherwise, the venue has a loyal following thanks to its hip exposed brickwork walls, vaulted ceilings and evocative candles. Snacks are served and cocktails are excellent, though pricey. And a little known fact about Bar Mizu is that the River Stein, a subsidiary of the Liffey, runs

Cocktail Bars

If you're hitting the town for cocktails ICE bar (see p.375) in the Four Seasons, or The Horseshoe Bar in the Shelbourne (see p.375) are good bets. For celeb-spotting, The Clarence Hotel (see p.377) is perfect. For those on a stricter budget, keep an eye out for special deals early in the evening, as most clubs will have a decent range of cocktails, and check out Captain America's on Grafton Street (01 671 5266, www.captainamericas.com) for cocktails by the pitcher.

underneath the premises and is supposedly visible through glass panes in the floor – a little known fact because it's not that visible. Oh well. They tried.

The Bernard Shaw

11-12 South Richmond St
Dublin 2
Map 416 B4 **377**

085 712 8342 | *www.bodytonicmusic.com*

This is a quirky, old-school pub named after the irrepressible playwright – ironic, really, since in life he was a teetotaller. Something of a hidden gem, the 'spit and sawdust' Bernard Shaw is thankfully devoid of the usual Irish pub trappings yet still retains an air of traditionalism perhaps due to the topsy-turvy layout, which, if you're on the right 'path' will lead you out to a beer garden and smoker's den with retractable roof and garden bench seating. Inside, the furniture is no more sophisticated, but comfy all the same, and chances are you'd be stood up nursing a pint anyway because this place is rammed on weekends. The jukebox is also a novelty, unless of course one person hijacks it the whole night – and there are regular DJ nights.

Bia Bar

Drury Court Hotel
28-30 Lower Stephens St
Dublin 2
Map 430 A1 **384**

01 405 3653 | *www.drurycourthotel.com*

This vibrant but tastefully decorated bar is adjacent to the Drury Court Hotel and has a penchant for retro and vintage grooves – and students, but don't let that put you off. One wall has a pop art Che Guevara print, the bar is beautifully curved, and there's a lovely side room that hosts a roaring open fire during winter. From Monday to Thursday there are 'buy one, get one free' pizzas, and the fries are marvellous. There's also free WiFi access. Alas, the beer garden had disappeared at the time of writing, but one can hope that it – and the crowds – come back with a vengeance. Weekends are often buzzing, when the sun has gone down and the beats are cranked up.

The Bleeding Horse

24 Camden St Upper
Dublin 2
Map 430 A3 **382**

01 475 2705

The Bleeding Horse is a fine trad-style pub and one of the oldest in the area. Built in approximately 1649 during The Battle Of Rathmines, the site has had several incarnations and extensions since then, but in the noughties it is a popular haunt for local residents and workers from nearby offices. Its proximity to the Pod, Tripod and CrawDaddy make it a natural spot for a pre-gig pint. There are snugs and stained glass galore, and live entertainment every Thursday to Saturday in the shape of DJs and bands plus pub quizzes midweek, and you'll find an Internet cafe upstairs.

The Brazen Head

20 Bridge St
Dublin 8
Map 425 E4 **379**

01 677 9549 | *www.brazenhead.com*

The Brazen Head is officially Dublin's oldest pub despite Conway's Pub on Parnell Street jostling for the same title. This eternally popular pub dates back to 1198, or at least what's left of its fortress-like façade does. Enhancing its already illustrious appeal, the pub was also frequented by Irish rebels Michael Collins, Wolfe Tone and Robert Emmet – indeed, it's alleged that earlier still in 1798 the United Irishmen plotted their rebellion here. It was also a favourite of James Joyce, who even references the watering hole in *Ulysses*. Unsurprisingly, you can't move for tourists, but staff are super friendly. Be sure to snub the upstairs dining room, though, whose menu is overpriced and sadly devoid of the excellent scampi and chips, fish and chips, and Irish stew that are served downstairs.

Late Date

The following outlets all serve food or drink later than average, so if you're faced with the final call, head off to:

371

Bruxelles

7-8 Harry St
Dublin 2
Map 430 A1 **396**

01 677 5362

This perpetually busy bar has crossover appeal thanks to its elegant chandeliers in the bar juxtaposing with the two grotty-but-fun basement clubs – one for Goths and rockers, the other for indie-heads. Naturally, the weekend crowds tend to be pretty lairy and finding a seat is akin to finding a shamrock in a haystack. But good times are to be had here, if, that is, you don't mind joining the jostle at the bar (although staff are pretty good at putting through orders). There is also outdoor seating at the front of the premises for maximum cigarette-smoking sub-culture fun.

Bruxelles

Café en Seine

40 Dawson St
Dublin 2
Map 430 B1 **389**

01 667 4567 | www.capitalbars.com

Deceptively large cafe-bar-restaurant exquisitely fashioned circa Paris in the 1800s. If Marlene Dietrich, Noel Coward and Edith Piaf were alive today, they'd all be propping up the central bar drinking a bellini, so opulent is the decor with the huge gold gilded mirrors, stained glass ceiling panels and Art Deco sculptures. Lunch snacks are dull and overpriced and the cafe staff surly, but come nightfall when the dinner menu comes out (and staff rotate), things take a tastier turn; check out the smoked haddock and cod fishcakes, and also Sunday brunch. The stereo's playlist wavers from Ella Fitzgerald to Celine Dion but, regardless, both the daylight and twilight hours have atmosphere in droves. Never mind that the night-time crowd can border on poncey – revel in the unashamed ostentation, enjoy that bellini, and to hell with the price.

The Clarendon

32 Clarendon St
Dublin 2
Map 430 A1 **385**

01 679 2909 | www.clarendon.ie

Informal but sleek'n'stylish bar in a prime location between St Stephen's Green and, funnily enough, Clarendon Street. Its window-fronted facade sets it apart from many other venues, the upper level having the added bonus of table seating actually set into the bay windows. Despite having the two floors (and a third for private parties), The Clarendon is rather snug hosting up to about 60 persons at any one time. This means it gets very full very quickly, although there is outdoor seating during the warmer months. Food is excellent, with an all-day menu every Monday to Saturday (until 20:00) and a brunch on Sunday with the usual hangover-joe suspects such as eggs benedict and french toast. Otherwise, you can't fail to be impressed by the chorizo pasta, crab spring rolls and chips with aioli. Yum.

Cocoon

Royal Hibernian Way
Dawson St
Dublin 2
Map 430 B1 **407**

01 679 6259

Any nightspot that is owned by a) a famous person (in this case F1 driver Eddie Irvine) and b) considered the 'in place to be' is often a bit too big for its Prada boots. Divided opinion remarks that Cocoon is a perfect example of style over substance, while also being comparable in vibe to bars in New York or London. Ultimately, such conclusions largely depend on where you stand on dress code policies and whether or not you want to visit a bar that bans trainers. Cocoon's clientele is as easy on the eye as its streamline interior – cue lots of models and *Fair City* actors, but as is to be expected, drinks prices are not so easy on the pocket (nor the head – the cocktails are rather moreish).

Dakota Bar

9 South William St
Dublin 2
Map 430 A1 **399**

01 672 7696

You can't move for hip bars on South William Street these days and Dakota is considered to be one of them. Open-plan but for a raised area that extends towards a back entrance, the hotspot has absolutely no affinity with its US-state namesake – this Dakota is way too trendy. Half-moon leather couches make for good booths and the long bar is perfect for rubbernecking. Service can be dicey but the combination of wall-to-wall hipsters, a good selection of draught and bottled beers and ambient tunes ensure an atmospheric night out. There's also a bar menu which is largely unremarkable thanks to paltry portion sizes of dishes and inappropriate pricing.

Davy Byrnes

21 Duke St
Dublin 2
Map 430 B1 **381**

01 677 5217 | www.davybyrnes.com

Famous for being the place where James Joyce's Leopold Bloom took a pit-stop for a gorgonzola sandwich and a glass of Burgundy, trad pub Davy Byrne's is as much a Dublin institution as the Windmill Studios. It has had a succession of decorative makeovers since its 1898 origins (it was first licensed in 1789 but by a different vintner), but its historical scope is echoed with replica Art Deco furnishings including three Joycean wall murals, one dating back to the 1940s by Cecil French Salkeld, father of the 20th century playwright Brendan Behan. Aside from its literary heritage, seafood is their house speciality, in particular oysters, but there are also more orthodox dishes such as soup and sandwiches. Oh, and the Bloomsday Special – gorgonzola and burgundy. In short, a delightful pub.

Dylan Bar

Dylan Hotel
Eastmoreland Pl
Dublin 4
Map 431 E4 **16**

01 660 3000 | www.dylan.ie

Overlooking the Still Restaurant, Dylan Bar is quietly making a name for itself on the Baggot Street drinking scene. Gorgeously decorated from the funky long chrome curved bar to crescent moon shaped plush couches, the beautiful hotel's bar serves over 200 wines from around the world and an extensive range of cocktails. But don't be fooled by the decadent design – the vibe is surprisingly relaxed. There's also a lovely outdoor terrace for those admittedly rare hot summer days and nights – fortunately it has gas heaters.

Enoteca Delle Langhe

Blooms La
Ormond Quay
Dublin 1
Map 425 F4 **400**

01 888 0834

A little slice of Little Italy, this charming Italian-owned wine bar has the added authentic bonus of being on Bloom's Lane, which is peppered with Italian cafes, al fresco seating and quirky shops – very continental. However, do not expect mountains of spaghetti; Enoteca only serves salad, cold cuts, cheeses and crostini. Thus, Enoteca is one for informal and light eats only, and of course a veritable wine list. Over 75% of the 200 odd wines here are sourced form the Langhe region with the rest mostly from other Italian districts. A 12-strong 'wine of the day' list changes daily and there's also a takeout service that won't break the bank.

The Foggy Dew

1 Fownes St
Dublin 2
Map 426 A4 **376**

01 677 9328 | www.thefoggydew.ie

This traditional Irish pub provides a haven from the hurdy-gurdy of Temple Bar. Despite its proximity to the area, The Foggy Dew is thankfully mostly devoid of Hen and Stag parties – more like a diverse cross-section of residents who are loyal to its lively-but-not-maniacal overtones. Given the tourist-toting area, pints are competitively priced, and staff are very friendly and efficient even during 'rush hour', which is any time from 18:00 on Friday and on into Saturday night. The layout is gleefully oddball – nooks and

373

crannies, plus the odd piece of rock memorabilia – and the *craic* can often be seen spilling out on to the street during busy periods. There's live music on weekends.

The Front Lounge

33 Parliament St
Dublin 2
Map 425 F4 38

01 670 4112 | www.frontloungedublin.com

From the outside, the gay-friendly Front Lounge is all 1920s understated glamour. Inside, though, is another story, with casual but contemporary furnishings and changing artwork on the walls. There's a small bar on entering which extends into a wide seated corridor and then up a few stairs to a second bar and, usually, noisy throngs. Music can get ridiculously loud, so if you're looking for a quiet night out then you're in the wrong place. As a general rule of thumb, no one really goes here for a bite to eat – it's all about the boozy evenings – but there is a snack menu comprising burritos, paella, scampi and sarnies. Open Monday to Thursday from 16:00 to 23:30, Friday and Saturday from 12:30 to 02:30, and Sunday from 12:00 to 23:00. See also p.383.

The Globe

11 South Great George's St
Dublin 2
Map 430 A1 39

01 671 1220 | www.globe.ie

Reminiscent of bars in the East Village, New York, The Globe attracts the unpretentiously hip thanks to its polygamous marriage of effortlessly trendy design, decent pricing and guest DJs and bands. Ordering a drink here can be a bugger when the venue is busy – which it is, every weekend – but staff are generally friendly enough. The Globe often hosts live music from jazz bands to DJ Gilles Peterson, and also conjoins with basement club Ri-Ra which is accessible from both inside and out the back. Food is not exactly the venue's reason for being, although it does the job and makes a decent accompaniment to laptop lunches (there's free WiFi access all day) and lost moments playing chess with your pal. Open Monday to Wednesday from 12:00 to 23:30, Thursday to Saturday from 12:00 to 00:00, and Sunday from 16:00 to 23:30.

The Hairy Lemon

42 Lower Stephen St
Dublin 2
Map 430 A1 390

01 671 8949

A traditional pub with quite possibly the best name in town. Popular with students, tourists and suburbanites in equal measure, the Hairy Lemon pleases for its tavernesque cosiness, stylish wooden interior and laidback background music. There's also an upstairs, which can become a sanctuary at weekends when a lot of the action is happening downstairs. The menu won't give Chapter One sleepless nights, but should you wish to indulge your stomach lining, then stick with the finger food rather than the main courses. The service is good though – quick and affable – and the atmosphere spot-on. Open Monday to Wednesday from 10:30 to 23:30, Thursday to Saturday from 10:30 to 01:00, and Sunday from 12:00 to 23:00.

The Harbourmaster

Custom House Dock
Dublin 1
Map 426 C3 401

01 670 1688 | www.harbourmaster.ie

In the cold light of day, The Harbourmaster is in dire need of a refurbishment from its peeling paint to smelly loos. But come nightfall when all the IFSC types surge in for a post-office pint, such details are quickly forgotten. The atmosphere usually disappears along with the suits though so expect to be one of very few punters after 22:00.

Sports Bars

Most pubs will show matches on their TVs with the sound low, but some places with big-screen TVs will advertise this heavily and draw big crowds for important games. The Goat Grill in Goatstown, Dublin 14 (01 298 4145), is a well-known sports pub in south Dublin. For something closer to the centre, Renards (also a nightclub, see p.387), Buskers in Temple Bar (01 677 3333) and Frezers (01 878 7505) on O'Connell Street are good spots. Check out www.sports-in-bars.ie for more.

Bars & Pubs

35 South
Great George's St
Dublin 2
Map 417 E4 25

Hogan's
01 677 5904

Fancy a quiet pint? Don't come to Hogan's. The word *craic* could've been invented for this immensely popular bar, a magnet for Dublin's affluent twenty and thirtysomethings – and the fact that it's open until 02:30 from Thursday to Saturday speaks volumes. The venue may be big – it's spread over two floors – but is almost always full every evening and inevitably livelier than a leprechaun on acid. During the day, you'll see its softer side, and maybe even notice the elegant wooden bar and panelled flooring. But once that sun goes down it is mayhem, with chatter almost as loud as the eclectic music. Open Monday to Wednesday and Sunday from 11:00 to 23:30, and Thursday to Saturday from 11:00 to 02:30.

The Shelbourne
Dublin 2
Map 430 B2 9

The Horseshoe Bar
01 663 4500 | www.marriott.com

Named after its curved shape, the Horseshoe Bar is nestled in Dublin's landmark Shelbourne Hotel which dates back to 1824, and in March 2007 reopened following a major refurbishment over an 18-month period (in a reputed 40 million euros makeover). Interestingly, in a previous, pre-renovation guise, it won a mention in James Joyce's Ulysses. Boy, did that man love his pubs. Naturally, then, the Horsehoe is as plush as you fancy with its deep red walls and dark wooden veneers. The clientele ranges from politicians and business executives to curious tourists who can afford to splash their cash on a G&T. Suitably splendid.

Four Seasons Hotel
Ballsbridge
Dublin 4
Map 811 E4 25

ICE
01 665 4000 | www.fourseasons.com/dublin

This super sexy bar displays dynamic Irish artworks, as per the Four Seasons' international manifesto to showcase works by local artists in each of their properties. Its name is also appropriate – ICE Bar is ice cool. From the white marble walls to the ambient illuminated bar, ICE oozes elegance and begs smart casual attire. You can bet that anywhere that is this hip will attract hipsters – and vodka, for this bar boats more flavours and varieties than you can throw an eastern European at. The hotel also has a resident sommelier, who in addition to wine tends to the 50 something brands of Irish whiskey – the largest collection in Ireland. Emphasis is mostly on sophisticated supping but rumbles in the tum can be sated by either the assortment of sushi or equally Japanese-oriented light bites: endamame, miso soup, sashimi carpaccio.

Jct of Mary St
& Jervis St
Dublin 1
Map 425 F3 404

John M Keating
01 828 0102 | www.jmk.ie

If a church has to be resurrected, then it could do a lot worse than being turned into this bar. Dating back to 1627 and originally christened St Mary's Church, the building hosted the baptisms of both Wolfe Tone and Sean O'Casey, and also the marriage of Arthur Guinness to Olivia Whitmore in 1763, which, incidentally produced 21 children. The church is now a stylish watering hole comprising the main bar, Cellar Bar and Tower Bar, resplendent with some original features – the galleries, altar, organ, and replica stained-glass windows. There's even an outside terrace, plus (mediocre) casual dining in the main bar and also in the upstairs Gallery Restaurant. Don't bother asking for a side dish of chips with your pint, though – they 'don't do fries' but they do produce bowls of 'panache' potatoes. Meanwhile, DJs play in the evening, a classical string trio is on every Saturday afternoon and live bands play every Sunday evening. Open Monday to Wednesday from 12:00 to 21:30, Thursday to Saturday from 12:00 to 22:00, and Sunday from 12:30 to 20:00.

Kehoe's

01 677 8312

There's no such thing as a quiet drink in this much-loved establishment. The city's last reputed resident publicans moved out a good few years ago now much to the chagrin of Dublin's drinkers who feared gastropubdom or worse. Thankfully, though, the 'new' owners have kept Kehoe's spirit intact, from maintaining the deep red interiors to the oh-so-lovely-and-thus-highly-coveted snug – in short, it's like being in a wonderful time warp. The upstairs area has since been opened up, although it has done little to accommodate the plethora of punters on your average night – expect revellers to spill outside during those, er, sultry Irish summer evenings. Kehoe's is open Monday to Thursday from 10:30 to 23:30, Friday and Saturday from 10:30 to 00:30, and Sunday from 12:30 to 23:00.

The Long Hall

01 475 1590

A noble institution if ever there was one, The Long Hall is delightfully stubborn at not keeping up with the Joneses. And why should it? This uber traditional pub appeals right across the board, from dads to students, artists to bankers. Quintessentially victorian, its all dark red walls, wooden bar, chandeliers, vaulted ceilings and mirrored walls, having retained much of its original character. There are also curios everywhere from oriental knick-knacks to muskets – the cleaner must have their work cut out for them. Of an evening, you'd be very lucky indeed to grab a table although daytimes are fairly chilled and perfect for browsing the broadsheets with yer pint.

Market Bar

01 613 9090

Renovating old buildings isn't a new thing, but you've got to hand it to the Market Bar for its inventive use of clogs – check out all shelves upon shelves of Dutch footwear (plagiarised from a London pub, apparently, reports Explorer's mole. Cheeky). Redesigned to the highest standard, the Market Bar retains its previous incarnation's, er, charms as the old arcade's sausage factory – with exposed redbrick walls, lofty ceilings and gothic windows. Fortunately you won't be waiting for the cows to come home at this efficient establishment – staff are genuinely lovely – although you may have to wait for a table, as the Market Bar gets packed. Inhibitionists beware, though – the mighty open-plan setting means that theoretically everyone can watch your every move. Food-wise, there are tapas and mezze dishes in different sizes but consistently decent prices, and the best patatas bravas in town. Open Monday to Thursday from 12:00 to 23:30, Friday and Saturday from 12:00 to 00:30, and Sunday from 16:00 to 23:00.

No. 27 Bar and Lounge

01 663 4500 | www.marriott.com

At the esteemed Shelbourne Hotel, there's the reinvigorated Horseshoe Bar and the premises' newest bar on the block, the No. 27 Bar and Lounge. Elegant and classic in a completely different way, there are chandeliers and drop-crystal lampshades galore, plus an ebony grand piano that echoes the jet-black stone bar. Cold winter nights are thawed by the roaring fire, which, trivia fans, burns peat, while chilly bodies can huddle up on the victorian couches. On the walls are a series of paintings depicting the adjacent St Stephen's Green by Irish artist Victor Richardson, and where food is served, a collection of etchings by fellow Irish artist Charles Cullen inspired by the ubiquitous Ulysses. Open daily from 12:00 to 00:30.

The Octagon Bar

The Clarence
Temple Bar
Dublin 2
Map 425 F4 **3**

01 407 0800 | www.theclarence.ie

Love U2 or loathe them, there's no disputing that The Octagon Bar's cocktails are among the best in town. Co-owned by Bono and The Edge, The Clarence wears its art deco origins well, and its signature bar is no exception. Literally in the shape of an octagon, this understated bar is flanked by tall wood panelling which dips into small seated alcoves and lends a studious, almost library-style mood. There's also an extended room to the side, which roars with an open fire during winter. Drinks are expensive, and the predominantly foreign staff can be a little flaky but they're friendly nonetheless, and, hey, you never know what celebs you may bump into – although chances are they'll be nondescript young professionals. Oh well.

Odeon

57 Harcourt St
Dublin 2
Map 430 A3 **394**

01 478 2088 | www.odeon.ie

Odeon is a beautifully restored and renovated bar that in its former life was the entrance to the Harcourt Street railway station. Thankfully there's not a Dart to be seen in this present reincarnation, although the art deco flourishes, lush potted plants, glass lampshades and ornamental bar hark back to its former heyday. Otherwise, though, The Odeon is thoroughly modern, with plush orange and black armchairs, dark walls and guest DJs at the weekend. Lunch is served Monday to Friday from 12:00 to 15:00, making it a hotspot for hungry business types from the surrounding offices, and there's also free WiFi access for those busy 'working' lunches. Sunday brunch, meanwhile, attracts a fair crowd although the absence of egg dishes is quite inexplicable. Cocktails are cheap though. Odeon is open Monday to Wednesday from 12:00 to 23.30, Thursday from 12:00 to 00:30, Friday and Saturday from 12:00 to 02.30, and Sunday from 12:00 to 23:00.

The Port House

64a South William St
Dublin 2
Map 430 A1 **395**

01 677 0298 | www.porthouse.ie

This charming tapas bar is tucked away on South William Street, its tiny facade indicated by large glass windows and a few outdoor chairs and tables. Inside is not much bigger, but for what it lacks in space it makes up for in atmosphere, its rustic brickwork and mismatched furniture barely exposed by evocative candlelight – and that's during the day. The word snug fits this intimate and romantic place like a glove, and is all the better for it – even on a school night there's usually a table queue, since you cannot pre-book. Staff are helpful, though, and will give you a phone call when a table is free. As its name suggests, the bar is from the same stable as the aforementioned Porterhouse, and has an abundance of port to wash down the patatas bravas, garlic gambas, paprika almonds and piri-piri chicken wings to name but a few quirky Spanish-inspired dishes. There's a decent wine list also and not just with Espanol varieties. Open Monday to Wednesday from 16:00 to 23:00, Thursday to Saturday from 11:30 to 00:00, and Sunday from 11:00 to 11:00.

The Porterhouse Central

45-47 Nassau St
Dublin 2
Map 430 B1 **392**

01 677 4180 | www.porterhousebrewco.com

Dublin's first microbrewery is almost always thronged due to a) it's novelty factor and b) because it's just so darn nice. Like stepping into a tardis, you're transported onto a long, meandering dark floor and bar which leads to a tiny outdoor smoking area. As one would expect, the beer here is excellent and includes many an eccentric variety from Porter House Red to the delightfully monikered 'An Brain Blaster' – an oyster stout (yes, it's made from real oysters), all brewed on the premises. There are 10 resident beers in all, plus the usual bottled and draught suspects for those shy on trying new ales. There is also a bevy of wine and a fair few cocktails – just name your vice, et voila. Food is also above your average pub grub, with hearty home-made burgers, casseroles and fresh seafood dishes on offer. Open Monday and Wednesday from 12:00 to 00:00, Tuesday from 12:00 to 23:30, Thursday from 12:00 to 02:00, Friday and Saturday from 12:00 to 02:30, and Sunday from 12:30 to 23:30.

Lower Liffey St
Dublin 1
Map 425 A4 405

Pravda

01 874 0090 | *www.pravda.ie*

Meaning 'truth' in Russian, the trendy Pravda crowd may not reveal much over a pint – nay, vodka – although good *craic* is guaranteed day or night. A hit in particular with students and young arty types, the revolutionary theme is not just in name only, permeating into the premise's split-level design: agit-prop murals galore. The raw brickwork and dingy lighting provokes a feeling of Soviet speakeasydom, although Mr Stalin might turn his nose up at the rather cosmopolitan food menu – pizza, paninis, beef burgers and bangers and mash (he would probably approve the blue collar prices though – the cod in beer batter is a steal at €9.50). Pravda's film nights and live music and DJs, though, are the main draw of an evening. Open Monday and Tuesday from 12:00 to 23.30, Wednesday to Saturday from 12:00 to 02.30, and Sunday from 12.30 to 23:00.

South William St
Dublin 2
Map 430 A1 406

Rush Bar

01 671 9542

Contrary to its name, the red-fronted Rush Bar is seldom as frantic as its noisy sound system would probably like to be. Still, Rush Bar is a fair option if its arguably more superior neighbours – the South William, Spy Bar and Dakota are full. Thursday to Saturday nights often fill up though, thanks to resident DJs on rotation playing late into the night with no cover charge. Snack-wise, it's crepes-a-go-go, wraps and sandwiches.

28 Parkgate St
Dublin 8
Map 424 A3 383

Ryan's

01 677 6097 | *www.fxbrestaurants.com*

It's the million dollar question: where in Dublin serves the best Guinness? Popular opinion nods to Ryan's; a traditional public house as legendary for this moot point as its fine pub grub. Perhaps it's its close proximity to the Guinness Storehouse, which is just a bridge away over the Liffey? A fine example of Victorian drinking

Ryan's

SamSara

dendom, Ryan's wears its vintage well, with a lovingly restored exterior and equally magnificent mahogany interior. There are also four oak-panelled snugs, which were originally used by female punters in an era when public drinking was distinctly unladylike (indeed, access to the snugs is to this day run by the barman who controls the latch. Want a drink? Ring thy bell). From its stained glass windows to vintage mirrors, no wonder Ryan's sometimes gets a shout-out on the open-top tour buses as it snakes around Phoenix Park. Ryan's is open Monday to Thursday from 12:00 to 22:00, Friday and Saturday from 17:30 to 23:00, and Sunday from 17:30 to 22:00.

La Stampa Hotel
35 Dawson St
Dublin 2
Map 430 B1 **17**

SamSara Café Bar

01677 4444 | *www.lastampa.ie*

SamSara is the opulent cafe and late-night bar located in the gorgeous depths of La Stampa boutique hotel, and a great spot for either an aperitif or after-dinner cocktail when dining at Balzac or Tiger Bec's restaurants. Or neither – when interiors look this fancy, propping up the bar for its own sake is good too and rest assured there will be plenty of other fancy-pants doing the same. Eclectic or just plain confusing, you decide, SamSara's decor ranges from a series of star-shaped paper lanterns to Moroccan furnishings set against an aural backdrop of house and moody electronica. Behind the bar is a wooden screen of complex Moorish patterns infused by ambient lighting, while brick pillars extend to a lofty vaulted ceiling. In terms of food, there's Thai food every evening from 17:00 and the cocktail list is not to be sniffed at either. SamSara is open Monday to Thursday from 19:30 to 02:00, Friday and Saturday from 17:00 to 02:30, and Sunday from 17:00 to 02:00.

42-44 Baggot St Upper
Dublin 2
Map 431 E4 **39**

Searsons

01 660 0330 | *www.searsons.ie*

Once upon a time when Landsdowne Stadium was still standing, Searsons was particularly jumping given its reasonable proximity to the sporting arena. These days, typical clientele include local professionals desperate for a lunch away from the desk or a few cheeky jars after work. Deceptively long, the dusky bar is peppered with yellow lanterns and reaches back into different seated areas and beyond that, a smoking area. There are DJs playing every Friday and Saturday and pub food served from 12:00 to 15:00 and 17:00 to 20:00. There's also free WiFi access, which is mighty generous but, alas, there have been instances of flat draught beer. Meanwhile, if anyone knows why there's a funny smell emanating from the back rooms, answers on postcard please. Searsons is open Monday to Thursday from 12:00 to 23:30, and Friday to Saturday from 12:00 to 02:30.

17 Chatham Row
Dublin 2
Map 430 A1 **378**

Sheehan's

01 677 1914

Regulars flock here in their droves, particularly on a Friday after work and throughout the weekend when you'll be hard-pushed to get a table. Traditional in character but with souped-up, plush furnishings following a renovation, another string to the pub's bow is that it also hosts regular stand-up comedy nights and live jazz during the week. There's also just one singular sports-showing TV screen – not too distracting, but enough to attract the odd football fan who knows that they won't get a look in elsewhere. Pub grub is good value for money, especially given the competitive location, with dishes ranging from soup of the day to chicken and leek pie to sandwiches, paninis and wraps. Sheehan's is open Monday to Thursday from 10.30 to 23.30, Friday and Saturday from 10.30am to 00.30, and Sunday from 12:00 to 23:00.

South William St
Dublin 2
Map 430 A1 375

South William

01 672 5946

Bar of the moment the South William is not just trendier than thou, attracting as it does affluent creatives and those who know their Roots Manuva from their roots reggae, it also purveys the most excellent pies. Contrary to the nasty steak and kidney football stadium types with which they are synonymous, South William's pies are largely very inventive and hugely filling despite their size and small knoll of side salad: bacon and cabbage, duck and red cabbage, beetroot and lentil, Guinness-braised beef shin. But that's just part of it. Mismatched tables and chairs exude a kitsch chic, and beside the tiny dancefloor are some couch-style benches. Upstairs is a wee bar accessible both at front and back – and good job, since this gets packed at weekends – and also a smoking area. Some punters find the clientele and staff somewhat cliquey but for its fat pies and phat tunes, this bar (sorry, 'urban lounge') truly deserves its hip reputation.

Powerscourt House
South William St
Dublin 2
Map 430 A1 22

Spy Bar

01 677 0014

All the bars on South William Street tend to follow the same design template – long double-storey bar that leads to small dancefloor. Spy Bar, despite being effectively in the Powerscourt Centre, is no exception since it's on the same strip of Georgian terraced buildings. Like its geographical peers, it has an equally up-for-it vibe AKA 'The *Craic*'. Spread across three floors, Spy is sometimes accused of being style over substance, but even cheesy electro remixes of pop tunes are to be had past the witching hour. Mostly though this place is aimed at thirtysomethings with a serious penchant for house music and a bit of contemporary melodrama – check out the Greco-Roman friezes. Well, if it's good enough for Hilary Clinton, REM, Sandra Bullock and Drew Barrymore who have all allegedly graced this hallowed venue…

7-9 Exchequer St
Dublin 2
Map 430 A1 397

Uki Yo Bar

01 633 4071

Dublin's first and only sake and karaoke bar. Marrying together those two highly fraught-with-danger Japanese pastimes – too much of either can be VERY BAD – Uki Yo has a loyal and trendy following. There's an entire menu dedicated to sake (rice wine) and over 3,000 karaoke ditties in English, Chinese, Japanese, Korean, Spanish, Filipino and Italian. Up to 10 friends can book a private room and 'sing' until hearts are content, with prices starting at €25 per room. As per the Japanese and Korean aesthetic, the decor is minimalist and contemporary, with screens set around black tables. Authentic, mid-priced food is available at lunch and dinner, plus there's a supper menu until 23:00 on weekdays and 02:00 on weekends. There's also brunch every Saturday and Sunday from 12:00 until 16:00. Uki Yo is open Monday to Wednesday from 11:00 to 03:00, Thursday from 12:00 to 01:30, and Friday to Sunday from 12:00 to 03:00.

34-35 Lower Ormond St
Dublin 1
Map 426 A4 386

Zanzibar

01 878 7212 | *www.capitalbars.com*

This colossal bar and club is spread over two floors, with an opulent Tanzanian theme – cue oversized velvet cushions, tented alcoves, hanging drapes, potted palm trees and 'exotic' lanterns. The snow white beaches, clear-blue oceans and warm climes of its namesake are sadly lacking, but nights out at Zanzibar are rarely dull. Resident DJs favour house and ambient global beats, while occasionally guest DJs will turn up the heat to scalding point. Fans of intimate, informal venues may not be impressed by Zanzibar, but those that like to get dolled up and don't mind queuing to get in at weekends will not bat a heavily eye-shadowed eyelid. Open Wednesday to Saturday, 17:00 to 03:00.

Not big, but very clever…

Perfectly proportioned to fit in your pocket, this marvellous mini guidebook makes sure you don't just get the holiday you paid for but rather the one that you dreamed of.

Paris Mini Visitors' Guide
Maximising your holiday, minimising your hand luggage

Gay & Lesbian

Gay Days

Dublin plays host to several very popular festivals on the annual gay calendar, including Gaze: The Dublin International Lesbian and Gay Film Festival (first weekend in August, www.gaze.ie), the International Dublin Gay Theatre Festival (first two weeks in May, www.gaytheatre.ie), the Lesbian Arts Festival (last weekend in May, www.alafireland.com) and the Pride Festival (last two weeks in June, www.dublinpride.org).

Although homosexuality was decriminalised in Ireland a relatively short time ago (1993), the capital's gay scene is thriving, as commercially savvy as you will find in any evolved European capital, and unlike gay social circuits in most cities, comfortably assimilated into the mainstream. This stems from pre 1993, when the city had only a couple of underground gay bars and people of a queer persuasion openly mixed in more liberal straight bars and clubs. Today, nestled among a compact, if diverse, gay scene, you'll find straight bars that positively welcome gay clientele and gay bars playing happy host to hetero couples who just want to get away from

Pride flag hanging over the George

the straight and narrow, particularly south of the Liffey, which divides the city into two distinct halves.

Another difference in gay Dublin stems from the fact that since 1929 no new licences for bars have been released, and a bar licence just about covers any pub of any size. This means that bars in the city just keep getting bigger and bigger, to pack more paying punters in. Gay Dublin is dominated by three 'super pubs'; The George, The Dragon and The Front Lounge, all within a few minutes walk of each other. A weekend trawling between the three might give the impression that the scene is a lot larger than it actually is, considering each of these pubs could – and regularly do – pack thousands of happy homosexuals in on any peak performance night.

There are no specific gay clubs in the city, although two of the aforementioned bars have substantial dancefloors and resident DJ's, so you will find regular gay nights in many of the straight clubs dotted around the city. The most popular of these right now is an alternative indie event called Q+A, which regularly takes place in the Temple Bar Music Centre (www.tbmc.ie) and for the ladies, Kiss at the same venue.

The ever-evolving gay one-nighter club scene is difficult to keep tabs on, but if you pick up the city's free gay publication, GCN, in any gay venue, you'll quickly get a handle on what's happening in the here and now. Websites like www.gcn.ie and www.queerid.com have daily updates as to what's happening on the social and community scenes, while the pocket-sized Little Gay Map of Dublin, which can be picked up in most hotels and tourist centres, tells you where everything is and features details of the city's many gay-friendly restaurants.

Life for gay people in Ireland today is good, if not exactly legally on par with straight society. While there is protection from discrimination at work and access to goods and services enshrined in equality law, there still is no legislation for gay partnerships. A new government was elected this June, and legislating for civil partnerships for same sex couples has been committed to in their programme for government. There was no mention of timing.

6 Parliament St

Dublin 2

Map 425 F4 **450**

The Centre Stage

01 670 3390

An antithesis to the super pub era of Dublin's gay scene, The Centre Stage is more like a quirky little wine bar you might find in Barcelona or Paris. Despite its minute size, however, this popular bar has big ambitions and regularly hosts shows from solo singers, mostly of the camp diva ilk. In between show times, televisions screen clips from musicals and as the night rolls on, you'll hear locals singing along. The all-day food menu is pretty standard fare and is served with a lack of polish, but their cheap and cheerful cocktail, the Kylie, is served by the jug and is just as adorable as its antipodean namesake. Open from 11:00 to 00:30.

Straight Or Gay?

Dublin's complicated licensing laws mean that there are not that many gay restaurants or bars - but there are plenty of gay-friendly ones. These are outlets like The Front Lounge (p.383 and p.374) and Cornucopia (p.383 and p.363), in which gay and straight people are both heartily welcomed.

Cornucopia
19 Wicklow St
Dublin 2
Map 430 B 7
01 677 7583

Popular with eco-gays and lesbians, Cornucopia is one of Dublin's oldest and best-loved vegetarian cafes. Reminiscent of the kind of veggie eatery that was popular in the 80s, you have to queue for your food here, choose from a limited menu and sit where you can find a space. This makes for a friendly, chatty spot where strangers in sandals mix with ease. While the fare is wholesome, featuring bean stews, lasagnas, salads and specially cooked breads, the overall effect of a Cornucopia meal can be starch overload, so it's wise to stay away from their potato salad sides.

The Dragon
64-65 South Great George's St
Dublin 2
Map 430 A1 448
01 478 1590 | www.capitalbars.com

Currently the most popular place to see and be seen in by the city's most beautiful boys and girls, The Dragon's decor is a strange mix of opulent oriental and sleek post-modern minimalism. The contradiction works, however, as do Dragon's cocktails, which are a pretty popular post-work appointment. Dragon's dancefloor tends to be overwhelmed with cheesy house and pop that isn't to everyone's taste, but upstairs on Friday nights you can really get down to a set played by the drag queen of Dublin, Miss Panti. Oh, and check out the mega-busy outdoor smoking area. It's where everyone hooks up.

The Front Lounge
33 Parliament St
Dublin 2
Map 425 F4 38
01 670 4112 | www.frontloungedublin.com

Peppered with comfy couches and featuring regular art exhibitions, The Front Lounge's (or the Flounge, as referred to by gay Dubliners) clientele is stylish, but wide ranging in age group and you'll find plenty of lesbians mixing among the gay boys. Although it's a big venue, there's a local feel to it, probably because it's a place where everybody knows your name. There's a great DJ at weekends playing eclectic, nostalgic pop until 02:00, and Casting Couch, a high-camp karaoke night on Tuesdays, is hugely popular. A mediocre menu of oddly devised dishes is served until 16:00 (20:00 on Sundays), and their early cocktail menu is popular.

The George
89 South Great George's St
Dublin 2
Map 430 A1 449
01 478 2983 | www.capitalbars.com

Once a corner barfly joint, Dublin's oldest gay haunt has expanded over the past decade to become mega-pub and club over two floors, with three bars, a dancefloor, stage area and chill-out zone. The corner bar is still there, now nicknamed Jurassic Park because of the general age of its particular clientele. The main venue has resident DJs playing different styles of music on different nights for a party-on crowd and is open until 02:00 (03:00 at weekends). Dublin's cluster of drag queens perform there most evenings, the most popular being Shirley Temple Bar's Bingo! on Sundays, which has become a Dublin legend.

Gruel

168a Dame St
Dublin 2
Map 426 A4 **447**

01670 7199

You might be forgiven for thinking you had stepped into an Eastern Block café on your first encounter with gay-owned and run Gruel. It's higgledy-piggledy decor, complete with mismatching chairs, tables and linoleum floor scream Moscow, circa 1979. The regularly changing menu, written on big blackboards, however, is top-notch and cheap, always including staples like succulent bangers, mash and caramelised onion and scrumptious Thai fish cakes. This is where the hippest of Dublin's gay population go to eat in the early evening, casually prepared for an otherwise unmentioned 10% service charge.

Juice

9 Castle House
73 South
Great George's St
Dublin 2
Map 430 A1 **31**

01475 7856 | *www.juicerestaurant.ie*

Situated slap-bang in between two gay mega bars, The George and The Dragon, Juice is a mid-market vegetarian restaurant with a steady gay clientele, friendly staff and a somewhat hit and miss menu. But then again, it's only hit and miss because Juice, unlike other veggie restaurants, dares to experiment and tries to deliver interesting alternatives for non-meat eaters. Sunday brunch is a good time to check the bright, airy and relaxed Juice (and its clientele) out. Go for their french toast topped with organic maple syrup and their corn fritters. You won't be disappointed.

L'Ecrivain

190a Lwr Baggot St
Dublin 2
Map 431 D3 **35**

01661 1919 | *www.lecrivain.com*

Situated about a 15 minute walk south of the city centre, L'Ecrivain is a restaurant for those who like their food served up formal and French, using only fresh Irish ingredients. One of the highest end restaurants in the city, it has consistently courted a loyal gay clientele who aren't short of pocket. It features a sleek and chic bar downstairs where you can enjoy an aperitif from a state of the art wine list that comes with its own wine waiter, while the dining room upstairs is luxuriously warm and glowing, serving chef and owner Derry Clarke's much loved dishes. It's a Dublin treat well worth paying for.

Lemon Jelly

10/11b East Essex St
Temple Bar
Dublin 2
Map 426 A4 **446**

01873 5161

On a sunny Dublin afternoon as you stroll down the cobbled streets of Temple Bar, you might notice some chilled-out beautiful people sipping lattes outside under the awnings of a tiny cafe. This is Lemon Jelly, an eatery which has become a staple with Dublin's gays. So popular has it been that another, large, sleek and modern branch has been opened across the river on Blooms Lane. It serves the best bagels in Dublin – their BLT, complete with crispy American bacon, is to die for – and they know how to do good, strong Columbian coffee, which is a turn up for the books in this city.

Gruel

Lemon Jelly

Nightclubs

While Dublin is undoubtedly a pub-goers' paradise, the number of established nightclubs in the capital has remained all but static in the last two decades. A new lease of life has been apparent very recently, however. Several long-loved clubs have been given extensive makeovers and a small number of very new and very shiny nightclubs have popped up to cater for the capital's glamorous and demanding twentysomething set.

Door policy is dependent on the kind of club experience you're hoping for. Security at VIP clubs around the Grafton Street strip is notoriously tight. If you are a determined type, however, the best advice is to leave the trainers at home and strut to the club door with confidence. It is also always a good idea to bring identification with you to avoid disappointment.

You can expect to pay in the region of €10 admission, but bear in mind that varies greatly, depending on both the night of the week and the particular acts or DJs scheduled. Concessions and drink promotions are common, with the city's vibrant student network ensuring that club owners are forced to entice business with midweek price promotions when the more affluent working crowd are tucked up safely in their surburban beds.

With a little prior planning, you will find the club experience you want in Dublin, with musical tastes from commercial house to hip hop and jazz to techno each catered for. The savvy visitor reads nightclub reviews in the freesheets found throughout the city in pubs, cafes and restaurants. You can also buy tickets for many clubs at www.ticketmaster.ie, while www.entertainment.ie and www.dublinks.com each offer comprehensive and up-to-date listings.

Drink It Quick
The majority of nightclubs open between 22.00 and 23.00, but locals do not generally hit clubs until after midnight, which is something of a shame, as all nightclubs are required by law to stop selling alcohol at 02.30. This law is often criticised, but it does mean that time spent in a nightclub is spent to full effect: the atmosphere tends to be as highly charged as the drinks!

Club 92

Leopardstown Racecourse
Dublin 18

01 289 5641 | www.leopardstown.com

Outside of the city centre, nightclubs are thin on the ground but Club 92, the Club of Love, is an institution on Dublin's south side. Playing a strictly commercial mix of hits, Club 92 attracts a loyal following among the glossy south county Dublin twentysomething set. Go to the adjoining Fillies Cafe Bar first for a couple of drinks, pick up some concession passes and then stroll down to Club 92 around 23:00. Admission costs €12.

Club M

Cope St
Temple Bar
Dublin 2
Map 426 A4 40

01 671 5622 | www.clubm.ie

Club M has an unpretentious reputation and caters for a more mature crowd. The music is standard chart fare with the odd cheesy classic thrown in for good measure. Admission costs €5 to €15 depending on the night, but keep your eyes peeled for concession flyers. Door policy is strictly over 20s and smart dress is essential. Inside, the dancefloor is the focal point of attention complete with neon lights and podiums, while a second level overlooks the dancefloor. There is also a VIP Champagne Bar called Elysium. The whole room can be hired for private parties and is popular for corporate events. Prices start at €75 for a bottle of Piper Heidsieck and a bottle of Krug Clos Du Mesnil will set you back a cool €1000! While far from cutting edge, Club M proudly appeals to the mass market.

dtwo

60 Harcourt St
Dublin 2
Map 430 A3 455

01 476 4603 | www.dtwonightclub.com

The ever-popular dtwo has built up a solid reputation on the Dublin club scene since it opened in November 2006. Open from Wednesday to Sunday, it hosts one of Dublin's top student nights on Wednesdays (admission €3). The rest of the week caters to an older after-work crowd (admission €6 with a concession and €10 without). Sundays is devoted to live music. Door policy is over 21s only (over 19s on Wednesdays) and if you have been drinking in the adjoining dtwo bar, admission is free before midnight. The eye-catching heated beer garden complete with retractable roof acts as a chill-out zone and is a great place to meet people.

Gaiety Theatre Club

South King St
Dublin 2
Map 430 A2 440

01 679 5622 | www.gaietytheatre.ie

The Gaiety Theatre has been a Dublin landmark since 1871 and has a great over-the-top interior with red velvet seats and baroque touches. The Gaiety Theatre Club has been going strong on Friday and Saturday nights for over a decade and has one of the latest licences in Dublin. Admission costs €12 on Fridays and €15 on Saturdays. The crowd tend to be slightly older: late 20s to 30s. The line-up here is truly eclectic with live jazz, salsa, funk and a northern soul night. The main auditorium acts as a cinema with offbeat movies screened on the main stage. There are four other rooms: two with live bands and two with DJs. An original spot and a refreshing change to the standard Dublin nightclub.

Krystle

Russell Court Hotel
21 - 25 Harcourt St
Dublin 2
Map 430 A3 460

01 478 4066 | www.krystlenightclub.com

Since Krystle opened in 2006, it has made a big splash and is challenging both Lillie's and Renard's for the crown of top VIP club. Billed as Dublin's elegant alternative, Krystle attracts a disproportionate number of models, popstars and rugby players. The music is an upbeat mix of house, hip-hop, funk and rock. The decor is modern and stylish with solid wood flooring. The large outdoor smoking terrace, which is heated and sheltered, is one of Dublin's best. Door policy is strictly over 23s and dress to impress: think Roberto Cavalli and sky high Jimmy Choos.

Lillie's Bordello

Adam Ct
Grafton St
Dublin 2
Map 430 B1 457

01 679 9204 | www.lilliesbordello.ie

Lillie's is an exclusive club just off Grafton Street. While under new management, the door policy remains as tough as ever and is definitely not for the fainthearted. Gold membership costs €500 and €42 monthly thereafter, while Platinum membership costs €2000 and €85 monthly thereafter. Admission is free for non-members from Sundays to Tuesdays and varies between €5 and €15 on other nights. Once inside there are three separate areas where you can swill champagne and spot celebrities to your heart's content. The most exclusive area is the Jersey Lil private room, reserved for members. There is a new terrace upstairs for smokers, which is a great place to eavesdrop on all the latest gossip. People come here to be seen and are generally dressed up to the nines. The crowd includes plenty of media types and music industry insiders. Expect to bump into a celebrity or three, especially on a Saturday night. Thursdays are a good night to go for a more chilled out slant on Dublin's beautiful people.

Club M

POD

Old Harcourt St
Train Station
Dublin 2
Map 430 A3 459

01 476 3374 | www.pod.ie

The Pod has maintained a dedication to providing the best live acts and international DJs for over 10 years. It's all about the music, with big names from Grandmaster Flash to Boy George having appeared here. It boasts three clubbing experiences in one club. Tripod is for dance music fans – it's slick, hot and trendy. The door policy is quite strict, so dress smart. Entry runs from €10 up to €30 for a specific gig. CrawDaddy is the cool choice for intimate gigs in retro surroundings. Adjacent to CrawDaddy is the straight up and stylish Lobby Bar. On weeknights it tends to act as a pre-amble or indeed overspill area to the main event at CrawDaddy, while at weekends it is populated with a mix of relaxed yet refined urbanites hoping to meet similar souls. In essence, the Pod is a somewhat pretentious but ultimately enjoyable slice of what clubbing is all about.

Renards

South Frederick St
Dublin 2
Map 430 B1 461

01 677 5876 | www.renards.ie

Although similar to Lillie's, Renards takes itself less seriously. Anything goes in this place and there is a great mix of people. Music is standard chart fare. There are three levels: the main dancefloor is open to all. The upstairs and downstairs levels are more exclusive and are reserved for members and their guests. Downstairs has something of a wild party atmosphere with a champagne bar and later opening. Upstairs attracts an older crowd and the reserved tables are very popular. Staff are friendly and particularly talented at mixing a mean cocktail. Renard's is unashamedly hedonistic and attracts its fair share of local celebrities, including U2, The Corrs and Colin Farrell.

Ri-Ra

Dame Ct
Dublin 2
Map 430 A1 39

01 671 1220 | www.rira.ie

Ri-Ra's tunes are less chart and more DJ-centric, and people come here for the music rather than the people watching. There is a fairly relaxed door policy, and admission costs €5 to €10 depending on the night. It is good to go midweek as the dancefloor tends to be less crowded, and admission is free before midnight. Strictly Handbag on Mondays, one of Dublin's most popular club nights, has been going strong since 1994. Dance to an eclectic mix of 80s and early 90s tunes. Funk Off on Thursdays is another great night out for all hip-hop devotees.

Sin

17-19 Sycamore St
Temple Bar
Dublin 2
Map 426 A4 451

01 633 4232 | www.sintheatrebar.com

Sin combines a lounge bar, club and venue over two floors and is open seven nights a week from 19:00 to 04:00. The decor is modern and fresh with white leather seating and wooden flooring. The mezzanine lounge overlooks the dancefloor and serves as a VIP area, which can also be hired out for private parties. Sin is always lively with a mix of commercial house and R&B. Fridays are devoted to club classics, Saturday to R&B and Sundays to progressive house. On Tuesdays there is an Asian night called 'Crazy Dragon' for which there is no entry fee and the entertainment changes weekly. Admission costs €10 after 23:00 on Fridays and Sundays and €15 on Saturdays. Door policy is strictly over 21s and dress code is smart-casual. Sin is an extremely popular spot among the 25 plus crowd who enjoy an unpretentious night out.

Spirit

57 Middle Abbey St
Dublin 1
Map 426 A3 454

01 877 9999 | www.spiritdublin.com

Spirit is unique on the Dublin club scene for its holistic slant that combines spiritual healing with hedonism. This destination club has hosted some of the top names in dance music such as David Morales, Paul Oakenfold and David Guetta. There are three

387

distinct areas in this superclub: Mind, Body and Soul. Mind is a holistic healing area, offering reflexology, reiki, massage, temporary body art and tarot reading. Body is the main dancefloor level, with a stage complete with showgirls to really get the crowd going. It also contains a mezzanine with a VIP bar and seating area. Soul is the ground floor bar area, which blasts soulful, funky beats. Spirit is Dublin's biggest and brashest club. Although it's a little pricey, Spirit really does have to be seen to be believed. Admission costs between €10 and €20 depending on the night.

The Sugar Club

8 Lower Leeson St
Dublin 2
Map 430 B3 **456**

01 678 7188 | www.thesugarclub.com

The Sugar Club inhabits the premises of the former Irish Film Theatre. It has kept the tiered seating layout and updated the decor with wood panelling, opulent velour and low lighting to give an intimate and decadent atmosphere. Unlike many overcrowded Dublin clubs, the emphasis is on comfort with table service and award-winning cocktails. The Sugar Club bills itself as Dublin's arts alternative and plays host to live music (blues, jazz, funk, salsa, rock), installations, exhibitions, comedy, quizzes and world cinema. Friday and Saturday nights are devoted to on-trend club nights with admission costing €15. Sassy Sue's GoGo Inevitable on Fridays is a retro night of 60s and 70s tunes that is one of the most popular in Dublin. Saturdays play host to guest DJs, so check out the website for current listings. The Sugar Club has something for everyone and stands out from the crowd with style.

Twenty One Club

21 D'Olier St
Dublin 2
Map 426 B4 **452**

01 671 2089 | www.21.ie

The Twenty One Club, Dublin's sexiest club, goes down a storm with the 18-25 crowd. The music is a mix of commercial house and R&B with Robbie Dunbar on the decks every Thursday and Saturday night. Door policy is strict; bring your ID and dress up. Admission costs €6 with a concession and €8 without. Thursday is ladies night with free admission for ladies all night. Mondays, Tuesdays and Wednesdays are hospitality nights and draw a big crowd with all drinks at only €3. Cutting edge DVD technology beams the video for each song onto giant plasma screens around the club. The stylish VIP room is more intimate with a capacity of 30-40, and is available to hire at a cost of €500 a night. Sign up to the Club 21 website to receive exclusive promotions and concessions.

Voodoo Lounge

39-40 Arran Quay
Smithfield
Dublin 7
Map 425 D4 **453**

01 873 6013 | john@emeraldmusicmanagement.com

While not strictly a nightclub, the Voodoo Lounge hosts several alternative music nights and is a must if you are a fan of heavy metal, goth or indie music. Owned by Huey from the Funlovin' Criminals, this hip spot in Smithfield is a little out of the way but worth the trek. Top international names, including Juliette Lewis, Gavin Friday and Shaun Ryder, have performed at Voodoo. Find out more by visiting their MySpace page: www.myspace.com/voodooarranquay.

Wax

Powerscourt
Townhouse
South William St
Dublin 2
Map 430 A1 **22**

01 677 0014 | www.spydublin.com

This dark, cavernous space oozes urban cool. The location, just off Grafton Street, could not be more convenient. Admission costs anywhere between €5 and €12, depending on the night. The music is first rate with a mix of house, electro and techno. Banter on Wednesdays is perfect for gown-ups who like to party mid-week. The Electric City crew are on the decks on Thursdays. Hospital takes up the reins on Friday with more pure dance. Saturdays is Family with top DJs such as BBC Radio 1's Annie Mac heading to Wax to play in a more intimate setting. A favourite among a hip, mid-twenties set.

Parties At Home

The smoking ban, early closing hours and the spiralling cost of city-centre socialising make inviting friends around an appealing option. If you are living in an apartment, you may have access to a roof garden. Hanley Event Group (01 269 3865, www.events.ie) in Donnybrook are tops for party planning, themed parties and marquee hire. They will work to your budget, and also have a fully stocked party shop for balloons, costumes and prop hire.

For bar-related needs contact Wunderbar (01 825 9854, www.wunderbar.ie) who have a selection of bars, coolers, taps and icemakers to buy or rent, as well as supplying kegs of beer. For wine, WineOnline deliver all over Ireland. Check out www.wineonline.ie for their monthly special offers. For children's parties, Harry Potter and Barbie themes rule the roost. The Birthday Yokes online store supplies every kind of themed partyware imaginable and offer next day delivery (086 172 7061, www.birthdayyokes.com). Bouncy castles are always popular and have become astonishingly elaborate over the years. Make sure the company you hire prioritises safety. Adventure Bounce is one of the most well established companies in Dublin (01 845 0992, www.adventurebounce.ie). Puppet shows and the traditional Punch and Judy have made a comeback. The Lambert Puppet Theatre (p.395) in Monkstown is run by Ireland's best-loved puppeteer family. This fantastic venue is available to hire for very special birthday parties only. A package for 15 children and two adults costs in the region of €300.

Parties At Home

Adventure Bounce	01 845 0992	Bouncy Castles
Artzone	01 499 0614	Art Parties
FitKids	01 484 7211	Gymnastic Parties for 2-8 year olds
Hanley Event Group	01 269 3865	Party Planning, Themed Parties, Lines, Marquees, Pipe & Drape, Ballons, Fancy Dress, Prop Hire
Katie Bonner	087 969 9147	Entertainer
Paul Redmond	087 888 7171	Magician
SoJo Kidz	087 299 9559	Face Painting, Arts & Crafts, Puppets, Organised Games
WineOnline	01 886 7732	Wine
Wunderbar	01 825 9854	Bar hire

Caterers

For dedicated foodies, how about hiring a professional chef to come and show you how to prepare a mouth-watering menu, which you can then devour? Alix Gardener (01 668 1553, www.dublincookery.com) is one of Ireland's top cookery teachers and offers a private dining service from €360. For a stylish dinner party, get in touch with an upscale deli such as Butler's Pantry (01 276 1431, www.thebutlerspantry.ie); with seven locations around Dublin and 20 years experience behind them your guests will not be disappointed. Their extensive range of menus includes 'My Nosh' – perfect for older children's birthday parties. Supper's Ready (01 475 4556, www.suppersready.ie) in Clontarf is another safe bet. They provide honest-to-goodness, home-cooked food at reasonable prices for a range of events. For larger scale events, Feast Catering (www.feast.ie, 086 384 4377) is a popular option. Run by Domini Kemp, the brainchild behind the Itsa Bagel chain and the Itsa 4 restaurant in Sandymount, the food is straight out of the pages of a Nigella Lawson cookbook. If you really want to push the gravy boat out then Cooke's Restaurant (01 679 0536, www.cookesrestaurant.com) on South William Street and its innovative blend of Mediterranean-Californian cuisine is the top choice. Cooke's has a proven track record in providing innovative and original catering for private buffet and formal dining, providing a tailored service of specially created food, a team of experienced chefs, professional servers and bar staff.

Caterers

Butler's Pantry	01 276 0185
Cooke's	01 679 0536
Feast Catering	086 384 4377
Supper's Ready	01 475 4556

389

Cabaret & Strip Shows

Dublin's strip scene is a relatively new phenomenon with 10 clubs in the city centre. The clubs tend to be small and open seven days a week from 20:00 to 03:00. Entry costs anywhere between €10 and €30, and dances cost €30 and upwards. Club Lapello (01 679 0514, www.lapello.com) on Dame Street is Dublin's best-established club. Entry costs €15 and dances are €30. A stretch limo service is available for stag parties and groups. The Barclay Club (01 670 6500, www.barclayclub.ie) on South William Street styles itself as an exclusive bar, restaurant and gentleman's club with fully clothed podium dancing in the main bar and lap dancing in semi-private suites. Upmarket and classy it may be, but the prices are steep – 30 minutes in a semi-private suite costs €400. For something a little more playful, check out the Tassel Club. This cabaret and burlesque revue (www.thetasselclub.com) has regular performances in the Sugar Club, as well as festivals and private parties. The Tassel Club is a unique blend of burlesque striptease, swing, jazz, circus performance and old school glamour. For something more risqué, Nimhneach is Dublin's only fetish and bondage night and is held monthly in the Voodoo Lounge. Dress code applies – check out www.nimhneach.ie for more details.

Cinemas

James Joyce opened Dublin's first cinema on Mary Street in 1909 – the enterprise failed and Joyce left Ireland, never to return. One hundred years on, the cinema scene in Dublin is dominated by multiplexes showing Hollywood movies. In the city centre, the Savoy on O'Connell St is Dublin's best known cinema and boasts Ireland's biggest screen. On Parnell St, Cineworld is Ireland's largest cinema. Average prices to catch a movie in Dublin are €9.50 for adults (€7 for the matinee show), and €6 for children, pensioners and students. The Cineworld Unlimited Card is perfect for cinema buffs: €17.50 a month gets you unlimited access to any of their cinemas in the UK and Ireland (www.cineworld.ie). Most of the suburban cinemas are located in shopping centres. Vue in Liffey Valley is particularly popular due to its extra comfortable seats and large screens. The UCI in Tallaght (www.uci.ie) runs a Kid's Club on weekend mornings and during school holidays – admission costs €3 per child and is free for accompanying adults. The MoviesCinema chain with branches in Dundrum and Swords have 'Reel Parents' mornings that welcome adults with babies and young children into their cinemas to catch the latest blockbuster. Admission costs €7 and baby-changing facilities are available. Check out their website for current listings (www.movies-at.ie/reelparents.tpl).

Cinemas			
Denzille Private Cinema	Dublin 2	01 676 8609	www.13denzille.com
Irish Film Institute	Dublin 2	01 679 3477	www.irishfilm.ie
Santry Omniplex	Dublin 9	081 871 9719	www.omniplex.ie
Cineworld Parnell St	Dublin 1	1520 880 444	www.cineworld.ie
Dun Laoghaire IMC	Dun Laoghaire	01 230 1399	www.imc-cinemas.com
Movies@ Dundrum	Dublin 14	1520 880 333	www.movies-at.ie
Movies@ Swords	Swords	1520 880 333	www.movies-at.ie
Savoy Cinema	Dublin 1	081 877 6776	www.savoy.ie
Savoy, Balbriggan	North Coast	01 690 5379	na
Screen Cinema	D'Olier St	01 872 5500	www.screencinema.ie
Stillorgan Ormonde Cinema	Stillorgan	01 707 4100	www.ormondebookings.com
UCI Blanchardstown	Dublin 15	1520 880 000	www.uci.ie
UCI Coolock	Dublin 17	1520 880 000	www.uci.ie
UCI Tallaght	Tallaght	1520 880 000	www.uci.ie
Vue, Liffey Valley	Clondalkin	1520 501 000	www.myvue.ie

There are a couple of independent cinemas, such as The Screen on D'olier St and the Irish Film Institute in Temple Bar, which show a more offbeat selection and more foreign language options. The Irish Film Institute runs a large number of events throughout the year. Examples include a French Film Festival, an Italian Film Festival, a Gay and Lesbian Film Festival, as well as retrospectives of the works of cinema greats

390

and educational talks. The Irish Film Institute's film shop is stocked with hard-to-find books and DVDs. There is also a bar and restaurant that attract an arty crowd. To support the Irish Film Institute's work, consider purchasing yearly membership (€20).

Comedy

Dubliners are renowned for their wit and Dublin's vibrant comedy scene is testament to this. Dublin has produced some comedy geniuses over the years, such as the late, great Dermot Morgan of Father Ted fame. Venues vary from tiny bars to purpose-built clubs. Get to a couple of open mic nights and when that nervous guy who keeps stuttering metamorphoses into the hottest talent around – you can always say you saw him back in the day! The Bulmers International Comedy Festival (www.bulmerscomedy.ie) takes place every September over three weeks and is now one of the largest comedy festivals in the world. Further afield is the Smithwick's Cat Laughs Comedy Festival (www.thecatlaughs.com), which takes place every Summer in Kilkenny. Perfect for a fun-filled mini-break in this enchanting, medieval city.

42 Wellington Quay
Temple Bar
Dublin 2
Map 426 A4 **428**

Ha'penny Bridge Inn

086 815 6987 | www.battleoftheaxe.com

The Ha'penny Bridge Inn is a traditional pub which has been hosting regular comedy nights in its upstairs room since 1996. The most infamous of these is Battle of the Axe every Tuesday and Thursday at 21:30 (doors open at 21:00). Comedians, singers or anyone else who feels like it is welcome to get up on stage and do their thing. At the end of the night, the audience vote for the best act, who then receive the prestigious Lucky Duck award. Much hilarity guaranteed but remember you may be laughing at how bad some of these acts are. Admission costs €8 or €6 with concession. The Capital Comedy Club runs every Wednesday and Sunday at 21:30 (doors open at 21:00) and features up-and-coming comedians, as well as the more established names. All these nights are popular so get there early. See also www.capitalcomedyclub.com for more.

23 Wicklow St
Dublin 2
Map 430 A1 **445**

The International Bar

01 677 9250 | www.theinternationalcomedyclub.com

The International Bar is a piece of comedy history. Downstairs is a popular spot for a pint and the bohemian crowd often spills onto the street outside. Upstairs is where Dublin's finest comedy talent is showcased five nights a week with a break for Jazz on Tuesdays. Mondays is the Comedy Improv, a five-piece ensemble who have been going strong since 1992 – be warned audience participation is encouraged! Admission costs €8 and doors open at 21:00. Wednesdays is the Comedy Cellar, which nurtures up-and-coming talent. This is where Ardal O'Hanlon, Dylan Moran and Tommy Tiernan cut their teeth. Admission costs €10 (€8 for students) and doors open at 21:00. Thursdays, Fridays and Saturdays is the International Comedy Club which features more established names and is hosted by the American comedian Des Bishop, a regular on Irish TV. Admission costs €8 (€6 for students) and doors open at 20:30 for a 21:15 show. Other websites with useful information are www.dmcwebs.com/improv and www.dublincomedycellar.com.

4-8 Eden Quay
Dublin 1
Map 426 B3 **430**

The Laughter Lounge

1800 266 339 | www.laughterlounge.com

The Laughter Lounge recently underwent a €6 million redevelopment and now boasts a full stage, two bars, a VIP area and a nightclub. This is undeniably Dublin's premier comedy venue and attracts top names from home and abroad, including Bill Bailey, Dara O'Brian and Johnny Vegas. Four comedians strut their stuff every Thursday, Friday and Saturday meaning there should be something to suit all tastes. Platters of food

(€10-€20) are available but must be pre-booked. The cocktail list is good and a free cocktail is on offer if you arrive before 19:30. The party continues after the gig with admission to the After Lounge nightclub included in the entry price. Sign up to the Laughter Lounge website for promotions and special offers. The Laughter Lounge is available for private hire from Sunday to Wednesday. Timings: Thursday, Friday & Saturday 19:00 – 2:30 (Private hire Sunday to Wednesday). Admission is €25-€30 for individuals and €20-€25 for groups of 30 people or more.

Concerts

Dublin has a lively music scene with great local talent. Dublin's largest venue is the Point Depot (01 836 6777, www.livenation.ie) with a capacity of 8,500 people. The Point is located on North Wall Quay just beyond the IFSC and be warned it is a bit of a trek down and back! Another venue, which often hosts big-name acts is the Olympia Theatre (01 679 3323, www.mcd.ie/olympia) on Dame Street. Fans of rock and metal should check out Eamonn Dorans (01 679 9114) in Temple Bar. Bleu Note (01 878 3371, www.bleunoteclub.com) on Capel Street is where you will find jazz and blues in Dublin. Every Summer, Dublin Castle plays host to the Heineken Green Energy Festival. Previous acts include Sinead O'Connor, Iggy Pop and Snow Patrol. Bud Rising (www.budrising.ie) is another summer festival held in Marley Park, which has in the past seen acts such as The Foo Fighters, The Chemical Brothers and Franz Ferdinand.

Curved St
Temple Bar
Dublin 2
Map 426 A4 **436**

Temple Bar Music Centre

01 670 9202 | www.tbmc.ie

With a great location in Temple Bar, this funky, modern venue is instantly recognisable with its giant images of Irish music legends displayed on the venue's exterior. Names such as Van Morrison, Ash and The Strokes have performed here in the past. More than just a venue, the Temple Bar Music Centre also houses a sound training centre and rehearsal studios, and it also hosts diverse club nights and big-name DJs.

58-59 Thomas St
Dublin 8
Map 429 D1 **431**

Vicar Street

01 454 5533 | www.vicarstreet.com

Vicar Street is a modern venue that plays host to live music, comedy and theatre. It was conceived by the late Jim Aiken, who was one of Ireland's most successful promoters. Vicar Street was designed with the audience's listening and viewing pleasure in mind with a state of the art sound system and great lighting. Unusually for a venue the floor area has table service. Artists as diverse as Marianne Faithful and Belle and Sebastian have performed here. A must-see for music lovers.

26 Wexford St
Dublin 2
Map 430 A2 **426**

The Village

01 475 8555 | www.thevillagevenue.com

The Village on Wexford Street is a live music venue, club and bar spread over two floors. It offers the opportunity to see big names such as Public Enemy, Scissor Sisters and The Kooks in an intimate setting. As well as live music, the Village plays host to club nights on Friday and Saturday nights with admission costing €7 and €10 respectively. Downstairs is a funky bar, which turns clubbier after 10:00 with DJ's every night. The Village attracts a cool but unpretentious crowd who know their music. Open from 19:00 to 02:30, seven days a week.

25 Wexford St
Dublin 2
Map 430 A2 **424**

Whelan's

01 478 0766 | www.whelanslive.com

Here you will find a traditional pub and a legendary live music venue combined with aplomb. Whelan's is an institution, which has attracted acts of the calibre of Jeff

Buckley, Nick Cave and the Artic Monkeys. While big names play here, Whelan's also has a reputation for promoting new, upcoming talents. The venue's sense of space is accentuated by high ceilings, which make you appreciate the acoustic sounds even more. Admission generally costs around €15 but this varies. Check out www.whelanslive.com for up-to-date listings.

Fashion Shows

Dublin Fashion Week (01 643 2801; www.dublinfashionweek.com) is the brainchild of former model Sonia Reynolds and has been going strong since 2005. Dublin Fashion Week showcases both emerging and established Irish designers. The concept attracted some criticism at its inception but has proved a great success with Brown Thomas now stocking a line from new designers showcased at Dublin Fashion Week.

Billion Dollar Babes (www.billiondollarbabes.ie) is an invitation-only, sample sale featuring top designers such as Prada, Armani, Valentino and Jean Paul Gaultier among others. Clothes, shoes and accessories are discounted by up to 80%. You will also find discounted wedding dresses and accessories in the Billion Dollar Brides section. To receive an invitation, all you need to do is register on their website. On the day, get there early to grab that elusive bargain.

Theatre

Other options **Drama Groups** p.236

As with any self-respecting metropolis, Dublin has a strong theatre scene – and then some, thanks to Ireland's esteemed literary heritage: playwrights Samuel Beckett, Oscar Wilde, George Bernard Shaw, John Millington Synge, Sean O'Casey and Brendan Brehan. And that is just the tip of the cultural iceberg, what with contemporary movers and shakers such as Mark O'Rowe, Jimmy Murphy and Peter Sheridan shaking up the limelight.

From period plays in old theatres to period plays in new theatres via contemporary dance in arts centres and stage schools, there's something for everyone and at varying prices. City centre restaurants too have cashed in on the scene, offering many a Pre-Theatre Menu to drama-oriented diners.

Annual drama events include the Gay & Lesbian Theatre Festival (May), Dublin Fringe (September) and the Dublin Theatre Festival (September/October).

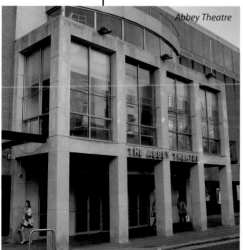
Abbey Theatre

The Helix

393

26 Abbey St Lower
Dublin 1
Map 426 B3 `425`

Abbey Theatre & Peacock Theatre

01 878 7222 | www.abbeytheatre.ie

Comprising two theatres – the Abbey and smaller sibling the Peacock – this venue is a stalwart on the theatre scene and quite right too; its mixed programme of old classics and daring repertory have moved and inspired since its 1966 opening at this particular site.

78/79 Grafton St
Dublin 2
Map 430 B1 `432`

Bewley's Cafe Theatre

086 878 4001 | www.bewleyscafetheatre.com

This is a charming makeshift theatre located in the former Oriental Room of Bewley's Café. Built with lunchtime theatre in mind, this tiny venue features table-and-chair seating so the audience can sup soup while watching 45 minute productions. It also hosts the odd live music night.

The Square
Tallaght
Dublin 24

Civic Theatre

01 462 7477 | www.civictheatre.ie

The Civic Theatre's multi-purpose auditorium presents a range of entertainment from popular dance shows to new drama, and from comedy to live music. The theatre also hosts reglar amateur dramatic workshops for aspiring thesps over the summer holidays.

Blanchardstown Centre
Dublin 15

Draíocht

01 885 2622 | www.draiocht.ie

This eclectic arts centre is incongruously located next to the mall, housing two theatres, two galleries, an artists' studio, and arts and craft workshop rooms. Emphasis is on creating a family-friendly community feel, as illustrated by its annual Spreacha Festival aimed at children.

Pembroke Pl
Off Pembroke St
Dublin 2
Map 430 C3 `442`

Focus Theatre

01 676 3071 | focustheatre@eircom.net

Founded by the late Deidre O'Connell who trained under Lee 'Actor's Studio' Strasberg in New York, this small but respected theatre and performance school is committed to Stanislavski's 'Method'. Expect serious plays that explore the human condition.

King St South
Dublin 2
Map 430 A2 `440`

Gaiety Theatre

01 677 1717 | www.gaietytheatre.ie

Dublin's longest-established theatre, the three-tiered Gaiety, has retained its character since opening its doors in 1871. Resplendent with cloakroom queues, chandeliers and boxes, the venue has hosted a plethora of performances including musicals, dance, pantomimes, burlesque drama and gigs. The Red Room Bar also doubles up as a late-night nightclub at weekends.

1 Cavendish Row
Dublin 2
Map 426 A2 `423`

Gate Theatre

01 874 4045 | www.gate-theatre.ie

Established as a theatre in 1892, the hallowed Gate successfully juggles plays, musicals and dance by Irish writers with those recognised internationally, with relationships burgeoning with new Irish playwrights Mark O'Rowe, Conor McPherson and Bernard Farrell to name but a few. In its long and interesting history, theatrical greats such as Orson Welles and James Mason treaded the boards here.

DCU
Collins Av
Dublin 9
Map 408 B2 `437`

The Helix

01 700 7000 | www.thehelix.ie

This large and versatile arts centre has three different performance venues – Mahony Hall seats over 1,200 people, The Theatre seats 450 and The Space seats an

394

intimate 150 – making it an ideal venue for musicals, orchestra performances, jazz sessions, Shakespearean plays, children's theatre and even ice extravaganzas. There is adequate parking at the Helix, but you can also take a number of different buses from the city centre. Buses 4, 11, 11A, 11B, 13, 13A or 19A will all take you to the right place.

Clifton La
Monkstown
Map 423 D4 **434**

Lambert Puppet Theatre

01 280 0974 | www.lambertpuppettheatre.com

This is a family-run, child-friendly theatre out of town that creates and presents its own productions. It also plays host to touring puppet companies and the Annual International Puppet Festival. Most productions are suitable for children aged 3 and up, and if they love what they see, they can buy their own puppets from the on-site shop. To get there, take the Dart to the Salthill and Monkstown station, or take the 7/7A bus from O'Connell Street to Monkstown Road.

Dundrum
Town Centre
Dublin 14
Map 814 D4 **24**

Mill Theatre

01 296 9340 | www.milltheatre.com

Nestled at the back of the shopping mall, just a script's throw away from Harvey Nics and the foodcourt, the Mill Theatre has been presenting a variety of plays and comedy for all ages since its opening in May 2006. There's also a gallery space for exhibiting artists.

43 Essex St East
Dublin 2
Map 426 A4 **429**

The New Theatre

01 670 3361 | www.thenewtheatre.com

Hidden at the back of the Connelly Bookshop (refurbished in 2007), the New Theatre provides an inclusive platform for emerging and established writers, professional theatre companies, directors and performers. It is one of the venues used for the Dublin Fringe Festival and the Dublin Theatre Festival.

Marine Rd
Dun Laoghaire
Map 423 F4 **441**

Pavilion Theatre

01 231 2929 | www.paviliontheatre.ie

Opened to the public in 2000, the theatre is in the prime location of the Pavilion complex, just a short walk away from the Dun Laoghaire Dart station. It runs a diverse selection of events from plays and traditional Irish music, world music and lunchtime children's theatre, and includes an art gallery upstairs.

39 Essex St East
Temple Bar
Dublin 2
Map 425 F4 **427**

Project Arts Centre

01 881 9613 | www.project.ie

This artist-driven arts centre is made up of two theatres, a gallery and a bar, and it showcases contemporary productions in the visual arts, music, dance and theatre categories. Productions are largely experimental, and are aimed at nurturing new and exciting talent.

Trinity College
Dublin 2
Map 426 C4 **444**

Samuel Beckett Theatre

01 896 2461 | www.tcd.ie

After a lovely walk through Trinity College grounds, you'll find the intimate Samuel Beckett Theatre. This is the home of Trinity's drama department, and during term time, you can catch works by Trinity students. Outside of term time, the theatre hosts a range of international and local acts, including the Dublin Fringe Festival and the Dublin Theatre Festival.

Culture Club

After a cultural experience at the theatre, head off for an equally cultural dinner at one of Dublin's fine Irish restaurants. You'll certainly find the best of Irish cuisine at Chapter One Restaurant (p.352) and at The Winding Stair (p.353).

395

DIGITALGLOBE™

C L E A R L Y T H E B E S T

61 cm QuickBird Imagery is the highest resolution satellite imagery available. We offer products and resorces to both existing GIS users and the entire next generation of mapping and multimedia applications.

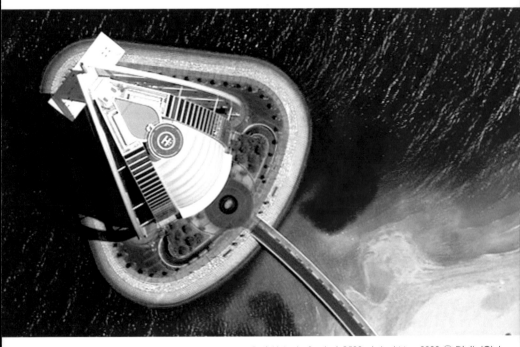

Burj Al Arab, Scale 1:2500, dated May 2003 © DigitalGlobe

MAPSgeosystems

DigitalGlobe's Master Reseller serving the Middle East and East, Central and West Africa

MAPS (UAE), Corniche Plaza 1, P.O. Box 5232, Sharjah, UAE.
Tel : +971 6 5725411, Fax : +971 6 5724057
www.maps-geosystems.com

For further details, please contact quickbird@maps-geosystems.com

Maps

Maps

User's Guide

This section has a series of detailed maps (see the Map Sheet Index on p.402 and p.403) of Dublin city. These are intended to help you get your bearings when you first arrive, and give you an idea of where we're talking about in the main chapters of the book. The street grids are blown up nice and big, at a 1cm=220m scale. We've also included the main hotels from the General Information chapter (see p.30 onwards) along with schools, hospitals, embassies, shopping centres, heritage sites and parks (see the legend below). We've also marked the Luas Red and Green Line stations and the Dart stations along the coast, for which you'll find a map on the inside back cover, along with some helpful information on the extensive bus network. You may have noticed that some of the areas covered in the Residents, Exploring and Going Out chapters have map references. They refer to maps from p.406 to p.431. For the bigger picture, the map on p.400 helps you to pinpoint Dublin's exact location, as well as some of the city's outer suburbs and neighbouring counties. It also defines the main roads leading out of the city to help you escape on that weekend break.

Street Talk

Navigating your way back and forth across the Liffey is as easy as ABC: just flick to the index at the back for a full listing of the main streets in Dublin's city centre. If all else fails and you're just no good with maps, work that Irish charm and ask for directions.

Need More?

We understand that this residents' guide is a pretty big book. It needs to be, to carry all the info we have about living in Dublin. But, unless you've got the pockets of a clown, it's unlikely you're going to carry it around with you on daytrips. With this in mind, we've created the **Dublin Mini Map** as a more manageable alternative. The Mini Map packs the whole city into your pocket and once unfolded is an excellent navigational tool. It's part of a series of Mini Maps that includes cities as diverse as London, Dubai, New York and Barcelona. Wherever your travels take you, you'll never have to ask for directions again. Visit our website for details of how to pick up these little gems or nip into any good bookshop (www.explorerpublishing.com).

Online Maps

There are a few websites that have searchable maps of Dublin: www. dublinmapped.com lets you click on the bits you want to see enlarged while you can use the mini map in the corner to navigate your way around. Another handy site is www.softguide-dublin.com. Hardcore map fans tend to like Google Earth (download from http://earth.google.com) for its satellite images, powerful search facility and incredibly detailed views, but the street directory isn't very detailed.

Map Legend

Ⓗ Hotel/Resort			Motorway
Education			Major Road
Park/Garden			Secondary Road
✚ Hospital			Other Road
Shopping		)═ ═ ═(	Tunnel
Heritage/Museum		⌷	Railway Station
Water		⌷	Dart
Industrial Area		Ⓛ	Luas Red Line
Agriculture		Ⓛ	Luas Green Line
Cemetery		**RATHGAR**	Area name
Stadium		M7	Road Number
Pedestrian Area		❶	Tourist Info
Built up Area/Building		✉	Post Office
Land		♟	Church

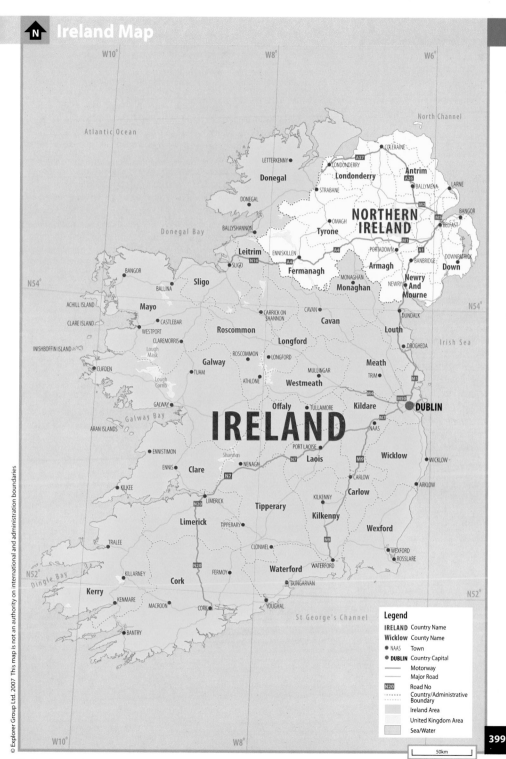

The Complete **Residents'** Guide

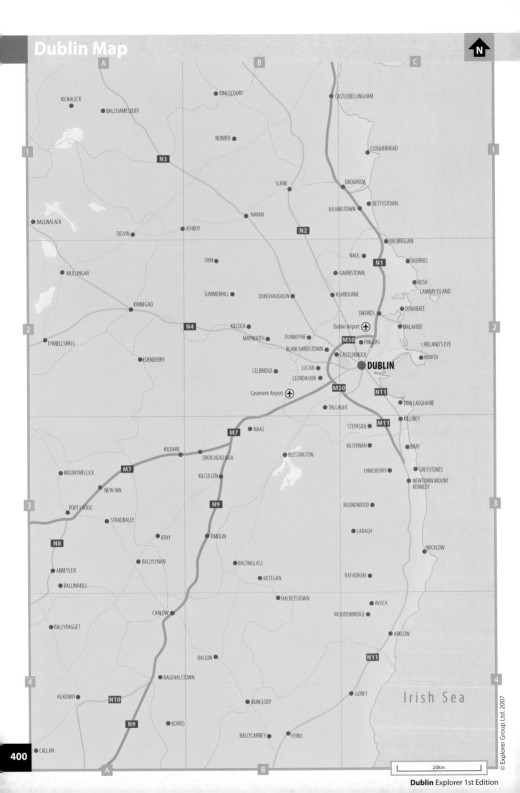

N

A   B   C

1

KILNALECK
BALLYJAMESDUFF
KINGSCOURT
CASTLEBELLINGHAM
NOBBER
N3
CLOGHERHEAD
SLANE
DROGHEDA
BALLINALACK
NAVAN
JULIANSTOWN
BETTYSTOWN
DELVIN
ATHBOY
N2
BALBRIGGAN

2

MULLINGAR
TRIM
SUMMERHILL
DUNSHAUGHLIN
NAUL
GARRISTOWN
ASHBOURNE
N1
SKERRIES
RUSH
LAMBAY ISLAND
KINNEGAD
SWORDS
DONABATE
TYRRELLSPASS
N4
KILCOCK
MAYNOOTH
DUNBOYNE
Dublin Airport ✈
M50
FINGLAS
MALAHIDE
EDENDERRY
BLANCHARDSTOWN
CASTLEKNOCK
IRELAND'S EYE
CELBRIDGE
LUCAN
DUBLIN
HOWTH
CLONDALKIN
M50
N11
Casement Airport ✈
TALLAGHT
DUN LAOGHAIRE

3

NAAS
STEPASIDE
M11
KILLINEY
KILDARE
M7
KILTERNAN
BRAY
MOUNTMELLICK
M7
DROICHEAD NUA
BLESSINGTON
ENNISKERRY
GREYSTONES
NEW INN
KILCULLEN
NEWTOWN MOUNT KENNEDY
PORT LAOISE
N9
ROUNDWOOD
STRADBALLY
N8
ATHY
TIMOLIN
LARAGH
WICKLOW
ABBEYLEIX
BALLYLYNAN
BALTINGLASS
RATHDRUM
BALLINAKILL
KILTEGAN
HACKETSTOWN
AVOCA

4

CARLOW
WOODENBRIDGE
BALLYRAGGET
ARKLOW
BALLON
N11
BAGENALSTOWN
Irish Sea
KILKENNY
N10
BUNCLODY
GOREY
N9
BORRIS
BALLYCARNEY
FERNS
CALLAN

20km

© Explorer Group Ltd. 2007

Dublin Explorer 1st Edition

Written by residents, the London Explorer is packed with insider info, from arriving in the city to making it your home and everything in between.

London Explorer Residents' Guide
We Know Where You Live

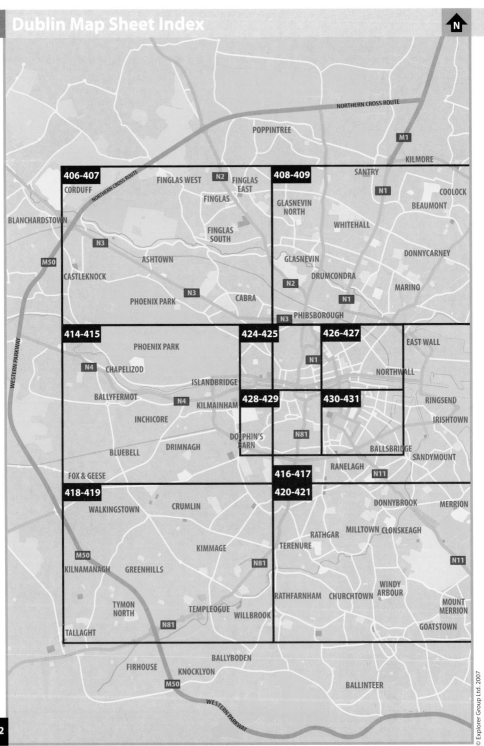

Dublin Explorer 1st Edition

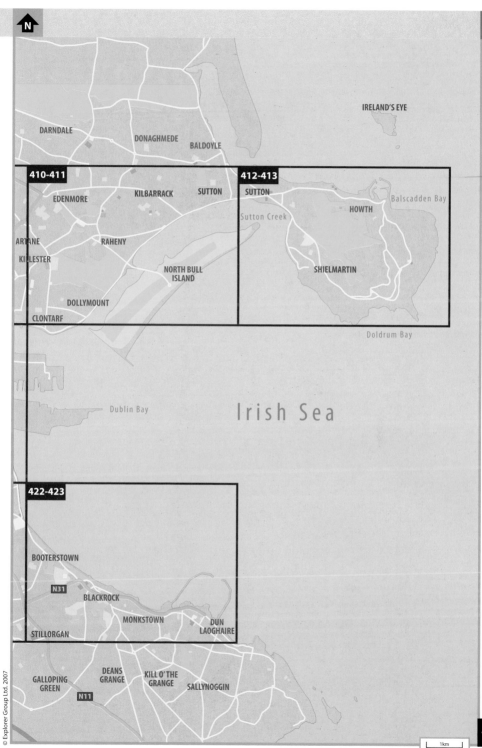

IRELAND'S EYE

DARNDALE

DONAGHMEDE

BALDOYLE

410-411

EDENMORE

KILBARRACK

SUTTON

412-413

SUTTON

SUTTON

HOWTH

Balscadden Bay

Sutton Creek

ARTANE

RAHENY

KILLESTER

NORTH BULL ISLAND

SHIELMARTIN

DOLLYMOUNT

CLONTARF

Doldrum Bay

Dublin Bay

Irish Sea

422-423

BOOTERSTOWN

N31

BLACKROCK

MONKSTOWN

DUN LAOGHAIRE

STILLORGAN

GALLOPING GREEN

DEANS GRANGE

KILL O' THE GRANGE

SALLYNOGGIN

N11

© Explorer Group Ltd. 2007

1km

The Complete **Residents'** Guide

Street Index

Street	Map Ref
Abbey St	425 F4
Abbey St Middle	426 A3
Abbey St Upper	425 F4
Adelaide Rd	430 B4
Allingham St	428 C2
Amiens St	427 D2
Anglesea St	426 A4
Anne St South	430 B1
Anne's La	430 B1
Arann St	425 F3
Arbour Hill	424 B3
Arbour Pl	424 C3
Ardee St	429 D2
Ard Ri Rd	424 C3
Arran Quay	425 D4
Arran St West	425 D4
Aston Quay	426 A4
Aughrim St	424 B1
Aungier St	430 A2
Bachelors Walk	426 A4
Baggot Ct	430 C3
Baggot La	431 F4
Baggot St Lower	431 D3
Baggot St Upper	431 E3
Ball's La	425 E3
Barrow St	431 F2
Basin St Upper	428 B1
Bell's La	430 C2
Belvedere Ct	426 B1
Benburb St	424 B3
Beresford St	425 E3
Bessborough Av	427 E1
Bishop St	429 F2
Blackhall Pl	425 D3
Blackhall St	425 D3
Bloom La	426 A4
Bonham St	424 C4
Bow La West	428 A1
Bow Lane East	430 A2
Bow St	425 E3
Boyne St	431 D1
Braithwaite St	429 D2
Bride Rd	429 F1
Bridge St Lower	425 E4
Bridgefoot St	425 D4
Brunswick St North	425 D3
Buckingham St Lr	427 D2
Bull Alley St	429 F2
Burgh Quay	426 B4
Burlington Rd	431 D4
Byrne's La	426 A4
Caledon Rd	427 F1

Street	Map Ref
Camden Row	430 A3
Camden St Lower	430 A3
Camden St Upper	430 A3
Canal Rd	430 A4
Canon Lillis Ave	427 E2
Capel St	425 F3
Cardiff La	427 E4
Carman's Hall	429 E1
Cathal Brugha St	426 B2
Cathedral St	426 B3
Cavalry Row	424 B3
Chamber St	429 D2
Chancery Pl	425 E4
Chancery St	425 E4
Chapel La	426 A3
Charlemont Mall	430 A4
Charlemont Pl	430 B4
Charlemont St	430 A4
Charles St Great	426 C1
Charleville Mall	427 D1
Charlotte Way	430 A3
Chatham St	430 A1
Christ Church Pl	429 F1
Church Rd	427 F1
Church St	425 E4
Church St East	427 F2
Church Street Upper	425 E3
City Quay	427 D4
Clanbrassil St Lower	429 E3
Clanbrassil St Upper	429 E4
Clarence Pl Great	431 E1
Clarendon St	430 A1
Clonmel St	430 A3
Coleralne St	425 E3
College St	426 B4
Cornmarket St	429 E1
Commons St	427 D3
Constitution Hill	425 E2
Cook St	425 E4
Cope St	426 A4
Cork St	428 C2
Cranmer La	431 F2
Creighton St	427 D4
Crown Alley	426 A4
Crumlin Rd	428 A4
Cuffe St	430 A2
Cumberland Rd	430 C3
Custom House Quay	426 C3
Dame Court	430 A1
Dame St	426 A4
Dartmouth Square	430 B4
Dawson St	430 B1

Street	Map Ref
Dean St	429 E2
Deans Ct	429 E1
Denmark St Gt	426 A1
Denzille La	431 D1
D'Olier St	426 B4
Dolphin Rd	428 A4
Dolphin's Barn St	428 B3
Dominick Pl	426 A2
Donore Av	428 C2
Dorset St Lower	426 A1
Dorset St Upper	425 F2
Dowling's Ct	427 D4
Drury St	430 A1
Duke La Lower	430 B1
Duke St	430 B1
Dunne St	427 D1
Earl St North	426 B3
Earl St South	429 D1
Earlsfort Tce	430 B3
Echlin St	428 B1
Eden Quay	426 B3
Elgin Rd	431 F4
Ellis Quay	424 C4
Ely Pl	430 C2
Erne St Upper	431 D1
Ernst St Lower	427 E4
Essex Quay	425 F4
Essex St East	426 A4
Eustace St	426 A4
Ewington La	428 B1
Exchequer St	430 A1
Fade St	430 A1
Fenian St	431 D1
Fishamble St	425 F4
Fitzgibbon St	426 B1
Fitzwilliam La	430 C2
Fitzwilliam Pl	430 C4
Fitzwilliam Sq North	430 C3
Fitzwilliam Sq South	430 C3
Fleet St	426 B4
Flemmings Pl	431 D3
Foley St	426 C2
Fownes St	426 A4
Francis St	429 E1
Frederick St North	426 A1
Frenchman's La	426 C3
Gardiner La	426 B1
Gardiner Pl	426 B1
Gardiner St Lower	426 C2
Gardiner St Middle	426 B1
George's Quay	426 C3
Golden La	429 F1

Street	Map Ref
Gordon St	431 F2
Grafton St	430 B1
Grand Canal Pl	428 B1
Grand Canal Quay	431 F1
Grand Canal St Lower	431 E1
Grand Parade	430 B4
Grant's Row	431 E2
Grattan Bridge	425 F4
Grattan St	431 E2
Gray St	429 D2
Greek St	425 E3
Green St	425 F3
Grenville St South	426 B1
Guild St	427 E3
Haddington Pl	431 E3
Haddington Rd	431 E3
Halston St	425 F3
Hammond La	425 D4
Hanbury La	429 D1
Hanover La	429 E1
Hanover Quay	427 F4
Hanover St East	427 D4
Harcourt Rd	430 A4
Harcourt St	430 A2
Hardwicke St	426 A1
Harmony Row	431 E1
Harpenny Bridge	426 A4
Harry St	430 A1
Hatch Pl	430 B3
Hatch St Lower	430 B3
Hatch St Upper	430 A3
Hawkins St	426 B4
Hawthorn Tce	427 F2
Hendrick St	425 D3
Henry St	426 A3
Herbert Pl	431 E3
Herbert St	431 D3
Herberton Rd	428 A4
Heytesbury La	431 E4
High St	429 E1
Hill St	426 B1
Hogan Av	431 E1
Holles St	431 D2
Hume St	430 C2
Infirmary Rd	424 A3
Inns Quay	425 E4
Island St	424 C4
James Joyce St	426 C2
James's St	428 C1
James's St East	431 D2
James's Walk	428 A2
Jervis St	425 F3

Street	Map Ref	Street	Map Ref	Street	Map Ref	Street	Map Ref
John St South	429 D2	Moland Pl	426 C3	Phibsborough Rd	425 E1	Strandville Av	427 E1
John's Rd West	424 A4	Molesworth St	430 B1	Poolbeg St	426 B4	Strangford Rd	427 F1
Kevin St Lower	429 F2	Molyneaux Yard	429 D1	Portland Row	427 D1	Suffolk St	430 B1
Kevin St Upper	429 F2	Montague St	430 A3	Portland St West	428 C1	Summer St North	426 C1
Kildare St	430 B2	Montpelier Hill	424 A3	Power's Ct	431 E2	Summer St South	428 C2
Killarney St	427 D1	Montpelier Gardens	424 A3	Prince's St North	426 A3	Summerhill	426 C1
King St North	425 D3	Moore La	426 A2	Prussia St	424 B1	Summerhill Parade	427 D1
King St South	430 B2	Moore St	426 A3	Queen St	425 D3	Summerhill Pl	426 C1
Lad Lane	431 D3	Moss St	426 C4	Quinn's La	430 C3	Sussex Rd	430 C4
Lamb's Alley	429 E1	Mount Brown	428 A1	Railway St	426 C2	Swifts Alley	429 E1
Landsdowne Pk	431 F3	Mount St Lower	431 E2	Rainsford St	428 C1	Talbot Pl	426 C3
Leeson St Lower	430 C3	Mount St Upper	431 D2	Reuben St	428 B2	Talbot St	426 B3
Leeson St Upper	430 C4	Moy Elta Rd	427 F1	Rialto Cottages	428 A2	Temple Bar	426 A4
Leinster La	430 C1	Nassau St	430 B1	Rialto St	428 A2	Temple St N	426 A1
Lemons St	430 B1	New Bride St	429 F2	Richmond St South	430 A4	Temple St W	424 B3
Lennox St	430 A4	New Market	429 D2	Ringsend Rd	431 F1	The Coombe	429 D2
Lisburn St	425 E3	New Row South	429 E2	Robert St South	428 C1	Thomas Ct	429 D1
Loftus La	425 F3	New St South	429 E2	Rosary Rd	428 B2	Thomas La	426 B2
Lombard St East	427 D4	Newcomen Av	427 E1	Ross Rd	429 F1	Thomas St	429 D1
Loreto Rd	428 B2	Newport St	428 C1	Russell Av East	427 F2	Townsend St	426 C4
Lotts	426 A3	Nicholas St	429 E1	Rutland Pl	426 A1	Upper Jervis La	425 F3
Lourdes House	426 C2	North Circular Rd	424 B1	Rutland Pl North	426 C1	Upper Liffey St	426 A3
Lourdes Rd	428 B2	North Gt George's St	426 A1	S Cumberland St	431 D1	Usher St	425 D4
Lower Abbey St	426 B3	North Strand Rd	427 E1	S Frederick St	430 B1	Usher's Island	424 C4
Lower Basin St	428 B1	North Wall Quay	427 E3	Sth Great Georges St	430 A1	Usher's Quay	425 D4
Lower Jervis La	425 F3	Northumberland Rd	431 E2	Sandwith St	431 D1	Verschoyle Pl	431 E2
Lower Liffey St	426 A4	O'Connell St	426 B3	School House La East	430 B2	Vicar St	429 D1
Lower Rutland St	426 C1	Oliver Bond St	425 D4	School St	428 C1	Victoria Quay	424 B4
Macken St	431 E1	Oriel St Upper	427 E2	Seaview Av East	427 F1	Viking Rd	424 C3
Magennis Pl	427 D4	Ormond Quay Lower	426 A4	Seville Tce	427 D1	Warbington Pl	431 E3
Malborough St	426 B2	Ormond Quay Upper	425 F4	Seville Pl	427 E2	Waterloo La	431 D4
Manor St	424 C2	Ormond St	429 D2	Shaw St	426 C4	Waterloo Rd	431 E4
Mark St	426 C4	Ossory Rd	427 E1	Sheriff St	427 D2	Watling St	424 C4
Mark's La	426 C4	Ossory West Rd	427 E1	Sheriff St Upper	427 F3	Wellington Quay	426 A4
Marrowbone La	428 C2	Our Lady's Rd	428 B2	Ship St Great	429 F1	Wellington Rd	431 E4
Mary Little St	425 F3	Parkgate St	424 A3	Ship St Little	429 F1	Werburgh St	429 F1
Mary St	425 F3	Parliament St	425 F4	Smithfield	425 D3	West Rd	427 F1
Mary's Abbey	425 F4	Parnell Rd	428 C4	South Circular Rd	428 A3	Western Way	425 F1
Mary's La	425 E3	Parnell Square	426 A2	South Dock St	431 F1	Westland Row	431 D1
Mayor St	427 D3	Parnell St	426 B2	St Andrew St	430 A1	Westmoreland St	426 B4
Mayor St Upper	427 F3	Patrick St	429 E2	St Augustine St	425 D4	Wexford St	430 A2
Mayor St Lower	427 E3	Pearse Square	431 E1	St Bricin's Park	424 B3	Wicklow St	430 A1
McDowel Av	428 A1	Pearse St	426 B4	St James Hospital	428 A1	William St North	427 D1
Meath Pl	429 D1	Pembroke La	431 E4	St John's Tce	428 A1	William St South	430 A1
Meath St	429 D1	Pembroke Rd	431 E4	St Mary's Rd North	427 F1	Wilton Pl	431 D3
Memorial Row	426 C3	Pembroke Row	431 D3	St Mary's Rd South	431 E3	Wilton Tce	430 C4
Mercer St Lower	430 A2	Pembroke St	430 C3	St Michan's St	425 F4	Winetavern St	425 E4
Merchant's Quay	425 E4	Pembroke St Lower	430 C3	St Stephen's Green	430 B2	Wolfe Tone Quay	424 C4
Merrion Row	430 C2	Percy La	431 E3	Stephen St Upper	429 F1	Wolfe Tone St	425 F3
Merrion Square	431 D2	Percy Pl	431 E2	Stoney Rd	427 F1	Wood Quay	425 E4
Merrion St Upper	430 C2	Peter Row	429 F2	Stoneybatter	424 C2	Wood St	429 F2
Military Rd	424 A4	Peter St	429 F2	Strand St Great	426 A4	York St	430 A2

405

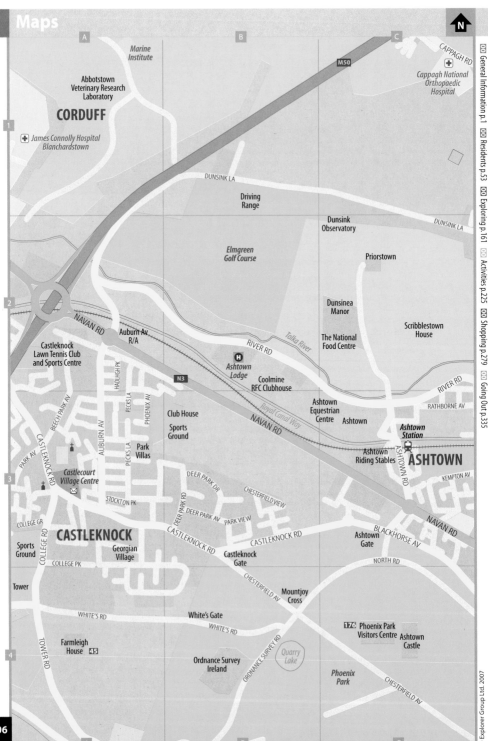

Marine
Institute

Abbotstown
Veterinary Research
Laboratory

CORDUFF

James Connolly Hospital
Blanchardstown

CAPPAGH RD

M50

Cappagh National
Orthopaedic
Hospital

DUNSINK LA

Driving
Range

Dunsink
Observatory

DUNSINK LA

Elmgreen
Golf Course

Priorstown

Dunsinea
Manor

Scribblestown
House

NAVAN RD

Auburn Av
R/A

RIVER RD

Tolka River

The National
Food Centre

Castleknock
Lawn Tennis Club
and Sports Centre

HADLIGH PK

PECKS LA

PHOENIX AV

Ashtown
Lodge

N3

Coolmine
RFC Clubhouse

Royal Canal Way

Ashtown
Equestrian
Centre

Ashtown

RIVER RD

RATHBORNE AV

BEECH PARK AV

AUBURN AV

PECKS LA

Club House

Sports
Ground

NAVAN RD

Ashtown
Station

PARK AV

Park
Villas

ASHTOWN

Ashtown
Riding Stables

ASHTOWN RD

CASTLEKNOCK RD

Castlecourt
Village Centre

STOCKTON PK

DEER PARK DR

CHESTERFIELD VIEW

KEMPTON AV

COLLEGE GR

COLLEGE RD

CASTLEKNOCK

Georgian
Village

COLLEGE PK

DEER PARK RD

DEER PARK AV

PARK VIEW

CASTLEKNOCK RD

CASTLEKNOCK RD

Castleknock
Gate

Ashtown
Gate

NORTH RD

BLACKHORSE AV

NAVAN RD

Sports
Ground

Tower

WHITE'S RD

White's Gate

WHITE'S RD

CHESTERFIELD AV

Mountjoy
Cross

TOWER RD

Farmleigh
House 45

Ordnance Survey
Ireland

ORDNANCE SURVEY RD

Quarry
Lake

176 Phoenix Park
Visitors Centre

Phoenix
Park

Ashtown
Castle

CHESTERFIELD AV

© Explorer Group Ltd. 2007

414

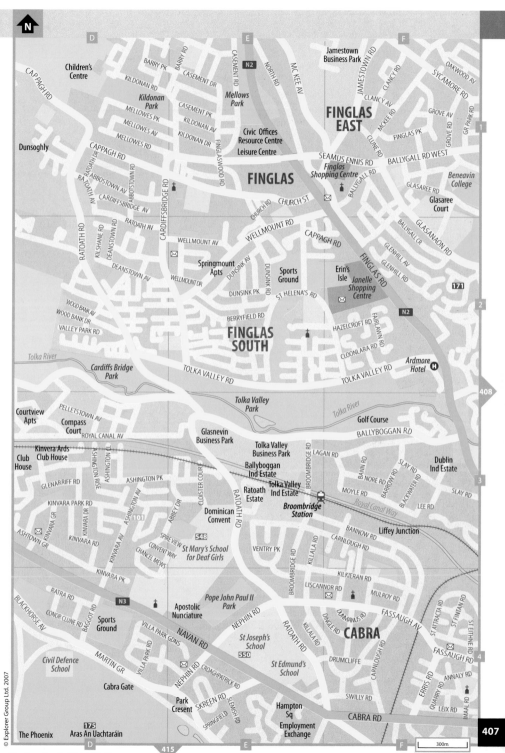

300m

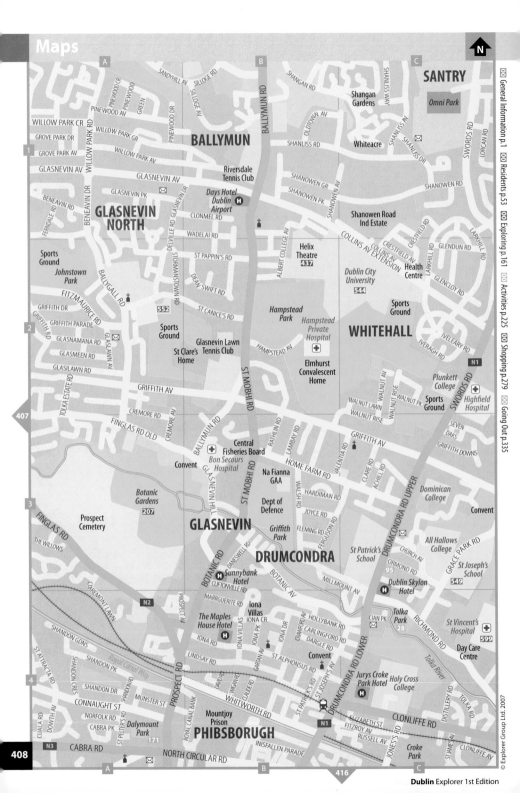

SANTRY

Omni Park

Shangan
Gardens

Whiteacre

BALLYMUN

Riversdale
Tennis Club

Days Hotel
Dublin
Airport

Shanowen Road
Ind Estate

GLASNEVIN
NORTH

Helix
Theatre
437

Dublin City
University
544

Health
Centre

Sports
Ground

Johnstown
Park

Hampstead
Park

Hampstead
Private
Hospital

WHITEHALL

Sports
Ground

Sports
Ground

St Clare's
Home

Glasnevin Lawn
Tennis Club

Elmhurst
Convalescent
Home

Plunkett
College

Sports
Ground

Highfield
Hospital

552

GRIFFITH AV

N1

407

Central
Fisheries Board

Bon Secours
Hospital

Botanic
Gardens
207

Na Fianna
GAA

Dept of
Defence

GRIFFITH AV

Dominican
College

Convent

Convent

All Hallows
College

Prospect
Cemetery

GLASNEVIN

Griffith
Park

DRUMCONDRA

St Patrick's
School
95

St Joseph's
School
549

Sunnybank
Hotel

Dublin Skylon
Hotel

N2

Iona
Villas

The Maples
House Hotel

Tolka
Park
28

St Vincent's
Hospital
599

Day Care
Centre

Convent

Jurys Croke
Park Hotel

Holy Cross
College

N1

Mountjoy
Prison

Dalymount
Park
171

PHIBSBOROUGH

Croke
Park

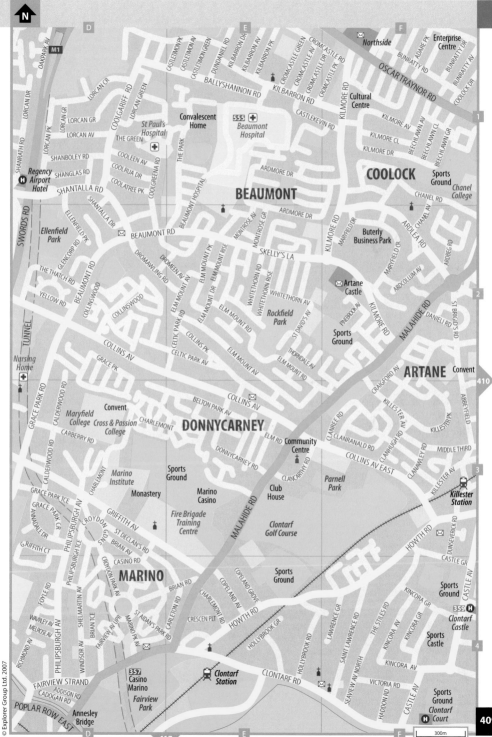

N

A | B | C

GREENCASTLE PARADE
GREENCASTLE RD
MALAHIDE RD
AYREFIELD DR
RATHVALE AV
RATHVALE PK
RATHVALE DR
AYREFIELD RD
SLADEMORE AV
SLADEMORE AV
FOXHILL AV
FOXHILL RD
FOXHILL PK
MILLBROOK RD

Sports
Grounds

ARDARA AV
GRANGE RD
CARRABROE AV
STREAMVILLE RD
THE BEECHES
MILLBROOK AV
SAINT DONAGH'S RD

Leisureplex
UCI
Cinema

1

LIMEWOOD AV
LIMEWOOD RD
TONLEGEE RD
TONLEGEE DR
TONLEGEE AV
GLENFARNE RD
GLENWOOD RD

Youth
Centre
WOODBINE RD
TONLEGEE RD
MOUNT OLIVE RD

MALAHIDE RD
ST BRENDAN'S AV
ST BRENDAN'S AV
MOATFIELD RD
MOATFIELD AV
ST BRENDAN'S PK
ENNEL PK
ENNEL DR

EDENMORE

Health
Centre

WOODBINE CL
WOODBINE DR
WOODBINE AV
RAHENY RD
WOODBINE RD

Kilbarrack
GRANGE PARK GR
GRANGE PARK AV
GRANGE PARK RD
GRANGE PARK VIEW
GRANGE PARK RISE
SWAN'S NEST RD

Mercy
College
MCAULEY RD
MCAULEY PK
MCAULEY AV
MASK AV
MASK DR
MASK RD

SPRINGDALE RD
EDENMORE AV
EDENMORE GDNS
EDENMORE DR
EDENMORE GR
EDENMORE CR

Edenmore
Park

Shieling Hotel
Hilltop
GRANGE PARK RD
BELMONT PK
GRANGE PARK
BRIARFIELD RD
FOXFIELD GR
FOXFIELD AV
FOXFIELD RD

2

GRACEFIELD RD
MCAULEY AV
Youth
Club
MCAULEY PK
McAuley
Park
LEIN PK
LEIN RD
RIBH AV
RIBH RD

St Malachy's
SPRINGDALE RD
HARMONSTOWN RD

St Joseph's
Hospital

Grange
Hall Apts

St Francis
Hospice

Raheny
Station
STATION RD
ST ASSAM'S RD W
ST ASSAM'S PK
SAINT ASSAM'S AV
ST ASSAM'S RD E
MAYWOOD RD

BROOKWOOD HEIGHTS
ROSEMOUNT AV
BROOKWOOD AV
GRACEFIELD AV
BROOKWOOD RISE
ABBEYFIELD

Harmonstown
Station

Rosevale
Mansions

ENNAFORT RD
ENNAFORT PK
HOWTH RD
MARYVILLE RD
BETTYSTOWN AV
WADE'S AV
ALL SAINTS PK
ALL SAINTS DR
WATERFALL RD
ST ANNE'S DR
ST ANNE'S RD
MAIN ST
AVONDALE PK
WATERMILL RD
WATERMILL AV
WATERMILL PK
WATERMILL DR
RAHENY PK
MAYWOOD AV
MAYWOOD PK

RAHENY

409

KILLESTER

HOWTH RD
ALL SAINTS RD

Sports
Grounds

224

Football Grounds

3

Deer Park
Hotel
FURRY PARK RD
FURRY PARK RD
Convent
St Paul's
College

St Anne's Park

DUNLUCE RD
DUNLUCE RD
SYBIL HILL RD
VERNON AV

Central
Remedial
Clinic

Sports
Grounds

Orthopaedic
Hospital of
Ireland 143
HAMPTON CT
BLACKHEATH DR
BLACKHEATH CT
MOUNT PROSPECT AV
BLACKHEATH PK
VERNON PK

MOUNT PROSPECT DR
MOUNT PROSPECT AV
MOUNT PROSPECT AV
MOUNT PROSPECT AV
BAYMOUNT PK
MOUNT PROSPECT AV

Manresa
Retreat House

JAMES LARKIN RD

4

SEAFIELD RD WEST
VERNON AV
SEAFIELD ROAD E
SEAPARK RD
SEAPARK RD
SEAPARK RD
SEAPARK DR
SAINT GABRIELS RD
DOLLYMOUNT AV
SEAFIELD ROAD E
CLONTARF RD

DOLLYMOUNT

KINCORA RD
KINCORA PK
BELGROVE RD
VERNON GR
VERNON AV
KINCORA GR
KINCORA RD

CLONTARF

Wooden
Bridge

410

A | B | C

© Explorer Group Ltd. 2007

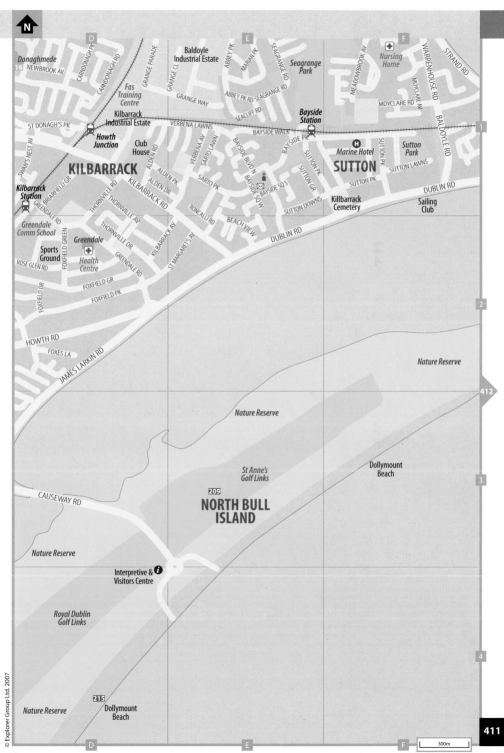

16

Donaghmede
NEWBROOK AV

Baldoyle
Industrial Estate

Seagrange
Park

Nursing
Home

Fas
Training
Centre

Kilbarrack
Industrial Estate

ABBEY PK RD SEAGRANGE RD

SEACLIFF RD

Bayside
Station

St DONAGH'S PK

VERBENA LAWNS

BAYSIDE WALK

KILBARRACK

Howth
Junction

Club
House

Marine Hotel

SUTTON

Sutton
Park

Kilbarrack
Station

SUTTON LAWNS

Killbarrack
Cemetery

DUBLIN RD

Greendale
Comm School

Sailing
Club

Sports
Ground

Greendale
Health
Centre

DUBLIN RD

ROSE GLEN RD

FOXFIELD GR

FOXFIELD PK

HOWTH RD

FOXES LA

JAMES LARKIN RD

Nature Reserve

412

Nature Reserve

St Anne's
Golf Links

Dollymount
Beach

CAUSEWAY RD

209

**NORTH BULL
ISLAND**

Nature Reserve

Interpretive &
Visitors Centre

Royal Dublin
Golf Links

Nature Reserve

215
Dollymount
Beach

300m

The Complete **Residents'** Guide

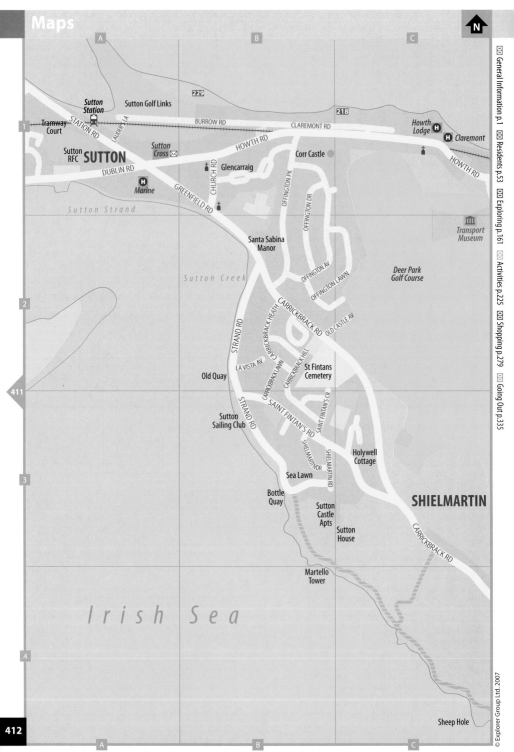

A · B · C

Sutton Station

Suttton Golf Links

229

218

BURROW RD

CLAREMONT RD

Howth Lodge H

Claremont H

STATION RD

LAUDER LA

Tramway Court

1

Sutton RFC · **SUTTON**

Sutton Cross ⊠

HOWTH RD

HOWTH RD

Corr Castle

DUBLIN RD

Glencarraig

Marine H

GREENFIELD RD

CHURCH RD

OFFINGTON PK

OFFINGTON DR

Transport Museum 🏛

Sutton Strand

Santa Sabina Manor

OFFINGTON AV

OFFINGTON LAWN

Deer Park Golf Course

Sutton Creek

2

CARRICKBRACK RD

OLD CASTLE AV

STRAND RD

CARRICKBRACK HEATH

CARRICKBRACK HILL

CARRICKBRACK LAWN

Old Quay

LA VISTA AV

St Fintans Cemetery

411

SAINT FINTAN'S RD

STRAND RD

SAINT FINTAN'S CR

Sutton Sailing Club

SHIELMARTIN DR

SHIELMARTIN RD

Holywell Cottage

3

Sea Lawn

Bottle Quay

Sutton Castle Apts

SHIELMARTIN

CARRICKBRACK RD

Sutton House

Martello Tower

Irish Sea

4

Sheep Hole

A · B · C

Ⓒ General Information p.1 · Ⓒ Residents p.53 · Ⓒ Exploring p.161 · Ⓒ Activities p.225 · Ⓒ Shopping p.279 · Ⓒ Going Out p.335

© Explorer Group Ltd 2007

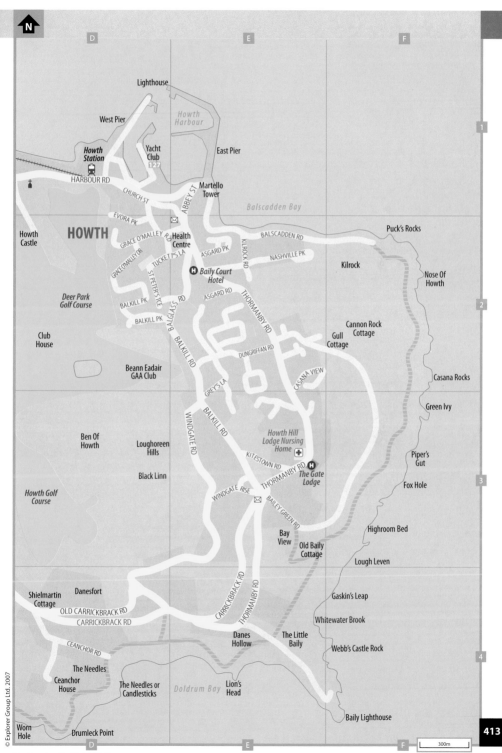

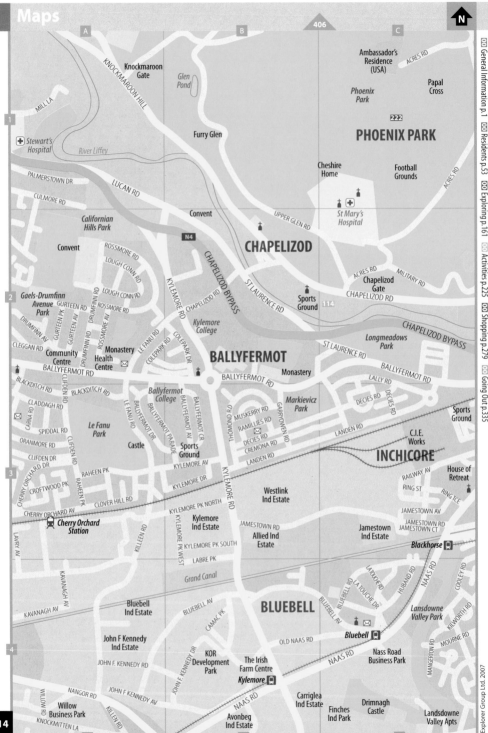

406

General Information p.1
Residents p.53
Exploring p.161
Activities p.225
Shopping p.279
Going Out p.335

A   B   C

1

Knockmaroon Gate

Knockmaroon Hill

Glen Pond

Ambassador's Residence (USA)

ACRES RD

Phoenix Park

Papal Cross

Furry Glen

PHOENIX PARK

Stewart's Hospital

MILL LA

River Liffey

Cheshire Home

Football Grounds

ACRES RD

PALMERSTOWN DR

LUCAN RD

CULMORE RD

Convent

UPPER GLEN RD

St Mary's Hospital

2

Californian Hills Park

N4

Convent

CHAPELIZOD

Convent

ROSSMORE RD

LOUGH CONN RD

ACRES RD

MILITARY RD

Chapelizod Gate

CHAPELIZOD RD

Gaels-Drumfinn Avenue Park

GURTEEN RD

DRUMFINN RD

ROSSMORE RD

LOUGH CONN RD

KYLEMORE RD

CHAPELIZOD RD

CHAPELIZOD BYPASS

ST LAURENCE RD

Sports Ground

114

CHAPELIZOD BYPASS

GURTEEN PK

GURTEEN AV

DRUMFINN AV

CLEGGAN RD

Community Centre

Monastery Health Centre

Kylemore College

BALLYFERMOT

Longmeadows Park

ST LAURENCE RD

BALLYFERMOT RD

BLACKDITCH RD

CLIFDEN RD

BLACKDITCH RD

COLEPARK DR

LE FANU RD

COLEPARK DR

BALLYFERMOT RD

Monastery

BALLYFERMOT RD

LALLY RD

DECIES RD

DECIES RD

3

CLADDAGH RD

CARNA RD

SPIDDAL RD

ORANMORE RD

CLIFDEN DR

Le Fanu Park

Ballyfermot College

Castle

LE FANU RD

BALLYFERMOT DR

BALLYFERMOT CR

BALLYFERMOT PARADE

Sports Ground

THOMOND RD

MUSKERRY RD

RAMILLIES RD

DECIES RD

CREMONA RD

GARROWEN RD

Markievicz Park

LANDEN RD

LANDEN RD

Sports Ground

C.I.E. Works

INCHICORE

RAILWAY AV

RING ST

House of Retreat

RING TCE

CLIFDEN RD

RAHEEN PK

KYLEMORE AV

KYLEMORE DR

Westlink Ind Estate

JAMESTOWN AV

JAMESTOWN RD

JAMESTOWN CT

CHERRY ORCHARD DR

CROFTWOOD PK

RAHEEN PK

CLOVER HILL RD

CHERRY ORCHARD AV

Cherry Orchard Station

LAVRY AV

KILLEEN RD

KYLEMORE PK NORTH

KYLEMORE RD

Kylemore Ind Estate

KYLEMORE PK WEST

KYLEMORE PK SOUTH

LABRE PK

Allied Ind Estate

JAMESTOWN RD

Jamestown Ind Estate

Blackhorse

4

KAVANAGH RD

KAVANAGH AV

Grand Canal

Bluebell Ind Estate

BLUEBELL AV

CAMAC PK

BLUEBELL

OLD NAAS RD

BLUEBELL AV

BLUEBELL RD

LA TOUCHE DR

Bluebell

LA TOUCHE RD

HUBAND RD

NAAS RD

COOLEY RD

KILWORTH RD

Lansdowne Valley Park

John F Kennedy Ind Estate

JOHN F. KENNEDY RD

KOR Development Park

JOHN F. KENNEDY RD

The Irish Farm Centre

Kylemore

NAAS RD

Nass Road Business Park

MANGERTON RD

MOURNE RD

WILLOW RD

NANGOR RD

JOHN F KENNEDY AV

KILLEEN RD

Willow Business Park

KNOCKMITTEN LA

Avonbeg Ind Estate

Carriglea Ind Estate

Finches Ind Park

Drimnagh Castle

Landsdowne Valley Apts

414

A   B   C

418

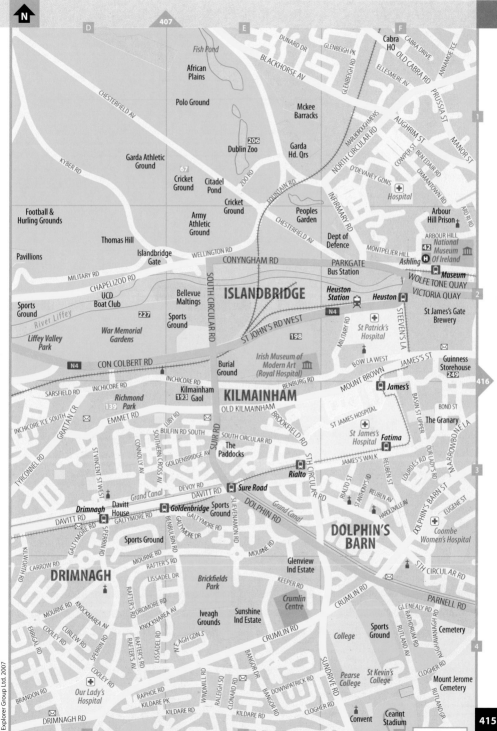

407

D E F

Fish Pond

African Plains

Polo Ground

CHESTERFIELD AV

DUNARD DR

GLENBEIGH PK

BLACKHORSE AV

GLENBEIGH RD

Cabra HO

CABRA DRIVE

OLD CABRA RD

ELLESMERE AV

ANNAMOE TCE

PRUSSIA ST

MANOR ST

1

Mckee Barracks

AUGHRIM ST

206 Dublin Zoo

Garda Hd. Qrs

ZOO RD

NORTH CIRCULAR RD

MARLBOROUGH/MENS

COWPER ST

BELCLAIR RD

OXMANTOWN RD

ARD RI RD

KYBER RD

Garda Athletic Ground

67 Cricket Ground

Citadel Pond

O'DEVANEY GDNS

Hospital

Arbour Hill Prison

ARBOUR HILL

42 National Museum Of Ireland

Cricket Ground

Army Athletic Ground

Peoples Garden

Dept of Defence

INFIRMARY RD

MONTPELIER HILL

Ashling

H

Museum

WOLFE TONE QUAY

Football & Hurling Grounds

Thomas Hill

Islandbridge Gate

WELLINGTON RD

CHESTERFIELD AV

FOUNTAIN RD

Pavilions

CONYNGHAM RD

PARKGATE Bus Station

VICTORIA QUAY

2

MILITARY RD

CHAPELIZOD RD

UCD Boat Club

Bellevue Maltings

SOUTH CIRCULAR RD

ISLANDBRIDGE

Heuston Station

N4 Heuston

St James's Gate Brewery

Sports Ground

River Liffey

227

Sports Ground

ST JOHN'S RD WEST

198

MILITARY RD

St Patrick's Hospital

STEEVEN'S LA

JAMES'S ST

Guinness Storehouse

416

Liffey Valley Park

War Memorial Gardens

Burial Ground

Irish Museum of Modern Art (Royal Hospital)

BENBURG RD

BOW LA WEST

MOUNT BROWN

James's

BASIN ST UPPER

249

N4 CON COLBERT RD

INCHICORE RD

Kilmainham 193 Gaol

KILMAINHAM

OLD KILMAINHAM

BROOKFIELD RD

St James Hospital

BOND ST

The Granary

NARROWMONE LA

3

SARSFIELD RD

INCHICORE RD

Richmond Park 139

EMMET RD

LUBY RD

BULFIN RD SOUTH

SUIR RD

SOUTH CIRCULAR RD

St James's Hospital

Fatima

OUR LADY'S RD

INCHICORETCE SOUTH

GRATTAN CR

ST VINCENT ST WEST

SOUTHERN CROSS AV

CONNOLLY AV

GOLDENBRIDGE AV

The Paddocks

JAMES'S WALK

REUBEN ST

LOURDES RD

DOLPHIN'S BARN ST

EUGENE ST

TYRCONNEL RD

Grand Canal

DEVOY RD

DAVITT RD

Sure Road

STH CIRCULAR RD

Rialto

RIALTO ST

ST ANTONY'S RD

REUBEN AV

HARDLMILLEAN

Coombe Women's Hospital

Drimnagh

Davitt House

GALTYMORE RD

Goldenbridge

Sports Ground

GALTYMORE RD

DOLPHIN RD

Grand Canal

DOLPHIN'S BARN

DAVITT RD

Sports Ground

BENBULBIN RD

SLIEVENAMON RD

STH CIRCULAR RD

KILWORTH RD

S PERRIN RD

MOURNE RD

MOURNE RD

MOURNE RD

Glenview Ind Estate

KEEPER RD

PARNELL RD

4

CARROW RD

DRIMNAGH

RAFTER'S RD

LISSADEL DR

DROMORE RD

Brickfields Park

Crumlin Centre

CRUMLIN RD

CRUMLIN RD

College

Sports Ground

GLENEALY RD

RATHORAM RD

RUTLAND AV

AUGHAVANAGH RD

Cemetery

MOURNE RD

KNOCKNAREA AV

CURLEW RD

SPERRIN RD

RAFTER'S RD

RAFTER'S AV

KNOCKNAREA RD

LISSADEL RD

Iveagh Grounds

Sunshine Ind Estate

BANGOR DR

CLOGHER RD

Mount Jerome Cemetery

ERRIGAL RD

COOLEY RD

COOLEY RD

BRANDON RD

Our Lady's Hospital

RAPHOE RD

KILDARE PK

WINDMILL SQ

RALEIGH SQ

NF SAGH GDN S

CLONARD RD

DOWNPATRICK RD

BANGOR RD

SUNDRIVE RD

Pearse College

St Kevin's College

Convent

Ceannt Stadium

DRIMNAGH RD

KILDARE RD

KILDARE RD

CLOGHER RD

415

300m

© Explorer Group Ltd. 2007

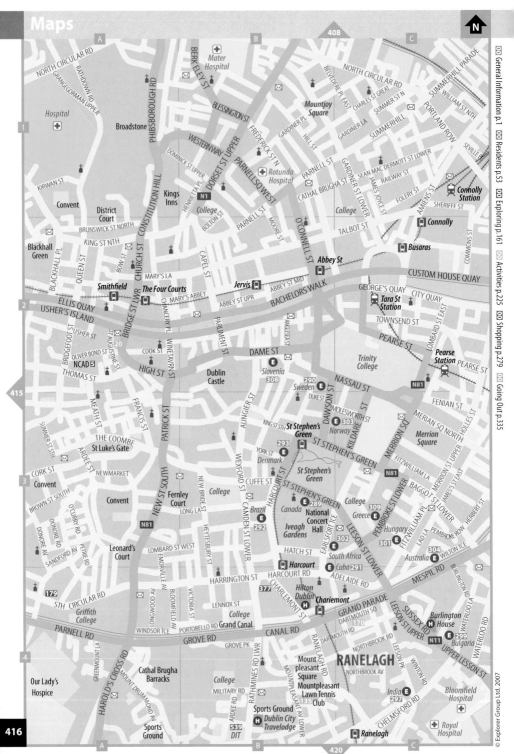

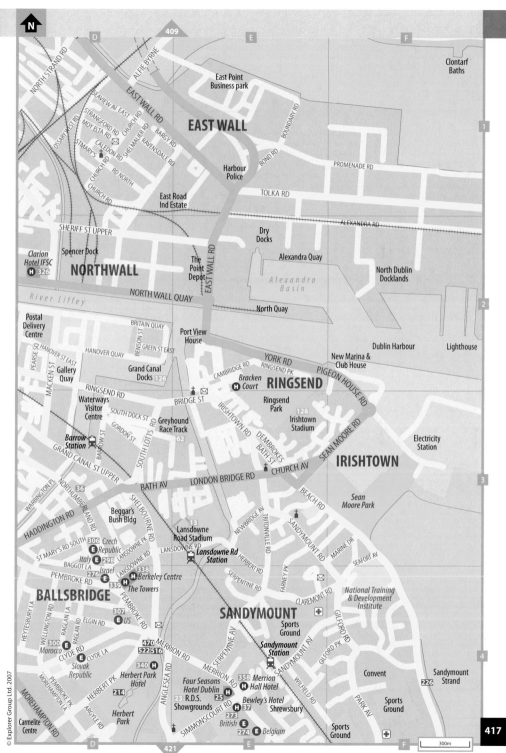

N

Clontarf
Baths

East Point
Business park

EAST WALL

NORTH STRAND RD

SEAVIEW AV EAST
STRANGFORD RD
MOY ELTA RD
CALEDON RD
ST MARY'S
RD NORTH
CHURCH RD

EAST WALL RD
BARGY RD
SHELMALIER RD
RAVENSDALE RD

CHURCH RD

ALFIE BYRNE
OSSORY RD EAST

Harbour
Police

BOUNDARY RD
BOND RD

PROMENADE RD

East Road
Ind Estate

TOLKA RD

ALEXANDRA RD

SHERIFF ST UPPER

Dry
Docks

Clarion
Hotel IFSC
H 326

Spencer Dock

NORTHWALL

The
Point
Depot

Alexandra Quay

North Dublin
Docklands

*Alexandra
Basin*

River Liffey

NORTH WALL QUAY

EAST WALL RD

North Quay

Dublin Harbour

Lighthouse

Postal
Delivery
Centre

BRITAIN QUAY

Port View
House

PEARSE SQ
HANOVER ST EAST
HANOVER QUAY
BENSON ST
GREEN ST EAST

YORK RD

New Marina &
Club House

PIGEON HOUSE RD

Gallery
Quay

Grand Canal
Docks 126

CAMBRIDGE RD
RINGSEND PK

*Bracken
Court*
H

RINGSEND

MACKEN ST

Waterways
Visitor
Centre

RINGSEND RD

BRIDGE ST

Ringsend
Park

Irishtown
Stadium 128

SEAN MOORE RD

Electricity
Station

SOUTH DOCK ST

*Barrow
Station*

GORDON ST

Greyhound
Race Track
62

IRISHTOWN RD

DEMBROKES

BATH ST

CHURCH AV

IRISHTOWN

GRAND CANAL ST UPPER

BARROW ST

SOUTH LOTTS

BATH AV

LONDON BRIDGE RD

*Sean
Moore Park*

WARRINGTON PL
NORTHUMBERLAND RD

36

HADDINGTON RD

Beggar's
Bush Bldg

SHELBOURNE RD

13

BEACH RD

SANDYMOUNT AV

ST MARY'S RD SOUTH
306 Czech
E Republic

Lansdowne
Road Stadium

LANSDOWNE RD

*Lansdowne Rd
Station*

NEWBRIDGE AV
TRITONVILLE RD

FARNEY PK

*National Training
& Development
Institute*

BAGGOT LA

Italy **E** 298

LANSDOWNE PK

Israel
276 **E**

338
Berkeley Centre

339 **H** The Towers

HERBERT RD

SERPENTINE RD

CLAREMONT RD

GILFORD RD

PEMBROKE RD

BALLSBRIDGE

PEMBROKE RD

SANDYMOUNT

Sports
Ground

MARINE DR

SEAFORT AV

HEYTESBURY LA
WELLINGTON RD
RAGLAN RD
RAGLAN LA

307
E US

ELGIN RD

SERPENTINE AV

*Sandymount
Station*

SANDYMOUNT AV

GILFORD PK

Convent

Sandymount
Strand

300
Morocco **E**

CLYDE RD

CLYDE LA

470
522 516

MERRION RD

358 Merrion
H Hall Hotel

226

Slovak
Republic **E**

340

Herbert Park
Hotel

MERRION RD

WILFIELD RD

PARK AV

Sports
Ground

PEMBROKE PK
MOREHAMPTON LA

HERBERT PK

214

ANGLESEA RD

SIMMONSCOURT RD

Four Seasons
Hotel Dublin
R.D.S.
23 Showgrounds
25

*Bewley's Hotel
Shrewsbury*
37 **H**

MOREHAMPTON RD

ARGYLE RD

*Herbert
Park*

273
British
274 **E** Belgium

Sports
Ground

Sports
Ground

Carmelite
Centre

© Explorer Group Ltd. 2007

The Complete **Residents'** Guide

300m

417

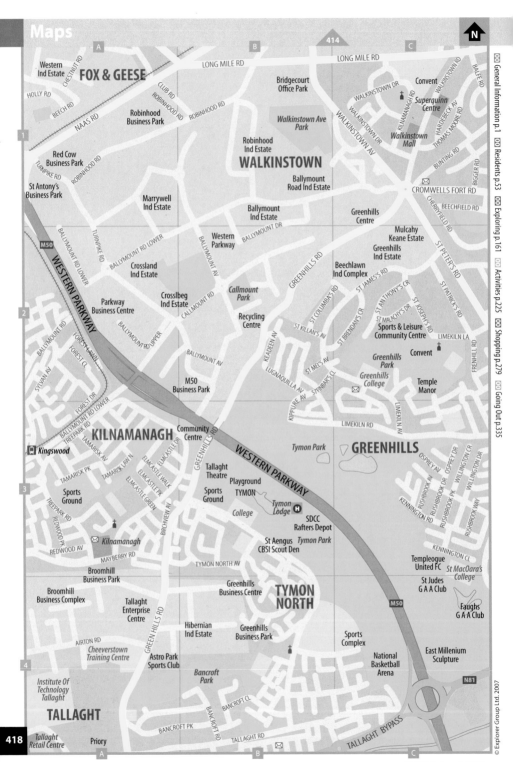

414

N

FOX & GEESE

Western Ind Estate

HOLLY RD

BEECH RD

NAAS RD

CHESTNUT RD

CLUB RD

ROBINHOOD RD

ROBINHOOD RD

Robinhood Business Park

Red Cow Business Park

TURNPIKE RD

ROBINHOOD RD

St Antony's Business Park

BALLYMOUNT RD LOWER

M50

WESTERN PARKWAY

BALLYMOUNT RD LOWER

TURNPIKE RD

Marrywell Ind Estate

BALLYMOUNT RD LOWER

BALLYMOUNT AV

BALLYMOUNT RD UPPER

Crossland Ind Estate

Parkway Business Centre

Crosslbeg Ind Estate

CALLMOUNT RD

BALLYMOUNT AV

Western Parkway

BALLYMOUNT DR

Callmount Park

Recycling Centre

M50 Business Park

LONG MILE RD

Bridgecourt Office Park

Walkinstown Ave Park

Robinhood Ind Estate

WALKINSTOWN

Ballymount Road Ind Estate

Ballymount Ind Estate

GREENHILLS RD

LONG MILE RD

WALKINSTOWN DR

WALKINSTOWN AV

WALKINSTOWN DR

Convent

KILNAMANAGH RD

Superquinn Centre

Walkinstown Mall

HARDEBECK AV

THOMAS MOORE RD

BUNTING RD

BALFE RD

BIGGER RD

CROMWELLS FORT RD

Greenhills Centre

CHERRYFIELD RD

BEECHFIELD RD

ST PETER'S RD

Mulcahy Keane Estate

Greenhills Ind Estate

Beechlawn Ind Complex

ST JAMES'S RD

ST ANTHONY'S DR

ST JOSEPH'S RD

ST PATRICK'S RD

ST COLUMBAS RD

ST KILLAN'S AV

KEADEEN AV

ST BRENDAN'S CR

ST MALCHY'S RD

Sports & Leisure Community Centre

LIMEKILN LA

FRENHILL RD

Convent

Greenhills Park

Greenhills College

Temple Manor

LUGNAQUILLA AV

ST MEL'S AV

STENBAR'S CL

LIMEKILN AV

LIMEKILN RD

KIPPURE AV

LIMEKILN RD

KILNAMANAGH

Kingswood

Community Centre

WESTERN PARKWAY

GREENHILLS RD

Tallaght Theatre

Sports Ground

TYMON

College

Playground

Tymon Lodge

Tymon Park

SDCC Rafters Depot

St Aengus CBSI Scout Den

Tymon Park

GREENHILLS

OSPREY AV

OSPREY DR

RUSHBROOK DR

WILLINGTON CR

WILLINGTON DR

KENNINGTON RD

RUSHBROOK RD

RUSHBROOK PK

RUSHBROOK WAY

KENNINGTON CL

Templeogue United FC

St MacOara's College

St Judes G A A Club

Faughs G A A Club

TAMARISK AV

TAMARISK PK

TAMARISK LAWN N

ELMCASTLE DR

ELMCASTLE WALK

ELMCASTLE PK

ELMCASTLE GREEN

BIRCHVIEW AV

FOREST CL

FOREST LAWN

SYLVAN AV

TREEPARK RD

REDWOOD PK

REDWOOD AV

MAYBERRY RD

Sports Ground

Kilnamanagh

Broomhill Business Park

TYMON NORTH AV

Greenhills Business Centre

TYMON NORTH

Broomhill Business Complex

Tallaght Enterprise Centre

Hibernian Ind Estate

Greenhills Business Park

AIRTON RD

GREEN HILLS RD

Cheeverstown Training Centre

Astro Park Sports Club

Bancroft Park

Sports Complex

National Basketball Arena

East Millenium Sculpture

M50

N81

Institute Of Technology Tallaght

TALLAGHT

Tallaght Retail Centre

Priory

BANCROFT PK

BANCROFT RD

BANCROFT CL

TALLAGHT RD

TALLAGHT BYPASS

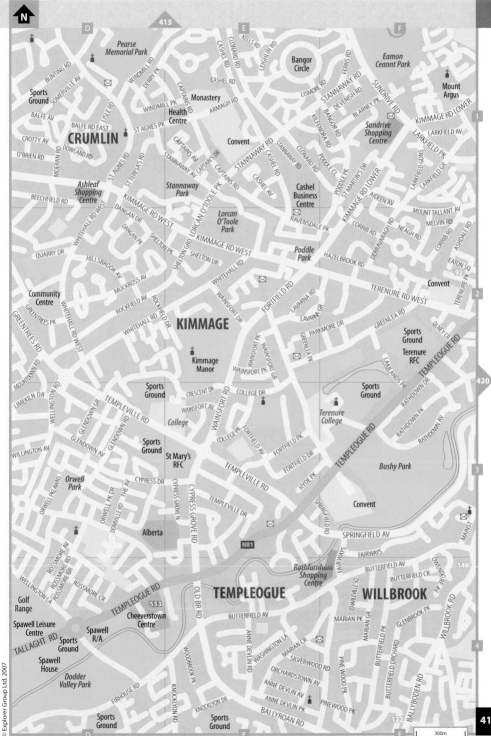

N

‡

Pearse
Memorial Park

D

WINDMILL RD
DERRY PK
WINDMILL PK
BLUNTING RD
SOMERVILLE AV
BALFE AV
LISLE RD

Sports
Ground

St AGNES RD
St AGNES PK
BALFE RD EAST

CROTTY AV
O'BRIEN RD
MOERAN RD
DOWLAND RD

CRUMLIN

KELLS RD
CLONARD RD
CASHEL RD
CASHEL RD
LEIGHLIN RD

E

CAPTAINS RD
CAPTAINS AV

Monastery

Health
Centre
ARMAGH RD

Convent

CAPTAINS DR
CAPTAINS RD

Bangor
Circle

Eamon
Ceannt Park

F

Mount
Argus

LISMORE RD
FERNS RD
STANNAWAY RD
DEVENISH RD
BANGOR RD
KILLENORA RD

SUNDRIVE RD
BLARNEY RD

KIMMAGE RD LOWER

‡

KIMMAGE RD LOWER
LARKFIELD AV
LARKFIELD GDNS
LARKFIELD PK
LARKFIELD GR

1

Ashleaf
Shopping
Centre

St AGNES RD
St TERESAS RD
STANNAWAY AV

Stannaway
Park

KIMMAGE RD WEST
DANGAN DR
DANGAN PK

LORCAN O'TOOLE PK
SHELTON PK
SHELTON DR
SHELTON GRO

Lorcan
O'Toole
Park

STANNAWAY RD
STANNAWAY RD
CASHEL RD
CASHEL AV
CLONARD RD
PODDLE CL

Cashel
Business
Centre

St MARTIN'S DR
PODDLE PK
KIMMAGE RD LOWER
AIDEEN AV
CORRIB RD
DERANARRAGH RD
NEAGH RD

MOUNT TALLANT AV
MELVIN RD
CORRIB RD
ASHDALE RD

BEECHFIELD RD
KIMMAGE RD WEST
WHITEHALL RD WEST

KIMMAGE RD WEST
WHITEHALL RD

RAVENSDALE PK

Poddle
Park

HAZELBROOK RD

Convent

EATON SQ

92

QUARRY DR
HILLSBROOK AV
ROCKFIELD AV
ROCKFIELD DR

WAINSFORT DR
FORTFIELD RD

TERENURE RD WEST

GREENLEA RD

TERENURE PK

2

Community
Centre
GREENTREES PK

WHITEHALL RD WEST
MUCKROSS AV

KIMMAGE

WHITEHALL RD

LAVARNA RD
LAVARNA GR

PARKMORE DR
GREENLEA PK

GREENLEA RD

Sports
Ground

Terenure
RFC

OLNEY CR
TEMPLEOGUE RD

GREENTREES RD
MOUNTDOWN RD

‡
Kimmage
Manor

WAINSFORT PK
WAINSFORT GR
WAINSFORT RD

LAGELANDS PK

Sports
Ground

RATHDOWN DR
RATHDOWN PK
RATHDOWN AV

420

LIMEKILN DR

WELLINGTON RD

TEMPLEVILLE RD

GLENDOWN GR
GLENDOWN AV
GLENDOWN RD

Sports
Ground

CRESCENT DR
WAINSFORT AV

College

COLLEGE DR
WAINSFORT RD

‡
Terenure
College

TEMPLEOGUE RD

Bushy Park

3

WILLINGTON AV

Orwell
Park

ORWELL PK DR
THE AV
DOMVILLE RD
CYPRESS DR
CYPRESS GROVE N

Sports
Ground

St Mary's
RFC

COLLEGE PK
FORTFIELD AV

TEMPLEVILLE RD

FORTFIELD PK
FORTFIELD DR
HYDE PK

SPRINGFIELD RD

Convent

‡

MAIN ST

149

ORWELL PK AV

Alberta

CYPRESS GROVE RD

TEMPLEVILLE DR

N81

SPRINGFIELD AV

Golf
Range

ROSSMORE RD
ROSSMORE GR
ROSSMORE CR
ROSSMORE LA
WELLINGTON LA

TEMPLEOGUE RD

553
Cheeverstown
Centre

OLD BR RD

TEMPLEOGUE

Rathfarnham
Shopping
Centre

FAIRWAYS
FAIRWAYS

BUTTERFIELD AV
BUTTERFIELD CR

WILLBROOK

CHARLEVILLE RD
GLENBROOK PK
BUTTERFIELD PK
WILLBROOK RD
OWENDORE AV

4

Spawell Leisure
Centre

TALLAGHT RD

Spawell
R/A
Sports
Ground

Spawell
House

Dodder
Valley Park

FIRHOUSE RD

WOODBROOK PK

KNOCKLYON RD

BUTTERFIELD AV

ANNE DEVLIN RD
WASHINGTON LA

MARIAN PK
MARIAN CR
MARIAN GR

SILVERWOOD RD
ORCHARDSTOWN AV

PINE WOOD PK
PINEWOOD PK

BUTTERFIELD ORCHARD
BALLYBODEN RD

Sports
Ground

Sports
Ground

ANNE DEVLIN AV
ANNE DEVLIN PK
‡
BALLYROAN RD

KNOCKLYON DR

122

F

419

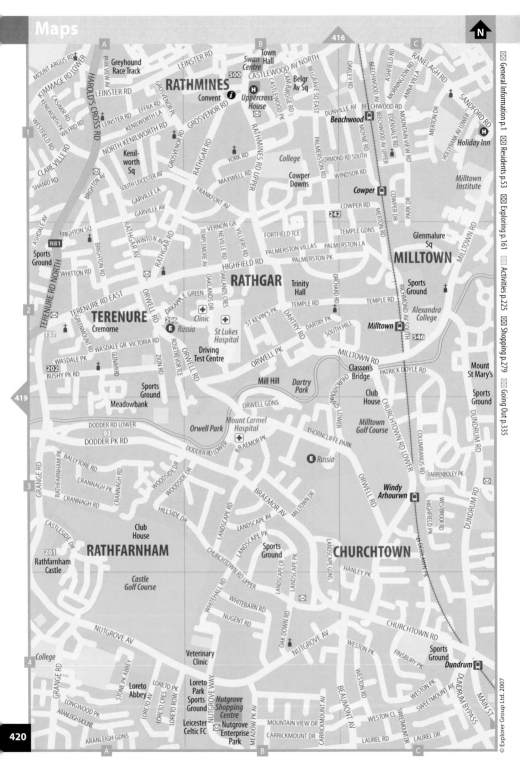

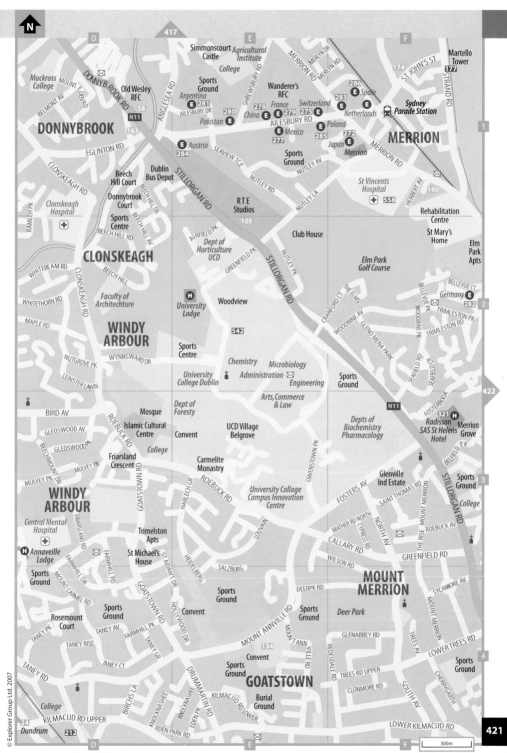

© Explorer Group Ltd. 2007

300m

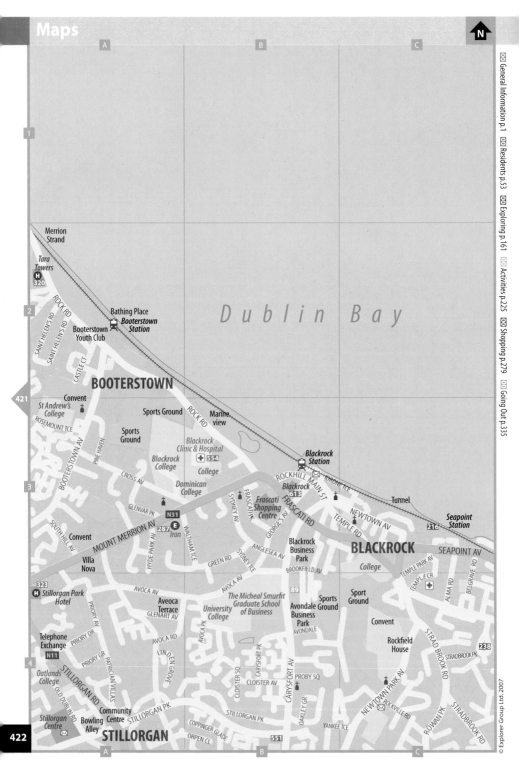

General Information p.1   Residents p.53   Exploring p.161   Activities p.225   Shopping p.279   Going Out p.335

A   B   C

1

Merrion
Strand

*Tara
Towers*
H
320

2

ROCK RD

SAINT HELEN'S RD
SAINT HELEN'S RD

CASTLE CT

Bathing Place
*Booterstown
Station*
Booterstown
Youth Club

D u b l i n   B a y

BOOTERSTOWN

Convent
St Andrew's
College
ROSEMOUNT TCE

Sports Ground
ROCK RD
Marine
view

Sports
Ground

PINE HAVEN

Blackrock
Clinic & Hospital
554
Blackrock
College
College

CROSS AV

*Blackrock
Station*

ROCKHILL MAIN ST
IDRONE TCE

Blackrock
613

Tunnel

BOOTERSTOWN AV

Dominican
College

GLENVAR PK

N31

287 **E**
Iran

SYDNEY AV

FRASCATI PK

Frascati
Shopping
Centre

GEORGE'S AV

FRASCATI RD

NEWTOWN AV

TEMPLE RD

*Seapoint
Station*
216

SOUTH HILL AV

Convent

MOUNT MERRION AV

HYDE PARK AV

WALTHAM TCE

ANGLESEA AV

SYDNEY TCE

Blackrock
Business
Park

BLACKROCK

SEAPOINT AV

Villa
Nova

GREEN RD

BROOKFIELD AV

College

TEMPLE PARK AV

TEMPLE CR

ALMA RD

BELGRAVE RD

323
H Stillorgan Park
Hotel

AVOCA AV

PRIORY AV

Aveoca
Terrace
GLENART AV

University
College

The Micheal Smurfit
Graduate School
of Business

89

Avondale
Business
Park
AVONDALE

Sports
Ground

AVOCA RD

AVOCA AV

Sport
Ground

Convent

STRAD BROOK RD

Rockfield
House
STRADBROOK RD

238

Telephone
Exchange
N11

PRIORY DR

PRIORY GR

LINDEN GROVE

PATRICIAN VILLAS

CARYSFORT SQ

CLOISTER SQ

CLOISTER AV

CARYSFORT AV

PROBY SQ

OAKLEY GR

NEWTOWN PARK AV

ROCKVILLE RD

STRAD BROOK RD

ROWAN PK

STRADBROOK RD

4

Oatlands
College

OLD DUBLIN RD

STILLORGAN RD

OLD DUBLIN RD

Community
Centre
Bowling
Alley

STILLORGAN PK

STILLORGAN PK

COPPINGER GLADE

ORPEN CL

551

YANKEE TCE

Stillorgan
Centre

STILLORGAN

A   B   C

© Explorer Group Ltd. 2007

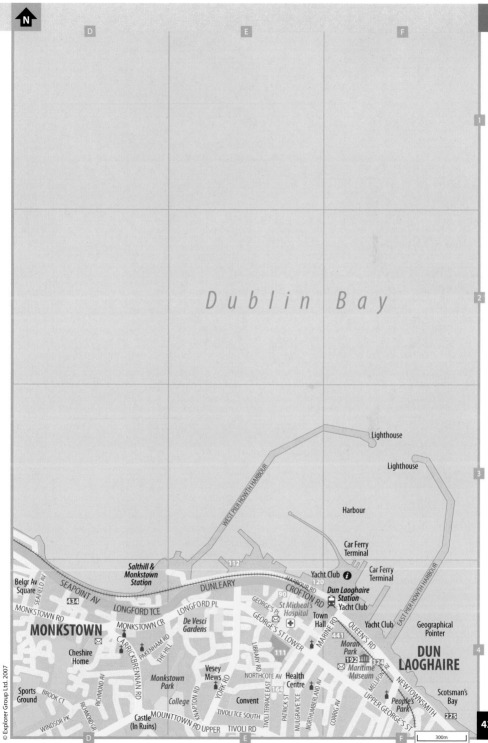

N

Dublin Bay

Lighthouse

Lighthouse

Harbour

Car Ferry
Terminal

WEST PIER HOWTH HARBOUR

EAST PIER HOWTH HARBOUR

Car Ferry
Terminal

112

Salthill &
Monkstown
Station

Belgr Av
Square

SEAFELD AV

SEAPOINT AV

434

DUNLEARY

LONGFORD TCE

HARBOUR RD

CROFTON RD

Yacht Club
120

Dun Laoghaire
Station
Yacht Club

MONKSTOWN RD

MONKSTOWN

LONGFORD PL

George's PL

90

St Micheal's
Hospital

Town
Hall

MARINE RD

Yacht Club

Geographical
Pointer

DUN
LAOGHAIRE

MONKSTOWN CR

De Vesci
Gardens

GEORGE'S ST LOWER

441

QUEEN'S RD

CARRICKBRENNAN RD

OAKENHAM RD

THE HILL

Cheshire
Home

LIBRARY RD

111

Moran
Park

192

324

Maritime
Museum

MELLIFONT

NEWTOWNSMITH

RICHMOND AV

Vesey
Mews

YORK RD

NORTHCOTE AV

Health
Centre

People's
Park

Scotsman's
Bay

Monkstown
Park

KNAPTON RD

College

PATRICK ST

164

Convent

TIVOLI TCE SOUTH

TIVOLITERRACE EAST

MULGRAVE TCE

NORTHUMBERLAND AV

CORRIG AV

UPPER GEORGE'S ST

225

Sports
Ground

BROOK CT

RICHMOND GR

WINDSOR PK

Castle
(In Ruins)

MOUNTTOWN RD UPPER

TIVOLI RD

300m

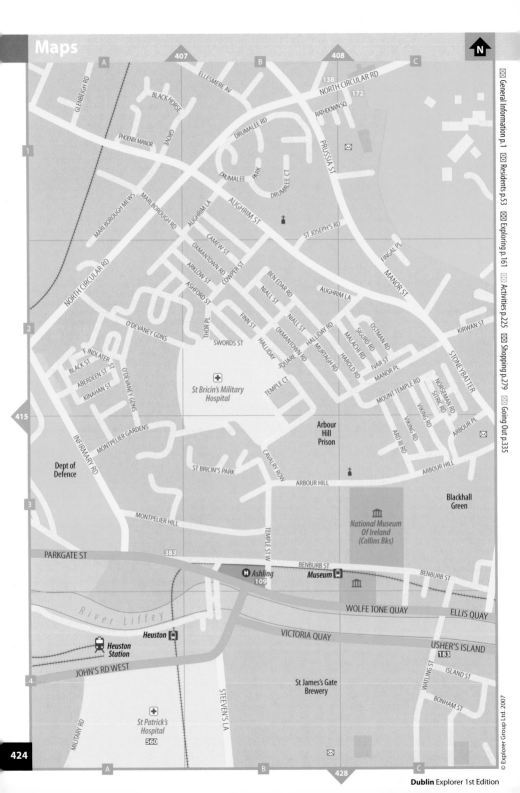

© Explorer Group Ltd 2007

General Information p.1   Residents p.53   Exploring p.161   Activities p.225   Shopping p.279   Going Out p.335

N

GLENBEIGH RD

BLACK HORSE

ELLESMERE AV

407

408

138

NORTH CIRCULAR RD

172

GROVE

PHOENIX MANOR

RATHDOWN SQ

DRUMALEE RD

PRUSSIA ST

DRUMALEE PARK

MARLBOROUGH MEWS

MARLBOROUGH RD

AUGHRIM LA

AUGHRIM ST

DRUMALEE CT

CAMEW ST

ST JOSEPH'S RD

NORTH CIRCULAR RD

OXMANTOWN RD

COWPER ST

ARDLOW ST

BEN EDAR RD

AUGHRIM LA

MANOR ST

ASHFORD ST

NIALL ST

FINGAL PL

O'DEVANEY GDNS

THOR PL

FINN ST

NIALL ST

OSTMAN RD

SIGURD RD

KIRWAN ST

SWORDS ST

HALLIDAY

OXMANTOWN RD

HALLIDAY RD

MALACHI RD

IVAR ST

MANOR PL

STONEYBATTER

F INDLATER

BLACK ST

SQUARE

MURTAGH RD

HAROLD RD

MOUNT TEMPLE RD

NORSEMAN RD

STIRL RD

ABERDEEN ST

O'DEVANEY GDNS

⊕ St Bricin's Military Hospital

TEMPLE CT

VIKING RD

VIKING RD

ARD RI RD

ARBOUR PL

KINAHAN ST

INFIRMARY RD

MONTPELIER GARDENS

St Bricin's Park

CAVALRY ROW

Arbour Hill Prison

415

Dept of Defence

ARBOUR HILL

ARBOUR HILL

Blackhall Green

MONTPELIER HILL

383

🏛 National Museum Of Ireland (Collins Bks)

PARKGATE ST

TEMPLE ST W

BENBURB ST

BENBURB ST

H Ashling 109

Museum 🏛

WOLFE TONE QUAY

ELLIS QUAY

River Liffey

Heuston 🚊

VICTORIA QUAY

USHER'S ISLAND

183

🚊 Heuston Station

WATLING ST

ISLAND ST

JOHN'S RD WEST

STEEVEN'S LA

St James's Gate Brewery

BONHAM ST

MILITARY RD

⊕ St Patrick's Hospital 560

424

428

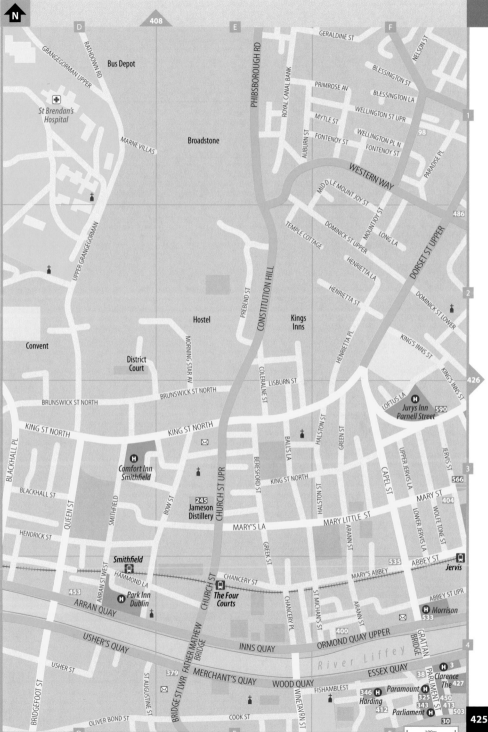

N

D | **E** | **F**

Bus Depot

GRANGEGORMAN UPPER

RATHDOWN RD

St Brendan's
Hospital

MARNE VILLAS

Broadstone

PHIBSBOROUGH RD

ROYAL CANAL BANK

GERALDINE ST

NELSON ST

BLESSINGTON ST

PRIMROSE AV

BLESSINGTON LA

AUBURN ST

MYTLE ST

WELLINGTON ST UPR

FONTENOY ST

WELLINGTON PL N

FONTENOY ST

PARADISE PL

1

98

WESTERN WAY

MIDDLE MOUNT JOY ST

MOUNT JOY ST

LONG LA

486

DORSET ST UPPER

UPPER GRANGEGORMAN

TEMPLE COTTAGE

DOMINICK ST UPPER

HENRIETTA LA

DOMINICK ST LOWER

2

Convent

Hostel

District
Court

MORNING STAR AV

PREBEND ST

CONSTITUTION HILL

Kings
Inns

HENRIETTA ST

HENRIETTA PL

KING'S INNS ST

KING'S INNS ST

426

BRUNSWICK ST NORTH

BRUNSWICK ST NORTH

COLERAINE ST

LISBURN ST

LOFTUS LA

Jurys Inn
Parnell Street

590

BLACKHALL PL

KING ST NORTH

KING ST NORTH

Comfort Inn
Smithfield

BLACKHALL ST

BOW ST

CHURCH ST UPR

BERESFORD ST

BALL'S LA

KING ST NORTH

HALSTON ST

GREEN ST

HALSTON ST

CAPEL ST

UPPER JERVIS LA

LOWER JERVIS LA

JERVIS ST

3

566

MARY ST

404

WOLFE TONE ST

QUEEN ST

SMITHFIELD

245
Jameson
Distillery

MARY'S LA

MARY'S LITTLE ST

GREEK ST

ARRAN ST

HENDRICK ST

Smithfield

HAMMOND LA

CHANCERY ST

MARY'S ABBEY

ABBEY ST

Jervis

535

ARRAN STREET WEST

453

Park Inn
Dublin

ARRAN QUAY

CHURCH ST

The Four
Courts

ST MICHAN'S ST

CHANCERY PL

ARRAN ST

ABBEY ST UPR

Morrison
533

GRATTAN BRIDGE

USHER'S QUAY

INNS QUAY

ORMOND QUAY UPPER

400

River Liffey

4

BRIDGEFOOT ST

USHER ST

ST AUGUSTINE ST

379

FATHER MATHEW
BRIDGE

BRIDGE ST LWR

MERCHANT'S QUAY

WOOD QUAY

WINETAVERN ST

FISHAMBLE ST

ESSEX QUAY

38

Clarence
The

3

427

346
Harding

Paramount

PARLIAMENT ST

450

325

343

413

503

OLIVER BOND ST

COOK ST

412

Parliament

30

425

100m

D | **E** | **F**

429

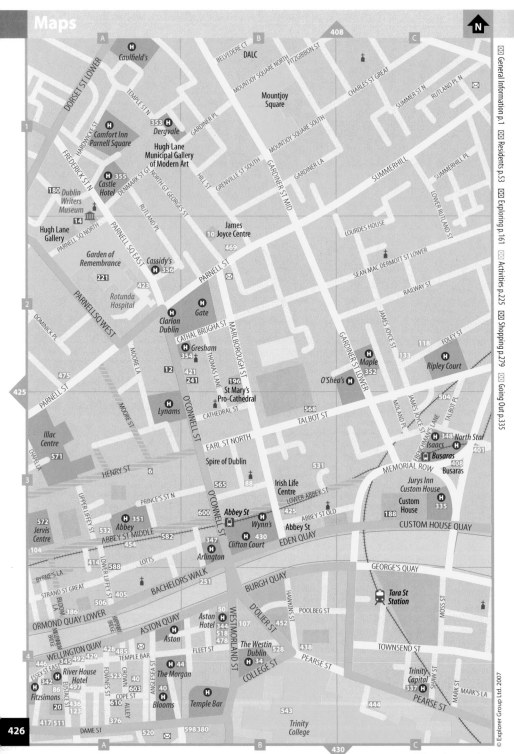

Explorer Group Ltd. 2007

General Information p.1 · Residents p.53 · Exploring p.161 · Activities p.225 · Shopping p.279 · Going Out p.335

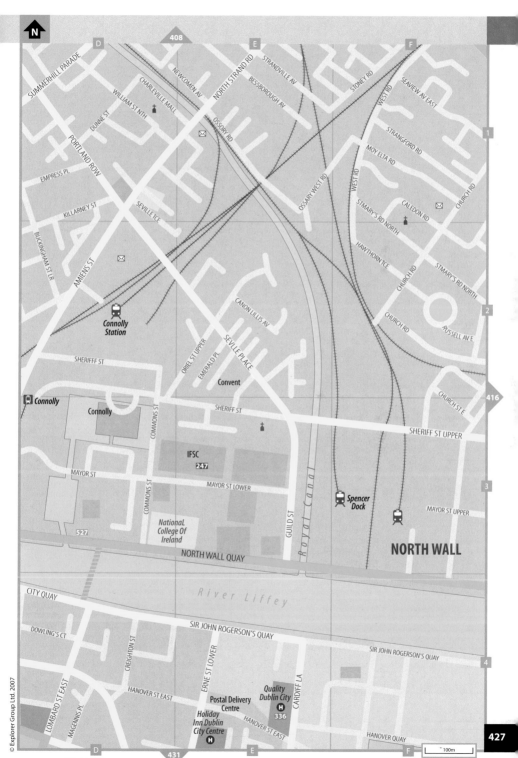

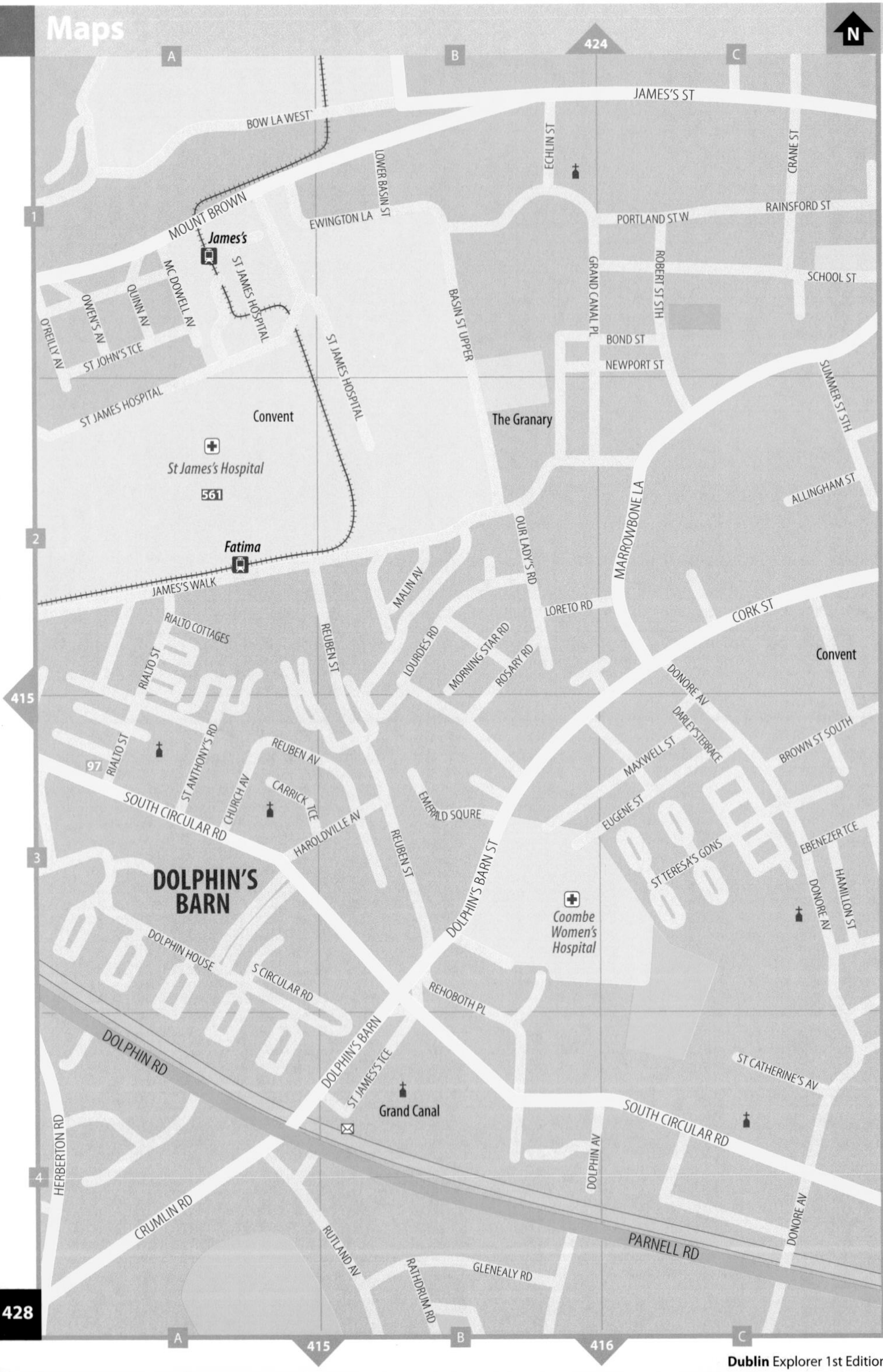

N

A   B   C

JAMES'S ST

BOW LA WEST

LOWER BASIN ST

EWINGTON LA

MOUNT BROWN

James's

ST JAMES HOSPITAL

MC DOWELL AV

QUINN AV

OWEN'S AV

O'REILLY AV

ST JOHN'S TCE

ST JAMES HOSPITAL

BASIN ST UPPER

ST JAMES HOSPITAL

Convent

St James's Hospital

561

Fatima

JAMES'S WALK

RIALTO COTTAGES

RIALTO ST

RIALTO ST

97

ST ANTHONY'S RD

SOUTH CIRCULAR RD

CHURCH AV

REUBEN AV

CARRICK TCE

HAROLDVILLE AV

REUBEN ST

REUBEN ST

MALIN AV

LOURDES RD

MORNING STAR RD

ROSARY RD

EMERALD SQURE

DOLPHIN'S BARN ST

DOLPHIN'S
BARN

DOLPHIN HOUSE

S CIRCULAR RD

DOLPHIN RD

DOLPHIN'S BARN

ST JAMES'S TCE

REHOBOTH PL

Grand Canal

HERBERTON RD

CRUMLIN RD

RUTLAND AV

RATHRIM RD

GLENEALY RD

PARNELL RD

DOLPHIN RD

ECHLIN ST

PORTLAND ST W

GRAND CANAL PL

ROBERT ST STH

BOND ST

NEWPORT ST

The Granary

OUR LADY'S RD

LORETO RD

MARROWBONE LA

CORK ST

DONORE AV

DARLEY'STERRACE

MAXWELL ST

EUGENE ST

ST TERESA'S GDNS

Coombe
Women's
Hospital

BROWN ST SOUTH

EBENEZER TCE

DONORE AV

HAMILTON ST

ST CATHERINE'S AV

SOUTH CIRCULAR RD

DOLPHIN AV

DONORE AV

CRANE ST

RAINSFORD ST

SCHOOL ST

SUMMER ST STH

ALLINGHAM ST

Convent

415

415

416

© Explorer Group Ltd 2007

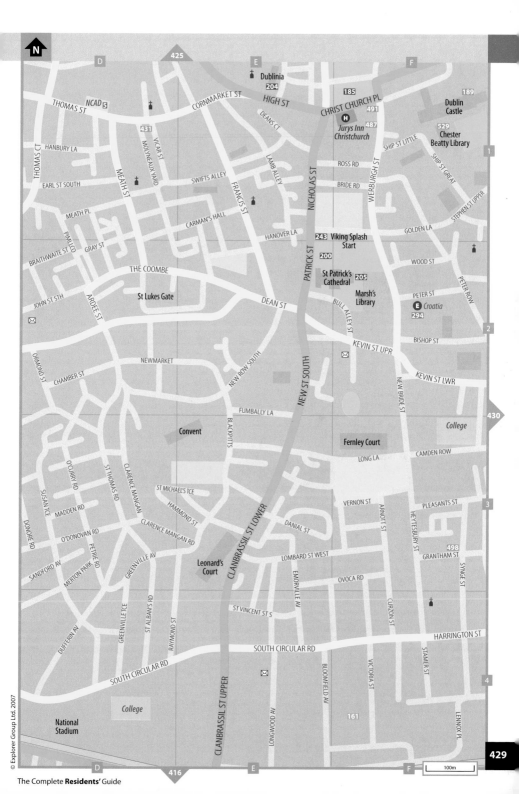

© Explorer Group Ltd. 2007

N

General Information p.1   Residents p.53   Exploring p.161   Activities p.225   Shopping p.279   Going Out p.335

426

Adams Trinity
448 31 474 519 513 525 39 465

250 499 609 41
SUFFOLK ST
472

GRAFTON ST

NASSAU ST

College Park

Dental School & Hospital

EXCHEQUER ST
484 31 100 15 482

476 496 397 524 583 466 445
ANDREW ST LANE
ST ANDREW'S LANE
WICKLOW ST
155 410 502 608 159
457 411 392
144 584
589
96
84
129
National Library

LEINSTER LA

Central
341 399 468
596 507 586 167 393 384 403 395 11 567 22 526

7 569 432
43 599
564 402 237
509

DUKE ST
580 407
381

611 169
Buswells
MOLESWORTH ST
461

461
194
Leinster House

197
National Gallery

MERRION SQ WEST

Brooks

Grafton Capital
375 385 495 52 396 404 390 165

ANNE'S LA
LEMONS ST
398 521 158 184
17 587 605 394

153

42
National Museum

254

Dnwy Centre Hotel
328 505 378 406

CHATHAM ST
530 440 166 534

National History Museum

190
Mansion House

SCHOOL HOUSE LA E

St Stephen's Green Centre
26

KING ST SOUTH
156
Browres Hotel
536 360 481 581 490

KILDARE ST
489
9

MERRION SQ UPPER
488

Mercer
331
32
The Fitzwilliam Hotel

St Stephen's Green

ST STEPHEN'S GREEN NORTH

The Shelbourne
MERRION ROW
471 477 473
29
Merrion

FITZWILLIAM LA

The Georgian

AUNGIER ST
MERCER ST LOWER
YORK ST
479

ST STEPHEN'S GREEN WEST

St Stephen's Green
228

HUME ST
Skin and Cancer Hospital
BELL'S LA
ELY PL

512
BAGGOT LA
PEMBROKE LA

WEXFORD ST

CUFFE ST

ST STEPHEN'S GREEN SOUTH

ST STEPHEN'S GREEN EAST

178

PEMBROKE ST LOWER
FITZWILLIAM ST LOWER

181
Fitzwilliam Square

429 424

HARCOURT ST
E 295
Finland
480 394 460

333
O'Callaghan Stephen's Green

332
Conrad Dublin

QUINN'S LA
LAVERTY CT

FITZWILLIAM SQUARE N

85
FITZWILLIAM SQUARE S

CAMDEN ST LOWER

MONTAGUE ST
CLONMEL ST

Jackson Court Hotel

Iveagh Gardens

456
Premier Suites Dublin

PEMBROKE ST
PEMBROKE PLACE
442
CUMBERLAND RD

49 612
CAMDEN ROW
Harcourt
217

National Concert Hall

EARLSFORT TERRACE

HATCH ST LOWER

LEESON ST LOWER

FITZWILLIAM PL
540

455 459
HATCH ST UPPER

HATCH PL

WILTON TCE

CAMDEN ST UPPER

CHARLOTTE WAY
382
Camden Court
330
Harcourt

HARCOURT RD

ADELAIDE RD

Royal Victoria Eye and Ear Hospital

RICHMOND ST SOUTH

LENNOX ST
Portobello
329
597

CHARLEMONT ST

Hilton Dublin

CHARLEMONT PL

GRAND PARADE

DARTMOUTH SQ

LEESON ST UPPER

SUSSEX RD
45
Burlington

CANAL RD

Charlemont

416

Dublin Explorer 1st Edition

A   B   C

1   2   3   4

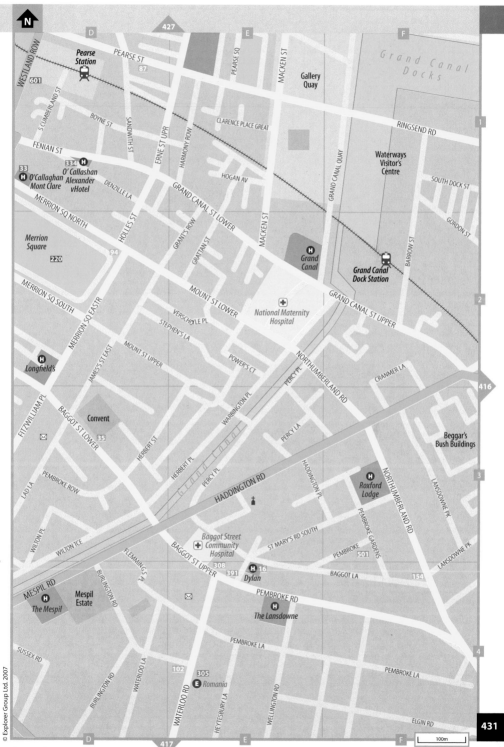

Planning an event

in Dubai?

Look no further.

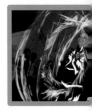

M.I.C.E. Events ◆ Corporate Events ◆ Teambuilding Events
Corporate Family Days ◆ Themed Events ◆ Entertainment
Balloon Decoration ◆ Event Rentals ◆ Mascot Fabrication
Keeko Kids ◆ Royal Events ◆ Product Launches

**Talk to us and discover the many ways we
can bring your event to life.**

Flying Elephant

The region's largest supplier of family and corporate entertainment.

For more information contact
Tel: +9714 347-9170 Fax: +9714 347-9171
info@flyingelephantuae.com • www.flyingelephantuae.com

We're on the lookout for talent!
If you are a multi-skilled entertainer, interested in working in sunny Dubai
on short and long-term projects, email your details to careers@flyingelephantuae.com

Index

Index

Index

Index

Index

_____

_____

_____

_____

_____

_____

_____

_____

_____

_____

_____

_____

_____

_____

_____

_____

_____

_____

_____

_____

_____

_____

_____

_____

Residents' Guides
All you need to know about living, working and enjoying life in these exciting destinations

Mini Guides
The perfect pocket-sized
Visitors' Guides

Mini Maps
Wherever you are,
never get lost again

Photography Books
Beautiful cities caught through the lens

Calendars
The time, the place, and the date

Maps
Wherever you are, never get lost again

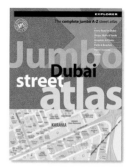

Activity and Lifestyle Guides
Drive, trek, dive and swim... life will never be boring again

Retail sales
Our books are available in most good bookshops around the world, and are also available online at Amazon.co.uk and Amazon.com. If you would like to enquire about any of our international distributors, please contact retail@explorerpublishing.com

Bulk sales and customisation
All our products are available for bulk sales with customisation options. For discount rates and further information, please contact corporatesales@explorerpublishing.com

Licensing and digital sales
All our content, maps and photography are available for print or digital use. For licensing enquiries please contact licensing@explorerpublishing.com

Ahmed Mainodin
AKA: Mystery Man
We can never recognise Ahmed because of his constantly changing facial hair. He waltzes in with big lambchop sideburns one day, a handlebar moustache the next, and a neatly trimmed goatee after that. So far we've had no objections to his hirsute chameleonisms, but we'll definitely draw the line at a monobrow.

Bahrudeen Abdul
AKA: The Stallion
Having tired of creating abstract sculptures out of papier maché and candy canes, Bahrudeen turned to the art of computer programming. After honing his skills in the southern Andes for three years he grew bored of Patagonian winters, and landed a job here, 'The Home of 01010101 Creative Freedom'.

Ajay Krishnan R
AKA: Web Wonder
Ajay's mum and dad knew he was going to be an IT genius when they found him reconfiguring his Commodore 64 at the tender age of 2. He went on to become the technology consultant on all three Matrix films, and counts Keanu as a close personal friend.

Ben Merrett
AKA: Big Ben
After a short (or tall as the case may have been) career as a human statue, Ben tired of the pigeons choosing him, rather than his namesake, as a public convenience and decided to fly the nest to seek his fortune in foreign lands. Not only is he big on personality but he brings in the big bucks with his bulk!

Alex Jeffries
AKA: Easy Rider
Alex is happiest when dressed in leather from head to toe with a humming machine between his thighs – just like any other motorbike enthusiast. Whenever he's not speeding along the Hatta Road at full throttle, he can be found at his beloved Mac, still dressed in leather.

Cherry Enriquez
AKA: Bean Counter
With the team's penchant for sweets and pastries, it's good to know we have Cherry on top of our accounting cake. The local confectioner is always paid on time, so we're guaranteed great gateaux for every special occasion.

Alistair MacKenzie
AKA: Media Mogul
If only Alistair could take the paperless office one step further and achieve the officeless office he would be the happiest publisher alive. Wireless access from a remote spot somewhere in the Hajar Mountains would suit this intrepid explorer – less traffic, lots of fresh air, and wearing sandals all day - the perfect work environment!

Claire England
AKA: Whip Cracker
No longer able to freeload off the fact that she once appeared in a Robbie Williams video, Claire now puts her creative skills to better use – looking up rude words in the dictionary! A child of English nobility, Claire is quite the lady – unless she's down at Jimmy Dix.

Andrea Fust
AKA: Mother Superior
By day Andrea is the most efficient manager in the world and by night she replaces the boardroom for her board and wows the pants off the dudes in Ski Dubai. Literally. Back in the office she definitely wears the trousers!

David Quinn
AKA: Sharp Shooter
After a short stint as a children's TV presenter was robbed from David because he developed an allergy to sticky back plastic, he made his way to sandier pastures. Now that he's thinking outside the box, nothing gets past the man with the sharpest pencil in town.

Derrick Pereira
AKA: The Returnimator
After leaving Explorer in 2003, Derrick's life took a dramatic downturn – his dog ran away, his prized bonsai tree died and he got kicked out of his thrash metal band. Since rejoining us, things are looking up and he just found out he's won $10 million in a Nigerian sweepstakes competition. And he's got the desk by the window!

Iain Young
AKA: 'The Cat'
Iain follows in the fine tradition of Scots with safe hands – Alan Rough, Andy Goram, Jim Leighton on a good day – but breaking into the Explorer XI has proved frustrating. There's no match on a Mac, but that Al Huzaifa ringer doesn't half make himself big.

Enrico Maullon
AKA: The Crooner
Frequently mistaken for his near-namesake Enrique Iglesias, Enrico decided to capitalise and is now a regular stand-in for the Latin heartthrob. If he's ever missing from the office, it usually means he's off performing for millions of adoring fans on another stadium tour of America.

Ieyad Charaf
AKA: Fashion Designer
When we hired Ieyad as a top designer, we didn't realise we'd be getting his designer tops too! By far the snappiest dresser in the office, you'd be hard-pressed to beat his impeccably ironed shirts.

Firos Khan
AKA: Big Smiler
Previously a body double in kung fu movies, including several appearances in close up scenes for Steven Seagal's moustache. He also once tore down a restaurant with his bare hands after they served him a mild curry by mistake.

Ingrid Cupido
AKA: The Karaoke Queen
Ingrid has a voice to match her starlet name. She'll put any Pop Idols to shame once behind the mike, and she's pretty nifty on a keyboard too. She certainly gets our vote if she decides to go pro; just remember you saw her here first.

Hashim MM
AKA: Speedy Gonzales
They don't come much faster than Hashim – he's so speedy with his mouse that scientists are struggling to create a computer that can keep up with him. His nimble fingers leave his keyboard smouldering (he gets through three a week), and his go-faster stripes make him almost invisible to the naked eye when he moves.

Ivan Rodrigues
AKA: The Aviator
After making a mint in the airline market, Ivan came to Explorer where he works for pleasure, not money. That's his story, anyway. We know that he is actually a corporate spy from a rival company and that his multi-level spreadsheets are really elaborate codes designed to confuse us.

Helen Spearman
AKA: Little Miss Sunshine
With her bubbly laugh and permanent smile, Helen is a much-needed ray of sunshine in the office when we're all grumpy and facing harrowing deadlines. It's almost impossible to think that she ever loses her temper or shows a dark side... although put her behind the wheel of a car, and you've got instant road rage.

Jake Marsico
AKA: Don Calzone
Jake spent the last 10 years on the tiny triangular Mediterranean island of Samoza, honing his traditional cooking techniques and perfecting his Italian. Now, whenever he returns to his native America, he impresses his buddies by effortlessly zapping a hot dog to perfection in any microwave, anywhere, anytime.

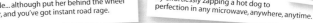

Henry Hilos
AKA: The Quiet Man
Henry can rarely be seen from behind his large obstructive screen but when you do catch a glimpse you'll be sure to get a smile. Lighthearted Henry keeps all those glossy pages filled with pretty pictures for something to look at when you can't be bothered to read.

Jane Roberts
AKA: The Oracle
After working in an undisclosed role in the government, Jane brought her super sleuth skills to Explorer. Whatever the question, she knows what, where, who, how and when, but her encyclopaedic knowledge is only impressive until you realise she just makes things up randomly.

Jayde Fernandes
AKA: Pop Idol
Jayde's idol is Britney Spears, and he recently shaved his head to show solidarity with the troubled star. When he's not checking his dome for stubble, or practising the dance moves to 'Baby One More Time' in front of the bathroom mirror, he actually manages to get some designing done.

Johny Mathew
AKA: The Hawker
Caring Johny used to nurse wounded eagles back to health and teach them how to fly again before trying his luck in merchandising. Fortunately his skills in the field have come in handy at Explorer, where his efforts to improve our book sales have been a soaring success.

Kate Fox
AKA: Contacts Collector
Kate swooped into the office like the UK equivalent of Wonderwoman, minus the tights of course (it's much too hot for that), but armed with a superhuman marketing brain. Even though she's just arrived, she is already a regular on the Dubai social scene – she is helping to blast Explorer into the stratosphere, one champagne-soaked networking party at a time.

Katie Drynan
AKA: The Irish Deputy
Katie is a Jumeira Jane in training, and has 35 sisters who take it in turns to work in the Explorer office while she enjoys testing all the beauty treatments available on the Beach Road. This Irish charmer met an oil tycoon in Paris, and they now spend the weekends digging very deep holes in their new garden.

Kiran Melwani
AKA: Bow Selector
Like a modern-day Robin Hood (right down to the green tights and band of merry men), Kiran's mission in life is to distribute Explorer's wealth of knowledge to the fact-hungry readers of the world. Just make sure you never do anything to upset her – rumour has it she's a pretty mean shot with that bow and arrow.

Lennie Mangalino
AKA: Shaker Maker
With a giant spring in her step and music in her heart it's hard to not to swing to the beat when Lennie passes by in the office. She loves her Lambada… and Samba… and Salsa and anything else she can get the sales team shaking their hips to.

Mannie Lugtu
AKA: Distribution Demon
When the travelling circus rode into town, their master juggler Mannie decided to leave the Big Top and explore Dubai instead. He may have swapped his balls for our books but his juggling skills still come in handy.

Maricar Ong
AKA: Pocket Docket
A pint-sized dynamo of ruthless efficiency, Maricar gets the job done before anyone else notices it needed doing. If this most able assistant is absent for a moment, it sends a surge of blind panic through the Explorer ranks.

Grace Carnay
AKA: Manila Ice
It's just as well the office is so close to a movie theatre, because Grace is always keen to catch the latest Hollywood offering from Brad Pitt, who she admires purely for his acting ability, of course. Her ice cool exterior conceals a tempestuous passion for jazz, which fuels her frenzied typing speed.

Matt Farquharson
AKA: Hack Hunter
A career of tuppence-a-word hackery ended when Matt arrived in Dubai to cover a maggot wranglers' convention. He misguidedly thinks he's clever because he once wrote for some grown-up English papers.

Matthew Samuel
AKA: Mr Modest
Matt's penchant for the entrepreneurial life began with a pair of red braces and a filofax when still a child. That yearning for the cut and thrust of commerce has brought him to Dubai, where he made a fortune in the sand-selling business before semi-retiring at Explorer.

Michael Samuel
AKA: Gordon Gekko
We have a feeling this mild mannered master of mathematics has a wild side. He hasn't witnessed an Explorer party yet but the office agrees that once the karaoke machine is out, Michael will be the maestro. Watch out Dubai!

Pamela Grist
AKA: Happy Snapper
If a picture can speak a thousand words then Pam's photos say a lot about her - through her lens she manages to find the beauty in everything – even this motley crew. And when the camera never lies, thankfully Photoshop can.

Mimi Stankova
AKA: Mind Controller
A master of mind control, Mimi's siren-like voice lulls people into doing whatever she asks. Her steely reserve and endless patience mean recalcitrant reporters and persistent PR people are putty in her hands, delivering whatever she wants, whenever she wants it.

Pete Maloney
AKA: Graphic Guru
Image conscious he may be, but when Pete has his designs on something you can bet he's gonna get it! He's the king of chat up lines, ladies – if he ever opens a conversation with 'D'you come here often?' then brace yourself for the Maloney magic.

Mohammed Sameer
AKA: Man in the Van
Known as MS, short for Microsoft, Sameer can pick apart a PC like a thief with a lock, which is why we keep him out of finance and pounding Dubai's roads in the unmissable Explorer van – so we can always spot him coming.

Rafi Jamal
AKA: Soap Star
After a walk on part in The Bold and the Beautiful, Rafi swapped the Hollywood Hills for the Hajar Mountains. Although he left the glitz behind, he still mingles with high society, moonlighting as a male gigolo and impressing Dubai's ladies with his fancy footwork.

Mohammed T
AKA: King of the Castle
T is Explorer's very own Bedouin warehouse dweller; under his caring charge all Explorer stock is kept in masterful order. Arrive uninvited and you'll find T, meditating on a pile of maps, amid an almost eerie sense of calm.

Rafi VP
AKA: Party Trickster
After developing a rare allergy to sunlight in his teens, Rafi started to lose a few centimeters of height every year. He now stands just 30cm tall, and does his best work in our dingy basement wearing a pair of infrared goggles. His favourite party trick is to fold himself into a briefcase, and he was once sick in his hat.

Noushad Madathil
AKA: Map Daddy
Where would Explorer be without the mercurial Madathil brothers? Lost in the Empty Quarter, that's where. Quieter than a mute dormouse, Noushad prefers to let his Photoshop layers, and brother Zain, do all the talking. A true Map Daddy.

Richard Greig
AKA: Sir Lancelot
Chivalrous to the last, Richard's dream of being a mediaeval knight suffered a setback after being born several centuries too late. His stellar parliamentary career remains intact, and he is in the process of creating a new party with the aim of abolishing all onions and onion-related produce.

Roshni Ahuja
AKA: Bright Spark
Never failing to brighten up the office with her colourful get-up, Roshni definitely puts the 'it' in the IT department. She's a perennially pleasant, profound programmer with peerless panache, and she does her job with plenty of pep and piles of pizzazz.

Sean Kearns
AKA: The Tall Guy
Big Sean, as he's affectionately known, is so laid back he actually spends most of his time lying down (unless he's on a camping trip, when his ridiculously small tent forces him to sleep on his hands and knees). Despite the rest of us constantly tripping over his lanky frame, when the job requires someone who will work flat out, he always rises to the editorial occasion.

Shabsir M
AKA: Sticky Wicket
Shabsir is a valuable player on the Indian national cricket team, so instead of working you'll usually find him autographing cricket balls for crazed fans around the world. We don't mind though – if ever a retailer is stumped because they run out of stock, he knocks them for six with his speedy delivery.

Shawn Jackson Zuzarte
AKA: Paper Plumber
If you thought rocket science was hard, try rearranging the chaotic babble that flows from the editorial team! If it weren't for Shawn, most of our books would require a kaleidoscope to read correctly so we're keeping him and his jazz hands under wraps.

Shefeeq M
AKA: Rapper in Disguise
So new he's still got the wrapper on, Shefeeq was dragged into the Explorer office, and put to work in the design department. The poor chap only stopped by to ask for directions to Wadi Bih, but since we realised how efficient he is, we keep him chained to his desk.

Shyrell Tamayo
AKA: Fashion Princess
We've never seen Shyrell wearing the same thing twice – her clothes collection is so large that her husband has to keep all his things in a shoebox. She runs Designlab like clockwork, because being late for deadlines is SO last season.

Sunita Lakhiani
AKA: Designlass
Initially suspicious of having a female in their midst, the boys in Designlab now treat Sunita like one of their own. A big shame for her, because they treat each other pretty damn bad!

Steve Jones
AKA: Golden Boy
Our resident Kiwi lives in a nine-bedroom mansion and is already planning an extension. His winning smile has caused many a knee to weaken in Bur Dubai but sadly for the ladies, he's hopelessly devoted to his clients.

Tim Binks
AKA: Class Clown
El Binksmeisterooney is such a sharp wit, he often has fellow Explorers gushing tea from their noses in convulsions of mirth. Years spent hiking across the Middle East have given him an encyclopaedic knowledge of rock formations and elaborate hair.

Tom Jordan
AKA: The True Professional
Explorer's resident thesp, Tom delivers lines almost as well as he cuts them. His early promise on the pantomime circuit was rewarded with an all-action role in hit UK drama Heartbeat. He's still living off the royalties – and the fact he shared a sandwich with Kenneth Branagh.

Tracy Fitzgerald
AKA: 'La Dona'
Tracy is a queenpin Catalan mafiosa and ringleader for the 'pescadora' clan, a nefarious group that runs a sushi smuggling operation between the Costa Brava and Ras Al Khaimah. She is not to be crossed. Rival clans will find themselves fed fish, and then fed to the fishes.

Zainudheen Madathil
AKA: Map Master
Often confused with retired footballer Zinedine Zidane because of his dexterous displays and a bad head-butting habit, Zain tackles design with the mouse skills of a star striker. Maps are his goal and despite getting red-penned a few times, when he shoots, he scores.

The *Dublin Explorer* Team
Lead Editor Jane Roberts
Deputy Editor Katie Drynan
Editorial Assistants Ingrid Cupido, Mimi Stankova
Designer Shefeeq Marakkatepurath
Cartographers Noushad Madathil, Noufal Madathil,
Ramlath Kambravan, Rasheena Palakkodan
Photographers Pete Maloney, Jane Roberts
Proofers Jo Holden Macdonald

Publisher
Alistair MacKenzie

Editorial
Managing Editor Claire England
Lead Editors David Quinn, Jane Roberts, Matt Farquharson,
Sean Kearns, Tim Binks, Tom Jordan
Deputy Editors Helen Spearman, Jakob Marsico,
Katie Drynan, Pamela Afram, Richard Greig, Tracy Fitzgerald
Editorial Assistants Grace Carnay, Ingrid Cupido, Mimi Stankova

Design
Creative Director Pete Maloney
Art Director Ieyad Charaf
Senior Designers Alex Jeffries, Iain Young
Layout Manager Jayde Fernandes
Layouters Hashim Moideen, Rafi Pullat,
Shefeeq Marakkatepurath
Junior Layouter Shawn Jackson Zuzarte
Cartography Manager Zainudheen Madathil
Cartographers Noushad Madathil, Sunita Lakhiani
Design Admin Manager Shyrell Tamayo
Production Coordinator Maricar Ong

Photography
Photography Manager Pamela Grist
Photographer Victor Romero
Image Editor Henry Hilos

Sales & Marketing
Area Sales Managers Laura Zuffa, Stephen Jones
Corporate Sales Executive Ben Merrett
Marketing Manager Kate Fox
Marketing Executive Annabel Clough
Retail Sales Manager Ivan Rodrigues
Retail Sales Coordinator Kiran Melwani
Retail Sales Supervisor Matthew Samuel
Merchandiser Johny Mathew
Sales & Marketing Coordinator Lennie Mangalino
Distribution Executives Ahmed Mainodin, Firos Khan, Mannie Lugtu
Warehouse Assistants Mohammed Kunjaymo, Najumudeen K.I.
Drivers Mohammed Sameer, Shabsir Madathil

Finance & Administration
Finance Manager Michael Samuel
HR & Administration Manager Andrea Fust
Accounts Assistant Cherry Enriquez
Administrators Enrico Maullon, Kelly Tesoro
Driver Rafi Jamal

IT
IT Administrator Ajay Krishnan R.
Software Engineers Bahrudeen Abdul, Roshni Ahuja
Digital Content Manager Derrick Pereira

Contact Us

Reader Response
If you have any comments and suggestions, fill out
our online reader response form and you could win prizes.
Log on to **www.explorerpublishing.com**

General Enquiries
We'd love to hear your thoughts and answer any questions
you have about this book or any other Explorer product.
Contact us at **info@explorerpublishing.com**

Careers
If you fancy yourself as an Explorer, send your CV
(stating the position you're interested in) to
jobs@explorerpublishing.com

Designlab & Contract Publishing
For enquiries about Explorer's Contract Publishing arm
and design services contact
designlab@explorerpublishing.com

PR & Marketing
For PR and marketing enquries contact
marketing@explorerpublishing.com
pr@explorerpublishing.com

Corporate Sales
For bulk sales and customisation options, for this book or
any Explorer product, contact
sales@explorerpublishing.com

Advertising & Sponsorship
For advertising and sponsorship, contact
media@explorerpublishing.com

Explorer Publishing & Distribution
PO Box 34275, Dubai
United Arab Emirates
Phone: +971 (0)4 340 8805
Fax: +971 (0)4 340 8806
www.explorerpublishing.com

Main Hotels

Bewley's Hotel Ballsbridge	01 668 1111
Burlington Hotel	01 660 5222
The Clarence	01 407 0800
Clontarf Castle Hotel	01 833 2321
Conrad Hotel	01 602 8900
The Fitzwilliam	01 478 7000
Four Seasons Hotel	01 665 4000
La Stampa Hotel & Spa	01 677 4444
Merrion Hall	01 668 1426
Merrion Hotel	01 603 0600
The Morgan	01 679 3939
O'Callaghan Davenport Hotel	01 607 3500
Schoolhouse Hotel	01 667 5014
The Westbury Hotel	01 679 1122
The Westin	01 645 1000

Airport Information

Aer Arann	01 844 7700
Aer Lingus	01 886 8888
Dublin Tourism	01 605 7700
Dublin Airport:	
Lost Property	01 814 5555
Airport Information	01 814 1111
Ryanair	818 303 030

Useful Numbers

AA Roadwatch	1550 131 811
Directory Enquiries	11811
Dublin Area Code	1
Garda Station, Pearse Street	01 666 9000
Ireland Country Code	353
Missing Persons Helpline	1800 616 617
Northern Ireland Area Code	44
Police & General Emergency	999 or 112 (Toll Free)
Speaking Clock	1191
St James Late Night Pharmacy	01 473 4022
Traffic Hotline	1800 872 345
Walsh's Late Night Pharmacy	01 492 3769
Weather Forecast	1550 123 854
Women's Refuge & Helpline	01 496 1002

Main Hospitals

Beaumont Hospital	01 809 3000
Mater Misericordiae University Hospital	01 803 2000
St James's Hospital	01 410 3000
St Vincent's University Hospital	01 221 4000
Adelaide & Meath Hospital	01 414 2000
James Connolly Memorial Hospital	01 288 3144
Our Lady's Children's Hospital	01 409 6100
The Royal Victoria Eye & Ear Hospital	01 678 5500
St Colmcille's	01 282 5800

Tourist Information

Tourist Information Centre	01 605 7700

Banks

Allied Irish Bank (AIB)	01 679 3211
Anglo Irish Bank	01 616 2000
Bank of Ireland	01 677 6801
National Irish Bank	01 484 0800
Permanent tsb	01 677 0425

Public Holidays

New Year's Day	1 January
St Patrick's Day	17 March
Easter Monday	Monday following Easter Sunday
May Holiday	first Monday in May
June Holiday	first Monday in June
August Holiday	first Monday in August
October Holiday	last Monday in October
Christmas Day	25 December
St Stephen's Day	26 December

Embassies & Consulates

Argentina	01 269 1546	421-E1
Australia	01 664 5300	416-C3
Austria	01 269 4577	421-E1
Belgium	01 205 7100	417-E4
Brazil	01 475 6000	416-B3
Britain	01 205 3700	417-E4
Bulgaria	01 660 3293	416-C4
Canada	01 417 4100	416-B3
China	01 260 1119	421-E1
Croatia	01 476 7181	429-F2
Cuba	01 475 0899	416-B4
Czech Republic	01 668 1135	417-D3
Denmark	01 475 6404	416-B3
Finland	01 478 1344	430-A2
France	01 260 1666	421-E1
Germany	01 269 3011	421-F2
Greece	01 676 7254	416-C3
Hungary	01 661 2902	416-C3
India	01 496 6792	416-C4
Iran	01 288 0252	422-A3
Israel	01 230 9400	417-D4
Italy	01 660 1744	417-D3
Japan	01 202 8300	421-F1
Mexico	01 260 0699	421-E1
Morocco	01 660 9449	417-D4
Norway	01 662 1800	416-C3
Pakistan	01 261 3032	421-E1
Poland	01 283 0855	421-E1
Portugal	01 289 4416	na
Romania	01 668 1085	431-E4
Russia	01 492 2048	420-A2
Slovenia	01 670 5240	416-B2
South Africa	01 661 5553	416-B3
Spain	01 283 9900	421-F1
Sweden	01 474 4400	416-B2
Switzerland	01 218 6382	421-E1
The Netherlands	01 269 3444	421-F1
USA	01 668 8777	417-D4